BREAKING FREE

Edward I. Halliday
1954

BREAKING FREE

GERARD MORGAN-GRENVILLE
with pen and ink drawings by the author

MILTON MILL PUBLISHING

Published by Milton Mill Publishing
Milton Mill, West Milton,
Bridport, Dorset DT6 3SN

By the same author
Barging into France (to be reprinted)
Barging into Burgundy (in print)
Barging into Southern France (in print)
Cruising the Sahara (out-of-print)
Holiday Cruising in France (out-of-print)

First published in 2001

Typeset by Milton Mill Publishing
Set in Bembo 11.5/14pt
Printed and bound in Great Britain
by R Booth Ltd, Mabe, Cornwall

ISBN 0-9540570-0-7

A CIP catalogue record for this book is
available from the British Library

Frontispiece: the author aged 21, reproduced
from a portrait by Edward Halliday R.A

CONTENTS

This book is dedicated to my wife Margaret
without whose unflagging encouragement and considerable
computer skills, this book would not have been published.

It has been written especially for my grandchildren,
Hector, Oscar, Rosie, Selina, Hamish and Harry
and also my step-grandchildren, Alexander and Toby
as my contribution to the history of our family, with the
expectation that in due course they will add their own.

PREFACE

He who longs to strengthen his spirit
must go beyond obedience and respect
He will continue to honour some laws
but he will mostly violate
both law and custom, and live beyond
the established and deficient norm.
Pleasure will have much to teach him.
He will not be afraid of the destructive act;
one half of the house must be pulled down.
This way he will grow virtuously into knowledge

C. P. Cavafy

WHY WRITE an autobiography?

Had I tried to answer this question before doing so, I would have given 'an addition to the family archives' as my reason. My father wrote a slim volume of memoirs when he turned ninety. My brother (and only sibling) wrote his reminiscences when he turned sixty-five and also wrote a book celebrating our mother's life. They were privately printed and I therefore saw this volume as completing an account of two generations of our family.

Now that I have written it, I would answer differently. The process of writing it enabled me to relive periods of my life and to recall events and people that I thought vanished from memory. That, by itself, made the effort extremely worthwhile. Those people, probably now quite aged, who used to develop their own black and white photographs, will recall the fascination of seeing the image gradually appear on a previously blank piece of photographic paper. The recollection of times past can be similarly intriguing: each scene remembered seems to release another so that small details reappear as if by magic.

I have since been encouraged to share this story with a wider audience because of the suggestion that beyond any intrinsic interest in the narrative itself, there may exist a more useful relevance. Leaving aside the purely anecdotal, there are aspects of the story which may hopefully encourage others who are hesitant to spread their wings through lack of resources or lack of self-confidence. For this is partly a tale of various endeavours that many people might rightly judge to be out of all proportion to the economic or educational abilities of the author.

It is my sincere hope that some of the activities recorded here will induce other potential venturers to break free.

For much of my life I have been involved in more than one occupation at the same time. In this account, I have followed the evolution of each for longer than is justified by strict chronology so as to avoid jumping back and forth.One of the pleasures of writing is the chance to air personal opinions and obsessions without the risk of being taken to task: this work is no exception!

I am greatly indebted to a number of people who helped me in putting together this book, especially to Juliet Vibert, Jennie Makepeace, Dick Worcester, Sara and John Hudston whose comments on the manuscript have been invaluable. Sarah Jenkinson at the Centre for Alternative Technology helped with photos and Peter Harper kindly allowed me to quote from his history of CAT.

'Strengthening the Spirit' by C P Cavafy is reproduced by permission of the Estate of Cavafy, c/o Rogers, Coleridge & White Ltd., 20 Powis Mews, London W11 1JN

CHAPTER I

My beginnings and the staff that peopled my early years - scenes that have vanished forever - formative journeys abroad - an eccentric godfather - Stowe and the rise and fall of the Grenvilles - parental influences

THE HOUSE in which I was born was full of clocks. Longcase, mantel, bracket and wall, they chimed the hours with a sudden cacophony for my father had succeeded in synchronising them precisely. Any which exhibited the least independence instantly had their deviant behaviour corrected.

At noon on Thursday, 26 March 1931, an *ensemble* of these discordant clocks announced not only midday but my simultaneous arrival into a world, a world still stunned by the Great Depression.

Hammerwood House, my home, was a late Georgian country house in West Sussex. The name derived from the adjacent Hammer Woods, the scene of early iron-smelting activities: nuggets of deep brown iron ore peppered the soft yellow sandstone banks that lined the sunken and still untarred lanes.

My parents' bedroom looked out to the south, across the hamlet of Iping toward the grey-blue horizon of the South Downs. For many years, these hills, five miles distant, remained the outer edge of my world, infinitely remote and mysterious. Across the entire panorama only the square church tower reached up through the trees to suggest human habitation.

In this church, a few weeks later, I was christened; Gerard Wyndham. The rim of the font was massed with primroses and narcissi were ranged against the base. Great branches of bird cherry stood against the wall in huge rectangular glass battery cases, borrowed from the electric light plant that lit the house and established my father as a *grand amateur* of electrics.

The name Gerard crops up at irregular intervals in the Grenville family tree ever since the twelfth century. My godfather, Sir Percy

Wyndham, evidently gave me my second name but naught else. There must have been expectations, never fulfilled. I do not believe he ever saw me again, nor do I recall his name being mentioned. But for sixty-nine years, I have been stuck with an empty name, unhappily but appropriately adapted during prep-school days to Windy.

In my early years, my mother kept photograph albums erratically annotated with my weights and measurements.

I look now at the first album and see a photograph of Sir Percy, much darkened with age, in which a tall and grave middle-aged man, in stiff collar and great-coat, stands in the church porch. He wears a trim beard and looks exactly like George V on the postage stamps that I later collected. Standing next to him my diminutive godmother, 'Bee' Goschen. Short of sight but long on generosity, she fulfilled her godmotherly duties to perfection and was the first outside adult with whom I felt comfortable. Between accidents, she drove herself in a dwarf Morris car with a huge silver bumble-bee fixed to the radiator: it was generally believed that this mascot marked her extreme limit of clear vision.

My parents were far from wealthy, in comparison to most of those of similar background, so it is all the more surprising to recall the extent of the staff that peopled my early years.

'Ninny' was my nanny: she stayed for twelve years and when she left my world tottered. Reuben was the head gardener and the object of a love-hate relationship, its course determined by how often I was caught stealing fruit. His wife Blanche was huge and kind and although these times were sadly before the era of deodorants, I relished being picked up and pressed to her great bosom. There was a chauffeur, Eastes, whom I scarcely recall and a very dear nursery maid, Emmie, who still spoils me with an extravagant tea if I visit her now, nearly seventy years on. I visualise Mrs Stocker (I never heard her addressed by a Christian name), the cook, standing by the kitchen table with a tray of Victoria sponge buns, stuffed with red glacé cherries which I extracted whenever I thought her attention was diverted. 'Ooh, Master Gerard, you'll get me into trouble you will, you naughty monkey, off with you!' There seemed to be little love lost between her and the black-coated, silver-haired and red-nosed butler, Passingham. I wonder what he could possibly have done to fill his days. He spent eons of time polishing glasses and silver in the sunless butler's pantry and I

recall his round-shouldered stoop as he shuffled in and out of the dining room with the dishes. Somewhere, well hidden, there was a bottle in his life. My indoor existence revolved around the day and night nurseries. Ninny, dressed always in mauve with a white apron and starched head-gear, was a model of responsibility, always punctual, never spoiling, always at hand.

Now and then, I would be decked out in my best clothes and trundled out of the nursery wing to be exhibited to visitors: I suspect that these performances gave me a life-long dislike of formal clothes. I dreaded the facile comments of strangers believing themselves obliged to say something. 'He's got your eyes Betty and Bill's figure, hasn't he? Not quite grown into his nose yet but I expect he will.' (He didn't) 'He *has* grown since I last saw him, hasn't he?' Had they expected me to shrink? 'Oh well, I expect you want to go back and play.' And then the inevitable 'shake hands and say good-bye' and, on being trundled out again a half-heard, 'What a dear little chap he is.'

Looking at these photographs it seems one endless summer, padding round the ten acres of garden, peering into sheds, smelling flowers, pushing a flimsy looking horse-on-wheels. There I am, looking anxious, sitting at a long table beneath the cedar tree, spread with a white cloth and piled high with sandwiches and cakes. It is a children's tea party, sixteen children, ten uniformed nannies. A *cordon sanitaire* divides this table from another: a few grown-ups, inhabitants of an alien world, are busy talking, facing away from the children.

Now, aged two and a half, I am playing with a pile of conkers; a year later, paddling at Trevenwith in Cornwall; it is July and the long beach is quite deserted. There was no road to the house then and I see a pile of cabin trunks and suitcases waiting to be carted across fields. King Arthur's Castle was here and there is a photograph of my brother John, born three years before me and then aged six, looking terminally bored; the caption reads *Morte d'Arthur* being read to John'. And now here's a photograph of a place I can actually remember - just - Garvocks, a family shooting lodge in Scotland.

There is the loch set in bleak moorland. At the water's edge, a tent, us two boys and half a dozen grown-ups; one seems to be slapping midges, another is delving into a huge wicker hamper. A moment in time and all those people now gone, except me. Even the loch has become a fenced reservoir for Glasgow. I remember my brother picking up empty cartridge cases from the grouse butts; red, green, blue, orange and all with the same captivating smell of exploded powder. And I recall being rowed across the loch in a heavy wooden boat that smelt strangely of something wonderful I later found to be varnish. Best of all, I recollect trying to dam up a lochside burn with my brother - an activity which never lost its magic.

It's the backgrounds of these photographs that especially engage my attention. Untarred roads, coppiced woodland, an absence of people, heavy elm wheelbarrows, old oak gates with solid ironwork, every workman wearing a waistcoat and tie and the women in hats.

I begin to see that I really belong to another age. These pictures evidence in every detail a conspicuous absence of prosperity. Even more noticeable is the scarcity of traffic, of posts, signs, aerials and ugly clutter. Village architecture has scarcely altered for a century or more; a few solid Victorian houses and shops are superimposed on Georgian streets. Town pavements seem almost deserted. Hedges are cleanly cut or laid and richly studded with tall trees, now mostly gone.

Chestnut coppicing was a common sight in West Sussex and hurdles were a local export. Every locality had its specialisation and communities were largely self-sufficient for meat and vegetables, butter and cheese. Carpenters and blacksmiths were plentiful and, between them, could make and repair almost anything. Horses still pulled carts and ploughs and there is a photograph of a Downland shepherd wearing a smock, a garment worn continuously since Saxon times. In those days, tithe barns and churches were excitingly large buildings which dominated the local view. Water mills were places of penetrating interest; the deep rumble of mysterious machinery, the rushing water of the tailrace and the occasional sight of a flour-covered miller were all grist to the imagination. There was no rubbish collection because households had so little. A broken jug, patent medicine bottles or a leaky bucket would lie half-buried at the end of the garden: the throwaway society was not yet even in sight. Electricity, with its hated pylons, was just beginning to disfigure the landscape. Early tractors and a few remaining traction engines attended the threshing of corn.

On Sundays, squires sat in their special pew at the head of the congregation. It was an ordered, disciplined society and the countries coloured red on the revolving globe in the nursery showed that my compatriots ruled a quarter of the world. The long shadow of the Emperor-Queen still influenced the parameters of my upbringing.

Summer. The day starts with my running round the house six times, followed by a cold bath and 'drying' with some kind of non-absorbent material which, via simple skin-chafing friction, is supposed to warm the body. In winter, no cold bath but porridge for breakfast. Disgusting retch-producing porridge. As the Frenchman said in his first encounter with it, 'am I supposed to eat this or has someone already done so?' Repeated refusal to eat the foul stuff results in being sent out. Being found by my father outside in the passage results in a beating. Similarly, all other food, no matter what, which is presented to us on a plate, must be eaten; eaten or beaten was the general rule. 'Waste not, want not' was the guiding principle of life, later much reinforced by wartime food shortages. It is with mixed feelings when nowadays I regard the plates of children with mounds of rejected food yet feel compelled to empty *my* plate whether or not I want the food.

Another photograph: I am on a horse, aged six and looking most unconfident, a situation that has never altered. The same year, I am in a pedal car, an open Vauxhall, with two little doors, a running board and, joy of joys, a klaxon. Another: I am on a haystack. And in them all I wear a tie. The next year finds me in a group of four, a music class consisting of drum, tambourine, cymbals and for me, a triangle: the sound must have been appalling.

Christmas Day. Every year a different tree but *never* a conifer with its German connotations. This year it is an apple tree and it is in full blossom; each leaf, each flower has been made and fixed to the branches by my mother, behind the locked doors of the drawing room. As soon as it is dark, the multitude of candles are lit: my brother and I, together with the people of the little village, are invited in. I hold my breath in wonder at the splendour and the magic. A tall Father Christmas hands us all presents and, accompanied on the piano by my mother, we sing Christmas carols. The grown-ups have rum punch and begin to talk. Father Christmas becomes too hot, removes his hat and beard and I am astonished and hugely disappointed to see that it is my father.

Every year until the war we went on holiday, piling into a large car with luggage stacked on a rack behind the boot. The cases were secured with leather straps, the surplus length being neatly coiled: I still have those straps, mouldering and stiff with age.

Each year my parents 'took' a house. When I was five, they hired the Manor House at Field Dalling in Norfolk. The photographs show immense beaches at Holkham, peopled solely by us two boys and a (still) uniformed Ninny, her shoes submerged.

In 1937, when I was six, they rented the Villa Küpelviese at Pörtschach on the shore of Lake Werthersee in Austria. Hitler must have been casting a dark shadow but I remember nothing of this. It was a *fin-de-siècle* wooden villa with balconies, finials and fretted barge-boards and in the garden was a fir tree which dropped long sausage-like cones with smooth scales. Meals were taken outside on a tiled terrace whilst black squirrels ran riot in the trees. There were toadstools, red with white spots and a lovely unmown lawn. It was here that I encountered bath sheets, rectangles of linen used to line the bath so that we didn't 'catch anything'. Brahms had lived in this house and for some reason, that impressed me deeply even then. The place excited me vastly and must have awoken me to the delights of 'abroad'. These were increased still further by the arrival of Lisa, the *première* ballerina in Vienna. She was stunningly beautiful, had long golden hair and wore Austrian national dress in which she cart-wheeled and cavorted across the grass, seemingly weightless. The following year she fled the Nazis and arrived unexpectedly at Hammerwood and a photograph shows her teaching me to stand on my head. I wonder what happened to her. Amongst the Austrian souvenirs packed into the car for the return journey was Eleisa, a maid selected by my mother to give to an aunt.

... balconies, finials + fretted barge-boards.

In those now far-off days, driving on the Continent was itself an adventure. The minor roads were often unsurfaced and progress was accompanied by a cloud of dust which gave advanced warning to village children who would line the road and wave frantically. To them a car was an event, a foreign car a big excitement. Village doorsteps provided seats for black-clad women who would sew, shell peas and perform a large range of domestic tasks all within gossiping distance of neighbours. Punctures were not infrequent and we travelled with two spare wheels. Petrol was of varying quality and regular stops were made to clean carburettors of water and dirt. Continental maps were poor, the roads often unsigned and much time was spent in asking directions, a thing which sometimes resulted in long exchanges between my mother and the stranger from which she would glean an extraordinary range of information to be translated and shared amongst us passengers as we sped on our way.

At seven, they took La Roche at Plougrescant in Brittany. My strongest memory is of the earth-closet which spanned a usefully deep cleft in a rocky bluff. Inside was hung an orange stuffed with cloves. The lavatory paper, Bromo, had come out with us. This came in individual sheets packed into primrose yellow boxes on which were printed the numerous medals won by the makers, and I remember wondering how lavatory paper competitions were organised. I still wonder. Half a century later, I found another box of Bromo in an abandoned British station in Antarctica and even in that far-off place, in freezing isolation, the image of that earth-closet and the smell of the pomander returned in force.

... The earth
closet spanned
a usefully
deep cleft ...

These photographs in Brittany show, once again, deserted beaches; black-dressed peasant women with the white coif of their region, wheeling massively built carts with iron-hooped wheels; kneeling to wash clothes in the stream and carrying tall and heavy buckets of water from the distant village pump. Their faces, craggy, weatherbeaten and prematurely old, speak of continual heavy toil. Blissfully unaware, I dug immense canals in the sand and sailed my model yacht. I also loved drawing: just recently I came across a sketch I made then of the little church at Port Blanc and a photograph shows it to be encouragingly recognisable. In the background is the American Buick car in which my father drove us here.

Then, at eight, just one month from war, we go to Amroth Castle near Tenby. War, or its prospect, means to me the continual and increasing anxiety stamped on the face of every adult. Conversations suddenly seem stilted: war must be a bad thing. We return early. Talk seems to stop when I enter a room. War must be a very bad thing. I wonder what it is. Yet people seem to be kinder to me, more forgiving than usual. Maybe it's a good thing after all.

The failure of Sir Percy to perform as godfather resulted in due course in his replacement by a man named James Robertson Justice, a successful actor, who for many years played rumbustious parts in films of dubious cultural value.

The world of actors was entirely alien to the social circle surrounding my parents and he was therefore a most unlikely choice of god-parent. They had met him many years earlier whilst returning to England on a small steamer from Capetown. One evening after dinner, as they were sailing along the Skeleton Coast off Namibia, my parents were having a romantic stroll on deck under a full moon before turning in for the night. They somehow strayed into an area intended only for crew. A burly stoker, black of face and in sooty overalls was declaiming from memory in the direction of the moon, the whole of Milton's *Paradise Lost*. My mother, astonished, introduced herself: the stoker gave his name as James Justice, explaining that he was working his passage home having lost his all in South Africa.

There were several subsequent literary vigils on the after-deck. Shortly before landing at Southampton, James asked to borrow five pounds 'to see him home'. They did not expect to see it again.

One afternoon, a few years later, there was a knock at the front door. It was James who had walked the six miles from Liphook Station to Hammerwood. In his hand he held five £1 notes and an old leather-bound copy of Milton, inscribed to my parents.

I only ever saw him once, many years later. Without prior warning, he appeared in an open silver Rolls-Royce, a falcon perched on the back seat. Godfather though he was, he had to be introduced to me. As he drove away, he threw a scrumpled up ball of paper at me. Idly I unscrumpled it: it was a five pound note, a large white sheet with black print promising to pay me five whole pounds. As the deep note of the exhaust faded into the distance, I was left jumping for joy.

I have reached my ninth year and have scarcely mentioned my parents. Though they were later to become the closest of friends, my early years were lived largely via parental proxy.

Encounters with my father were, in principle, to be avoided. Although no doubt he tried, he was not a born lover of small children. A generation later and still at one remove from daily contact with them, I found myself similarly distanced. He had an all-seeing eye for misdeeds and a memory to match. He escaped his children and also - as soon as good manners permitted - the stream of guests invited by my mother, for the further reaches of the large garden which was his earthly paradise. He and my mother had created it from scratch. I can see him now weeding, watering and pruning with ceaseless activity. The garden grew larger every year. The lawns alone entailed following a huge Dennis motor-mower some twenty miles for a single cut. If one of our games resulted in a broken twig, it was certain to be noticed until my brother and I became expert in the art of camouflage. One day, however, we incurred such colossal damage that it could not be concealed. I had persuaded my brother to curl himself up inside an old motor tyre which I then rolled down the long and sloping lawn. It soon arrived, at speed, at the principal shrubbery through which it crushed a path like a small tank, but the explosion of anger which we expected never happened, something we pondered for weeks, even years afterwards.

Another escape for him was the workshop where he delighted in mending engines and tinkering with cars. It was here that I made my first real contact with him: he enjoyed explaining the workings of the internal combustion engine and found me a willing pupil. But his safest bolt-hole was the electricity generating building. This housed his pride and joy, a Ruston-Hornsby diesel generating set, its larger components painted green with an inset red line. The huge engine possessed a great flywheel and to start it each morning (there was no electricity at night) my father would climb the spokes of the wheel, ever faster, like a hamster on a treadmill, as the engine coughed its way into life. Entry to this sanctum was utterly forbidden and I had to content myself by looking through the window at the whirling wheel and the spinning governors as my father did his rounds with oil can and rag. Next door was the abandoned gas plant by which means the house had been lit earlier in the century.

My mother, although invariably sweetness and light, inhabited another world; social, charitable, musical and busy with an abundance of entertaining. Thus it was, in various forms, in country houses up and down the land until the war. But the genes of my parents and the events of their lives impacted upon me in numerous ways. They still do.

The Grenville family-tree goes back, with the imaginative assistance of the College of Heralds, to Rollo and the Duke of Normandy in the tenth century. It is probable that a Grenville came over from Normandy at about 1066 though not with William the Conqueror's invasion. The name is untraceable since the numerous variants over the years make precise geographical location a matter of guesswork. Although the historian A. L. Rowse believes the Grenvilles originated in Upper Normandy, I think it more likely that the name derives from either Grandeville (large town) or Grainville (grain town). In Lower Normandy, around Caen, there are permutations aplenty: Granville, Grinville, Grainville, Grenteville. (State papers of Elizabethan days show the family name spelt variously Greenfield, Greynvile and Grynvile.) When half a century later, by coincidence I found myself living in that region, I half expected to experience a sense of belonging; it was remarkable for its absence!

The family took root in England and at an early date, acquired ownership of an estate on the borders of Oxfordshire and Buckinghamshire at Wotton Underwood. There, the oldest family burial chapel in Britain houses Grenville tombs from the twelfth century. The estate was in the continuous possession of the family until early last century.

For hundreds of years, the Grenvilles pursued the even tenor of their way as country gentlemen, taking no important part in public affairs. In the sixteenth century, a branch of the family was established in Devon. Sir Richard Grenville, a cousin of Sir Walter Raleigh and the most illustrious of this branch, was famed for the epic destruction of the Spanish Armada in 1588 and was also the first man to *found* a colony in North America (1585 on Roanoke Island). It is ironic that his kinsman George Grenville, when First Lord of the Treasury, was author of the Stamp Act in 1765 which led directly to the *loss* of the American colonies. Sir Richard lived at Stow near Kilkhampton (since demolished) and it is a curious coincidence that, via marriage to the Temple family, Stowe (near Buckingham) became the main Grenville family seat as well as the largest house in Britain.

The influence of Stowe is hard to exaggerate. It became an immensely powerful political base. From the 1730s, Grenvilles frequently held Cabinet office, providing two Prime Ministers, a Home Secretary, a Lord Privy Seal, a Foreign Secretary and a First Lord of the Admiralty. They acquired an Earldom, a Marquessate and in 1822, the Dukedom of Buckingham and Chandos. By this time, the estate extended to 70,000 acres of which 9,000 formed a 'managed' landscape surrounding the house. Today, on fewer than 700 acres, it remains the finest landscape garden in Europe, now magnificently cared for by the National Trust.

Via judicious marriages, political alliances, government sinecures and innate shrewdness, the family acquired colossal power and wealth. They also acquired a degree of avarice and ostentation which led directly to financial disaster. Both the First and Second Duke were fond of 'shopping' – a painting here and a statue there. Constant attempts to raise money involved shuffling assets, negotiating loans, delaying payments and selling their heritage – a single consignment to be sold at Christie's lists 1,000 pictures. Vast sums were spent entertaining Queen Victoria and others in princely style. In 1848, the Second Duke went spectacularly bankrupt. This entrained the sale of the century, a five-day bonanza for collectors. Though he died in penury, his funeral was not unlike that of a monarch: troops and tenants lined the route, guns were fired and the ducal coronet was borne on horseback before the carriages of the mourners.

My great grandfather, Richard Plantagenet Campbell Temple-Nugent-Brydges-Chandos-Grenville, the third and last Duke (whose five-barrelled name entitles him to an entry in the Guinness Book of Records) was a hard-working and supremely honest steward of a ruined estate. He saved both Stowe and Wotton, as well as 10,000 acres, but failure to produce a male heir, even with two wives, terminated the dukedom. His eldest daughter, Baroness Kinloss (my grandmother) married Louis Morgan (of nearby Biddlesden Park) hence the name Morgan-Grenville. After her eldest son (my uncle Richard) was killed in the Great War, Stowe and its still fabulous contents was sold in 1921, a sale which lasted an incredible nine days.

Although partially denuded of content by forced sales in the previous century, the remaining inventory was quite remarkable. Besides numerous paintings by great masters, superb statuary, furniture and tapestries, a magnificent library and a vast array of *objets d'art*, there was also a staggering quantity of virtually everything else: a glance at the sale catalogue reveals, for instance, over 500 bottles of sherry, more than 100 ormolu ornament brackets and 350 flint-lock rifles.

In the four years following the First World War about a quarter of the landed area of England changed hands: Stowe was but a part of this avalanche. In 1923, the house became Stowe School.

Even though sale prices were depressed at the time, it is a source of surprise to say nothing of regret, that so very little remained to the family thereafter. The crash of a pre-eminently powerful and aristocratic family was absolute. I have often been asked whether an awareness of such ancestral distinction has in any way influenced my life. I think that perhaps it has: a kind of 'been there, done that' consciousness has allowed me to view conventional achievement from a fairly detached standpoint.*

My father was born in 1892 at Biddlesden, (Stowe being let to the Comte de Paris until 1896). The family then returned to Stowe where with greatly reduced staff, palatial life was resumed. The table in the state dining room seated 100 and in various roof spaces, there was a warren of servants rooms yet by 1920 there were only four indoor staff left. Funds were swiftly running out.

My grandmother, a stern character of unbending moral rectitude, was distant to her five children. She placed a cane inside my father's school trunk: attached to it was a note to the Housemaster recommending its use. Back at Stowe for the holidays and judged to have told a lie, my father was made to walk through the streets of

*See *The Rise and Fall of the Grenvilles* by John Beckett

Buckingham wearing a huge red tongue bearing the words 'I am a liar'. These and other unkindnesses left him with a stammer for life.

After being wounded at the second battle of the Somme and having convalesced, he became an instructor for the newly formed Royal Flying Corps. After the War, he returned to discover the family exchequer empty and soon found himself trying to make ends meet working in a Cornish tin mine. He married in 1916 but his wife, Irene, died in childbirth. Their son, Robert, my half-brother, was fifteen years old when I was born. He became a farmer in East Africa when I was eight; I scarcely knew him.

In succession, my father drilled for oil in Romania (where a doorless lorry he was driving through a forest - and which was only firing on three of its four cylinders - was chased for miles by a pack of wolves); mined for diamonds in Afghanistan (driving the first ever car, a Model T Ford, into Kandahar); panned for gold in East Africa (and was pushed across much of Kenya on a bicycle) before returning to England and involving himself as an adviser in the electrification of private houses. But by this time, he was married to my mother to whose origins I will now turn.

My mother's maternal grandparents, the Stoddards, both came from Massachusetts. Although themselves of Pilgrim Father origins, they reversed the flow and ultimately settled in Scotland, Arthur Stoddard having rescued the Glenpatrick carpet works near Glasgow from the edge of bankruptcy. Arthur was a merchant and entrepreneur of vast energy. In pursuit of his business, he crossed the Atlantic more than fifty times in sailing ships that often took thirty to forty days to make the east to west crossing - the equivalent of over two whole years spent on just one leg of his commuting life. If American get-up-and-go genes have survived, they can be traced to Arthur Stoddard and his wife who frequently accompanied him. Undoubtedly from the same source, my mother inherited a strong love of family, tempered with a puritanical streak, a fondness of adventure, a sharp mind, an artistic bent and an unflagging confidence in the Almighty.

Sir Charles Renshaw was my mother's father. He had married one of Arthur Stoddard's daughters, Mary, and in due course acquired and ran the substantial Stoddard carpet works. He was also Chairman of the Caledonian Railway Company. Rare for his day, he treated his employees as fellow human beings and later, when a Member of Parliament, his constituents as genuine and equal friends. He was a keen sportsman and was noted for his sense of fun. From Sir Charles, my mother inherited his liberality of spirit and natural ebullience.

The twin streams of character from the two sides of her family were combined, without loss, in my mother's make-up. I realise full well, that for a son who adored his mother, it is inevitable that she will be viewed through rose-tinted spectacles. Yet it is still possible to be objective since her life was chronicled in many ways.

I have a vignette of her at eighteen (in 1910), living in the family castle Barochan in Scotland. She wrote excellent English, could speak fluent French and German, good Italian and a little Gaelic, was conversant with the classics in English, French and German, was an accomplished poet, a first-rate pianist, a good violinist, a competent artist, a fearless side-saddle rider-to-hounds, an enthusiastic fly-fisher, a proficient botanist (her collection of East African flowers is in the Natural History Museum) and ornithologist, as well as an outstanding epée fencer in which she might have represented the country had not her father prevented her so doing. She had an intense appreciation of the beauty of nature. It is also clear that hers was a wild spirit. She was forever climbing trees, running along burns, sitting in a drifting rowing boat on piles of cushions beneath a parasol, devouring book after book or sewing clothes for 'adopted' children in London's East End. But she was also mercurial and given to quick bursts of temper. She never wasted a single second. Photographs show her to have been a beautiful girl, as does a portrait by the society painter de Laszlo. In later life, she undoubtedly became over-protective of her children but, this apart, it is difficult not to admire her extraordinary range of accomplishments or her virtuous and loving character, forged on the anvil of tragedy when her adored husband, Frank Gull, was killed in 1918 at Favreuil, shortly before the Armistice, in an action for which his Divisional General had recommended him for the Victoria Cross.

My mother and father married four years and six years respectively after the deaths of their first spouses. My father and my mother's husband had been in the same regiment, the Rifle Brigade, and knew each other quite well. Both my parents had been deeply in love and found it extremely difficult to adjust to the new situation, in spite of each having the utmost regard for the other. It took them many years to become the devoted couple of their later lives.

CHAPTER 2

A war-time child – evacuees and evacuation – I discover my mother - an idyllic countryside – tutors – destruction of a tutor's car – derailing a train - a fearful prep school – Eton – tea with two Queens – last days of freedom – spectre of the Army – a sudden revelation about knowledge

THE THIRD of September 1939.

'Come along boys: hurry up, the car's waiting!' Ninny is standing at the bottom of the back stairs shouting up at us. 'Don't worry about your laces, I'll see to them in the car.'

What's the hurry I wonder?

My brother John and I are driven off to the house of a prosperous neighbour to play with the children, boys exactly our age. I feel disadvantaged: they have a huge playroom, masses of lead soldiers and spring-loaded field guns firing hard little pellets to knock them over. I am never allowed the guns so I busy myself standing the soldiers up ready to be knocked down by my seniors. Two more children arrive, girls - irrelevant.

In the nursery, three nannies sit round a table on which stands a large and shiny wooden box with a rounded top and, on one side, an illuminated dial and three knobs. In this wealthy household, the nanny has her own wireless set. I go in and am signalled to shut up; a man's voice issuing from the box has the three nannies spellbound. They stare at the wireless as though expecting him to emerge from it. I have never seen Ninny look so solemn and am at once alarmed. The announcer says something about a 'state of war existing' at which all the nannies gasp, look at each other and two of them hurry from the room. Ninny remains, sees my alarm and says:

'Nothing to worry about, dear. Pull up your socks and go back and play with Jimmy there's a good boy.'

It's definitely this word 'war' which is bugging them all. Although the grown-ups all look as though they've seen a ghost, they also become inexplicably indulgent. *This* now becomes a worry.

For months, things carry on much as normal including the conversations suddenly truncated when I or my brother appear. Christmas comes and goes, leaving me with a second-hand bicycle.

Then one day, Ninny says:

'Tomorrow some evacuees are coming to stay. They come from the East End. You must be very nice to them: they've left their Mummies and Daddies behind and haven't ever been in the country: they'll feel lost so you must help them.'

East End of what, I wonder. And why have they left their mummies and daddies; it seems odd and adds to my general anxiety.

They come, about half a dozen of them and about my age. They wander about silently in a tight bunch with expressionless white faces. Two of them defecate on the terrace in front of the drawing room window. They seem short of shoes: some of mine disappear to make good the deficiency. We stand, the evacuees and me, a fair distance apart and stare. 'Why don't you play with them?' says Ninny, ashamed at my unfriendliness. But how can I? They are from another planet, speak a different tongue, have very short hair, funny clothes and have begun to play with my toys. We circle each other at a safe distance, mutual dislike clouding the air. The same week, my father and Reuben the gardener dig a huge pit, 100 or so yards from the house, futilely attempting to do so unobserved. The Crown Derby dinner service, the Worcester armorial plates, the Sèvres tea service, Dresden figurines and loads of silver are buried in a pit of sand. Immediately after this, two air-raid shelters are constructed, one for the staff and one for the family: this last in due course collapses under its own weight. But the first bombshell to land is verbal: we are called into the library - an unusual and sinister event. My father looks tired and somehow different, and my mother looks as though she has been crying. There is no preamble.

'As you know' says my father, repeatedly trying to smile but failing 'there's this war. I've been trying to join the army to do my bit but they won't take me; say I'm too old. Instead we're all going to Gloucestershire. I've got a job making aeroplanes. We're going in a week's time. Ninny's coming too. We've found a house in a village. The evacuees will stay on here in the care of another family to whom we've let the house. As soon as the war's over, we'll come back.'

An impenetrable fog of gloom descends as the packing begins. Drawn faces and hurrying steps. My questions go unanswered: I seem always to be in the way. Sudden insecurity steals up behind me. I go quiet and this seems to add to the tension.

Almost immediately it is my ninth birthday. When I was seven, I had a cake in the shape of a steam engine, at eight it was the figure eight and now, a van arrives from Searcy Tansley in Sloane Street bearing a magnificent cake in the shape of a house and decorated in icing so that it has dark blue windows with pale blue shutters, pink hollyhocks against the wall, red roses over the dark blue front door. The whole stands on a board which has a lawn, a path and a vegetable garden.

I remember this because it was half-eaten when we left and it was the first thing I ate when we arrived at the new house, a moment characterised by the deep dejection of the party, exacerbated by my unbounded excitement at exploring a new place, small though it seemed.

The Court at Withington, some nine miles south of Cheltenham, housed us for a year. My Mother succeeded in turning, seemingly overnight, into an accomplished cook and housekeeper. Now, for the first time, I saw her daily. We went on walks and bicycled on the empty roads. She taught me the names of flowers and trees in both Latin and English, read me stories and played with me. Suddenly I found myself possessed by a most loving and protective mother and was deeply happy. Too happy perhaps.

The war remained a distant and vague idea. But one night a jettisoned bomb landed a few fields away although near enough to bring the ceiling down on the gardener and break his nose. As there was mutual loathing, I was delighted! The war lurched a little nearer. A dog-fight in the sky above brought it nearer still. Food becomes scarcer; sugar, chocolate, butter gradually disappear. Then come the deaths of individuals known to my parents. Civil Defence, talk of invasion and their reluctance to open *The Times* and read the latest shipping losses all contribute to the scales falling from my eyes, yet it is still all at one remove from me.

I am sent to a prep school already evacuated to Padstow in Cornwall, accompanied by my brother John, now in his last term there. It is hateful, in spite of brotherly protection, but I am saved by the sudden bankruptcy of the school, caused, I learn later, by a general parental fear that a German Invasion will cut off the Cornish peninsula. An American godmother of my brother offers to have us both for the war. My parents decline which was as well - the ship on which we would have sailed was sunk. Instead a tutor arrives. He has an Austin Seven and parks it on the sloping circle of gravel in front of the house. I hear a clicking sound and observe that with each click, the wheels turn the merest fraction. There is no one looking so I give the car a helpful push and it starts forward slowly, gathering speed. Appalled, I try to pull it back but it runs faster and falls from sight over a terrace wall. The next morning, the tutor leaves but without his car. Suspicion centres on me but since it's clear that no-one saw me do anything, there seems no point in owning up.

The good ladies of the Withington Women's Institute rise in unison to face the food shortages which daily become more serious. They toil through the summer to lay by a store of jam with the last of the sugar, the entire stockpile being stored in our cellar. These jam pots are sealed with a taut cellophane cover. It so happens that by chance, I discover that if the cover is pierced, there is a satisfying 'pop' which is a source of mild pleasure. With the aid of a table knife and in the spirit of the times I therefore bomb all the pots. Some months later, with food even shorter, it is decided to distribute the jam. Every pot has grown a luxuriant grey mould. The culprit is identified and to his infinite embarrassment made to appear before a plenary session of the Institute and blurt out an apology.

My brother and I hear a story about the French Resistance derailing German trains. This really ignites the imagination. Only one field distant is a branch railway line running along a steep embankment. We place a penny piece on the rail, wait for the train and hunt for the flicked off coin once it has passed: it is twice the size. We do it again and again and although expensive and wildly time-consuming, we create some immense pennies, the Victorian ones, being the softest, become the largest, saucer-sized. Since this does not derail the engine we place a large stone on the line and hide 100 yards back. Putting our ears to the rail we hear the train approaching about a mile away, then we see the moving column of steam, hear a hoot and a goods train thunders round a bend toward the stone. I am suddenly aghast at what we have done but it is too late. A steel deflector in front of the bogies flicks the stone off the line. But the driver has seen it and soon the policeman does a round of the village asking questions which are surprisingly easy to answer evasively. The age of innocence is over.

In rural Gloucestershire, in the early years of the war, there was almost no traffic on the roads. This is my abiding memory of that period. Out there beyond the confines of the garden was a world to be explored, a world whose limits were defined by the distance I could propel my bicycle and return by the appointed hour. Signposts had been removed or turned around to confuse potential parachutists. Grass grew in an endless strip along the middle of the lesser lanes - successive pot-holes caused one to cross and recross, a small bonus to the excitement of cycling. Farmers had not yet grubbed out ancient hedges which divided the small valley fields nor cut down the hedgerow trees which in so much of lowland Britain gave the landscape the appearance of an endless forest.

All hands helped at harvest to stook the sheaves and load the cart. The reward for helpers was to shoot the rabbits from the ever-diminishing area of standing corn, and glean the fields for any remaining ears with which to feed the chickens. In bad weather, a field might only have been partly laid, then being beyond the reach of the reaper-binder machines, it became a gleaners' paradise.

Tractors were small and unintimidating except when it came to starting them with the handle: then they could kick the unwary by a sudden counter rotation and break a hand or fingers. Fuel for tractors was very precious; so many tankers running the gauntlet of German U-boats in the North Atlantic had been torpedoed, leaving their crews to jump into the burning seas or fill their lungs with crude oil. The sight of a fuel can was inseparable from such dark images and once when I knocked one over and lost a pint or two into the dry stubble, I could feel the unexpressed anger of those around me, silencing me into shame for lighthearted carelessness.

Yet, as I look back, I am conscious of a golden era, untroubled by the hideous events and nameless fears which those of an older generation took such care never to mention in front of children. In my mind's eye, I see only two kinds of weather, constant sunshine or deep snow, the background to a time overflowing with possibilities of pure enjoyment. Other than a bicycle I needed few toys (more or less unattainable in the War anyhow) for the countryside around yielded up treasures of many kinds. To poke around in a nettle-covered scrap-heap and discover a bent wheel or temporarily divert a small stream to create an island kingdom or listen to a story from an elderly council lengthsman clearing ditches - such ploys filled hours of carefree existence.

Occasional tractor sound apart, the countryside was silent, if in this silence you include, as I do, the irregular calling of farm animals, the singing of the birds and the hum of insects. It was unimaginable then that I was to witness the end of quiet and the dimming of the starry firmament. Half a century later, millions of cars, lawn-mowers, strimmers, chain saws and aeroplanes have seen off the silence, just as street lights have become the enemy of the stars.

In those days, the villages were largely peopled by labourers and their families, living on earnings which left little or nothing for hard times. They mostly spoke with strong regional accents and in Gloucestershire quite a few nouns had genders. For example, a tap for hot water was 'she' and for cold, 'he'. They inhabited damp cottages that might now be condemned. These homes of weathered stone and rusty corrugated iron sheds were bright with flowers from wicket-gate to front door and flanked with unsprayed vegetables that proclaimed the earthy skills of their owners. In spite of their relative poverty, there was never a lack of hospitality for us boys nor were there accusations of patronisation when my mother brought soup to sustain the sick.

In the intervening years any negative aspect there may have been to country life as it then was, has erased itself from memory and I look back on that period of my life as a blissful era, untouched by the horrors of war or the least realisation that Britain was within weeks of starvation, such were the shipping losses.

Not long ago, I went back to the Gloucestershire of my childhood. I found it violated by the chemical farmers who have poisoned the wild flowers, snatched out the hedges and despoiled the fragile landscape. Cattle and pigs have been imprisoned in batteries, the small-holdings are gone as have so many of the little wayside ponds. Swarms of immigrants now populate vast acreages of almost identical homes in artificial stone, whilst many of the wealthy have spent their fortunes ruining dilapidated old manors with pretentious and inappropriate alterations. Much the same is to be found across the country today. It is heart-rending for those who knew another Britain, a far, far cry from the Britain of today. In so many ways it was truly a different country. Too many people, this is the problem; a population of about twenty million seems to me to be about right for these islands.

Eventually the war edged into my life. A young man from the village whom I knew by sight was killed in action. Air-raids on Gloucester brought staccato replies from anti-aircraft guns and searchlights scoured the skies. Blackout was rigorously but politely enforced by the elderly village policeman. Distant barrage balloons were sometimes to be spotted which gave rise to the accurate proverb: 'When balloons be high no rain be nigh'. These were the occasional encroachments of war into the deep peace of those first years.

One winter's night, the sound of far-off explosions took us outside the house. The horizon toward Gloucester was lit with a pinkish and flickering glow. To save petrol and time, my father sometimes spent the night at the aircraft factory: this was one such night. My mother telephoned the factory switch-board and there was no answer. For some time it proved impossible to find out what had happened to my father and my mother's anxiety was terrible to witness.

Every Thursday, Mr Midwinter, the carter, whose large and jolly wife ran the village shop, set off with his horse and cart for Cheltenham and a round of deliveries and collections. I only accompanied him once but the memory of that eighteen mile round trip has never faded. On that occasion, there was a package to be collected from Cavendish House, Cheltenham's Department store, and included in it were some gramophone records. A night or two later, shortly after the light had been put out in my bedroom, I heard music of a kind that was new to me and which I found enchanting. I crept downstairs and listened at the door of the sitting room, entranced, rushing back to bed the instant it stopped, for to be caught meant paternal trouble. The next day my mother told me that it was a recording of Elgar's Enigma Variations. From that day forward, I had an insatiable appetite for classical music.

An aunt, whose children were much older, passed on to us a very large set of Hornby 'O' gauge model railway. There was far too much of it to lay out inside the house so, with my brother, I painted the rails to prevent them rusting, and created a railway network in the garden. With the expenditure of much imagination, this miniature railway seemed almost real and provided *huge* enjoyment. In the midst of this experience, my mother gave the lot to some neighbouring evacuees, in accordance with her belief that, in order not to become too attached to things material, one should always give away one's most treasured possession. This she always did but on this occasion, the model railway was ours, not hers. I felt deeply deprived and some forty years later, this railway deprivation was appeased only when I began to play instead with full-size trains.

Although whole days were squandered in damming up a tributary to the River Colne, sailing model boats on the resultant 'lake', fishing for crayfish and shooting the Rector's chickens with a home-made bow and arrow, education could not be entirely avoided. There were several tutors and governesses who attempted the forlorn task of teaching me. I was not a natural learner of the regimented information required for exams, a fact rendered in stark relief when my lessons were joined by the grand-daughter of the then Archbishop of Canterbury who was not only precocious but never, under any circumstances, did anything naughty. This painful disparity made lessons disheartening for me and put the instructors under pressure to improve my performance, though the lot of the tutors was precarious. One was dismissed because he was confused over the difference between blackthorn and hawthorn which, to my mother, marked him out as a simpleton and a second dear old man went when he was caught with his hand stuck up my shorts. The tutors were replaced by Miss Dodsworth, a sour spinster, who achieved the summit of human unpleasantness. She resembled a larger version of Queen Victoria, with her hair parted centrally, a mean mouth and hawkish eyes. Her secret key to education was intimidation and her methods included rapping the knuckles with the edge of a ruler, pulling hair, boxing ears and kicking shins. She amplifed these inducements to learn nothing with shouted sarcasm and unfair comparisons. She was a woman so foul that if I met her today I would enjoy slowly torturing her to death but alas she is already dead. Just recently, I met another of her victims whose feelings were identical. Why I never told my mother or why she did not see the situation for herself I shall never know.

Top left. Now six and the proud owner of the Vauxhall pedal car.
Top right. Aged 18 months, I am being held by Ninny, my nanny, in uniform as always.
Right. 1938, in Brittany, flanked by my brother John and my father.
Below left. Gas-mask parade summer 1939 at Hammerwood.
Below right. Lisa, the Austrian ballerina who taught me to stand on my head.

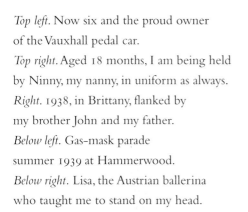

Top left. Claude Beasley-Robinson, my first Housemaster, managed to combine a deeply spiritual and austere lifestyle with that of a rich eccentric. He later became a monk.

Top right. Francis Cruso, my second Housemaster. Intellectual, musical and wonderfully indulgent, he shared my antipathy for team games.

Below left. Aged 13, my first year at Eton.

Below right. My brother John, at 19 during his National Service.

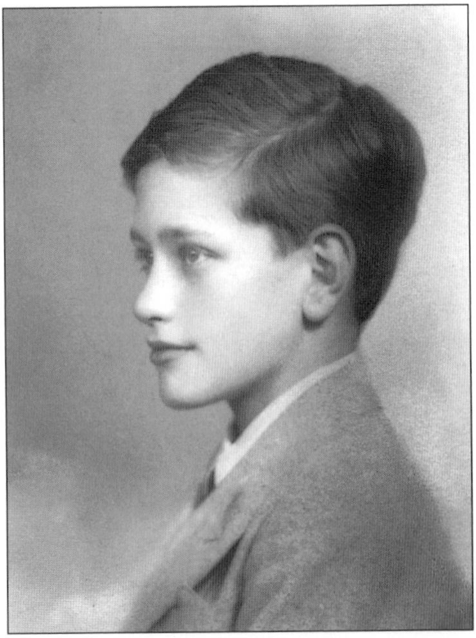

But worse was to come. The belief that I might not pass the Common Entrance Exam and therefore be ineligible for Eton projected me, aged eleven and a half, to a preparatory school, Heatherdown, which had been evacuated 'for the duration' to Downton Hall, a large late Georgian house near Ludlow in Shropshire. The stone parapet to the South Front had been sculpted with a huge Latin inscription meaning 'All good things come from God'. It soon became clear that God had therefore had nothing to do with the school. The drive was a mile long and the full horror of my being abandoned by my adored mother struck me with force when a petrol-starved taxi deposited us both at the entrance to this drive. I screamed and howled with spasms of unimaginable grief and begged to be taken home again. It was to no avail and I cried most of the time for the first three days. This and the fact that I was joining contemporaries now in their fourth year at the school, ensured that I would be bullied mercilessly. It took me two terms to work out how to hold my own and to make any friends. The staff, all of whom had avoided the war on one pretext or another, ranged from the unpleasant to the horrible. But at least I passed the exams.

The experience of Heatherdown did little to encourage my hopes of Eton. But my first term there coincided with my brother's last, as it had at my first prep school, and since we boarded in the same house, I had the prospect of some fraternal protection. But I need not have worried; after the horrors of my preparatory school, Eton, if not actually enjoyable that first year was easily endurable.

My Housemaster, until he retired three years later, was Claude Beasley-Robinson, a deeply religious man who subsequently became a monk. He created an oratory in the house and daily attendance for compline was obligatory. Unusually for someone of his calling, he tore around Eton in an open yellow Vauxhall, built in the late twenties and known as the Yellow Peril. He also hunted and employed a large black horse on which to ride the Thameside towpath to coach the house oarsmen with the aid of a large megaphone.

The war was in its last year and various missiles landed in the vicinity of the school. The blast from one - or was it fright I wonder now - capsized my slender boat as I sculled up the Thames. On many nights in the winter of 1944, we had to dash to the shelter where the damp fog of the Thames valley seemed to have its origin. Hours spent in its narrow confines gave me both pleurisy and pneumonia.

Eton was tolerant of those who disliked sport which was fortunate, for then as now, I found team games involving a field and a ball boring and, dare I say it, rather mindless. I suppose I should also add that I was fairly useless at them anyhow. The heterogeneous culture of Eton came to my rescue. With a friend, Christopher Cory, I made a roof garden on top of our House: it subsequently featured in an article in *Country Life*. We hauled up tons of earth and even made a pond with a fountain. Just after we both left, the roof collapsed, adding, no doubt, a fair sum to the school bills.

One winter, the Thames flooded and parts of Eton were submerged. As this threatened the functioning of the drainage system a notice was sent to each house warning boys not to put anything down a drain that could possibly cause a blockage. Naturally no time was lost in doing just this and the following day we were all sent home, leaving miles of drainpipe hopelessly clogged with pages from Homer.

Our corporate ability to avoid being taught was formidable. Masters (or 'beaks' as they were known) who could not keep order or who were elderly or unsuspecting almost invariably had cruel advantage taken of them. One tall, charming and frail man who tried to teach me history suffered a broken toe when the heavy blackboard, which had been set by a boy on the extreme edge of the easel pegs, crashed down on to his foot as soon as he applied the chalk to its surface. We thought it hilarious as he limped back to his desk, his jaw clenched in pain.

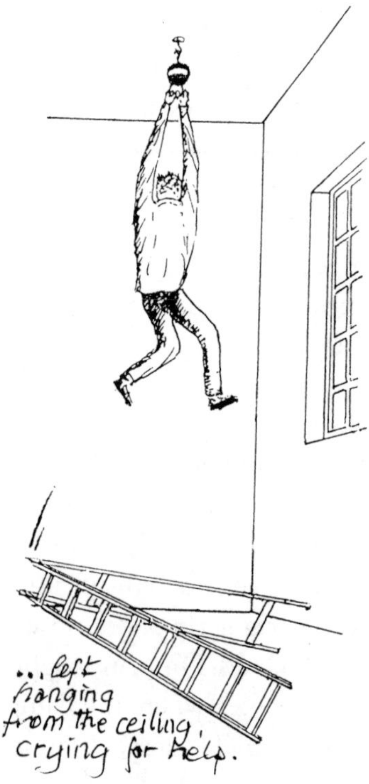
... left hanging from the ceiling, crying for help.

Another, whilst attempting to demonstrate atmospheric pressure with the aid of Magdeburg Hemispheres, climbed up some tall steps in order to hang the device onto a ceiling hook. At the instant he raised his weight off the steps (to show that atmospheric pressure kept the evacuated hemispheres together) the steps were 'accidentally' tripped over and the man was left hanging from the ceiling crying for help. Eventually he fell to the ground, hurting himself sufficiently for the class to be dismissed.

The tutor who taught me German was the victim of an old trick which required for its execution two half bricks. As soon as he faced away to write something on the blackboard, at a signal from the ringleader, one boy would chuck his half brick out through the closed window and the other would throw his at the master. Simultaneously, the boys would yell 'I'll get him, Sir' and rush from the classroom into the street, shouting 'there he goes' and, of course, running straight to the tuck shop.

For most of the time at Eton I remained something of an academic dullard, seldom scoring even average marks. My reports were all of the 'could do much better if he tried' category. One master wrote 'Try as I might, I have been unable to penetrate the woolly vacuousness of this boy's mind'. Another wrote damningly 'Although he is invariably polite when I speak to him, he doesn't seem to have the least perception of the purpose of education'.

I do not doubt that these reports were fairly accurate: Eton reports generally were. They reflected not only a slowness to mature but a positive instinct to ignore subjects which I believed I would neither need in the future nor could fully comprehend. My list included algebra, Latin, biology and chemistry and these omissions have proved to be appropriate for me. The teaching, certainly at that time just after the war, was not imaginative. Much of it, especially languages, was taught by the most tedious methods imaginable. (I recall my French tutor amazing us with the advice that the only way to learn the language was to have a French girlfriend.)

The privacy provided by our individual rooms, the houses being run by the boys rather than the housemasters, and the acceptance of unconventional behaviour were all trump cards in the Eton pack. It was this last feature that years later persuaded me that my two sons should also go to Eton, an undertaking only made possible by the great generosity of a friend. In my subsequent life, the fact of my having been to Eton was never advantageous in any business relationship but it has certainly been beneficial socially.

In my last year at Eton, at the end of each term (or 'half' as they were known there) my seventeen year old contemporaries left to start their obligatory National Service. As far as I know, they all went into the Army except for a very few who had chosen the Navy. I knew no-one then, nor did I ever know anyone in the following half century, who had joined the Air Force: some complex form of snobbery may have been partly responsible but I think it was more to do with the fact that most of our fathers had served in the army during the Great War, and the Regimental Tradition was still extremely strong. Families 'belonged' to particular regiments and it was widely assumed that succeeding generations would not voluntarily defect. A small remnant of the myopic, obese or flat-footed, escaped the call-up altogether and lingered on into their eighteenth year, thus occupying many of the most privileged positions in the school to the dismay of the rest of us. They then seemed to drift on into University where they were already well-established by the time their peers were demobilised.

The boys who left for military service seemed to disappear into a black hole: nothing was heard or seen of them for the remainder of my school days. Occasionally younger brothers, of which I was one, would receive letters reporting grisly details of the brutal army training which awaited us. So I did my best to draw an opaque curtain across all thought of the future and settled down to extract as much enjoyment as possible from the shrinking sum of months remaining.

In this endeavour I met with much success, living in a whirl of activity tailored as far as possible to the exploration of forbidden territory beyond the school boundaries and to the avoidance of academic effort. With the silent connivance of my warmhearted and courageously tolerant housemaster, Francis Cruso, I kept a motorbike (actually something called an 'autocycle', a forerunner of the scooter) in his distant garden shed, and was thus enabled to roam the Great Beyond.

One day my father collected me from Eton and took me to Langley Park, a large house near Iver in Buckinghamshire which my elder half-brother (still living in Kenya) had inherited from his deceased mother's family. The house had been built for the Duke of Marlborough as a reward for his successful campaigns. He turned it down as being far too small, thus securing Blenheim. Only a few miles from Eton, though quite out-of-bounds, Langley served for several years as the destination for many an expedition. With one or two friends we would sneak over and, with the connivance of the keeper, shoot duck in the winter, or in the summer swim in the lake or raid the hot-houses for grapes. An unusual feature at Langley was the family pew in the parish church. A door led into an adjacent library to which the Sunday papers were delivered. These could be read before a blazing log-fire during the rector's sermon.

The house and contents were to be sold and Queen Mary, the acquisitive wife of George V, wanted to see what was on offer. Together with the present Queen Mother, the two Queens arrived and were given tea. Before being 'presented' to them, I had been instructed that under no circumstances must I ever turn my back toward a Queen. The door to the drawing room was centrally placed and on entering I found to my dismay that the two Queens were at opposite ends of the room. I endeavoured to walk sideways towards the tea table with its single Queen, caught my foot beneath a rug and fell flat. The Queen Mother thought it hilarious; Queen Mary looked unamused.

In the dog-days of the last summer, I would scull up the Thames to Queen's Eyot, a slender island owned by the college on which was a kind of pub which dispensed a famously watered beer. But the hours toiling upstream engendered a huge and wonderful thirst so that even watered beer guaranteed a carefree return and, on hot days, an 'accidental' swamping.

Friends and numerous small celebrations formed the structure of this final year. As the hours passed ever faster, Eton exerted a strange and unexpectedly strong hold upon me. The old college buildings, even the lanes and paths, seemed to radiate their sense of history. Five hundred years of their accumulated wisdom reached out to me. I felt myself to be on the threshold of adventure, and there began an intensity of consciousness which was hugely exciting and which has never really disappeared.

Suddenly, I found myself actually *wanting* to learn. Years of boredom in hopeless confrontation with seemingly useless and badly taught subjects had dulled my modest mental powers. But now, quite unbidden, a bright new inquisitiveness possessed me. I scurried round the magnificent school library plucking books at random, igniting curiosities left and right; so much now seemed fascinating. I found myself memorising such entities as the manufacturers' marks of English china, the Orders of Greek architecture, the recognition of English period furniture. Yet, even as I rejoiced in this new consciousness and indulged myself as widely as I knew how, there lurked in the background a growing sense of approaching danger. The curtain I had raised against the thought of National Service was becoming transparent. I dashed to Luxmoores Garden, a then idyllic retreat beside the river, full of seats, bowers and small vistas, drank it all in and hurried onto the next escapist rendezvous.

I stood on the roof of my House at sunset and stared so hard at the dark silhouette of the neighbouring buildings that I remember it now fifty years on. I was in the double grip of a sudden nostalgia for Eton, and a potent awareness of an electrifyingly interesting world beckoning me forward. But between me and that lay the spectre of the Army. As the escaping months shrank to weeks and then to days, I crammed in every experience possible.

The Eton Cadet Force represented a beginner's version of army training. There were several hundred members and via a process I no longer recall, I found myself to be the senior cadet-officer. I strutted around with a swagger stick under my arm and surveyed my army. This ephemeral, unexpected and certainly undeserved command proved of some assistance a little later in the highly competitive scramble for the 'right' regiment.

CHAPTER 3

National Service training as officer cadet - discovering limits of ability - arrested - commissioned into Coldstream Guards - disillusion - transferred to Rifle Brigade in Germany - I lose my men - the dawn of Hope

THE CURTAIN was abruptly snatched aside. A brown envelope: "You will report to the Brigade of Guards Training Depot at Caterham, Surrey at 1600 on 2 September 1949".

The chestnuts outside the Depot were already turning golden yellow. A few freshly opened and sweet smelling conkers lay in the gutter. It was a cloudless autumn day, its perfection punctured by shouted commands flying over the barrack wall. There was still a good hour before the deadline of four o'clock. I turned to walk away, thought again and decided it might be wise to forego those final minutes of freedom in order to beat any last minute rush.

With sinking heart, I stood before the Guard Room at the entrance. An immense and impressively vertical soldier with a red sash across his khaki uniform, peered down at me, his eyes half obscured by the peak of his service cap. I stopped and stared. Then, drawing a deep breath I walked in, setting my suitcase down silently on the lower step in a calculated gesture of humility. Instantly, there was a roar:

'You there, what do you think you're doing?'

'I've come to report.'

'Well, report then! Get inside and look sharp.'

'Name?'

'Morgan-Grenville.'

'Sergeant! You call me Sergeant! Got it?'

'Yes, Sergeant.'

'Which is your surname Morgan or Grenville?'

'Both, Sergeant.'

'One of those with a fancy name are you? Spell it!'

'M-O-R-G-A-N-hyphen-G.'

'Hyphen! What's that? Three names then, very fancy!'

A soldier flew out of an inner room.

'Take this man to his barrack room. Now! At the double!'

It was the first time I had run with a suitcase and the first time I had had a soldier inches behind me shouting Left turn, Right turn, Get your knees up, Halt! Now *I* was in that black hole, lost to family, friends and the tantalising delights of civilisation that had been opening before me like a lotus-flower.

I entered a vast barrack room with, on each side, five open windows and eight bare beds. In just ten minutes I had become a gibbering recruit.

'That's my f...... bed' said the Trained Soldier, indicating the one nearest the door. 'If you've any sense, you'll choose one as far away from me as possible. My f...... feet smell and the man in the bed nearest me gets to wash them. Now get your f...... stuff stowed, make your bed and in five minutes, I'll march you to the f...... tailor's shop. Had any nice girls? I doubt it, you look like a mother's boy. Get a f...... move on, you look half asleep. Haven't you ever made a f...... bed before?'

As a matter of fact, I hadn't. Ever.

'Left-right, left-right, left-right-left! Swing your arms! Keep in line! Left-right, left-right, left-right-left! Look up! You're a f...... shower, you lot. You're a lot of f...... toffs. Corporal! Drill this lot till they drop. At the double! And if they can't march properly by the time I come back, you'll be doing it all night!'

With such sweet words of encouragement from the Sergeant, we learnt to march. We were each singled out in turn for our assorted failures, held to ridicule for our exaggerated antics. Round and round, up and down, back and forth across the square we went, in the cool of the morning and the heat of the day.

Twenty-six of us formed a platoon - we had all converged on this prison that fateful day. Twenty-six boys from public school pre-selected as potential 'officer-material'. We comprised one 'intake" and we were the focus of great attention, all of it exceedingly unwelcome. Issued with battledress, heavy boots, belts, anklets and beret, we were at once in the first stages of being de-personalised. Left-right, left-right, left-right-left permeated to our very souls. We marched and we marched.

Fatigue reduced us to automata. Tiredness and hunger ruled each moment. One day, when these thoughts occupied every available brain cell, I heard:

'You there, fifth rank, centre, you're out of line once again. Corporal! Give him an extra parade.'

Who's copped it this time I dimly wondered, then realised it was me. I began to think I couldn't survive another parade. There was no part of me that didn't ache or throb, no hidden reserves of strength, no fight left. We were standing to attention facing the Officers' Mess. Eyes Front. Motionless. The sun seemed to occupy the whole sky. Throats were like sandpaper. Trickles of dust-ridden sweat stung eyes.

The door of the Officers' Mess opened and a Captain sauntered out followed by a golden retriever. He approached our platoon. The Sergeant saluted.

'Sir! Platoon ready for your inspection, SIR!'

'Thank you' said the Captain with a quiet nonchalance. He walked slowly along the three ranks, his face perfectly blank, the dog at his heels, said 'Carry on Sergeant' and wandered back into the Mess. It was half past twelve and I imagined him downing a pink gin before lunch.

I decided then and there that I would bend every last bit of me into becoming an officer. A fresh layer of stamina mysteriously arrived. Later, much later, I wondered if this hadn't been the exact effect intended.

Rifle drill. Marching. Assault course. Marching. Machine-gun drill. Marching. On and on it went. Relentlessly. One man disappeared from our Platoon; he was there one moment and the next he was gone, never to be seen again. Another went sick for three weeks and was 'back-squadded' to the following intake in January. And then, on a parade at the end of a gruelling day, the man next to me fainted and fell forward onto his bayonetted rifle, slitting open a nostril and stabbing his head.

Every night we sat up polishing shoes, buckles, cap badges, 'blancoing' belts, anklets, cleaning rifles, laying out our battledress trousers beneath the three-part army mattress to ensure the requisite razor-edge crease. Often this went on after 'lights out' and it was common to fall asleep on the job. One day I argued, very mildly, with the Trained Soldier. He grabbed my highly polished boots and stamped on the mirrored toe-caps. It took me most of the night to repair the damage.

Life revolved around sleep and food and the total inadequacy of both. The barrack bed when first observed was clearly designed to create insomnia. The cookhouse food, when first sampled, was clearly not produced to eat. Within three days of arrival, I could have slept on a concrete floor and cheerfully eaten the disgusting food off the pavement.

Each morning there was a kit inspection and woe betide anyone with a 'deficiency'. Every item had to be set out in a certain way. The three sections that formed the mattress were piled on top of each other, the corners corresponding with absolute accuracy. Then the three, grey, Issue blankets had to be "squared', together with the sheets. Each piece of clothing was precisely folded, stacked. Mess tins, knife, fork, spoon, all must be gleaming and positioned exactly. In front of this bizarre display, we each stood at the foot of our bed, in perfect turnout, boot toecaps like black glass, webbing faultlessly 'blancoed', eyes to the front. As the inspecting officer approached with the accompanying sergeant and trained soldier, I would snap to Attention, barking the formula '22178217 Recruit Morgan-Grenville G. One pair boots at the Bootmaker, one shirt at the laundry otherwise all present and correct SIR'. This last bellowed at full voice. Simultaneously, the officer would look for irregularities: were there three blankets, was I properly shaved, hair of correct length? Then he might grab the rifle and peer into the breach and up the barrel. A speck of dust meant extra fatigues: a speck of rust something far worse. All of us learnt for the first time the meaning of the word 'clean'.

And then, after three months or so, a strange thing happened: it dawned on me one day that against all expectation, I was actually surviving; that for the first time in my life I was fit, that unbelievably, I was actually one of the more proficient at the dreaded assault course. Several of my companions were by now good friends. In short, I was coping. In a curious way I came almost to enjoy the marching; there was a corporate rhythm achieved by the precise timing of our movements quite as exact as that of a ballet troupe. It gave me a buzz to observe our proficiency as other, newer recruits shambled along in now laughable disorder.

I look back with the perspective of fifty years and realise that these months of 'basic training' were perhaps the most formative of my life.

If there was a moment when boy became man, it was then. The permanent hunger, the extreme weariness, the tedium, the occasional fear have all telescoped into irrelevance with the passage of time. But the self-reliance and sense of discipline which it engendered has remained. I realise now that this training was brilliant. Those responsible for carrying it out knew exactly how far to push each one of us. Whatever we were set to do *had* to be done. Excuses for failure were always counter-productive. Everything was subject to Regulations. A sleeve when rolled must have rolls of so many inches width. Barrack room windows must each be open so many inches according to season. A cap badge must be exactly over the left eye, not a fraction of an inch either side. Compliance with all rules was imperative since any neglect was certain to be noticed and disciplined. Those who have not experienced the army tend to ridicule the idea of such enforced uniformity; those who have 'done their time' know that it works.

To understand what it is like to feel fit was itself a revelation. To know that you are capable of climbing a rope, descending a drainpipe or scaling a high wall was not only most agreeable but as I found in later life, in socially delicate circumstances, potentially something of a lifesaver.

Then came a week of field training at Pirbright. Much of this was in 'full kit' an assortment of heavy packs, pouches, water bottle and steel helmet. A more challenging assault course awaited us. We crawled, with the heavy and bulky encumbrance of our kit, through claustrophobic drainpipes: learnt to tie a stone to the end of a rope, throw it over a high wall and then climb the free end. Using a branch of a tree, we would swing across water in the same fashion. There was a high beam which must be walked along; probably it was only ten or twelve feet from the ground but it felt like a hundred. There were gaps in its length which had to be stepped across, and those who suffered from vertigo fell into the sand below. Thus encumbered, we 'fought' our way through an assortment of obstacles which included the black depths of the Basingstoke Canal - three foot of mud and one of water - and terminated in an 'assault' on a steep hill. This incident has remained clear in my memory since it involved, whilst already exhausted, soaking, and heavily laden, picking up a supposedly wounded man, heaving him onto my shoulders and attempting to run uphill through deep soft sand. Some reached the top but I was not among them.

There were enjoyable interludes of rifle shooting at targets. Then there was bayonet practice on straw-filled 'German' dummies carried out to the obligatory accompaniment of blood curdling shrieks. It was especially repellent having to put your boot on the recumbent 'body', and twist the rifle in order to extract the steel blade from the 'rib-cage'. I found it all too easy to imagine being at the receiving end.

Next came several weeks at Eaton Hall, the Duke of Westminster's gloomy and hideous mid-Victorian Gothic pile, near Chester, which was requisitioned by the army, allowed to deteriorate and then thankfully demolished. The parades and marching continued apace, but were alternated by intensely boring lectures on subjects such as Fire Orders, foot inspection and, worst of all, TEWTS (Tactical Exercises Without Troops) which was as illuminating as a meal without food.

The pressure was relentless. There was never enough time allocated for any task, or even for getting from one place to another. This was doubtless intentional but resulted for me in a spell in a guardroom cell. Between a lecture and a parade, there was a five minute gap to get from one place to another as well as to change. One of my boots had a knotted lace that, in the time available, I could not undo. Was it better to spend more time undoing the lace and being late for parade (certain punishment) or risk being detected wearing one boot and one shoe? I chose the latter. As I walked out through the gate to reach the parade ground, I saw, to my horror, the Regimental Sergeant-Major (Ogre of Ogres) looking at each officer cadet as he walked through. It was essential to distract his attention, and to achieve this I could only think of repeatedly taking off and putting on my beret. It worked too well.

'You there! Come here! What's wrong with your beret?'

I stopped and moved towards the six foot six, 16-stone giant, coming to attention as close as possible, hoping thereby to make the disparate footwear less apparent. For several long seconds there was silence, then there was a gigantic roar.

'Sergeant! Put this man under close arrest!'

In the depths of winter, we went to 'battle-camp' at Okehampton. On the snowy slopes of Dartmoor, against an unremitting Siberian wind, we 'fought' our way ever upward, crawling under cover of live ammunition to encourage us to keep our bottoms down. After three days I found myself in the sick-bay with pleurisy. Two weeks out of training meant automatic back-squadding. With only hours to spare, I was pronounced fit and returned to duty.

At the end of seven months, I was commissioned into the Coldstream Guards and after a short leave, reported for duty at the barracks in Birdcage Walk, London. Joining this elite Regiment as a newly fledged ensign was a humbling experience. Resplendent in my new service dress, Sam Browne belt and Officer's cap, I walked, proud as a peacock, past the saluting sentry at the entrance, and made my way to the Officers' Mess. I could see platoons of soldiers being drilled and I remembered that officer I had seen amble out of the Mess at Caterham. I lacked the retriever, but I enjoyed a fleeting moment of exhilaration as I paused in the doorway to the Mess. I had made it.

It was about two o'clock in the afternoon. As instructed, I asked a Mess Servant to take me to the Adjutant, expecting to be shown the ropes, and introduced to my brother Officers. The Servant took me into the Mess where numerous Officers were drinking their after lunch coffee and reading. I was ignored, totally ignored. The Mess Servant indicated the Adjutant. He was seated in a deep leather chair reading *The Field*. 'Hullo' I ventured uncertainly. Not a flicker of movement. 'Hullo' I said again, a little louder. Without looking up he said: 'I don't know who you are but if you open your eyes you'll see I'm reading'. I backed off in a state of embarrassment and edged toward a table set out with newspapers and magazines, selected one, and sat down in another arm chair, one of the few left unoccupied. I buried my head inside the pages; almost at once someone passed, flicked at the paper saying: 'Commanding Officer's chair' and walked on. No-one, absolutely no-one said anything more to me. I got up and stood by the table with the papers. The Officers gradually disappeared, including the Adjutant, and soon I was alone in this huge room hung with portraits of the Regimental Great. It seemed that I was unwanted. What did unwanted Officers do?

Although the Coldstream Guards is one of the most celebrated regiments, and I had thought myself exceedingly lucky to have been commissioned into it, it had, nevertheless, been my second choice. I had applied for the Rifle Brigade (which, with the 60th, formed the Greenjackets Brigade). My father had fought in the Rifle Brigade in the First War as had two uncles, one of whom had been killed. My mother's first husband had also fought with the Rifle Brigade, and he too had been killed. It was most definitely my Family Regiment. There were, alas, no more vacancies for new Officers at that moment in either of the two Greenjacket Regiments.

I was pondering my immediate situation when the Mess Sergeant came up to me.

'Mr Morgan-Grenville Sir? The Commanding Officer wishes to see you at once.'

This was ominous.

He introduced himself unsmilingly and left me standing.

'Well Morgan-Grenville, how long have you been serving here as an Officer of the Coldstream Guards?'

'I've, er, just arrived, Sir.'

'An hour or so ago?'

'Yes Sir.'

'Well I hope you enjoyed your time in my Regiment. I have received a signal from the War Office. I am instructed to inform you that you are to be transferred to the Rifle Brigade. You will proceed to their First Battalion in Germany. You are to report to the RTO (*Railway Transport Officer*) at Harwich Docks tomorrow at 1600 to escort a draft to Minden. I suppose you are to be pitied on serving in the Coldstream Guards for less time than anyone else. That's all. You may go.'

No smile. Fury. For him it was a personal insult. (Later it occurred to me that the Adjutant had also seen the signal and was similarly annoyed.)

I needed no second bidding. I leapt into a train and rushed home with the news which greatly cheered my father. Although it was thirty-four years since he had served with the Rifle Brigade, he assured me I would not meet with such stuffy indifference in the regiment that he revered above all others.

The next morning found me on my way to Harwich and my draft of twenty soldiers. I had no idea what I was meant to do with them but when I eventually found them, I was told testily by their accompanying Sergeant that I need do nothing whatever, except enjoy travelling first-class as an officer to Minden; he would look after them all the way. I did exactly as he proposed.

That was the last I ever saw of my draft for when the train reached Minden, I was the only person to 'detrain'. I walked the length of the train but they had simply vanished. It seemed an appalling start: to lose twenty men committed to my charge was surely a matter for a Court Martial.

A Corporal was there in a jeep to meet me. He said not a word about the draft. At least *I* was expected. It was late evening when I was delivered to the Mess, and the Officers, having finished dinner, were leaving the dining room. I braced myself to be ignored again.

'Hello' said someone. 'You must be Gerard Morgan-Grenville: I'm Colin James, the Adjutant. I expect you're starving; we'll get hold of some food - the dining room is upstairs. D'you mind if I join you? Mess Waiter! Get a bottle of hock, please. Have you had an awful journey? There's a few people still in the dining room, I'll introduce you so at least you'll know some faces. They're looking forward to meeting you; we've never had a Coldstream Officer before - most exciting!"

My integration with the Officers was swift and painless. They were - to a man - friendly and markedly informal. The Colonel did not have his specific chair but one or two of the Officers' dogs did.

I decided not to say anything about the lost draft - at least, not yet. The following day it seemed a bit late to mention it so I still said nothing. Neither did anyone else, ever. It was most curious and I have often wondered where they fetched up. Perhaps half a century later they are still in transit somewhere.

CHAPTER 4

A military blunder – appointed mines and demolitions officer – blowing up the Regiment – high spirits – catching a vehicle in a tank-trap – manoeuvres in a pastoral scene – staying at Grand Admiral Raeder's castle

MINDEN LAY on the banks of the River Weser, surrounded by flat hedgeless fields, much given to the growing of roots. The middle part of the town was medieval with timber-framed buildings and narrow cobbled streets - some inset with tramlines. At that time there was almost no civilian traffic, though the trams were frequent and I can still hear that shrill squeak and heavy clanking as they negotiated points and curves.

The inhabitants were markedly unfriendly even allowing for the fact that they had just lost the war. In a drab middle-class suburb was located the Officers' Mess, the former home of a local industrialist. An adjacent row of ugly but solid villas had been requisitioned as Officers' quarters.

The villa allocated to me and three other junior officers had a small garden, and in this grew several well-established lilacs which were in full flower. The scent was almost overpowering: it penetrated into my subconscious for, even now, when I sniff lilac, I am instantly transported back half a century to the garden of that dismal villa.

Shortly after my arrival, the whole Battalion - all 700 or so - was to march through the centre of Minden in order to remind the citizens of their victorious existence, though the occasion was advertised as being in honour of the King's Birthday.

The first adaptation I needed to make in the transition from Guardsman to Rifleman was in the speed of marching. Rifle Regiments have a much faster step which entrains a number of problems for those used to a slower pace. Ceremonial of this kind has never been the speciality of Rifle regiments in general and the Rifle Brigade in particular. Nevertheless, without benefit of much rehearsal, the regiment marched swiftly out of barracks and down the cobbled road into the old town. Leading this very long column was the regimental band in its finery, with instruments polished and bandmaster out in front setting a cracking pace to the beat of a Sousa march. Immediately following the band was the Company to which I had been posted, and leading this was the Company Commander. Just behind him, leading my platoon, I was finding that my training with the Red Coats had sunk in so deeply that I was unable to adapt quickly enough to this new fast pace. Although I kept in time, it was at the expense of a sufficiently long pace. In consequence, the gap between me and the Company Commander started to widen in a most unmilitary manner. The Company Commander, seeing out of the tail of his eye that he was too far in front of his Company, started to shorten his pace, the effect of which was of course to create an ever-lengthening gap between the band and the rest of the column.

The climax to this situation occurred in the centre of the old town when a large number of citizens decided to take advantage of the gap in order to cross the street. By the time they were across, the Band had vanished. It then became apparent that the ceremonial route had not been confided to the Company Commanders, a detail which was in any case of seeming unimportance since all they had to do was to follow. The Band, happily unaware that they had become uncoupled, played on ceaselessly, a sound which could be plainly heard but whose direction was a matter of guesswork: the only person needing to make the guess was the leading Company Commander immediately in front of me and it was a guess that needed to be made quickly but, as he explained later, every few paces the sound seemed to be coming from somewhere different, such were the mercurial accoustics of the ancient streets. Alas, he guessed Left when it should have been Right.

The error was quickly realised but it was impossible to turn a marching column around within the confines of a narrow street and, in any case, it would have looked ridiculous. So on we marched sometimes going right and sometimes left according to the dictates of the treacherous sound. Then, quite suddenly, the Band ceased playing.

The Bandmaster had observed that he had mislaid his regiment. He had halted the Band and silenced the music. Finding that the Battalion did not immediately reappear, he listened for the resounding percussion of 1400 boots striking cobblestones but being at the mercy of similarly deceitful acoustics set off in the wrong direction. For a long time, to the ribald amusement of the citizens, Band and Regiment independently explored the narrow streets of Minden until, quite unexpectedly, they came face to face round a bend. A somewhat undignified series of movements were made to reposition the Band in its rightful place, after which we set off for home to lick wounded pride and launch a Colonel's Inquiry as to how it came about. As a result of this, I was offered some practice drill.

Shortly after this embarrassment, the Battalion received a signal advising that some busybody from on high was coming to check stocks and satisfy himself that there were neither too few, nor too many of any item which formed part of our vast inventory. This was clearly a blow since not only did the stocktaking require a lot of time, but our excellent Quartermaster, Charles Sandle had, like all good quartermasters, accumulated a huge 'buckshee' collection which, of course, needed to be hidden. Most of this extra stock had been noiselessly acquired by one means or another so that when a soldier accidentally lost or damaged something, it could often be replaced quietly, thus obviating the need for tedious inquiries. It was a practical example of 'problem minimising', a Regimental speciality.

However, there was one vexatious problem for which there was no easy solution. It concerned the stock of explosives. These, which were allocated to the Battalion annually, had accumulated for several years and this was strictly against Regulations. The surplus could not be hidden since it needed to be contained in a special underground store. The reason for the large stock was that there was nobody in the Battalion trained either in its use or its disposal. This was, of itself, an infringement of Standing Orders. As a matter of urgency, someone had to attend a course to learn the necessary skills. It was my misfortune and, as it turned out many other people's also, that I was detailed to take the course, though at the time it seemed to promise a deal of fun.

I spent a happy but deafening week learning about detonators, primers, guncotton and plastic explosive. I learnt about mines, how to place them and how to disarm them - this last being a terrifying task as it is a very tricky business and a single error results in being blown to bits. (The mines on the course were only dummies, but I came away with a vast respect for the courage of those who volunteer to do this.) Finally, we learnt about booby traps, a source of seemingly endless entertainment – in peacetime.

And then I returned to Minden, the living example of how a little learning is a dangerous thing.

I was at once instructed to get rid of the surplus stock, via controlled explosions, and also to give a few lectures to others so that there would be several 'experts' instead of only one.

It was with undiluted joy that I took possession of the key to the explosives store. I couldn't believe my luck. There were boxes and boxes of booby traps, smoke bombs, fuses, trip flares, detonators and all the fascinating things about which I had been learning. There was enough explosive to blow up *anything*. And it was all mine to play with.

I started with the booby traps. These ingenious little devices could be easily placed in almost any situation where, when an object was moved, they would fire a detonator. In field use, the detonator would ignite a fuse which would then set off some explosive but if unconnected to anything else, the detonator made a bang as loud as a shot-gun cartridge and, if a foot or so from a person, would be likely to make them jump but unlikely to cause any injury. I therefore saw these gadgets as the ideal means of perpetrating practical jokes on brother officers of the similar lowly rank of Second Lieutenant.

I commenced a reign of terror in my villa by inserting these detonating devices into the hinges of bedroom doors and then exiting the room via the window. An officer returning to his room would receive a major fright. In this, I was entirely successful. I therefore enlarged my repertoire to include lavatory seats, car doors and sundry items such as a table positioned inconveniently so that it would be moved. I noticed people were beginning to get jumpy. But it was all in the name of Education and I proceeded blithely on to bigger things.

The first of these was a neat arrangement whereby via a remote control, I could set off a smoke bomb beneath a car parked outside the Officers' Mess. The car selected belonged to Alan Leslie-Melville, since I had identified him as having an advanced sense of humour – apart from the fact that in those days only a very few officers had cars.

Satisfying myself that Alan was in the Mess, I placed the smoke bomb under the engine, activated the device, entered the Mess, walked quietly to the window and observed a most satisfactory cloud of smoke enveloping the car.

Alan' I shouted 'Your car's on fire!'

He unburied himself from a newspaper, looked out and saw smoke billowing up from his precious Volkswagen.

'Get the fire hose!" he shouted, rushing from the room. Enjoying the joke, I didn't move. Other Officers poured out of the Mess grabbing buckets of water and sand. Then to my dismay, I saw flames streaming out from under the engine: the car really was on fire.

... some oaf had put a smoke bomb beneath the car

By the time it had been extinguished, it was clear that there was substantial damage. It was also clear that some oaf had put a smoke bomb beneath the car. I then discovered the limit of Alan's sense of humour. By general agreement, that was the last of the practical jokes.

I now turned my attention to educating the soldiers. When on my course, I had observed the interesting effect of an underwater explosion and I was most anxious to share the experience. A platoon was instructed to gather around the swimming pool, my preferred demonstration site since everything could be plainly seen in the clear water. It was now high summer and there was a heatwave. With 600 or so people wanting to use the pool, it was difficult to find a 'slot' when it would not be in use and I was under pressure to perform my demonstration as fast as possible. This constraint led to me taking an unfortunate shortcut.

I decided to illustrate the remarkable force exerted by an exploding guncotton primer - itself only about the size of a golfball. We had been shown this on the course and it had sent a plume of water shooting far into the sky. It was sure to impress.

The soldiers listened attentively. I flew through the preparations and lit the fuse. Seconds later, water cascaded, not vertically as intended, but sideways and several of my pupils were drenched.

The next morning the pool was empty, a crack running the length of the bottom. There was no more swimming in the pool that hot summer. I was summarily ordered to take all the remaining explosives, the flares, the detonators and, saddest of all, the booby traps, and blow the lot in one great explosion.

At that time, six years after the War, it was possible, though not actively encouraged, to regard the surrounding lands as one's own. Accordingly, I set about selecting a site, well away from anything fragile, where the Great Explosion could be safely executed and observed by the Battalion.

My full expertise was now to be put to the test. I soon found what I was looking for, a small group of trees which I intended to flatten in, what I now realise, was a shockingly unecological but highly dramatic manner. The centrepiece of this spinney was a stout oak tree and it was against the butt of this that I piled the entirety of my stock. Although total destruction could be achieved with far less explosive, since I had been ordered to blow the lot and since my reputation could not afford a further failure, I proceeded on the basis of the more the merrier. When all was in place, I 'tamped' the charge, as set out in my instructional handbook, connected an electrically fired detonator, and paid out a roll of wire into the middle of an adjacent field. To the end of this I connected the electric plunger, a gadget which I had only read about and whose function was to ignite the charge.

I went back into the spinney, checked everything with great care, made a loud noise to drive out any birds and returned to the plunger well satisfied with my preparations. This would *really* impress. Even senior officers might not have seen anything quite so dramatic since the end of the war. All was now ready for the spectators.

At the appointed hour, a column of 'three tonners' arrived bearing the greater part of the Battalion. The track along which they halted was about 150 yards from the spinney. My plunger was half-way between the two. The soldiers, with their officers, lined up along the track. This was my big moment and I made the most of it.

With the aid of a megaphone, I shouted an explanation of exactly what they were about to witness. Their absolute silence indicated again that I had their entire attention.

'Now' I said. 'When I press this plunger, you will see that spinney fall flat.' There was a ripple of excited comment.

I pressed the plunger. Nothing happened. Again and again I pressed it. Still nothing. A great merriment broke out in the audience. I was non-plussed: perhaps some animal had tripped over the wire and pulled it apart. I started to walk toward the spinney to investigate. Suddenly there was an earth-shattering roar, a mighty blast, and I was knocked flat, winded, deafened and disorientated. The oak tree remained standing but the tree next to it shot into the air, passed over my head in sections, and landed just in front of the Battalion. One of the trucks was damaged and numerous windows in a village some way off were shattered. The whole of the rest of the spinney remained precisely as it was. The soldiers were miraculously unscathed and returned to barracks wildly jubilant. Thus ended my career - and almost my life - as a mines and demolition officer.

If, in recounting the incident of the march through Minden I have given the impression that the Rifle Brigade was a shambles, I hasten to correct it.

Unlike the Brigade of Guards, one of whose functions was Public Duties involving Ceremonial, the Rifle Brigade concentrated on being highly professional in its soldiering. There was an entirely different ethos. Things were done in as relaxed a way as possible with a minimum of bullshit; it was the military result which counted. Huge Regimental pride was shared by all ranks and it has remained with me ever since. This was a regiment which had fought with the greatest distinction in most theatres of war, from the Peninsula campaign onwards, earning more Victoria Crosses than any other.

It was in the Officers' Mess that this ethos was most apparent. There was much friendliness and mutual support. Everyone seemed to have that rare quality of being able and willing to make the least of difficulties, no matter what they were, and this saved my bacon on many occasions. Officers never threw their weight around on those junior to them. Their overriding priority was to look after the men they commanded before they looked after themselves. The *esprit de corps* from top to bottom was formidable. Amongst these Officers I made and kept many friends. And as I became more aware of how things stood in some other units, I realised just how fortunate I had been to find myself in this very special regiment in which such informality and excellence prevailed. I learnt quickly that this informality did not exclude respect for one's seniors, and that orders were sometimes charmingly disguised as suggestions, or even floated as ideas.

A few weeks after my arrival, the Colonel-in-Chief, the Duke of Gloucester, came to visit the Regiment and dined in the Mess. Our Colonel at the time, Freddie Stephens, was sometimes vague about names. Introducing his Officers to the Duke, he fumbled for mine.

'May I introduce, er, our most recent, er, arrived officer, er, er, just arrived, er Jeremy, Jeremy, er, er ,er, Stopford-Sackville.'

'Stopford-Sackville!' said His Royal Highness, focusing on me. 'Tell me, how's your father? What's he up to now? How's he keeping?'

I looked at the Colonel: he was examining the ceiling.

'He's very well, thank you sir. Doing more of the same sort of things.'

'Is he now. Good, good.' And they moved on.

He was the first of a number of dignitaries and Generals whose visits often ended in after-dinner high spirits, such as descending the stairs on a toboggan.

An evening which ended rather differently saw the Officers of some neighbouring units invited to a buffet supper in a marquee on the lawn. In due course, the senior officers departed, but many of the remaining guests had drunk too much and were outstaying their welcome. Four of us decided to put an end to the party. We went outside and removed all the guy ropes on one side of the marquee. Quite slowly, the huge tent keeled over; as it did so there was a crescendo of fuddled voices, the sound of broken glass and much swearing. Since the sides were still pegged to the ground, there was no easy escape and the sight of heaving bodies crawling beneath the canvas afforded profound satisfaction. It was, of course, an accident.

During the summer we made an excursion to Soltau for manoeuvres on the vast Lüneburg Heath south of Hamburg, some eighty miles from Minden. We drove up in a convoy of half-tracked vehicles which were the standard carrier for motorised infantry. This sandy training area, previously used by the German army and dominated by a tall tower from which Hitler watched his army in training, was home from home to many professional soldiers since it closely resembled the training area near Aldershot.

We slept under canvas which the men greatly preferred to being in Barracks. It was possible to make oneself very comfortable, so long as it did not rain. My platoon had been assigned the 'defence' of an area surrounding a sandy track. All we had to do was to dig in, camouflage our vehicles, read or sunbathe, and wait for the 'enemy' who were eventually expected to approach in their half-tracks.

By the second day, we were getting bored. Then I had an idea which would employ my thirty riflemen and might provide some amusement. I decided to divert the sandy track along which the 'enemy' were expected, in a loop through some adjacent trees. In the new track, we would dig a great pit, five foot deep and ten foot square, and cover it over with a web of branches and turf. On this new track, we would lay sand and gravel to replicate the original route. Meanwhile, we would cover the real path with turf and heather and, for greater realism, 'plant' trees in it.

The men thought this to be a promising idea and they set to with a flurry of activity. By the end of the day, all was in place. I still have a photograph of the finished work, and I have to say it looked very convincing indeed. Now all we had to do was to wait and with luck, the next day we might catch an 'enemy' vehicle in our trap.

The following morning, a radio message indicated the approach of 'enemy armour'. We did not have long to wait before a half-track came lumbering along. From our various points of concealment, we had the thrill of seeing it steer onto the false road and then go crashing into the pit. Its occupants sustained some nasty bruises and they climbed out in a state of shock which quickly turned to anger and a search for the culprits. By good luck, a general in a jeep appeared at that very moment. I emerged from my hide.

'Hullo there! What's happened to that half-track?'

'It's fallen into a trap, Sir.'

'Did you make the trap for the purpose?'

'Yessir!'

'The occupants don't look pleased.'

'No, Sir.'

'Good show, bloody good show, young man. That's the spirit. Well done. On you go driver and watch out for traps!'

He drove off without my knowing who he was. This was most

unfortunate as some days later our Colonel was informed that the vehicle was ruined with a twisted chassis, and that a Court Martial was being considered. (It seemed that in the peacetime army, everything had to be simulated or pretended. I never really saw the point of training in this dull and parsimonious manner and did what little I could to make our field manoeuvres more realistic, often I fear at the expense of the taxpayer.) The matter of the wrecked 'half-track' was eventually put to rest by the mysterious production from nowhere of an entire buckshee vehicle.

In the early autumn, we went on more interesting Divisional manoeuvres in the hills thirty miles south of Minden.

I retain vivid memories of this landscape, especially the Weser valley with its fertile meadows rising up from the river toward the forests which covered the sides of the valleys. Early one morning, emerging from my tent, I remember looking down from the forest edge onto a sea of mist. Gradually the red-tiled roofs of the ancient timber-framed houses emerged into the clear September sun. Family farms, with eaves strung with corn-cobs, were centres of activity from first light.

We were witnessing the final flowering of a quietly prosperous peasant economy. The production of food was the central activity and if this meant the village street was covered with mud and cow-pats, so be it. Chickens, ducks and geese seemed as free-ranging as the inhabitants. Piles of steaming manure were heaped against farm walls. Long and narrow carts pulled by huge horses criss-crossed the landscape. Some had rubber-tyred wheels but most still had the large iron-hooped and spoked wooden wheels of a bygone age. They creaked and rumbled along the stony tracks, a country sound that has since gone for ever. From each house, blue smoke dissolved into the pale morning sky. The hauntingly wonderful aroma of wood-smoke and sun-dried manure has proven unforgettable. Behind the houses, the rich black soil bore row upon row of luxuriant vegetables and the apple orchards were laden with fruit.

As we looked down from the woods above, the village came to life. Occasional shouts, dogs barking, children laughing, cocks crowing: these were the centuries-old sounds of village life. How had it come to pass that these inoffensive farmers had been dragooned into fighting their peaceful neighbours? But it *had* happened and thoughts of forgiveness vied with those of revenge. If, in the process, we captured a hen or two, well, it was hardly surprising.

There was little fight left in these people. But occasionally, some small act of hostility would occur. One night as I walked (I expect noisily) through a village in the company of my platoon sergeant, a window opened and a bucket of slops was poured over us. With lightning speed, the sergeant fired a Verey pistol into the open window. The incandescent magnesium pellet ricochetted round the bedroom. There were shouts and screams and then smoke started to pour from the window. It seems to me now that both actions were entirely appropriate!

It was not only the German peasantry who were busy producing food. The Battalion produced for itself, in odd corners of the barrack enclosure, pigs, geese, chickens and vegetables, as well as flowers for the various messes. There was even a grocer's shop to provide the married families with food at a much cheaper price than was otherwise available - a far cry from the cost-strapped Army of today in which the dead hand of political correctness has made it hard for initiative to flourish or even for the Army to operate effectively.

Germany was an extraordinarily good posting for a young officer five or six years after the war. The country was pretty much at one's disposal. As 'Motorcycle Officer', for example, I would identify a circuit of roads on which to race and simply close them off without reference to higher authority. Or we would go out with rifles hunting for wild boar without asking anyone's permission. Similarly, we could sweep the fields of roots for partridge or the lakes for duck.

Leave was remarkably plentiful and we took ourselves off to distant places. Four of us went by rail to Venice, travelling on our driving licences (for which neither before nor since did we take tests) and shouting down any ticket inspector who dared to question its validity as a travel document.

In the winter there was skiing in the Harz Mountains. It was on my second ever skiing descent that I mistakenly chose a *piste* that suddenly turned into a bob run. There was no escape. I sat on my skis and gathered speed relentlessly. I tore round the ice-embanked bends in a state of terror lest there be someone or something blocking the run. A recent fall of snow slowed my progress sufficiently to avoid being thrown out at the corners, and I emerged at the bottom shocked but whole.

My numerous leaves were made vastly more interesting due to my having a car. My elder brother, with huge generosity, had lent me the funds to acquire the small Ford, a 'Popular', knowing how priceless mobility was in that situation. This loan had meant that he was carless for the time being and for this munificence I remain forever grateful. A godmother, who had made many visits to assorted castles of the Continental aristocracy before the war, now furnished me with introductions. The first and perhaps most memorable was to the wife of Grand Admiral Raeder, the Grand Admiral himself being 'detained' after Nüremberg. The Raeder Castle was improbably immense and in full working order. I invited myself.

Driving up with a brother officer, Toby Gore, there were - drawn up in a line on the top step of a broad flight up to the entrance - five uniformed male servants. The moment I stopped in the diminutive car, all five descended; two opened the doors, bowed as we emerged and the other three removed our scanty belongings from the boot. As soon as we stepped out, the car was driven away to be washed and the Admiral's wife stood at the entrance to welcome us. Behind her were a group of uniformed maids. Two of these escorted us to our adjacent and vast tapestry-lined bedrooms. Two more appeared with our 'luggage' - they looked as though they were more used to handling cabin trunks. Then yet two more came bearing a hip bath and huge cans of hot water. One of these remained. She stood to attention looking straight ahead at the end of the bath, holding aloft an unfurled towel. She said nothing. I looked at her inquiringly but there was no response. We concluded there was nothing for it but to strip off and bath ourselves. Ablutions completed, there was a brief tug-of-war for the towel: it was evident that she was used to assisting the drying of her charges.

When we descended, we were shown to an immense library and introduced to Count Schassburg. 'Ah' said he 'I see you wear ze Old Etonian tie: vee do not haf ze zame skul ties heer. Bad, very bad, how do you tell who you meet, hein? Tell me, do you know Lord Chester? He haf very good shit you know. I shit everywhere you know. I hope to shit at Lord Oxford's soon. You say shit? Or is it shoot?'

It was my first introduction to someone of his kind. Frontiers, politics and even war seemed but an occasional impediment to the width of his social territory which was more or less Western Europe. They must have found us very dull. At least we succeeded in not asking after our absent host.

Girls were at a tremendous premium. The bachelor officers, of which there were many, searched far and wide and mostly without success. A few rather senior officers serving in that part of Germany had eligible daughters but obviously great care was needed if anything went wrong! Something had to be done. It was decided to give a Great Ball. The RAF arranged an aeroplane at Blackbushe: it was filled to the ceiling with girls and there followed a joyful weekend.

By this time the Battalion had moved to Celle, a most attractive town north of Hanover. The ancient timber-framed houses, carved with figures and mottos, were painted in bright colours and were reminiscent of Hans Andersen's tales. But I was not destined to continue my service there, my life having taken a most unexpected turn.

CHAPTER 5

Become ADC to a fierce General – talk of war – Paris and the birth of NATO – fall under spell of Eisenhower – learn to dislike Montgomery – the General shut up in a chicken house – a flaming row and fear of arrest – inspecting French officer cadet school with the General stuck in a taxi – sudden promotion – memorable dinners with Prince Chavchavadze – travelling Europe with a polymath – offending Monty

THE ADJUTANT, Colin James, leant across the dining room table one lunchtime, looking vaguely in my direction.

'General Frankie Festing's here to choose an ADC. Colonel Mike has selected three Second Lieutenants - presumably ones he's happy to lose - for him to choose from. He's interviewing the three of you this afternoon, you're the last one. Good luck. I've heard he's a very fierce man, he certainly looks it!'

Panic. Who was the man anyway?

I looked him up in various volumes of the Rifle Brigade Chronicle. There were many references. Known as 'Front Line Frankie' from his habit of leading from the front in battle, he had seen much war service in Burma and had led the capture of Madagascar. A photograph showed a huge moustachioed man apparently dodging bullets, a broad smile across his face: the caption read 'Festing was everywhere the fighting was fiercest, encouraging his men by Christian name'. Even in the most appalling conditions he actually seemed to enjoy himself. I learnt too that in battle he preferred a walking stick to a rifle and that the American General, Stilwell, considered that the three best British Generals in action were Montgomery, Slim and Festing. He was the son and grandson of a General. He was a fervent Catholic and a noted collector of Japanese swords. And then I came across something he had said about civil servants: 'The world is full of boring jobs and boring people do them best'. I warmed to him instantly!

I was ushered into the presence - the first General I had met face to face. He was indeed a huge man, six foot four inches tall and broad with a craggy face and shortish hair which tended to stand up, adding to his apparent height. He wore tweed plus-fours, a baggy and very shabby tweed coat, and on the desk was a threadbare tweed cap. A faint smile crossed his face as I entered.

'You must be Morgan-Grenville and you've come to look me over, haven't you? Sit down if you want: I'll go on standing as I've got piles. We'll leave early tomorrow morning. I presume you can drive: difficult for me with these bloody piles. You'll drive me to my home in Northumberland to get my gear then we'll go to Paris together. Oh yes, there were problems of one sort and another with the other two so I'm having you as my ADC. I hope you don't mind. You'd better get your bits together and say your goodbyes. See you at 0800 tomorrow. Any questions?'

'No Sir.' My mind was utterly blank.

I stumbled out into the warm afternoon air, my head spinning. ADC? What did this involve? Paris? What the devil did he mean with *Paris*? Drive his car? What about *my* car? If he was a General, why didn't he have a driver? And why was he dressed in old tweeds as though for a day's pheasant shooting?

That evening, in the Mess, I received a great quantity of advice, mostly bad. The new job was generally considered to be enviable. But I was less sure. I suddenly realised how much I was enjoying regimental soldiering and I had many plans for forthcoming leaves. And it was plain that my new master had a reputation for not suffering fools happily. I took some comfort from the thought that I would probably find myself 'returned to unit' within a week.

The next morning, punctually at 0800, we started. That is to say I climbed, awkwardly, into the driver's seat of the General's large and ancient Vauxhall and he climbed, painfully, into the back where he sat askew, holding on to a tall stick with both hands.

'Off you go, then, no point in hanging around in this bloody countryside.'

I pressed the starter. The engine remained indifferent.

'Pull out the choke. Come on.'

I pulled the choke and pressed again. The engine responded and settled down at a fast speed. Many hands were waving. Gingerly I put the car into gear. It leapt backwards like a wounded kangaroo.

'Ow! Blast you! I told you I've got piles! And anyway, Northumberland is in the other direction.'

At intervals, in the mirror, I glimpsed a miserable, irritable face which grimaced at every bump. If, for a stretch there were no bumps, it was 'Faster, drive faster!' Then when the next bump came it was, 'Drive slower, you're killing me.'

It was not a happy drive, a fact that became increasingly clear with each passing hour. The General was in pain and seemed much preoccupied. As for me, I was already pining for my new friends and the fun I had been forced to abandon so abruptly. Mercifully, on the ferry, he disappeared to private quarters. Then the long drive north. Quite suddenly, as we approached the Northumbrian hills, he seemed to change persona.

'This is the only place to live in Britain. Great hunting. Great shooting. Great people. You can't imagine how I miss it when I'm away. I forgot to tell you I'm an irritable old bugger. I also forgot to tell you that we'll be living in Paris with my wife, my four children, the Nanny and my collection of Japanese swords. I've been summoned to the War Office the day after tomorrow. We're then taking the Golden Arrow night train over, so meet me at Victoria Station. There'll be reserved accommodation. Do what you like till then. By the way, we're going to Paris to set up SHAPE - Supreme Headquarters Allied Powers Europe, silly name but probably the most significant thing happening in the world at this time. My job is to co-ordinate the organisation and training of the armies of the eight participating countries, sounds deadly doesn't it but it wouldn't surprise me if we have a lot of fun. Can't you smell this air? Better than champagne! Ow! Watch out for pot-holes, blast you!'

I deposited the General, met his family, was driven to the station and went as fast as British Rail permitted back to my home in Sussex. There I announced the news of my new posting to my parents, arranged for someone returning on leave from Minden to bring back my car, and rushed back up to London to the Golden Arrow.

The reserved accommodation, blinds drawn and a soldier standing guard over the General's luggage, was impressive. But there was no General. And only minutes to departure time.

At the very last moment he appeared, walking oddly as though stepping over invisible obstacles. He was wearing a crumpled service dress, breeches, boots and he held a shepherd's crook. The two senior Officers accompanying him saluted and withdrew. He seemed in high good humour.

The train started and I was suddenly conscious of being closeted alone with this intimidating man; his presence seemed to fill the compartment. I had not the least idea of my presumed responsibilities. What task was I about to be ordered to undertake? I felt my range of abilities to be gravely limited. I could have put the luggage away but the soldier had already done this. Should I have bought a newspaper or a flask of coffee? I felt myself surplus to the situation and sat meekly in the corner.

The General slammed the door of the compartment and threw open the window.

'I need fresh air. That War Office is crammed full of the most dreadful bores, ugh! They always ask me if I've read the stuff they sent me but of course I haven't - it's unreadable most of it - a single paragraph would suffice but nobody there seems able to summarise anything.'

I made nervous throaty sounds intended as affirmation of this intelligence. The General placed his stick on the rack, threw off his belt and service dress jacket and sat down carefully.

'Your job' he said smiling 'is to see that I never leave my stick behind.'

I wondered briefly if this was to be my full time job. He removed his boots and handed them to me. What was I to do? Store them, polish them? I decided to put them in the rack then gazed out of the window at the sad houses that lined the foot of the embankment. The General rearranged his huge frame aslant on the seat, coughed and fixed me with a penetrating gaze. He looked terrifying.

'You're my ADC,' he began.

'Yes Sir!'

'As such, I shall expect you to be there when I need you.'

'Yes Sir!'

'I don't need you now so do what you want.'

'Thank you Sir.'

'Don't call me Sir all the time, you're not a butler. Draw the blinds on the corridor side, I don't want to be seen.' I obliged.

'Now listen to me.'

'Yes Sir, I mean, yes.'

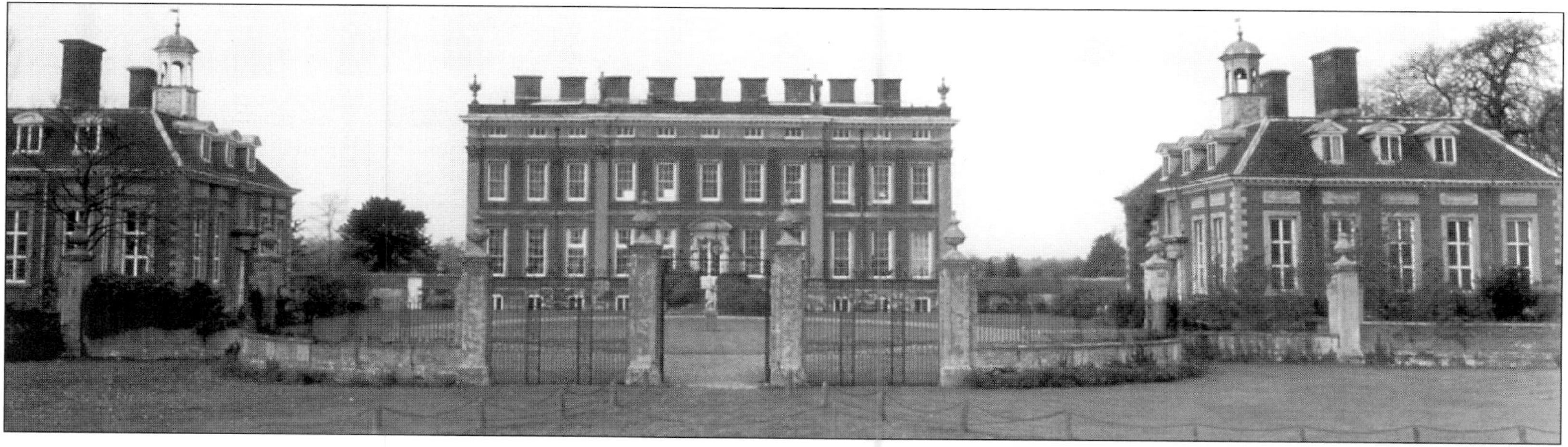

Above. Wotton House, Oxfordshire. Site of the Grenville home from the 12th century. Latterly the dower house for Stowe.
Below. Stowe, Buckinghamshire. Britain's largest house and the family home until it was sold in 1921 to become a public school.

My mother at 24, from a painting by de Laszlo.
Inset, a photograph taken when she was 65.

My father, at 80, on his only visit to Henbant:
he hated leaving his garden.

'There's something you should know. What I am about to tell you is absolutely secret. You must tell no-one under any circumstances whatever. I've been at an emergency meeting of the Defence Chiefs. The situation in Berlin is critical. As you know the Russians are trying to squeeze us out. They have a stranglehold around the city. The US Government and our Government expect that war may have to be declared against the Soviet Union within seven days. When we reach Paris I may hear that I've been given a different job, a command. If so, you'll come with me. You'd better find yourself a tin hat! It's a difficult situation for which, as usual, we are ill-prepared. Now I'm going to try to go to sleep so keep quiet and keep everyone, I mean *everyone,* out of this compartment.'

I sat next to the door, ready to repel intruders. Gradually the full weight of what I had just heard pressed heavily down upon me.

War. It was unthinkable. I was aware of the Berlin crisis, but only as the current political football match between East and West. I shut my eyes and tried to envisage what this actually signified for me. What was expected of an ADC in war? I thought of a painting I had seen of Napoleon sitting astride a white horse on the crest of a hill, surrounded by a couple of Marshals and a group of Aides-de-Camp. I presumed they were there to gallop off with messages. I was hopeless on a horse. And then I thought of tanks, Russian tanks, whole divisions of tanks racing across the German plain, overrunning our thinly spread forces. I saw myself in a trench, beside this now snoring giant opposite, as a T-34 tank bore down on our command post: the caving trench and the merciless steel track pounding us flat into the soil.

... merciless steel track pounding us flat into the soil

This scene I must have imagined with great force as variants of it formed recurrent nightmares for years to come.

Gradually, helplessly, I dozed off.

Startled into wakefulness by the angry shout of my master, I looked up and saw some kind of uniformed official asking for a travel document. I confessed to having nothing.

'Haven't you?' said the General 'How funny, neither have I.'

And then to the official – 'Ask the RTO in Dover. If you don't like that, telephone the Prime Minister. But whatever you do, I don't advise coming back in here again. Good afternoon.'

The man backed out.

'I told you to keep the door SHUT! I expect you want to tell your family about what I just told you - well you can't.'

A dead weight settled on my stomach and a fearful dread dominated all my thoughts. I looked at the General. Unbelievably he was chuckling to himself.

'You know, I think this could be huge fun. But you look as though you've seen a ghost!'

At the Gare du Nord, a French Colonel quickly identified the General.

'*Bonjour mon Général. Je suis Colonel Tharaux: à vôtre disposition! Vous êtes le bienvenu*! These soldiers will see to your baggage. The car is waiting. We will go to the Hotel Scribe where we have found you a suite.'

The Colonel looked harassed, an impression amplified by his hunchback caused, I later learnt, by his having been hung on a butcher's hook by the Germans, in case he had anything to tell them - a thing he had declined to do.

The baggage, of which I felt part, was piled into the staff car. Suddenly 'Where's my stick? WHERE'S MY STICK?'

The Colonel looked horrified. I bolted back to the train. It lay along the bottom of the rack. I had failed in my single responsibility.

The Hotel Scribe, just off the Champs Elysées, had been taken over for senior staff. I had been allocated a diminutive room somewhere within the sloping mansard roof, probably reserved in normal times for maids or nannies accompanying their employers: it seemed entirely appropriate. The General disappeared to a conference and I was instructed to be standing by the Reception Desk at eight the following morning. Having satisfied myself that the stick had been delivered to the General's suite, I emerged into the street and took a deep breath. Suddenly on my own again, I began to take stock. Here I was, at large in Paris. Everything I saw filled me with a wild excitement. The numerous smells of a Paris street in autumn were as the scent of a fox to a hound. Here I was being paid to be a tourist, and at a time when it was difficult for most people to travel anywhere. Yet I appeared to serve no serious purpose and the intelligence I had received from the General suggested that I might be dead in a few weeks.

I set off in search of a meal. It was then that I realised I had no French money. There was no-one to ask and the Dining Room of the Scribe looked far too intimidating to enter. I went to bed hungry and deeply anxious.

The next morning at eight, I heard the tap, tap, tap of an approaching stick along the marble corridor. At the same moment, Colonel Tharaux entered the lobby. Looking excited, the General addressed the Colonel in what passed for me as fluent French. I was dismayed as, no doubt, a working knowledge of French was also expected of me. My abilities were sadly limited but at least I hadn't put myself forward for the job.

A staff car deposited us at the Hotel Astoria, a stone's throw from the Arc de Triomphe. This hotel had been requisitioned for the embryonic team which in due course became NATO. Standing at the entrance were two American servicemen who managed a smart salute as the General unrolled himself from the car. Between them appeared a face I instantly recognised - that of General Eisenhower, Ike himself. He gave his famous ear-to-ear smile to Frankie Festing and the warmest of handshakes. After a brief exchange, Ike detached himself and to my acute embarrassment, extended a similar welcome to me. Here was one of the most celebrated soldiers in the world actually greeting *me*. I had met charisma face-to-face for the first time in my life. From that day to this, I have kept him as my yardstick for that elusive quality which secures instant adherence. When, a few days later, I received from him a personal letter informing me that my presence was 'proof of my country's confidence in me' and requesting my co-operation in this great venture which was 'of a gravity without precedent in the history of free peoples', I felt myself at least half-way to becoming a world leader!

For several weeks the Hotel Astoria provided cramped accommodation for the SHAPE staff whilst the new headquarters at Rocquencourt, a few miles to the west of Paris, were being finished. Festing's 'suite' comprised a bedroom furnished as an office, with an outer room painted in grey, equipped with two grey steel desks, one of which was designated for his ADC. The room looked out into a dark ventilation well. The office exactly matched my state of deep gloom at being thus confined.

The second desk was occupied by a Gibralterian secretary who, though no longer enjoying the bloom of her springtime, found, to her undisguised delight, that her free time had been 'requisitioned' by a randy Scandinavian Major further down the corridor.

There was a buzzer; one ring for the secretary's attendance, two for me. Seldom were there two buzzes. I sat behind my metal desk supposedly guarding the entrance to my master's lair. In this function, I was as much use as a toy poodle. Visitors were all senior officers unused to being detained by an extremely young second-lieutenant. They simply barged in. Every now and then documents, some of which were marked Cosmic Secret, were delivered to me by Antonio, a bubbly corporal in the fancy dress of the Italian Carabinieri. My ignorance of army shorthand and the significance of numerous acronyms rendered these signals meaningless, but it was still evident that the prospect of a confrontation remained. Meanwhile, the Berlin Airlift commenced.

Antonio brought me cups of coffee in order to ogle the secretary: he was desperate for female company.

With the success of the Berlin airlift, the threat of war receded and with it a great anxiety. Equally soon, I became bored, lonely, and resentful at my enforced idleness. I saw little of the General and when I did it was usually in the company of senior officers. At this juncture the General acquired *a fin-de-siècle* villa which had been rented for him in a quiet street in the westerly suburb of Vaucresson.

The Villa Lumen stood in a large garden, part of which had, surprisingly, been turned into a chicken run with some twenty birds in residence. With the villa also came a cook-housekeeper, Madelaine. She prepared breakfast, attended to the housework, went home at midday, and reappeared in the evening to cook and serve dinner for two. When we were absent she locked up the house, closed shutters and removed the eggs from the chicken house. I was given a key to the villa. 'Don't you dare lose it!' barked the General.

I now acquired a second responsibility. It was the ordering of a staff car whenever the General wished to commute to and from Paris. The two calls required daily to discharge this function did not significantly reduce my frustration. I had therefore decided to approach the subject when there occurred an incident which unexpectedly changed my circumstances.

My master had been invited to attend a 'gala' performance at the Opera. He decided to go, in spite of disliking opera, and instructed his secretary to secure a second invitation for me, 'in case anything should go wrong.'

I ordered a staff car to collect us from the Villa Lumen in good time. Festing had donned his full dress uniform, the car arrived and we set off. I was greatly looking forward to the event but he was dejected.

'Don't like opera, don't know why I agreed to go. The seats will be too cramped, the plots are stupid and the female singers fat. But I suppose it'd be rude to turn back.'

We drove on in gloomy silence. Arriving at the Opera, it was soon evident that the General was the only person in military uniform. He looked uncomfortable and angry. The seat was indeed too small for him and he was obliged to sit sideways. I could feel him fulminating like a faulty firework.

It was the usual mixture of popular excerpts. One such was from Mozart's *Magic Flute*, the scene in which the bird man, Papageno, dressed entirely in feathers, sings an irritating aria, accompanying himself on a tin whistle. It was the last straw and as soon as the interval came, I was told to go out and have the car brought to the door.

It was raining. The car was not to be found. 'Well find a blasted taxi then and find it quickly.' When eventually I found one, I was soaked, Festing was in a rage, and neither of us addressed a word to the other. It was only as we approached the Villa Lumen that I realised I had not brought the key of the front door and that Madelaine would have locked up and gone home. I felt sick with apprehension but decided to say nothing just in case Madelaine was still there or had by chance left a door unlocked.

There was a thunderstorm accompanied by a violent cloudburst.

We both ran to the front door as the taxi drove away. It was locked. There was no porch.

'Open the door man, what are you waiting for!'

'I'm afraid I've forgotten the key Sir.'

'Get into this house or you're fired!'

'I'll try the other doors.'

I ran round. Everything was locked and steel-shuttered. No ladder to reach the upper floor.

'You blithering idiot, double off to the housekeeper's place and get a key. I'll give you three minutes!'

By now the General was getting very wet and very irate. I ventured to suggest that he'd be better off inside the chicken house. He shot me a venomous look but made off towards it. As I ran out of the gate I heard a noise of panicking, flapping birds as though a fox had got inside.

I knew the street where Madelaine lived but not the number. It took me not three but twenty three minutes to find the house, get the key and return. It had now almost stopped raining. I shouted to the chicken house that I was back with the key. As I unlocked the door, the General emerged, his uniform, complete with his decorations, was entirely covered with white chicken feathers which had stuck to the wet material. He looked exactly like the Papageno we had seen an hour or so before - but without the tin whistle. He was white with rage. I tried to apologise but I was shouted down. As an ADC I knew I was a failure, but quite suddenly, I felt I was being unreasonably abused. I lost my temper.

'Why don't you get someone who doesn't mind having nothing to do, who can look after your wretched stick and remember the house key. I'm useless to you and I'm bored out of my mind.'

I could hardly believe it was me speaking.

'I think you'd better go to bed, we'll talk about it in the morning.'

I went without saying goodnight. And I slammed the door.

I awoke early. The events of the evening lost no time in trampling through my mind. I had been disrespectful, insubordinate. I had failed (again) in my duties. I would be sacked, possibly arrested. I had not yet learnt that he regarded loss of temper as a sin and would therefore be full of remorse.

I heard Madelaine arrive with the croissants and soon the aroma of coffee ascended the stairs. Then began the banging and clumping that accompanied the General's levée. I went downstairs, sat down and began to toy with a roll. In a minute I would know my fate. I had no excuses. I was resigned.

The door was flung open. 'Morning!' said the General. He was chuckling again.

'I owe you an apology - my sense of humour failed last evening. It's a story I shall dine out upon. I told you we'd have a lot of fun but I hadn't envisaged anything quite like that. Couldn't stand up in the chicken house so I sat on a perch. It broke and I ended up on my back in the chicken shit. Your job today is to get my uniform cleaned. Now what about some coffee! And, oh by the way, I'm glad to have found out how far I can push you before you react: I don't admire people who let themselves be pushed around. Good for you! And when we get to the office, I'll see you're never bored again.'

From that moment on, we were good friends in spite of flaming rows at quite frequent intervals. A subsequent ADC, Paul Greenwood, experienced a loss of temper during a car journey. 'Stop the car,' the General ordered, 'I'll have to go into that church to seek forgiveness.'

Shortly after this misadventure, there occurred another with consequences that could not be laughed away, at least not immediately. The General's first 'away' engagement was to inspect the French Officer Cadet training school at St Cyr. This was an important event and one for which the hundreds of cadets had been rehearsing for some time. Several of the most senior French generals were to attend because of its significance - French soldiers being inspected by the new British chief for training was predictably an event which, for the ever sensitive French, needed to be conducted with a maximum of gravity and decorum.

I did not fail to order the staff car to arrive at the Villa Lumen at an appropriate hour. But it did not arrive. It was then too late to arrange another. Salvation lay in finding a taxi, something which took me half an hour and earned me severe verbal chastisement. Once again we drove in furious silence. The driver refused to hurry and we reached St Cyr twenty minutes late. Festing was afire with fury. To be seen to arrive in a taxi was exceedingly undignified; to arrive in a taxi and be late verged on a calculated insult. To save a few seconds, the taxi was ordered to drive almost to the saluting dais upon which stood the cream of the French military.

I sprang out, whipped round the taxi and opened the General's door and stood stiffly to attention. No General emerged. I peered in. He was struggling to disengage his Sam Browne belt from the armrest where the sword-fitting on the belt had somehow punctured the leather upholstery and become hooked within it. With an apoplectic lunge, the material tore and a somewhat disarranged General stepped out and presented himself at the dais. Simultaneously, the band struck up the British National Anthem, whilst the Officer-Cadets presented arms.

Meanwhile, the bad-tempered old taxi driver was hissing at me to pay the fare. I had no francs. I asked him to wait. He refused. I marched sedately onto the dais, slipped in next to the General, and under cover of the very loud band, managed to ask him without moving my lips if he had any francs with which to pay the taxi. No answer. Whilst pondering the problem, the driver started tooting the horn. This was disastrous. I went back. '*Payez*!' he said 'then I shall desist'. I offered him my watch. No interest. I offered him double the fare but after the parade. He refused. I said we wanted him to take us back. He spat. Then he started shouting abuse about *les Anglais*.

'I demand my money this instant,' and with a shouted '*Merde*!' he got out of his cab and walked briskly onto the dais, grabbed the General's arm and said '*Payez*!'

It was the ultimate indignity. Two French officers hustled him away, paid him and he drove off blowing a jig on his horn. At least I had the slender satisfaction of knowing his armrest was ruined.

The day was saved by Frankie Festing's trenchant sense of humour, his diplomatic skills and his ability in French. In the Officers' Mess after the parade, he somehow managed to make them laugh. As for me, I secured a large float of French francs.

SHAPE moved offices to Rocquencourt, just to the west of Paris. There were other ADCs - in rank all Captains or above. The General decided that I should also be a Captain: he felt his position to be undermined with so junior an ADC.

'Get yourself decked out as a Captain. I'll send the Paymaster a signal to have your pay adjusted.' I hadn't realised promotion could be so arbitrary. I would be by far the youngest Captain in the British

Army. In the French Army, there were Captains in their forties, even fifties. I was still only nineteen. With six pips on my two shoulders, I was three ranks up and only four ranks off Brigadier-General. I needed no second bidding.

There was an immediately hostile reaction from the War Office in which Festing was ordered to see that I was to be reduced at once back to the rank of Second Lieutenant. The General refused to act on the instruction. The exchange became heated. He sent a final signal to the War Office - 'Either my ADC retains his Captaincy or I resign my commission. It is clear that I do not enjoy your confidence.' A compromise was reached. I could dress as a Captain and could call myself a 'Temporary Acting Captain' but I would be paid as a Second Lieutenant. The General agreed so long as I received a special Paris allowance. This I did and my total pay equated with that of a Captain. Satisfaction all round.

We moved from the Villa Lumen to the Château de Breteuil, near Chevreuse, thirty miles south-west of Paris. The General sent for his family and we spread ourselves around half the vast house. 'These boys of mine,' announced their father, 'can get a bit obstreperous. If they annoy you, or don't do what you tell them, you have my full permission to thrash them.' In the other half of the château lived, from time to time, the Marquise de Breteuil, a former dancer in the Folies Bergère. The Marquis was nowhere to be seen.

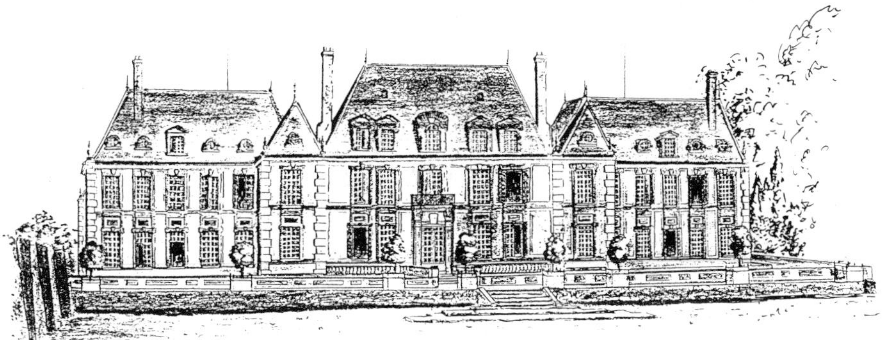

The chateau de Breteuil ... but the marquis was nowhere to be seen

In the long winter evenings, the General polished his collection of Japanese swords - he had collected one hundred and thirty (which he left in his will to the Ashmolean in Oxford). These swords were of surgical sharpness and one of his many mischievous delights was to pretend to be hiding a sword when passing through Customs posts in order to excite the officer into wanting to examine it, an act which usually afforded the macabre satisfaction of seeing him run his finger along the blade and cut himself to the bone.

General Eisenhower's deputy was Field-Marshal Montgomery. Festing had to report directly to him and he was not one of Monty's admirers, believing him to have become a conceited and dangerously megalomaniac general. When recounting his meetings to me, he referred to him as 'that arrogant little man' or 'that stupid pip-squeak' and Monty's insistence on sartorial correctness was anathema to him. Festing was incapable of looking smart. Rumpled and creased in uniform, he had the appearance of an unmade bed.

One day he went in to see the Little Man and minutes later reappeared, red of face and unbuttoning his service dress jacket. 'I've been told to polish my buttons, dammit. What's he think I am, a lance corporal? Infernal cheek! I suppose if I give them to you, you'll say you're not my batman and make a fuss. Hell!'

He then got down on all fours and pushed the buttons, one at a time, along the pile carpet, trailing a dark streak, but soon they shone. He sat in a chair, puffing.

'I'll keep that bloody dwarf waiting - I've polished them too quickly. In future I'll wear a service dress with the black buttons of the Rifle Brigade; that will fix His Highness. Damn and blast!'

The General acquired a French ADC, Le Capitaine Louis d'Estienne d'Orves. Louis' elder brother had been perhaps the most celebrated *résistant* during the war - a Paris *métro* station and adjacent *place* bears his name in testimony. Although twelve years older than me, he became one of my best friends and we saw each other often after we were both out of the Army.

At about this time, we embarked on a series of inspections of French military units. We were conveyed around France in a large American vehicle driven by a master-sergeant. I sat in a front seat, map-reading (I had many well-concealed failures) while Louis and the General discussed history, religion and food in the back: they were both deeply knowledgeable on all three subjects. At intervals, the General would point out some turreted medieval castle on a hilltop. 'Ah,' said Louis, 'it belongs to my cousin, shall we go and call, they will be delighted to meet you.' His family, distant and near, seemed to own hundreds of castles, wherever we went. When we did call, they *were* always delighted. Sometimes, on the way to some Inspection, the driver would suddenly be told to stop - the General had caught sight of a bric-a-brac shop. Not infrequently, he would come away triumphantly brandishing some antique weapon. He became the most highly regarded collector of old weaponry in Britain.

Louis invariably knew where to stay, choosing unremarkable little hotels with creaking beds, squeaky lino floors, distant lavatories and all illuminated with the dimmest bulbs, mostly on light switches calculated to leave one stranded mid-corridor. But the food was consistently outstanding. In 1951, the best food was to be found in small family run hotels with a tradition of their own *specialités*. It was my introduction to a lifelong interest in the pleasures of the table.

Louis had a fine house in the Rue Jacob in Paris and later - staying with him there shortly after I had been demobilised - I was taken several times to visit the Vilmorin family château at Verrières-le-Buisson. Louise de Vilmorin, who was a poet, occupied one wing, whilst her three brothers lived in another. Louise, tall and lame, held a salon reminiscent of Emerald Cunard's and dazzled her guests with witty conversation. She had been married to numerous titled Europeans and counted amongst her lovers Duff Cooper and André Malraux. It seemed that all her guests, apart from me, were famous. The film director of the day, the playwright, the choreographer of the Opera Ballet and a scattering of writers might comprise a typical gathering. They seemed to compete to outshine each other and were equally at ease doing so in several languages. They were much older than me, exceedingly accomplished and faultlessly mannered.

In these groups, I felt naïve and linguistically crippled; my hope was that no-one would talk to me or even notice my presence. Even so, it was at one of these parties, at a moment of near social paralysis, that I was introduced to a Princesse de Polignac, a beautiful girl of my own age. I think it was perhaps the first time that I experienced the bolt of electricity that announces instant compatibility between man and woman. We walked in the park, mostly in silence, stealing glances and returning tentative smiles. We returned much too quickly to the gathering and dumb with confusion failed to make any arrangement to meet again. In spite of the brevity of the encounter, it transformed my impression of females.

I bought, for very little, an American Hudson car discarded by a US Army private and I explored the countryside. But I was still lonely. Then one day, I heard that a girl whose family lived near mine in Sussex was coming to Paris for three months to learn French. We arranged to meet. Although by now I had turned twenty, I had never really had any opportunity to get to know girls in general and certainly not one in particular, but the experience with the Princesse filled me with a new-found expectancy. I knew this girl to be pretty, fun, and exactly my age.

We met at the Bagatelle in the Bois de Boulogne. She was indeed friendly and attractive. Moreover, she had time on her hands. She knew no other English people in Paris, and we should have had a lot of fun together. But to my great distress, I found myself tongue-tied, gauche and generally gormless. I was astounded at my own futility. We sat on a bench and eventually held hands. Unsurprisingly, I was soon abandoned in favour of someone more amusing. It was many months before I had a chance to try my luck again.

We travelled the eight Alliance countries - sometimes by car, sometimes by air. From time to time, we seemed to have a Dakota at our disposition and once even a Flying Fortress bomber. These visits were exhausting. Once, in Oslo, I retired to bed at the end of a very long day, having been instructed to be ready to depart at seven the next morning, at which time four Norwegian generals would be arriving at the hotel to collect us. At five past seven the next morning, the telephone by my bed awoke me. A thinly disguised voice said - 'The General Staff of the Norwegian Army wonder if it would be convenient for you to accompany them on a tour of inspection. They wish to depart in three minutes. Good morning.'

Back in France, Frankie generously did what he could to see that I was included in any interesting invitation. It was fascinating for me to witness entertainment - usually dinners - on a scale that I had never previously encountered. Everything was grand, the place, the people, the food. Hosts and guests seemed invariably to be multi-lingual, and able to toss clever and witty conversation back and forth like stars at Wimbledon. Successive dishes, often looking like an illustration from a Victorian edition of Mrs Beeton, were picked at frugally, so many were they. Tiered dishes in silver or gold were stacked with fruits and delicacies I had never before seen. Wines of great age and variety were constantly poured by the many uniformed footmen in attendance. The memory of one such host dominates the rest.

We were sometimes invited to dine at the vast Château de Dompierre, the 17th century seat of the Duke de Luynes, which was then tenanted by a Georgian Prince and Princess by the name of Chavchavadze. He was immensely rich and extraordinarily talented. He was one of the finest pianists of his generation. The château was extremely elegantly furnished and in the great *salle-des-fêtes*, with its murals by Ingrès, were several pianofortes, fortepianos, harpsichords, spinettes, all by the finest makers. The Princess had two blue-nosed whippets with diamond-studded collars. At the conclusion of dinner, the Prince would tap gently on the table and an immediate silence would fall. The guests knew this to be a signal for The Story.

Prince Chavchavadze was brought up within the ageless Georgian tradition of story-telling. The tales themselves were mostly contemporary; it was the manner of their telling wherein lay something magical. I have since heard a good many raconteurs exercising their art but none have been comparable. First of all the man had something magnetic about his personality. Then he was a master of facial expression, of split-second timing, of gesticulation. A story describing a thunderstorm was told without a single word. He had a voice with endless inflexions and eyes to match. He could imitate any accent, seemingly in any language. He knew how to maximise the drama with the alternation of sad with happy, slow with fast, loud with soft. Everyone present, young or old, at any of those dinners was in thrall, like children before a conjuror.

The story over, the Prince would ask if anyone would like to hear the work of any of the great classical composers for piano. Once he played a short piece by Bach on a grand pianoforte. Then he played the same piece on an instrument contemporaneous with Bach. After that, he played his own version of how Bach might have composed it had he been alive now. Finally he performed a version in which he had 'jazzed-up' the Bach original - it seemed to my untutored ear to be by far the best.

It was at one of these parties that the Prince asked me to accompany him, dressed as a page, to the great fancy-dress ball given in the Venetian

Palazzo Labia, by de Beistegui, a Mexican-Spaniard of vast wealth. It promised to be the ball of the century but alas, Frankie Festing counselled me not to go, in a series of cryptic warnings. Regretfully I made my excuses. I think he thought I would be raped by the Prince.

When I read of the extraordinary preparations for the party, the list of guests and the defenestration into the Grand Canal of photographers found hiding behind the ball-room curtains, I felt I had foregone an unusual experience. And then when I saw Cecil Beaton's photographs of the fifty gondolas filled with bejewelled guests, dressed as 18th century pashas and princesses, the most resilient of whom were still to be found dancing in the piazza the following morning, I knew I should have insisted whatever the consequences.

A little while later, Chavchavadze was killed in a car crash.

I soldiered for two and a quarter years. But it took many more before I realised just how privileged my service had been. Many contemporaries had a very different encounter with the Army yet I doubt that I could find any who would disagree that their experience was valuable to them. Since the end of conscription, it has been politically unfavourable to introduce any kind of national or even community service. In consequence, we have had four decades of youth, mostly unfit and without a sense of self-discipline, with results that have been painfully apparent.

I am forever grateful to Frankie Festing for the generous education of his fairly feeble and sometimes difficult ADC. He taught me many valuable lessons. Foremost of these was his measured approach to Important People. He was seldom impressed by Position, realising that those at the top often arrived by virtue of luck, favour, ruthlessness or dead men's shoes. I never saw him kow-tow to anyone nor denigrate his colleagues for reasons of personal preferment. Titles and wealth left him unmoved. He was a fervent yet humble Catholic. When the Prime Minister, Macmillan, summoned him to a Cabinet meeting during Holy Week, he refused with the words – 'I am not going to let the Prime Minister bugger up my Holy Week', a statement which soon permeated the dull offices of Whitehall.

He showed me that to follow a particular profession did not in any way limit one's potential in any other sphere. Apart from his interests and collections already mentioned, he was a connoisseur of paintings and of wine, he hunted, wove tapestry, took snuff, sailed the Atlantic single-handed, read prodigiously and was a genial host. At times, he seemed interested in almost anything *except* soldiering. Yet he rose to the highest military pinnacle, chief of the Imperial General Staff with the rank of Field Marshal. He died in 1976, rosary in hand.

I have dwelt on Frankie Festing at length but it was this man more than any other who set me on the road to independence in thought and action. It was the greatest gift to have received by the age of twenty.

On my last day at SHAPE, I was sent for by Monty.

'I hope you're going to stay in the army.'

'No, Sir.'

'Why ever not?'

'I think I've already seen the best of it.'

This naïve reply instantly offended the little Field Marshal and I was curtly dismissed.

CHAPTER 6

Demobilisation – indolence – debutantes and the spectre of a job – escape to America – apprenticed in a plywood factory – financial catastrophe in a boarding house – country house weekends – learning to fly a Tiger Moth

I HAD rejected the Army though I had given no consideration to any other career. Plenty of time, I thought.

I returned to England and was demobilised, a procedure which included the issue of an outsize 'civvy' suit in a nondescript brown material, black shoes with improbably thick soles and a near-cousin of the pork-pie hat in mid-green. This striking outfit was supposed to assist with job hunting, the solidity of the soles suggesting that success might not be immediate.

Returning home to a great welcome, I soon settled down to being looked after by a doting mother and, initially, a tolerant father. My elder brother, John, introduced a steady stream of girls into my life, mostly his rejects. Little by little I was becoming more confident in female company. They came to stay for weekends, characterised by their innocence and sociability within a local circle of families of broadly similar social background. There were days spent shooting and nights spent partying. Life was sweet and full of promise. Living at home, money was not an immediate problem.

Mothers, anxious to launch their daughters in the 'right' circles gave extravagant dances in London or in their country houses. In drawing up lists of 'eligible' young men to be invited, some of the more astute hostesses exchanged semi-informed rumours in code. One hoped never to find certain letters put against one's name – NSIT (not safe in taxis); MTF (must touch flesh); AP (absolute pauper) though this last, if not the others, would have been appropriate to me. Often we were billeted out for these dances on anxious neighbours whose kindness one took for granted. In the London season, there might be two, even three dances on the same night and there was a regrettable tendency to pass the whole evening at the party expected to be the most exciting, even though one had accepted the others. It was an unedifying time of much take and little give.

Debutante girls, resplendent in new dresses, did their best to accommodate my peculiarly inept dancing. Conversation was sadly ingenuous and boringly centred on dances previously attended. There was always a painful disparity between the pretty, sophisticated girls who had perhaps 'come out' a year or two before and the newly launched, plain, gauche girls who sat in agonised limbo, waiting to be claimed by someone, anyone. Sometimes, I would see a girl home but the rules, then still widely respected, inhibited any intimacy beyond a modest cuddle and a fleeting kiss.

One day, my father suggested that perhaps it was time to get a job. It was a rude shock: I had settled into an enjoyable way of passing the time, besides I found the thought of employment quite foreign to my purposeful drifting.

'Have you any idea what you want to do?'

I didn't want to do anything.

'No, not really.'

'Have you thought about Industry?'

What a ghastly thought.

'No not really.'

'Or the Civil Service?'

What was that, I wondered?

'No, not really.'

'Well I think it's time you did. You will need to earn money, you know. One day you'll have to buy a house. Think about it. We'll talk again in a week's time.'

It was just after this sobering interview that I received a most timely invitation. A friend from Eton, Ralfe Whistler, had a Canadian aunt, Mrs Wood, who was anxious to people the Dominion with Old Etonians. The aunt was exceedingly wealthy and uncommonly generous. She proposed to Ralfe that he bring a friend over to the country and have a good look round. And whilst there, we might as well look at the United States and, for that matter, why not include

Mexico too. How would we travel? She would give us a new Studebaker car. And a pile of money for our expenses.

This was not an invitation to be turned down at this tricky juncture. Thus the question of a job was shelved without loss of face.

On 17 June 1952 we took off from London in a Stratocruiser for which a First Class ticket had been provided. This was the age of civilised trans-Atlantic air travel - if you could afford it. We sat at a table for dinner, stopped briefly in Iceland to refuel and stretch the legs and then retired into full length and curtained bunks for the onward flight to Montreal. One arrived as fresh as the proverbial daisy.

Used as we were to the austerity of post-war Britain, North America burgeoned with everything; not just as a land of plenty so much as a land of excess. We were shocked by the waste. Seeing people abandon half-eaten plates of food struck us as wicked. But we had come to learn and remarkably soon were used to the all-encompassing extravagance.

The Studebaker car awaited us and in twenty-three days we arrived at the Texan-Mexican border via a meandering route that touched twenty-three States. Nine days later, having acquired a form of dysentery and after covering most of the length and breadth of Mexico, we were back in the United States. Another sixteen days and eight more States, we reached Vancouver. Two weeks more, and via all the remaining American States save six, we reached Toronto, our destination, a mere 300 or so miles from our starting point, Montreal. But instead of 300 miles, we had driven 13,000 miles, equivalent to half the Earth's circumference. The only problem was that we had somehow omitted to see anything much of Canada which had been the main purpose of the expedition.

mid-day Mexican

Enjoyable as it was to spend those weeks with a good friend, it was a ludicrous journey. We tore through so many places that they are now largely blurred in memory. I suppose I tasted the flavour of tourist America and after staying in forty-seven motels in succession, never wanted to stay in another. In Arizona, we drove off far into the arid desert without even a minimum of preparation except for a drum of Coca-Cola (which put me off it forever) but somehow found our way back to tarmac. A breakdown could have meant disaster. In Death Valley in California, we succeeded in frying an egg on the bonnet of the car; interestingly, it left a fried egg-shaped mark which proved to be indelible. And then in the small town of Kellogg in Idaho, we were both arrested for 'indecent exposure'; driving shirtless was considered suggestive. We spent a night in a most comfortable cell and were given a memorable breakfast after which we were released by a genial Sheriff.

We spent a few days in Canada reporting to the aunt. She was unexpectedly diminutive but highly animated, warm yet unclaiming of our time. Her generosity was prodigious and though I was a major beneficiary, I liked her for herself and her earnest passion for Canada. Yet in spite of this, she spent most of her life at sea, transferring straight from one cruise to another. She took with her a spirit lamp on which she would boil an egg in her cabin in preference to a meal in the dining saloon. She must have been a kind of marine hermit.

We returned to Southampton aboard the liner, *RMS Scythia*, one of Cunard's smaller liners which was nearing the end of her days. She was built and furnished to allow first-class passengers to travel as though they were staying in a particularly affluent and well-run country house and once again the aunt had provided first-class tickets. I was profoundly impressed by the experience; so impressed that nearly four decades later, I built a miniscule passenger ship, one-fiftieth the size, which broadly encapsulated the same concept. But more of this later.

I was also struck by something else. On the first day, Ralfe met a girl. I do not recall seeing either of them again until we reached Southampton.

Home again. This time the period of grace in which the matter of a career remained unmentioned was markedly shorter. My father returned to the attack.

'We love having you here but you simply can't stay around forever. Money *has* to be earned. No doubt you picked up some ideas in the USA!'

My mind was a perfect blank. I had never given it a thought. I could only think of the tassel-dancing women in New Orleans and the prototype Hippies on Fisherman's Wharf in San Francisco. Of the two, the second seemed more in line with my lack of qualifications.

'Not really.

'Well I've been thinking that either you should train as an architect, since you like drawing or maybe become a probation officer.' (No explanation for this last suggestion.) 'Do either of these ideas appeal?'

'No, not really.'

'You keep saying "not really". Isn't there a *single* thing you can think of which you'd like to do?' This said testily.

There wasn't. And looking back, it was scarcely surprising. I knew next to nothing about what any career actually meant doing. 'Industry' was often mentioned but what did it really mean? I hadn't the least idea. Of course I had seen illustrations of the insides of factories, of tired-looking men standing by a row of presses, of tired-looking women behind rows of sewing machines. From that day to this I have wondered how anyone ever managed to solve the problem of choosing a career from a state of ignorance. And then in desperation,

'Maybe you should try for a place at University. Do you think that would be useful as well as giving you more time to sort yourself out?'

'I don't know.' I didn't.

Shortly thereafter, it was arranged that I should go for an interview at Oxford University. Unsurprisingly, I was turned down. No-one said why. I have never regretted it.

It was then that my father remembered someone he had met in the war, Paul Irons (father of the actor Jeremy Irons) who was, at that time, the Financial Director of the Saunders-Roe group of companies. I remember seeing my father write to him. He wrote slowly and carefully at a large roll-top desk and I wondered what he was writing. Perhaps: 'I've got a problem with my twenty-one-year-old son,' or more likely: 'I've got a twenty-one-year-old son who's a problem.' Whatever he said, it resulted a week later in my travelling to their Head Office at Cowes on the Isle of Wight.

Saunders-Roe made flying boats. Both flying boats and the company were gradually on their way to becoming history and in order to accelerate the process, they were not only considering hiring me but constructing three gigantic aircraft called Princesses. These were fitted with no fewer than *ten* propellers. Only one ever rose off the water and that but briefly. They were finished two years after BOAC (the only likely customer) had decided against ever ordering flying boats. They were subsequently cocooned, and for many years became part of the floating scenery at Cowes. During this time the Government - unbelievably with hindsight - considered trying to power them with lightweight nuclear reactors, an experiment that mercifully never took place. They were broken up in the mid-Sixties.

In days gone by, flying boats were made of plywood. Hence Saunders-Roe had a local subsidiary making laminated wood products; at this time they consisted chiefly of plywood sheets faced with a veneer of exotic hardwoods. These were then being sold to the shipbuilding industry for lining-out cabins and saloons. An apprentice was needed in the veneer sorting department. The job was mine, whether I liked it or not, and it started in two weeks.

Donald Campbell, who was limbering up for the world speed record on water, wished to sell his 1926 Red Label, 3-litre Bentley. He wanted £250. I bought it on impulse with my Army gratuity. It was a truly wonderful car. It had a deep throaty roar, a leather strap over the bonnet, an exterior handbrake, a folding roof and a huge glistening radiator in German silver. It guzzled petrol but no matter; everybody was bright green with envy. Foolishly, and to my continuing regret, I sold it a year later for the same price, which I considered at the time to be a pretty good deal. Had I kept it, it would now be worth around 300 times that figure.

It was a truly
wonderful car

I contemplated my imminent employment with a total lack of enthusiasm and wondered, not for the first time, if I had made an error in leaving the Army. The job sounded despairingly boring, the pay was poor and people I had met when I went for interview were deeply unimpressive.

A booking had been made for me in a boarding house, The Cedars in Ryde. Piling my luggage into the Bentley, I crossed with the car to the Isle of Wight and soon identified my 'digs' - a Victorian bourgeois dream. A single Scots fir stood in for the cedars. Three bachelors were already in residence: they all worked at Saunders-Roe. My landlady was formidable; of the old school of boarding house proprietors, she governed from her lair in the basement, a dragon unchallenged. There were precise rules posted in each room about hours, lights, noise, hot water and use of the bathroom. Meals were served at an exact time and lateness meant starvation. The menu reflected the day of the week, unvaryingly. Monday, Brown Windsor soup (watery), two slices of mutton (leathery), cabbage (overboiled), potatoes (underboiled), tomato ketchup, sliced white bread and margarine; Bakewell tart and custard. Tuesday, minestrone (watery), two slices of beef (leathery), cabbage (overboiled), potatoes (underboiled), HP sauce, sliced white bread and margarine; steam pudding and custard. But I still had my Army appetite and I relished every mouthful.

The first day at work confirmed my worst forebodings. The factory, even to my inexperienced eye, was clearly rundown and poorly managed. The staff were unmotivated and demoralised. It soon became obvious that prospects for this company's future were dim and it was a depressing environment in which to begin what appeared to be suspiciously like an industrial career.

On the second day, I was shown the stocks of wood veneer. I was allocated three months in which to learn to distinguish the forty or so different woods. I learnt them all the same day. This may sound priggish but anyone could have done the same. Even so, Management came to hear of this as being a phenomenal achievement and thereupon made a rash decision as to my future employment.

On my first weekend at The Cedars I decided to carry out a service on the Bentley. The huge sump held a vast quantity of oil. It filled a bucket. Where to dispose of it? These were those halcyon days before

I understood the need to respect environmental and ecological imperatives. In consequence, the existence of an adjacent drain against the wall of the house was all I needed to solve my problem. I poured it in without feelings of guilt. The oil was gone, vanished. Seconds later, my landlady appeared; she seemed quite deranged: her mouth opened and shut but she remained speechless. She indicated with a stabbing finger that I should descend to her basement flat as a matter of urgency.

Streaming down the wall onto a new carpet was the oil; sticky, black, smelly. It had been a ventilator, not a drain and the financial consequences were calamitous.

From my first day at the factory, I had been aware of an unpleasant odour which pervaded the workplace. I asked the foreman what caused the smell.

'It's some chemical or other. Don't rightly know what and we're not s'posed to ask. Some secret new-fangled product 'tis. 'Course we *do* know summat, it's them plastics. Summat to do with roofing sheets. Now just you forget that young man. Haven't told you nothin' mind.'

At the back of the factory there was a yard which sloped down to a tidal creek on the River Medina, whose mouth is at Cowes. This yard was littered with rotting crates of plywood and the detritus of numerous failed experimental ventures, each of which had doubtless engendered a brief hope of commercial salvation.

In the lunch hour, I would escape thankfully from the gloom of the veneer sorting department into this sunlit yard to eat my sandwiches, the crusts of which sometimes went to a family of ducks which inhabited the reeds and the secret glories of the tall Indian balsam which, at the time, was a new immigrant to our shores and which now, half a century later, continues to work its way slowly up our rivers by means of its powerful spring-loaded seeds.

The rest of the workforce strangely ignored this quiet yard - with a single exception. A sickly-looking man in white overalls would appear at intervals holding a small square of a translucent plastic material, identified as the source of the smell, and affix it to a board which was angled toward the occasional sun. Some of the earlier ones looked as though they hadn't much enjoyed their exposure to the elements.

After a few weeks of chillingly boring employment, I was sent for by the Managing Director. I expected the sack for lateness, having overslept on several occasions.

'I've had a most encouraging report on your progress from your foreman.'

'Thank you, Sir.'

'I've decided to transfer you at once to the Sales Department. I want you to undertake a special job. You will not know this but we have been secretly developing a new product for which we believe there is a worldwide demand. This development is almost complete so manufacture will start soon. It is a major breakthrough.

Now listen carefully. All round the world, there are factories, warehouses, sheds and barns, roofed with corrugated iron, corrugated asbestos or corrugated aluminium. These buildings are mainly dark inside since there are seldom any roof-lights due to the expense and difficulty of installation. What we have secretly developed is a *translucent corrugated roofing sheet* in forms which match all other standard types of roofing sheet and which can just be inserted in place of an existing sheet. Since our product is low-priced, very strong, permanent and can even be made in a variety of colours, we think we've got something that can be readily sold everywhere. We have identified that the biggest potential for sales is in Australia and New Zealand. I want you to go there and sell it. But first you will need to understand export procedures. We have arranged for you to be attached to a firm of Shipping Agents in the City with a view to you passing, in due course after your return, the exam of the Institute of Export.'

My Guardian Angel had come up trumps.

Keen as I was to escape the dreary routines of the plywood factory, I was even less anxious to work in the City. But in an age of conformity, I was still conforming: bowler-hatted and rigged out with stiff white collar, tie-pin, rolled umbrella and gloves I joined the other similarly uniformed commuters in the twice-daily shuffle from the West End. It was now winter and the legendary fogs of London were still very much in evidence. On a really bad day with visibility down to a few yards, surface transport ceased. There was an eerie silence as one groped one's way along familiar streets. Smuts descended on everything; white collars became grey and many of the elderly expired.

From the start I felt there was something fundamentally unpleasant about the City. Of course, the vast majority of City workers were, then as now, but functionaries in the workings of Capitalism and seldom shared in the gross and, arguably, undeserved winnings of the few. There is perhaps an even more flagrant disparity now than there was then: the resultant fortunes of the few continue to create a social divide. I have never had reason to alter my view that the receipt of huge salaries and ridiculously large bonuses are extremely anti-social since the resultant spending power is upsetting to general values, especially in property. Perhaps I should add that it is not a matter of sour grapes since *nothing* would have tempted me to spend my life in the City.

I was allocated one side of a small desk. My mentor, Mr Davis, sat opposite. His life had been spent slowly climbing the short ladder of export and shipping documentation. He seemed saddened that I did not already know that FOB signified Free on Board or CIF meant Carriage, Insurance and Freight. Forms C&E, 246E and Letters of Credit, Forwarding Agents and Manifestos were the stuff of his life. But, alas, not mine. I never grasped anything at all and although his great patience was the equal of my stupidity, it was a futile endeavour. A few months after I had departed, to my utter astonishment, I received a Certificate incorporating me as a Member of the Institute of Export entitling me to the suffix M.I.Ex. after my name. I have often wondered who sat the exam in my name if indeed anyone - and why? Perhaps it was a booby prize.

The pace of my social life was now much accelerated.

On the top floor of a Victorian mansion in Herbert Crescent, off Sloane Street, I had rented a diminutive flat whose widowed and kindly owner spoilt me outrageously and charged me a pittance. Huge breakfasts served on Copenhagan porcelain were carried to my room and on the rare occasion I was in of an evening, I could count on her bringing me a delicious meal of several courses for which no payment was ever requested.

Many weekends were spent in country houses where servants seemed still to be plentiful. Carefully balanced house parties whiled away the hours with croquet, horses, visits to neighbouring house parties, lengthy meals, dancing to a gramophone and incessant trivial conversation interspersed with the odd practical joke. I never really felt comfortable on these occasions: they seemed contrived. I think I was more of an observer than a participant and probably appeared stand-offish. But it was the traditional way of life for the young in the privileged classes. It was a means by which their national network was passed from generation to generation.

Some such visits were followed by asking a girl from the house party to Hammerwood for a weekend - often quite far ahead since any girl worth her salt would be (or at least pretend to be) booked up for a couple of months or so. In the intervening period, it was possible that the chosen girl had lost her allure, either because another had appeared whose appeal seemed superior or because she had done likewise with some young man. I remember sometimes meeting these girls at the station on a Friday evening and wondering what on earth I could have seen in them; a prelude to a dismal visit.

Even when there was mutual compatibility, these girls had to run the gauntlet of parental approval. Seen in the context of my home, they often seemed strangely inadequate. Asked by my mother, for instance which was their favourite French poet, they might suddenly appear to be embarrassingly stupid and I lacked the social skills to deflect any such inquisition. The more my admiration for the girl was evident, the brighter the spotlight of maternal examination. Few were the maidens whose parents were untraceable by mine, via a couple of telephone calls - the sins of the fathers lived on. In some respects it was an effective filter and although it seldom appeared so, the social engineering could result in pairings not too distantly removed from arranged marriages.

The survivors may have been few but they were special. One such was Virginia, to whom I was becoming deeply enamoured. To be sure we had only met at weekends, mainly at my home, and it is impossible to think that we could have known each other well but the decisive alchemy had occurred and I soon found myself forming up to her Member of Parliament father and making a formal request for her hand. 'Too young and too poor!' he said, standing with his back to a blazing log fire, and I was dismissed with an invitation to apply again in a year's time.

It must seem strange to those born of a later generation that such a pronouncement by a prospective father-in-law could possibly determine our intentions for marriage - but it did. We therefore commenced a long unofficial engagement and embarked our frail ship upon the sea of strain which this involves.

I had not yet found the confidence to plough my own furrow.

On several successive weekends my brother and I learnt to fly. This we did at Portsmouth where an ex-World War I Royal Flying Corps Instructor, known as Mad Mitchell, had a rough and ready flying school which nevertheless boasted six Tiger Moths, antiques even then.

Mitchell's method of instruction was simplicity itself; just four hours of demonstration followed by trying to fly solo. There was no complicated theory to worry about, no meteorological wisdom to be imparted, no air law, no tests. Tiger Moths were bi-planes with fore and aft open cockpits for two aviators. The instructor sat in the aft position and shouted instructions at the pupil who might or might not be able to hear against the noise of the engine and the rushing air. There was a seat harness with which to anchor oneself to the seat. I had not mastered this simple device when the instructor, in hour three, decided to loop the loop. I shouted to him that I was unharnessed but he did not hear. There was, in the event, barely sufficient centrifugal force to prevent my falling to earth at the summit of the loop. The feeling I experienced at that moment has not dimmed with time.

The four hours completed, Mitchell called me over.

'Ready to go solo?'

'I think so.' I didn't, of course.

'OK. Take that one up.' He pointed to his most decrepit looking machine. 'Now remember, if you're going to crash, turn off the magneto switches before you do - less likely to catch fire. Do one circuit and land again. Off you go!'

With much trepidation, I climbed into the Instructor's cockpit. I set the controls, turned on the magneto switches (which for some reason were on the outside of the aircraft) and a man swung the propeller. 'Contact!' The engine burst into staccato life and I taxied to the far side of the field, turned the machine and faced a strongish wind. Opening the throttle fully the machine gathered speed, bouncing merrily over the uneven turf. With only one person to carry, the aircraft rose unexpectedly quickly. In a series of undulations I was soon at the required height of 1,000 feet, wobbling my way round the standard circuit. Then I commenced the descent, always the most difficult part. I approached the field with little enough confidence but, to my relief, I seemed to be well set for a perfect landing. The wheels touched down and just as I was about to cut the engine, the plane, caught by a strong sea-breeze, soared up to fifty feet or so and hung in the air, apparently stationary. With only seconds to spare before it stalled and crashed, I opened the throttle, put the nose down and gathered flying speed. Then I was over the perimeter fence and committed to another circuit.

Puzzled but not yet in a panic, I completed a further circuit and made a new approach. Exactly the same thing happened. I tried again. The aeroplane simply would not stay on the ground. By now, my puzzlement had turned to mild alarm. I noticed Mitchell gesticulating wildly in front of the hangar but his signals conveyed nothing.

The next time round, I managed three attempted landings, one after the other, as I flew up the runway. After each one, I found myself airborne again. There now seemed to be no particular reason to believe that I would ever succeed in landing this infernal machine. As I flew around yet again, the last dregs of confidence vanished as I beheld a fire engine drawing up alongside the landing strip. This was immediately joined by an ambulance. A small crowd was gathering.

I now learnt about fear. With the prospect of imminent disaster, muscles became taut, resulting in jerky, inappropriate movements. The inside of my mouth went dry, so dry that it was difficult to think of much else. My brain locked into a single idea - fly the Tiger Moth onto the field under power, instead of stalling it onto the ground as instructed. I knew this would be my last attempt. I touched down, threw the outside ignition switches, shut my eyes and awaited the crash. I had made a perfect landing.

I felt utterly drained and sat slumped in the cockpit. Mitchell came across.

'Didn't anyone tell you how to land in a wind?

'No.'

'You don't stall it, you fly it onto the ground.'

'So I found out.'

'You'll lose confidence if you do this sort of thing. It's the same as falling off a horse. Take off again at once and do a circuit or you'll never fly again.'

I felt I never wanted to fly again anyhow. But I did as he said. And made a good landing.

CHAPTER 7

A fairy godmother – become global super-salesman by accident – pioneer aviator Sir Gordon Taylor – assisting a kleptomaniac – joining the staff in a Malaysian brothel

THE REDOUTABLE Mrs Wood now came back into my life. She had focused on my brother John as a potential immigrant to Canada. Also briefly jobless at that period, he was a very willing explorer. It so happened that his invitation to cross the Atlantic coincided with my outward journey to Australasia to sell the translucent roofing sheets. Mrs Wood was anxious that John should also experience Canada and that, at a time when the British appeared so impecunious to North Americans, we should both be seen to be affluent, a view with which we had no quarrel.

John had gone on ahead and we met in Montreal. A suite had been reserved in the vast King Edward Hotel. It was bitterly cold and the hotel was superheated. In our heavy English tweeds, we were at once much too hot. I opened the windows of our rooms, then we went out to explore the town and returned much later to find the hotel in a state of crisis. The heating had gone off and the residents were buzzing with anger. It turned out that it was all my fault. The steam-heated radiators of our suite had frozen solid beneath the open windows and in some way I never quite understood, had necessitated closing the system for some repair.

It was here that we discovered the fun of launching paper aeroplanes from a high window - now only briefly opened for the purpose. The extraordinary air currents produced by the heating systems and the ice-cold ambient air, caused the planes to perform some amazing aerobatics and stay aloft for ages. Why, I wondered, were we the only people to do this – was everyone else bored by it?

Mrs Wood had by now been successful in luring her nephew Ralfe to Canada. Since our jaunt around North America, he had married a

Canadian, and moved out to Winnipeg, but was at this time temporarily acting as tax collector at Whitehorse in the Yukon. His wife Jane had given birth to a son on Christmas Day *on* the dining room table at the Governor General's house. Now she had returned to Winnipeg and we were headed to stay with her in their bungalow on the outskirts of the town, Ralfe being still in the Yukon.

We crossed Canada by train. To look from the window at the snow-covered and featureless landscape of the Prairies is to wonder how anyone would voluntarily wish to live there. If Mrs Wood's immigrant hopes for us were ever near to fulfilment, Winnipeg was the place where they met their end. The thickest British tweeds were of no more protection from the biting winter winds than a pair of summer pyjamas. Knee-deep snow was glazed with ice on which one might walk a good distance before falling through and grazing a leg. In winter, one remained indoors or in a car. In summer it was much the same regime to escape the awful heat.

Jane met us at the station and we threw our several suitcases into the back of her stationwagon. It was only when we reached her house and removed our luggage that we found we had piled them on top of a box containing her new baby, Hugh. A few weeks earlier, in the Yukon, she had looked out of a window to see a bear peering into Hugh's pram.

We made a brief stop in Banff where in the most dismal conditions, we hired skis and descended the lower slopes of Mount Standish, dressed still in our resilient but far from waterproof tweed suits. We became soaked and frozen and took ourselves to a bar to thaw out. We ordered beers, stood at the bar and started to drink. At once there was a cheer from twelve other drinkers. It was a law in Alberta that to drink, people had to be seated: it was therefore obvious that we were foreign. Each of the twelve stood us both a beer and it was not until we had downed the twenty-four glasses that we could leave without loss of face.

My first night at the ill-named Sunshine Lodge was different to any other so far experienced. The Lodge had only one room left. It had a single bed (which John won on a toss) and two bunk beds of flimsy construction. For reasons of overhead space, I chose the upper bunk. We put our luggage on the lower one and went to find something to eat. When we returned, the luggage was on the floor and a couple were 'busy' in the lower bunk. We retired discreetly and returned an hour later, having learnt from the crafty Management that they had hired us beds, not a room. When we came back the situation was unchanged. Without verbal exchange, we climbed into bed - in my case, one which rocked and pitched seemingly without respite the entire night. The next morning, I rose early, tired but deeply impressed.

The train continued its serpentine course, very slowly, through the thick snow of the Rockies to Vancouver where John and I parted, he to England and I to New Zealand, stopping on the way for a day in Hawaii, another in Tahiti and a third in Fiji.

Shortly I would be landing in Auckland. It was time to reflect: my relaxed and luxuriously subsidised travels to the opposite side of the world were about to end. I would step onto the soil in New Zealand in my new persona of 'technical sales representative'. I had no idea how I would fare in this capacity. I had a bag full of sections of roofing sheets in differing profiles and colours. I had price lists and pages of technical data. Now it was up to me.

I peered down at the outer suburbs of Auckland as we came in to land. It was clear that there were indeed any number of corrugated roofing sheets, mostly painted in green or dull red. And it was also true that few of these had roof-lights incorporated.

The Agents for the company in New Zealand were the Scott Timber and Hardware Company. Peter Scott was to meet me on arrival.

I liked him immediately. Not much older than me, it was soon apparent that he had a well-developed sense of fun. As we drove to his offices, I inquired somewhat anxiously how I was to get round New Zealand to make my calls on building material wholesalers.

'Quite unnecessary,' he said. 'All you need to do is to meet our branch managers in Auckland, Wellington and Christchurch. They already know about the product, they think it will sell and they just need the samples you've brought. The Auckland branch manager will spend a week on the road with the samples. Meanwhile, if you agree, we'll go up to the Bay of Islands, hire a boat, fish and have a good time. My wife Marilyn would like to come too if you don't mind. Then we'll see if the stuff has sold when we go back to Auckland. If they do get orders, you can send them to the factory as if *you'd* taken them.'

This was a most promising start.

The Bay of Islands in the north of New Zealand was most attractive. So was his new wife. It was a happy time during which I began to wonder whether New Zealand might be a good place to live and work – a thought that remained with me for many years. I liked the country and the few people I had met and I especially appreciated the slower pace at which life was lived. But there was a wind that seemed never to cease for a single minute.

We returned to Auckland. There was a huge stack of orders and much excitement. In Wellington and Christchurch, it was the same story. I posted them all back to the factory with a cover letter which did not go out of its way to prevent any assumption that I was a dream salesman. Peter's brother David decided to come over to England to see the factory soon after I was due to return.

I flew over to Sydney filled with the false confidence of a vicariously successful salesman.

Once again I looked down from the aircraft as we approached Sydney and was greatly encouraged to observe an even bigger sea of corrugated roofs. It had been arranged that the Saunders-Roe Agents would attend to the launch of this new product. For this purpose, they had assigned to me one of their team, Ron Hunter, who would make the necessary arrangements.

But first of all, I was to meet the Agent himself, Sir Gordon Taylor. I already knew something about the legendary exploits of this man, so well known in Australia. One of the great aviators of all time, he had made the first flight from Australia to America (1934), the first to Africa (1939), and the first to South America (1951). He had been knighted for his services to aviation. He had also won the George Cross.

Gordon welcomed me with solicitous warmth. He was one of those great and rare men who somehow managed to make the vast gap in age and achievement instantly disappear.

'I think you should spend a few days in Sydney, then a few in Melbourne. While you're in either city, you've been made a member of the Union Club, the nearest thing we have to a good London club. Australia is a great country and I want you to see as much of it as possible. I've got a new MG sports car which I don't really need yet so take it where you like and give it back to me when you finish. I've got good friends in the outback and I thought you'd like to meet some of

Louis d'Estienne d'Orves

Frankie Festing. Later to become a Field Marshal. He helped me greatly to put life into perspective whilst I was his ADC.

At 19, here in the full dress of the Rifle Brigade. I spent much of my National Service in Paris with the somewhat honorary rank of captain.

Top left. The incident of the veil at my wedding to Virginia
Top right. Virginia at the time of our wedding
Left. Hurst Farm in Sussex
Below. L-R, Laura, Roger (nephew), Joanna (niece), Hugo, George.

them. I'm an old boy but I recently married a girl of 26. She's getting desperate to go night-clubbing and I'm a bit too far gone to dance all night. So I'm counting on you. Feel up to it tonight? Yes? I'll pick you up at the Club at 7.30. OK? Good!'

At 7.30 he appeared and seemed to know everyone in the Club.

'Let's go quickly or I'll never get away; my wife's in the car and longing to meet you.'

In the front seat of the car sat one of the most attractive girls I had ever set eyes upon. I forgot how tired I was and danced the night away very cosily and apparently to the satisfaction of husband and wife.

Ron Hunter joined me for the long drive from Sydney to Brisbane. Five hundred and seventy-five miles in one day, through forests of blue gum, many of them on red laterite roads, trailing behind us an immense dust cloud. We spent a few days in the area visiting wholesalers of building materials. Ron took the orders and the results were phenomenal. They were falling over each other to receive early deliveries. We were never turned down. It was a salesman's paradise.

Ron let me into his darkest secret. He was a kleptomaniac specialising in hotel cutlery. He just *had* to secure a knife, fork and spoon, provided they were badged, from every hotel we visited. He was a charming man and as far as I know, this was his only vice. I suppose I should be ashamed of having helped him enlarge his collection but, alas, I am not, as I enjoyed seeing him get so much pleasure for such a small cost.

I drove to meet Gordon's grazier friends in the Australian Alps. These people flew light aircraft everywhere, even from one part of their farm to another. Then I stayed with another of his friends on a Murray River farm.

'I've got a horse saddled up for you,' said my host. 'I'll take you to see my boys rounding up cattle.'

I nodded assent, too abashed to admit that I was a hopeless rider.

'Now, whatever you do, don't fall off in this next bit near the river; it's carpeted with rattlesnakes so we'll go through it fast.'

I was a few hundred yards into it when I fell off.

'Thought you said you could ride: must have misheard.'

We returned to the farm, pride badly wounded.

In the Union Club in Melbourne, I was introduced to fried oysters. I ate them in dozens for breakfast, lunch and dinner. This passion for oysters came to a sudden halt when, later in London, I ate a bad one and was unconscious for three hours.

The wholesalers of Melbourne pressed orders continuously into my extended hand. Buoyed up by the illusion of my success, I hopped across to Tasmania where my ex-Rifle Brigade brother officer Roger Parker-Jervis was ADC to the Governor. Thence to Adelaide and the interminable trans-continental railway journey to Perth, across the endless emptiness of the Nulabor Plain with its choking red dust and sweltering heat. From Perth, I went by light aircraft to Darwin, stopping at various ranches on the way to pick-up or put-down farmers and all the while receiving more and more orders. These I posted back with covering letters which neglected to mention the extraordinary force with which they were heaped upon me.

My next stop was Singapore. The Saunders-Roe Agent had booked me into the Raffles Hotel - the old and now demolished Raffles. This was the ultimate experience in colonial comfort of a bygone period. Here I received a letter from the factory telling me that I had done very well indeed and that in view of the immense number of orders, several new production lines had been laid down and dispatch of the first orders had already taken place. I basked in the praise and flew on to Kuala Lumpur. More orders, ready and waiting. In my entire tour, I had not actually had to sell a thing myself.

The Malaysian Agent took me to a restaurant where the plethora of delicious dishes soon filled me to an uncomfortable extent.

'Massage Club!' pronounced the Agent rubbing his ample tummy. 'We go now. Yes? Very good. You like it, yes? Very good girls, very happy, you come, yes?'

Deeply apprehensive but not wishing to offend I agreed to go. I had vague notions about massage parlours in general and Eastern ones in particular but a wish to receive nothing more than a massage induced a reluctance to enter the place with enthusiasm.

I was led down narrow passages with a mounting sense of foreboding. Outside a red-painted door, the Agent stopped and beamed at me.

'Best massage in Kuala Lumpur! You see. You choose best girl. I follow.' I was tempted to make a run for it but I knew it would have been thought pathetic.

The door opened and we ascended a flight of stairs to a large hall lit by a skylight. Around the walls hung with dark red silk, there ran on three sides a kind of continuous ottoman. On this, in an assortment of alluring positions, sat about a dozen girls most scantily clad. On the fourth side was a raised desk and behind it sat a large woman, no longer young, the repository of numerous necklaces, bangles and miscellaneous adornments. To this woman, the Agent addressed himself in a low voice, turning to indicate me. Money appeared to change hands. I hung back, trying to look at ease and stealing furtive glances at this horde of girls. There was a smell of strong scent.

The Madam, for such she plainly was, turned upon me a beaming smile and with the sweep of an arm indicated the range of her merchandise. There was a sudden silence. The row of girls, their gaze fixed upon this tall, white and perspiring youth, sat immobile awaiting his pointing finger. Half paralysed with confusion, I stared at the ground. A light giggle rippled through the group. My companion was studying the ceiling, muttering something, whereupon the Madam got up, walked toward the bench and selected an item from her stock. This was presented to me and I was beckoned to follow her.

I lay upon a bed and was massaged. It was pleasant, efficiently performed and lasted all of ten minutes. But the dew of rosy freshness I had fleetingly observed along the settees was not in evidence in my attendant. It was clear that I had been allocated an experienced wench used to dealing with diffident cases. There followed a series of gestures, accompanied by pidgin grunts which attempted to elicit whether I was wanting to accept her other skills and if so, which. But mental turmoil prevented my giving a clear signal either way and much perplexed, she withdrew.

I dressed and made my way back into the hall. My entry was greeted by titters, bashful smiles and highly provocative body movements. The Madam indicated a vacant place between two girls on the bench. There I sat for over an hour awaiting the return of my companion, for all the world a part of the establishment. And when other clients appeared, casting an appraising eye over the bodies on offer, my humiliation was fathomless and enduring. At least I remained unchosen.

On to Rangoon: richly gilded pagodas and rats scuttling through the streets. Calcutta: pampered luxury rubbing shoulders with extreme poverty. London: icy rain, traffic at a standstill, frustrating my intended rush to see Virginia.

CHAPTER 8

Bankrupting a factory – honeymoon – joblessness – spree in Tiger Moth ends in official grounding – dirty job in the Black Country – a ghost – demonstrating grinders to Middle Eastern Arabs – defeat at Waterloo – sacked and escape from Birmingham

BACK TO The Cedars in Ryde. Somehow it looked a little shrunken and less forbidding; I had not yet learned that appearances are substantially a function of confidence. Travel, I found, had given me a new perspective. And, besides, was I not now one of the world's great salesmen returning to receive the homage of his colleagues?

At the factory, it was indeed a hero's welcome! I had, it seemed, saved the day. Declining turnover had been reversed. Plywood manufacture was being edged out, replaced by rows of moulds on which the glass fibre and polyester resin was made into corrugated roofing sheets. The smell was appalling. Extra shifts were being worked and production was impressive. A continuous stream of orders continued to pour in from the places I had visited. The factory was swamped. People looked at me appraisingly, uncertainly.

Promotion was immediate. I was to work in the London office and assume responsibility for export. My salary leapt up.

For a few weeks, it was a life of minimal activity: the last thing the factory needed was more orders. Then one day I received a letter from Ron Hunter enclosing a complaint from a grazier who had installed twenty four sheets in the corrugated iron roof of his shearing barn. They had come from the first consignment to be delivered. These sheets had crazed, then cracked: pieces fell out, the rain came through. Replacements had been supplied but the matter looked serious. The next week, a similar problem had occurred in New Zealand. After that, the deluge. *All* were faulty. The 'accelerated weathering tests' on the samples I had observed being angled to the winter's occasional sun had proved totally irrelevant to conditions actually encountered.

There was a Board Meeting. The situation was deemed to be hopeless, the Company was placed into liquidation and I, along with all the employees, was jobless, victims of my accidental success with an imperfect product.

I returned home to Hammerwood again. But it was only to be 'home' for one more week. On 27 April 1955 I married Virginia Peto at St Paul's, Knightsbridge. We took the night train to Paris, arriving in time for breakfast at the Hotel Tremoïlle. In retrospect, there are better ways of spending the first night of a honeymoon! As we walked up the nearby Champs Elysées, we stopped at a kiosk to buy a paper. *The Times* carried a photograph of us leaving the church; Virginia's long veil had been swept up in the wind to become wrapped round my forehead and stream behind *me*!

I had booked two seats at the Opera for a four-hour performance of Wagner's *Tristan and Isolde* that evening. Looking back, I find this even more extraordinary than the night train! After three days in Paris, we took the train to Lake Como. As we passed through the Alps, I recall our first behavioural divergence - Virginia read assiduously whilst I was spellbound by the spectacular alpine scenery: I remember thinking that it represented a difference that would be difficult to bridge. Of course it is unimportant but at the time, this preparedness to ignore the view to which I had drawn attention repeatedly, seemed a kind of sacrilege. In spite of such limitations, we spent five happy days at the rather grand San Georgio Hotel in Lenno. In early May, Lake Como was at its most beautiful and quite uncrowded for it was still well before the time when so many idyllic places lost their charm to mass tourism.

Virginia had been bribed by her father not to drink before she was 21 or married. Her tolerance of alcohol was consequently rather limited, a fact which was all too clearly demonstrated at the San Georgio after she had experimentally consumed half a bottle of wine. With the help of a steadying hand she had managed to leave the dining room more or less upright but at the foot of the staircase she decided to make the climb on all-fours which was briefly embarrassing since on each landing there sat a maid (a feature of grand hotels in those days) trying desperately to keep a straight face.

Although married, we had nowhere to live. Once again Mrs Wood, a true fairy godmother, came to the rescue. Having just purchased a Sickert painting in London and having nowhere to put it, she took a short lease on the top two floors of Number 44 Eaton Place and gave it to us on the condition we accommodated the painting. Although we had no carpets and almost no furniture, at least we had one notable painting.

Our ten days of honeymoon were now extended by a further 126 days whilst I looked in vain for a job.

The tedious process of answering advertisements and attending occasional interviews was characterised by the advertiser misrepresenting the 'opportunities' and by me misrepresenting my abilities. I recall struggling *not* to land a job selling soap powders in West Africa and another in which I was required to manage a team of door-to-door salesmen in shampoos. 'Just get your foot in the door and if you're any use, you'll soon move on to better things,' advised my father, perfectly reasonably, once again facing the prospect of an unemployable son. Of course he was right but I had only to enter the portals of some pretentious head office to be overtaken by a desire to rush back out into the sunlight. 'Mr Carter will see you now,' said the Receptionist, 'fourth floor end of corridor on the right'. My heart would sink as I made my way to the dingy office and then it would plummet when I saw what twenty-five years in the firm had done to Mr Carter. 'There's a lot in your CV about your time in the army but I'm afraid that doesn't cut much ice here.' Peering over his spectacles and inclining his balding head to my application, 'I wonder if you could tell me why it seems to be taking you so long to find another post - four months is a very long time indeed. Are you perhaps applying for jobs beyond your capability?'

It was disheartening interviews like this that planted the seeds of defection. They were slow to germinate but I began to know that one day I would abandon wasting my life in the idiotic pursuit of jobs I didn't want. I would break free. But now, right now, there was clearly nothing for it but find work and earn some money - for I had none. Partly as an economy, Virginia and I spent much of this time at Hammerwood. But this was also a reflection on how much I enjoyed being there, itself a product of powerful motherly influence. Both Virginia and I were still strongly under the sovereignty of home and looking back, this return to parents was a major error. We were two people who needed to shed these influences and to have struck off on our own. This failure contributed substantially to future disaster.

At weekends, I briefly resumed my interest in flying solo. I was joined in the first of these flights by my brother John and my father, each in other Tiger Moths. John had been learning with me but my father had not flown himself since the First World War. (After being wounded at the Somme, he had become a flying instructor in the newly founded Royal Flying Corps. Later, aged 95, he became its oldest member.) We made a single circuit in close convoy and landed safely. I have always regretted that there was no photographic record of such an unusual event. Within a few years, all six of Mitchell's Tiger Moths had crashed or become unserviceable.

We made a single circuit
in close convoy

The second flight was exhilarating; it was also my last solo flight. I had been told not to go for more than twenty minutes but when I rose into the air I felt freshly liberated, intensely joyful and filled with a new-found confidence - a potentially lethal mix. There was a deep blue sky dotted with small puffy clouds. I flew from Portsmouth up toward the South Downs and soon found myself above Uppark House. Two gardeners were at work in the walled garden. I decided to 'dive-bomb' them, roaring down then straightening up at the last moment. One lay down flat on the ground and another crouched under the wall, a most satisfactory result. I then hedge-hopped in a westerly direction. Seeing familiar places from a very low altitude I found fascinating and I sought various friends' houses to 'buzz'. In due course I arrived at the huge Fawley refinery on Southampton Water. The temptation to fly a slalom course in and out of the tall chimneys was irresistible. Unknown to me, my activities caused the general alarm to be sounded and fire engines readied. At once the aircraft's identification letters were traced by the Aviation Authorities in London. When, in a state of immense self-satisfaction I landed the machine, half an hour late, Mitchell came storming out to me to tell me I had been officially 'grounded' and would most likely be arrested. It was just as well as I wasn't very good at flying and I couldn't afford it anyhow.

It was not until September that I landed a job that promised well: I had not found the process easy. The only apparent drawback was that it meant working near Birmingham, the bleak industrial complex then known as the Black Country on account of the thousands of chimneys which used to belch soot into the air. On the western side lay Smethwick, my destination. In the intervening half century the forest of chimneys has mostly been felled. Indeed the town has been largely - though miserably - reconstructed. But in 1955, it was a kind of English Calcutta; huge numbers of diminutive factories of desolate appearance stood shoulder to shoulder along narrow streets. In those days, Britain still supplied vast quantities of manufactured products to much of the world.

One such factory made portable power-tools of an early variety. Its owner and managing director, who had built up the business from nothing, had decided to retire. Accordingly, he had advertised for a Personal Assistant to whom he might progressively delegate responsibility for the running of the firm. He had decided to hire me for the purpose.

Such was his eagerness to retire that he lost no time in handing over selected activities and from the start I was overfaced. The Sales Manager was constantly absent with chronic asthma and it fell to me to stand in for him also.

There were fifty or so employees. They stood at machines which rested on concrete plinths set into the oily earthen floor. Dimly lit sheds spread out behind the offices where the whirring of pulley belts and electric motors made it difficult to hear. A smell of cutting oil pervaded the place. In these insalubrious conditions, a workforce which was, to a man, cheerful, helpful and hardworking, turned out a useful range of products for which there was a modest demand worldwide. It now fell to me to maintain this demand against which foreign competition was making damaging in-roads, especially in the previously captive colonial markets.

In those days numerous factories required steam. The boilers in which the steam was generated were often rendered inefficient due to a build-up of limescale. To combat this, a device had been produced to chip the scale from inside the boiler. It consisted of a powerful electric motor which stayed on the ground outside: to this was attached a length of flexible drive on the end of which was the hand-held cutting head consisting of steel cutters which revolving at high speed were held against the lime-scale and scattered it far and wide. One of the world's nastiest jobs was to use this device, known as a 'Scatascalo'.

The boiler would be taken out of service for the minimum time. An access plate would be removed and the operator of the machine invited to enter. The noise of the cutters reverberating inside the still warm steel drum and the dust created by the flailing cutters defy description; it was hugely unpleasant, claustrophobic, dangerous and shockingly unhealthy.

A variant of this machine was one which, instead of a descaling head, had a grinding wheel and this was extensively used for removing the flash from welds. This was also noisy and could be dangerous as well due to the tendency for grinding wheels to shatter.

I was instructed to prepare leaflets in Arabic and then to make a sales tour of the Middle East to demonstrate personally the supposedly unique advantages of these devices.

Meanwhile, it was proving hard to find anywhere rural to live, within reach of the Black Country. In desperation, whilst Virginia spent the days looking for somewhere - anywhere - we stayed in the one remaining room at the Bell Inn in Belbroughton. I recall the landlady showing us into the depressingly furnished and stuffy bedroom. Behind the muslin curtains on the glass of the closed window were several dozen torpid bluebottles. Whilst informing us of the time she expected us for the evening meal and the times in which we were not permitted to use the bathroom, she proceeded to squash with her forefinger each and every bluebottle, leaving their remains on the linoleum below. The prospect of dinner seemed somehow less compelling.

Our room was adjacent, and separated by only the thinnest partition, to the room of a man who had a terminal pulmonary illness. His nocturnal noises combined with the disgusting food commonly served in pubs in the Fifties precipitated our immediate departure into the only other lodgings which could be found - the top floor of an enviably nice Georgian farmhouse owned by one of the most unpleasant couples ever encountered. It was to escape from this that we contemplated buying a house which seemed to be a bargain. It was the Old Rectory at Arley, near Bewdley, and we went to inspect it. As I walked up the rather grand Jacobean staircase ahead of Virginia, I was abruptly aware of a fearful - even terrifying - presence of such force that, quite involuntarily, I bolted to the top, rushed to a window and looked into the sunlit garden. I was joined a minute later by Virginia who had experienced precisely the same sensation. There had been no thought of the supernatural prior to that instant. Neither of us ever encountered anything similar before or since. But later we learnt that someone had been cut down and murdered on that staircase in the 17th century.

It is strange how many ghosts belong to an earlier century. How many ghosts, if any, are seen at Verdun or Stalingrad? I would be interested to know.

A short while later I embarked on the export 'sales drive' to the Middle East. The only way these machines could be sold to the Arabs was by means of demonstration, so in partnership with local agents I set up a stall in the *souk* of the capital city in each of nine countries and sheikdoms in the Middle East.

Sparks flew as we ground our way through inches of steel bar. Expressionless Arabs watched, inquired about prices, ordered. There was no bargaining, just a verbal order and a spoken address. When later these machines were delivered, there was not a single case of a bad debt.

It was on this tour that I met a man who greatly impressed me. He was the firm's appointed Agent for Egypt. He was a Christian Egyptian named, curiously, Israel. Married to a Greek, he had a powerful network of sub-agents throughout the Eastern Mediterranean. He decided to take my business education in hand.

Sitting at a massive desk, Dario Israel would lay before himself a single letter: nothing else remained on its polished surface. On this one letter, with whatever problem it contained, he would concentrate fiercely to the exclusion of all else, claiming that extraneous clutter surreptitiously dilutes concentration. I later found this to be true. Israel bargained ferociously with wholesalers but never beyond the point which he knew they could afford, having a deep-seated philosophy about 'good' and 'bad' money. Once, when he subsequently visited the factory in Smethwick, someone stole £500 in cash from his overcoat which he had inadvertently left for a few minutes in the cloakroom of the Plough and Harrow hotel. He forbade any pursuit of this money saying that the thief might have been in greater need of it for all he knew, and he did not wish to have the sum recovered as it might then be 'bad' money. In business his word was his bond. He committed most deals to his memory and seldom wrote out a contract. He was very widely trusted and this had led to a vastly successful empire.

Perhaps my most valuable lesson was that the conduct of a business must be enjoyable if it is to succeed. He himself found endless enjoyment in little things like a new foreign postage stamp, a mis-spelt letter, the street scene outside or a particularly good cup of coffee. His sense of fun was greatly endearing. He remained a good friend in the ensuing years.

I went from country to country, once again possessed of a product which proved easy to sell. In due course, I arrived in Iran. I had been given an introduction to the British Ambassador in Tehran who had kindly invited me to stay. When, the following morning, the ambassadorial Rolls Royce, sporting the Union Jack on its long shiny bonnet, deposited me at my metalworker's stall in the *souk*, adjacent stall holders were as much astonished as His Excellency's driver.

The owner of the Smethwick factory, in order to free himself still further, now hired an elderly Director of Engineering, one of whose tasks was to supervise me. We loathed each other on sight and I resented being supervised by someone who knew even less about marketing than I did. From the start we were on a collision course.

At this time, something happened which was seen to present the firm with a unique opportunity for huge sales. People of my generation all remember the familiar sound of railway carriages passing over the gaps between rails, da, da, da, der, da, da, da, der, on and on. This gap was deliberately incorporated into the laying of rails because in hot weather the rails expanded and the gap closed. Indeed accidents had occurred where insufficient space had been left and the rails had buckled but some bright engineer had recently discovered that only the last so many feet of a rail expanded lengthwise, the main extent of the rail expanded in *width*. Therefore, no matter how long a rail might be, only the last few feet needed to expand. And the effect of the wheels passing over the gap not only made this irritating sound but damaged both the wheels of the carriages and the rail-ends. Accordingly, it was decided to butt-weld the rails together to produce continuous lengths. This involved an almost unimaginable number of welding operations, each one of which left a seam of 'flash' which had to be ground away.

The new Director of Engineering designed a device for this purpose. It was large, heavy and expensive but it did the job, provided the rapidly spinning grinding wheel was lowered very slowly onto the rough weld. British Rail seemed excited by news of this invention and requested an immediate demonstration. It was assumed by the Director that only this apparent formality lay between the securing of a vast order and his obtaining a share of the accompanying profits. But he felt himself far too grand to give the demonstration personally.

Consequently, being reasonably proficient by now in the use of grinders, I was instructed to give it. It was to take place at Waterloo Station about 100 yards beyond the end of the last platform. The Regional Engineering Chiefs, their assistants and assistant-assistants were to attend.

The day chosen turned out to be wet, very wet. Traffic was reduced to a crawl and there were the usual parking problems. In consequence, I was a few minutes late as I arrived, puffing and sweating, pushing this cumbersome contrivance to the demonstration site at which the welders had created some extra-large welds for my benefit.

About thirty spectators all in mackintoshes and holding dripping umbrellas formed a half-circle around the welded rail. They had clearly not enjoyed the wait and I was requested to get on with the show as fast as possible.

I heaved the machine on to the rail and attempted to start its engine. It was wet and unco-operative. It coughed and spluttered then eventually burst into noisy life. Over the top of this and that of numerous passing trains, I addressed my damp-looking audience.

'Good morning gentlemen,' I said with as much bonhomie as I could muster. 'Here you see the latest invention to deal with the weld problem. I would like to assure you that this machine has been rigorously tested and in the hands of a skilled operator can remove a typical weld flash in a matter of seconds. It's a raily good machine.' My feeble pun left them looking blank. 'I will now demonstrate how even this extra large weld can be swiftly demolished.'

I lowered the grinding wheel, now turning at a ferocious speed, just a little too fast. There was a sound like a rifle shot and the wheel exploded into a 1,000 small, red-hot, flying fragments. It was as though I had tossed a grenade at my audience. There were no fatal injuries but most of the mackintoshes were punctured as were the protruding trouser legs. There were also some nasty skin grazes and someone ran for a first-aid box. The only person left entirely unscathed was the demonstrator who, in his haste, had omitted to turn the grinding wheel's half-guard away from himself and toward the audience!

The Engineering Director assumed I had deliberately sabotaged the demonstration and when a short while later it was learned that a competitor's machine had been selected by British Rail, his fury was cold and vengeful.

The weeks and months rolled on. I was well paid and had good prospects, moreover the job was interesting and I had considerable freedom of action. Yet I did not feel fulfilled. I was increasingly conscious of the fact that all my efforts were in support of someone else's business and someone who wasn't even there. I was giving of my best yet my efforts were not guaranteeing my own future security. I was, in short, an employee. The grass on the employer's side of the fence seemed a lot greener. The urge to break free was now stronger than ever.

Virginia and I often returned to one or other of our homes at weekends. One weekend at Hammerwood, I discussed these feelings with my brother. Although at the time he was, at an exceptionally young age, the Secretary to a major group of companies, he had been having parallel thoughts. We decided to form our own company there and then. But since we hadn't the least idea what it might actually do and since we had almost no capital, we opted for some kind of agency business in which we might earn a percentage on sales as commission. Thus was born a business whose trading style was entirely vague; Industrial Agencies Limited.

It was clear to us both that in view of the extreme uncertainties that would attend the development of this enterprise, it would be sensible to remain in paid employment for the time being. We then allocated as much income as we could spare to fund the company and set about finding a 'manager' whose task it would initially be to identify products to sell and on which we might take a commission. Although this was a rather naïve concept we soon found someone, Charles Broad, who having just recovered from TB, was keen to have a part-time job and whose business experience fitted him well for such a task. We returned to our jobs with lighter hearts.

The axe fell when Broad telephoned me to report being unwell and because I could not be immediately found, the call was put through to the Director of Engineering who was thrilled to discover that, apparently, I had a business on the side. It had occupied none of my time but it was for him a convenient *causus bellae*. I was sacked, and this in the days when legal protection from unfair dismissal did not exist.

A few days later, Broad learnt that he had a recurrence of TB, threw himself from a train and was killed. It was a deeply sad and inauspicious start to my taking over where he left off but being suddenly jobless again, and being by now quite unwilling to submit myself again to the dreadful interview process, it seemed the obvious thing to do. My brother would join me in a year's time if I could get the business launched.

Virginia was thrilled to be leaving the Midlands. We found a farm cottage down a rutted track near Loxwood on the Surrey-Sussex borders and with the help of a mortgage we purchased Hurst Farm for £2,000.

CHAPTER 9

Launch own company – make a profit of five shillings – on the road – crisis and lucky break – into production – saga of a suitcase – playing at shops – alias George Ross – swap cottage for a grand house at no cost – lose earth-mover in quicksand – obtain agency for new German aircraft and strike chimney whilst demonstrating

By now, in 1957, I was 26, married, discharged from two employments, unqualified, nearly without funds and on the verge of taking a potentially terminal financial risk. On the credit side, I had found that I could sell things, had a fair grounding in business (which turned out against all that I had been told to be largely a matter of commonsense), and had visited thirty-eight countries in five continents, thereby harvesting many contacts. Of greater value perhaps was the discovery that the business world was not full of genii nor even of people with much ambition. I was astonished by the way so many people wasted time. Indeed, I met many whose main occupation seemed to be to *kill* time, people who were delighted to be sent on missions unrelated to their own progress. Business life for many was something of a charade wherein success lay in one's *apparent* importance: improved office furnishings might be judged a more worthwhile attainment than the profitable development of the business. Hours were spent in talking inconsequentially and at the end of the day, pubs would fill with those not over-anxious to return home, their sad faces lined up behind the bar, seeking temporary oblivion.

All this was in the days when people held jobs for years on end, even for life; when competition was perhaps less fierce. Into this world I now stepped uneasily. It was like flying solo again. There was no-one to say 'stop, you can't do this' but there was also no-one to ask 'how do you do this?' Within a few days, I realised how piecemeal was my experience. We had decided that we wanted to trade but we had not the least idea in what. Or how. Or where. It seemed difficult to get a grasp on anything solid. But in the first six months, a number of wildly disparate opportunities appeared haphazardly via such business contacts as we had between us. There was a possibility of selling an ocean of creosote to Finnish Railways (unsuccessful); selling a petrol filling station in deepest Wales (unsuccessful); selling a £300 consignment of antique furniture in New Zealand (success - a profit of five shillings).

Then a modest break. I had met someone who manufactured cedarwood bungalows and who needed a documentary film made to show how they were built. I had an old (even then) 16mm cine camera and I offered to shoot the film. It brought me a good fee and, thus encouraged, I thought briefly of making films professionally.

A friend who visited Norway happened across a range of eight melamine kitchen tools in five bright colours. There was nothing like this on the British market and colour was just beginning to animate kitchens. I concluded an arrangement with the makers for exclusive import. Daringly, I placed an order for stock worth £26. I then sold a small part of this shipment to Selfridges for £10 5s 6d. It had taken six months to procure the company's first trading receipt. But this microscopic sale yielded a wildly disproportionate boost to my confidence.

A kindly buyer at a London store explained that if we were to provide display units for the melamine kitchen tools, hanging each tool on a rack and giving each a name (even if its function was perfectly obvious) sales would increase dramatically. Together with my brother and our two wives, we converged on Hammerwood and manufactured dozens of display units which were amateurishly flimsy but functional. We even made presentation boxes of cardboard with a cellophane window through which a set of tools was partially visible. Buyers assured us this would sell well for Christmas.

And so it proved. This relatively insignificant product determined our eventual field of operation. The display units yielded a rich harvest of orders and prospects justified the holding of a considerable stock. This was kept in an ancient slab-roofed grain store which sat on stone mushrooms adjacent to our new home. One side had sunk, so the whole building leant dangerously. Stock was placed carefully on the higher side but each time I entered, I half-expected the place to collapse and whilst assembling orders, I found myself tip-toeing silently from one type of spoon to another.

I would go to London and walk miles and miles with my bag of sample kitchen tools making 'cold' calls on store buyers, ironmongers and gift shops, picking up many orders. Then I would rush home, pack up the consignment, type out the invoice, load parcels and display units into the car, drive to London and make the deliveries. This experience of being salesman, packer, typist and delivery man stood me in good stead as the business developed. It was immensely hard work but strangely satisfying. And there was absolutely no-one to boss me around.

At the end of the first year, we had cash in hand of £59 12s 6d.

My brother John now joined me. His qualifications were in Accountancy and so we divided the business: I would see to sales and he to administration.

We began to find other Scandinavian kitchen products: a meat-tenderising hammer, mixing bowls, a knife sharpener, salad servers and a peculiar thing called a Hob-Nob which was of indeterminate function but somehow managed to look useful. We also obtained a small stock of plastic flowers from Italy - then all the rage. When these last arrived, we found the flowers had been liberally doused with a most pungent and horrible scent which made them unsaleable, a small disaster. A further set-back was an incoming shipment of a new kind of scraper-brush intended as an aid to washing-up. It was unmarked with its country of origin and therefore not in accordance with the Merchandise and Marks Act. I had to go to the docks, unpack the brushes and stick on each a label saying 'Made in Sweden' – 8,500 of them.

In those days, a central London address for a trading company was considered important if not vital. We were lent, very kindly and free of charge, a Victorian clerk's desk in a shipping office in the City - indeed the one where I had been 'indentured' to learn about export documentation. It had a high sloping top and was meant for writing on whilst standing. But at least it gave us an address and it was in Billeter Street which was 'respectable'. For £3 we purchased a typewriter which kept trying to slide off the sloping desk and which represented our total investment in office equipment. There was no telephone, nor was there room for us both together for by now my brother John had joined me.

A Victorian clerk's desk in a shipping office

We took a basement office at 9 Hertford Street in Mayfair which was available for a small rental, small because it was one gloomy room lit by a skylight above our desks. Four floors above the skylight was a flower pot a third of which projected over its windowsill. In view of this, £2 8s 6d was spent - after much debate - on a wire guard for the skylight.

Turnover gradually increased but there were now two of us needing money. We had also spent almost all our slender reserves. We gave ourselves a month in which to make some profits. I raced round Britain, scouring the town centres for potential customers from Penzance to Inverness with an ever-heavier bag of samples. More orders. But still not quite enough to break even. We gave ourselves one final month but unless we could turn in a profit, we would be obliged to cease trading. The future beyond that didn't bear thinking about.

Walking briskly along Piccadilly, I noticed some 'gifty' items of kitchen hardware in the window of Robert Jackson, an upmarket grocer now defunct, whose basement hardware department I had overlooked on my previous sales walks.

The buyer of this department had just returned from an alcoholic lunch, provided by a hopeful supplier, and this good man - for such he was - seemed eager to pass on a helpful tip. He fumbled in a drawer and found a business card bearing the name Clifford Harrington. This man, he explained, had called on him earlier that week with a sample of a spiked meat-carving dish, in stainless steel made at a factory part-owned by this same man whose name and Brighton address now held my full attention. Clifford Harrington was, it seemed, anxious to find an organisation to sell it. The buyer forecast good sales. I thanked him profusely and caught the next train to Brighton.

It was a meeting attended by Fortune. It was one of those rare instant-but-enduring friendships. Clifford was a Director of a coach-building works, Thomas Harrington, which was seeking to diversify, the sale of hand-made car bodies being in sharp decline. An exclusive distributorship was immediately agreed and I relieved him of the one and only sample carving dish.

Rushing back to London, I went round all my new buyer-contacts and quickly secured a huge pile of orders. Harringtons flew into production and we found ourselves possessed of a 'hot seller'. Shops we had never even heard of wrote to us for details of this new wonder-product which was, all said and done, a look-alike recreation of a Victorian meat dish but with spikes added and made of stainless steel instead of china. Stainless steel was suddenly fashionable. The carving dish made an ideal present for men - always in short supply - and it received much editorial publicity recommending it as a perfect wedding present. In consequence, a vast number of couples who married in the Sixties have one of these dishes, *our* dishes!

I was well aware that the amount of sales calls that could be packed into a day was crucial to survival. In major cities, I often ran from one call to another. I seldom made appointments, finding it more productive by far to rely on talking my way in to see the buyer. Frequently I would encounter salesmen sitting in some stuffy outer office awaiting an appointment perhaps an hour or so ahead. These patient time-unconscious salesmen could often be overtaken and sometimes they lost to me a good slice of the buyer's budget.

Selling is a skill, one which I found could be honed to produce astonishing results. Within my field, I learnt six rules as I progressed. The first is never try to sell a single product; it is too easy for the buyer to find a reason why he doesn't want it. The conversation must be switched from 'if' to 'which'. The second rule is never to produce your samples too soon. It is vital to build up a sense of excited anticipation before showing them. I have known buyers, after appropriate verbal preparation, seize a wrapped sample like a spoilt child at Christmas and unpack it for examination, unable to restrain their curiosity any longer. Rule number three is related; samples must be immaculate, un-fingermarked and wrapped in successive layers of high quality protective material - this engenders an air of status and prolongs the state of rising curiosity as the layers are progressively but slowly removed. A bit like Salome discarding her seven veils, I found it paid to delay the removal of the last layer whilst accelerating my 'patter'. As soon as, but not until, it was evident that the buyer was no longer listening - being desperate to see the sample - I took away this last wrap and awaited sounds of admiration. The fourth rule is to present your 'selling points' in inverse order to their strength. All buyers are looking for arguments in favour of rejecting your product. It pays, therefore, to open with a feeble selling point so the buyer can have the satisfaction demolishing it. The fifth rule is never to 'knock' your competitors' product: a buyer will rally to his defence and the atmosphere is soured. The last rule is to present oneself as smartly dressed as one can afford. In my sample bag, I also carried a duster for shining up my shoes between calls. I never ceased to be amazed by the number of company sales representatives who ignored these rules, greatly to their detriment.

In the winter we went to ski for the first time. It was then possible for one person to go free if a party of sixteen people could be put together. Taking advantage of this, we set off for the village of St Johann near Kitzbühel in Austria, which then boasted a single short ski lift and un-pisted slopes: skiing in the late fifties was still very much a minority sport. In those days, travel was normally by train which involved a largely sleepless night on couchettes. Such wagons had a well-deserved reputation as a breeding ground for colds and influenza, a free bonus now in the gift of airlines. Accordingly I arrived early at Victoria Station with a disinfectant aerosol to purge our reserved compartment of its bugs. I discharged the entire contents into the darkness, reclosed the door and retreated to the platform outside. To my dismay, I saw the door of the compartment suddenly open and four people stagger out in their pyjamas, coughing, gasping and filled with the spirit of retribution. I slunk away to check the compartment number again – right number, wrong carriage!

I sometimes wonder whether learning to ski then was possibly more pleasurable than now. To descend even a 1,000 foot in soft snow with long skis took much time and incurred many mishaps but it engendered a warm glow of achievement. As with so many other tourist-related experiences, the enjoyment is so often, if not always, in inverse proportion to the number of participants.

On the return journey, there was an absurd incident with an Austrian ticket inspector. Insufficient room in our compartment for all our luggage obliged me to put my suitcase in the corridor. The inspector said this was against the rules so I moved it to a large space at the end of the corridor. He returned to say, as rudely as possible, that this was also illegal and that I would have to sit with it on my knee. I ignored him. When we arrived in Innsbrück, where we had to change trains, the suitcase had disappeared. I found the railway police and reported the matter. Four months later, I received a letter from them informing me that the suitcase was now in their possession and would be returned on payment of 25% of the estimated value of the contents - by way of reward for the finder. The case had been thrown out of the train by the inspector. It had hit a telegraph post and burst open, scattering its contents into deep snow soon covered by fresh snow. In the spring thaw, someone had found it, collected everything, including two cuff-links packed loose and handed it all to the Railway Police to claim the reward - a system which demonstrably works.

The business was beginning to climb into profits. Paying ourselves the minimum, the rest was instantly ploughed back as we sought to reinforce the minor success so far achieved.

We hungered for new products. This was still a time of shortages and anything new and well made was exceedingly hard to find, but once found, it was relatively easy to sell. Our range gradually increased to include barbecues (a newly emerging fashion) insulated picnic containers (a failure), an onion chopper (still going after thirty years), a cast-iron boot remover in the shape of a huge ant (named the De-Boot-Ant and featuring in Christmas catalogues for years), a selection of rather horrible plastic dispensers for quickly squeezing huge quantities of ketchup onto platters of fish and chips (a one-season wonder) and a wine-making kit which was not only a commercial failure but tempted all concerned to waste a large amount of valuable time in private experiment!

To save time commuting to London, we decided to rent a diminutive office in the High Street of Haslemere not far from our homes. It seems an obvious decision now but at the time conventional wisdom held that provincial offices were death to a business. We found it to be our single best move; time, energy and quality of life all increased greatly.

... A diminutive office in The High Street...

Much amusement arose from an extremely small retail shop that we set out in one room nearest the street to dispose of unwanted stock. This shop was opened only if there was nothing else pressing, which was seldom, but on these occasions, the blind would be raised, the door opened and business done. One day, the blind jammed at an angle across the window and defied all efforts to raise or lower it. A collecting tin, labelled 'Fund for the Blind', was placed beneath it in a frivolous moment. To our surprise, it amassed many contributions which were duly passed on to the appropriate charity though we remained ignorant as to the donors' intentions.

By 1962, we had a staff of fifteen and the tiny offices were quite inadequate. We moved along the road to Tudor House. Built in 1580, the internal partitions of lath and cow manure had preserved a pungent Tudor smell which pervaded the building. It was said to be haunted and this deterred the female staff from working late in the evenings.

Tudor House …
… was said to be haunted

With our move, we subsequently found we had abandoned a way of life to which, alas, it was impossible to return. All members of the Company had been at that time associated with every aspect of the business and nothing was rigidly departmentalised. Expansion had to be paid for by giving up a certain light-heartedness that had carried us through some tricky passages. During the earlier years continuing trading losses made a blithe dependence on fate essential. With our move the business began to become compartmented – unavoidable but regrettable, for so often it is contact with every-day detail which provides the interest as well as the humanity.

Concurrently with this move, the name of the Company was changed from Industrial Agencies Limited to Dexam International Limited in line with the name previously given to a recently formed French subsidiary. The acronym, derived from *Distributeurs Exclusifs des Articles de Ménage,* seemed appropriate enough until we discovered that *Article de Ménage* could commonly mean a chamber-pot.

These were years of frenzied activity, not only for my brother and me but also for our small and dedicated staff. We worked as much as was necessary to achieve our aim of establishing a business which was both profitable and enjoyable for all concerned. Success was built on service, even if this meant giving up swathes of time or travelling to the far reaches of the country.

As the company gradually gained the representation of leading manufacturers of glass and china, so the team visited their factories to learn how products were made and put faces to names. This was fascinating and gave me, and most others, a lifelong interest in these fields. Some such visits were combined with a period of relaxation if opportunity permitted. A visit to a glass works in Austria found us all skiing. Most of the party were new to winter sports which produced an assortment of consequences. Clifford Harrington, who had now joined us as General Manager, demolished a ski school class whilst trying a ski bicycle. The newly acquired Sales Manager got wedged inside level crossing gates and was extracted from the path of an oncoming train with seconds to spare while Anne Mortimore, our one and only female representative, fell into a deep ditch and acquired frostbite. Despite the odd wound, these escapades welded together a first-class team with a common body of camaraderie.

The Duke of Richmond and his son, the Earl of March, were, from the beginning, our sleeping partners in this two-family company. Their corporate entity, The Goodwood Estate Company, now built a factory at Chichester for the production of stainless steel tableware and this was rented by Dexam. Under the pseudonym of George Ross, I designed a complete range of contemporary stainless steel tableware marketed under the name 'Chichester'. For many years it sold very well in several countries until, like everything, stainless steel tableware went out of fashion. Now I come across pieces quite often in junk shops or even continental antique shops. It gives me an odd Methuselah-ish feeling; almost as though I had lived an earlier life.

In 1958, our first son Hugo was born. A baby who initially took unkindly to joining us and gave loud and incessant vent to his feelings made it quickly apparent that our cottage was too small.

At about this time, the Duke of Westminster was selling an estate at Hascombe, near Godalming. The centrepiece of this sale was Burgate House, built in 1734 with a wing added later and a Gertrude Jekyll garden. In the same lot was a lodge, a large stable block and sixteen acres. The lot failed against its reserve at auction and was subsequently knocked down to me for £8,500. I resold the stables to my parents, for whom Hammerwood had by now become too large, and resold the lodge to Robin Goodwin (the painter nephew of the painting uncle Albert Goodwin). The difference was covered by the sale of our cottage. Thus for no additional cost, I now possessed a beautiful period house with fine panelling and staircase, eighteen bedrooms, walled gardens, fifteen acres of woodlands and an uninterrupted and unspoilt view across the whole of the Weald of Sussex.

But instead of being underhoused, I was now grossly overhoused. To my surprise, I found the materials used in the new wing were of such value to a demolition firm, the house could be shrunk to little more than its original size at no cost. The work was put in hand and the house greatly improved. The garden, in spite of its pedigree, consisted of a series of six rather featureless terraces falling away from the house. Gertrude Jekyll had designed it toward the end of her life when she was nearly blind. I took it upon myself to alter it. This required the use of an earth mover.

This huge machine excavated its way onto a sunken lawn towards the end of one day. The driver removed the ignition keys and went home, reappearing the next morning. No earth mover. It must have been stolen! But, wait, what was that small yellow object protruding from the earth. Quick, fetch a spade! It's the top of the driver's seat -

the highest bit of the machine: an hour later that too had disappeared along with the earth-mover to which it was attached, never to be recovered. It was my first - and the contractor's first - introduction to 'running sand'.

The house had been built on a projection of solid sandstone. But where the greensand borders the Wealden clay, there are pockets in the clay which are, in effect, covered ponds or quicksands. The covering can be surprisingly thin though this is not readily apparent until it is removed and an object is left standing on top. The garden was constructed on such a site. Once exposed, even a spade left stuck in the ground would slide, imperceptibly, into oblivion.

We heard through a friend in the aviation world that a German aircraft company had produced a prototype two-seater aeroplane of unusual design. Of light construction, it had the engine and propeller at the rear end of its short fuselage. The makers wanted to find representation in Britain, and the idea appealed to us in spite of it being nothing whatever to do with our business, an unwarranted diversion for which I nearly paid with my life.

I dashed out to Germany, negotiated a draft agreement and arranged for a demonstration to be held. This was convened in a month's time at Croydon Airport, an early airfield progressively encroached upon by housing. Substantially reduced capability meant it was soon closed for ever.

A press release was written and aviation trade journalists invited to attend.

A fine day dawned. I arrived early at Croydon and met the test pilot who had flown the machine over, apparently without misadventure, from Dusseldorf the previous day. He was tall as well as broad and had one of those Germanic bull necks.

'Good morning Herr Stumpfenagel. Nice to meet you!'

'Ja.'

'Did you have a good flight over yesterday?'

'Ja. How many kilos you?

'I don't know in kilos: about twelve stone.'

'Stone? Stein? Was ist das? You tall man also. Bad!'

'Bad? Why?'

'Kleine plane, grosse men. Bad!'

'You think I should come with you?'

'Ja. You kommen. Two-seat plane, müssen two men haben.'

'Oh.'

'You give me bad field. Keine raum. Houses, alles houses. Bad.'

'Oh.'

'No vind. Bad. Veeree bad.'

'Oh.'

Such was my preparation for the demonstration flight. Several journalists, cameras swinging, arrived in good time to partake of the expensive refreshments we had hazarded for the occasion. I handed out the Company's brochure, printed only in German, and introduced Herr Stumpfenagel to a perplexed-looking press. He said nothing: his attention seemed to be totally absorbed by the windsock which hung limply from its standard.

With one eye on the rapidly diminishing levels in the bottles I announced that we would now demonstrate the aircraft. The journalists followed me onto the tarmac and stared at the frail-looking machine, shooting questions at the pilot who remained mute and dejected. Gesturing frantically to him to get in and go, Herr Stumpfenagel climbed slowly and heavily aboard and lowered himself gradually into his cockpit, motioning me to do likewise in the rear seat. I had not practised this and it took me an unimpressive number of minutes to manoevre myself into the inadequate space, my knees pressed into the pilot's back.

'Ve go now, ja?'

'Yes,' I answered hesitantly, torn between my desire for a successful demonstration and fear that the machine was inadequate for the load it now carried. But immediately we taxied to the end of the short runway. I noted with rising concern that Herr Stumpfenagel positioned the aircraft so that the tail was almost touching the perimeter fence. Then we were off.

About three-quarters of the way across the field, we rose slowly into the air and continued a few feet from the ground towards the houses at the far end. We appeared to be flying straight towards someone's bedroom window. Herr Stumpfenagel's neck was a series of taut bulges. At the last moment we rose to rooftop level - rooftop but not chimney-pot level. There was a sharp jolt, a peculiar noise and a tall clay pot struck by a wheel went rattling down the slates to the ground. The aircraft dipped slightly, touched the top-most leaves of a tree, rose a little more and eventually completed a circuit never exceeding 100 feet. Herr Stumpfenagel remained slumped in his seat.

'Gott in Himmel!'

'Yes, we nearly met.'

'Mein Gott! Bad, bad. Mein Gott!'

'We need whisky!'

'Ja. Ja. Visky! Schnell!'

The journalists had gone, along with the whisky. It cost £12 to supply and fix a new clay chimney-pot. Nothing more was ever heard of that aircraft. Tail between legs, I slunk back to concentrate on our hardware business.

CHAPTER 10

Overhoused and overstretched – a frenetic DIY handyman – marriage problems – business forges ahead – merging two companies in the Moroccan desert – initiative test extraordinary – drama behind Iron Curtain – instant violin virtuoso – business booms and I lose interest

DESPITE A great deal of excitement and fun, for me the Sixties were a difficult decade. The business continued to grow rapidly. Yet although profitable, it needed ever increasing capital to sustain its growth. We therefore took minimal salaries and were constantly overstretched. The house and garden seemed in urgent need of maintenance and I was soon obliged to acquire the skills of the DIY amateur. Nothing ever seemed to work for very long. The roof leaked, a garden wall fell down, windows needed paint, rooms had to be decorated, the kitchen modernised, the car seen to, acres of grass mown and high yew hedges clipped. There never seemed to be enough time for relaxation or even modest cultural pursuits.

Our daughter Laura was born in 1961 and second son George in 1964. Barbara Crocker came to help look after them. She stayed for twelve years on a minimal salary and became a very close friend to us all, except Jemima, the Basset hound, with whom she maintained a mutual loathing. Without her constant and loyal support, life might have been very difficult for all of us. Hers was the prop that kept the edifice standing and for this she earned the undying gratitude of us all.

We turned the top floor into a flat and rented it to a sister-in-law who had just married a sailor, Ben Bathurst, who later became the last Admiral of the Fleet.

My father had converted the stables into a house and he and my mother, now both in their seventies, set about making a garden from scratch. It soon flourished and they were clearly relieved to have escaped the problems of being overhoused and overgardened. I envied them.

To have one's parents as neighbours is not a guaranteed formula for success, still less so in the case of in-laws. But sufficient time had passed to smooth out rough edges all round and their presence was delightful to me and mostly so for Virginia of whom they had grown extremely fond. They lived a quiet and contented retirement, centred on family and garden, yet they also observed with well-concealed concern the deteriorating condition of our marriage.

My mother had suffered from angina for some years. One night she had a stroke which left her unable to talk or walk. It was the start of several difficult years during which partial recovery and further strokes competed to raise and dash our hopes. Few people could have been less well adapted to the immobility enforced upon her. Although initially unable to articulate except in grunts, she remained mentally unimpaired and as soon as she had sufficiently recovered the use of a hand, indicated in the shakiest scrawl that she wished to learn Russian.

Two successive nurses who attended her after her first stroke both talked about her over her head as though she was already dead, leaving us all to wonder why such unfeeling people could ever adopt this profession. When she was later able to talk and write a little, she confirmed to us how diabolical this behaviour had been.

A final stroke in 1969 carried her away, doubtless to her great relief, as to find herself a burden to others was, for her, the ultimate affliction. I was glad to have been around for her final years; it remains my hope that I was able to give back a little of the ever-selfless love she had shown me throughout my forty-eight years. We had been very close. Almost every day throughout my time at school and, later, in the army, she had written to me; in bad moments, it had been a lifeline. She wrote to my brother likewise. She was buried at nearby Dunsfold where, eighteen years later, my father joined her on the opposite side of a shared tombstone.

In the mid-Sixties, our marriage started to fall apart. As in most such cases, the reasons were complex. Asymmetrical interests had helped to divide us and the background of overwork and financial struggle had not helped. But we continued for another ten long years leading lives which were increasingly independent. The reason for doing so was to provide a constant domestic background for the children in their early years. But the price we paid was heavy. Compromises, emotional strain and the impossibility of simultaneously creating another long-term relationship exacted a massive toll and, in retrospect,

I believe that it would have been better for all of us if we had gone our separate ways sooner. It is impossible to be sure. We succeeded in remaining civilised through this long and difficult period though the need for escape was sometimes dominant. (I recall, for example, that I rushed off to Crete with a friend where we bought a donkey of improbable contrariness, and walked the length of the island. We returned on a ferry in a tempestuous sea in the company of Archbishop Makarios whose staff and stovepipe hat seemed to preserve our safety until we all disembarked at Pireus. On its next voyage, the ferry foundered with all hands lost.) In many marriages which fail, there still remains so much that is good and which, released from daily irritations, can be salvaged. Even when divorced and after my re-marriages and, later, after hers, we continued to visit each other quite often and to enjoy family holidays together every single year up to the present, apparently to the astonishment of all!

By 1965 we had outgrown our offices at Tudor House. This reflected the rapid commercial success we were now enjoying. We acquired a large private house named Watchers, formerly the home of Stewart Grainger, the actor. Hitherto we had worked in offices with views of no more than twenty yards. Here there were extensive gardens looking on to National Trust land. It even had a swimming pool and a tennis court.

We built a huge showroom and grew vegetables which a skilled cook turned into high quality lunches for trade buyers. Soon we were deluged with customers as word spread that a day spent in the Dexam showroom was an enjoyable experience. The Company prospered even more.

Meanwhile, the subsidiary company in France was also growing apace. Yet progress was accompanied by constant misunderstandings, bureaucratic tomfoolery and the perverse nature of the Gallic character, disadvantages inadequately offset by the pleasures of Paris.

A further subsidiary in Holland soon revealed the peculiar difficulties of working with the ever-knowing Dutch. It was promptly closed on the precept that the unenjoyable is unprofitable.

In 1966 we built a warehouse in Midhurst, West Sussex. This, and our own transport, greatly helped the smooth running of the business. Ken Hammond, the warehouse manager, who had been responsible for organising everything with great efficiency and who had brought together a first-class staff, met an untimely death when his tie became enmeshed in a shredding machine and he was strangled. A much loved and ever cheerful man, this loss was keenly felt for a long time to come.

Soon we were deluged with customers...

In one market or another, we were now representing many famous companies: Wedgwood, Orrefors, Coalport, Lalique, Royal Copenhagen, Kosta Boda, Daum, Masons Ironstone, Johnson Brothers and Waterford Crystal to name but a few of the world leaders in glass and ceramics.

With the addition of ever more salesmen, it became apparent that further team-welding was needed so one day the eighteen Sales Representatives received a memorandum announcing flatly that a Sales Conference would take place at latitude 30°10'N, longitude 5°04'W. Dust was shaken from school atlases and the horrible realisation dawned that the sands of the Northern Sahara were the intended location.

Two Land Rover drivers, Doug and Jim, met the eighteen members of the expedition at Casablanca - together with their sixty-five pieces of baggage. Somehow, the twenty piled into the two vehicles. But four miles outside the city and at a speed of 60mph, samples, rations, tents and bedding fell from the over-piled roof-rack and spun away into the night. From an apparently empty landscape, Arabs suddenly appeared and quickly identified our new product samples (the essential component of the voyage) as being highly desirable. It needed all our powers of persuasion and a little money to negotiate their return.

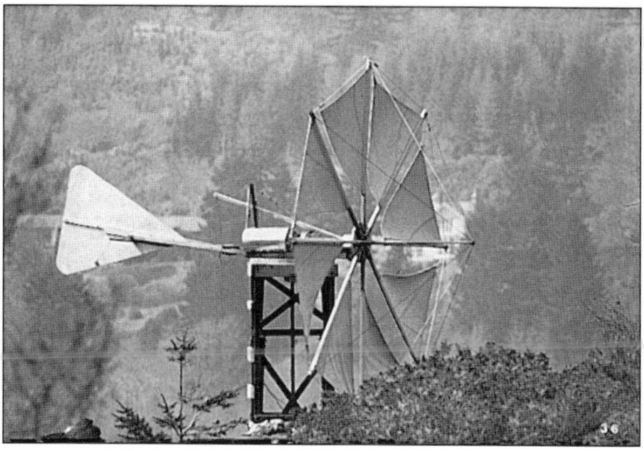

Top left. Prince Philip's visit to The Quarry. Things did not go quite according to plan!
Left. Diana, in the early days at The Quarry
Top Right. The cottages at The Quarry as we found them.
Above right. The 'Cretan' windmill. People loved it.
Below left. Barbara Crocker, with her much cherished cup of tea.
Below right. *S.S. Scythia*, which so impressed me, on one of her last Atlantic crossings.

Top left. Henbant Fach after the alterations, looking west.
Below left. Henbant looking east. Note the dormer windows which in the photo below are almost beneath a huge snowdrift. The winters could be severe and once we were marooned for ten days.
Bottom left. A neighbouring farmer taking stock to the market in Abergavenny six miles distant. Each animal had a name and were properly looked after - unlike so much stock today which is reared under battery conditions.
Bottom right. Robert.

After a noisy night in Marrakech, the following day saw us over the Atlas Mountains. Rough roads added to the discomfort of passengers whose heads became quite bruised. It was therefore a rather depressed party that finally arrived at the oasis of M'Hammid, site of the conference itself (which was subsequently the subject of a special report in *The Times*).

The sun went down during a desperate and unsuccessful struggle to erect tents before darkness was complete. The intense cold endured during the small hours proved the first blow to our physical well-being - it would have heartened our competitors to have seen us emerging from our tents in differing degrees of misery in the desert dawn. They would have been delighted to observe the Sales Force ailing from internal disorders, and severe chills, one of which turned to pneumonia. Medical stores consisted of the subsequently famous sulphaguanidine pill, which will long be remembered, and of which no less than 400 were issued during the course of the Directors' morning surgeries. A second pill designed to have the reverse effect found no demand. The only other medical stores, those acquired in the duty-free shop at Heathrow, were unfortunately appropriated and consumed shortly afterwards within a matter of minutes by the Caliph of M'Hammid and his bodyguard who, by means of some desert custom, considered it their due.

In this Oasis on the Moroccan-Algerian border, close to the last fortress outpost of the Camel Corps, and in the shade of huge date palms, the new products were presented to the Sales Force. It somehow added a degree of glamour to some quite prosaic items.

Suffice it to say that despite - or perhaps because of - an unquestionably rugged week, this expedition succeeded remarkably well in its primary job of welding new faces into the team.

Two years later, the Sales Force visited a Swiss manufacturer of fondue equipment (for which there was a vogue at the time). Following a toboggan race which had resulted in cuts and bruises due to one competitor trying to roll a cigarette while racing, the team thought they were headed for home. They were - but not in the manner they expected.

To the horror of all, the Sales Force were taken to a railway station and following the issue of a ticket, a very small amount of money and a sealed box (not to be opened until after departure), they embarked on the first ever Dexam Initiative Test. For the purpose of this test, the Sales Force had been divided into three teams and dispatched on different trains in different directions. These teams corresponded to the new sales areas and were under the command of newly appointed Area Managers. Once embarked on their trains, team leaders opened their boxes and read, to their dismay, instructions for the test. These called for the completion of fifteen tasks including the manufacture of a two-piece lounge suit for a member of the team (psychedelic suit material, scissors, thread and buttons provided), the suit to be worn on arrival at the Haslemere office; the assembly of a highly complicated and exceedingly delicate ship from a kit provided; the identification of a number of photographs; the taking of a photograph (cameras issued) of a team member performing various tasks such as milking a cow and kissing a French policeman, (bonus points being given for combining as many of the activities as possible in a single photograph); bringing back, still frozen in its original wrapper, a French ice-cream; and returning with the longest unbroken French loaf.

These requirements produced in anticipation a deep gloom. But within hours, situations varying from acute embarrassment to shaking hilarity replaced the initial despair.

When the groups had dispersed, the model boat builder of one team was crouching near a radiator far into the night, the pieces clamped between his hands when he fell asleep. On awaking in the small hours, he found himself superglued to both the model and the radiator. For a time it seemed that he was doomed to become a permanent fixture in the hotel. In due course Nature called and there was talk of dismantling the radiator so that he was free to accompany it, and the ship, to the WC and this manoeuvre was only avoided by a genius with a razorblade. One team obtained a fifteen foot long French loaf which met with disaster whilst travelling in the Paris Metro at rush hour. It was replaced by a nine foot loaf, tied to a plank. This endeavour started a correspondence in the French millers journal about how to produce such superloaves.

The return of the teams to Haslemere was exceedingly mirthful and boisterous. Once again shared fun and (relatively) harmless adventure had helped to create the remarkable spirit for which the company now enjoyed a reputation within its field that was - and hopefully remains - unique. Customers enjoyed a personal and genuinely friendly relationship with members of the company and they appreciated the sometimes huge efforts which were made to service their business requirements. As an example of this last, I recall an incident in which Percy Percival, a Sales Representative, had met with an accident. Before succumbing to the anaesthesia prior to an operation, Percy's last words to his wife were to try to hasten a delivery of 'seconds' to one of his customers.

There was, in this team-making endeavour, one further and rather more economical episode. It should be remembered that the salesman spends most of the year on his own with only occasional visits from Area Managers or senior staff. With only such infrequent meetings individuals accumulate a good bit on their chests and experience had shown that the safest place possible to let off steam was as far away from anything breakable as possible.

Pursuing this policy, a sales meeting was arranged at a point ten miles south of Ross-on-Wye. After checking into a hotel at Symonds Yat in order to give the illusion that the meeting was to be held in a nice, warm comfortable hotel - it being autumn - the Sales Force embarked on a sight-seeing trip down-river. Disembarking, a short walk led into one end of a pitch black, and puddle-ridden disused railway tunnel. Emerging at the far end the team found, to their horror, a small encampment of tents, kindly lent by the Ministry of Defence. At this moment and for most of the rest of the three-day conference, it rained incessantly. The whole area became deep in mud and the tents leaked. It says a good bit for the participants that the entire agenda started and closed on time and that the party ended in great spirits. The element of surprise - even unpleasant surprise - is a valuable weapon against boredom, the prime cause of disenchantment and collapse of morale.

Many visits were made to countries the other side of the Iron Curtain, principally Czechoslovakia and Hungary, in order to buy glassware. These journeys were always fascinating due to the first-hand chance to see Communism in action. Even at the humble level of a foreign glass-buyer, it was abundantly clear that inefficiency was rampant and that poverty and fear walked the streets. Occasionally the dramas of political knavery were played out before our eyes.

In Prague, before retiring to bed one evening, Clifford Harrington took a shower. He slipped and in falling grabbed a basin. It too fell to the ground shattering into jagged fragments. Clifford was badly cut and bleeding profusely. He shouted for help, repeatedly. Eventually, one of our party heard him and gave assistance. The next day, we found that both the occupants of the rooms adjacent to his had, of course, heard his shouts but had concluded that he was being hauled out by the secret police and did not dare to become involved. It is hard for us to imagine how terrible such a regime must be even for those who made no attempt to challenge it.

The head 'comrades' of the producing factories and the centralised selling offices never failed to entertain us lavishly. These exhausting banquets involved numerous toasts in slivovitch or vodka. For the comrades, such occasions enabled them to over-indulge at the expense of the state and not infrequently they became inebriated. At such moments, they were sometimes liable to become too free with their tongues. 'Minders' were everywhere and indiscretions could be fatal. Late one evening, at a banquet in our honour, during the reign of Bresznev, a factory manager, who spoke good English, rose unsteadily to his feet and entertained us with an hilarious characterisation of the Great Leader. He 'disappeared' a short while later. Another 'comrade' with whom I had become friendly shared my interest in music. He was particularly fond of Elgar's works but could not obtain any recordings. Subsequently, I sent him some and later heard that this simple act had resulted in his being demoted from all contact with foreign 'spies'.

If I had to encapsulate in two words the nature of life under Communism, I would choose *joylessness* and *fear.* Freedom at a personal level had been so effectively extinguished that there was no longer any point in trying to better one's position. To paint your front door, to grow extra food for your family or try too conspicuously in your job were all indications of non-conformity and all non-conformity was dangerous. Consequently, every business, every building and every person looked - and was - run-down and depressed.

Nobody trusted anyone else; often they could not even depend on their own family. People were spied upon by neighbours with a grievance and reported. The secret police had it all their own way.

Very occasionally, someone sufficiently senior and confident of his position in the hierarchy would chance his arm and try something different. There was one such occasion where it had been arranged that we should visit a winery situated in a cave. This was to be followed by a barbecue in a wooden chalet on one of the hills outside Budapest. We all emerged from the wine cave happily tipsy, having sampled several excellent dry Tokays and breathed deeply of the alcoholic fumes. It was a wonderfully warm night in late summer and an enormous orange moon was delightfully positioned over the hill. At the chalet a gypsy in embroidered jacket played heart-rending airs on his violin. A whole sheep was being roasted on a spit but it was far from being cooked so we sat on a verandah drinking Bull's Blood, sniffing the roasting mutton. By the time it was ready, I realised that I had consumed too much wine.

But the toasts were still to come and it was unthinkable not to participate. I became rather drunk. Then there was a rare and ancient sweet Tokay to be consumed: I had myself requested it whilst in the cave. This too must be imbibed.

The result was inevitable: I became completely drunk. But I was still articulate and, in fact, enjoying myself greatly. Whilst in this regrettable state, I heard myself have the following exchange with my host.

'Comrade, do you play the violin?'

'No Mr Grenwill, I not play wiolin.'

'Well *I* do. Please Comrade, will you ask the Gypsy to hand me his violin. I will play to you.'

I should have been warned by the expressions of alarm on the faces of my colleagues. The instrument was handed to me by an angry-looking Gypsy. Though I had never before held a violin, I put it to my shoulder in the manner of a maestro, seized the bow by the wrong end and immediately produced what I was subsequently told was a hideous grating sound.

I was at once convinced I was a genius. Not only was I a violinist of extraordinary talent but an outstanding composer into the bargain. Yet, disconcertingly, I received no acclaim - instead they were all looking at the moon with strained expressions. Then the gypsy, unable to restrain his anger, said something loud to my host who must have responded with the Hungarian equivalent of 'get lost' since he slunk off into the night.

I played on till, quite gradually, I began to slide beneath the table. As

I disappeared from sight, a hand relieved me of the instrument. I remember nothing more of that night but the shame of that incident haunts me still whenever I happen to hear a Gypsy violinist!

On these forays for new products we flew in a private aircraft, a twin-engined Aztec which, together with the pilot, John Gibbon, we shared with another company.

Trying to fly this machine myself convinced me that I was not a born pilot. I found I could quite easily forget to do essential things like putting down the undercarriage before landing. The ever-tactful John would interpose with a light touch - 'How about a bit of wheel before we land - only a suggestion!'

In eastern Europe, private planes were almost unknown. Approaching the airfield at Sibiu in Romania with none too much fuel, we found a flock of sheep, complete with shepherd, spread across the runway. Making two low passes, the shepherd got the message and very slowly moved his flock to one side whilst we repeatedly circled the airfield with the last of the fuel. We were informed that ours was the first private plane to land there since 1939.

When my brother and I had set up the Company, it was with a very definite object in view - financial security and independence. Although by the end of the Sixties we were a long way toward this goal, it turned out to be a seemingly endless struggle: always more and more capital was required to finance growth. My original aim was to have made enough money by the age of forty to retire from business and follow other pursuits. I did not want to go on doing the same kind of things year after year even if this was needed to be able, eventually, to retire a wealthy man.

My brother, however, increasingly enjoyed directing the company. He was an extremely gifted administrator and financier. He had a strong paternalistic outlook and felt that the large number of people we now employed and their numerous dependants were to a great extent his responsibility. He was happy, indeed eager, to follow the star of Dexam as far as it would take him.

I felt then, and feel now, that some people are better at starting enterprises and others at running them. I believed I belonged to the first category and he to the second. By now, I began to feel I had fulfilled my potential and had little left to offer the enterprise. I therefore began to mention these feelings and was vexed to find that my brother found them difficult, if not impossible, to understand.

It led, directly and unstoppably, to a cooling in what had for thirty years been a remarkably close relationship. But what was said was said. It was agreed that the following year I would take three months off in order to decide if my future lay in another direction. If I concluded it did not, I would return to the fold, all forgiven. If new pastures beckoned, then I would be supported by a continuing salary.

It was a formula designed to allow apparent uncertainty to ease the strain of my departure which, by now, we both knew to be definite and for the two of us these were sad and difficult months. I slowly realised that John saw my departure as bordering on treachery as well as threatening to the stability of the company. He had never seen himself as a salesman and he viewed the forthcoming void in this field with alarm. But I knew from my days in the army that the waters close rapidly over the heads of the departed: people *are* dispensable.

Towards the end of my time with Dexam, I went to a trade fair in Paris and came across a Spanish exhibitor displaying on a small table an array of porcelain figurines, mostly somewhat elongated and sentimentalised female forms. His company, then largely unknown outside Spain, was named Lladro. I obtained the distributorship for Britain. Over each year ahead, the quantity we sold increased exponentially. Eventually a vast container lorry would grind its way from Valencia to the warehouse in Midhurst every month, laden with an ever-expanding range of figurines. Thousands of people started collecting the pieces and aircraft were chartered by Dexam to fly trade buyers to the factory. Lladro was a very hot line indeed.

This was a fortunate find and it made a good leaving present for the company.

I find it difficult to express my regrets about leaving Dexam in the same breath as recording my wish so to do. There was much that I valued in the unusual ethos of Dexam. This had developed over the years and there was huge satisfaction in seeing the Company's growth from a vague idea to a major enterprise.

There was a spirit of hard work, professionalism, fun and comradeship: of challenge, sense of humour and open-mindedness: of mutual loyalty, friendship and much enjoyment. Laughter and wit were hourly events: seldom did one hear a raised voice. We always tried to give a service that competitors fell short of providing. I still remember, for instance, how Jim Emsley, a phenomenally successful salesman who joined us almost at the start, would - when necessary - rise at 3am on a winter's morning in Leeds to collect goods in Surrey and deliver them to customers in the north of England that afternoon. (In those days, over-night deliveries were unheard of.)

We were perhaps the first company in our field to move into a country house, the first to have sales meetings abroad and the first to become computerised. Yet at the offices in Haslemere, a visitor would still encounter a dog warming itself before a log fire.

CHAPTER II

Problems of an artist – uncontrollable urge to buy a barge – adventures on the waterways of Holland and France – a gendarme marooned – incidental life of a bargee – oh to be a lock-keeper – barging into business and the extraordinary consequences thereof

Some years before, whilst still at Burgate, I had experimented with oil painting and become excited in finding that I was not hopeless at it. I asked Robin Goodwin, the painter installed in the Lodge, if he would give me six lessons. In the course of these, I quickly discovered that I could paint, not brilliantly at all, but sufficiently well to extract a deep satisfaction.

I joined the Chelsea Art Society and exhibited. The canvasses sold for prices which encouraged the thought that I might make a living from painting. I spread my wings and showed in Paris a number of landscape paintings which I had done in France.

It was in France that I especially enjoyed painting - if indeed 'enjoy' is a word appropriate to an operation that is exhausting mentally and physically. But the painter of canvasses, in oil, especially large ones, faces great difficulty in returning these still 'wet' works in an undamaged state to his studio, especially when the painter is abroad.

It was this problem which gave rise to an idea which, in its fulfillment had extraordinary consequences.

One winter's day driving home from the office, the image of a motorised canal barge came floating into my mind. Simultaneously a barge combined all the advantages of a house with those of a mobile studio, a constantly changing scene before its windows. It offered complete independence of cars, aeroplanes, trains and hotels and an end to living out of suitcases. I should be able to travel in comfort and at my own leisurely pace. I should be able to sail through forests, valleys, fields and towns, step ashore and wander where I wished and all without so much as leaving home. We had been planning to buy an old barn near the river Lot in south-west France as a base for painting.

... an old barn near the river Lot...

This idea now suddenly lost its appeal.

I sat down and wrote to the editor of every paper and magazine to do with boats, to all the larger boatyards and to many names listed in the London telephone directory under Barge, Boat, Marine, Sea and Ship. I heard from just one firm that there were for sale in Holland three barges of the type and size that conformed to the specification I had given. A few days later I learned that one of the three had been sold and another withdrawn. I received a photograph of the third and knew at once that I *must* have it.

I hurriedly set forth to an address in Maastraat, Rotterdam, one day in January 1968 in a state of considerable anxiety lest 'my' boat should have been sold.

After a restless night in which confused dreams alternated with attempts to master the fierce heat of the radiators. I climbed out of bed and drew the curtains. A few small snowflakes drifted fast across the square and a strong wind chased litter through the herds of cyclists. I dressed quickly and set forth. Holding the lapels of my overcoat close about my neck, I hurried toward Maastraat. The already drawn faces in the tram queues stared unseeing through the struggling traffic.

Pressing the bell at the enquiry desk I waited impatiently. A girl emerged.

'May I help you?' she asked in English using the sixth sense that all foreigners seem to possess to unerringly determine nationality.

'Mr Overberg please.'

'I'm sorry, Sir, Mr Overberg is not here.'

'But I have an appointment with him,' pulling his last letter from my pocket.

'I'm sorry, Sir. Mr Overberg is not with the business any longer. He left yesterday and he is not coming back.'

'May I see the person who has taken over from Mr Overberg then?'

'I'm sorry, Sir, but no one has come to take his place yet.'

'I'd like to see the manager then,' I said a trifle loudly.

The Manager listened to my story with sympathy and surprise; evidently he had not known that he was in the shipbroking business. He rummaged amongst some files on the unfortunate Mr Overberg's desk. It was all there - the whereabouts of the barge and the address of the owner. I was bowed out into the freezing street.

My next appointment was with a surveyor. I hurried round to his office, got into his car and drove straight round to the address I had been given.

I saw the barge at least a mile before we reached her. She was moored on a canal high above the surrounding reclaimed land. It was love at first sight. The surveyor was sent on his way lest he might advise against purchase.

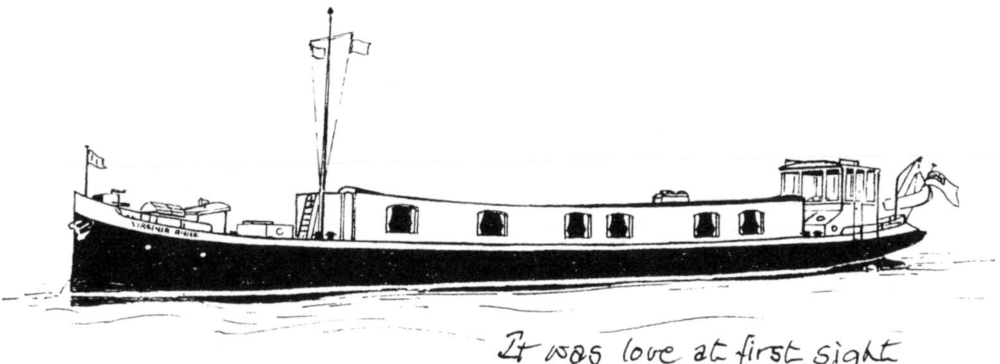

It was love at first sight

As I walked along the raised bank, the cutting edge of the wind was unblunted. But there she was! Beautiful and serene, and seeming to radiate a kind of peaceful timelessness. I walked over her in a kind of trance.

Two hours later I met the owner, a lady of great charm who spoke fluent English. From the first, it seemed decided that I was to have the boat and the possibility of my not wanting her was never mentioned. The owner had recently been widowed and the prospect of parting with the boat after sixteen years gave her much sadness. She and her husband had converted her after the war. Before that, she had plied up and down the Maas carrying sand for the estuary dykes ever since 1912, the year she was built.

We returned to the barge together. The temperature inside the saloon was well below freezing and soon we were utterly frozen. We hurried to a nearby restaurant to be revived with Dutch gin. By the end of lunch, negotiations had been concluded: we sent for paper, carbon sheets and stamps and there and then drew up our Bill of Sale.

I had anticipated weeks of haggling and legalities but instead, in less than two hours, the barge was mine. For better or worse. I was now committed and the exact nature of my purchase was to be revealed to me by stages. I had never previously owned or sailed a boat of any kind other than the slender matchwood 'riggers' at Eton.

The barge was named *Virginia Anne*.

A neighbouring shipyard was commissioned to inspect the hull and undertake some modifications including the provision of a central heating system, a cooker and a bath. As soon as the work was completed, I set forth to move the boat towards France accompanied by my father as engineer, and a neighbouring farmer as deckhand.

An effort was made to learn useful knots. These we practised on the train journey to Harwich with a guide book and a length of rope bought for the purpose. Holding up a large and neat noose for admiration, we became aware of a woman standing in the doorway of the compartment transfixed with fear. On our arrival, we found that our rope practice had secured us an otherwise empty compartment in a packed train.

The barge weighed 115 tons and was the length of three buses. Unfamiliar with any boat larger than a single-seat rowing boat, I realised that steering was likely to be problematical. We knew nothing whatever

about the rules of the waterways – in fact, we knew nothing about anything. Apprehension on this score resulted in us hiring 'Charlie' – his Dutch name was unmanageable. Recommended to us as a marine jack-of-all-trades, Charlie was ex-merchant navy, rather ancient and wore, at all times, inside and out, a black Homburg hat, pulled down over the tops of his ears: he also wore my overcoat to which he had taken an immediate fancy. It soon emerged that he was deaf in one ear and half-deaf in the other as well as almost blind. He was also exceedingly short-tempered. He was therefore virtually useless except as a close-range interpreter of conversations between ship and shore, in which he used the megaphone as an ear-trumpet so his contribution was marginal.

The first few miles of navigation was food for future nightmares. There seemed to be no relation between my activity with the huge wheel and the direction in which the bow chose to wander. Many were the moored barges into whose steel sides we banged. Very gradually I became used to the seemingly unnatural technique of steering well ahead of the intended turn but our progress remained serpentine for weeks.

The hapless Charlie involved us in a most unwelcome expense as I manoeuvred alongside a pontoon. He had been positioned so that he could place the loop of a mooring rope over a bollard. At one end of this long pontoon, a bargee was tarring his vessel. Charlie had successfully lassoed his drum of tar, mistaking it for the bollard. The tar was upset and so was the bargee. Money changed hands. Later that day, after he had started to use an electric razor on his still hatted head in the middle of dinner, he was sent in a taxi to the nearest station.

We entered the Rhine estuary. The river was in flood. It was snowing and visibility was poor. We missed the turning into the Afged Maas and found ourselves crossing flooded farmland toward a windmill. Only with difficulty did we find our way back to the river, collecting strands of barbed wire round the propeller as we did so. We could easily have come to rest far from the river, perhaps marooned high and dry for a few years until another flood might again have floated us. Such incidents punctuated an exceedingly exciting progress through Belgium and into France. Gradually, in spite of many near accidents and a number of real ones, we became accustomed to handling the barge in a variety of situations and were soon able to perform complex manoeuvres. Our greatest discovery was that the whole business of

... we found ourselves
crossing flooded farmland

'barging' along the inland waterways was delightful in the extreme even in the depths of winter. Now that we had left the busy canals of the dreary Dutch plains and passed through the pleasant but unexciting landscape of Belgium, we found ourselves in a continuous meander of pastoral beauty as we descended the French Meuse. Later, the almost deserted canals ran through scenery little altered for a century and except when they were crossed by a main road, tranquility was unbreached. We progressed at the speed of a fast walk.

To awake in the morning and see a kingfisher flying past the window is a rare delight. To travel along waterways is to relive the formative childhood years when new sights, sound and scents impress themselves indelibly on the memory. Who could forget sand martins skimming beneath a slowly rising mist to announce yet another fine day or the sound of a moorhen in the reeds at the water's edge; or the scent of the river itself, 'thrilling, sweet and rotten' as Rupert Brooke so exactly described it?

Casual exchanges with people walking the tow-path or going about their canal-side work added to the feeling of being a part of the local life. Often fresh produce was available from lock-keepers and every village had its bakery. For occasional longer journeys, we had bicycles. At the end of the first cruise we left *Virginia Anne* on the northern slopes of the Vosges in the care of a friendly lock-keeper who wrote every month to assure us that all was well. One day, an unscheduled letter arrived.

Panicky handwriting covered a dozen sheets. My immediate return was requested to deal with a triple *désastre*. I learned that a prisoner had escaped from gaol and found the barge a convenient place to shelter. He had filled himself up with a bottle and a half of whisky, taken a tin of *canneloni* and placed it on the pressure stove; *mais malheureusement* instead of paraffin (*pétrole*), he had filled the stove with petrol and produced a sizeable explosion. From carpet to ceiling, all was blackened with *canneloni*.

The day after the explosion while the *agent* was investigating the crime, a terrible wind had arisen and the barge had broken its moorings and drifted across towards the far side of the port where she remained grounded in soft mud some distance from the bank. The *agent* stranded, they were unable to pull her back, which event had given rise not only to the resentment of the *agent* but also to the third element of the disaster, *une catastrophe véritable*! Did I remember the details of the mooring? Then perhaps I could imagine the nature of the event. Indeed, I remembered all too well agreeing with the lock-keeper that as an extra precaution, we would tie a rope round the base of the sentry-box-like hut that the French find such an economical solution to the problem of indoor sanitary plumbing. *Hélas*, the distressed woman went on, the rope had failed to break under the tension and the uprooted *cabinet* had plunged into the canal. *Grâce au bon Dieu* it had been unoccupied at the time. Nevertheless they were all greatly inconvenienced.

The winter passed and I was already looking back over our gradual ascent of the Continental landmass with increasing nostalgia and longing for the next journey. I had become a dedicated bargee. Every mile of canal, every hour of each day held a fresh enchantment. I felt a kinship for the boat I could never have believed myself capable of forming; each part had its own identity, a special character that extended almost to the individual rivets. The texture of the wood, the feel of the tarred sides, the smell of the engine room, the creaking of a straining rope - all these had become symbolic of another infinitely varied and uniquely pleasurable life. Over the two and a half decades in which I owned her, the good ship *Virginia Anne* afforded intense pleasure. Each time I left her it was a severe wrench: I could cheerfully have lived aboard her for years. Although we sailed her thousands of kilometres and passed through hundreds if not thousands of locks, I found that the lure of covering big distances steadily diminished, so much so that I would be perfectly happy not to move at all. After all what could be more lovely than to find oneself living by the sandy bank of a peaceful river in Burgundy. On one side a buttercup-filled meadow merging with the blue-green of distant hills, on the other a wide breadth of still water with motionless white Charollais cattle standing knee-deep at the edge in the stippled shade of an ancient willow. It is the stuff of serenity.

I find it difficult to convey the essence of the barging life since it was never repetitious; it was more a succession of incidents. But in the hope of providing some colour, I have extracted a few excerpts from the *Barging* series which I wrote.

'For some days, we had not been conscious of any use being made of the towpath. For reasons which are unimportant, we decided to moor one night - in contravention of the rules of the waterway - on the towpath side of the canal. The mooring ropes spanned this almost unused path to trees on the far side at a height of two foot or so.

We were just sitting down to dinner when we heard the sound of an approaching *velomoteur*, or power-assisted bicycle. By the time I reached deck to shout a warning about the hazard, the man and his machine were upon the ropes.

An extraordinary thing took place. Owing to the elastic nature of the rope - which had made contact with the fork of the bicycle above the front wheel, the rider continued some way, still astride his machine, albeit at a rapidly diminishing rate. Then, very suddenly, the two parted company, the rider continuing for a short way in a sitting position along the towpath before glancing off the bank into the canal. The motor bicycle was subject to the effect of a vicious catapault action. It shot back along the towpath, from which it had so recently arrived and came to rest in some bushes at a considerable distance from the barge.

There was great difficulty in reuniting rider to mount since the former was disenchanted with his watery surroundings and the latter had assumed a curious shape.

It was a situation in which we were both in the wrong: I, to have moored on the towpath side, and he to have used a motor vehicle on the towpath. Both were forbidden. Our position was therefore one of stalemate. An hour of repairs, physical, moral and mechanical, saw machine and rider reunited and the barrage of early imprecations buried beneath a cheerful toast, accompanied by extravagant statements of mutual goodwill and longevity.'

'One day, I was attempting an awkward mooring, with a number of small fishing boats preventing a sufficiently close approach to permit a landing. The solution to this problem is, normally, to throw a rope to someone, but there was nobody to be seen. However, as we approached, the head of an elderly man appeared from the *Flying Dutchman,* an old sixty-tonne Dutch barge, sporting the remnant of a Red Ensign. I asked for assistance. The head disappeared to be replaced a few seconds later by an attractive girl wearing old blue jeans.

"Just a mo!" she said and disappeared. Five agonising minutes went by, as I struggled to prevent the *Virginia Anne* sinking the local fishing fleet, before she reappeared, this time most elegantly but quite inappropriately dressed.

"Would you like me to do something?" she asked in plummy accents, fluttering her eyelids.

"Yes! If we throw you the line, could you tie us up to that tree, please?" I said, indicating a stout willow growing from the side of a steep nettle-covered bank. I could see that conditions were not perhaps ideal but it was the only suitably strong mooring.

"Oh, I'd *love* to!" she replied gaily and tripped lightly ashore. The rope was thrown accurately so that the end lay conveniently close to her feet at the top of the bank. It was then that I saw she had no shoes. "Oh dear, the nettles are *awful*!" she cried as, very slowly, she made for the noose. Gradually the wind drifted the *Virginia Anne* out, and the line started to slide down the bank.

"Oh dear, the rope's going away... Ouch... these nettles *do* sting... Gosh... my poor feet. Oh *dear*!" Her lamentations continued as she crept delicately down the bank in pursuit of the escaping rope. Soon it lay at the water's edge and too distant to be thrown again. That's it I thought, as the rope floated out into the river. She's let it go and now I'm in a mess. But I was wrong. She may not have been quick but she did not lack resolution.

"Oooh the water *is* cold," she tittered as she came on in relentless pursuit. About twenty feet from the bank, she caught up with it, swam back and tied it round the tree.

"Sorry I was so slow. I'm rather wet - perhaps I'll change - see you in a minute - bye!" she called and vanished. Shortly afterwards she reappeared, this time in a bikini - although it was far from warm.

"I'm Sally," she said. "Do you mind if I come aboard?" The male members of the crew were unequivocally delighted. "Gosh," she said. "You don't know how pleased I am to see you." I assured her that it was mutual and asked her whither she was bound.

"I'm all mixed up," she started. "I've no idea where I am, really. You see, I answered an advertisement in *The Sunday Times* to act as cook on this man's boat. I've never been on a boat before, I've never been abroad before - I can't speak French and I'm getting desperate" she continued, without drawing breath. "You see I thought it would be a family or something with me just helping out a bit and that kind of thing but when I joined the boat in Brussels, it turned out to be just this old man you see, and he's really too old to manage at all because he can't see properly and he doesn't hear much either so I don't think I could help him even if I could, if you know what I mean. You see, I don't know at all where I am or anything really and there's never enough money to buy anything, we just eat sort of scraps - that is when I'm not pumping the water out - the boat leaks you see - and it gets worse all the time but he tells me that everything will be all right when we get to Paris, but you see I can't make head nor tail of the map so tell me *please*, do you think we're going in the right direction?" She blinked wide-eyed at us. "Perhaps I could telephone Daddy from there and he might send me some money to get back or come and fetch me."

Just then, we heard shouts: "Sally! Sally! Where *are* you? Come and help me with the pumps. Quickly!"

"Oh dear, now he's going to be angry with me again. I'll have to go: see you soon, bye!"'

'In our carefree navigation of the canal system, it was all too easy to forget that professional bargees depended on an unobstructed passage. But a laden barge would only make half our speed. Overtaking was always tricky especially as such barges needed to stay in the deeper middle of the canal. Once my efforts to pull ahead in an unexpectedly shallow pound resulted in striking a rock and causing a leak.

The barge I had been trying to put behind me, moored to a quay a short way ahead. The bargee walked back to see if he could help. It was the end of a long, hot day and I was touched by his concern: crawling through dark and airless bilges, shifting fifty kilo blocks of concrete ballast must have been the last thing he wanted to do.

The leak temporarily staunched, we invited the couple to a meal.

Our two guests had been married for six years. Both were the children, grandchildren and great-children of bargees. They had one child of five who lived with a parent because of a recent illness of *Madame*, and one of six months which was aboard with them. Neither the bargee nor his wife had had a holiday since they had married. All their earnings and leisure hours were devoted to their car, kept aboard, in which they drove about 30,000 miles a year mainly on Sundays to visit parents.

"Your life's a hard one but you have preserved your freedom," I said. "At least you don't have to be at a factory bench by a certain hour and spend the day doing a repetitive job. You have the fresh air and often glorious scenery."

There was a silence. It seemed that my remarks, intended to cheer them up, had somehow fallen wide of the mark.

At length, *Madame* said, "I don't think you really understand, *M'sieur.* When you work thirteen hours a day, six days a week and do housework like any other wife, plus helping with the front rudder every few minutes, chipping and painting, scrubbing decks, helping with ropes in locks, rushing to make purchases in the shops you pass, helping with the paper-work, carrying the sixty hold-covers every time you load or unload - when you're doing this you don't appreciate the finer points in life. It's perhaps difficult to imagine a life with a new place each day, never knowing where to get things or who to turn to if things go wrong. You can't make friends in a few hours and, anyway, what would be the use? You'd probably never see them again. Can you imagine just having one little room, smaller than this saloon, for everything? No bathroom, no washing-machine; no money to buy anything and nowhere to put them even if we could afford them? Can you *imagine* what happens when my husband or I are ill? We have to decide whether we can cope - the barge can't be managed single-handed. But if we stop, not only does it cost us our earnings but we get a bad name for late delivery. So, ill or not, the work goes on, winter and summer, freezing for three months and being cooked alive in that small cabin for another three. Can you imagine what it's like standing all day like my husband does, being vibrated and deafened by the noisy engine, never daring for a single instant to relax his concentration? And all the time living in the presence of danger. Do you know how many bargees and their families are drowned or injured? Every *week* we hear terrible stories. I am grateful if we get to the end of the week without being crushed. *M'sieur* I'm *not* complaining of my lot. Don't think I envy you, but I am explaining to you why the scenery we pass means little to us. How safe the waterways are, how co-operative the lock-keepers, how accessible the shops; these are the considerations which matter to us. By today's standards it's a hard life. Hard for a man, very hard for a woman."

She paused, suddenly looking more than her five and twenty years. Then, embarrassed at having made the conversation so serious, she smiled forcedly and added, "But it's nice for us to know that our efforts are appreciated at least by some people, and that our waterways are more than just main roads."

Incidents such as these were the substance of everyday cruising.

Punctuating a day, there would be continual exchange with lock-keepers. One such almost ended in tragedy. We had entered a lock and Virginia was seeing to the mooring rope at the bow. Throwing the end with a noose to the attendant, but out-of-sight lock-keeper, and

...unaware she had lassooed the lock-keeper

feeling it caught, she started hauling in the slack to make fast, unaware that she had lassooed the man who was now teetering on the edge of the lock struggling to free himself.

Perhaps as a reaction to my rather frantic lifestyle, I found myself envying these people. I always have it in mind one day to apply to the Authorities for the job of lock-keeper. It represents the ideal employment if one is prepared to subsist on a modest reward. I have calculated that, for me, three boats a day is the required work-load. More would be tedious and fewer would hardly justify the title.

To occupy the lock-keeper's house, set in a canal-side grove of fruit trees, and to move with calculated slowness from hoeing the *petit pois* to feeding dandelions to the rabbits, must be to live life as the gods intended. One could hardly stale of the company, meted out for twenty minutes at a time, of the passing bargees: whether through constant intercommunication or intuition, everything is known. And the prospect of selling a kilo of freshly-dug young turnips or a bunch of fiery radishes would ensure one's wits were kept constantly alert with the cut and thrust of commerce. The names of the locks themselves roll melodiously off the tongue: *Charmois l'Orgueilleux, Chavelot, Chaumousey, Bois l'Abbé, Pont Tremblant, Basse du Pommier* were but a few from a small section on the *Canal de l'Est.*

However, it will be recalled that the purpose of buying a barge was as a floating studio and so far the only paint applied had been to the barge. Yet it was becoming clear that although barging was more fun than painting, instead of it being a profitable hobby, it was becoming financially unsustainable. I was acutely aware that *Virginia Anne* was quietly rusting away at her moorings in France and continually making inroads into my now much reduced resources.

Jim Page, who had been one of the Land Rover drivers on our Sales Conference in Morocco, agreed to try his hand as skipper of the barge. His job would be to prepare the boat to receive paying passengers, welcome them aboard, buy provisions, cook meals, clean the boat, make the beds, act as guide and drive the barge for five or so hours a day, which was of course a hopelessly formidable task for anyone.

Jim struggled manfully to carry out a task that was humanly impossible and the first few cruises saw some reimbursement of the charter fees. A cook was therefore added and standards improved but the two were still overstretched. They were later joined by a deck-

lock houses

hand and a stewardess. This foursome was then able to provide an excellent and comprehensive service and I set my cap at the American market.

This modest undertaking turned into a pioneering venture which was to have the most far-reaching consequences. Although it had been started solely to staunch the outflow of expense on a boat that I was determined not to sell, it soon became clear that there might indeed be a good market for barge cruises where charterers could be fed, guided and generally pampered - though this last condition was conspicuously absent in the early days. The operation had more in common with upmarket camping than luxury cruising. But any deficiencies in this regard were largely offset by the element of adventure, the huge enthusiasm of the crew and the sheer beauty of the waterways. Gradually, we found increasing numbers of charterers and by the third season, the enterprise was marginally profitable. But the vessel remained internally spartan.

In these early days, passengers were expected to take the rough with the smooth. Equipment was often substandard, if not actually dangerous, though our awareness of this was only occasioned by unfortunate events. There were, for instance, no guard rails along the sides of the barge, resulting once in a passenger falling overboard when the boat bumped against a bridge abuttment. Two more passengers fell in when they crossed the ancient gangplank too close together so that it broke in half. One of the original lifebelts, thrown in to aid a struggling passenger, actually sank under its own weight. Any work done in a shipyard was ruinously expensive, so that 'do-it-yourself' alterations seemed the only solution even though they resulted initially in gimcrack cupboards, leaky plumbing and dust-laden varnish.

In 1975, there was, besides *Virginia Anne*, one other 'hotel-barge' in France, also in its first season. Neither of us could have then guessed the astonishing potential of this venture which in the next twenty years attracted some 150 barges, all offering cruises, albeit of greatly varying qualities, on the French waterways. Many of these barges were owned by members of the crew of the initial (British) pioneers, a kind of self-replicating process. It was the unlikely start of an enterprise that in two decades would see its participants earning collective revenues of around a billion dollars a year. On the back of this industry arrived whole fleets of self-drive mini-barges (*penichettes*) and a number of huge river-cruisers.

The word 'barging' now began to expand its meaning as a result, I like to think, of the three 'barging' books I wrote in this period, *Barging into France, Barging into Burgundy,* and *Barging into Southern France,* which recorded the many adventures of the *Virginia Anne*. Be that as it may, the word 'barging' has entered the holiday vocabulary and the cruises are now a mainstream item for a US travel agent. It remains a worry that although a barging holiday is itself environmentally excellent, the carriage of passengers across the Atlantic is certainly not. The fact that most of them were coming to Europe anyhow is at least a partial comfort.

There has however been a deeply rewarding aspect to this development which, at the time, I scarcely foresaw. Whilst *Virginia Anne* was thrusting her way into France, commercial barges were already in terminal decline as more and more goods were transported by lorry, in the name of speed - though greatly to the detriment of the environment, barges being around twenty times more fuel-efficient than lorries. Already some canals, such as the surpassingly lovely Nivernais, were on the threshold of closure. Indeed, as *Virginia Anne* nosed her way into the narrow upper reaches of that canal, we were lopping overhanging branches and constantly clearing weed from the propeller. Passenger barges, and the pleasure boats that followed in their wake, undoubtedly saved many canals. Without them, these waterways would have been progressively closed, becoming the undisputed preserve of the army of French fishermen, an army with immense political clout. Already lock-keepers' houses were being sold off, depths of canals reduced and leaking lock gates left unrepaired. The entire infrastructure was deteriorating fast.

I believe that, however fortuitously it may have happened, this endeavour helped decisively to preserve these magnificent waterways and also introduced tens of thousands of people to the peaceful beauty of rural France. The many vessels which now navigate the canals and rivers not only pay State dues but have brought a substantial and continuing economic gain to local commerce. Last but by no means least, it has given a new lease of life to an entire fleet of barges - many of vintage origin - which would otherwise have been broken up.

CHAPTER 12

Discontent – rampant environmental concern – staying with San Franciscan Hippies – Diana – the germ of an idea – interview with Roy Jenkins – a magical quarry in Wales – the strands of Green Fundamentalism – the truth about nuclear power – the beginnings of Something Significant

By now in my mid-thirties I experienced a growing unease. My outwardly visible circumstances were enviable. A successful business, a fine house and, by 1964, three healthy children. My parents were happily installed in the converted stables. There were friends aplenty, many opportunities to travel and my immediate surroundings afforded endless scope for creative enterprise.

Yet I was increasingly prey to a profound discontent which, initially I found hard to articulate. It lay beyond the frontiers of a failing marriage. It permeated my whole life and gradually threw into question all that I had been doing.

I began to perceive my existence against a global perspective and found it wanting in relevance. This perception was animated by the first stirrings of environmental awareness, then reaching the public domain through such seminal works as Rachel Carson's *Silent Spring* and via leading journalists such as Gerald Leach and Kenneth Allsop. That I was susceptible to this new awareness I can readily trace to my mother who had long preached the need for humanity to live within the finite resources of planet Earth. Increasingly the developed world was disregarding these limits.

Simultaneously, I began to see my social world as rather superficial. There were good friends whose company I greatly enjoyed and with whom conversation might be edged toward matters environmental. I would find sympathy or cynicism; contradiction or agreement. But what I did *not* find was a willingness to do much more than talk. Looking back, I see there was no particular reason why they should have done anything, yet at the time their reluctance to get involved seemed irresponsible. I edged away.

This was a time when the Hippie movement and Flower Power were securing a high public profile. My curiosity was awoken. Here were people who represented values which were opposed to those of my conventional background. They looked exceedingly scruffy, wore outrageous clothes, shunned the barber, held custom to ridicule, rejected Authority, placed a low value on wealth, favoured disarmament, renounced nuclear power and were prepared to live simply 'so that others might simply live'.

Of course, this movement of people, mainly in their twenties, comprised good and bad like any other group. But almost in spite of myself, I sympathised closely with the central gist of their direction. And the more they were mocked by the forces of tradition, the more I aligned myself to these values. Naïve they might be but wrong I thought they were not.

Because I was still unable to focus my feelings in any effective way, I experienced a deep restlessness, but I was effectively locked into a way of living, each part of which interlocked with the other parts. It seemed impossible to break out of this circle without catastrophic consequences to all around me and besides I was still unsure. I carried on.

One evening, we went to a dance in a large country house. The guests seemed uniform, not just in their dinner jackets but in their outlook - perhaps 'inlook' is a more appropriate word. I had just had a discouraging exchange with a friend whose right wing views I found exasperating. I wandered off in search of food. As I entered the dining room, I noticed a girl sitting by herself on the floor behind the door. Her expression suggested she, too, was not at ease in this circle. I talked to her and almost instantly we found ourselves on precisely the same wavelength.

Diana was the daughter of the head of a very large nationalised industry. She had broken away from a father whom she considered to be domineering and whom she believed was responsible for the first symptoms of anorexia she was then experiencing. She was what might now be termed a Green Fundamentalist. She earned her keep by cooking for parties.

My subsequent conversations with Diana convinced me that something needed to be done to break the mould: what this something was I had no clear idea. But I began to perceive that Fate intended for me an almighty change of course.

On my frequent visits to France, I kept noticing numerous empty plastic water bottles thrown into hedges and ditches. This seemingly insignificant observation set me reflecting again on the profligacy of the western world and our contempt for our surroundings. I was already alive to such issues but it was these water bottles being so routinely chucked out that triggered me into pondering lifestyles in earnest.

In the late Sixties, articles in the non-tabloid press questioned this profligacy and advanced the notion that resources were finite. We were squandering not only our birthright but also that of the less developed nations. The fact that waste also caused escalating pollution was another issue that received growing attention. Somewhere along the line, I had become sensitised to these problems. Perhaps I was even genetically programmed to become involved for both my mother, and her mother, were accurate forecasters of environmental decline. As far back as 1949, I recall my mother addressing a farmers' meeting and warning of the dangers of the 'new' chemical methods of agriculture.

My interest in this now reared up before me and began to dominate my life. I raged against the perpetrators of this destruction with the fervour of a new convert. Something *must* be done. But what, actually, could I do, could *anyone* do?

It was a massive question to which I had no immediate answer.

I took myself off to talk to the journalists and soon realised that their sources were largely American. It seemed that there, 'environmentalism' was becoming a sub-culture at least on the theoretical level. Public consciousness was only being scratched in Britain but in the hot spots of the United States, Green Fundamentalism had gained a firm foothold, especially amongst rebellious young students. I decided to go and see for myself.

I flew to San Francisco armed with introductions to a number of leading businessmen and several politicians.

I found a uniformity of opinion: yes, there were these problems and, yes, if they were not solved the world would enter terminal decline. As to the cure, my contacts fell into two principal groups; one, the larger, believed some future techno-fix would solve each and every problem. The other saw a need for a colossal shift toward simpler lifestyles. Yet both groups were agreed that no change would be possible in the existing order of things: was not consumerism the engine that maintained employment and created wealth? No Government would dare to tamper with that! Change could only occur via a vast 'bottom-up' public demand.

There was little enough visible evidence of any mood for such a change, so somewhat in desperation, I decided to talk to the Hippies, up in the surrounding hills.

Diana then arrived in San Francisco: she too was eager to meet them. We hired a car and, with difficulty, located several communities, each quite different to the other. Some embraced the need for organisation, for hard work to construct shelter, grow food, and project a positive face toward their brave new world. Others lived in rank squalor, devoid of imagination or leadership, dissolute, irrelevant to the outside world and ultimately to themselves.

Their membership was disparate. There were draft dodgers, unemployed university graduates a-plenty, lay-abouts living on state benefit, numerous girls of rich families living off their parents, writers and artists of every kind, and a plethora of guitarists. All welcomed us to their hearths and tried to articulate their emergent beliefs.

There was one thread common to all: they were passionately opposed to nuclear power. It represented all that was authoritarian and secret: it could be fatally dangerous to both man and nature and it was the mainspring of the nuclear weapons industry. There was much talk of alternative energy sources and in some communities there were primitive attempts to harness wind and sun to provide electricity and heat.

In spite of their genuine concern and reformist ardour, these groups were notoriously fragile. People came and went, some to find other groups more in sympathy with their particular outlook, some disenchanted with the simple life. There were also numerous attempts at communal living, mostly fragile, being frequently riven by sexual jealousies.

We both returned to Britain convinced of the need to alert people to impending environmental decline and the urgency of demonstrating safe practical steps, however small, by which humanity's impact on the earth might be reduced. This seemed to us to be the only way forward. The failure of the Hippy groups to have much positive interface with the public reflected their flight from the reality of ordinary life for ordinary people.

As I flew back, I felt the germ of an idea developing. It was to set up a centre where the need for simpler less damaging lifestyles could be explained and demonstrated to the public. The aim of greater self-sufficiency was also to be a principle of the project. It was only a vague idea but it was strong and persistent.

As the events of life recede into the distance, so our view of their significance alters. From the vantage point of the present, I can see more easily that the Green Fundamentalism which was beginning now to settle upon me was also in part a response to losing a sense of purpose, which my withdrawal from Dexam had caused and which events at home had helped to exacerbate.

I therefore threw myself into a new world, peopled as I then thought by those who had seen a great light. I turned myself into an informational vacuum cleaner, sweeping through papers, leaflets and reports, filtering in data and opinions compatible with my emergent beliefs. It was an unbalanced approach yet precisely what was required to generate a white hot zeal. The world was stuffed full of people whose views were perfectly balanced - 'I think he's a little unbalanced about it' was - and is - a sentence of death amongst those who top the pyramid of worldly success.

Although in time I realised that some of my early gurus were single-issue partisans, I also know that those who seek to implant a new consciousness upon the world cannot afford to dissipate the savage energy they need in taking too much account of the 'ifs' and 'buts'.

So with a fierce concentration, I focused on one central idea, the setting up of this centre where people, ordinary passers-by, might readily perceive the disastrous course on which our civilisation was set and be shown things they, *anyone*, might do to reduce their impact on the environment. Ways of life which the planet could sustain were to be suggested and some of the more obvious methods of achieving these would be demonstrated. It was intended to show a range of practices which would have minimal adverse consequences both environmentally and socially. It was also proposed that books and pamphlets would be available for sale, and finally that, both in order to put these ideas to the test and to gain public credibility, those who lived and worked there would be as self-reliant as possible.

There were just three difficulties; I had no staff, no place to put it and no funds.

I wrote to my much older half-brother, Robert Morgan-Grenville. He had farmed in the Aberdare hills of Kenya and had been forced to abandon his land and his home at the time of the Mau-Mau insurrection. Afterwards he lived on the coast at Malindi, spending much of his time fishing. He was seriously concerned by the decline in fish stocks. He had inherited a fortune many years before but because of his long absence in Africa, I hardly knew him. He had a reputation for being something of a recluse and careful with his money but I received a letter by return saying simply - 'I think it's a great idea. Let me know how much you want'.

I asked for £20,000 which in those days seemed a very great deal of money. It came immediately and without strings. Almost at once, I met an American post-graduate, Steve Boulter, a specialist in the study of ambient energy sources such as solar, wave, wind, biogas and hydro. He was very keen to become involved in a practical project in this field and as he was at a loose end I set him to find a site. It soon emerged that it is the hardest thing to find within Britain any site on which planning permission would be given for some experimental and unorthodox venture. At the first whiff of the unconventional or the politically controversial, most planners run a mile.

I saw that what I needed was a 'shop-front' which, by virtue of the presence of respectable names, would allay Establishment fears. I founded a charity, The Society for Environmental Improvement which had as its object Education. Under this banner, the centre would be launched. Within a month, I had secured the patronage of a dozen or so nationally respected individuals. The only person who actually asked to see me was Roy Jenkins so I presented myself at his office in the House of Commons.

Jenkins: 'So you want me to lend cwedibility to your pwoject? I'm not aware that I have much.'

Me: 'Your support would be immensely valuable. You are held in great esteem.'

Jenkins: 'It's nice of you to say so but I doubt it. I see fwom your letterhead that you want to impwove the enviwonment. Sounds like a good idea but *how* exactly?'

Me: 'Well, er, well...'

Jenkins: 'Never mind. It's a good idea, pwobably impossible to descwibe. I'll happily be a Patwon if I don't have to give money or time, especially the latter, starting now. Glad to have met you. Good luck. Goodbye.'

With a broad smile and a pat on the back, I was shown the door.

The telephone rang.

'Hullo?'

'Steve here. I've found a site.'

'Yes?' Cautiously. There had been several before, all hopeless.

'This one's different. It's perfect.'

'Then it'll be too expensive!'

'It isn't. Peppercorn rental. The guy's excited about the project. Says he thinks he remembers you at Eton. I've talked to the planners; they didn't say no.'

'Have you been drinking?'

'It's just precisely what you asked me to find. I've found it.'

'Where is it?'

'Wales.'

'Oh.'

'I have to go back to the States tomorrow. Grab a pencil. Here's how to find it. See if you can get up at once. There's someone else who has got the ear of the owner.'

I scooped up Diana and drove straight to the then unpronounceable Machynlleth in mid-Wales. I looked at my notes. 'Up the road toward Dolgellau for two miles, turn right at the bus stop, right again at an island tree, 100 yards and you'll be at the foot of a disused slate quarry. There's an overgrown track on the left hand side - it'll take you up to the quarry level. That's the site.'

We parked the car and emerged into silence, broken only by the murmur of a stream. Above us a precipitous bank of slate rubble rose to a line of trees. To one side was a tangle of wild rhododendron: into this led the track.

It took some time to clamber over or under the branches up the steep track. They ceased abruptly as we arrived at a broad and level expanse of slate waste dotted with birch trees. Beyond, the face of the

Top. The Saharan expedition Land Rover at the foot of sand-dunes. Such dunes only cover quite a small part of the Sahara.
Left. Jenny
Below. Rock paintings such as these adorn many caves and still continue to be discovered.

Above. The start of an adventure and the fulfilment of a railway passion. The Royal Scotsman's Directors and a Piper at Euston Station.

Below left. Margaret in 1992 in the garden at Le Manoir.

Below right. Having fun designing a decorative motif on the bow of *Fleur de Lys*. Why pay someone to do the thing one enjoys?!

quarry rose sheer to the grass covered hills above. There was a perfect stillness.

We found a terrace of three ruined cottages, two huge derelict slate cutting sheds complete with rusted slate guillotines, several small flat-bed rail trucks and here and there, lengths of rail. Vast chunks of slate lay scattered around us, drill holes on one side where they had been exploded away from the rock face. Elsewhere were piles of half-finished or broken slabs of pigeon-grey slate, marble smooth and sharp-edged.

We walked along the bed of a railway line, the rails partly vanished. It took us to the lip of this vast heap of spoil extending out toward the green valley far below. Beyond were the tree covered slopes of the Mynydd Du mountain in the Gwynedd National Park. There was not a building in sight, just thousands of acres of sheep-dotted grassland, moor and forest. It was a sensational view yet the quarry itself was hidden from the valley. We scampered back to explore the cottages. Though now the residence of numerous worms, beetles, mice and birds, I thought at least one could be made habitable quickly, ignorant as I then was of the annual rainfall of ninety-five inches.

...just thousands of acres of moor and forest...

The site indeed seemed ideal: no doubt about that. True it was miles away from the centres of population but it was close by a main road and if what we intended to do there was sufficiently momentous, people would beat a track to the door wherever it was. This settled, I hurried along the road to see John Beaumont, the owner. Although outwardly a highly conventional man, he quickly understood the idea and welcomed the prospect of something exciting on his doorstep. Within an hour, he agreed to rent the site for one shilling (5p) per annum on a 100 year lease.

Returning to the foot of the quarry, I gazed up at the edge of the tip and sensed that this was to be the beginning of something significant. Where better than this derelict but beautiful site to pioneer a way of life which could be lived without using up the capital resources of planet Earth or employing technologies that could be fatally dangerous to civilisation. Suddenly it all seemed so simple and so obvious.

Sitting here, in a Dorset garden, twenty-five years later, it is difficult to reconstruct precisely the cast of mind or the events which, collectively, combined to make of me at that moment, a single-minded environmental zealot. No doubt that, like all zealots, I must have been not only difficult to live with but, to most people, singularly awkward company as only an obsessive can be. Yet at the same time, I recognise that to establish a project such as I was envisaging would never have seen reality without an almighty push from someone prepared to devote concentrated bursts of energy to it. A passionate belief in the supremacy of its importance and a dogged refusal to accept rejection were essentials. It also required an ability to communicate and enthuse the essence of the idea to a wide spectrum of others; volunteer labourers, planners, corporate donors, local inhabitants and journalists.

What then were the strands which now united to make me this person? I have already referred to my mother's influence which via some slow (and subliminal) process, now blossomed into activism. This shift, accompanied by a growing awareness of at least the more cosmetic aspects of a polluted environment, provided a seedbed for other related ideas which quickly took root in this fertile soil.

Predominant amongst these was the issue of nuclear energy. This provoked the most passionate opposition and reinforced anger at other mainstream activities hostile to the public interest and threatening to environmental sanity. So it was for me and so it had been for the Hippies I had met in California.

The nuclear power tale is one of unprecedented technocratic arrogance founded on a heap of miscalculations, subsequently overlaid by an even bigger heap of lies. There are many books and films which chronicle the story and tell of truth distorted beyond belief, of known but unrevealed dangers, of cover-ups from Government downwards, of secret surveillance - even murder. Because civil nuclear power stemmed from its military cousin and is materially inter-related to this day, it was developed largely behind closed doors.

The nuclear boffins doled out attractive technological promises to successive governments who for forty years or so were, incredibly, all fooled by assurances on safety, then by the ludicrous forecast of 'power too cheap to meter', which would 'obviate striking coal miners, expensive and finite oil and gas'! They also took the opportunity to rubbish the idea of deriving energy from the sun or the wind. After this they managed to sell the laughable notion of perpetual motion with the Fast Breeder Reactor. With astonishing gullibility successive governments swallowed it all, finally endorsing the commercial nonsense of creating a national fortune via the reprocessing of spent nuclear fuel, a dangerous and highly pollutive charade that continues to this day quite unnecessarily.

All the time, vast sums of public money were poured into a public relations programme to reassure the public that nuclear power was clean, safe and economical. Although it was quickly apparent that it was the exact opposite of these things, because of the vast investment being made as well as the high level of individual credibility put on the line, the truth was continuously concealed. Even now, after half a century, we are supposed to believe that uranium can be mined without killing miners, that nuclear waste can be disposed of without danger, that time-expired reactors can be dismantled safely and economically, that the reactors are not in fact Trojan horses which could at any moment be blown sky-high by terrorist or enemy action with Chernobyl-type results. We, the public, are still not supposed to know that any one of them could so malfunction that if back-up systems and shut-down procedures failed to operate, radio-active fallout could devastate a vast area, killing, maiming or shortening the lives of literally *millions* of people. The nuclear industry, even in Britain, continues to release radioactive substances into the environment, continues to have accidents and continues to falsify records.

Variations of this nuclear saga occurred in every country whose Government had been hoodwinked by the nuclear Establishment. The 'incidents' (or malfunctions) which occurred - and they happened in their hundreds - were mostly downgraded in significance or even flatly denied. Outside the Communist countries, nowhere did this occur more than in France where one head of the nuclear power programme when asked why he failed to inform the public about nuclear accidents said, famously – 'You don't consult the frogs when you drain the marsh'. But gradually, the facts, along with nuclear radiation, seeped out from the power stations especially in the USA. Discontented staff at the Atomic Energy Authority leaked disturbing revelations and anti-nuclear campaigners world-wide gleaned corroborative information. It was soon apparent that in the nuclear sector, the principles of democratic government did not apply.

All over the country, there were people from every kind of background forming anti-nuclear groups - loose networks of people who did not like what they heard and, in varying degrees, were prepared to do something about it. Once alerted to the situation, many of these people observed other happenings - dangerous pollution by large chemical companies, the dumping of waste and the irresponsible transfer of hazardous substances by land, sea and air.

There was a heady mix of sympathisers and even if many of them were totally disparate in outlook and background, there was a powerful potential for support whenever a project provided a focus for action. As soon as the grapevine spread the word that something was happening in a disused slate quarry in Central Wales, volunteers started to arrive, unannounced, without tools, without skills and, mostly, without a penny to their name.

CHAPTER 13

The Quarry and the birth of the Centre for Alternative Technology – anarchists, communards and neo-primitivists – distrust of Government and subversion – pioneering in the rain – making pathetic devices which somehow capture public imagination – organic horticulture commenced – Prince Philip takes an interest with subsequent embarrassments – Government Chief Scientist defects to us – marching with Scargill – a crippling blow against nuclear power – Hilda Murrell joins and is murdered

MANY YEARS later, the story which unfolded in this quarry became the subject of a book, *Crazy Idealists**. It is introduced by Peter Harper with an historical perspective, from which I quote.

'The Quarry is the happy combination of a Vision and a Place. The vision... was based on a growing conviction that all was not well with the Onward and Upward march of industrial culture, and that some radical, even revolutionary, alternative was necessary for long-term survival. Looking back to that time, we can see that the sentiments and ideals of this vision were part of an anti-industrial tradition in Britain going back at least to the 16th century, tracing a line through the Diggers and Levellers in the 17th, the Luddites and Romantic poets of the 18th and social critics like Ruskin and William Morris in the 19th. In the middle of the 20th century the tradition emerged as an accumulation of overlapping movements critical of industrial culture: the New Left, the 'counterculture', conservation and environmental groups, the "organic" movement, cooperatives, spiritual and personal growth movements, women's liberation, de-schooling, the peace movement.

Underlying many of these movements was a hearty distrust of a faceless, mass society and its mega-technologies. If there were to be alternatives, they had to be human-scaled and run with gentler methods. But how, exactly? The dissenting culture tended to attract dreamers

*CAT Publications, Machynlleth, Powys, SY20 1BR

and idealists who would not have the first idea how to create effective practical alternatives, so were doomed to remain parasitic on the very mainstream society they were denouncing.

"Alternative Technology" was conceived as the body of genuine alternatives that would really work; it accepted the broad "alternative" critique but, crucially, did not throw out the methods of science and technology, the skills that went with them, and the fundamental insight that you have to do the sums and get the numbers right. In this sense it was a bridge between conventional and alternative worlds.

In the early Seventies, the Green Movement was becoming visible. Friends of the Earth had arrived from America and the Club of Rome had published *The Limits to Growth* which forecast that contemporary industrial society and ecological stability were incompatible. There were many apocalyptic visions of a post-nuclear war scenario which gave rise to the concept of a survivalist society which would lead to a reconstructed non-authoritarian, sustainable system, employing safe and simple technologies, being self-sufficient and intolerant toward a consumer-culture.

It was a multi-faceted dream, shot through with nostalgia for an imagined golden past and a belief that Arcadia was only just out of reach. There were as many solutions postulated as there were individuals to voice them.

Into this fiercely bubbling cauldron dropped the first volunteers, an uneasy mix of anarchists, communards and neo-primitivists. A faint but heady scent of revolution filled the air.'

It was autumn. On fine days, the place was magical. On wet days miserable. And wet days outnumbered the fine.

There was no waterproof shelter. One of the three cottages only needed limited work to be habitable by anyone who could tolerate extreme damp. For the rest of the 'workers', we needed caravans, but as yet the access was blocked by a rhododendron jungle. My first action was to buy picks and axes and distribute them to the volunteers. As soon as the road was cleared, a few about-to-be-scrapped caravans were procured for little or nothing and towed up to the site.

Diana set up a field kitchen and undertook on a microscopic budget, to feed the work force. Unpaid and asking no thanks she provided the motherly glue which kept everyone together. On one of the abandoned slate-cutting sheds, there remained an end still roofed with rusted corrugated iron. The sheets flapped and banged in the wind and occasional cascades of water would descend but it was better than the open. At this end, a great fire would blaze night and day to dry out sodden clothing. Late into the night, around a trestle table, by the light of a hurricane lamp, we would discuss the ills of the world, especially the iniquities of Government; our general purpose being to identify the means by which its policies might be converted or, if necessary, subverted.

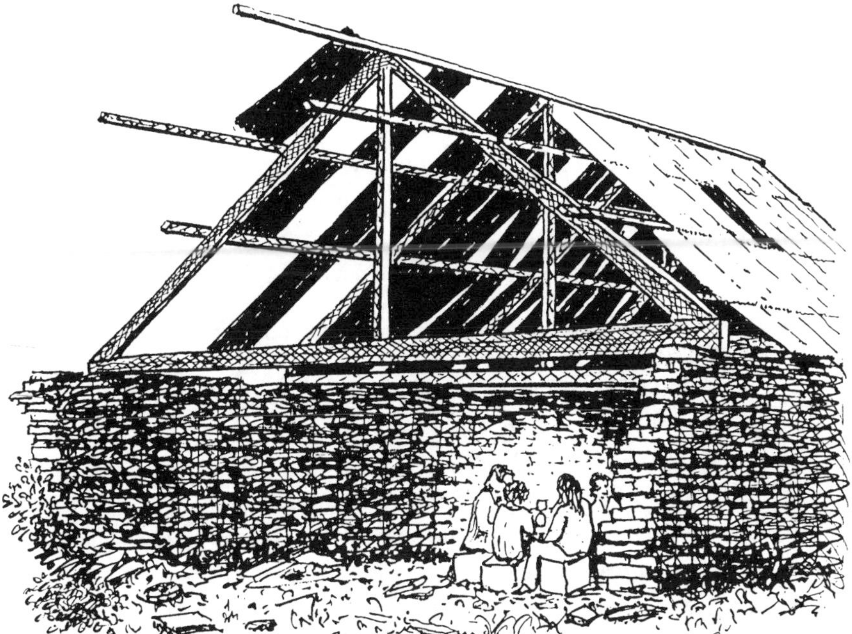

... The shadow of a threat to the established Order ...

I do not know whether it was the place or the strange circumstances which inspired discussions, quite often of a high intellectual calibre. Yet their content was sufficiently diverse, even abstruse that had there been a Government spy amongst us, it is doubtful if he could have discerned even the least shadow of a threat to the established order of things. Nevertheless, it was round this half-sheltered table in an abandoned quarry during wild and wet Welsh autumn nights that the first practical steps were planned. But almost a quarter century would elapse before the Prince of Wales declared that every British Planner should beat a path to this place, or that a Minister for Energy announced that his policies for the future of British sustainable energy supplies stemmed from a visit to this site.

Our vision of the Promised Land was now in place but the sea which must be crossed to reach it was uncharted and perilous. A thick fog of uncertainty swirled around us as each volunteer suggested a different way ahead.

At this early stage there were many moments when the task seemed hopeless. At a practical level there were continual set-backs due to lack of money, absence of skills, violent disagreements and appalling weather but we were all conscious of other well-intentioned projects which had sunk without trace, battered to bits by the realities of survival, so there emerged a dogged resolve to press on.

In February (1974) a full-time worker, Tony Williams was engaged on a miniscule wage. He kept a diary in which he recorded the successes and failures of each day as well as a continuous indictment of the weather. To impart the flavour of that moment, I shall quote a little of that diary which is now a sacred relic at The Quarry.

Friday 8th Feb: Heavy rain all day.

9th: Rain early, clearing later.

10th: Intermittent rain all day.

11th: Rain and wind all day.

12th: Rain early, clearing later.

13th: Fine and sunny early, but showers after noon.

14th: Intermittent rain.

15th: Showers.

16th: Intermittent rain...

Monday 4th Feb: We cleared the debris from the upper rooms in the cottage, noting that much of the structure is very damp, due to holes in the roof.

5th Feb: Pat has repaired the largest leaks in the cottage roof. The upstairs narrow window has been framed. Our work was interrupted during the afternoon by the arrival of two local press-men.

9th Feb: Diana as usual has been marvellous, keeping us well fed and never ceasing to work. She cleared the rotting wooden floor from the engine shed and cleaned the cottage interior, separating the tools from the catering, which makes life more tolerable.

15th Feb: Today we spent indoors pottering around the cottage. We are suffering from lack of materials. Cliff has removed much of the old plaster, revealing how damp the cottage really is, but the roof seems to be keeping most of the water out.

19th Feb: No visitors all day, thank God. A dirty day, digging, mostly with hands, to prepare a drain at the rear of the cottage.

21st Feb: Today I travelled to London for a short planning meeting with Gerard et al. I am disturbed by the proposed size of the project and that we seem to be split between those who think big, and those who are more down to earth. Pat was there, and I hope communicated some degree of reality to the gathering. Steve is still hung up on his exhibition hall, although no-one has any idea what use it might be.

24th Feb: The floor is going very slowly and I have become angry and frustrated at the slow progress. I was determined to finish it today, by candle light if necessary, but we were brought to a standstill after lunch by a succession of visitors, including Denis Humphries, the last resident of the cottage, who gave us much valuable information.

3rd March: This afternoon I visited the highest part of the Quarry for the first time, a most rewarding climb. On the way down I saw Steve in the Quarry, near where the ravens are nesting, removing vegetation. I was extremely angry, and threatened to throw him off the site. He is determined to go ahead with his Disneyland concept, and I am determined that he won't.

4th March: We have now moved in. We have set up three beds and mattresses given by Audrey and found that all the furniture fits quite nicely. We had to remove the upstairs window to get some of it in. It is cold and very damp, but habitable.

March 12th: Nigel, who has been lent some books on the subject by Audrey, has begun to dig the garden. I turned my attention to the plumbing, and as I feared, got nowhere. All the connectors are the wrong size or the wrong sort.

March 15th: I have rigged up a tarpaulin to keep the rain off the west wall. It also provides storage space for tools and a small work area. A long hard look at the collection of plumbing fittings gave me no clue as to how to connect it all up. I shall need some help.

March 21st: I finished connecting the plumbing and turned on the supply. Several leaks developed, requiring the system to be drained each time. I was using a Calor cooking ring as a blow lamp, which made soldering difficult. Several joints came unsoldered. Finally, after a very nervous day listening for leaks, the system filled and I was able to light the stove. Lo! Hot Water!

(Audrey was the wife of John Beaumont, our landlord. Over many years she provided generous material and moral support for the volunteers.)

Alas, Tony Williams proved unable to keep pace with the need to achieve results and two months later was replaced by Mark and Mary Matthews who managed the site until the following year when the strain proved too much for their marriage. Mark left and was replaced by an architect already living in the district, Roderick James, who with colossal energy, enthusiasm and practical know-how, propelled the project forward decisively. Without Roderick's outstanding contribution, sustained over many years, it is quite probable that the venture would have foundered.

Though still living at Burgate, I spent alternate weeks up at the Welsh slate quarry - now just referred to as The Quarry. By good fortune, I was lent a nearby house belonging to Eirene White, a Labour Peer and Minister of State for the Welsh Office. She had chanced upon the project and voiced enthusiastic support, almost the first non-Hippie encouragement which had come my way.

Throughout the summer of 1974, the first 'exhibits' were prepared. It is difficult in retrospect to understand how I or any of the others could have imagined that this embryonic display would be other than ridiculed. Neither is it surprising that the Nuclear Establishment did not immediately feel its existence terminally threatened, for our 'Alternative Technology', in so far as the generation of electricity was concerned, consisted of two ultra-primitive devices.

The first of these was a 'Cretan' windmill of a type in use for at least 1,000 years. Erected on a high bluff, the eight-sailed mill produced, in a good wind, enough electricity to light a few bulbs. A second and outstandingly pathetic exhibit consisted of a bicycle wheel incorporating a dynamo-hub. To this wheel were fixed aluminium vanes so that when mounted on a high pole it would sometimes turn in the wind and light a bicycle lamp. But surprisingly, as a demonstration of wind-generated electricity, these two devices proved instantly accessible to public understanding and through some alchemy of Fate struck a spark of enthusiasm for the potential of wind energy. One might think that this miniscule demonstration within the hidden confines of an abandoned slate quarry in mid-Wales would be unlikely to influence public opinion to any perceptible extent. But, apart from a few thousand visitors who found their way there, it became something of a focal point for media attention (which it has subsequently remained) and gained a huge number of 'column inches' and many hours of television coverage. At a time when opposition to nuclear power was burgeoning, the concept of safe energy from ambient sources exerted a strong appeal.

Twenty-five years later, numerous exposed hills in Britain are crowned with groups of large wind turbines producing safe, non-pollutive, electricity: to an extent, they owe their general public acceptance to the continuing demonstration of ever larger windmills at The Quarry and even more to the widespread publicity which they received. Wind generated electricity is now coming onstream globally faster than nuclear power, and the UK Government intends that it shall provide a steadily increasing fraction of electricity supplies. Wind power is a booming multi-billion pound industry. In due course, we may expect these turbines to be located at sea so that those who find their hill-top presence intrusive will have nothing to worry about: indeed at the time of writing this is happening with eighteen off-shore sites providing the potential needs of over a million homes.

To show the energy potential of waves from coastal installations, we built a large tank of water on which a hand-operated paddle created waves whose energy could be made to light a miniature lighthouse. It was another symbolic demonstration but by the same process helped to create awareness of the possibilities of this vast source of energy. Today wave technology, starved until recently by successive governments of significant development funds, has the potential to meet *all* Britain's electricity needs three times over.

The potential of solar energy was illustrated by circulating water in a coiled plastic pipe enclosed in a glazed box. The occasional burst of sunshine enabled visitors to experience tepid water running from a tap. Once again, the spark of public fervour was struck. Twenty years later, and with vastly improved technology, we installed the largest solar roof in Europe to demonstrate the full potential of solar heating. At the time of writing, the direct conversion of light to electricity (photo-voltaic solar power) is within sight of providing competitively priced electricity which (other than the environmental costs of manufacture) is non-pollutive. The first oil company to invest in this (rather than trying to stamp it out) is likely to strike a golden return.

Organic horticulture was problematic. There was almost no soil and the little there was had its nutrients leached out by the site's annual ninety-five inches of rain. This, together with the salt-laden wind, offered unpromising possibilities. But heroic efforts to compost leaves, bracken, newspapers and the contents of old mattresses produced, initially, some rather sickly examples of the vegetable kingdom of which we were inordinately proud. Now, twenty-five years later, organic horticulture is the fastest growing section of the food industry. And at The Quarry, a large and excellent garden now helps to feed the resident mouths with unpolluted vegetables.

Back in these early days in 1975, a few explanatory notices attempted to present our philosophy to visitors who started to arrive in ever greater numbers. Although collectively these visitors wasted much precious time, it was from them that we also harvested volunteers and the occasional donation. Gradually we were able to look for better and better qualifications, personal and professional, in the 'staff' that came. Today these qualifications are of a high order.

We needed ever-increasing quantities of tools, materials and food but our money was almost gone. I wrote to manufacturers all over Britain, begging donations in kind and it speaks volumes for their goodwill that almost one in three contributed something, gifts which ranged from a single hammer to a van-load of Digestive biscuits, which consequently became our staple diet for years to come!

Then a bombshell. The Duke of Edinburgh announced his intention of coming to visit our display in October. The Royal Train would come to Machynlleth. Suddenly we were Something and our local standing, hitherto a matter of disdain, leapt into an amazed ascendant.

Alerted by the impending Royal visit, the media circus arrived. Mostly uncomprehending and dismissive, they did not have to search hard at this very early stage of our evolution for an 'angle' from which to present the shambles which met their cynical eyes. Designations such as 'scruffy hippies', 'environmental fanatics' and 'middle-class visionaries' formed the average level of comment. I came in for particular derision as soon as my hyphenated name and Eton and Army background was discovered: one journalist renamed me Mr Mournful-Windmill. But the old adage that 'all publicity is good publicity' was once again proved true. People arrived. And all the while, as our ultra-simple exhibits were starting to show, there actually might be practical alternatives to such horrors as nuclear electricity or chemical farming. Very gradually it was taking root in the public consciousness. Meanwhile, the strength of the scorn which was heaped upon the project in general and me in particular by many Establishment figures, though irritating, was also proof that we were saying something that these people found threatening to their interests - and *their* interests were not ours. We felt that we were hammering some of the first nails into the coffin of the Old Order. As it turned out, we were, though not exactly in the way we imagined.

In anticipation of the impending visit of Prince Philip, British Rail had decided to paint the hitherto neglected Machynlleth station in some merry colours. Security men crept around The Quarry examining the exhibits with suspicion. Names of every person likely to be present were checked out and those with no fixed address, together with the self-confessed anarchists, were asked to find another interest for the day .

In the run-up to The Visit, we also acquired, free of charge, an electric pick-up truck and a magnificent narrow-gauge railway carriage for twelve people. To draw this last, we had been loaned for the occasion a small steam engine, though its real purpose was to demonstrate the vastly superior energy efficiency of rail transport and the environmental benefit of using compacted straw briquettes instead of coal or oil - the low-temperature burning of fields of straw being a pollutant as well as a waste. A short section of the original quarry's rail track was re-instated.

On the eve of The Visit there were animated discussions. The anarchists had taken themselves off in a spirit of extravagant disapproval but now it seemed that several of the remaining non-anarchist 'staff' were uncompromising Republicans. These too disappeared in a cloud of sarcastic reproach, reducing still further the people available to demonstrate our exhibits.

On the day of The Visit, the citizens of Machynlleth exhibited a muted enthusiasm for His Royal Highness since he had not previously shown a particular interest in the town. None-the-less finishing touches had been put to the station: flowers hung in baskets and the red carpet was ready to unroll across the platform.

Alas, he arrived, and left, by helicopter!

At the foot of the steeply sloping and still rough track up to the quarry level, I waited with the electric pick-up truck. It was to be our first demonstration of a supposedly less polluting transport. With a marked lack of excitement, His Royal Highness sat in the passenger seat bemoaning that he was not at the wheel and grumbling that the truck was unsuited to its intended task of climbing the track. Half way up, the main fuse blew. 'Told you so!' he said, scrambling out and striding up the slope by himself as I endeavoured to stop the heavy truck running back down the hill out of control.

fired up with straw briquettes...

At the top, the railway engine had a full head of steam. Delivered only the previous day, it had been fired up with the straw briquettes but they had given out insufficient heat to enable the engine to pull the carriage. In desperation, and unknown to me, a quantity of coal had been put in the firebox and a further quantity was stowed in the panniers, overlaid with the straw fuel.

'An example of making a more sensible use of resources,' said I a trifle smugly. Prince Philip strode over to the panniers and dug his hand beneath the straw briquettes, triumphantly holding aloft a lump of coal. 'Thought so!' he said. It was an inauspicious start and the photographers were having a field day. But at the end of his visit he proclaimed the project to be 'important' and 'most relevant' and earlier despondency reverted to hopefulness. In the following days not all the Anarchists and Republicans trickled back. Unrealised at the time, we had inadvertently taken a step toward more conventional behaviour and thereafter the faint scent of Revolution that had permeated our beginnings was increasingly hard to detect.

One month later, I answered the telephone back at Burgate. 'This is Buckingham Palace, Colonel Evans speaking. His Royal Highness,

Prince Philip, would very much like you to dine with him on 9 December. Would you be free to accept his invitation?' I was, and I did.

The work that was going on at The Quarry yielded results that encouraged me greatly. We began to attract helpers with useful skills. Gradually the cottages were restored, and with the caravans, they housed some of the volunteers. The planners were turning out to be unexpectedly helpful and the media had given up sniping.

Diana was performing miracles with the field kitchen and vegetable garden. Numerous wild plants, alleged to be edible, found their way into her legendary salads. Amongst these were young bracken shoots, delicious but later condemned as carcinogenic. She also acted as quartermaster, knew the whereabouts of everything, recycled nails, bolts and nuts and put the fear of God into any volunteer who lost a tool.

The indigenous Welsh sometimes affected not to understand English (especially in the pubs) and initially disregarded the project and its participants. They had, after all, endured centuries of English interference. Ignored, their grievances often disappeared. However the vogue for second homes in Wales was another matter, one addressed militantly by the Welsh Language Society. Many second homes were set on fire, lending a certain poignancy to the Gas Board's current slogan 'Come Home to a Real Fire'. To counter this threat of hostility, we made all signs bilingual and held open days for the locals. Very gradually, they became supportive, especially when they perceived that we were generally anti-Establishment and, in particular, strongly opposed to the nearby nuclear power station at Trawsfynydd which had been thrust upon the Welsh with a promise of numerous jobs, most of which were given to outsiders.

The Quarry opened to the public in July 1975 and by the end of the year had received 15,000 visitors, which allowed a degree of self-financing and set the scene for financial survival.

I began to spend less time there as the project rolled forward with its own developing dynamic. The focus was becoming clearer and real expertise arrived in the person of Bob Todd, a world-class electrical engineer. Over the coming years many first-class brains and hands were attracted to the place: a surprising number came for a visit and never left. Almost all abandoned promising careers and good salaries in favour of a way of life and an aim in which they *believed*. At an early stage, a uniform (and very modest) salary was agreed, irrespective of credentials or responsibilities, it being held that everyone had the ability, in one way or another, to make an equal contribution. The place is still run as a cooperative; all are involved in planning decisions which are made by consensus, and management is via an elected group.

The evolution of The Quarry (alias the Centre for Alternative Technology or CAT as it is now generally known) has been a continuous process. Its early revolutionary ferment has given way to a more measured approach based on facts as well as 'gut beliefs'. During much of this period I was but an occasional visitor. From a relatively early stage the project stood on its own feet, economically and philosophically. The extraordinary achievements of the Centre in succeeding years will be touched on later.

Amongst the visitors to CAT were many snoopers who were occasionally unmasked: one such turned out to be a Director of the Central Electricity Generating Board. This seemingly insignificant incident was interpreted as confirmation that we must be saying something that was holding their attention.

Royal encouragement was plentiful and valuable: a visit from the Duke of Kent was followed in 1978 by the first visit of Prince Charles. Nowadays the Royal Family are constantly criticised as anachronistic but back then they were certainly far ahead of Establishment thinking in matters environmental and the lead currently being given by Prince Charles is both courageous and far-sighted.

The nuclear issue was central to the evolution of the Centre. Almost everyone involved formed part of some anti-nuclear network. I formed close links with Friends of the Earth in London and Paris; with the Sierra Society in the US and many other regionally active groups. We amassed a great deal of information about nuclear accidents around the world.

A former Government Chief Scientist, Sir Kelvin Spencer, who had himself helped to create the nuclear power generating programme and who was now much shocked by the developing culture of deceit, suddenly 'defected' and threw in his lot with us. During his retirement, in Devon, we met frequently and soon became possessed of priceless first-hand evidence.

One evening, I attended a debate in which the Chairman of the

Central Electricity Generating Board, Sir Walter Marshall, attempted to justify nuclear electricity. Opposing him was Gerald Leach, *The Observer's* environmental reporter, who had cancer. Marshall became aggressive and tried to push Gerald away from the microphone. I leapt on to the stage and punched Marshall in the chest. It was a declaration of war.

At once I decided to campaign far more vigorously against the nuclear programme. My first stop was General Sir Frank Kitson, who had been in my regiment, and was then responsible for counter-insurgency measures. I alerted him to the terrorist potential of the civil nuclear programme. This, and other initiatives, resulted, I believe, in many expensive but necessary counter-terrorist precautions being enforced. The significance of 'expensive' was that one of the ways we thought we could get rid of nuclear electricity was by proving it to be uncompetitive. Still then being branded as the 'cheapest', we knew that costs were being ruthlessly massaged. Today it is acknowledged to be the most expensive commercially available electricity produced anywhere.

I teamed up with Arthur Scargill, the much maligned miners' leader, so loathed by the Establishment. He arranged an anti-nuclear march in Durham and invited me to join the front rank, remarking that I would almost certainly be the first old Etonian ever to do this! After the march, I addressed 3,000 miners and experienced for the first time the dangerously powerful kick obtained from knowing that you have the enthusiastic support of a militant crowd.

The previous year I had joined Ecoropa, an 'ecological think-tank' which had been set up by a leading Bordeaux wine merchant, Edward Kressman, and had attracted a miscellany of disaffected Establishment individuals, one or two from each western European country and mostly people with some 'clout'. I made use of this 'umbrella' to create a network of several thousand environmental activists in Britain. With the help of dissident nuclear physicists, we printed a powerful anti-nuclear leaflet entitled 'Nuclear Power - the facts they don't want you to know' and launched its national distribution through this new network.

The leaflet was a sell-out. Within weeks we were reprinting by the *million*. Pubs, doctors' surgeries, even public libraries displayed the leaflet. Volunteers distributed them door-to-door. It also appeared as a poster and was soon plastered over bus-stops and telephone poles. Since the leaflet was purchased by the volunteer distributors, the whole campaign cost nothing.

This leaflet so gravely damaged the nuclear image that the Government took the highly unusual step of authorising a counter-leaflet which attempted to refute the allegations we had made. It was long, boring, evasive and poorly distributed. It failed utterly.

We had helped to deal a major blow against the spread of nuclear power stations.

There was, at this time (1984), a Public Inquiry into the proposed Sizewell Nuclear Power Station. Hilda Murrell, the famous rose grower of Shrewsbury, was a powerful opponent of the nuclear industry. She had, although in her late seventies, taken a course in nuclear physics at the University of Wales to help make certain that her facts were unassailable. She asked me if she could present her evidence against Sizewell under the Ecoropa umbrella. I agreed and in the weeks that followed had many telephone conversations with her about this evidence. It has since been established that all the principal objectors were under surveillance and therefore both our lines were tapped.

Her evidence was devastating. In the last conversation I had with her, she concluded with the words – 'If they don't get me first, I want the world to know that one old woman has seen through their lies'. She did not enlarge on what she meant by the 'don't get me first' but four weeks after this exchange, she was viciously stabbed to death.

It so happened that Hilda's nephew, Robert Green, a naval Commander at the Northwood Operations Centre during the Falklands War, was inevitably privy to the details surrounding the sinking of the Argentinian training ship *Belgrano*. Information about this appalling and unnecessary act was leaked and Robert was an initial suspect. Although it was later shown that, whatever his feelings about it, he had leaked nothing, the connection was made with Hilda and her 'anti-state activities'. Downing Street was desperate to discover - and stop up - the source of the leak and MI5 was immediately involved.* No one was ever accused of her murder. I believe she was killed because she knew too much and when interviewed for television news, I said so.

*See *Unlawful Killing. The Murder of Hilda Murrell* by Judith Cook

Public Inquiries on major issues which are politically sensitive have too often had much in common with the show trials of the Communist era. The notorious Windscale Inquiry seemed to be a prime example. Selectively chosen evidence on one side and largely disregarded evidence on the other, enable the Inspector (also selectively chosen) to produce findings in line with Government policy. It can be a tilted playing field in which objectors, usually impecunious, fight the State with its virtually limitless funding. When this occurs, it is a system that is contemptible and, as in the case of Windscale, destroys confidence in the workings of democracy. The very name of Windscale became so synonymous with accident, deceit and cover-up that it was renamed Sellafield.

One day, I was crossing to France on a British Rail car ferry. When the ship docked in Calais, there was the usual twenty minute delay while the cars slowly exited. In this time, the car-deck was blue with the exhaust fumes of engines needlessly started ahead of time and the extraction fans were hopelessly inadequate to deal with the problem. It so happened that I had with me an American Mail Order catalogue which included details of an affordable gadget for measuring carbon monoxide levels. I sent for one and used it when I next crossed. Needless to say, the levels recorded were rated as exceedingly dangerous. Under threat of publicity, British Rail re-organised procedures immediately and greatly reduced the problem. Other ferry companies followed suit within the year.

This little incident encouraged me to the view - still firmly held - that direct action, based on solid information and the certainty of public support, if needed, is - *by far* - the most effective way to secure environmental improvement as Greenpeace demonstrate so effectively to this day.

CHAPTER 14

Interviewing the world's environmental gurus – become a workaholic - escape to the Sahara Desert – account of double crossing with assorted incidents – a practical joke – our marriage ends – decamp to the Black Mountains – become lonely

IT WILL be recalled that my marriage to Virginia was effectively over though we remained nominally together. This situation brought with it numerous problems and many agonizing conversations of a kind that will be known to many readers. We did our wobbly best to minimise the strains and let each of us go our own ways.

I experienced an overwhelming need to escape these pressures and quickly became a workaholic. I have looked at diary entries for the early Seventies and am astonished by the hyperactivity they reveal. Unhappiness is father to action. The happy man is relaxed and in less hurry to achieve his perceived ambition because to a large extent it is happiness itself that is every person's goal.

Though setting up The Quarry in deepest Wales, I was still running the sales and marketing side of Dexam part-time and also scouring Europe and the United States for new products. At the same time, I was talking to anyone who seemed to be saying important things about the environment: Barbara Ward with *Only One World*, Barry Commoner with *The Closing Circle*, Teddy Goldsmith with *Blueprint for Survival*, and Gerald Leach with his epic series in *The Observer*, *Spaceship Earth*. I was also maintaining a presence with Virginia and the concomitant social life was still considerable. There were dinners, dances and visits to Covent Garden and Glyndebourne, painting and exhibiting, writing (and illustrating) several books on 'barging', one of which I dictated to a secretary in ten days, much of it whilst travelling. In this frenzied period, I used to send for the barber to cut my hair whilst working at my desk at Dexam, just to save twenty minutes travel time. I tried to visit my father most days when I was at home.

Meanwhile the garden needed maintaining and the house repairing; one task alone involved removing, scraping, preserving and replacing thirty-six exterior shutters and since money remained a major constraint, we could seldom afford to employ tradesmen to make or mend. In this period, I acquired the basic skills of a jobbing builder and handyman which enabled me, amongst numerous other tasks, to build a two-story 'Swiss Chalet' for the children and, more daringly, a zip-wire from the top of the hill behind the house, a descent of 150 feet. On my first test run, the braking mechanism failed and I slammed into a tree shattering an ankle, leaving me to drop from the wire onto the undamaged leg in the centre of a bramble thicket!

Inevitably there came a moment when it was all too much. I needed to flee my own workaholic therapy. I considered sailing the Atlantic or crossing the Sahara Desert. As I had never sailed anything, I chose the desert and immediately set about making arrangements.

As it happened there was a man in the adjacent village of Dunsfold who specialised in adapting Land Rovers for expeditions. I immediately ordered a long-wheelbase vehicle from the appropriately named Mr Bashall, specially kitted out for desert travel.

This involved the fitting of special springs and tyres, a sump guard, an elevated air intake, side panniers for storage, a winch, sand-ladder fixings, many racks for jerry cans, extra lights, a vice fitted to the bumper, pig wire over side windows, a roof-rack extending the length of the Land Rover and (my innovation!) a permanently erected canvas canopy above the rear of the roof-rack to provide intruder and scorpion-proof sleeping quarters. To these modifications were added a large box of spare parts and a mechanic's instruction manual.

The problem of paying for the expedition was happily resolved by my publishers who commissioned a how-to-do-it book, sold as *Cruising the Sahara*.

Two female companions volunteered to participate in this venture, one dropping out before departure. With the remaining one, Jenny, I set about preparing for what would be a serious expedition. It was an immensely diverting activity as we projected in our minds every conceivable situation and set about providing ourselves with the relevant material, being still happily ignorant about the overriding need to travel light. There are few things more satisfying than addressing an entirely new venture, finding out everything about it you can, then plunging in. It adds a fresh dimension to life - and so it turned out with the desert.

Towards the end of February 1973, we set off, a half-century after the first ever motorised crossing of the Sahara. The famous Citröen half-tracked vehicles which succeeded in the original expedition at least had the benefit of a convoy of similar vehicles fully equipped with all spares, mechanics and guides. In contrast, our self-contained expedition felt a bit vulnerable to possible mishap.

We had accumulated so much gear and so many provisions that the vehicle was full even before we started. We had succumbed to luxuries such as a refrigerator, a lavatory seat on a stand and a canvas bath - though where we thought we would get water from for this last item I haven't the least idea. In addition, we had two spare wheels, fourteen jerry-cans for water and petrol, a folding kitchen table and a cabin trunk containing useful items such as clothes pegs, compass, nylon cord, distress flares, presents for the natives, water-sterilising tablets and over 100 other items weighing over a ton, all considered indispensable at the outset.

We rumbled slowly and heavily across France and boarded the ferry in Marseilles for Algiers. After a turbulent crossing and an interminable time passing through Customs (a pan-African speciality), we drove slowly up the Atlas Mountains into deep snow and groves of cedar. Crossing the watershed we quickly entered a warmer climate: flowering almond trees and prickly-pear cactus lined the road. Streaks of orange marigolds and white marguerites alternated with the emerald green of the spring grass as we descended the twisting road toward the barren plain that separates the Tellier Atlas from the Saharan Atlas.

Somewhere in this region, the starter motor failed. We didn't have a spare but, as it happened, we found ourselves outside the main gate of an oil-drilling camp. Driving in and out constantly were Land Rovers. I dispatched Jenny to talk to the camp manager and see what could be done. With the triple assets of fluent French, strikingly good looks and much charm, she had secured within forty minutes a brand new starter and a mechanic to fit it, all for nothing.

On the third day, we reached Ghardaia, one of a string of oases that flank the north of the Sahara. We stocked up with fresh vegetables and hundreds of oranges which were piled in huge pyramids along the streets.

Driving across the open desert, miles from anything marked on even the largest scale maps, perhaps not seeing another vehicle all day, was intensely exciting and therapeutic. The frenzied pace at which I had been living slowed rapidly. The sheer beauty of the landscape dominated the mind and was deeply calming. I had not been prepared for this: although I knew that most of the desert was neither flat nor sandy, I had not envisaged the grandeur or the drama in these vast multi-coloured landscapes dotted liberally with stunted acacia trees. I had, I think, expected repetitive scenery but the mix of rocky plateaux, gravel plains and curvaceous sand dunes was infinitely varying and wonderfully satisfying visually.

I could feel myself sloughing the accumulated stress of recent years. I looked at my co-driver who felt she was doing the same. Companionable, competent and fun, Jenny was proving an ideal 'co-expeditioner' - a role for which the qualifications are many and rare. The nights were cooler than expected and the days hotter. By early afternoon, the floor of the Land Rover was so hot that the passenger had to travel with his or her feet in a bowl of water. Any exertion was draining and we soon developed techniques for driving which helped us to avoid getting bogged down in soft sand; repeated use of the sand-ladders and the digging which their use entailed was so fatiguing we would sometimes walk ahead to reconnoitre the worst places. Even so we occasionally became seriously stuck in sand up to the axles. Dealing with this was exhausting. A spare wheel would have to be rolled thirty or so yards ahead of the vehicle, then after being attached to the hook of the winch, it would be buried in a hole so deep that when the winch was engaged, the Land Rover moved forward rather than the wheel moving backwards.

A mere 800 miles or so brought us to the Tassili Mountains where extraordinary rock formations contain numerous caves decorated with perhaps the finest and least visited rock paintings of pre-history. Many caves were hard to reach, we had to scramble up rocky hills in the intense heat of the sun. There are hundreds of such caves now known and probably hundreds more still undiscovered. The dry desert air had helped to preserve these painting perfectly.

200 more miles of mountainous track took us to Djanet, the last oasis before the perilous crossing of the Tenéré Desert, 1,000 miles of

intermittent piste, irregularly marked by the remaining stakes from the trans-Saharan Berliet lorry expedition of long ago. In the course of this run, one crosses the frontier between Algeria and Niger but the respective customs posts are over 500 miles apart. About half-way along this leg of our journey, we arrived at Bilma, the point of departure for immense camel caravans carrying rock-salt mined by hand from waterlogged pits in this desperately poor, scorpion and fly-ridden mid-Saharan oasis, virtually cut-off from the world.

Two days further on, we stopped at the legendary Tree of Tenéré, then perhaps the most famous tree in the world, yet rarely seen because of its extreme isolation. Standing by itself, quite alone, in thousands of square miles of barren desert, it was a valued landmark, being adjacent to a 150 foot well, and an object of veneration to desert travellers. A few years later, it was cut down by a group of passing soldiers and used for firewood. It has recently been replaced by an artificial tree of tubular metal.

Only 100 miles or so from Agadez, I drove over a ledge, dropped two or three feet and broke a half-shaft. There are two half-shafts in a Land Rover, one long, one short: it is almost always the long one which breaks and we had a spare. But here it was, of course, the short one. Lying under the vehicle on scorching sand, peppered with grit from a rising storm, attempting to unbolt the differential, effected a rapid transition from the sublime to the hellish.

At that time, Land Rover spare parts were sometimes stocked by the 'locals' as a form of investment. After waiting a few hours, a lorry appeared travelling towards Agadez. Consulting the mechanic's manual, we gave the driver the part number and a few hours later, another lorry appeared with the appropriate spare. It goes without saying that if you happen to live in a Saharan oasis and you have put your savings into Part No 123456 and somebody else, stuck in a potentially life-threatening situation, actually needs Part No 123456, then it is not the list price on which negotiations open. In such a situation, it is difficult to negotiate at all and it was only the arrival of another lorry driver who stopped to see whether there was business to be done and found there was, which caused the original vendor to back-track to a slightly lower but still astronomical price. Unexpectedly, we found we held an ace in our hands, our twelve-volt refrigerator, as much of a status symbol to locals as a Rolls Royce in Europe. Its departure was regrettable but it drew the sting from the bill.

We encountered many of the 'blue' men, Tuareg tribesmen whose indigo-dyed attire and black headscarf is so distinctive. Their language, Tamashek, is written in a script called Tifnak which has the unique characteristic that it can be written in any direction.

Outside Agadez, there used to be a campsite called Joyce's Garden. Joyce, a German, catered for the desert weary. His ramshackle establishment, grandly titled Hotel de l'Aïr, was the first post of civilisation for those coming south across the eastern route. Its fame rested largely on the provision of ice-cold beer and a swimming pool - actually a smallish tank of greenish water, possibly infested with bilharzia and much else, but no turquoise pool of crystal purity has ever come within measure of this filthy, stagnant, blissful place.

As we crossed the southern edge of the Sahara toward Niamey and Gao, we began to see a surprising amount of wildlife; antelope and gazelle, hyena, giraffe, desert fox and the desert gerbil of pet-shop fame. Birds too were plentiful, especially bee-eaters, wheatears and desert bullfinches while a bustard took shelter beneath the Land Rover during a sandstorm. Then there were the reptiles; geckos, lizards and the more sinister sand-vipers. Worst of all were the scorpions of which there are sixty species. These have an uncanny habit of hiding in shoes and a sting is a serious and occasionally fatal, event. Much of the desert fauna has camouflage colouring. Many birds walk more than they fly and all species can survive for long periods without water - some thirty species are more or less independent of water for their entire lives.

In Niamey, we could have (illegally) sold the Land Rover to the Chief of Police for sufficient profit to pay for a return flight and the cost of the expedition.

In Gao, I went to redeem a Poste Restante letter for which there was a charge. I only had a relatively large denomination note. The clerk refused to give me change and adopted a bullying tone, then when I became angry said he could only give me change in hundreds if not thousands of ultra-low-value postage stamps. I took the stamps, quietly wetted them and stuck them over every surface within reach. Having lost 'face' the clerk became enraged and there followed a shouting match which electrified the other customers and nearly ended in a fight. I reflect now that my action was entirely justified since it is indeed a civic duty to combat bureaucratic absurdity whenever found!

We now set out to cross the Western Sahara, more precisely the Tanezruft Desert, almost 1,000 miles of sandy piste largely devoid of markers. Occasionally there was an empty oil barrel or a post, erected by the Berliet lorry company, but for most of the way, one needed to stick to the tracks of preceding vehicles – if any! Sometimes after a sandstorm, the track would be invisible for long stretches and it was entirely possible to wander off into the trackless desert without any certainty of re-finding the route - ever. Now and then we would see the wreck of a vehicle stripped bare of every component, or the wreck of a camel, a whitened skeleton. Our journey predated satellite navigating equipment which now removes the uncertainty from locating position. It also removes a great part of the excitement.

Some way into this desert is a control post, Bordj-Moktar, marking the frontier between Mali and Algeria. Here there were many sad sights, vehicles hopelessly broken down, their penniless owners begging for a lift and travellers without the correct documents trying to bribe their way through (always successful at a price).

I had an interesting exchange with the resident bureaucrat in charge of stamping the vehicle carnet. To appreciate this little incident, it is necessary to know that the Land Rover had previously belonged to the Southern Electricity Board, that I had omitted to update the registration document with my name and also that my passport photograph was not a good likeness.

Customs Man: *'Montrez-moi votre passeport!'*

Me: *'Voila!'*

Customs Man: *'Montrez-moi le carnet de la véhicule!'*

A long silence while he scrutinises both documents repeatedly

Customs Man: *'Vous avez volé la véhicule!'*

Me: *'Non, Monsieur'*

Customs Man: *'Alors vous avez volé votre passeport!'*

Me: *'Non, Monsieur.'*

Customs Man: *'Vous n'êtes pas Monsieur Grenville, Gerard Wyndham Morgan. Je suis bien sûr que vous êtes Monsieur Board, Southern Electricity! Avouez! Vous êtes Monsieur Board!'*

In the middle of the Tanezruft, an exhaust valve burnt out and it looked as though our vehicle might become one more desert wreck but we continued slowly with much reduced power and greatly increased petrol consumption. Although we were equipped with long-range fuel tanks and carried six jerry cans of fuel as well, we had also added a sixty-gallon barrel, after much agonising over the weight and the expense 'just in case' before we left Gao. In the event, it was this extra supply which saved us. We reached Reggane, the first outpost north of the Tanezruft - just.

After that, the last 1,000 miles back to Algiers was an anti-climax and the return to civilisation was surprisingly jarring. We took the ferry to Genoa and just after disembarking, the clutch 'went'. But experience with my 1926 Bentley, which only had a dog clutch, meant that I could happily change gear clutchless - it was simply a knack of judging engine speed against road speed and starting each time in gear. We limped back, both immensely pleased with the adventure, a feeling which the passage of years did nothing to diminish.

Many people have since asked what possible attraction there could be in travelling thousands of miles across a desert. To such people the Sahara is doubtless the place of legend: foreign legionnaires paraded before their desert fort, murderous Tuareg tribesmen armed with antique muskets mounting a camel charge, sun-crazed men in shorts and topee staggering drunkenly towards a fatal mirage, endless rippled dunes of scorching soft sand rendering each short step a terrible exertion, whitened bones on yellow sand, swarming flies that drive you insane, scorpions beneath every stone, the legendary Timbuktu forbidding entry to the infidel, camel caravans padding silently through the moonlight in hopeless search of wells which have not dried.

So firmly do many people cling to their fantasies that they find it hard to realise that there is another Sahara as alluring as theirs is frightening. This is the real Sahara: the greatest desert on earth. To explore its expanse is to become acquainted with the surface of the moon or the bed of the oceans. It is to experience a solitude and tranquility that is unknown in Europe. It is to see the earth on the day of Creation in all its nakedness. To stand on virgin desert beneath stars of incredible brightness, in a silence which is absolute, is to undergo a profound experience. To stare across golden sand, under the blue hemisphere of each day, towards the rose-coloured hills of a distant horizon, or to contemplate the voluptuous curves of rising dunes or the sudden emerald of a verdant oasis is to be recharged spiritually.

Have you seen birds that are ludicrously tame? We found them greatly attracted by music. A tape of Sibelius' Violin Concerto would have even astonished St Francis by their corporate enthusiasm. Had you thought of a Sahara of flowers or of rocks carved by the wind with such consummate skill as to make the works of abstract sculptors seem sadly contrived? Of combing the markets for fragrant spices at give-away prices? Or of simply making off towards the horizon to stand where perhaps no man has ever stood before?

Lest you think that I romanticise the desert, I will be more objective. When the winter fogs or cold spring winds afflict our island, even the northern Sahara enjoys the best weather of a British July not just one day between wind and rain but a whole string, each and every one predictably fine, clear and hot. Even in March, you may eat fresh pineapple, mango or strawberries and buy the most succulent vegetables. You can join the relatively few who have seen the greatest rock paintings in the world, works of magnificent simplicity and astonishing elegance. There are countless mud-built edifices of striking architectural beauty. Two people may stand in the North African desert separated by 3,000 miles of emptiness without a single metalled road between them. You can be below sea level or 11,000 feet above it. You may travel 500 miles across open desert and not see a living soul.

Britain is one of the most densely populated countries on earth. The effects of this overcrowding impinge on us from all directions and affect our bodily and mental well-being. We are almost never out of the sight, sound, or smell of traffic, aircraft and the Great Industrial Machine. What better reason, therefore, to visit the loneliest place on earth?

The Sahara had me in its grip and two years later, I temporarily withdrew Hugo from Eton and made two more crossings with him.

I have often found that the saying 'as one door closes, another opens' is true. Returning from the Sahara it was suddenly plain to me that the compromises which had for so long concealed the deepening cracks of domestic life were no longer supportable. With much sadness, we decided to go our separate ways and to sell the house. It was especially hard for my father who lived next door but he too recognised that the issue could no longer be fudged.

The house was advertised. I was so confident of a quick sale and so desirous of a new base that I unwisely took out a loan from the bank and scoured estate agents in the Welsh Marches; a longed-for area in which to live. Almost immediately I found an enchanting place in Herefordshire. It was a small 17th century farmhouse surrounded by aged pear orchards. The River Arrow flowed quietly past the small garden. I fell in love. Its owner was an elderly maker of violins and the part-finished products of his craft hung from the black beams. I bought it in haste; then repented at leisure for Burgate did not sell. I was obliged to re-market the gem that I had found and with its sale went a small piece of my heart and a large slice of money.

The housing market was in the doldrums and as week succeeded week, hope began to falter. Then one day I received a telephone call from a London agent who said that he had an Arab oil Sheik he was certain would pay the asking price. An appointment was made. It was winter and the house was notoriously cold. Two days prior to the visit, I turned on all the antiquated radiators and pressed the boiler into performing a miracle. The house actually became warm; exotic flowers decorated shining rooms and the dining room table was laden with delicacies for a sweet-toothed Arab. At the appointed hour, I was ready and waiting to welcome this wealthy man. I felt it was now or never.

Punctually, a huge and shiny car appeared and drove slowly into the courtyard. A tall man in a suit – the agent I presumed - stepped out, followed by a soldier with a rifle who stood to attention as the Sheik, in robes and head-gear, eased himself slowly from the back seat. A second car appeared and from it emerged an impressive number of yashmaked females from the Sheik's harem.

I advanced sedately toward his Excellency who acknowledged me with a cursory flick of the wrist. Walking slowly backwards across the courtyard, I delivered a short speech of welcome, interlarded with Arab greetings such as 'May your shadow never grow less' and, as he entered the house, 'My threshold is greatly honoured' and such-like formulae. Then, to my astonishment, as the hitherto silent Sheik reached the inner hall, he burst into uncontrollable mirth. All was instantly revealed: the 'Sheik' was none other than my disguised neighbour and very close friend Simon Heneage whose retinue comprised his family and other local friends. It was a masterly practical joke which remains to be avenged!

Eventually, Burgate sold and Virginia and I divided the disappointingly meagre proceeds. We achieved an amicable divorce, thanks to my brother John replacing solicitors, whose settlement techniques would indubitably have proven highly divisive and ludicrously expensive. Divorce solicitors can be the source of copious misery, mostly unnecessary and often incurred in the pursuit of outrageous fees which can of course be greatly swollen by getting their clients into heated dispute.

In early 1976 and with cash in hand, I hurried back to the Welsh Marches and once again scanned the windows of the estate agents. I swiftly found myself under the spell of a primitive sheep farm on the southern slopes of the Black Mountains in Breconshire. Whereas my previous choice had been in a sheltered valley, this was one of the highest farms in the county. Its price exactly matched my share of the proceeds and I soon found myself the owner of Henbant Fach and its seventy-five acres.

The house, above Crickhowell, was a fifteenth century longhouse, complete with original oak screen and damp stone floor. In the seventeenth century, a massive chimney had been added and later still an upper floor had been crudely inserted beneath the heavy stone roof. On the ground floor there was a stable and a single room with a huge fireplace and, opposite this, a stone bench beneath the panelled screen: beyond was a minute kitchen. Water was from a distant spring and electricity was represented by two shadeless bulbs and lengths of meandering cable looped from nails.

Facing the house, across a small grass-covered yard, were two old stone barns, both roofed in rusty corrugated iron which emitted eerie sounds in a wind as the sheets vibrated on rusty nails.

In 500 years of occupation, it seemed that no one had done anything to achieve even a modicum of comfort or convenience. There was no vegetable garden, no steps up the steep slope on which the house was built, no source of heat beyond the one fireplace. The house was damp, dark and almost derelict but its situation was incomparable. On one side it looked down across the valley below to the Sugar Loaf Mountain, on the other toward the Table Mountain. In all this panorama, there was not a single eyesore. Above the house, numerous small fields, edged by stunted thorn trees and wind-swept ash trees, rose 600 feet to the heather and bracken-covered expanse of the Black Mountains.

There was a neighbouring sheep farm, as well kept as mine was disordered. Ron Thomas, the elderly farmer, had lived in this place almost all his life and was deeply scornful of my predecessor when I went to introduce myself.

'Very lazy was Ifor Williams, see. Fond of a drink or two, or three like. Didn't fancy the early mornings like. Well, well, I mustn't tell tales though I knows some, mind. They say the house is haunted,

... fell under the spell of a primitive sheep farm

see. Some woman who, then, well, well, it's not for me to say, is it, you'd be best asking Ifor, mind, it's not my business, isn't it. T'is a lovely place to live I tell you but a bugger of a place to make a living, see. I 'spect you knows about sheep and will soon make a tidy job of it but if you needs for anything, you just ask me or get your missus to ask mine, look you."

'I'm afraid I'm not a sheep farmer and I'm not married, but thanks all the same.'

'Ah...Er...Oooh. 'Course, not my business like but what would you be a-wanting with a sheep farm if you're not a sheep farmer, I'm asking myself, like. Well, well, well, whatever next?' And he limped off to tell the Missus about their peculiar new neighbour.

For the first few days in these unfamiliar surroundings, I experienced a sense of liberation that I found strangely exhilarating. Answerable to no one, I could ignore the clock and keep my own hours and I revelled in this lively independence, pausing repeatedly to drink in the extravagant view. All the fields had age-old names which Ron Thomas translated for me: they included the Field of the Rowan Trees, Fox's Field, the Lamb's Field, the Field of the Lone Ash Tree, Round Meadow and the Field where the Devil hung his Mother-in-Law. Each had an entirely distinct character and for a few days I toyed with the idea of keeping sheep simply so that I could range back and forth across this paradise, for such it was.

Day after day I would see no one. The house was so gloomy inside that I postponed efforts to improve it. Instead, I found much happiness in climbing to the top of the land and repairing the much fallen dry-stone wall which formed the boundary between farm and open mountain. The work was arduous and virtually irrelevant but as a therapy, both mental and physical, it can have no equal. My divorce had left me shattered, far more so than I initially realised. But gradually I began to look outward again and when I did so I found that I was lonely. I had also begun to feel the pinch from a total inexperience of cooking, washing or ironing; sewing on a button and all housework was virgin territory.

I began to experience that most dangerous feeling - that I needed a woman in my life. And so, in the time-honoured tradition of human beings who have found their Eden, I took the first steps toward its destruction.

Top left. Self as chauffeur delivering Laura to wedding of Prince Charles and Diana.
Top right. Cutting the 25th anniversary cake at CAT.
Below left. With my honorary brother Sasha somewhere in Georgia.
Below right. Hugo, James Heneage, George and Laura involved in some game aboard *Virginia Anne* in the late seventies.

Virginia Anne
A family holiday in progress, one of many over a period of a quarter century.

Fleur de Lys
This was the first ever super-luxury barge (for just six passengers) and the first with a swimming pool.

Napoleon
Seen here passing the Papal Palace in Avignon, this barge was the most comfortable small river cruiser in Europe.

CHAPTER 15

A fresh start – open a shop and am instantly bored – Robert and the building of a Great Hall – making clocks - attempt to launch a new Green party in British politics – founding the Green Alliance – punishment of a parking warden – creation of first private train in post-war Britain – a ghastly accident in Spain

MY MANIFOLD failings in the domestic sphere, combined with a sense of post-divorce loneliness, became acute, a condition which, I later learnt, is a frequent source of subsequent marital blunder. And so it was for me.

After many weeks of bachelordom, I invited Fern Roberts, who had previously been my personal assistant at Dexam, and was herself going through a divorce. She came just for the weekend. The all-round quality of life was dramatically improved. A second weekend followed. Further improvement. Then a whole week. Marvellous. Then a week with Garth, her three-year old child, and Tarquin, her three-month old baby. Patchy.

Someone with more prudence might have drawn a line at this point. But I was busy and my loneliness was unalleviated. Besides, I was fond of Fern and grateful for the domestic support so willingly given. A while later, she moved in. We lived together quite happily and we formed an efficient unit: Fern was a capable secretary and competent house-keeper.

She bought a shop in Crickhowell, The Cheese Press which was simultaneously a bookshop, a gift shop and a coffee shop. I enjoyed choosing and setting out the merchandise the first time but the novelty wore off very soon. I was still to learn that a shop can swiftly become a kind of open prison to its owner. The tables in the café quickly became the residence of those who hadn't anything much to do and the gift shop became a shop-lifters' paradise but in spite of these many drawbacks the enterprise made a modest profit. This, together with my Dexam salary, represented our total income and it was not enough.

The house remained unimproved and to make anything of it required substantial funds. After much heart-searching, having decided against sheep farming, I sold fifty of the seventy acres to a nearby farmer, engaged a local one-man builder and advertised in the personal column of *The Times* for an assistant who wished to learn the building trade - this last intended as an economical solution for the continual labouring which would need to be done and, besides, I also hoped to find an individual whose company I might enjoy.

The successful applicant was Robert Hammond who managed, within a short time, to be as skilled as a professional. Immensely strong, careful, intelligent and possessed of an excellent sense of humour, he ached to do something more substantial than house renovation and I happily agreed to upgrade my simple plans for the house to include a Great Hall incorporating a 'medieval' tower, the whole being about the size of a small parish church.

We decided we could build this ourselves without further professional help and that we could do so almost entirely with recycled materials.

We scoured the mountains in my Saharan Land Rover, retrieving enough stone to build the entire extension. Then we recovered enough used timber for the roof structures and floors. Whilst extracting a beam from the roof of a barn which was due to be demolished I broke three ribs. This accident introduced me to the staggering inefficiencies and callousness of the National Health Service, as then exemplified by the Nevill Hall Hospital in Abergavenny.

Although it had a reputation for discharging patients in coffins, the locals were loathe to criticise it openly for a deep-seated fear that when their turn came merciless revenge would be taken upon them. My turn having now come, I found myself in urgent need of pillows, as anyone who has broken their ribs will confirm. I was given one and one only: nothing I could say would procure more. It seemed true that nobody cared whether one lived or died. In great discomfort I got up, presented my one pillow to the ward sister, and shuffled myself to the front door. The moral is that inaction by dissatisfied 'users' results in an ever-worsening performance. It is a constant truth whether applied to hospitals, hotels, councils or governments. If the performance isn't good enough, make a fuss.

In the event, Robert completed the building almost by himself in a little under a year. In the lunch break he would find a sheltered corner, sharpen his chisels and planes, and spend a quarter of an hour reading Maupassant and other enlightened authors.

The wiring and the plumbing were undertaken by a remarkable man from one of the mining valleys. At once an accomplished engineer, an electronics expert and the repository of numerous shocking confidences which he disclosed daily, he was also an alcoholic and an immensely skilled forger of car licences which he sold to his friends for half the official rate.

The wet days were a problem and there were many of them. Building in the rain is no fun and building *should* be fun. A solution soon came in sight, one which solved the boring problem of paying the mortgage which I had been obliged to take out.

I had noticed that nobody seemed to be making the kind of mahogany kitchen wall-clocks with Roman numerals that used to hang on Victorian kitchen walls. I was put in mind of this when a year or two before I had chanced upon one of the last makers of enamelled clock faces, in the Vosges Mountains in France. In Crickhowell, there was an ailing machine-shop for mass-produced wooden boxes and its owners were keen to turn out the clock frames whilst the French enameller produced the faces. A clock trade-fair yielded up makers of brass bezels, clock motors, hands and glass and in a few weeks all the components for clock-making were to hand. On the first rainy day, we went into production. Under the name Celtic Clocks we sold into the gift trade. Soon there were not enough rainy days for Robert to keep up with demand. A mail-order catalogue took them and the orders came in such a continuous stream that house building had to be abandoned to fulfill them. A small cascade of money rolled in until a Japanese factory copied them for sale at half our price and so we cheerfully reverted to house building instead, though sadly it spelled the end for the factory in Crickhowell. But it had been a most rewarding commercial excursion and the mortgage was paid off.

Although I was living in isolation from contemporary politics, I became increasingly aware of the need for a political face to the 'environmental movement' as it was being termed. I believed that a Parliamentary party with a 'green' agenda would ensure that major issues were properly debated. Green parties were being formulated across Europe and there was a general view they might become a powerful force.

It was a case of wishful thinking laced with political naivety. Subsequent events have amply demonstrated that the way forward is to have the principal parties compete with each other for green credentials.

Together with Maurice Ash (then Chairman of the Town and Country Planning Association), I invited members of all the environmental organisations we could think of to attend a meeting at Conway Hall in London, which we had hired for the purpose of seeing if a potentially effective political alliance could be formed, leading to the establishment of a Green political party in Britain.

The event was educational to its politically innocent organisers. Although all the participants shared entirely the same general concerns, there was absolutely no consensus about any proposals and the meeting broke up in heated disarray. I realised then that ideals and politics were uneasy bed-fellows and that I was temperamentally ill-equipped to compete in political chicanery.

In spite of this crashing failure, we formed an entity called The Green Alliance Trust, which adopted a valuable and enduring role in publishing a Parliamentary newsletter. Now, every two weeks, whilst Parliament is in session, this is an effective tool for keeping political track of the major green topics as well as the MPs who support or oppose them - a service now widely used by MPs, journalists, the environmental lobby and major corporations. In 1999, Dr John Reid (then Minister for Transport) proclaimed - 'This Government recognises the debt we owe Britain's environmental organisations, at the forefront of which is, of course, Green Alliance.' The Minister for Environment (Michael Meacher) added - 'Green Alliance is in the forefront of the relationship between government and NGOs and has contributed significantly to policy development over the years. You have been influential on greening government. You paved the way in the 1980s for the *rapprochement* between business and environmentalism. And, of course, you were working on biotechnology in those happy, far off days when most of us did not need to spend half of every day talking about GMOs. Being able to pick the issues of the future is an important skill and one the Green Alliance has demonstrated it possesses in abundance.' In November 2000, Tony Blair launched Labour's environmental agenda to Green Alliance. (Green Alliance, 40

Buckingham Palace Road, London, SW1W ORE.)

A Dutch film company made contact with me. They were producing a series of documentaries on individuals involved in the environmental field, and wanted to come to Henbant and make one on me. We had an enjoyable week shooting it, which once again made me half-regret that I had not gone into the film business. I never saw the resultant product - it was shown in Holland, Belgium, Germany and Canada, but instead I received a sackful of letters which took ages to answer.

In July 1981, the wedding of Prince Charles to Diana Spencer took place at St Paul's Cathedral. My daughter Laura (who had worked with Diana) and son Hugo (who was a friend of Diana) were both invited to attend. Since I was not, I offered to act as chauffeur. The car had its annual wash, I dressed up in a dark suit, borrowed the postman's cap and bought a yellow duster. It was fun driving through the streets filled with cheering crowds with a police escort in front. After depositing my 'fares' at the Cathedral, I was directed to a special car park where I made free with the duster and shared coffee from a Thermos with my co-chauffeurs.

At Henbant, the extension of the house was now complete. A Welsh flag flew from the staff atop the tower and thereafter I was known locally as Morgan-the-Flag.

The former cowshed had been converted to holiday accommodation to provide a modest income. The barn had been re-roofed and now housed my Holzapfel ornamental-turning lathe on which, after a gap of many years, I again set to work. My father had inherited such a lathe and taught me the complex skills needed to employ its numerous chucks and tools. I had bought this second lathe years before for rather little money in a sale and subsequently found it to be very valuable. It appeared there were only twelve in Britain, one of them in the Science Museum. A Victorian gentleman's pastime, they enabled a skilled operator to produce highly ornamented turnery, often executed then in ebony or ivory. Some of the pieces made were so complex they might easily not be recognised as turnery, especially as pieces could be oval or even square. I once saw a replica of the Albert Memorial made on a similar lathe: it was of course quite hideous. With a disciplined approach, pieces could be lovely but, alas, discipline was rare. It proved simply too tempting for operators to use the many fascinating chucks and apply decoration to any remaining plain surface.

Robert, the builder, had left for another job and whilst I was still in building mode I set to work constructing a medieval gatehouse, of which the low but attractive arch effectively prevented subsequent access by any large vehicle, resulting in considerable inconvenience! A small garden and the planting of many trees brought all the component parts into a delightful whole. In the two years or so in which the building operations had been carried out, the place had not lost its feeling of antiquity, and one day I had the great satisfaction of hearing the leader of a guided walk pointing out to his party the rarity of such a 'medieval' tower – then less than a year old.

I set to work constructing a medieval gatehouse

Down below in Crickhowell, the shop which had by now started to prosper mildly was suffering a set-back due to the arrival of an officious parking warden who did his best to prevent would-be shoppers parking nearby. This man, known as Dai-Book-and-Pencil, was believed to accept gifts in return for leaving trader's vehicles unmolested. One very hot day, Dai went into the butcher's shop outside which was parked, as usual, the refrigerated delivery van.

'Your van is causing an offence, look you; I'll have to book you, see.'

The butcher leant over the counter and hissed into Dai's ear.

'No need for that Dai. Hop in the back and choose yourself a nice cut, like.'

In hopped Dai, out came the butcher and shut the door on him. Dai was then driven to the summit of the pass between Crickhowell and Talgarth and released freezing onto the shimmering road.

'Put you your smart hat on Dai, and your jacket, and get you walking back to Crick. And if you take anything off, or stop, I'll run you round to the Chief Constable, see.'

Dai did as he was told and sweltered and puffed his way back the thirteen miles. He was never seen again, shamed into self-exile. This little incident afforded pleasure out of all proportion to its importance. I have long thought that parking wardens, all of them, being only at one remove from the 'people's police' of the Communist era, should be painlessly extinguished.

I began to receive letters from some of the charterers of *Virginia Anne*, saying how much they had enjoyed their cruise and what suggestions did I have for their holiday next year? As I had none, it was clear that I was missing an opportunity.

I was reflecting on this one day in 1982, driving to the north of England. I had reached Carnforth in Lancashire when I saw a sign advertising Steamtown - a private museum of old steam engines and carriages. On impulse I turned off and two hours later had half-persuaded the owners to hire two of their most interesting carriages. For I had found myself possessed of an idea: I would try to persuade British Rail to couple these two coaches onto scheduled trains travelling the Highlands of Scotland, and thus enable my much-indulged barge passengers to travel in similar luxury through that magnificent scenery.

One coach had once formed part of the Royal Train. It possessed beds, bathrooms with baths, and accommodated just six people. The other coach had a comfortable observation saloon, an open verandah, a dining saloon, as well as a kitchen and crew accommodation. As a plan it seemed simple enough but, when approached, British Rail did not welcome the idea of pulling private coaches around Britain. Beyond the doctrinaire policies of a nationalised industry that private enterprise should be excluded, there was, it appeared, every kind of practical difficulty. The coaches I wanted had an incompatible braking system, the buffers were of slightly different heights and the couplings were not of a standard type. In an attempt to change problems into solutions, I invited the relevant manager to a meeting aboard a steam launch on Lake Windermere and an hour or so after a memorable and largely liquid lunch, he came to the view that it might just be possible to oblige.

a liquid lunch aboard a steam launch seemed to improve matters...

The resulting engineless train - hooked on to scheduled services - was christened *Highland Belle*. An itinerary covering over 1,000 miles of highly scenic rail travel included an excursion in an elderly motorboat to Kinloch Castle on the Isle of Rhum. A crew of four were engaged, a brochure printed and the American agents advised. It was, I believe, the first commercial private train in post-war Britain and it was an instant success. One of the first charterers was a travel writer for *The New York Times*. The train was given a whole page in the travel supplement and the attempted bookings which followed would have filled the train for ten years, but we only had use of the carriages for two. It was necessary to find others, but meanwhile the money was rolling in fast.

As an alternative holiday for the growing clientele, I started a new activity which traded under the name of Holiday Castles. I found seven private castles in Britain and another seven châteaux in France where our passengers would be regally housed and divertingly entertained. This venture never really took off: perhaps it was a few years ahead of its time since now there are several companies offering something similar.

...the first private train, christened Highland Belle...

Both these projects were a lot of fun to set up. The first introduced me to the world of grown-up railways which were even better entertainment than the model ones of which I had been prematurely deprived four decades earlier and the owners of the castles vied with each other to compete on hospitality of which I was the beneficiary.

Fern and I went with my brother and his wife for a long weekend in Venice and travelled in the Venice-Simplon Orient Express (VSOE) which had been heavily advertised. I found it vastly disappointing and as I was unable to sleep much due to the numerous noisy stops made throughout the night, I lay awake pondering whether I might not create something of the kind but according to a better formula. Indeed the staccato progress of the train, the cramped cabins and the lack of ventilation encouraged me to think I could hardly produce a worse result. By the time we reached Venice, I had made up my mind to try. Just one problem: where to find the vintage carriages, each now being a 'collector's piece'.

'Where can I find them - any ideas?' I said to my brother. 'Not a clue,' he said, 'but I expect they'll just turn up like things do.'

Sometimes, on impulse, I reach for an atlas and open it at random. Studying a page is always interesting and often awakes a deeper curiosity. It was this habit which found me looking at a map of Northern Spain and observing there was an area about which I knew nothing. It was a mountainous region called the Picos de Europa and it looked intriguing.

A few weeks later, Fern and I found ourselves enjoying the comfort of the local Parador. On the second day, we set off to climb a minor peak - in reality more of a very steep hill. The alpine meadows were full of flowers; it was the kind of day that made the heart leap for joy. In my case, alas, it was not only the heart that leapt, for on the descent I felt like practising jump turns of the kind normally performed on skis when on a snow-covered slope. I had found this to be an effective way of descending a steep hill quickly. Carried away by the rhythmic satisfaction of this tactic, I failed to notice a minor precipice. Seconds later, I was on my back with a double spiral leg fracture.

I did not know that anything could be so painful. I counted to 100 then started again in French and then again in German. Fern arrived. I pointed to my leg. She pulled up the trouser and her expression jumped from one of mild concern to one of extreme horror: the bones were sticking out of the leg.

We were near the top of the hill, several thousand feet up and a good two hours walk from the nearest help. Above, there were eagles wheeling in slow circles. I was starting to shiver uncontrollably and I was wet from having landed in a bog.

At such moments of disadvantage it is tempting to leave matters to someone else, but I have found it is preferable to try to take command since the effort takes the mind off the pain and if mistakes are made, they are your own. So I asked Fern to drag me onto some dry grass, spare me surplus clothes and build a shelter of branches to protect me from the sun and the inquisitive gaze of the possibly hungry eagles. Fern was not possessed of a good sense of direction so my major concern was that she and the rescue party would never re-find me. I asked her to go down slowly marking the route every fifty yards or so. After she went, I spent a lonely five hours studying the grasses nearest my head and pondering the busy movements of numerous small insects. I began to wonder if I would die of exposure that night and deeply regretted that I had neither paper nor pencil with which to record thoughts of seemingly boundless importance.

The sounds of approaching voices are with me still. Two men of the mountains, brown-faced, taciturn and sure-footed, heaved me onto a canvas stretcher as though collecting a dead sheep, then trundled me jerkily down the mountain with Fern trotting along after them. On the road, a small van awaited me. Without benefit of a splint, cushions, blankets or other material to stabilise me, the stretcher was placed on the metal floor of the van.

Some twenty inches of leg and stretcher projected beyond the open doors of the van and once we set off the feeling of vulnerability increased sharply when a car, driven by a *desperado* with a villainous grin, kept pulling out and then suddenly swerving back again, only inches from my extremities.

We climbed a steep hill. Every time the driver changed gear, the van lurched and the stretcher slipped slightly further through the open doors towards the road. Judging that another lurch or two might see me run over by the closely following car, I let out a primaeval cry. The driver looked round, sized up the situation and, without slowing up, yanked the stretcher back by grabbing my arm and pulling.

The *ospedale* in Potes looked unlike any hospital previously encountered. It was a small building with a single cavernous room and was guarded by a sloppily-dressed soldier. I was carried in from the blazing sunshine and laid to rest on a cold table. My bearers disappeared and gradually it dawned upon me that this was no hospital but a mortuary. Nothing happened, no one came. Outside I could see a busy street and what appeared to be the aftermath of market day. Then, apparently with nothing better to do, one or two people drifted in, unchallenged by the soldier, and attempted to satisfy their curiosity by leaning over me, shooting incomprehensible questions and leaving a small cloud of vapourised garlic and alcohol to add to a growing nausea. Soon there was a small crowd examining with a macabre interest the internal workings of the human leg. Nature was calling urgently and I wanted, most desperately, to oblige but circumstances could not easily have been less propitious. The crowd became first fascinated then hilarious at my frantic miming of my need. No one did anything. Eventually, and at the cost of hideous embarrassment and a decapitated plastic bottle, the problem was publicly solved to the vast amusement of all. Fern, who had collected our car, reappeared.

Meanwhile a man who seemed to have taken charge was handing a wooden box, recovered from the vegetable market, to the soldier on the steps. Shortly, silhouetted against the blinding light through the open door, I saw this man smash up the box with the butt of his rifle. He brought the pieces in. The more promising bits were selected and a primitive splint was constructed. Our car was by now outside the mortuary and since no ambulance was apparently available, the seating was undergoing partial removal. The stretcher was meanwhile placed beyond the car more or less in the centre of the busy road so that traffic tearing down the street had to swerve to avoid the obstacle. Watching the tyres screeching inches from my head proved a brilliantly effective distraction from my physical problems. Not for the first time, I wished that at Eton I had learned a little live Spanish instead of a lot of dead Latin.

Minutes later, Fern was driving me the seventy or so miles to the general hospital at Santander. The discomforts of this journey were relatively easy to tolerate in the expectation that, within a couple of hours, I would be fixed-up.

Arrived at the hospital, I took my place on a wheeled stretcher in the queue of those awaiting repair. Children inspected me, dogs sniffed at me and the odour of the human throng on a hot day bore heavily upon me. Eventually, I was wheeled into a small and stifling room and unloaded. Several people and a cat came in. A uniformed nurse was painting her nails. The bone-setter appeared with his pupil for whom I was to act as a model on which to practice. No mention of anaesthetics.

What followed, without anaesthetics or analgesics of any kind, in spite of many spirited requests, would be good to erase from the memory. Suffice it to say that years later, the unsmiling olive-skinned face of the bone-setter with the rolled cigarette dangling from his lower lip has not entirely disappeared. Neither has his last remark, accompanied by a sudden raising of his black eyebrows and a look of feigned shock – 'Dios, I 'ave fixed ze foot on backwards!'

His black humour was not so far from the truth and back in England, it had to be reset.

Every experience in life is supposed to have some value; I have often wondered what was the value of this – other than as initial practice for a student bone-setter.

CHAPTER 16

Become a Countryside Commissioner and refuse to sign Official Secrets Act – a calamitous event – surprise discovery of antique rolling stock inside straw stacks - creation of Royal Scotsman train - embarrassing drama at Edinburgh station – Margaret enters my barging life – design world's most luxurious barge – excursion to Rajasthan with three wives betrayed by bank manager – revenge – Fleur de Lys launched in triumph

IN THE vicinity of Henbant, there were no fewer than four Cabinet Ministers with weekend houses. Old Etonians all, they were remarkably sociable, and it was instructive to observe how they behaved toward each other - a clear pecking order was always apparent. One who was Secretary to the Treasury came on the *Virginia Anne*, and had an exhilarating time squirting the bikini-clad girls on the boats we passed with giant water pistols. Telephoto lenses were mercifully absent.

Another, who was Secretary of State for Wales proposed that I should be appointed a Countryside Commissioner. 'Only provided it has teeth to enforce its remit,' I replied. Assured that it did, I agreed. In the following three years, as a Commissioner for England and later, for Wales, I learnt a lot about Quangos, for such it was, and the personal politics quietly played out within their sphere. I should have been warned when the Secretary of State said to me – 'you're a controversial character and I'm taking a risk in appointing you' - but I failed to realise that the risk he was taking was simply that I might disagree with the way decisions were made.

The remit of the Commission was to advise Government on countryside policy. In addition, it had a large budget to carry out schemes for the improvement of the countryside. The Commissioners were mostly intelligent and successful individuals, who cared about the countryside and attended the meetings unpaid. Yet it seemed to me that on many issues we were looked to merely for rubber-stamp approval. I did not like this and I liked still less being asked to sign the

Official Secrets Act. I refused point-blank and thereafter was considered a threat. The Commission's reluctance to stand up and be counted at Public Inquiries, and to speak out on issues which might lead to criticism of Government policy, confirmed my worst fears. After a few years, and after hearing once too often the Chairman say, 'you're on your own again Gerard', I resigned.

There are few worse things than Government-appointed bodies created to take care of a particular public concern but fearful, for political reasons, of real confrontation. In consequence, the public believe their concerns are being defended, and do nothing. I have even known chairmen of such bodies seek to avoid a necessary confrontation in the private expectation that it would improve their chance of a knighthood or some other honour. Quangos can be kept on a short lead by these means.

After such encounters and others too boring to relate, I have come to realise, a little belatedly perhaps, I am simply not a committee man. Even a parish meeting puts me in mind of those endless hours at school in which a shaft of sunlight entering the classroom would induce in me a wild longing for fresh air and escape from the boa-constrictor of boredom induced by those who love the sound of their own voice.

At Henbant life was outwardly normal. People came and went, their arrival and departure silently observed by neighbouring eyes in true Welsh tradition. The elderly pair next door had sold up and the place bought by a friendly young couple. The slight twitch of a muslin curtain had been replaced by a frank stare. The young farmer, Owen, was fascinated by attractive girls and whenever one turned up, would find an excuse to drop in. Learning that Julie Christie had volunteered to help pack the Ecoropa anti-nuclear leaflets, his interest shifted into top gear. Then one day the actress Susannah York came to stay, though her arrival after dark had been undetected by Owen. The following morning I saw him driving sheep from one field to another. I called over to him and told him the good news.

'If it's Susannah York staying with you, then I am the King of Wales.'

A little later, as Susannah and I walked up the track towards the mountain, we met Owen coming down with his tractor. I effected an introduction. Owen's mouth opened and shut soundlessly, and when we looked back several hundred yards further up, he hadn't moved. Subsequently, his attitude toward me underwent a subtle change that seemed to be an emulsion of deep respect and rank envy!

Diana, who had been obliged to give up her post as 'House Mother' at The Quarry, due to her anorexic condition having worsened, came to stay for a few days. I was deeply shocked at her dramatic loss of weight and even more so by her evident feeling of helplessness, if not hopelessness. It was difficult to know what to do for the best. After some days, she went home and to her utter dismay her parents had her 'sectioned' - that is locked up in a supposedly secure institution of the kind that used to be known as a 'loony bin'. Used to a free-range life lived out of doors, she soon became deeply despondent and felt that she had been abandoned. Clad only in a dressing gown and slippers, she escaped one wet winter's night from a bathroom window and hitchhiked from Shrewsbury to Abergavenny, arriving at Henbant on foot, frozen, sodden, exhausted and in despair. She weighed a little over five stone and was clearly sinking. She begged not to be returned.

In Wales then - and hopefully now - there was a network of 'safe houses' and experts in this and that who would, if necessary, perform their function outside the law. There were some 300 police looking for her but availing myself thus of a doctor, Diana was coaxed back a little way toward recovery. But she learnt of the search for her and after a week or so, having gained some strength, she elected to go home again. She left by taxi and when she arrived home found her parents away. A few days later, in a paroxysm of wretchedness, all hope forsaken, she hanged herself in the stairwell.

It is not hard to imagine the self-questioning which followed this tragic event. Her state, mentally and physically, was so calamitous that I think the end, whatever we had done, might not have been so very different. There is no way of knowing and her loss remains a source of constant grief – just as the contribution she made remains a source of constant inspiration. I think of her often and wonder if I should have let her go. There is no knowing.

Later, at her favourite spot at The Quarry, a great seat was built in slabs of slate and on the back a brass plaque was affixed; it was cast on the spot, and recorded the fact that without her singular contribution the project might never have succeeded. In an article by Peter Harper on the early days of CAT he writes:

'Without doubt Diana kept the show on the road, and it was with great sadness that we learned of her tragic death in 1986. Many of her old friends came to the Quarry to build a seat in her memory, in a quiet corner of the garden she started; a spot where the garden ends and the wild woods begin. It does not "command" the garden: it is almost invisible until you come upon it. It is oriented rather strangely, slightly to one side as if listening for something. It is solid, enduring, comforting. It is Diana's place.'

It was now 1984 and my daughter Laura was due to be married in September. A former neighbour, Simon Heneage, the man responsible for the Arab practical joke at Burgate, had generously offered his house for the Reception. This property was on the side of a steep hill and had minimal parking. At the foot of the hill was a large flattish field and I eyed this as potential parking space. I had met the farmer who owned it a few times but hardly knew him.

I walked down to the farmyard, a place surrounded by a surprising number of stacks of straw bales. Protruding from one was a length of railway line.

'Whatever's that rail doing there?'

'Minding its own business.'

'You interested in railways?'

'Why? Are you?'

'Yes. I have two carriages running round Scotland.'

'You're joking! You mean you've done a deal with British Rail?'

'Well, yes, sort of. But I've only rented the carriages and I have to give them up next month. I need to find replacements. Know of any vintage rolling stock anywhere?'

No answer: just a penetrating look. Then

'Are you *serious*?'

'Yes.'

'Then climb the ladder against that straw stack.'

I did and found myself looking down on to a vintage steam engine.

'What's behind the other straw stacks?'

'More! I've got engines: a friend of mine has carriages - the cream of what is left in Britain. People are so nosey and the planners so suspicious I decided they'd be better hidden.'

The friend, Rick Edmondson, was but a telephone call away.

'You want to put a vintage train together for paying passengers?'

'Yes. But better than the VSOE train.'

'They'll need to pay thousands of dollars for a ticket.'

'They will. Give me the carriages and I'll do the rest.'

'*I've* been longing to do this. Are you sure you can get the passengers?'

'Yes.'

'It's a deal! When do we start?'

Thus was born the *Royal Scotsman.* I approached two friends, Fergus Hobbs and Michael Ryan who were also in the 'barging' business, and a short while later, together with Rick Edmondson, we formed the Great Scottish and Western Railway Company Limited of which I was the Chairman.

Our train was able to sleep and feed twenty-eight passengers. It had the oldest dining car in the world built in 1891 and used as part of Earl Haig's headquarters during the First World War; an observation car built in 1892 (and coincidentally used by my grandfather when he was Chairman of the Caledonian Railway); a saloon car built in 1912 for the Great Northern Railway and several old coaches converted during the winter to provide luxury cabins, each with its own bathroom. There was also a coach with a place for playing cards, a small library and writing desks. Staff carriages, a kitchen and generator cars completed the train

During the winter, a team of cabinet makers fitted out the coaches luxuriously. Carpets with the company's logo were specially woven, a huge dinner service was made by Royal Worcester, complemented by the finest silver and crystal. A crew of eleven were carefully selected; amongst these were two chefs capable of turning out the best meals to be found anywhere in Scotland.

There was no doubt in our minds that the train we had put together would be the best in the world. I had not needed to put up any money. It just remained to work out an itinerary and secure the full co-operation of British Rail.

After my experience of the VSOE, I was anxious the train should not move at night. Fergus and I went to Scotland and worked out a tour that included a quiet siding or a country station for each night. A comfortable bus would accompany the train and take passengers to visit private houses and gardens, a distillery, a smokehouse, and other Scottish delights as well as places of historical importance. It would be a six-day tour from and to Edinburgh. A steam engine would haul the train on the scenic line to Mallaig.

The train was completed on schedule and one day in March 1985 was quietly shunted into Euston Station for a press launch. It looked fabulous and received Press reviews that corresponded. Then after some rehearsal it was hauled up to Edinburgh for the start of its first season on 6 May.

The scene at Waverley Street Station that afternoon will not readily be forgotten. Even an hour before departure, scores of train buffs from all over Britain had come to witness the launch. The passengers, who had mostly come from the USA specially for this occasion, were busy with batteries of cameras. The crew, smartly attired, were standing by their carriages. A large contingent from Scotrail walked up and down the platform checking couplings and staring in at the windows. To complete the small crowd were dozens of citizens who, passing by, had seen something interesting and, with nothing better to do, were also inspecting the train. The band of the Black Watch was assembling as were two television crews. In the centre of the platform was a raised dais banked up with potted hydrangeas.

I was introduced to the Chairman of Scotrail. He and I were to stand on the daïs and after his speech of welcome, he would turn to me: then with a few more words, I would step forward and vigorously wave the green flag. The train would depart to the strains of massed bagpipes. The rolled up flag was thereupon handed to me. This was railway history in the making!

The platform was rapidly becoming crowded with the curious. About five minutes before the departure, we took up our position on the daïs. The band of the Black Watch struck up with a Highland air. The passengers were busy on the platform taking last minute photographs. A television cameraman came across to me and asked to be shown how the departure would be signalled. I demonstrated with a low and furtive wave of the now partly unfurled flag. Immediately whistles blew, doors slammed and, dumbfounded, I saw the train start.

There was pandemonium. The train was now full of casual sightseers whilst the actual passengers were still on the platform. Everybody was shouting, 'Stop the train, stop the train!' The only person not to hear the shouts was the engine driver who was steadily applying power. Doors re-opened, a few sightseers jumped off, one or two passengers managed to scramble on: the rest flew along the platform, some with their cases, scattering the band of the Black Watch more decisively than in their entire history. The television crews were having the time of their lives. The Chairman turned to me.

'Well it's saved me having to make a speech but I wouldn't wonder if you haven't got some angry passengers, or rather non-passengers, on your hands.'

'How soon can you stop the train?'

'There's no radio in the cab. We could try telephoning ahead and maybe we can get some signals set but they are apt to be in places where you cannot embark passengers; a problem I'm afraid.'

'Oh dear. I've got a feeling I've made a bit of a blunder.'

'You could say that.'

Quite a lot of people did. It made the national news. The train carried on blithely until it reached Oban, four hours later where the town band played welcoming music to the infuriated sightseers of Edinburgh streaming down the platform.

In spite of such an inauspicious start, the train went from strength to strength. From *The Los Angeles Times* to *The Washington Post*, from *Harper's Bazaar* to *Travel & Leisure*, the *Royal Scotsman* received rave reviews. The food was indeed considered the best in Scotland and the train the most luxurious in the world.

And so it remains to this day.

In 1982, I advertised once again in the Personal Column of *The Times*, this time for a deckhand for *Virginia Anne*. There were only four replies of which three were clearly hopeless. The fourth, a twenty-five-year-old girl called Margaret Doyle seemed vaguely hopeful but in the event she took to barges as a duck takes to water, and two years later took over as skipper with an all female crew.

With Margaret in place, the operation went smoothly, but by this time competition (much of it provided by previous deckhands-turned-entrepreneurs) was beginning to hot up. I decided that our barging business would only succeed if we kept 'ahead of the game' and, to this end, I conceived a plan for a barge to out-barge the competition. In due course I found myself walking alongside a canal in Ghent,

Belgium, where I noticed a 'For Sale' sign on a barge of appropriate size. It was soon purchased, taken to Bruges and moored alongside a shipyard, which with the falling-off of barge traffic was one of the few left and was itself in slow decline.

Meanwhile, I had made detailed drawings for the conversion of the ship, agreed a price for the steelwork and obtained bank agreement to borrow a great deal of money. Putting a 360-tonne vessel in dry dock for many months, and using the services of a shipyard to build a steel superstructure, is an expensive pursuit.

A continental barge of 'full' size is a hefty object - 139 foot long by 16 foot wide, some ten times more capacious than a typical English narrow-boat. Into this cavernous space were to go, on two decks, three luxury suites of bedroom, bathroom and dressing room; a large saloon, dining room, sun deck and swimming pool. There was also to be crew accommodation for six and the many other spaces that are required for preparing food, laundry, making electricity, providing numerous services and piloting the barge. Fitting everything together without waste of any space is a fascinating exercise, made all the harder by the numerous rules applicable to passenger boats.

Throughout the winter work proceeded in conditions of bitter cold. Ships' carpenters were brought from England and gradually the barge took shape.

I had been deeply impressed by Margaret's attempts to smooth out the continual problems, both human and technical, which accompany any such project. Her positive stance and willingness to work all hours commended itself to me mightily and I began to rely on her contribution increasingly. Procurement of the thousands of bits and pieces needed - and usually needed instantly - became Margaret's speciality and there cannot have been a street in Bruges which did not yield up something, even if it was only a carton of Belgian *pommes frites* which are second to none!

In the middle of that winter I took a party of six to Rajasthan in India. It was, I suppose, an unusual party as it included my ex-wife Virginia, my present partner Fern and - although I had no idea of it at the time - my future wife Margaret. It seems strange looking back but it was greatly enjoyed by all of us - which says a lot for the delights of Rajasthan!

One object of this journey was to buy unusual furnishings for the new barge, an aim which was suddenly fulfilled when we accidentally encountered a kind of Aladdin's cave in Jodhpur. There we purchased numerous 'antiques' and also bought some genuine ones: our order provided a great deal of local employment in the following weeks.

Returning to Bruges it was clear that in our absence the barge had begun to slip seriously behind schedule: it was also substantially over budget. Yet if we were not ready to carry passengers at the start of the season there would be grave financial consequences and loss of marketing confidence. We increased the number of workers on the barge to a peak of thirty-six.

At the same time, I went to see the Manager of the National Westminster Bank who had provided the loan and asked him for an increase, a sum which was well covered by securities. Allowing himself to be liberally entertained at my expense in the best local restaurant, he concluded the meeting by withdrawing the entire loan at thirty days notice in the full knowledge of the appalling difficulties which were almost bound to ensue. Trying to raise money on a half-built ship is legendarily difficult. He no doubt hoped that the Bank would soon possess a potentially valuable asset obtained by him at a knock-down price.

The man was a worm. Back in his office I lost my temper, and leaning across his desk shouted in his ear my opinion of him and his employers and then as a gesture of the utter contempt I felt for both him and his bank I swept everything off his desk including the telephone, the lamp, the photographs of his ugly wife and weedy-looking children - whereupon he pressed his panic button. I removed myself smartly into the street, kicking the door as I went. The sound of angry buzzing followed me down the street. Later, in order to improve my humour, I collected a bag of dog turds and deposited them in the night-safe labelled – 'For the attention of the Manager'. As it turned out, by a stroke of luck, I ran into a regional director of Lloyds Bank who picked up the loan and thereafter financed the business with much friendliness and enthusiasm for what we were doing. Alas he was one of the last of his kind, now displaced by the tyranny of ice-cold accountancy, suffocating to the entrepreneurial spirit.

Although work was proceeding on the barge almost round the clock, it was clear that I had allowed insufficient time for all the finishing that was required. We had a deadline at the end of March for a Press launch in Paris, a journey that would take a week or more. In the end we set sail for Paris with the workers still on board, arriving just in time for the launch, with the work completed literally minutes before the appearance of the journalists.

The barge looked magnificent. The cabins were fitted out with huge four-poster beds hung with splendid fabric. Throughout the barge was a wonderful assortment of quirky things. In the saloon were rich furnishings from Rajasthan, a grand piano, stone pillars from a redundant church in Herefordshire, a ship's female figurehead sporting generous breasts and a magnificent ship's control in brass which I had spotted being carried along a street whilst in Nairobi. The Dining Room was pure Rajasthani, the sundeck a mass of flowers and the swimming pool, seven foot deep and aquamarine, looked hugely inviting. The crew were resplendent in blue and white uniform as they poured the champagne.

There was just one problem: there had only been time to paint one side of the hull: precautions were taken to ensure that the Press only ever saw that one side!

We christened her *Fleur de Lys*. And the journalists loved her.

CHAPTER 17

My second marriage terminates – retreat to France – interlude in Burgundy – land world's best job – death of my father – descent of the Danube – a candlelit paradise off Turkey – buy Le Manoir in Normandy – echoes of D-Day – my relationship with the French – Italian rail project frustrated by incarceration of Directors

THE IMPETUOUS pursuit of objectives close to the heart leaves little enough time or inclination to ponder the imperfections of marriage. But as I turned fifty I became, as many of us do, a little more introspective. At the same time I was under family pressure to 'tie the knot' of the hitherto informal and somewhat erratic partnership with Fern. I was instinctively reluctant to do this but also loath to disappoint my father, now in his ninetieth year, who minded a great deal about the propriety of living together unmarried. Since Fern was positively on the side of marriage, as were my family generally, we pottered off to the Brecon Registry Office and married.

Fern is no longer alive to correct any errors in this narrative and besides, no point is served in raking through the memories of failure. For whatever reason, our relationship went into slow but steady decline almost at once. Perhaps it signalled the end of trying to make it work, perhaps it was the coincidence of an ill wind: I do not know. Within two years it was effectively over, and was subsequently to become the subject of an acrimonious divorce.

One day, I woke up with the realisation that not only was the marriage over but my future did not lie at Henbant either. I was marking time pointlessly and both Fern and I had nothing left to say to each other. I thought of the tremendous efforts put in to making Henbant the very special place it had become, but came to realise they had been valid in themselves -the *doing* of it inspired the satisfaction I had experienced. Taking a deep breath, I decided to leave.

Robert had returned briefly to complete a small addition. Fern's children were at boarding school. I packed a case and put it in the car. Then I said goodbye to Fern, to Robert, to the dog and to the house. I drove slowly down the hill and I did not look back. Deeply shaken, I fled to France.

In the course of the ensuing year, Fern developed cancer. A few months later, Tarquin fell from a cliff at his school in Wales and was killed. Shortly after, I heard that Robert also had cancer. Fern died first, then Robert. The ages of all three totalled less than 100 years.

On the slippery pole of human happiness, I had again descended.

It is at such vexing times that I have learnt to expect the unexpected. Driving through France I experienced a strange and illogical sense of exhilaration, a kind of spiritual freedom that seemed to purge my being of the accumulated grief and angst of a second broken marriage. It was as if some higher power had uplifted the dead weight of my distress and cast it to one side. This feeling of liberation became so intense that on sudden impulse, whilst threading my way through the backwoods of Burgundy, I stopped the car, climbed out and shouted for joy. Then I rolled on the ground and kissed the grass. Against all odds, though physically exhausted, and circumstantially undone, I found myself filled with happiness. The sheer beauty of my surroundings overwhelmed me with such force that it displaced my distress. I knew with certainty that I had made the right decision.

At this time, Margaret was temporarily renting lockhouse 52 on the Burgundy Canal. It was to the deep seclusion of this former lock-keeper's house that I now made my way. Two up and two down, damp and only partially furnished, permeated with the sound of water cascading over the lock gates, it was for me at that moment a haven of calm. Unexpectedly the happiness which had eluded me in past months came flooding back.

In those far off days Margaret's culinary skills were still evolving and there was a tendency for things to burn on the fierce gas jets of the cooker. In consequence I found myself, most mornings, chipping away at burnt residue on the pans. Sitting by the lockside absorbed in this homely task I became aware of Margaret's ability to put me back together again. No questions asked, no expectations expressed, she set me back gently on my feet. It was a brief interlude: she had her job

Lock No 52 on the Burgundy Canal

with the barges and I mine - much of it in England - and it was not until the season ended that we addressed the possibility of a future together.

The *Fleur de Lys* was a difficult barge to winterise. There was so much to protect from frost and make vandal-proof it seemed obvious that since we were both now homeless, we should live there during the winter and do the many jobs which required attention before the following season. Working on a boat in peaceful surroundings is deeply pleasurable. I had found that I resented paying others, often at an exorbitant rates, to do jobs which I really enjoyed doing. Margaret felt the same. Between us we acquired many practical skills which stood us in good stead in the following years and which greatly increased the profitability of the operation. The vessel was therefore moored in a peaceful pound at Tonnerre in Burgundy, and connected to the electricity supply. Ensconced in the ship's luxurious interior, we set to work.

An exceptionally cold winter closed in, and although generously equipped with radiators, the windows iced over *inside* and for many weeks there was no view at all. The heating oil actually froze. Survival began to be an unexpected struggle and before long I found myself looking once again in the windows of estate agents. Although I had at that moment insufficient funds to buy the house of my dreams, I considered there was no point in looking at houses which did not rank high on the scale of desirability, believing that in some way, the necessary funds would appear.

We began to look at some enticing châteaux. At the first one, we encountered a large mongrel sitting near the front door. As we approached, he wagged his tail and actually managed a broad smile. The owners who were moving to Paris were looking for a home for Filou (thief) so, inevitably, he joined us and subsequently became part of the crew. A dog of determinedly independent character, he wandered; one day, to our great sadness, he was run down by a lorry and killed.

Fortunately, we did not find the ideal house, so in the following season whilst Margaret skippered the *Fleur de Lys*, I rented a house in the small village of Montillot near Vézélay. This was almost the only house available to rent in the district: its owner had run short of funds before completing its renovation so largely in lieu of rent I set to work to finish it. Whilst doing so I learnt what it was like to live in the centre of a dying French village, a timely experience that prevented a repetition later on. The muslin curtains pushed aside at each arrival or departure, the ceaseless barking of chained dogs (here, as everywhere else in France) and the pre-dawn clatter of the village baker, two doors along, were strong deterrents to prolonged occupancy.

Margaret was able to escape her duties from time to time and we used often to visit nearby Vézélay, the lovely hill-top village with the famous Romanesque Basilica. It was from Vézélay that one of the principal pilgrim routes set off to Santiago di Compostella. The huge all-round panorama from the summit must be one of the great views in Europe - thousands of acres of meadow and woodland totally unbesmirched by a single eyesore.

The Basilica had a reputation for miracle cures. I had been long suffering from a bad back, much worsened following a surfeit of plastering, and for some days was almost unable to walk. I drove myself to this church mindful of its reputation and with the aid of a stick and the speed of an aged snail, I descended into the crypt. No sooner had I arrived in this empty chamber than I heard a gaggle of chattering Japanese tourists starting to come down the steps. As a kind of reflex, I leapt for the second flight of steps to escape them and, as I hastily reached the top, realised with utter astonishment that I was cured. I think, perhaps, it was another little miracle: I wish I could feel more certain.

Whilst at Montillot, I discovered cross-country bicycling and explored widely in the vicinity. In May the woods were carpeted with lily-of-the-valley and whilst pedalling along the rides on a warm evening the air was heavy with their scent.

Alas, the deep peace of a Burgundian summer was interrupted by an impending divorce and the concomitant need once more to earn a good living, a need which had resulted in my accepting a Consultancy with a major international travel company operating at the top end of the market.

My brief was to conceive new ideas in the field of luxury travel and to this end, I was given *carte blanche* to roam the world, provided I undertook to do so in the style to which the very well-heeled would expect to journey! There were no deadlines, no targets and no limits on cost, but there was to be a share in the winnings from any resultant project which proved successful.

As jobs go, it promised extraordinarily well!

My father died in February 1988 - he was 95. Until his last year he had enjoyed remarkable health, and although extremely deaf he was more or less game for anything. He had tried skiing, on a local hill, for the first time in his seventies. He worked at Dexam one day a week until he was ninety and for his ninetieth birthday-treat chose a balloon ride. At ninety-two, he wrote a monograph *The First Ninety Years* which neatly skirted anything he minded about; his account of soldiering through the Somme in the First World War occupied but a few lines.

His life had witnessed so many huge transformations: late feudalism to socialism, the horse to the supersonic airliner, the pen to the computer, a deeply rural countryside to a creeping suburbia. He had survived two world wars in which so many of his friends had died. He had adapted to all these changes, welcoming what he believed to be good but the values he grew up with before the Great War remained with him all his life. At the end of his book he questions the drift away from those values and, in spite of his optimistic nature, remains consumed by doubt. He abhors the erosion of the countryside and the maltreatment of the land by contemporary farming methods, the disappearance of the rural craftsman and the neglect of woodlands. He saw patriotism and tradition as having become matters of contempt and authority as an object of derision. He related the increase in social violence to a general lack of discipline, especially in the home. The disproportionate valuation of 'a splash of paint on a canvas' and a fine piece of furniture he saw as symbolic of an age that was losing its way. He concludes, 'A nation, that by hard work and sound moral character, having achieved its ambition, tends to relax into a state of apathy and degeneration; only further challenge will reawake the spirit that once made it so great.'

Although disappointed not to make his century, he began to hint that he was ready and willing to depart this life as soon as he entered a serious decline. He seemed suddenly to lose almost all his strength and one evening when my brother and I went to visit him, he made his situation crystal clear. 'You wouldn't keep a dog in this condition, you'd have it put down. Think about it.' We dropped hints to the doctor, then requests to hasten the end. Yet, being a courageous fighter unused to giving in, he hung around on the threshold of death for several weeks. One day, when he was barely alive, I was with him alone. I knew that he wanted to die but that he was holding back. I said to him – 'you may go now: we all want you to go and be in peace: there is no reason to stay with us: we'll catch you up soon enough: go now with our love.' His eyes flickered briefly and I think I saw the vestige of a smile. Within a few seconds he was gone.

He was quite unsure about life after death but he hoped with every cell of his being that he would be reunited with the two loves of his life, his first wife and my mother.

In the years that followed his death, I came to realise how little I knew of his life and its emotional peaks and troughs. I wish he had volunteered more and that I had asked more but now it is too late. So seldom does it seem to be the right moment to ask difficult or private questions: still more is it difficult for an older person to volunteer information not requested. With benefit of hindsight, I should have overcome the scruples of privacy and thus have been able to share the wisdom of his years. I miss him greatly. His was a solid and courageous character. Our views often differed but he was always supportive of my endeavours and I am enduringly glad to have seen much of him toward the end of his life

My first endeavour in the field of luxury travel was to assess the feasibility of putting a luxury cruiser on the Danube: no such vessel then existed. In order to do so, I booked onto a German river cruiser for a passage from Passau to Budapest, to sample the best on offer at that time.

It was a lovely journey, somewhat marred by my co-passengers, almost all German, since their main interest appeared to be eating for the sake of eating. Filling the stomach commenced with a vast *Frühstück* which made a 'full English' breakfast look like a miniscule snack. At eleven there was hot soup, biscuits and coffee; at one, as big a lunch as anyone could possibly eat; at five, tea with pastries, cakes and tarts; at eight, a gigantic five-course dinner and for those who still had a cubic centimetre of space left to fill, more soup and biscuits at eleven. Each of these occasions found a complement of the ship's company present, chomping determinedly in silence. In the short spaces between meals and snacks which I suppose were regarded as fasts, coach trips were organised to nearby places of interest.

One of the few other non-German passengers was an elderly lady from Belgravia, plainly used to a life of comfort in which foreigners seldom featured. Disembarking in order to see the wondrous monastery of Melk, this lady turned to me as she saw three huge coaches parked on the quay. Drawing herself up and pointing with her stick, she said slowly and loudly – 'Do you suppose I am expected to enter a charabanc with all these Huns? I prefer to remain on the quay.' She did so.

My client subsequently decided to order a luxury ship for cruising the Danube. I therefore designed a 2,000 tonne river cruiser for seventy passengers looking for the utmost comfort, and found a shipyard in Holland keen to build it. Just as it was to be ordered, the good ship *Mozart* made an unexpected appearance on the Danube; we had been pipped to the post.

An ex-MacBraynes paddle-steamer, past its days for ploughing through the turbulent waters off Western Scotland, had managed, nevertheless, to paddle its way to the south coast of Turkey, where in the ownership of a formidably wealthy newspaper proprietor, it had undergone a major face-lift and was to be offered for ultra-luxury cruising in sheltered waters. An opinion of its suitability for the purpose was asked of me. Together with a Director of the travel company, we set forth to test it.

Whilst there, we were invited to a party on an island owned by the sister of the newsprint magnate. It was a memorable evening. The paddle steamer waddled slowly toward the island, just after darkness had fallen, bearing a load of pampered guests, most elegantly attired. It was a balmy night and the stars were on full display. As we approached, I saw that the entire length of the quay, and the whole of the garden which separated the sea from the palatial house, was lit with thousands of candles placed inside glass globes. Somewhere beyond, a group of stringed instruments were creating sensuous sounds. Flunkeys with laden trays were circulating with vintage champagne and the most succulent morsels of this and that. The scent of wood-smoke permeated the warm air.

It was almost unbearably romantic and I confess to having been momentarily shot through with bright green envy and crimson regret that I was unaccompanied by one of the female Turkish delights whose expensive scents added fuel to my internal fires.

Living aboard the *Fleur de Lys* became diminishingly attractive. We began to feel the need for a home which did not have to be abandoned during the chartering season. Money was now starting to roll in from various projects and we set no immediate limit on what might be spent on a house. In consequence, we found ourselves looking once again at châteaux in the Burgundian region, an area to which we were both much attached.

French châteaux are, at first sight, extraordinarily good value for money. But they tend to reach the market only after they have been stripped of anything saleable. Often the subject of long and fierce family squabbles, the château itself may remain unsold until agreement can be reached by all the family members to whom, under the Code Napoleon, it usually belongs equally. Meanwhile, a pressing need for money results in the piecemeal sale of surrounding lands (sometimes even up to the front door), dependent dwellings and adjacent buildings and, of course, in the abandonment of major repairs.

As things turned out, nothing appeared which was even remotely practical so our search gradually widened to include much of France. We saw many wonderful properties but those which were not fatally disadvantaged by the process just described were either hopelessly remote, in dreary surroundings or disproportionately expensive.

We decided eventually that we wished to be within easy reach of England and extended our search to Normandy. Of all the areas in this region, there was one, the great plain of Caen, that we rejected in advance for its bleak horizons and vast chemically-farmed prairies. Needless to say, it was precisely in this area that we were sent details of an attractive 16th century presbytery, Le Manoir de l'Eglise, which by all accounts did not suffer from any of the usual problems. We went to see it, lost our hearts to it and purchased it on the spot.

Situated near the beautiful town of Bayeux, it lay on the floor of a shallow valley just sufficiently deep to mask the somewhat dreary surroundings, so its immediate outlook was pleasant. The house formed part of a huge 16th to 18th century farm courtyard, composed of beautiful stone barns and stables. Within this sheltered yard were lawns, flowerbeds and trees. There was one building missing to this enclosure, only the base of the former walls remaining. Some years earlier, when it had been stacked high with straw, the farmer's wife had found her husband atop with the dairy maid and, without so much as a word, put a match to the straw, leaving them to make a fiery escape.

The manor was built on an island between river and mill-leat and possessed several riverside water meadows. The lush grass in these meadows should perhaps have warned us that winter flooding was habitual and we did not have to wait long before the rising waters

The creeper-clad Manoir in Normandy

crept up to the ground floor. On the first of these occasions, we were due to attend a meeting with my client in the travel business who had appointed a venue interestingly positioned in the depths of the Kenyan bush. We left for the airport by boat!

Adjacent to the house was the village church. It had been installed with an automatic electric bell-ringing device which hammered at the great bronze bell 144 times at seven in the morning, noon, and seven in the evening. At first we thought we would never become used to the fearful din but we did so surprisingly soon and - unlike our guests - scarcely noticed it.

In the churchyard was an English soldier's grave from the Second World War, maintained by the War Graves Commission. He had been killed at the bridge leading to the house and I felt grateful to him, as if he had personally made it possible for us to live in this peaceful place. This feeling of being the undeserved beneficiary of all the courage, the deaths and the bitter tragedies of the Invasion of Normandy remained with me always. I often thought of the simple inscription on a Singapore war memorial.

When you go home
Tell them of us and say
For your tomorrow
We gave our today

In one of our fields was the base of an anti-aircraft gun emplacement and just over the river was the rubble-strewn site of a château demolished by the Allies, which had been the regional Wehrmacht headquarters, visited by Rommel whenever inspecting the coastal defences. I never quite got used to the feeling that half a century after being at the receiving end of Hitler's armaments, I now owned part of his former arsenal.

Aged thirteen at the time of the Invasion, I well recall the intense anxiety stamped on every face those first days after the Landings. I had just come in from playing in the garden when two days after the Landings, my mother met me in the hall, looking radiant with excitement. 'Bayeux has fallen, undamaged.' I had to wait fifty years to appreciate the full significance of the last word. The architectural splendours of this small town never ceased to please.

We were but a few miles from the beaches of D-Day 1944, as the British cemetery in Bayeux with almost 5,000 graves, and the 9,000

GARDEN FOLLIES

Self-build structures which provide a focal point for the eye, Mostly of marginal use, they all gave great satisfaction in their building and are as much appreciated by children as adults.

Top. A pavillion on stilts, combining a mixture of architectural features.
Middle. A kind of *dacha* built on piles in a lake and constructed of straw bales rendered in lime mortar.
Below. A life-size *trompe-l'oeil* boathouse which 'disappears' as it is reached.

THE DOGS OF
MY LIFE

All but Jemima were rescue dogs and mongrelish.

Top left. Sophie
Middle left. Mutt
Bottom left. Rolo
Top right. Jemima
Middle right. Filou
Bottom right. Ben

US graves just along the road at Omaha, testified so forcefully. We became deeply interested in the remaining vestiges of the Invasion and put together a series of tours for our American clients.

In the seven years that we lived at Le Manoir, we extended and greatly improved the house, created a garden and planted trees. But we never came anywhere near to integrating in the village. We heard the same story repeatedly from British settlers in France. It was not especially the fact that we were foreign: the French simply keep themselves to themselves - their focus is family, not neighbours. The friends that we made were almost all English or of mixed nationality. Our neighbours made no effort to make us feel welcome nor unwelcome; we were simply ignored.

Even after many years in France, I find it difficult to be consistent in my feelings for the French; my observations are full of paradox and ambivalence. Most British settlers will admit to a love-hate relationship - a condition that time spent in France often seems to exacerbate. There have been extreme moments when I have wondered whether the invasion should have included France within its remit, yet others when it seemed natural that the two countries should peacefully merge. French arrogance, bureaucracy, dishonesty and political chicanery have encouraged the former whilst ordinary, friendly, hard-working natives have encouraged the latter.

But of the French countryside, the architectural and cultural heritage, it is only possible to be wildly enthusiastic.

The success of the *Royal Scotsman* train had awoken a new interest in luxury hotel trains and it looked as though I was to be invited to repeat the trick in Indonesia and Mexico. Although these projects never materialised, I had meanwhile targeted Italy as my preferred site. After much discussion, there emerged a scenically and culturally mouth-watering itinerary.

There were, it turned out, no suitable carriages in Italy but a series of meetings with the Wagons-Lits company in Paris ended with a potential train of great allure. It only remained to persuade Italian Railways of the financial benefits of running the train along their track and integrating it into their schedule. Preliminary inquiries elicited encouraging replies and a date, some weeks ahead, was fixed for a meeting with the relevant board members.

I flew out to Rome on the appointed day and presented myself at the head office. The entrance hall was alive with men in dark suits bustling in all directions. There was also a posse of uniformed *carabiniere* near the door. I announced myself at the desk.

One of the dark suits approached.

'Can I help? You want Il Signor Peruzzi? He not here, he not able to see you, he is, is, absent, you understand?'

I didn't but I had one other contact.

'Is Il Signor Mattei here? I have a meeting arranged with him, il Signor Peruzzi and the other directors.'

'No Signor Mattei, no *Direttori*. Absent. Gone.'

'It cannot be possible: this meeting has been arranged for weeks.'

'*Mi dispiace*, you not hear? No tell you?'

'No.'

'*Direttori,* in, how you say, *prigione,* all *Direttori* et signori Peruzzi e Mattei, all in *prigione. Finito*!'

And with a quick throat-slitting mime, he bowed and went.

It soon transpired there had been a scam involving commissions on the sale of railway property and more commissions on the purchase of replacements for which the *Direttori* were now under lock and key. It would be months or years before a new board would convene to discuss a side issue such as mine. Weeks of work down the drain; too bad - but that is the lot of the entrepreneur!

CHAPTER 18

Mission to Moscow – life under Communism – I fall in love with Russia and Sasha becomes an honorary brother – Russian ministerial wonderland – I acquire a private railway carriage and take it to Siberia - Lake Baikal – a banquet among Buryats – Heaven and Hell in Siberia

DESPITE THE setback resulting from the temporary indisposition of the Directors of Italian Railways, interest in luxury hotel trains continued to rise.

My next attempt was in the Soviet Union. The potential for a five-star mobile hotel in a country which spread across eight time zones, yet lacked, at that time, a single first-class hotel, seemed limitless. Though still under the yoke of Communism, things were beginning to quietly thaw through the remarkable skills of Comrade Gorbachov.

There was immediate interest. Together with a colleague, I flew to Moscow where we were allocated rooms in the National Hotel, supposedly Moscow's best at that time. My palatial room overlooked Red Square. I watched the scene from the window with fascination. It was December and continuous mounds of mud-splattered snow separated the uneven pavements from the pot-holed roads. Fur-hatted Muscovites picked their way carefully past numerous obstacles of holes half-dug, pavements half-mended, and the uniformed police stationed more or less everywhere. Outside the hotel there was a line of large Volga limousines, engines running, and half-uniformed chauffeurs in their seats either asleep or chain-smoking. Across the square, almost in silhouette against the grey sky, the astonishing outline of the Cathedral of St Basil.

I turned to examine the doubtless heavily bugged room. There was a black grand piano and next to it a large and ancient refrigerator in full rumble. I glanced inside, hopefully expectant of vodka. Empty. I sat at the piano, lifted the keyboard cover and started to play; only half the notes responded, all wildly out of tune. There were two huge plywood cupboards without either shelves or hangers, twin beds with plywood heads and plywood bedside tables fitted with disfunctional radios. Luxury was represented by an armchair with bright orange upholstery placed next to the cerise curtains, one of which hung limply from a dislocated track. There was a parquet floor but no carpet. The room above must have had similar flooring; steps resonated loudly from over my head. Two bentwood chairs and a plywood coffee table completed the inventory. Every item was boldly marked with a five-figure reference number, painted in white, even the poor piano, no doubt a relic of some pre-revolutionary drawing room. The room was an appropriate introduction to the nature of Communism.

I had thought I was prepared for the bathroom, having been warned to bring my own 'universal' plug. But I had not been told that the tap would emit, in equal quantities, boiling water and scalding steam - or more often nothing at all.

If this was the best hotel in Moscow, it would not be difficult to better it even if it was to be on wheels, or so I thought, in total ignorance of the Soviet system.

The first instance of this was the need to buy meal-vouchers; these had to be purchased with foreign currency. Eager for dinner but as yet without vouchers, we presented ourselves at the hotel restaurant. A large and dragonish matron in a once-white housecoat was standing at the door.

Dragon: 'Voucher!'

Me: 'We have no voucher. We pay.'

Dragon: 'Nyet! Voucher.'

Me: 'OK. We buy voucher. How much?'

Dragon: 'No voucher, no meal.'

Me: 'How much? We buy voucher.'

Dragon: 'No much, nyet voucher meal.'

Me: 'Eh?'

Dragon: 'Sit on table!'

Me: 'But we have no voucher.'

Dragon: 'Nyet! No voucher. Meal.'

Me: 'Thanks.'

We selected a table and sat down. After twenty minutes or so an unsmiling waitress came and hovered by the table.

'May we have the menu please?'

'Voucher!'

'We have no voucher.'

She disappeared and was presently replaced by an elderly waiter wearing army boots and a melancholy air.

'The menu please.'

'No menu. Other table,' and he indicated the adjacent table, identical in every way to the one we were sitting at.

We repositioned ourselves.

'Here is menu! Voucher!'

'Steak and dumplings please.'

'No steak, no dumplings.'

'Goulash and kasha then please.'

'No fish, no kasha.'

'Then caviar, toast and champagne!'

'Voucher!'

Half and hour later, steak and dumplings arrived, tepid, and no voucher was ever again demanded.

Such was the nature and the pace of life under a system where all incentive was absent, all creativity discounted and all effort kept to a minimum. To the foreigner, it was an Alice-in-Wonderland existence where the consequences of any request or any action were entirely unpredictable, except that they were almost always disappointing.

Next morning, the Soviet Tourist agency - the imaginatively named Intourist - had been mobilised to show us the sights. These are, as many readers will know, remarkable even by world standards and we were duly impressed. We were allocated a special guide, Nadia, who possessed some magic formula which enabled us to see everything ahead of everybody else waiting in the endless queues. We got off to a bad start when we did the unthinkable and declined to visit Lenin's tomb. The line of the faithful awaiting a glimpse of the old rogue went as far as the eye could see. I could imagine being one of them queueing all day and having at last reached the head, being displaced by foreigners. I did not wish to be one of those and besides, appearing to pay respects to the scoundrel was odious.

We were whisked out to the north of Moscow in a black Volga car. Suzdal, Yaroslavl and Zagorsk. By the evening I was in love with Russia. The vast horizons with dark threatening skies, the wooden peasant houses (izbas) with fretted barge boards - wooden lace they call it - and simple paling fences, the rich colours of the monasteries with their gilded onion domes and finials, the muddy rutted roads. Above all, it was the people: faces so extravagantly different and so packed full of character; old faces which had witnessed and survived purges, war and starvation.

... the monasteries with their gilded onion domes.

That evening, there was a banquet in our honour. The caviar, the Georgian champagne, the red wines and most of the food were all excellent. But the necessity to receive and propose endless vodka toasts throughout the meal was a sore but entirely necessary trial and one that was to be repeated relentlessly.

At this meal, I met Sasha, a senior railway timetabler with a splendid sense of humour and a robust ability to quietly rubbish the system. His family had been relatively prosperous before the Revolution. We struck up an immediate friendship which many visits later led to him becoming my honorary brother.

At nine o'clock the next morning, we joined a large assembly of the senior personnel in the Railway Ministry, the Minister himself, Comrade Krapski presiding. My eyes were glued to this man, sporting a well-cut dark suit, a diamond tie-pin and gold chain across his waistcoat. He actually arrived in a bowler hat, a cartoon image of a reactionary fat-cat capitalist.

Minister: 'Welcome. How can I help?'

Me: 'We want you to build a luxury hotel-train, which we will market.'

Minister: 'No problem.'

Me: 'We will need to find out approximate costs.'

Minister: 'We fix the cost now. How much?'

Me: 'It depends on how luxurious the train is and how long the journey is.'

Minister: 'We fix cost now. Train no problem. You allocate passengers to fill it!'

Me: 'We cannot *allocate* passengers. We have to sell tickets to people who will want to know exactly what they will get for their money. There is a limit to what people will pay and we must be sure that the price we pay you permits us to make a profit.'

Minister: 'Profit? What is profit?'

Me: 'The difference between the buying price and the selling price.'

Minister: 'There is no difference. It is the same.'

Me: 'May we talk about the train? We need a bathroom with every sleeping compartment.'

Minister: 'No problem. We have built it already.'

Me: 'Very good! May I see the plans?'

The plans are produced and I see there is one bathroom between *two* cabins.

Me: 'We need a bathroom for *each* compartment.'

Minister: 'There is one.'

Me: 'According to the drawing, there is one between two.'

Minister: 'You are wrong. When the passengers of one compartment are using the bathroom, it is the bathroom of their compartment. When the other passengers are using it, it is their bathroom. So, each compartment has a private bathroom.'

It was hard going; there was no common ground and their argumentation was often specious. This was the command economy in operation. Allocations, norms, and prices unrelated to costs. However at the end of the visit, things looked up. A few years earlier, the Praesidium of the Soviet Union had ordered some luxury railway coaches from East Germany. There was one allocated to the Chief Minister of each of the fifteen Soviet Republics. Gorbachov had commanded that these carriages were to earn foreign currency. One was to be placed at my disposal, for I needed to become acquainted with the country.

'We go to see it, yes?' said Sasha.

'Can't wait!'

'I think you will like it.'

'Where can I take it?'

'Anywhere you wish. There are 92,000 miles of railway line in the Soviet Union. Go more or less where you want. We just hook it on to a scheduled train and unhook when you want to look around.'

'Can I go to Siberia?'

'Of course! There's a train of some kind every few minutes. Nine days from Moscow to the far end.'

'What about meals?'

'We've arranged for an embassy cook, a supply of special food and a steward to serve it.'

'Caviar?!'

'As much as you want!'

'Can you come too to make the arrangements?'

'Of course. And Nadia also.'

'Accommodation?'

'One large twin bedroom with its own bathroom complete with a very large bath; a saloon and dining table.'

'Sounds wonderful! What will it cost?'

'Nothing!'

Things were definitely looking up.

A little research indicated that the Siberian region around Lake Baikal was potentially of interest to experienced travellers. Accordingly we asked Sasha to have the carriage moved to Irkutsk in Eastern Siberia. Some weeks later, Margaret and I returned to Moscow and went through the usual charade of trying to retrieve baggage before it was put on a flight to some distant destination. Then entrusting ourselves to Aeroflot, flew to Irkutsk where Sasha, Nadia and the private carriage and crew awaited us.

It was formidably comfortable and the crew most friendly. It was also clear, from our first meal, that the stocks of caviar were plentiful and the 'cellar' was well supplied. The only setback, which we somehow learned to survive, was the steward's sadness that he had not been issued with white gloves for the service of meals!

To reach Lake Baikal, the carriage was hooked onto a train to Slyudyanka and then shunted sixty miles up a side line to the lakeside village of Baikal. The line had not seen much use in recent years: branches reached across it and young birches were shooting up between the rails.

Lake Baikal is vast, considerably larger than the whole of Wales. It is, in fact, the world's deepest lake (almost 5,000 feet) and contains no less than one fifth of the world's fresh water. Of the 500 plants and 1,200 animals found in and around the lake, two-thirds are found nowhere else. Amongst these are Arctic seals, the world's only fresh water seals. The water is of an extraordinary clarity although paper factories at the southern end are doing what they can to pollute the lake irreversibly.

In my mind's eye, I see the place now as though I am alighting from my carriage on arrival. It is a warm day in mid-September. The sky is without cloud and the forest which slopes down to the lake is the yellow-gold of autumnal birches.

Margaret and I wander off along a dirt road which leads up a shallow valley. The grass is mostly brown from the heat of the brief Siberian summer. Small fields are enclosed with old fences of wooden poles. On either side of the valley forested hills rise gently toward rounded summits. The silence is absolute; to the noise assaulted Westerner, this silence seems strange, almost disturbing.

A mile or so on we come to the first *izba* of a village. This is even more beautiful than the ones we have seen near Moscow. Here the log cabins have fretwork on the elaborate window surrounds and along the eaves. All the houses are much the same size but the detailing always differs. Some are washed over in an acid green, a Wedgwood blue or a pale terracotta. Here and there the roofs of corrugated iron are painted a dull red. All are set back from the track and are irregularly spaced. The wide village 'street' wanders between swards of grass, cropped short by sheep. Poles, seldom vertical, suspend an assortment of wires that meander from house to house. Behind each *izba* is a strip of land that joins it to the forest above: each strip is about an acre and all look as though they have just been ploughed and harrowed.

There is a light rumbling sound and a young girl appears, pushing an ancient hand-cart on which is balanced a much-battered milk churn. She stops, waves and smiles and calls out a greeting. Alas, we can only counter with a Russian 'Good-day'. Then we meet a dog, two chickens scratching in the grass, and behind her paling fence, a stout headscarfed woman in a flower-print skirt hacking at the ground with a hoe. There must be the prospect of frost at night; the window-boxes are empty, the geraniums are inside the glass. We pass the village post office. It is painted in two shades of blue and the filigree shutters lend it an unthreatening, unofficial air. The wooden post box looks home-made and in the window are the notices of villagers offering items for sale or exchange. We arrive at the yellow-painted wooden church, its short steeple projecting from an octagonal tower with fretted galleries. Inside is the smell of incense: four soldiers are standing before the iconastasis, hats in hand, motionless.

It is all so peaceful, so still, so lovely. I feel I could live here.

Early the next morning, we were uplifted by a huge and deafening military helicopter and flown 150 miles north, deep into the territory of the Buryat tribe. These people live in solid-looking log huts, octagonal with a heavy turf roof and one window. A single hut was open for our inspection: I remember the interior darkness and the strong animal smell. Meanwhile the helicopter crew set about preparing lunch. A fire was lit, a trestle table erected beneath the birch trees, a white cloth laid over it and set with solid porcelain tableware. Soon there was a popping of corks - and it was another banquet; just that it happened to be in the Siberian backwoods.

The very name of Siberia evokes dreadful images of the millions dispatched to exile in these vast territories, yet it was hard in these exceptionally privileged circumstances to understand the full horror of being sentenced to work here. It was another perfect day: leaves fell slowly to earth and the eternal comfort of the woodsmoke lent the place an air of calm serenity. Deportation to Siberia became a frequent punishment from the end of the 16th century. It was an effective, if extremely ruthless means of getting rid not only of convicts but social misfits and even those who had committed no crime except to quarrel with someone in a position of power. In proportion to the demand for workers in the Siberian mines, so were even the most trifling misdemeanours met with sentences of exile. Crimes for which deportation might be ordered included drunkenness and any political activity - or even *suspicion* of such activities. An army of 'convicts' slogged their way to Siberia to work as slave labour under the harshest conditions. Their heads half-shaven, they were fettered and branded with a mark indicating their 'crime'. Civil rights and all property were forfeit. It was a one-way journey. Vast numbers exiled had helped to build the trans-Siberian railway on which we were about to travel.

Opposite our quiet siding at Baikal we could see the old trans-Baikal ferry and ice-breaker, Angara. We climbed aboard and were astonished to see she was built in 1898 in Newcastle-upon-Tyne. We learnt that she had been dispatched in thousands of parts and assembled on the lakeside. At that time, this was the terminus of the trans-Siberian railway. When the ice was too thick for the ferry, passengers were wrapped in sheepskins and pulled by horses the forty miles across the lake on sleighs. Some 2,000 such sleighs jingled their way across the ice from one side to the other at an average speed of seven miles an hour. Now the Angara was laid up - a piece of floating history which looked as though she might not be floating much longer.

We could have cheerfully spent weeks in this region but we had seen enough already to make a positive judgement on its potential.

Quite without warning, the sky clouded over, the temperature plummeted and a blizzard battered against the carriage window. Abruptly winter had arrived in Siberia: it was 20 September. Now I understood the misery of the convicts. And then I remembered that the *average* winter temperature in Eastern Siberia is minus 40°C. Perhaps I would not like to live in that village after all.

CHAPTER 19

Journey to Antarctica – a Welsh tea-party near Cape Horn – attempt to make Government change policy on Antarctica – design a new vessel for the Rhône – take up sand-yachting – break a military curfew in Azerbaijan – acquire a silver samovar and steam engine – climb up monument in darkness and am machine-gunned – arrive in private carriage in Tbilisi (Georgia) and given State Reception due to mistaken identity – visit Stalin's home – Big Boss loses dignity

MY NEXT commission was to go to the South Pole - or to be precise, an area 1,200 miles to the north of it in Antarctica.

The aim was to establish whether tourism there was something to be encouraged or not. At the time, there were plans to make the entire polar ice-cap an international 'Park', inviolate for all time – an idea vigorously opposed by the USA and the UK. This was a subject of great importance for Antarctica represents ten percent of the Earth's total land surface. The largest animal on the continent is a wingless fly but the sea is teeming with life with some thirty million seals and 100 million sea birds. Krill provide the staple food for half a million whales. Toward the end of the 19th century, whaling stations were established by the Norwegians and British. The rusting remains, along with the huge vertebrae and ribs of the processed whales are a monument to this exploitation which decimated the whale population. Deserted scientific bases testify to the rigours of survival in the world's coldest place.

The ship, *Ilyria*, (which, worryingly, had not been ice-hardened) was due to leave from Ushuaia at the extreme southern end of Argentina and cruise across the notoriously un-level Drake Passage to the 'panhandle' of Antarctica. The passengers were almost all American. In the ship's saloon meetings had been organised to test opinion and weigh the obvious disadvantages of uncontrolled exploitation against the less obvious potential disadvantages of tourism.

Margaret and I met in Buenos Aires as I had first to go to the USA. We stayed in Buenos Aires just long enough to be mildly mugged, then flew south to join the *Ilyria*.

Antarctica, a black and white wonderland of pristine beauty held us in thrall. Cathedral-sized icebergs towered above the deck, seals lazed on fragments of sheet ice. Penguins slid down icy gullies just for the fun of it. It was impossible not to be deeply moved by the majesty of the scenery and the profusion of wildlife.

abandoned whaling station in Antarctica

On the return journey, emergence into the Drake Passage succeeded in emptying the ship's dining saloon with sudden co-ordination. Once returned to the calm of the Beagle Passage, the ship was stopped and with the aid of inflatable boats, we visited the tiny port of Harberton and were invited to tea at the *estancia* of third-generation Welsh immigrants. In extreme isolation and over the span of a century, they had succeeded in preserving intact the wondrous spread of a Welsh tea party. We were sad to leave their warm hospitality and the loveliness of an austral summer's day adorned by sheets of multi-coloured lupins.

It seemed obvious that Antarctica had to be saved from indiscriminate exploitation by the many countries whose governments were staking claims to parts of it. There was already talk of oil and minerals. The passengers, including me, were mostly in favour of attempting to achieve a form of controlled tourism and passionately supportive of international 'park' or World Heritage status. It is possible that these Americans, many of whom wielded much 'clout' in the United States, were collectively responsible for bringing about a change of policy by the US administration.

I decided to do what I could to help change the view of the British Government on this issue. I wrote to Douglas Hurd, the Foreign Secretary (we were at Eton at the same time), putting the case for preservation as forcefully as possible and offering him a visit to Antarctica at my expense. Alas, he sat on his hands, just as he did so catastrophically and shamefully over Bosnia, but in the end the UK Government was obliged to fall in line with the USA and the other claimants to Antarctica, all of whom had voted in favour of preservation. It was yet one more damning example of wilful, even cynical environmental disregard by that disastrous Conservative Government.

It may be recalled that in earlier life I had crossed the Atlantic on the Cunard liner, *RMS Scythia* and that I had been much struck by the 'floating country house' effect of the First Class accommodation. I now decided to replicate this in microcosm.

We needed something new in the barging business and once again we set out to achieve new standards. We calculated that if we put a 400-tonne barge on the River Rhône, it would just be possible, having regard to depths and bridge heights, to build on three decks. This would allow a vessel to carry twelve passengers in extreme luxury, attended by a crew of seven.

We retraced our steps to Ghent, found a barge which conformed to our needs and had it delivered to the shipyard in Bruges (where we had converted *Fleur de Lys*) now in the final stages of decline. There were no suitable shipyards nearer to the Rhône. It was agreed that they would do the steelwork but all the fitting out would be done in their wood-working factory with our shipwrights. We were by now much more confident as 'converters' of barges. We knew how long it took to do things, where to buy components and how to allocate space to the nearest centimetre. The prospect of spending more time in Bruges was also welcome: we had become wedded to the place, especially during the winter when we had the lovely town much to ourselves.

The new ship, to be called *Napoleon*, was a much more ambitious vessel than the *Fleur de Lys*, and because she was to navigate the Rhône - the most difficult river in Western Europe - her construction was subject to stringent rules. There were four large engines to install, numerous pumps, kilometres of wire and masses of pipes. There were three separate systems for steering and something of a novelty, the pilot house situated toward the bow. It presented a formidable challenge. I was at the limits of my technical and design capability, at the brink of bank lending, committed to working for the travel company at the same time, rushing from one country to another (almost always with Margaret), working against the clock and loving every minute of it in the special way that living 'on the edge' ensures.

We returned regularly to Bayeux to receive many family visits and, at the same time, try out a new interest, sand-yachting. We were well positioned for this with the long and generally smooth sandy beach of Arromanches. We bought two sand yachts and had a great deal of fun as well as some spectacular accidents. There can be no way of getting wetter or more thoroughly plastered with sand than with *les chars-à-voiles*.

spectacular accidents and plastered with mud and sand

Shopping on Saturday mornings in the great open-air market place in Bayeux became something of a ritual for Margaret who would return laden with good things. Back now in Dorset, this is something we miss (though the Bridport Farmers' Market is rapidly catching up!).

On one of our journeys to Bruges, I went to visit the graves of my uncle and my mother's first husband, who were both killed in the

First World War. It was a deeply saddening experience to drive through that war zone and see the vast number of graveyards, all immaculately cared for by the War Graves Commission. It changes familiar statistics into the grim reality of human beings, each with his individual hopes and loves, individually slaughtered. Row upon row, cemetery upon cemetery: each life reduced to a name, a regiment, a date and an inscription. Afterwards, I felt that this sacrifice of the 'flower of Britain' should be seen by every Briton. It is less easy to forget once the scale of the massacre is observed with your own eyes.

The next journey in the Soviet Union was not one that could be easily forgotten. Margaret and I joined our two Russian 'colleagues' Sasha and Nadia at Moscow and flew down to Baku on the Caspian Sea. Here, in Azerbaijan, we were to take the private carriage, issued to the Chief Minister of that country and, crossing Georgia, continue onto the Turkish frontier.

Closed frontiers and border disputes between Azerbaijan and its two neighbours, Armenia and Georgia, to say nothing of other disputes between all three and the Soviet Union, had made such a journey impossible, more or less continuously, ever since the Revolution in 1917. Now there seemed to be a moment when tourism to this region was - and might remain - possible in the years ahead. As it turned out, this moment was shortly followed by the demonstrations which preceded the break-up of the Soviet Union, which entrained a succession of other disputes, so that we may have had the luck to make this journey by private carriage at perhaps the only moment since the Revolution. That we made it at all was, in the event, a close-run thing.

Our first evening in Baku found us sitting under vines on the pleasant terrace of a restaurant. Our pale-skinned group was instantly identified as foreign and quickly became the focus of attention. Many of the diners, though Moslem, were happily drinking wine and in the spirit of spontaneous hospitality they bought champagne for us. Margaret and I were subjected to the good-natured questionings of our self-appointed hosts and their rather less good-natured remarks to our Soviet colleagues. Quite soon and rather suddenly the restaurant emptied and we found ourselves alone and slightly inebriated. We decided to stay for a meal and an hour or so later, thought it time to return to the hotel.

There were just two uncertainties; we could not quite remember where the hotel was, or its name, and Nadia was very drunk. We asked for a taxi. No taxis. We paid up and set off in the direction we believed the hotel to be. The streets were completely deserted which was as well since Nadia was becoming loudly indiscreet about the natives as she clung to my neck for support. Eventually, we chanced upon the hotel but our entry, involving much unlocking and unbolting, seemed to cause considerable surprise. The following day we learnt why. There was a state of martial law and a curfew: anyone out after the deadline risked being shot. Nobody had quite liked to mention it in case, I suppose, it gave us a bad impression of Azerbaijan!

The following day, we were introduced to Comrade Tofeck (the head of Azerbaijani Railways) and the Minister for Transport. We soon found this Comrade to have charm, intelligence and modesty in equal proportions, which was pleasing as he was to accompany us as far as the Georgian border.

As the train was not due to leave until that evening, we had most of the day to look around. It was very warm so we took ourselves off to the Caspian Sea and plunged in. The rather unattractive beach was of grey pebbles. Suddenly there was a shout from Sasha.

'Gerard! Look what I've found!' He was holding aloft a pebble, which looked like any other.

'It's got a hole through it!' I stared blankly. 'Don't you know what it means? A pebble with a hole through it means you will return to this very spot at some time in the future. It is *very* lucky.' His face glowed with pleasure. I was not at all sure I wanted to return to that particular beach.

'If you don't want to return, can you just fill the hole up with something?' I ventured. Sasha looked crestfallen. It was too late to unsay what I had just said. My quip had translated itself falsely into – 'I'm not enjoying either the place or the company'. Thereafter, I was much more careful not to offend unwittingly. The Russian temperament, as I had indeed been warned, lives on the edge, ready to go either way and to ignore this is to court disaster.

Later, we wandered into the old part of Baku and I was surprised to come across an antique shop. In the whole shop there were only *two* items for sale, both priced at twenty dollars apiece, a gaudy painting and a large Russian samovar in German silver. We left with the samovar, and when later we flew back, we were obliged to have it on our knees all the way. It lives on in a largely ornamental capacity, an elegant monument to an extraordinarily inefficient method of heating water!

As soon as we boarded our carriage in the evening, it was clear that dinner was going to be yet another banquet. From that evening forward, every dinner and most lunches were banquets so that soon we felt unable to do justice to any of the meals.

The next day found us halted near Kirovabad. We had expressed a wish to do some walking to work off the effects of the huge meals. Accordingly, a car took us to some grass-covered hills studded with limestone rocks. The short turf grazed by flocks of sheep was wonderful to walk upon and interesting too since some of the rocky outcrops contained natural caves which had been home to early man.

We were just beginning to feel that the exercise had begun to counter the effects of forced feeding when, to our horror, the next cave, although far from civilisation, contained a table set for a further banquet.

Not far away from our carriage was a huge and ancient steam locomotive looking sadly derelict. I drew Comrade Tofeck's attention to it.

'When,' I asked 'did that engine last pull a train?'

'You like steam engine?'

'Yes, I think they are wonderful machines and it is sad they are all now abandoned.'

'Not abandoned! Very good Azerbaijani engine! You like to have engine? Yes? I command engine tomorrow. No like diesel. No. Yes?'

Early next morning, unusual sounds drew me to the window. There was the rusty engine with steam issuing from numerous apertures and a dense column of black smoke rising vertically above the funnel. A man in black overall, with a black face, was climbing into the cab. Almost at once, it began to move with a great wheezing and clanking and a minute or two later, a sharp jolt announced its rendezvous with the carriage.

Soon the engine was hissing and puffing its way westward with just our single carriage. Clouds of steam and smoke obscured vision first one side and then the other, sometimes both. Smuts from the soft coal entered eyes and nose. Every now and then, the driver blew the shrill whistle which, only feet away, made me jump. I regretted my sudden enthusiasm for the steam engine. When visible through gaps in the smoke the scenery was interesting although seldom beautiful. In due course we arrived at Akstafa, our destination for the night, shortly before the border with Georgia. Our arrival coincided with the merciful conclusion of another specially large 'farewell' meal aboard the carriage.

'I command engine tomorrow!'

We stepped onto the platform and were immediately introduced to Comrade Sorbak, deputy Minister for Railways.

'Welcome Meester and Meesis Grinwell to Akstafa; my home, I here born. Ha!'

'I look forward to seeing the place.'

'I take you my home: we make big dinner for you, come!'

'How kind, but ...'

'Akstafa very good town. I show you all, you like. Ha! You hungry?'

'Well actually we have ...'

'Azerbaijan wine very good, ha, ha!'

'Yes, so we have found, but we...'

'Look! There is car: I take you my home my wife wonderful with kitchen. She make great dinner, much wine, yes? Very good, yes, we go, we have good time, yes, no?'

There was nothing for it in the cause of *la politesse* but to submit. And submit we did. Course after course, wine after wine. Sometime after midnight at a point when all I could think of was sleep, Comrade Sorbak said:

'The great poet of Azerbaijan lived near Akstafa. You not see my country if not see monument for him. It is very near. We go, yes?'

'It is a great idea but maybe tomorrow when it is light.'

'No need light we have car light, you must see, our hero-poet, yes? We go. Now!'

We went. And we kept going for a long time. Eventually we came to a large car park. At the far side was a huge stone monument built up on a series of courses, each set perhaps an inch or so in from the course below. Many feet up was a narrow ledge, where plaques were inscribed with quotations from the poet's works. Comrade Sorbak insisted we scramble up the plinth, via the miniscule projections of stone, and stand with him while he gave a rendering of the famous lines. To this end, the car headlights flooded the edifice: even in our debilitated state, we all somehow managed to make the ascent clinging on to odd bits of stone. The chauffeur remained in the car.

We had just gained the ledge and Comrade Sorbak had cleared his throat before attempting to translate the stirring words, when out of the darkness behind the car came a burst of machine-gun fire toward the monument: the rounds were mixed with tracer. We must have made a tempting target but before the gunner could readjust his aim the chauffeur turned the car lights out, started the car and disappeared.

At this moment, in the small hours of pitch darkness, whereabouts unknown, abandoned by our driver, half-way up the almost sheer side of the monument, adhering to it like flies on a wall, half-drunk, exhausted and in fear of our lives, I was partially consoled by the thought that at least we would probably now be spared a lengthy translation of the poet's works in pidgin English.

The next morning, we crossed the border into Georgia and soon found ourselves arriving at the capital Tbilisi - bygone Tiflis. We had been hooked onto a longish train and, being at the tail end, our carriage had not reached the platform. I looked out of the window and noticed a large number of flashing blue lights of police vehicles around the station - more trouble no doubt. I was wondering whether we should jump down into the grass, when the train started forward: then as our carriage reached the centre of the station, it stopped with a sudden jolt which caused me to fall flat, a most undignified occurrence as it happened, for at that point a red carpet had been unrolled for *our* dismounting. At the far end of the carpet a group of officials was lined up. Police had cordoned off the platform.

I picked myself up, doing my best to assume an air of dignity, and stepped out onto the carpet - a new but strangely agreeable experience! An official came toward me.

'Meester Mogram Greenwheel, welcome to Tibilisi! We are much honoured for your wisit. I am Comrade Chkhzhkzchkvadze. I wish you wisit joyous to Soviet Socialist Republic of Georgia'.

'Thank you Comrade. May I introduce you to Margaret?'

'Meesis Magrill Grimwel, welcome! We go now to Ministry, Comrade Minister waits.'

Outside the station, a large black saloon. In front, several police cars: on either side and behind, police motorcyclists. All had flashing blue lights and as we drove off to the accompaniment of sirens, the leading police cars signalled all other traffic into the side. Pedestrians and cyclists were waved into the ditch where they froze to the spot as we passed.

Slowly I began to ponder the question, who did they think we were? *Who* did they imagine we represented? It was clear that in some way they must consider the future of Georgia to depend upon the visit of whomever we had been mistaken for. We never discovered the answer to this question. We did however ascertain that the previous week an identical reception had welcomed the US Secretary of State Schultz to Tibilisi and if they believed I was some European statesman of equal status, who was I to correct them?!

We were taken straight to see the Minister. His office, not a lot smaller than a tennis court, had at its far end a raised platform with a colossal desk of shiny plastic. On the broad expanse of its surface were seven telephones of different colours. Enthroned behind this desk sat the diminutive Comrade Minister in a sky-blue suit.

'Comrade Minister, I present you to Meester and Meesis Mogwol Gremlin.'

'Welcome comrades!'

This evidently represented the extent of his English and an interpreter stepped forward to receive a lengthy declamation from the Minister whose podgy hands pointed at intervals to all points of the compass.

'The Comrade Minister wishes to know whether you intend to continue on the railway to Batumi on the Turkish frontier.'

It seemed a good idea.

'Yes please.'

At once there was an agitated discussion between the Minister and his advisers. It was clear there was a difficulty. Perhaps they had discovered we were imposters. The interpreter stood up.

'There is no problem. It will be arranged. But not tomorrow. In two days. Now we show you Georgia!'

While this exchange was taking place, Sasha was talking quietly in Russian to one of the officials who spoke a little of the language. He came over to me and whispered into my ear.

'The line has been sabotaged and they need two days to mend it. It's the Abkhazians. There's been a bit of shooting.'

We drove off into the mountains, the police escort now much reduced but no less aggressive. They seemed to have guessed that we were not of Foreign Secretary status.

We stopped at a village restaurant. In the yard was a table laid for a banquet. My heart sank but I was determined this time not to be filled to bursting with food and drink. But I did not know the Georgians, whose hospitality is as pressing as are their arms and legs towards members of the opposite sex: as many emotional signals are exchanged beneath the table as above it.

That evening at dinner, yet another gigantic meal, I proposed a toast to our Georgian hosts. The toast in reply indicated that whilst we, the British, were most welcome, our Soviet colleagues were not.

The blue touch paper was lit. There was a furious exchange of recriminations in Russian and I thought a fight inevitable. But silence suddenly fell and we sat in a pool of embarrassment. There were no more toasts that evening.

While the line was being repaired we were taken to see Stalin's home and his personal railway carriage at the appropriately named town of Gori. They were both extreme in their austerity; if they had belonged to some saint they could hardly have been more revered. It was continually astonishing to find such enduring awe, sometimes bordering on veneration, for a man who had caused the death of at least 20 million people. Soon we were in the carriage belonging to the Georgian Government, and accompanied by the chief of the Georgian Railways. It was not long before he brought up the subject of steam locomotives. There was apparently an interesting engine, which could be fired up, at the very next junction where the train was scheduled to stop. I was determined to see that it stayed where it was.

'There it is!' announced the Chief on arrival. 'We go look.'

We climbed out and sauntered over to the huge and rusting locomotive. As we stood there, talking, I noticed that all the other passengers had climbed back in the train which looked to me as though it was about to depart. I said so.

'Meester Mugrat-Gravel, train no go without me! I am Big Boss.'

The words were no sooner pronounced than the whistle blew and the train started. The Big Boss ran like the proverbial cat, all dignity abandoned. He was hauled aboard by his coat collar, clutched by an immense female train attendant standing in the doorway, who next turned her attention to pulling us aboard in a similarly unseemly manner.

We arrived in Batumi to see people scattering flowers over bloodstains on the road, the result of a shoot-out earlier in the day. Perhaps, after all, this was not an itinerary to be recommended!

CHAPTER 20

Hunting a paddle-steamer on the Volga – Sasha discovers the West – USSR falls apart – pleasures of avoiding Mrs Thatcher – delights of the table – married again – cycling for business – an extraordinary meeting – walking the Pyrenees – relief convoy to Croatia – 'Napoleon' crosses Europe – fulfilment and crisis – buying a French castle – selling up

WHEN LAST in Budapest, I had caught sight of an aged paddlesteamer, the *Petöfi*, moored rather too permanently to the quay, suggesting that she was no longer in commission. The memory of her lying there in a state of neglect occasionally returned to my mind, so that when casting around for a luxury passenger ship to put on the upper reaches of the Volga in Old Russia, I thought I would investigate her potential.

Back in Budapest, I found her State-run owners suspiciously keen to discuss the possibility of a sale. We walked down to the quay and as I approached her elegant hull with its huge sloping funnel, I experienced a similar feeling to being in a home for rescued dogs - a sort of recognition of a desperate plight, compelling one to try to save a stricken creature, in this case, 190 feet of quietly rotting paddle-steamer. Built in 1920, she had plied the Danube with up to 1500 passengers yet her power was only half as much again as our six passenger barge *Fleur de Lys*.

It was a sad half-hour, for that was all it took to see that her rescue would be commercially unrealistic. It was not just that she had been vandalised for any component which could be used in a house, such as light fittings, neither was it the sheet of willow-herb which made a roof garden of the upper deck but, through a total lack of maintenance, the steel structure was fatally rusted. It was a peculiar characteristic of the Communist states that little or no effort was made to maintain old structures, whether ships, monuments or great houses.

Shortly after this, I heard of a paddle-steamer of similar size which was still in service on the Volga. We flew to Moscow, picked up Sasha and Nadia and flew on to Kazan, 500 miles to the east, to meet the

Chief of Soviet River Transport, an organisation seemingly willing to form a Joint Venture Company for the project.

On arrival we learnt that the ship had set off for somewhere else.

'Not problem, we go in big car, very fast, we find ship at Zelenodolsk, not problem but first we drink to project', said the Chief, whereupon he showed us into a room clearly set out for serving yet one more banquet.

'Comrade Golikov, we look forward to celebrating our meeting but we have come 2000 miles to see this ship and have to return to Moscow early tomorrow morning. Maybe we should move now to be sure of finding the ship at her next port.'

'My friend, we must eat and drink! Ship go v-e-r-y slow. Car go v-e-r-y fast. At Zelenodolsk we wait long time for ship.'

I believed him. And so we ate and drank. And then we were driven off in the Chief's big black car, we arrived in time to learn that the steamer 'had just left'.

'I tell you not problem Comrade, we go now to Cheboksary. I telephone. I command ship stop for night. We go fast. We arrive before ship.'

The next delay was in crossing the Volga on the ferry: loading was slow since many of the lorries trying to board seemed to be in a state of mechanical distress. Eventually we landed on the far side and within a few miles the road had deteriorated to a condition which in Western Europe would be considered impassable. It started to rain and speed was reduced yet further. We bounced and slithered from pothole to rut and only arrived at nine in the evening. The ferry 'had just left'.

'Now we go find restaurant.' Seething with rage, I set off with the others. There was only one restaurant and it was open: as we stepped towards the door, it was banged shut in our faces.

'We go now. My friend here is boss. He has hydrofoil. Very fast. We go after steamer. We see steamer v-e-r-y quick. We go whoooosh!"

Just for a moment, I stupidly allowed myself to think we might actually reach the ship after all. Then we met the regional chief. Mr Golikov translated.

'Steamer here two hours ago. Comrade Captain he say passengers to stay here night. Passengers say to Captain if stay night he go in river - plop - Captain say passengers no stay night, go to Gorky.'

Although we were now aboard the hydrofoil, not only was it pitch dark but the Gorky region was closed to foreigners.

'Not problem, I send photograph! My friend make good meal. If problem, then drink! Come comrades, we have good time!'

In a white fury, dejected and full of self-blame that I hadn't overcome scruples of politeness and insisted that we forewent the meal at the airport, I even began to wonder whether the ship actually existed but given the reality of our situation, expressing such thoughts was unlikely to improve matters. I decided there was nothing for it but to swallow anger, force my face into a smile and hope that something could subsequently be salvaged. We sat down and waited while the 'chief' looked for food on the hydrofoil. He found a bag of tomatoes, the end of a cucumber and a large bottle of vodka.

The circumstances could hardly have been less propitious for 'good cheer' but, once ignited, Russians have an extraordinary ability to sweep all before them in a cascade of boisterous good humour, at once sympathetic and perceptive, endearing, uninhibited and direct. Within minutes I was thoroughly enjoying myself: I saw once again why Russians find Westerners so turgid.

We reached the ferry on our return journey at four in the morning. There was a queue of lorries about a mile long waiting to board when the service started later that morning. The ship was at the jetty, tied up for the night. Comrade Golikov told his chauffeur to climb aboard and wake up the crew. Gradually lights started to come on, the hugely noisy engines were fired up and the ramp slowly descended. This encouraged all the lorries to start up but we drove on and the ramp was immediately raised. As we drew away, the flashing of lorry lights and irate blowing of horns made me glad there was about to be three miles of water between us and an army of infuriated lorry drivers. It was yet one more example of the extreme license enjoyed by the bosses of the Soviet system, where privilege and raw power for the *nomenklatura* existed to a degree unheard of in the capitalist countries.

We were no sooner home in Normandy than Sasha, by now my honorary brother, announced his intention of visiting us. Travel abroad for Soviet citizens was still very difficult but the prospect of a Joint Venture Company with a western partner made his permit possible. We met Sasha's plane at Paris. It was his first visit to the West. His colleagues at the Railway Ministry were agog to learn more about life beyond the Iron Curtain and gave him a video camera. Starting at one end of the Champs Elysées, he walked very slowly to the other end recording everybody, each building and all the traffic. Later, when we brought him to Bayeux, we took him to a supermarket where he started to record the entire inventory until the Manager accused him of spying for the competition. He was astonished by almost everything he saw so that we too began to see France and Western lifestyles through his eyes. On one hand he envied the efficiency and the convenience of Western life but on the other was disgusted by the excess and the waste. Most of all he deplored the lack of human contact in any kind of transaction and was permanently in a state of readiness to down tools and embark on a heart-to-heart discussion. Attempting this with the girl at a busy supermarket checkout convinced him that the West had lost its way.

Shortly after this visit, Sasha and a Soviet 'lawyer' came to London to negotiate a contract for the railway project. They were accommodated in the St James Court Hotel and were clearly stunned by the comparative luxury. A month later we received a supplementary bill from the hotel, some £600 for the minibar. They had thought the miniature bottles of spirits were free samples and either drank them or put them in their luggage. Each time they returned to the room, as if by magic, they found the minibar recharged!

We had now negotiated the use of the private ministerial railway carriages but they needed refurbishment. As there were no suitable materials in Russia, they were moved to Finland, the only western country which had the same wide-gauge railway as the Soviet Union. Shortly after this, the Soviet Union started to fall apart and most of our endeavours came to naught. It was deeply frustrating but I cannot deny that for me it had all been hugely enjoyable! At least these private carriages are still available for charter.

One of the many pleasures of living in France was the avoidance of Mrs Thatcher whom I considered odious. Never had I experienced any British politician for whom I felt such loathing. Most of her utterances made me cringe with revulsion at their sanctimony and contemptuousness. I could not accept her hectoring attitude and to me Thatcherism epitomised the most repugnant aspects of Conservatism: Conservatism that was based on naked capitalism and not a million miles from Fascism. It seems entirely in character that she took tea with General Pinochet to show her support for the Chilean ex-dictator charged with mass torture of dissidents. She was indeed responsible for reining in the runaway unions but that is about all I give her credit for. Her time in office saw Parliamentary tolerance much reduced and the country become dangerously and unpleasantly divided. Along with a large majority, I threw my hat high in the air when she was toppled and felt a great deal happier at the possibility of returning to Britain.

There was an aspect to living in France that came upon us unexpectedly. We found that the island mentality, the hall-mark of the British, is gradually replaced by a Continental identity. Instead of the perception that whatever happens across the Channel is possibly irrelevant, one slowly becomes aware that the event has actually taken place 'down the road'. It may sound a trifling difference but it is one that grows progressively until the British appear as isolationist and somehow out of step. One does not have to be French to observe this.

Another, and very positive pleasure, was the need to sample many of the finest restaurants in France. I say 'need' for such it was - our American passengers expected us to know which actually lived up to their reputation. We soon came to know the limits of French cuisine. It was often over-rated and infrequently sublime. The colossal expense of running an establishment that achieves, day after day, the summit of excellence, and the great commercial temptations offered by the deep-freeze and microwave, have thinned substantially the number of reliably pre-eminent restaurants.

Sadly many people cannot equate the prospect of a fabulous meal with the potential cost: they simply cannot imagine that the pleasure could be proportionate. But I would urge those who have never entered one of the great temples of gastronomy to gather up courage along with their savings, and experience one of mankind's major achievements - the consummate orchestration of superb ambience, refined service, oenological and culinary perfection. Yes, there is a risk that it will be an off-day but if lucky it is an event that will not be forgotten.

On one side of our Manoir was the Mairie, the administrative and mayoral office found in every village or town in France. Next door to the Mairie was the Mayor's farm. One day, when Hugo and some friends were staying the weekend, Margaret and I decided to entice the Mayor into his Mairie and marry us. This time I had absolutely no doubt that it was the right step to take.

'Special Interest' holidays had long been a developing market. One of the fastest growing was walking and bicycling tours and perhaps the most popular destination for these was France.

My client in the travel business now decided to enter this market and I was asked to put together a range of tours. I had never really done any serious cycling but to see what was required, Margaret and I booked with an American company already offering tours in Burgundy.

To prepare, we bought two bicycles and pedalled our way round the level lanes of the Norman countryside near Bayeux. But when we presented ourselves at Chablis for the start of the tour and met our co-cyclists, we realised that we were gravely outclasssed. Most of the party had come as a group from Houston, Texas and the men had spent many winter evenings cycling up and down a multi-story car park. They had all the latest gear and we were novices.

We were saved by the wives who, very sensibly, had not spent their winter cycling up ramps so that in the event we achieved an average time for the eighty kilometre circuit, much of which was hilly. We had never cycled anything like this distance in our lives and when we arrived at our destination, none other than the renowned establishment of Monsieur Meneau's *L'Esperance* at Vezelay, we collapsed onto deck-beds by the pool and fell asleep.

This experience led me to suspect that most desk-bound people would be better off walking for their holiday. Since we had already done a number of walks in various parts of France, we decided to open our research by exploring new territory. We chose the Pyrenees. This is, of course, a vast area and it was important to find someone who knew the region. A certain Monsieur Langlois emerged as the expert. He had apparently walked every path in the mountains and produced a number of printed guides. However, neither Monsieur Langlois nor his guides could be located. So we flew to Toulouse, hired a car and aimed at the middle of the line of mountains.

After a series of minor foothills, we came to the first major climb. Half-way up, we saw a man pushing a bicycle: he looked very hot.

Margaret insisted that we offer him a lift to the top. It is perhaps hardly necessary to add that our passenger was none other than the elusive Monsieur Langlois.

At the top of the hill, we reunited him with his van. In this were all the maps and guides which he now freely dispensed. We then embarked on a trek of astonishing beauty along the Spanish side. The skies were blue, spring flowers massed in prodigal extravagance and streams of crystal waters cascaded down the rocks. It was elysium and not another soul did we meet.

It was this walk which ignited in us both the wish to explore Europe on foot more extensively. In the ensuing years, we travelled many hundreds of miles along footpaths, almost always deserted, in the hills and mountains of France, Spain and Italy. Hardly ever have we been rained upon and if necessary there is usually a barn in which to shelter.

a barn for a picnic

In 1992, the Balkans descended into conflict: Serbia, Croatia and Bosnia commenced an orgy of 'ethnic cleansing'. At an early stage in this abominable struggle, it seemed that the suffering inflicted by the Serbians on Croatia called for practical action in their support - the Western Allies being, as usual, long on rhetoric and short on deeds. Inland from the town of Split, on the Adriatic coast of Croatia, the town of Sinj had been blasted by Serbian shells. The Humanitarian Centre for refugees had been destroyed, as had the bus depot. There was therefore an immediate need for food and clothing as well as transport.

We decided to help supply a few of these needs, albeit in microcosm. Together with Roger Collins, the manager of our barge business, and Lado Ciechanowski, a friend and neighbour in Normandy, we set about collecting as much largesse as we could cram into three minibuses. With red crosses affixed to the vehicles, we drove from Bayeux to Croatia. As we approached Sinj, the roads were largely deserted and the sound of shelling became louder.

Our contacts in the stricken town received our consignment with expressions of great warmth. We also bequeathed them two of the minibuses, one of them procured by Roger Collins. To our embarrassment we were invited to a lunch as a mark of thanks but the huge spread laid out for us, which could be so ill-spared by our hosts, worried me profoundly.

The military situation in that part of Croatia was deteriorating rapidly and for a moment our return was less than certain. In the event, we got the remaining minibus onto the last ferry from Split to Ancona in Italy. Sitting in the dining saloon that evening as the cork was pulled from a flask of Chianti, we reflected on the fine line that divides people between poverty and affluence, war and peace or oppression and freedom.

After our return, the Balkan situation steadily degenerated. Over three months, I exchanged a personal correspondence with Douglas Hurd, the Foreign Secretary. Re-reading this now, I am appalled afresh by the hollow assurances, the continual and cowardly temporising and the passing of responsibility for action elsewhere. The UN looked to Britain for a lead: Hurd had every opportunity and every reason to initiate appropriate measures and stand by the promises made of 'safe havens' but neither he nor John Major's feeble Cabinet were prepared to do anything except look for reasons why they should do nothing. At the same time they connived in allowing the British Forces in Bosnia to be put into an impossible situation on the ground. It was a shameful and profoundly unwise episode in our history which lead directly to the next Balkan war in Kosovo, for which that Cabinet must bear a large measure of responsibility.

I had picked up a another commission to design a small ship for the Danube. In due course, it was completed and we went to the river for the trials. It was during this journey we discovered the cycling path built along the length of the Danube through Austria. We tried a section of its smooth surface and decided to return one day to pedal our way the 150 beautiful miles from Passau to Vienna.

By early 1991 the new barge *Napoleon* was now nearing completion in Bruges and we were faced with the problem of moving her to the Rhône. The very careful calculations we had made required the structures on the top deck to be demountable. They also called for a great tonnage of ballast to be loaded. Only then would she make it to the South of France through the canals and rivers. She would have as little as an inch or two under some of the lowest bridges and minimal clearance over the canal bottom.

We settled for Belgian patio tiles as a dense ballast and as a commodity which might make a profit in St Jean de Losne, our destination. In this small town, home to many retired bargees, which lies at the cross-waterways of the Saône river, the Burgundy and the Rhône-to-Rhine canals, arrangements had been made to reconstruct the upper deck and have the necessary stability tests without which we would not receive an operating certificate. In the event, to our immense relief, the journey proved the calculations correct and I believe that *Napoleon* made waterway history by being the largest vessel ever to have crossed inland from northern to southern Europe.

Soon after our arrival the quay was piled high with patio tiles. In consequence, part of this mariners' town are now laid with a particular type of Belgian tile not to be found elsewhere in France!

The upper deck reassembled, the tests completed and passed, I now set about furnishing the interior as sumptuously as space would permit. The entire ship was panelled in ash wood. Tony Oakshett, the portrait painter, applied his skill to reproducing portraits of the Rhône valley famous. Provençal furniture was found or commissioned. The saloon was vastly comfortable and the stairwell was lined with rich hangings and opulent use made of gilt and marble; a chandelier hung in its centre. I think it is fair to say that the ship looked hugely attractive – at least I thought so!

Piece by piece the jigsaw was completed and we set sail for Arles at the foot of the Rhône. At Lyon, we picked up members of the family for the maiden cruise and put boat and crew through their paces.

Above. One of the numerous water tournaments on the river at Le Manoir.

Below left. In 2000, CAT received the Prince of Wales award.

Below right. Ballooning from the deck of the *Fleur de Lys.* Balloon journies were almost always delightful but if an unexpected wind got up, landing could be problematic.

MY CHILDREN AND GRANDCHILDREN
Left. L-R Hugo, Oscar, Sophie, Hector
Middle. L-R Laura, Selina, Hamish, Rosie, Euan
Right. L-R Caroline, Toby, George, Harry (Alexander absent)

We were anxious to avoid replicating the multiple disaster which befell a competitor on their maiden voyage down the Rhône not long before. The Captain of the *Fleur du Rhône*, (luckily without the complement of a 100 or so passengers) hurrying downstream in flood conditions, decided that the bridge at La Voute was too low, attempted to turn and struck the bridge abeam, breaking the vessel in two. It so happened that the local *Sapeurs Pompiers* were having their annual lunch in a restaurant overlooking the river. Abandoning their *entrecôte et frites* they rescued the crew but the bridge which carried the main railway line was put out of commission and because of the sunken vessel, navigation was suspended. The resultant bill was enough to finish off any company.

For us, this project had been ambitious: the design work had been voluminous, embracing every cubic inch of space, all sixty million of them: technically, *Napoleon* was by far the most complex ship we had built and, from the standpoint of the passengers, much the most comfortable river ship in France. As I floated down this great but perilous river, sitting in a warm jacuzzi on the open top deck, sipping champagne, and watching the sun sink behind the terraced vineyards, I knew one of those rare and fleeting moments - perhaps lasting only a few milliseconds - when I felt suffused with a sense of profound gratification. It was some forty years since I had been so impressed by Cunard's *Scythia*. The idea of creating something similar, perhaps better, even if only a mere fraction of the size, had at that instant become a reality. For that one fugitive but priceless moment, all the work and all the worry were as nothing. It had been worth it all a thousand times over. Shortly after this brief moment of fulfilment, the Fates decided, as they usually do, to deal any tendency to self-satisfaction a resounding thump. Just before Arles, the Mistral had started to blow with its accustomed violence. About a mile before an arched bridge, the main engine suddenly stopped. Steerage was still possible with the bow-thruster. It failed to start. Pushed by the following wind, the stern started to slew broadside on: the strong current and the Mistral appeared to have every chance of making *Napoleon* replicate the disaster of the *Fleur de Rhône*. Only a few hundred yards separated the ship from the bridge when the main engine was re-started. The moment of fulfilment had belonged to another epoch!

By 1993, we had been at the Manoir for some seven years and in a sense, there was not much left to do. This, together with a recurrent desire to live in deeper countryside, gave me itchy feet. It was a condition which Margaret only partially shared but, supportive as ever, she soon picked up on the excitement of thumbing through magazines filled with photographs of houses and castles, many of which, as usual, looked irresistible. By now, we were both old hands at interpreting the brazenly dishonest descriptions which French estate agents so recklessly apply. But even so, the allure that some of the photographs produced was overwhelming. From time to time, we simply jumped in the car and went to look. Gradually, as disappointment succeeded disappointment, we went further and further afield, regarding one third of France as potentially 'liveable'. We saw many beautiful but inherently defective properties and finally came to rest with a château perched on a rocky bluff high above the Dordogne River, near Sarlat. It was not its size, nor the fact that it was open to the public nor even the labyrinthine complexities of disputed ownership that made us think again: it was the simple thought that living so far south we would be largely out of visiting range to family and friends. Somehow it had not impinged upon us with sufficient force until actually confronting purchase. We began to see how easily we could have become ex-patriots, mouldering in a distant corner of someone else's

a chateau perched on a rocky bluff above the Dordogne

country: it seemed better to moulder in one's own! However, running a business spread across France from the other side of the Channel seemed impractical and it was this that gave rise to the thought that perhaps now we had 'done' barging. We had been in at the beginning and our fleet was the best. But we were now competing with 150 other barges 'plying for hire' and French officialdom was becoming ever more grasping and objectionable.

We resolved to sell up and go whilst still enjoying it.

It is always easier to buy things than to sell them and, in France, this is particularly so with houses as so many people have found to their cost. We allocated a year for the purpose. I took photographs and advertised Le Manoir directly, cutting out house agents with (in France) their fat commission. Six people wrote for details, three came to see the house, two were not interested. This left just one but it was someone desperate to buy. We received a good offer and since at the time the exchange rate was almost fifty percent more favourable for us than when we bought the house, we agreed to sell, even though it was clear we would not find anything in England by the time we would need to move out.

Next we put the barge business up for sale. Only one company was eager to buy. We sold it to them at once.

Now we could relax. A French friend had a small house to let in the middle of the great plain south of Caen and into this we went whilst we scoured the English property press. It was the end of a wonderful chapter but now our eyes were turned northward to England to a destination and an occupation unknown.

CHAPTER 21

Coming to rest in West Dorset – collecting yew clippings – raising funds for charity – Stowe again – follies – a final cruise – a painter discomforted - designing a new kind of boat for the sea – become a publisher

TO HAVE no house to call your own, to have no job and no particular objective in sight is to many people the stuff of nightmares. I have, however, come to see it as a form of liberation, a new canvas on which to create a fresh image. There is so much to explore in life and to be locked fast in a single endeavour is to limit severely the range of its potential. When the pattern of life becomes repetitious, I feel it is sometimes best to decamp and see what is on offer.

In 1994, there was a lull in the British market for houses. People with homes to sell were waiting for the market to pick up and consequently, there were few properties available. Mainly by process of elimination, we soon confined our research to the south-west and West Dorset became a preferred area. When therefore a Mill in a village near Bridport, came on the market, we lost no time in going to see it. It was the first place we had come across which aroused feelings of 'recognition'. A second visit confirmed those feelings, shared as it emerged, with another 400 people who had sent for the brochure. An agonising negotiation followed but success was ours at last. When I found that the Mill had been the home of Kenneth Allsop, an environmentalist guru of a quarter century before, I began to wonder if Destiny had a hand in the negotiations!

In the Exeter Cathedral library, the 11th century regional Domesday inventory lists a mill here, though the main part of the existing house is 18th century. Between the rounded hills of grass that rise up on either side, there is a level garden enclosed by old yew hedges. At the end of a no-through road, surrounded by stone barns and a cottage, it is a kind of earthly paradise situated, as we slowly discovered, in one of the most beautiful and unspoilt parts of Britain, an area peopled, as we

... agonising negotiations followed but success was ours at last

also soon learned, by an abundance of friendly and, not infrequently, richly-talented people, a few of whom are delightfully eccentric.

It was the yew hedges, just mentioned, that gave rise to the next project. A friend in France, Juliet Vibert, who visited the Mill soon after our arrival, noticed in a French newspaper that a pharmaceutical company in Le Mans was offering to clip yew hedges in France in return for the clippings. She suggested that we write to the company to ask if they would like to clip our hedges here in England. We did - and they said they might be willing to do so.

It was obvious therefore that the collection of yew clippings must be a potentially profitable business. We suggested that we became their agents in Britain and that we set up a system for gathering the clippings which, we learnt, were being processed into an anti-cancer drug. They agreed. Together with a neighbouring couple, Kirsty Fergusson and Chris Norman, we established a company to provide this service and we soon found 3,000 gardens from which we could obtain worthwhile quantities of yew. The business was run from the Mill and not only provided an income but in the first five years raised over £120,000 for Macmillan Cancer Relief and Marie Curie Cancer Care through the generosity of garden owners who allowed us to pass on their payments.

Stowe now came back into my life. The National Trust invited all the descendants of my grand-mother to a lunch. Eighty-one members attended and we were introduced to the extraordinary plans to restore, with meticulous attention to detail, and to maintain, in perpetuity, the landscape gardens and the thirty or so temples, grottos, monuments and bridges. For the last 150 years, these buildings had struggled to survive amidst collapsing family fortunes and a cash-hungry school which had nevertheless done its impoverished best to look after them. Two years later, I was asked to join the Trust's Advisory Committee for Stowe. I find it difficult to think *only* in terms of restoration, my instinct being to add yet more architectural touches to this, the finest landscape garden in Europe!

My urge to embellish gardens with structures of superfluous function is perhaps the manifestation of some dominant gene. At Burgate it accounted for a bridge that spanned a gully and which carried a line of convincing *trompe l'oeil* balusters; at Henbant there was the gatehouse which severely limited access to the house; at Le Manoir there was a folly-summer-house and at the Mill, a pavilion on stilts embracing seven architectural styles from around the world and a kind of Russian dacha, built on piles in the lake, and constructed of straw bales rendered over in lime mortar. The actual building of all these structures, their contemplation when finished and their occasional use gave the greatest pleasure imaginable. The British are great creators of gardens yet so many fail to provide a focal point or the interest of the unexpected which *can* be achieved simply and cheaply.

Five months after we moved to Dorset, my brother John died from cancer for which he had an operation five years before. In the intervening years, he lived an active life which included being a High Sheriff and Deputy Lieutenant for West Sussex. He was shooting pheasants only two weeks before he died. I was glad to be in England and to have seen something of him. We had grown much closer in the final years of his life but it is a matter of lasting regret that for so many years, we had become distanced for reasons I was never able to fully comprehend.

We went on a final family cruise aboard the *Virginia Anne* in the middle of the winter in 1994. For a quarter century, year on year, we had cruised the waterways of France: *Virginia Anne* had seen the children become adults and now, all three were living their own lives. Independent all, they seem happily married and productive of my many grandchildren. Hugo is now a leading professional artist; Laura seems, at least to me, to be a model mother and wife and George is now a managing director in the very successful international travel business to which I was formerly a consultant.

With our impending return to Britain, we felt the moment had come to relinquish possession finally of this our first and best loved barge. She was so much part of my life - and indeed Margaret's too after twelve years - that it was a very sad parting. There was no rivet, no nut or bolt that we did not both know intimately. Every square foot of her had associations of some kind, some disastrous, some hilarious. We had all learnt to manoeuvre her with varying degrees of precision that we could never have believed possible in the early days. Many years earlier, in an ultimate test of this skill, my brother John and I hung eggs fore and aft on the rubbing strake on both sides and challenged each other to enter the 115 tons and the ninety-six feet length of barge into a lock without crushing any of them. With only a few inches clearance either side, this was no easy feat!

On the first day of this last cruise, I painted a landscape in oils. As it progressed on the canvas, I became rather pleased with it, then as so often happens, I made some fatal error and in a moment of extreme irritation, threw the painting into the canal. Thinking better of it, I fished it out and hung it up on a wall in the adjacent village, happy to give it away: I pinned a large card bearing the word *gratuit*. When we returned a week later, it was still there; a humiliating experience!

The lot of a landscape painter can be quite humbling. Once I was painting the scene at a medieval farm. Now most painters see themselves in an interpretive role, presenting their own impression of a given scene. As I painted this farm, I was altering slightly the position of some of the buildings as well as excluding certain unwanted features. An old man came up to me.

'*Bonjour, M'sieur,*' he said, eyeing me up and down suspiciously and looking at the canvas. After some minutes, he observed, 'You have made several mistakes in your painting - do you wish me to tell you what they are?'

'Yes.' I said, thinking mistakenly to humour the man.

'In the first place, you have forgotten to put in the electric poles.'

'That's true but I left them out on purpose because I thought they were ugly.'

'Ugly? To me they mean electricity and electricity is beautiful. It means I no longer have to milk by hand. But you are also wrong about other things. For example, you have put these buildings too close together. Like that we couldn't get the big cart through the door on to the road.

'I realise that,' I said. 'But it doesn't matter because the road isn't included in the canvas.'

'You have not drawn it as it is and therefore it is not right.'

After this condemnation there was a lengthy pause during which I felt the extent of his disapproval spreading back and forth from omission to alteration. Then suddenly:

'I know what it needs! My tractor in the middle! Yes that will certainly improve it; I will fetch it and put it there for you.'

Soon, the tractor in position, the old man came back, bringing with him most of his family, the smallest member of which spread his hand on the centre of my palette and with fingers well and truly loaded with the colours of the spectrum, transferred them to my trousers. After studying the picture for a few minutes, Madame observed in a low voice to her husband

'I think he is painting our farm but I cannot be sure. If it is not the farm, why does he stand there?'

Grandmère who had by now shuffled onto the scene said in a querulous voice, 'Is he painting those crumbling buildings?'

On receiving confirmation from Monsieur, she said,

'It's a disgrace! It's bad enough that anyone should have to live in them let alone that people should come and paint them.' Then addressing me, 'When you have finished, perhaps you would do us the favour of taking yourself off with your canvas and showing it to the landlord from whom we rent these miserable buildings. Not that he cares whether we are wet or dry,' she added shrugging her old shoulders.

'When are you going to put the tractor in?' asked M'sieur, a note of irritation in his voice.

'The light is getting poor,' I parried. 'I think it will have to be tomorrow.'

'That is too bad because tomorrow I shall be using it all day.'

The eldest boy who had been studying the painting with great attention then asked

'What purpose does it serve, your picture?'

My various attempts to provide him with a convincing answer to this perfectly reasonable question left him unsatisfied and left me feeling unsure!

In the months following the sale of the barge business, much as we had enjoyed so many of the activities associated with it, we experienced a palpable sense of relief to be disengaged from the responsibility of running a cruise business whose passengers were usually from the ranks of the very rich. Any failure was potentially expensive. We were wholly and vulnerably dependent on the crews and their ability to resolve problems as they arose. But sometimes it was beyond their power to deal with an incident and then the skipper would telephone, sometimes waking us from a deep sleep.

'Sorry to tell you, the chef's done a runner. We can deal with lunch and take them to dinner at a really good restaurant but we must have a replacement within twenty-four hours. Sorry!'

It was not easy in the middle of the season, when any chef worth his salt was already employed, to locate, interview, persuade and transport to a moving destination a new candidate, all in a matter of hours.

'Sorry to tell you, the Rhône is in flood, we're moored up against piles, no one can get ashore and the forecast is that we'll be here for several days. The level of the river is above that for which the insurance holds so we can't move. If we're here for forty-eight hours, we'll be out of water and fuel for the generators is getting low! Any suggestions?'

'Sorry to tell you, the electrics have gone down. The main fuse board's burnt out. There's a man coming from Valence in the morning but the air conditioning is out and it's 38°. Any ideas?'

'Sorry to tell you but that new chef has gone beserk. Passengers were seated in the dining room waiting for dinner last evening when he raced in, stark naked, told them to cook their own f...... dinner and dived through the window into the river. The police want him for suspected drugs. Need another by tonight. Sorry!'

While it was peaceful to be spared such difficulties, we were conscious of simply missing *boats*. Once they have worked their way into your system, it seems they are there forever. But we felt we had 'done' canals. There remained the sea.

As someone who hates being cold and wet, I was extremely dubious about sailing and I suspected that in approaching seventy years of age, I would be too wobbly to cope with flapping sails on lumpy seas. But the alternative of motor cruisers did not commend itself either. We examined several and thought them ill-designed for doing much more than being moored to a pontoon and providing their owners with a place on which to drink several gin-and-tonics at a weekend, in the company of adjacent boat owners doing just the same. We noticed that in almost every case, the engines had only run for very few hours.

These motor cruisers seemed mostly pretentious, with their working parts largely inaccessible, slow-moving and ill-designed for even a moderate sea. But there was an exception, the Rigid Inflatable Boat (RIB) much in demand by the Lifeboat Service and this seemed a good commendation. These boats, as their name suggests, are of rigid construction, and their 'rim' is surrounded by a large air-filled tube to give them huge lateral stability. But they are open and therefore wet.

I decided to design a super-structure which could be built on to a large RIB. Then I found a RIB manufacturer in Bridport. Although on its last legs, the factory promised the skills and facilities necessary. The initial delivery forecast of two months became extended to seven and with the completion of the boat, the company went bankrupt.

We launched 'Salamander' (for she is yellow and black) at Weymouth. She achieved thirty four knots and gave a relatively comfortable ride in a choppy sea. Gradually we took her out in bigger seas. Twice, due to the malfunction of a new type of engine, we needed - to our embarrassment - rescue by the ever-ready RNLI. On the second of these occasions, back on land again and towing a trailer, I took a corner too close and destroyed a piece of someone's house. Whilst surveying the damage, the door of the house opened to reveal the self-same crew member of the RNLI lifeboat who had rescued us at sea an hour or so earlier! Nothing daunted, he fetched tools and straightened out the damage whilst somehow managing to conceal his feelings.

So what next? Well, if this book is to be published, it will need a publisher. Now *there's* an idea!

REFLECTIONS

Between the covers of this book lies the story of a life. Yet, in truth, it is little more than a fragment of that life and touches only the outward and visible part. As I go back to read what I have written, it is plain to see that the emotional and the spiritual have only surfaced between the lines. Yet it is these invisible elements which have nudged me toward the paths that I have chosen.

I have found it a struggle at times to keep in touch with myself, to identify the sound of the trumpet that resonates for me, to be true to myself. It is all too easy to become embroiled in activities which are alien to one's nature.

The holy writ of the career ladder somehow got lost along the way and, mercifully, was never refound.

I have not mentioned the many friendships that have allowed me to 'warm both hands before the fires of life' and which have given me an immeasurable richness of experience and a profound happiness. They have proven the most enduring elements in the changing fortunes of a varied life.

What have I achieved? It is a fair question to ask of oneself, yet it is one which I cannot answer.

Achievement is relative, transient and quite unquantifiable. From the projects recorded in this narrative, other ventures have spun off and they in turn have given rise to yet others. The waves spread ever outwards, touching distant shores that will remain forever unknown to us.

I do believe, firmly, that powers unidentified, but not unrecognised, take a hand in advancing a cause honourably founded. It has been a source of astonishment to observe the way that things fall into place largely by themselves once the personal commitment has been made. Achievement seems attracted by hard work, determination and a preparedness to take risks. Fortune really does seem to favour the bold. She seems also to smile on those who hang on, limpet-like - when the opposition seems overwhelming.

As to the distillation of my experience of life, perhaps the question is best approached by asking another. 'What, if I had my time again, would I do differently?'

Many things.

I would hope to waste far less time for I have spent too much of it unproductively; it is so much easier to say Yes instead of No.

On another round, I would hope to be more skilled at avoiding situations, or people, to whom I have little or nothing to give: much energy has been squandered needlessly and to no-one's advantage.

I would hope to break free sooner of any restrictive aspects of the era into which I was born, to shed the shackles of pointless conformity and to challenge the 'established and deficient norm'.

I would like to think that I would dare to make more mistakes, for I have sometimes been too concerned to ensure that I had a parachute.

I would take fewer things seriously and relax more readily. I would aim to travel less but see more.

I would devote more time to looking at beauty, and to the observation of nature.

I would always keep a notebook and pencil in my pocket.

Next time I hope that I could feel satisfied that I had stopped whatever I was doing long enough to give a leg-up to at least as many people as had given one to me.

I wish most of all that I could have learnt earlier that nothing is for ever, that the tide turns and the sand-castles of life are washed away. Failure to accept this can lead to much sadness.

Life is a personal evolution. It is scarcely possible, aged twenty or so, to have more than a hazy idea of our potential. Ten years later, our outlook and understanding may have altered completely. In consequence, there are depressingly huge numbers of people living discontented lives, stuck with the wrong career in the wrong place or the wrong spouse, or all three, and I have come to think that this is not only sad but often unnecessary. Life is short and to endure real and continued distress seems pointless and wasteful of the manifold benefits - including health – which fulfilment bestows.

Many people frown at the idea of a pluralistic approach to one's working life. They seem to feel that a 'serious' person cannot chop and change activities or pursue several simultaneously. I have never understood this point of view. It seems to me that people should engage in what they believe in, what they are any good at and what they enjoy. How else can they live a satisfied existence?

The resource to be husbanded with the utmost care is *time*. We know not how much we have and to be profligate is to throw away handfuls of one's own life. To be in a situation where fulfilment is absent or where boredom is the dominant feeling should be to question being there at all. Time spent thus is crushing to the spirit and snuffs out the feverish excitement of Life.

I have failed to bash enough officious bureaucrats, insincere politicians and assorted pompous idiots in this round and I have failed to create enough waves when the hard-won and infinitely precious freedoms of our civilization have been put at risk by successive cowardly governments. Freedom is not won and forever possessed. It must be re-earned every day, in every generation.

People (including me) often hold back from taking action on an issue of great importance. They see the problem but do nothing. 'What,' they say, 'is the point of one person trying to reverse the flow; how can I make the least difference, I am one of sixty million in this country and six billion beyond.' To say this is to forget that to fill the bucket you need many drops of water – *each drop counts*.

In this imperfect world, there is an endless and urgent need to improve conditions - human, animal and environmental. I have been much encouraged to find that quite often a single well-aimed letter to an appropriate individual or to a paper can achieve substantial and occasionally dramatic improvement. It is infinitely worth the effort.

I have learnt gradually to distrust the assertions of scientists with their tunnel-vision specialisations, the contents of newspapers, Governmental reassurances to the public on matters of safety and any pronouncement about anything by the French Administration!

We live at a time when our environment is being destroyed from every angle. Much of the destruction is in the cause of promoting rampant consumerism and thus creating profits for the shareholders of international corporations; a less compelling reason for potentially terminal decline it would be hard to find. Many activities of the World Bank and the International Monetary Fund are designed to facilitate Globalisation - an almost wholly disastrous concept created to favour these organisations. They must be opposed. Globalisation favours the worst aspects of capitalism leading toward an homogenised world in which the poorest are the most exploited, the environment is disregarded and the fundamentally sane concept of regional self-sufficiency is abandoned.

The collapse of British farming is but a symptom. Small farmers who have looked after their piece of countryside for years, even generations, are falling victim to international agri-business, a system which forces the production of the cheapest food, vegetable or animal, sprayed or drugged and sold to rapacious supermarket chains.

At every level of Government the formula of the short-term fix is applied; the future remains unaddressed. Uniformity and mediocrity are the norms within which we are supposed to exist. 'Political correctness' is supposed to paper over social divides and typifies the cosmetic approach to the concealment of problems. Governments seem to have no aims (beyond their re-election) than to satisfy an apathetic public by the encouragement of consumerism and of increasingly trivial, violent and sex-laden television programmes with which to anaesthetise their minds.

There is a need in all of us to feel a sense of pride in our country, something which I find increasingly difficult now and it saddens me greatly. To me, England means the English countryside, its villages and market towns. It also means those people who are its long-term inhabitants and the way of life that they have evolved over the centuries. This is the England that is now disappearing as we watch. What remains I wish to defend with any weaponry that comes to hand. The piecemeal destruction of the country and the rural culture in which I grew up and have loved ever since is fuelled by the urbanised majority here and across Europe. Their understanding, sympathies and values are not rural and they are not mine.

Criticism has been levelled at me from time to time for blowing loudly the trumpet of environmentalism, then engaging in an activity seen as incompatible with the principles expressed.

It is a fair judgement if the critic is an environmental purist. I believe the way to a sustainable world is to encourage people to do *less* of the things which are damaging. Less, much less but not zero. To tell people they must not use cars or they should only have two inches of bath water is, however desirable environmentally, simply not a 'saleable' proposition to most people. But we can all lessen our impact on Earth by employing less damaging ways of doing things. This said, I admit to not having done anything like enough of 'less'.

To those born of a later generation, it may come as a surprise to learn that in my childhood there was no television, frozen foods, contact lenses, mobile phones, ballpoint pens, credit cards, fast food, radar, dishwashers, videos, t-shirts, air-conditioners, photocopying, yogurt, microwave cookers, FM radio, 'disposable' nappies, software, lasers, electric blankets, MacDonalds, oil heating, instant coffee, jeans, supermarkets, dating agencies, plastic, split atoms, men on the moon or men wearing earrings!

Desirable as some of these things may seem, they come with a heavy price. The self-reliance and the stillness of country life seven decades ago has vanished.

Our most precious resources are clean air, clean water and clean soil. These are our birthright and yet they are all under threat. Those who contaminate them are our certain enemies and it is the duty of every citizen to fight them. What kind of health can we expect with the pollution we already have? What kind of inheritance will our children have? Isn't this a world worth saving?

I am aware that there is a Cassandra-ish slant to these closing pages but a recitation of the ills of our time is a necessity if we are to address them positively.

I am increasingly encouraged by the spread of understanding, especially among the younger generation that is now in evidence not just in Britain but around the world. The ease of communication and the emergence of shared beliefs in a fairer and environmentally-conscious society is likely to bring great benefits to Mankind in the next few decades though the process of adaptation may prove to be a challenge to capitalism that it will find difficult, even impossible, to accept.

If only I was half a century younger, if only..!

OFFICE of ARCHITECTURE in BARCELONA

CARLOS FERRATER & PARTNERS

ACTAR

Office of Architecture in Barcelona

Xavier Martí, Alberto Peñín, Carlos Ferrater

Borja Ferrater, Núria Ayala

Lucía Ferrater

This book represents a time for reflection. Since 1970, after forty years of combined professional practice and academic experience, I will attempt to think out loud – not loudly – to step beyond the concerns of everyday work. The document that follows attempts to define a new approach to the architectural project that is both personal and professional.

Until recently, my studio carried out its work in a small office with just four or five employees. Occasionally we collaborated with other studios and contracted specialists to offer their expertise during design and construction phases.

The development of the Office of Architecture in Barcelona (OAB) grew out of these relationships. OAB was established in 2005 by Carlos Ferrater, Xavier Martí Galí and Lucia and Borja Ferrater as a collective platform informed by our past experiences.The early results of this new entity, including projects conceived and completed by the studio in the five years since its founding, are presented in this publication.

OAB draws on the collaborative nature of my previous studio, incorporating new ways of understanding the contributions of each team member to generate richer, more varied, prepared and flexible projects. The creation of this new platform attempts to tackle the challenges that contemporary architecture has raised in intellectual and social, technological and environmental spheres.

Inspired by the social nature of group work and the personal style of the studio's contributors, this book is organized into a collection of chapters; the projects and recently built works convey a willingness to work in different scenarios, expanding and enriching the range of propositions in the pursuit of new avenues of formal expression. The book covers the theoretical aspects of each project, focusing on innovation, research, and the application of new technologies. At the same time, as we explore each project's development, emphasis is placed on context, the building's objectives and the social roots of the architect's work.

OAB has experimented with many aspects of architectural intervention, working on buildings of different sizes and budgets, public spaces, interior spaces, and ephemeral or themed installations connected to the landscape. In each case, we strive to integrate the collective international perspective of our studio. A diverse set of contributors makes our work possible. Individuals work along side collectives – often, we work in partnership with the offices of our former associates, including Alberto Peñín, Joan Guibernau, and Elena Mateu and Juan Trias de Bes. Young architects and architecture students hone their skills under the guidance of Núria Ayala, our project director, and in small groups with OAB's full-time architects.

A series of circumstances led to the birth of this new platform and along the way we have maintained the position that each new project represents a different experience and requires a tailored approach. Furthermore, the platform is built on several basic tenets: embracing innovation and experimentation, conceptual flexibility, and a willingness to offer alternative architectural propositions. Throughout the development of the publication, we must address what we have already learned and remember that the essence of the architect does not lie in language, delineation styles, or process methodologies. Rather, it lies in the architect's unique ability to respond to the conditions of the site and the city, to recognize the social complexity of program organization, to harness the use of light as a raw material of design – with its capacity to generate space and emotion – and to affect sensory perception through materiality. When these skills are harnessed and harmoniously combined, the architect can bring the architecture closer to future users and residents.

I will attempt to explain the circumstances that led to the formation of OAB. First came the decision from a group of young architects, members of my own family, who decided to turn the work of a studio into a collective experience.

Second, the new studio was conceptually enabled and strengthened through the development of a cohesive theoretical corpus, culled from the knowledge we gained from previous project experiences.

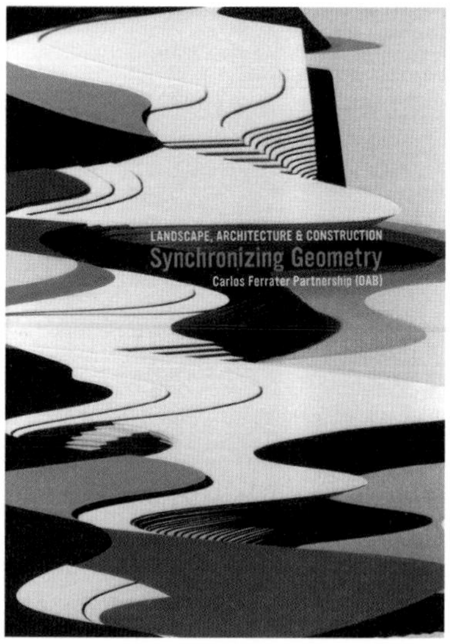

This knowledge is compiled in *Synchronizing Geometry*, an exhibition that documents preparatory procedures for our projects. Our use of open and flexible complex geometries as instruments capable of probing the intellectual conditions and cultural history of places and landscapes allows us to create varied and pointed responses. This instrumentation, from the use of geometry, shapes the organizational and programmatic framework while providing constructive mechanisms that make it possible to convert initial ideas and original concepts into constructed realities.

Following an invitation from the IIT (Illinois Institute of Technology), OAB exhibited documents and models that illustrate theoretical concepts, while arguing for different empirical approaches to architectural inquiries. Exhibited in the lobby of Mies van der Rohe's Crown Hall, the show has since been expanded with new documents and additional models of experimental projects. They are now exhibited in the Schools of Architecture in Barcelona and Madrid, the Bezalel Academy of Arts and Design, Jerusalem, Tel Aviv University and the Museum of Fine Arts Bilbao, among others. The roaming exhibition is continually updated, and will continue to travel to different institutions and universities worldwide.

The third circumstance came about from the importance and necessity of simultaneously designing both the architectural and structural solutions.

In almost all projects covered in *Synchronizing Geometry*, structure is understood as the spatial support of the project, sometimes the structural skeleton is even conceived as a final form of the construction. Thus the reinforced earth walls in the Botanical Garden of Barcelona, the "load bearing" membrane as an urban façade on the Mediapro building, the reinforced concrete sheet that fuses the shapes of the seafront Promenade in Benidorm, the topographic roof of the Science Park in Granada, or the light diaphragm on the roof of the Zaragoza-Delicias Intermodal Station, among other projects, have led us to establish a synchronous collaboration with Juan Calvo, an engineer, whose experience in large civil engineering works, particularly bridges and long-span structures, has given us the opportunity to incorporate our own solutions in to the engineering of the building.

Highly complex post-tensioned membranes such as that of the AA house, the solution of random shells in Benidorm or the actual foundation structure in

the distribution of axial forces in the skeleton of the Mediapro building, have all become both intellectual and constructive proposals. The majority of good Modern architecture, the symbiosis between form and structure, owes a great deal to new methods of calculation for finite elements and the capacity of new computers. These two factors combine to shrink the traditionally strained relationship between form and construction. Though it is sometimes very difficult to understand how structural systems work to support the designed form, an internal structural logic must always be present and understood. How could Louis Kahn design the false vaults of the Kimbell Museum without the cooperation of August Komendant or Jørn Utzon or the sails of the Sydney Opera House without the help of a very young Peter Rice who years later would reappear more mature with Renzo Piano in the Pompidou Centre in Paris? The symbiosis between architecture-engineering that SOM achieved in skyscrapers like the Sears Tower in Chicago, or the works carried out at the end of the century by Ove Arup architects and engineers and especially Cecil Balmond's collaborations with different architects, such as those with Shigeru Ban and Toyo Ito. How do we understand the feat of Sullivan in the Chicago Auditorium Building, at the time the tallest building in the world with an extraordinary constructive and noise resolution, without the help of Dankmar Adler.

The fusion between architecture and engineering can be found in many accomplishments throughout the twentieth century in the work of Eladio Dieste, Felix Candela, Eduardo Torroja, Morandi, Fuller, Tange, Saarinen and so many beautiful pieces that make up a substantial part of modern architectural heritage.

We decided to situate the new studio in Barcelona city centre in the Ensanche Cerdà district, in Carrer Balmes and Còrsega, near Avinguda Diagonal. establishing activities in two different locations.

The first, on Carrer Balmes 145 is destined to house the professional structure and the second on Carree Còrsega 254 is to accommodate cultural activities and academic research. This functional separation allows parallel developments while minimizing interference.

In Carrer Balmes the studio concentrates on initial ideas, models and drawings, the basic structure of the design projects, competitions and sometimes the technical solutions for these works. Here, we try to avoid those cumbersome and bureaucratic aspects that hinder and undermine the fragility of the creative process, encouraging collaboration with partner studios and connections with the work teams who develop the construction on-site, always directed by one of the main architects. This organization allows for greater agility, flexibility and interaction between teams.

The Gallery on Carrer Còrsega receives groups of architects visiting Barcelona, and there are expositions of our model collection, illustrating the moments of greatest creative tension that forms the basis of experimental geometry. In addition, temporary presentations and exhibitions of topics related to the culture of architecture can be found in the Gallery. For example the *Arqtopsias* exposition, the paintings of the "water front" in New York by Maria Rubert or space sculptures by Miquel Planas, also the launch of the book *Las cosas del Señor Tomasso* (The things of Mr. Tomasso) by Juan Carlos Arnuncio who narrated the final days of agony of the architect Borromini, among other activities.

It is also a documentation center that collects and codifies publications, monographs, brochures and videos dedicated to the work of the studio, or an imprint in co-edition with Actar that has published books like *Synchronizing Geometry*, *Casas y habitantes* (Homes and inhabitants) or monographs of buildings like the Catalunya congress center, the Science Park in Granada or the Sunset Beach Promenade in Benidorm.

Finally on the top floor, Borja Ferrater leads a group that carries out research on issues that deal with geometric processes such as complex geometries from the twentieth century, isometries etc.

This working structure allows great flexibility, good relationships between members of the team and it facilitates the inclusion of issues unrelated to the world of architecture that help to enrich the project process. Therefore it is the above-mentioned substantive and structural issues that have led to the creation of OAB as a platform to address the architectural challenges of this new century.

The studio's work can be understood through the concerns, proposals and achievements that travel across the publication's chapters.

Carlos Ferrater Lambarri

Menorca, April 1, 2010

OAB
Office of Architecture in Barcelona

BALMES

OAB

1

Revisiting the Barcelona Botanical Garden. 1989–1999–2009

Carlos Ferrater

The Barcelona Botanical Garden is located on Montjuïc, between the castle and the Estadi Olímpic Lluís Companys, on a site with uneven terrain (altitude between 140 metres and 100 metres). Its shape is reminiscent of an amphitheatre facing the northwest and has an area of about 14 hectares. For years it has been a municipal waste landfill that has been converted into one of the largest green spaces in the city. It offers magnificent views over the Llobregat delta, the Olympic Ring and much of the metropolitan area of Barcelona, with the mountains of the Garraf massif and the Sierras de Collserola and Marina as a backdrop.

The most immediate reference is the Historic Botanical Garden, founded in 1930 by Dr. Pius Font i Quer in the quarries of La Foixarda, Montjuïc and reopened to the public in October 2003. The need to build entrances to the new Olympic facilities in 1986, seriously affected it. This situation helped push forward the proposal to build a new botanical garden in Barcelona, which would house a new building for the Botanical Institute and its collections. It would become a reference centre for the preservation of Mediterranean flora.

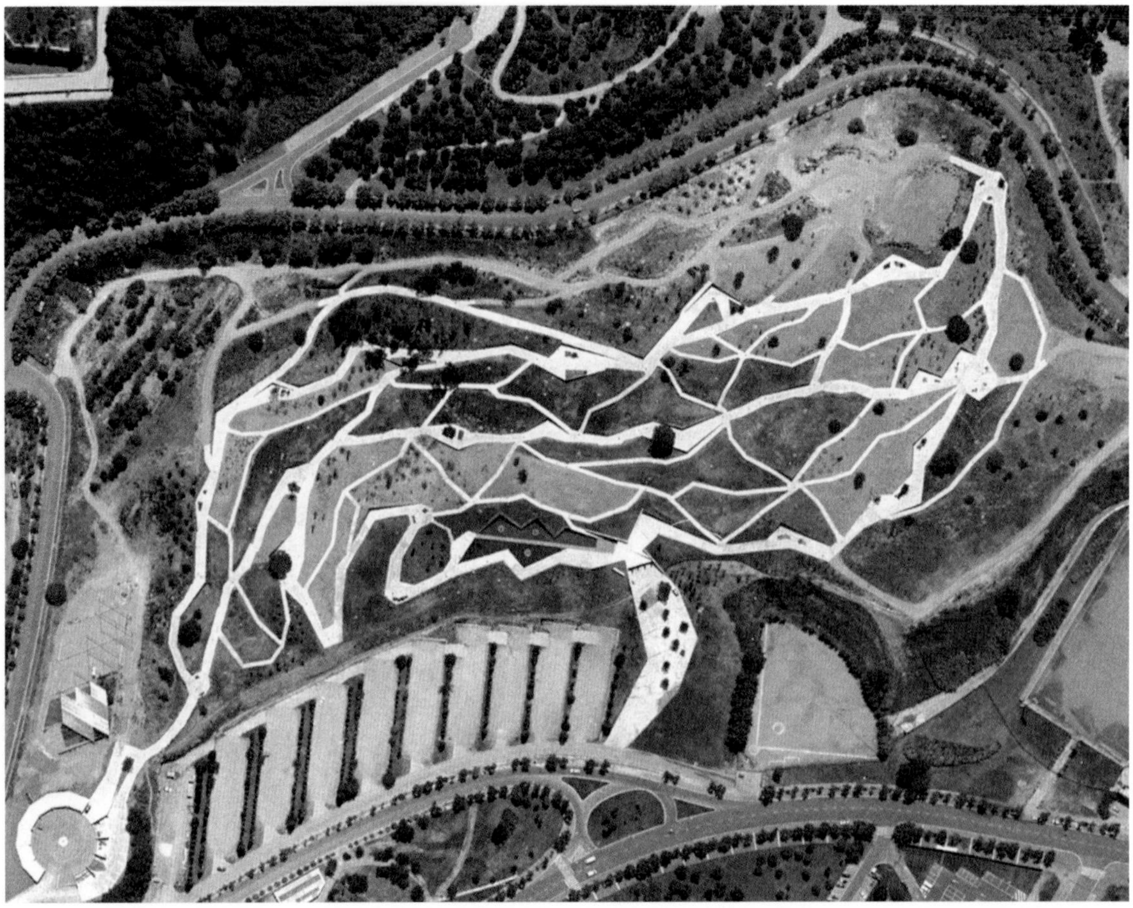

It's been 20 years since 1989 when an international design competition to build a new botanical garden in the mountain of Montjuïc was held.

The proposals had to be developed by interdisciplinary teams consisting of architects, landscape architects, botanists, biologists, engineers, etc. In the failure of a unanimous agreement by the jury, the remark by Maria Aurèlia Capmany on the fractal and Mediterranean condition of our proposal played in our favour, a view that was the deciding factor for the jury, declaring us the winner of that competition.

It has been more than 10 years since 1999, the year in which construction of the garden was completed and the first plantings were carried out. I think the time has come to intellectually and physically compare and analyse if that first abstract proposal to superimpose a grid on the land, to work scale-free and to incorporate a few certain constructive mechanisms, operating on sustainable principles, has allowed us to create a new landscape on that landfill. And, on account of the transverse nature of the proposition, which in principle could be regarded as the structure of the garden, i.e. the network of paths, walls and interstitial spaces, today forms the shape and decoration of the gardens, while on the contrary, the vegetation and plant communities today make up the scientific structure of the garden. The original grid has been visually diminished but it still remains as an intrinsic and natural order of a new landscape. At the end of the intervention, the boundary between natural and artificial, between structure and ornament, has gradually become undetectable.

In recent years, a series of new additions, further expansion of the network of paths, plantations in the areas of Australia, California and the Mediterranean as well as new infrastructures such as the multipurpose outdoor space, have completed the former intervention.

It is for all the abovementioned reasons that 20 years since that first competition and 10 since the construction of the garden, it is appropriate to revisit and review those principles, as well as the method for approaching a project and how to proceed in terms of construction.

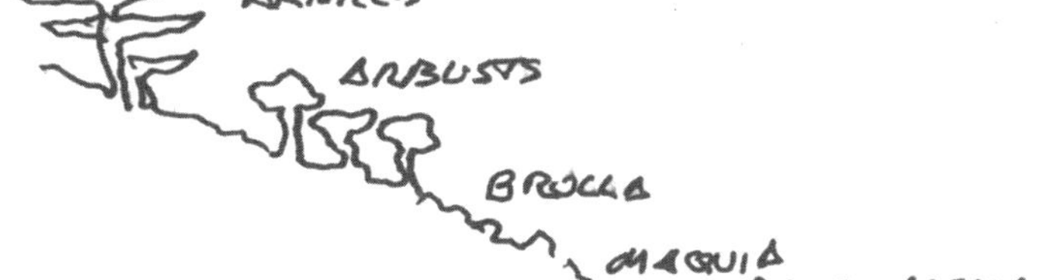

Fractal construction of the landscape

When an interdisciplinary team consisting of biologists, botanists, landscape designers and architects initiated the project for the Barcelona Botanical Garden, on the mountainside of Montjuïc, we raised two key considerations:

The first consideration was how to achieve a project argument in which the actual site provided the construction guidelines, placing emphasis on the morphological and topographical conditions of the new landscape. Unlike other urban and architectural interventions carried out at Montjuïc, this project is totally different and has been based on universal exhibitions, Olympic Games or other unique events.

The second consideration involved the structure of the new garden, which had to include the Mediterranean flora as well as those from other homoclimatic areas, California and part of Japan in the northern hemisphere and in the symmetrical parallel of the southern hemisphere, a part of Chile, South Africa and a small region of the Australian coast. The layout of the new garden would be based on botanical and ecosystem issues, as well as the use of the convergence concept of plant morphology, becoming a tool of high scientific value and a part of the future of twenty-first century botanical gardens.

The synthesis of these two intentions would only be possible if we were to have an instrument capable of promoting dialogue and the joint work between the different disciplines, an impossible task in the early days of the project. This is how the idea of a triangular grid on the site emerged. The grid would have to adapt to all unevenness, fraying at the edges and increases or decreases in the surface according to the varying topographic slope. The guidelines of the triangular grid would follow the three main directions of the contour lines, thus ensuring that two vertices of each triangle were at the same level, slope line 0. Other subdivisions of the grid in accordance with the concepts of accessibility, plantation, etc. would maintain the same structure.

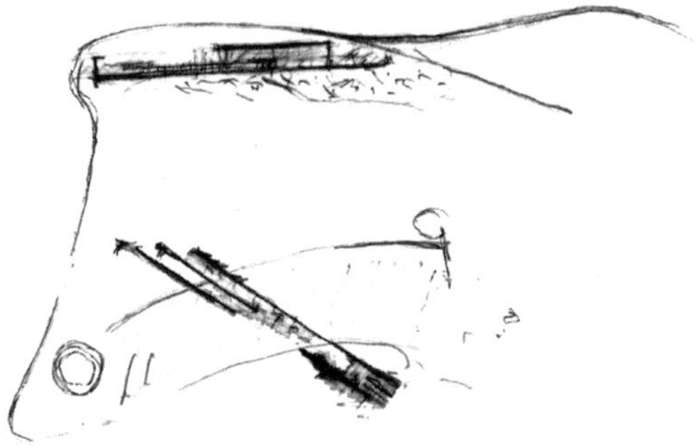

This irregular and variable geometric order according to its situation on the ground would permit us to:

—Simplify the hidden infrastructure networks, drains, irrigation, computerisation of the garden, etc.

—Give the territory a hierarchical network of routes, depending on the use and the slope, establishing primary or secondary routes, relating to work in the garden, etc.

—Provide order to the territory that would make it possible to use the garden for scientific, educational and leisure purposes in the future, ordering the mosaics of the various plant communities.

—Prepare the fundamentals of the project simplifying the organisation of future constructions: herbarium, greenhouses, shade houses and research and services buildings, following the same logic of intervention.

Using a personal computer we put together a programme through which we could visualise the grid, identify any triangle and the species planted within. All this was displayed with photographic evidence so that finally we could attain the specific or detailed file of any of the species in the triangle. This project mechanism would allow us to achieve a certain level of control over the form of the future landscape, which was our primary goal.

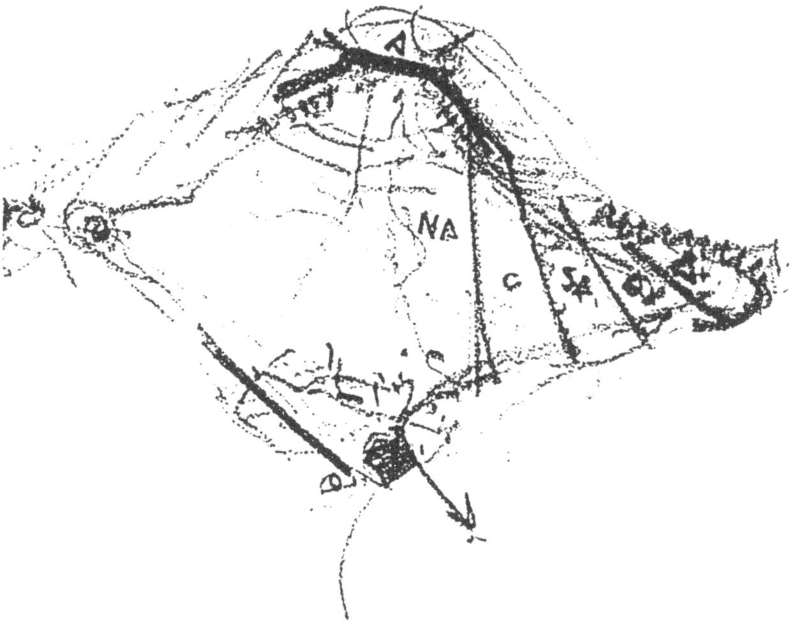

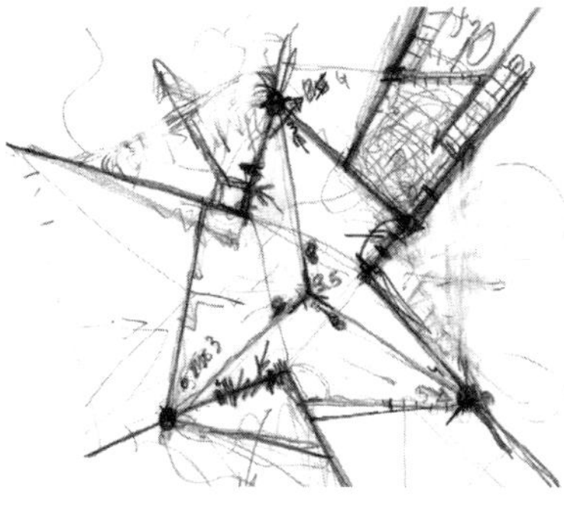

Slightly altering the heights of the vertices of the triangles, the grid becomes fractured and the land begins to unfold new planes, so that every piece of the ensemble has a unique orientation and slope. There is also information on the requirements of sun, water quantity, ease of planting and relationship with other species in these files.

The construction system that will make it possible to fracture the grid, will consist of a set of double concave or convex triangular walls that vary in height, length and turning radius. These walls will enable the landscape to acquire order and a fractal dimension, organised on the basis of irregular and segmented forms. After the planting is carried out the excessive initial virtuality will subside, remaining only as an inherent order to the construction of the garden. This method with an ultra artificial component from the outset, will eventually take on its own fractal dimension of nature, achieving, in the words of J.M. Montaner, a future synthesis between the ecological balance of the plantations and the artificiality that the constructed infrastructure gives the area.

The logic of the intervention occurs in the scale-free dimension, in the project mechanisms used, which is distant from final size of the interventions. The initial outline and measures will not be necessary to delve deeper into the project. It will be the use of the triangular grid which will divide and fragment the landscape, while solving the complex demands of the project.

Carlos Ferrater

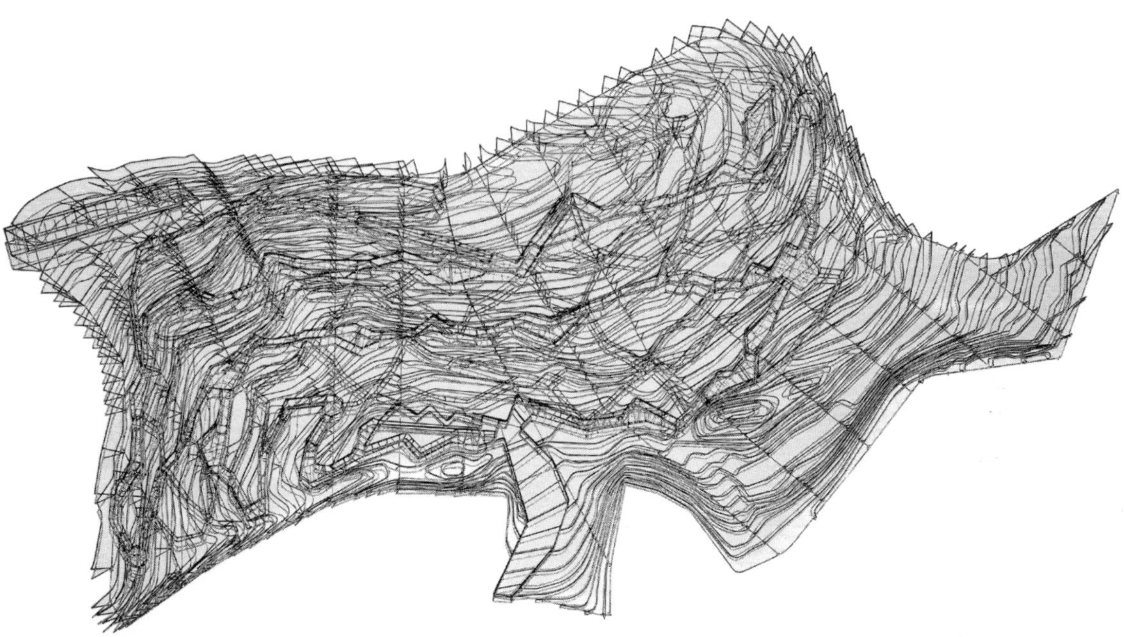

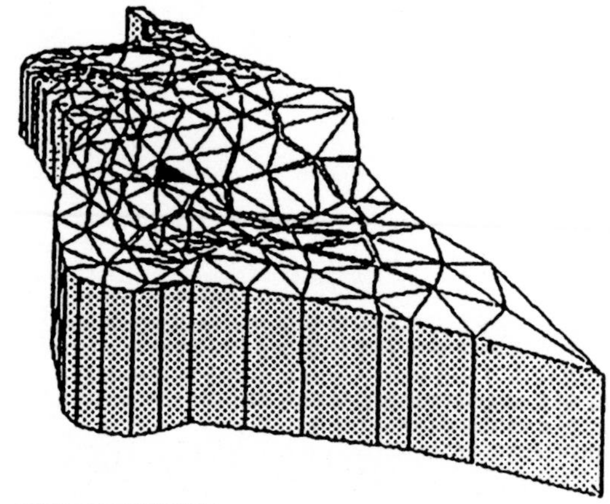

Generatrix

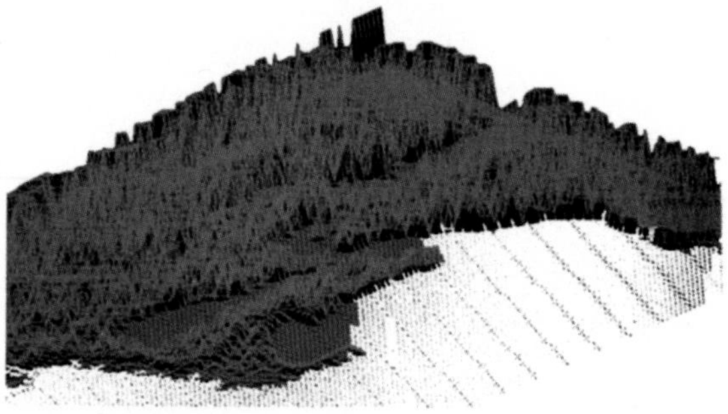

Vertex elevation

The Garden project employs a triangular grid structure fractured with concrete paths that adapt to the terrain and arrange the routes, the construction and infrastructure, while allowing the harmonious distribution of vegetation units.

The Garden displays a representation of the flora from regions around the world with a Mediterranean climate. Mediterranean vegetation is considered one of the richest in species diversity. It is estimated that only 1.7 percent of the Earth's land surface has a Mediterranean climate, but those regions account for 20 percent of the world's flora and more than half are endemic. Today, Mediterranean vegetation is severely threatened mainly due to human activity. For this reason, the Garden has two main objectives: to contribute to the preservation of plant species and to create awareness, increasing public respect for nature and the value of biodiversity.

The Mediterranean basin (between 30° and 45°N latitude) is not the only region with a Mediterranean climate. There are other areas of the planet, located at the same latitude in the northern hemisphere or an equivalent latitude in the southern hemisphere, which also have this climate. These areas include south and southwest Australia (between 27° and 37° S latitude), the south of South Africa (between 30° and 35° S latitude), central Chile (between 30° and 37° S latitude) and eastern California (between 30° and 42° N latitude). Together they form the Mediterranean biome, a set of remote plant and animal communities far apart in terms of space but with similar characteristics due to climatic similarities.

The floral richness of these areas and the similarity of their plants and landscapes are the main source of inspiration for the Barcelona Botanical Garden.

Botanical Garden
Barcelona

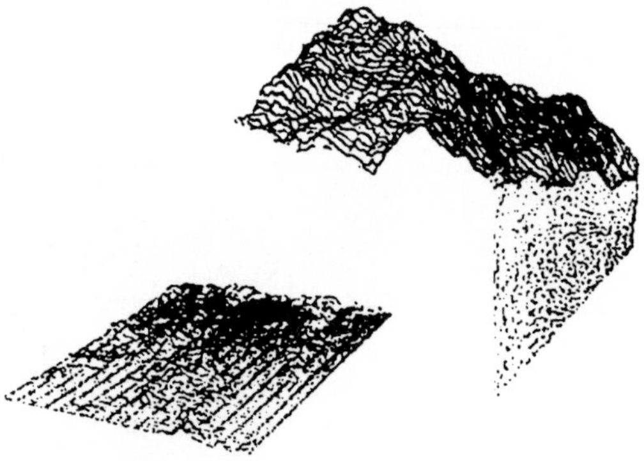

Fractal islands

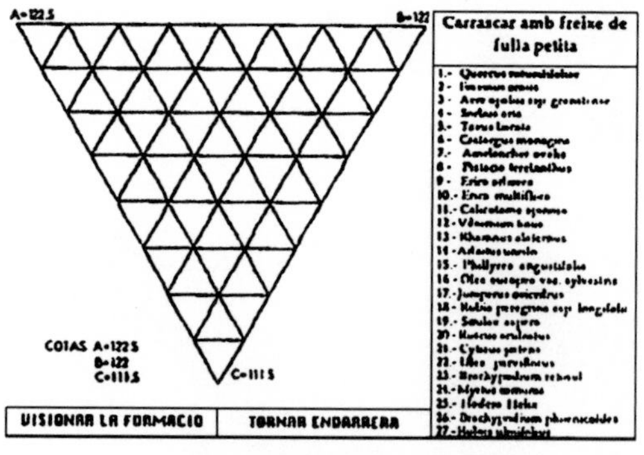

Plant community programme

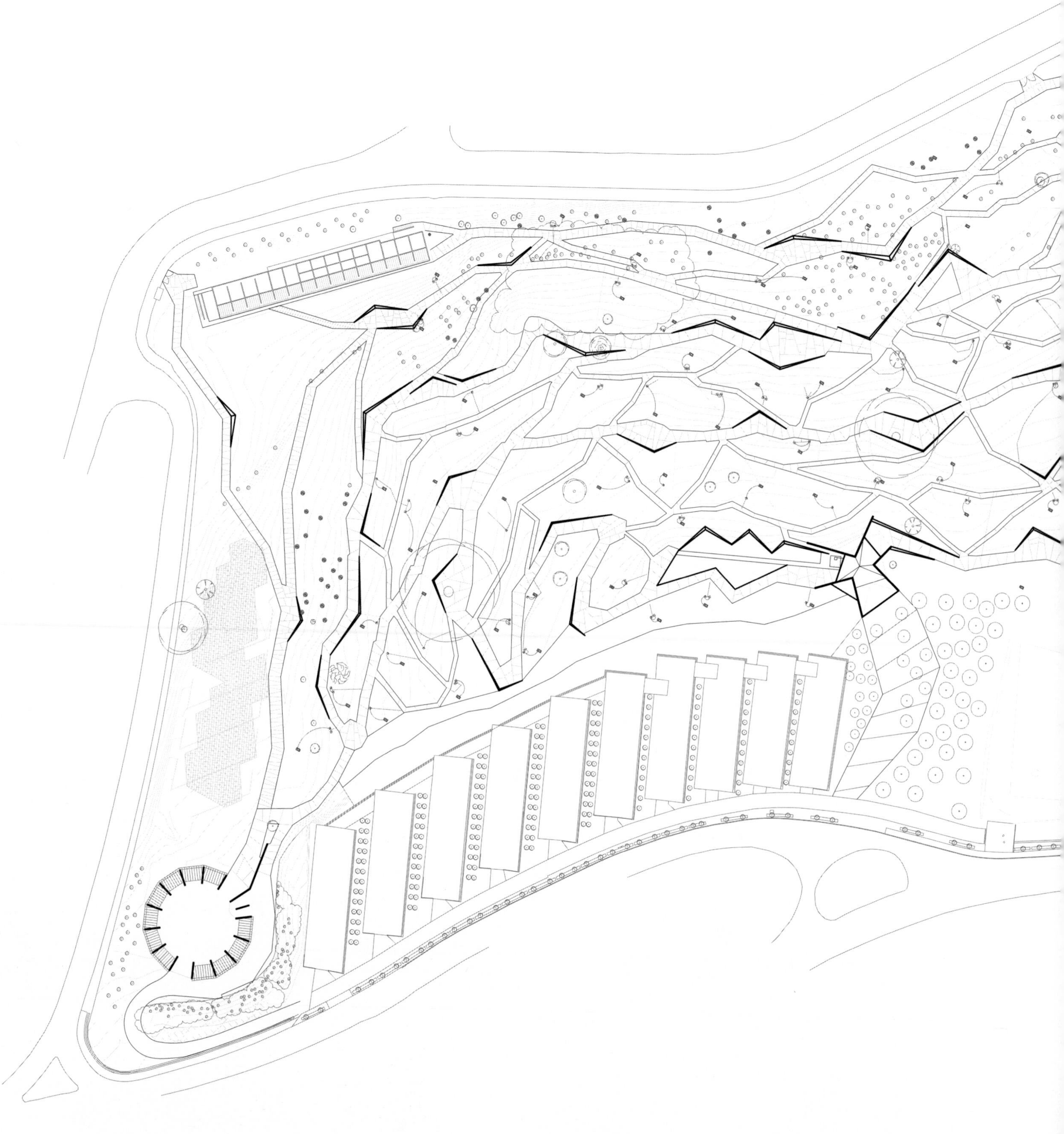

General plan

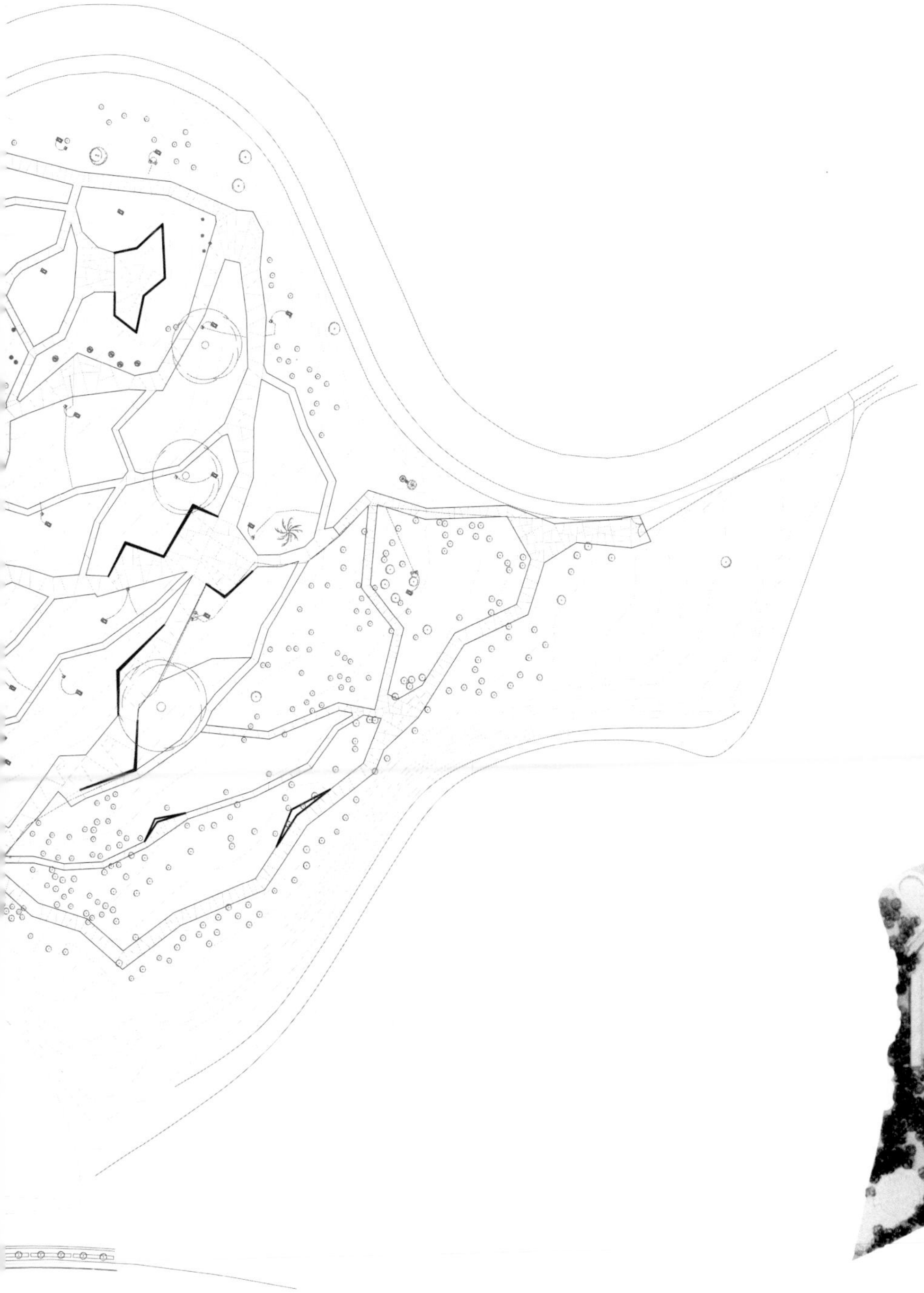

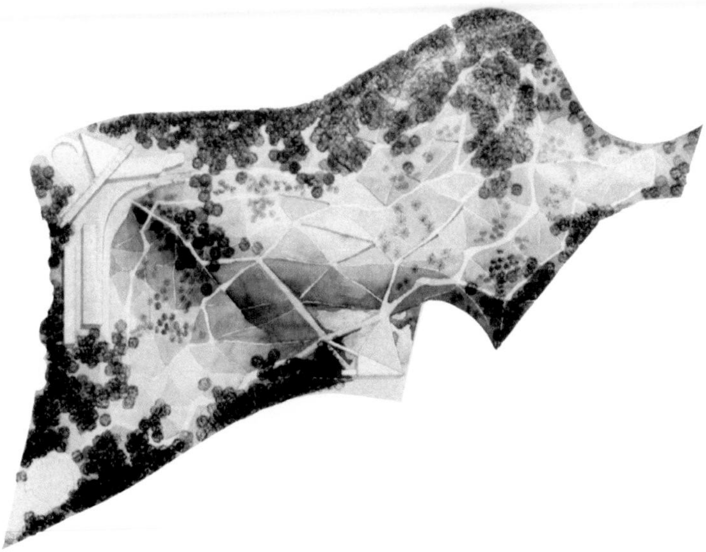

Watercolour drawing (80 x 65 cm)

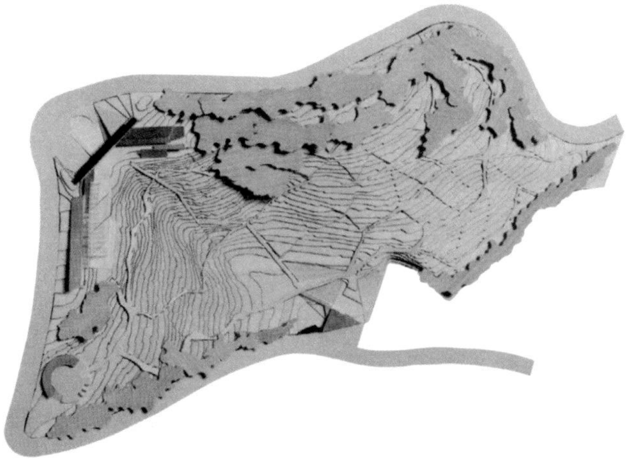

Scale topographic model made with different types of wood (50.5 x 70.5 cm)

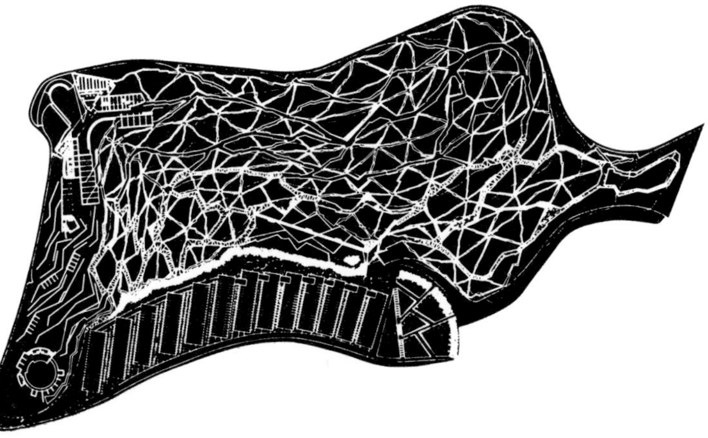

Original grid

The Garden offers collections of Mediterranean plants distributed according to geographical areas (Australia, Chile, California, South Africa and the Mediterranean basin) and, in turn, grouped according to the landscapes that they form in nature. These groupings, called phyto-episodes (plant communities) are the exhibition and management units of the Botanical Garden. There are currently 87 phyto-episodes. The forests communities are located in the highest areas and those dominated by shrub-like plants can be found in the central and lower areas.

Australia. The Australian Mediterranean region, with 700,000km², is the second largest (accounting for just over 20 percent of the biome). It is formed by two separate sectors, located in the southwest and south of the continent. There are some 8,000 known species, 75 percent of which are endemisms. The climate is Mediterranean with some tropical influence due to the proximity of the ocean monsoons, so the summer drought is not as rigorous as in our Mediterranean area, but even so the frequency of fires is high.
In the Australian area of the Garden, in addition to its characteristic Mediterranean flora, warm flora from the southwest of the continent are also cultivated (the states of Victoria and New South Wales). Both the tree-like and shrub-like plants are dominated by a large number of species from few families, such as the mimosa (Acacia), Myrtaceae (Eucalyptus, Melaleuca, Callistemon) and Proteaceae (Hakea, Banksia, Grevillea).

Chile. The Mediterranean area of Chile is a narrow coastal strip of about 100 kilometres corresponding to the region of central Chile. Its area is 140,000km² and it represents less than 5% of the biome. Climatically, it has a rather cool character marked by the influence of the ocean, with plenty of coastal fog. There are some 2,400 known species, 23 percent of which are endemic. An important ecological feature of this area is the historical absence of fire, and a marked presence of herbivores, in particular camelids (llamas and guanacos). There is, therefore, an abundance of thorny bushes and plants are not adapted to fire.
The Chilean Mediterranean area has a variety of sclerophyllous landscapes (plants with stiff and rigid leaves), with woodland and shrub formations including the sclerophyll forest to the coastal scrubland, and including "el espinal" or spiny hillside scrublands. Many Chilean plants have the names of Iberian plants as early settlers compared them to those they were familiar with.

California. The Mediterranean area of California occupies a narrow coastal strip from Cape Blanco, in the United States, to Punta Baja, Mexico, with the centre more or less in San Francisco. To the east, the strip extends about 100 or 200 kilometres inland. Despite its small size (about 10 percent of the total biome), it is the area with the largest continuous expanses of unchanged Mediterranean landscapes. There are some 4,300 known species, 35 percent of which are endemisms. Climatically, the seasonality is very pronounced as 85 percent of the rainfall is concentrated in the winter.

The summer droughts are very severe but the coastal fog partly relieves this contrast.

South Africa. The South African Mediterranean area is the smallest of all and represents just 3 percent of the biome. There are some 8,550 known species of which 68 percent are endemic. Rain is most intense in the cold season however it is never very abundant. Moreover, due to the summer influence of tropical monsoons, there is no completely dry season. Despite the presence of the Mediterranean climate at the two ends of the African continent, the flora of this region has few genera in common with the Mediterranean basin. The diversity of soils, climate and topography, together with geographical isolation and the recurrence of fires, have led to very high diversity and to the proportion of endemic and rare species making it, along with the southwest of Australia, the highest of the Mediterranean areas and one of the richest in the world.
In the Garden, the Mediterranean area of The Cape, the subtropical territories of Karoo and Savannah and temperate zones of the south-eastern forests are represented.

Mediterranean Basin. The quintessential Mediterranean area is the Mediterranean basin, i.e. the lands surrounding the Mediterranean Sea. It stretches across European, Asian and African territories and has an area of 2,300,000km^2. There are some 25,000 known species, of which 50 percent are endemic. Mediterranean flora has many solutions to adapt to the ecological factors that have influenced its evolution. Rigid and persistent leaves to resist the dry summer, spikes, thorns and toxic substances to defend themselves against herbivores, low plants in the form of a pin cushion, or shrubs that lose their leaves in summer to reduce transpiration. The great capacity for the regeneration of plants in the Mediterranean basin (five times higher than those of the California chaparral, which is the area it most resembles) clearly shows the importance of centuries of human intervention. Humans, with the help of ploughs, fire and cattle have profoundly shaped Mediterranean plants and landscapes.
The flora of the Mediterranean basin has been distributed in the Garden in four bio-geographical sub-regions: eastern Mediterranean (between Italy and the Caucasus), western Mediterranean (Iberian Peninsula and Balearic Islands and Tyrrhenian), northern Africa (from Morocco to Tunisia) and the Canary Islands.

The Botanical Institute of Barcelona is located within the Garden, it a research centre with a long tradition in Catalonia, which maintains the main scientific collections created in the country for more than three centuries. The current building, opened in 2003, includes an exhibition hall open to the public, where you can visit the Cabinet of Natural History. The Salvador Museum was the first museum open to the public in Barcelona.

Text taken from the *Col·lecció de Parcs i Jardins de l'AMB*

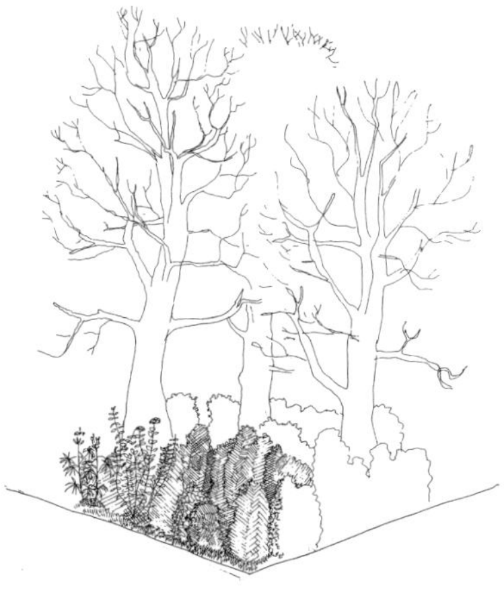

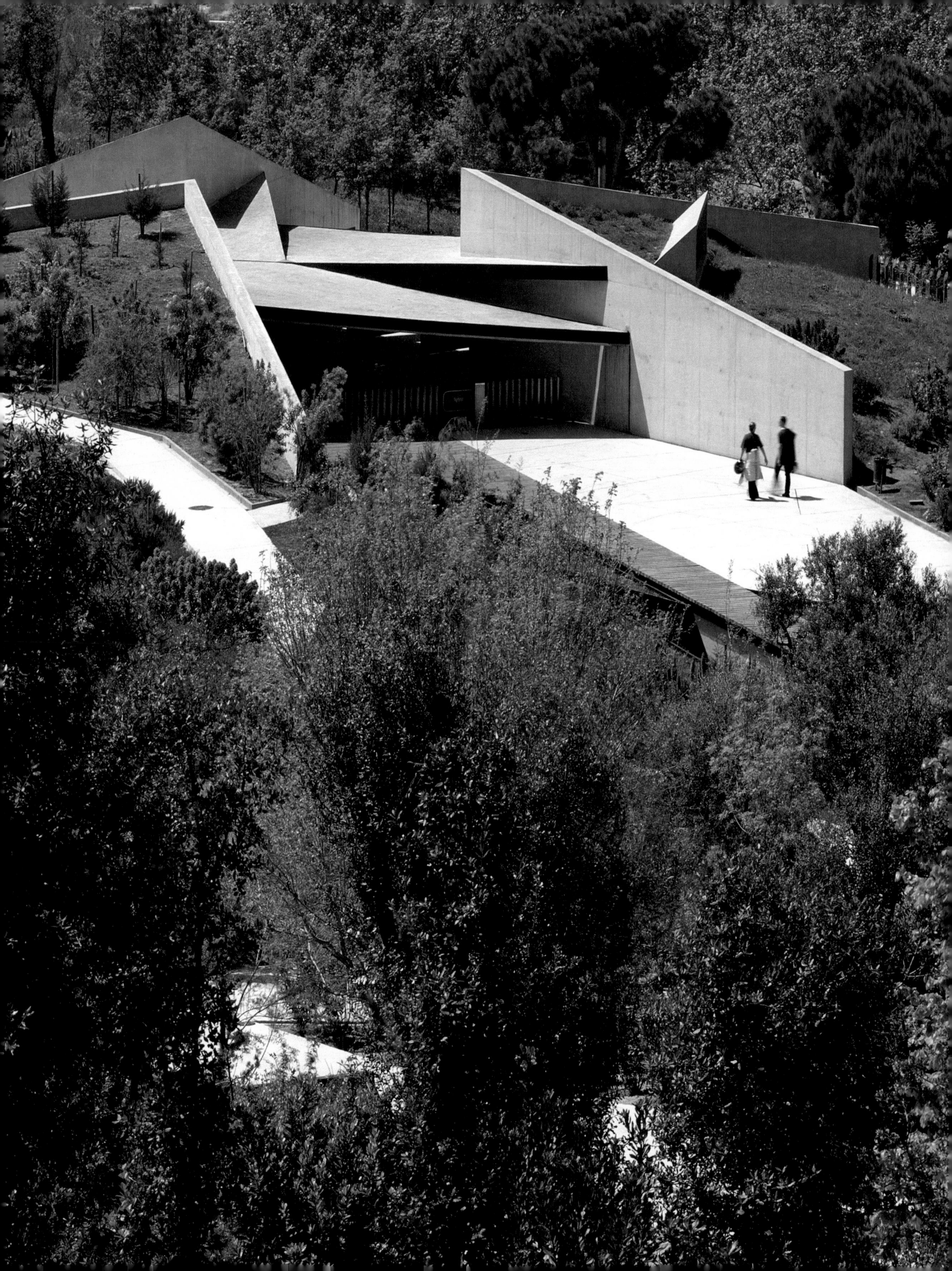

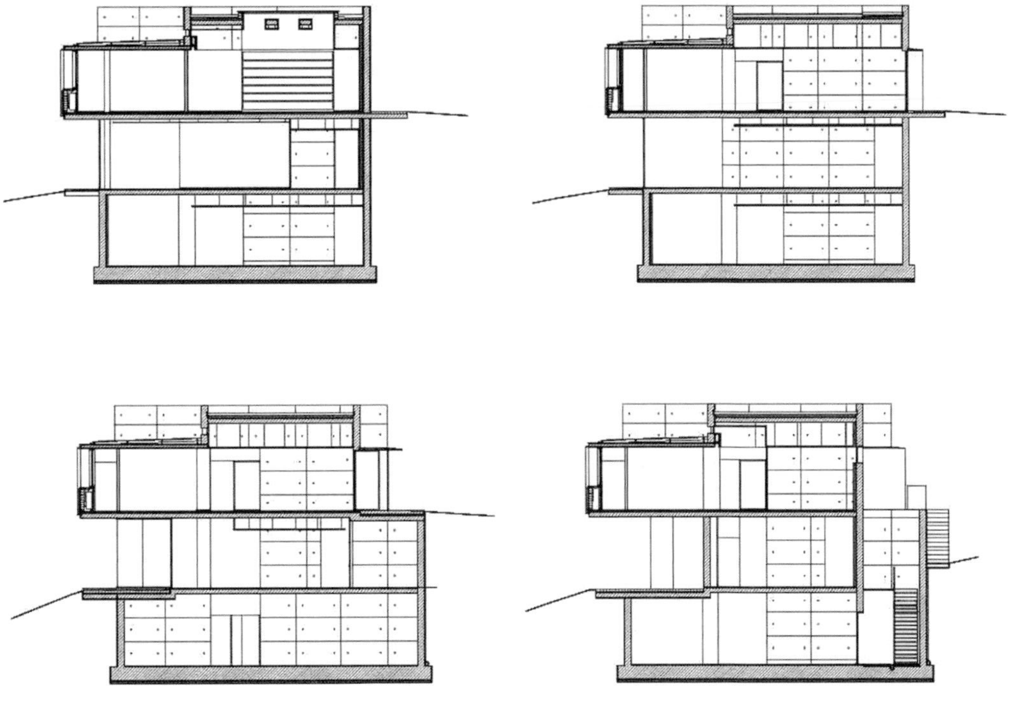

Cross sections

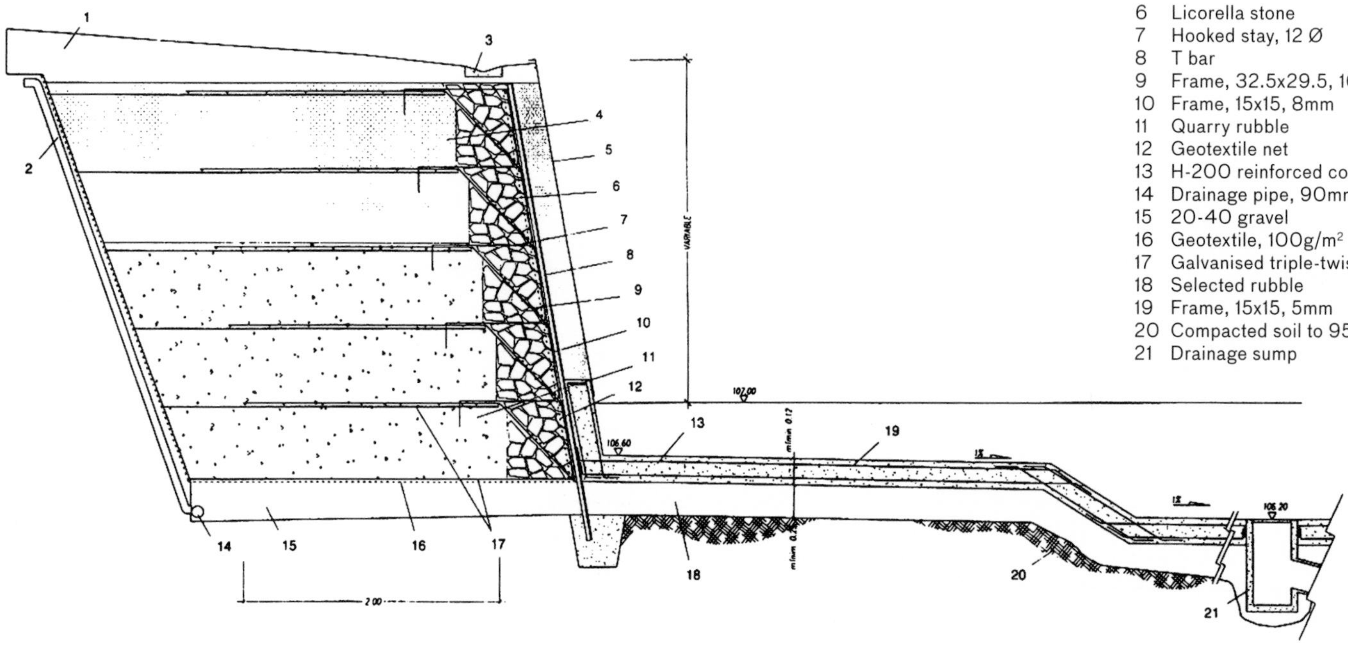

1 Compost
2 Drainage
3 Concrete ditch
4 Selected soil
5 3mm corten
6 Licorella stone
7 Hooked stay, 12 Ø
8 T bar
9 Frame, 32.5x29.5, 10mm
10 Frame, 15x15, 8mm
11 Quarry rubble
12 Geotextile net
13 H-200 reinforced concrete
14 Drainage pipe, 90mm
15 20-40 gravel
16 Geotextile, $100g/m^2$
17 Galvanised triple-twisted mesh
18 Selected rubble
19 Frame, 15x15, 5mm
20 Compacted soil to 95% avg. porosity
21 Drainage sump

Section of reinforced wall

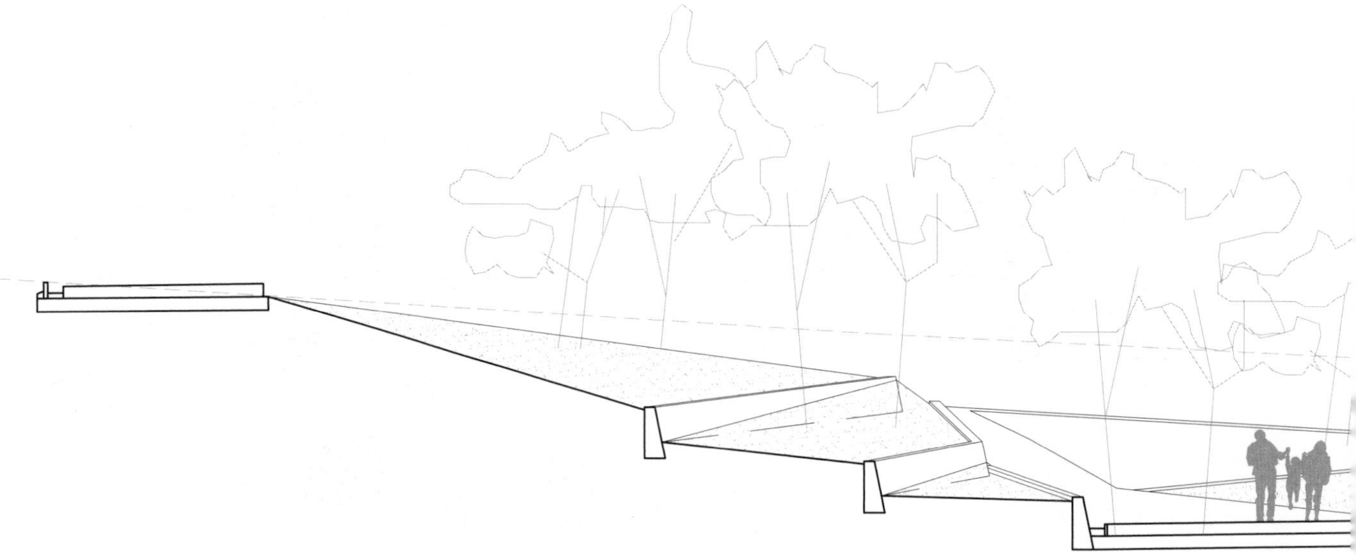

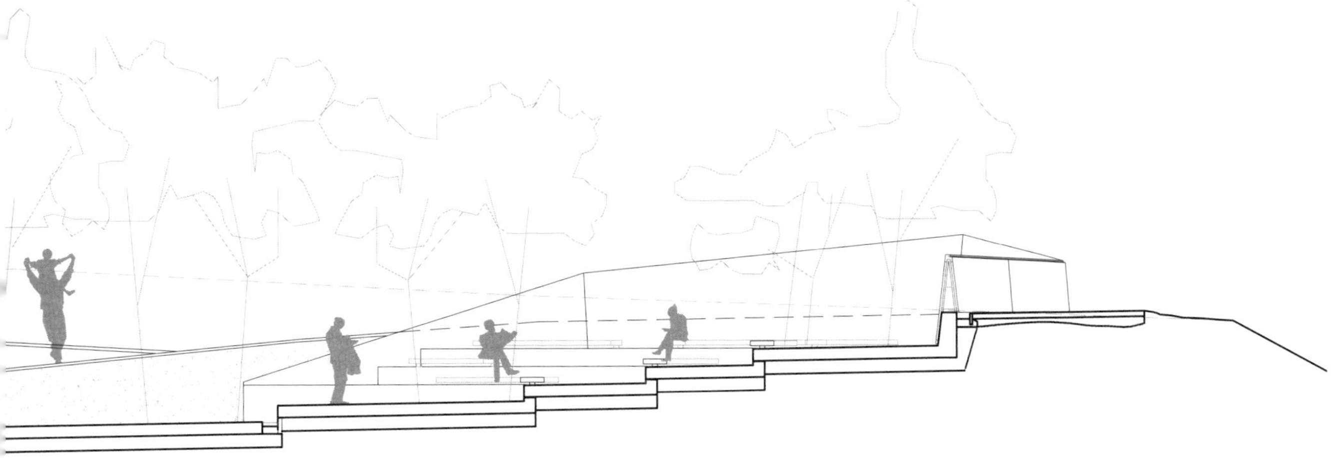

Carlos Ferrater

"Rascahorizontes"

The eastern side of Montjuïc facing the Ronda del Litoral and the port has a steep cliff and a profile degraded by erosion. It passes between the beautiful cemetery and the themed gardens of Costa i Llobera. You could say that it is the contrasting section or the extrados of the Botanical Garden's transept.

The actual geology of the stone of Montjuïc, its almost vertical section and coastal horizon, encouraged me to apply for the international with competition in which Barcelona City Council requested a solution to "els cims de muntanya de Montjuïc" to literally attach a group of buildings to the mountainside at different heights using cantilever construction in which different activities had to be located: from a centre of worship next to the cemetery, programmes for city and port facilities, to horizontal structures to support the gardens as an extension of those existing in the Eastern sector.

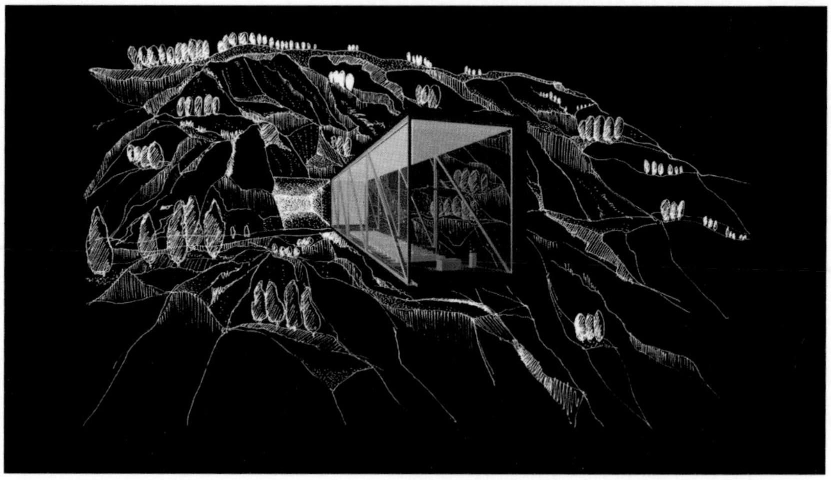

The term "rascahorizontes" (horizonscrapers) known more commonly as "rasca-suelos" (landscrapers) challenges the term skyscrapers, although from a structural point of view they have a similar root. Both are two cantilevered corbels subjected mainly to the lateral force of the wind as the weight of a skyscraper creates a smaller force compared to buckling due to slenderness or horizontal forces.

We had to make the most of the stone support of the mountain as had to be done in Manhattan with the granitic subsoil to find structural mechanisms that made it possible for bracket structures to perform efficiently. With the help of Juan Calvo, our regular co-worker, we devised a system that would strain the upper part of the large central support beam making it work in tension and tighten deep anchorages while the lower section was compressed against the rock mass distributed over a large surface. A ring system distributed throughout the large central bracket helps to distribute the force while the outer shell that forms the living areas of the building is reinforced. All the installation networks and services are located longitudinally inside this large central beam while an exterior linear corridor is embedded and suspended in the lower section of the "horizonscraper" resolving the escape route that continues along the emergency staircases which are also suspended. A large column contains the lifts that ascend from the base of the mountain acting as a strut that secures the cantilever.

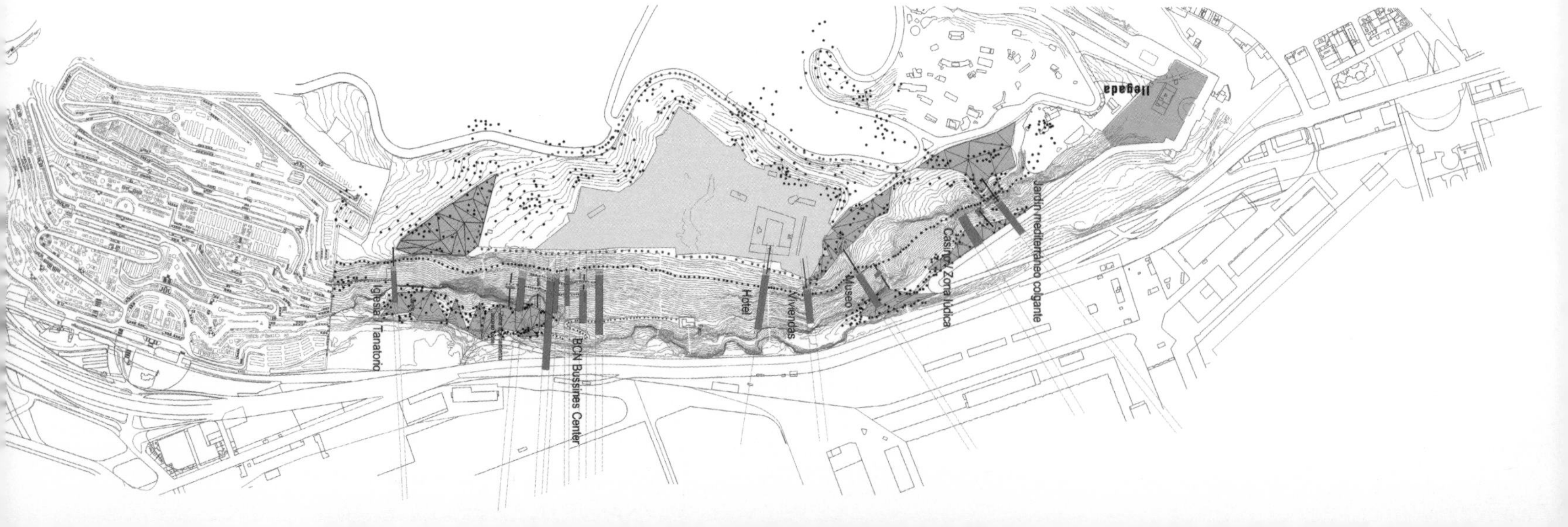

With a 12 x 12m useful section, the programme is structured on three levels and is organised around two fire compartments. The first in the cantilever and the second inside the mountain, both converging at the meeting point of the vertical communications and horizontal and vertical escape routes. Beyond the formation itself and its interest as a structural or constructive piece, the idea and concept is to propose to the city of Barcelona a coastline where "horizonscrapers" with different lengths of up to 150m and different altitudes create a scene of complementary activities for the coastline giving the city a distinct and original character avoiding competition between cities that build their "skylines" based on skyscrapers that are increasingly higher and more technologically complex.

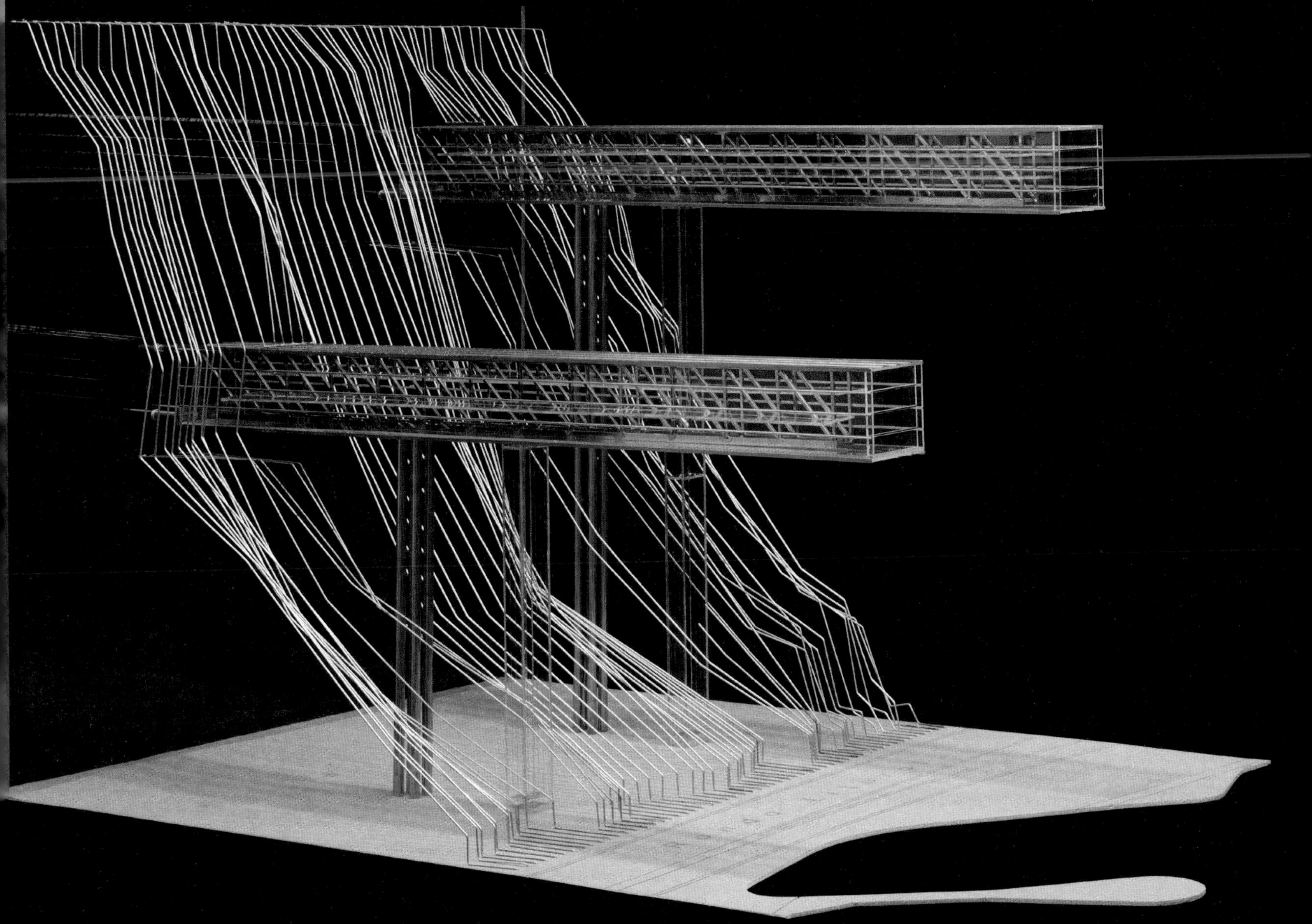

2

Residential architecture and the city

Carlos Ferrater

This chapter addresses the issue of multifamily housing, showcasing two buildings simultaneously over time that respond to different typological programmes, small apartments in the case of the Vertix Diagonal building, and larger-scale housing in the M3 building in Plaza Lesseps. Two spaces in transformation in the city of Barcelona, the first in the recently created Diagonal, and the second in an area that has undergone many changes in recent times.

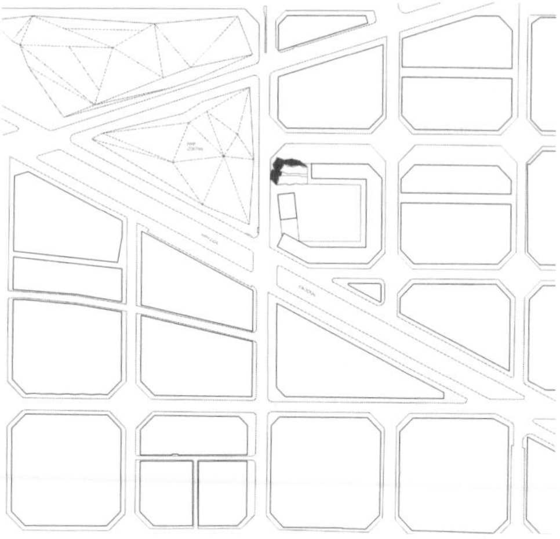

Vertix Diagonal building

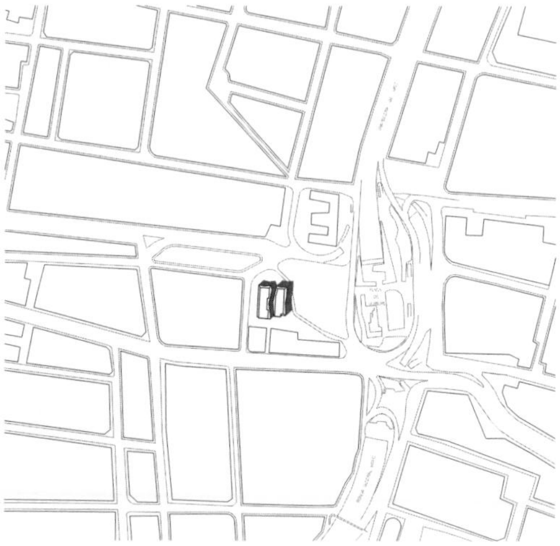

M3 Lesseps building

Both buildings pose questions that deal with the construction of the city, defining urban areas from the architectural project, while raising substantive issues on typological diversity and the construction of flexible and lightweight façades that encompass sustainability, environmental control and Mediterranean traditions.

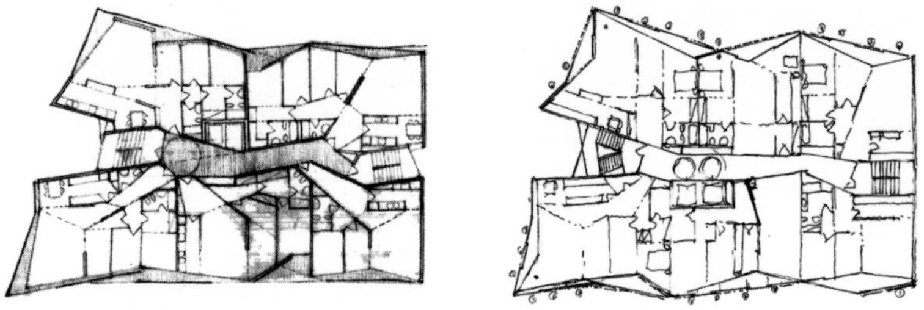

Sketch for Vertix Diagonal building

Carlos Ferrater Xavier Martí Galí

Vertix Diagonal building

In Barcelona's new Diagonal, opposite the Central Park designed by Jean Nouvel at the end of the north arm of the block, there is a residential building with a twofold purpose, first as the façade of the open block of the Cerdá Plan, and secondly, that of an autonomous piece.

Six apartments per floor organised around a zigzagged corridor that links the two vertical circulation cores and designs the communal space and light towards the exterior.

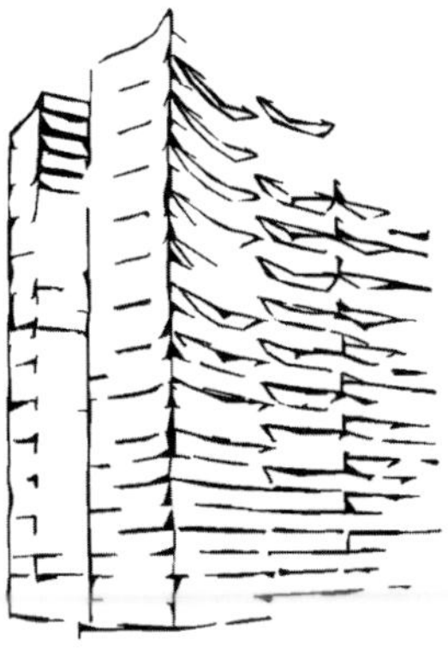

The houses have intermediate spaces that are obtained on the basis of the winding, different levels of the façade, where the sliding blinds are arranged on the interior and exterior thereby maintaining privacy and light control but at the same time helping to create open spaces that link the exterior and the interior, making the separation walls of the homes unnecessary.

The configuration of the building allows for a variety of typologies. This versatility is reflected in the development of 1, 2 and 3 bedroom apartments on one floor.

The dimensions are defined by the treatment of the outer skin. Black-painted steel ribs form the skin of the building, while solving the intertwined form of the metal slats and interior glass around the perimeter of the façade. Fractures in the skin are found in spaces housing stairs.

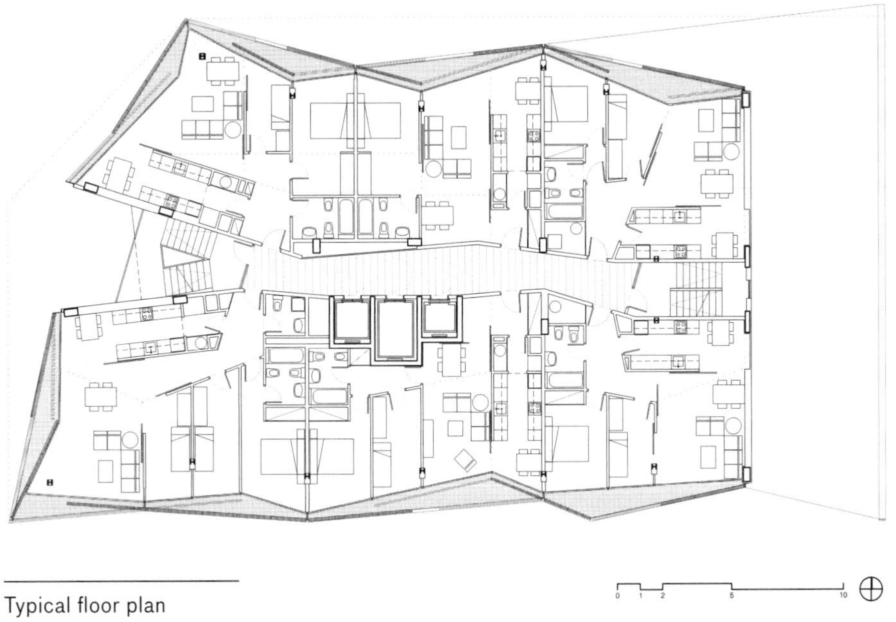

Typical floor plan

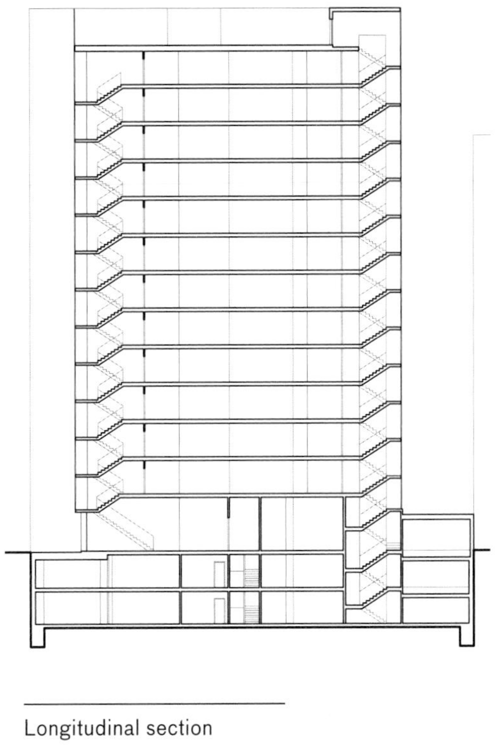

Longitudinal section

The projects presented in this chapter experiment with the intermediate space that is formed at the boundary between the exterior and interior areas of the home. The mobile or fixed shutter elements help to create a place that acts as a climate filter, regulating the level of privacy and solar control, creating spaces that become an extension of the house, something that José Antonio Coderch de Sentmenat experimented with when he built houses for fishermen in 1955, on Paseo de Juan de Borbón, in Barceloneta, opposite the port of Barcelona.

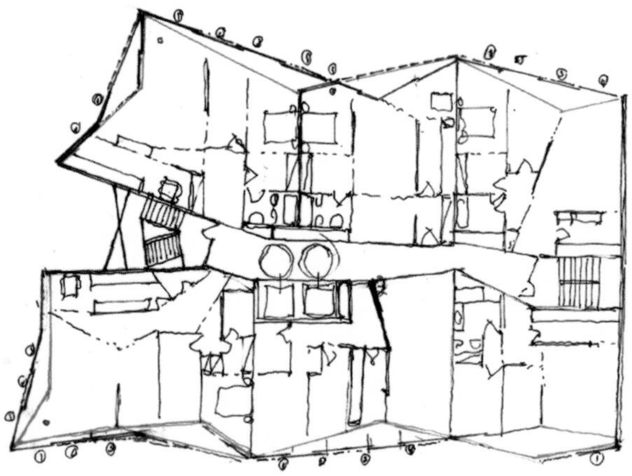

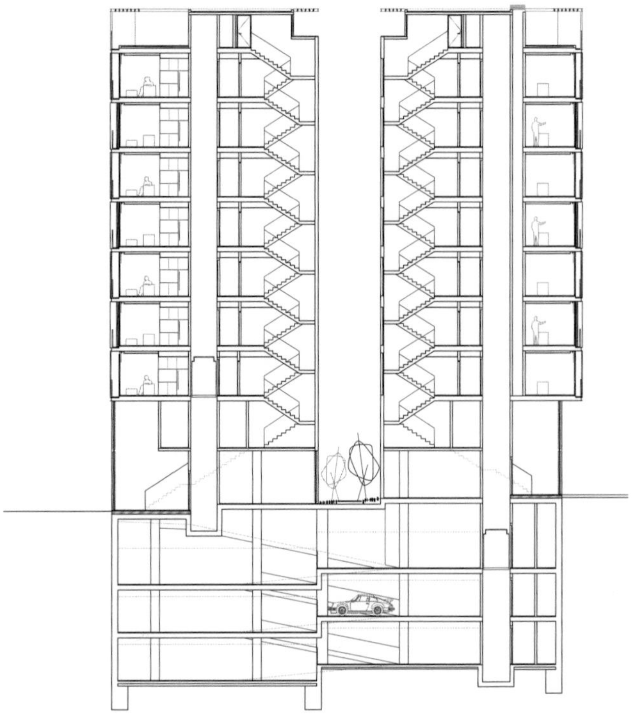

Typical floor plan

Cross section

Carlos Ferrater Lucía Ferrater

Lesseps Metro-3 Building

This building adheres to the specific volume criteria outlined it in the city of Barcelona's new metropolitan plans. The opening of a new passage and the expansion of the Avinguda del Hospital Militar shape the physical framework and regulations of the intervention.

The project proposes the division of the building into two separate volumes with an open space as a continuous courtyard. This decision makes full use of the space with lights reaching 2.5 metres, allowing all the rooms to be naturally ventilated.

The open space setting of the building between blocks in a longitudinal direction, allows for a shift in the corner that contains the double wall of the building, emphasising the fracture volume.

Access to the premises on the ground floor is created by the space between the blocks and also from the streets. The car park is divided into three basement floors accessed via a ramp next to the party wall with access from Carrer Riera de Vallcarca, this being the lowest point of the site. There are four different entrances to the apartments, two located on the north façade and two on the south.

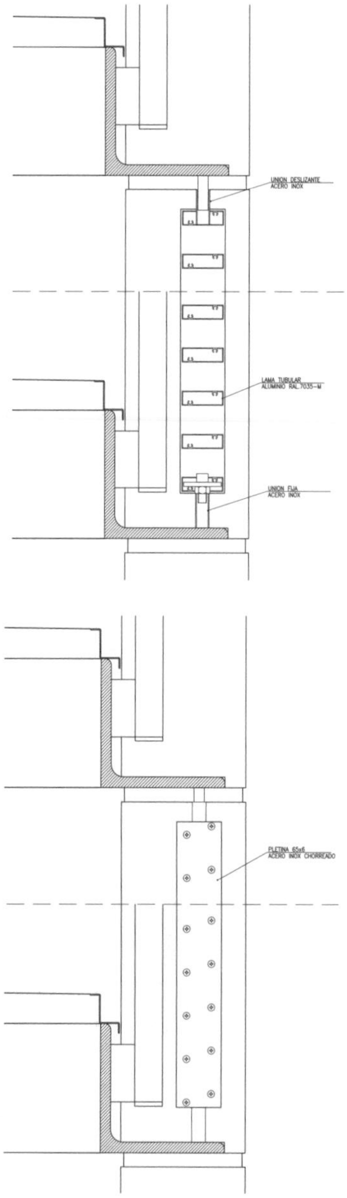

Wall detail

The façades offer a set of fixed and sliding metal shutters that open and close the terraces and allow for better integration of indoor-outdoor spaces, regulating daylight. These shutters, made of stainless steel, transverse tubular crossbeams lacquered in pearl grey. They are framed by fine steel railings forming a grid where the vertical bars create a rhythm and the horizontal beams refine the pace of the framework. This latticework façade, along with the interior glass planes, wind around the entire perimeter creating interstitial spaces, transition areas between the city and the interior inhabited space, a heritage of Mediterranean architecture.

The building, next to the Joan Fuster library, has been constructed as a symbol of the new Plaça Lesseps in Barcelona.

3 Intermodal

Carlos Ferrater

Zaragoza-Delicias Intermodal Station

The international design competition for the Zaragoza-Delicias Intermodal Station, which the Ministry of Development convened among a selection of Spanish and foreign architects including Norman Foster, Santiago Calatrava, Ricardo Bofill, Richard Rogers, Rafael Moneo and Ábalos & Herreros, allowed us to work in and explore a field that until a few decades ago was exclusively reserved for the world of transport infrastructure engineering.

The TWA terminal in New York and the Foster Dulles terminal in Washington, both projects designed by the Finnish architect Eero Saarinen were milestones in airport architecture and in recent times we have witnessed extraordinary airport projects designed by architects such as Stansted by Norman Foster or Kansai airport by Renzo Piano.

Working with large flows of people, mobility limitations and Intermodal connections between different transport modes are all fundamental points: High speed trains, buses and coaches, large changeover areas and car parks for public and private vehicles demand the effective management of changing between different modes of transport making the process more fluid, more agile and quicker.

Departures lounge

Arrivals lounge

This was one of the challenges raised by the Zaragoza-Delicias Intermodal train station, a city in a blurred territory, with the high speed train it has become an important node located 75 minutes from Barcelona and Madrid and in the future Valencia and Bilbao making it a key station for connections with Europe. This meant that the design of the station had to allow for a quick and efficient connection from all means of transport to the high speed train. For this reason the station is equipped with double arrivals and departure halls as well as a transfer hall that lies below the tracks, although it is assisted by natural light and in a few minutes via remote-doors allows private car users, public transport, coaches or trains to access the high-speed trains. This layout is similar to how an airport operates; a typological experimentation for new twenty-first century stations.

Intermodal Train Station Zaragoza

Delicias station is structured as a major hub of growth in the city as was El Pilar in its day. Delicias station helps to merge two districts, it is the backbone for the Expo towards the river Ebro and it has become a nucleus for the services sector and installations, which are all located around the large 40,000m^2 structure (equivalent to the size of eight football fields). The station has a roof suspended by large arches and a tetrahedron mesh that offers natural light, good acoustics and a good level of environmental comfort while retaining the spatiality of the traditional station.

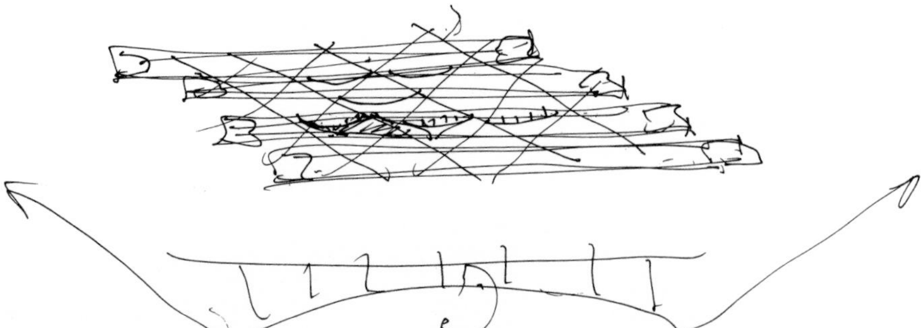

Altaria

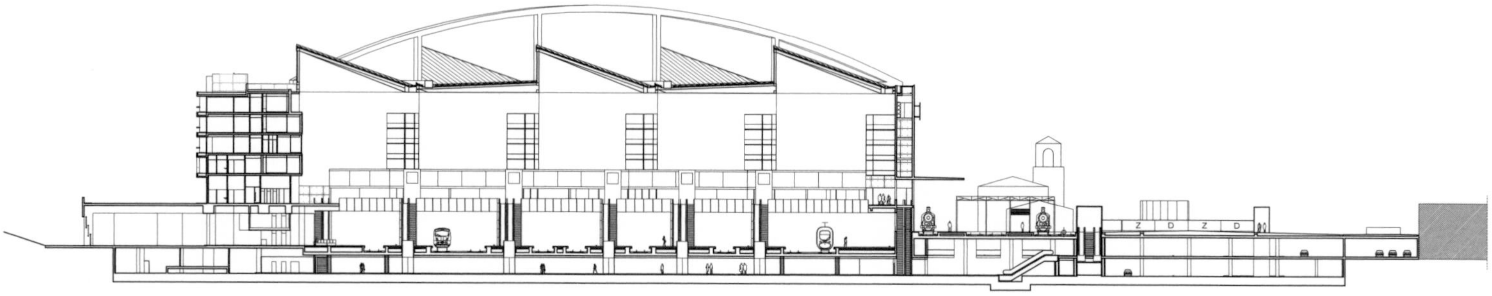

Cross section

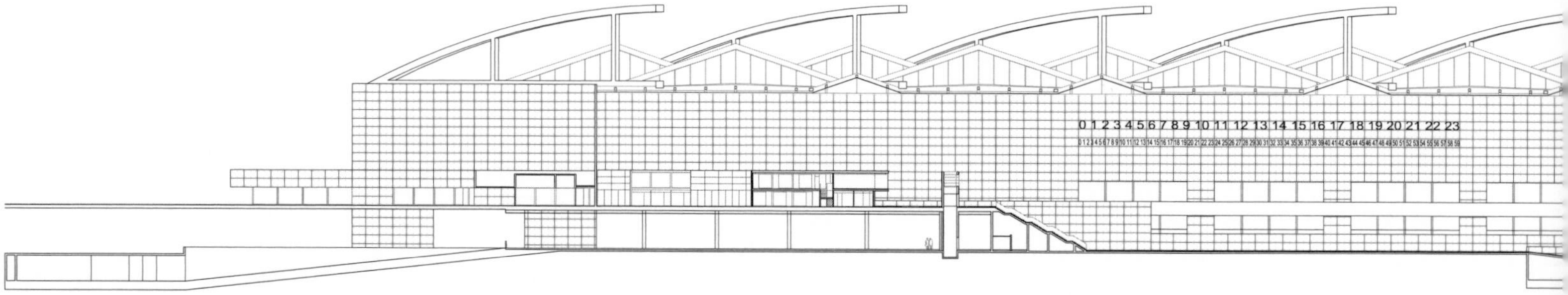

Longitudinal section

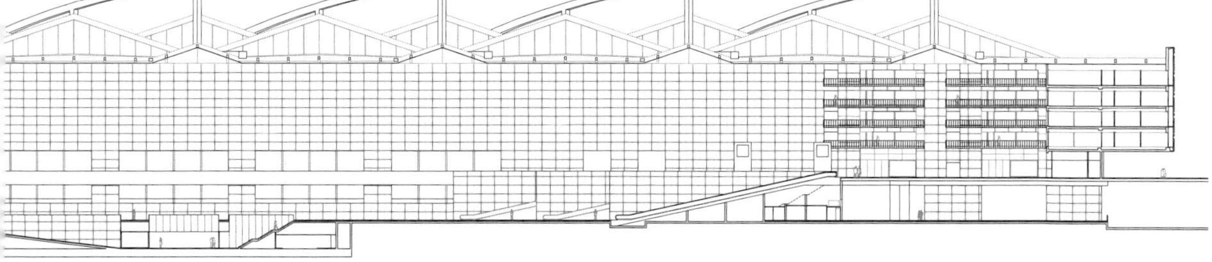

Intermodal Building at Barcelona Airport

After the experience in Zaragoza and being named finalists of the competition for the new terminal at Barcelona Airport, we decided, along with Ramon Sanabria and J.M. Casadevall, to set up a studio to develop projects in the field of transport infrastructure collaborating with various engineers. This has allowed us to carry out several projects in the airport of Barcelona such as the multimodal building, which we are currently working on, the façade of the new city airport and the Line 9 station at terminals 1 and 2. We are also working on the construction of Murcia airport after winning the competition organised by the Ministry of Infrastructure in 2008. Though perhaps to date, our greatest achievement has been the completion of the Intermodal building at Barcelona airport. The project has a neutral and opaque façade built with sleek aluminium profiles and the frieze by Joan Miró put the finishing touch to the enclosure between the old terminals A and B.

The building, an independent volume with glass skin on its four faces provides the gradual fusion of natural and artificial light by giving this new space a floating and apparently empty sensation even though the building is full of travellers.

Both the train station in Zaragoza, which earned the 2004 Brunell award, and the Intermodal building for the airport of Barcelona that earned the Flight International Award, raise questions about generic space. A station that becomes a micro indoor city where hotels, restaurants, office buildings, convention centres, shops or cultural activities, transmits a hybrid co-existence between the traditional public space and generic space advocated by Rem Koolhaas.

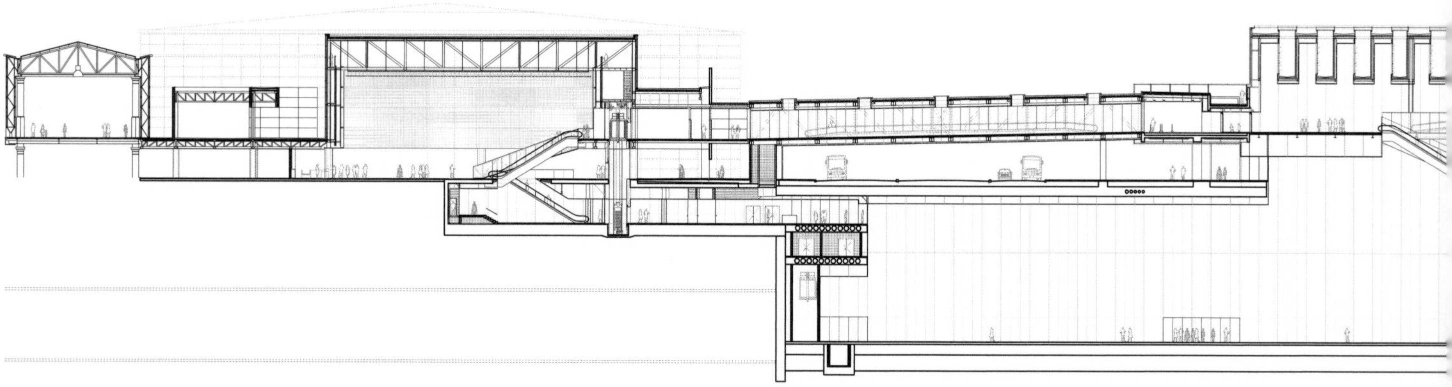

Longitudinal section

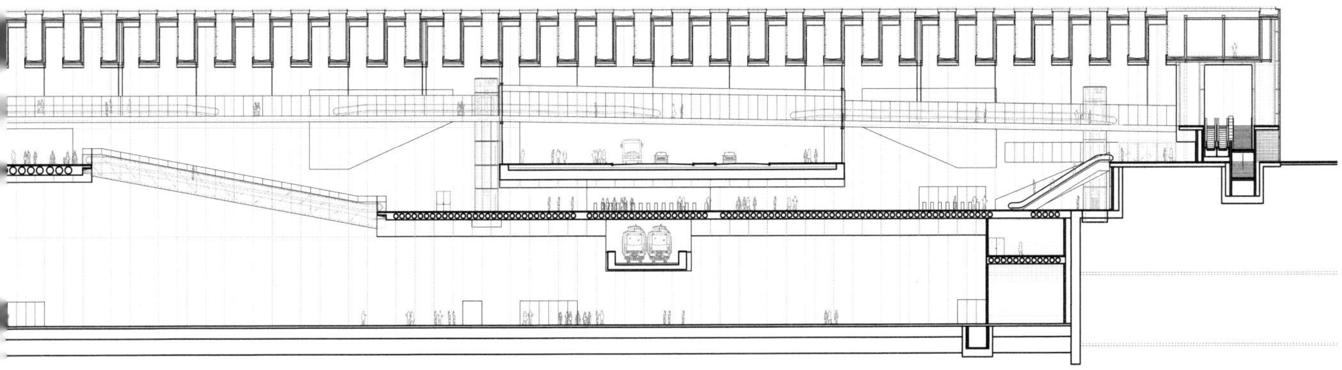

4

Rediscovering the Eixample morphology

Joan Busquets

The development of the Eixample Cerdà has become a laboratory for the evolution of architectural and urban forms.

We could say that the special contrast between the geometric rigidity of the Cerdà Plan and complexity of the geographical order of the "Llano de Barcelona" – formed by a system of roads, drains and properties – resulted in the morphological development of the Eixample, which at first sight seemed contradictory, but perhaps it is one of the reasons for the great spatial richness and diversity of its built-up and functional system.

It is common knowledge that the initial hypothesis of Cerdà to reserve much of the centre of the blocks as free and collective spaces was immediately overturned after its approval due to the increasing need to fill these spaces for industrial and large services. This initial proposal has been solved by recent activities, such as the new city ordinance of 1985 to free up the centre of the block for landscaped areas and, in some cases the block's courtyard has been reserved for public use.

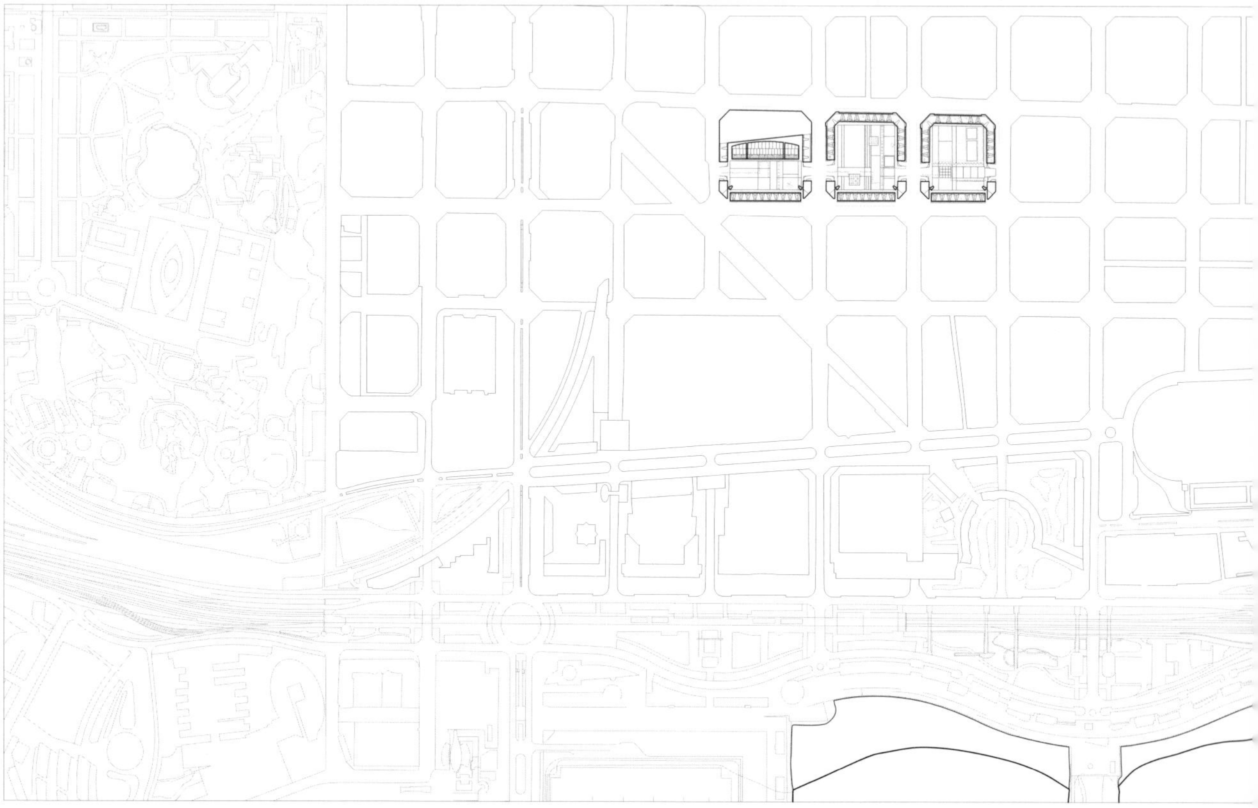

Three blocks in the Eixample, 1992

The development of Eixample for over more than 150 years has consolidated a model of the closed block building, concentrated in the membrane of the block by establishing two well-defined situations: streets and corners. This has established a fairly constant system that different generations of architects have gradually used less frequently with many different stylistic hypotheses and programmes. As we celebrated the 150th anniversary of the Cerdà plan at the exhibition in the CCCB, we tried to investigate this hypothesis of mapping relevant examples following those two situations: either in a line i.e. following a street, or on a corner, i.e. solving the encounter between perpendicular streets. This exercise tests the richness of this typological laboratory i.e. the Eixample, in which it is clear that the stylistic conditions are nothing more than an accompaniment in regards to other crucial dimensions such as the insertion of the functional programme and/or the width of the plot on which the architecture is developed.

This recent research reveals the series of proposals by Carlos Ferrater and his team in the formation of a universe of typological proposals of great interest in both the situations mentioned above: whether “corner” or “line” that following the tradition already established by the MBM office in the sixties. These efforts are of great value because they are limited to private promotion operations and therefore are rarely given to research projects involving any risk. Several proposals for in line buildings and especially corner decomposition forces are particularly praiseworthy as in most cases they are infill operations within the existing structure and therefore subject to the residual logic of some of these plots.

Semi-open blocks with houses inside

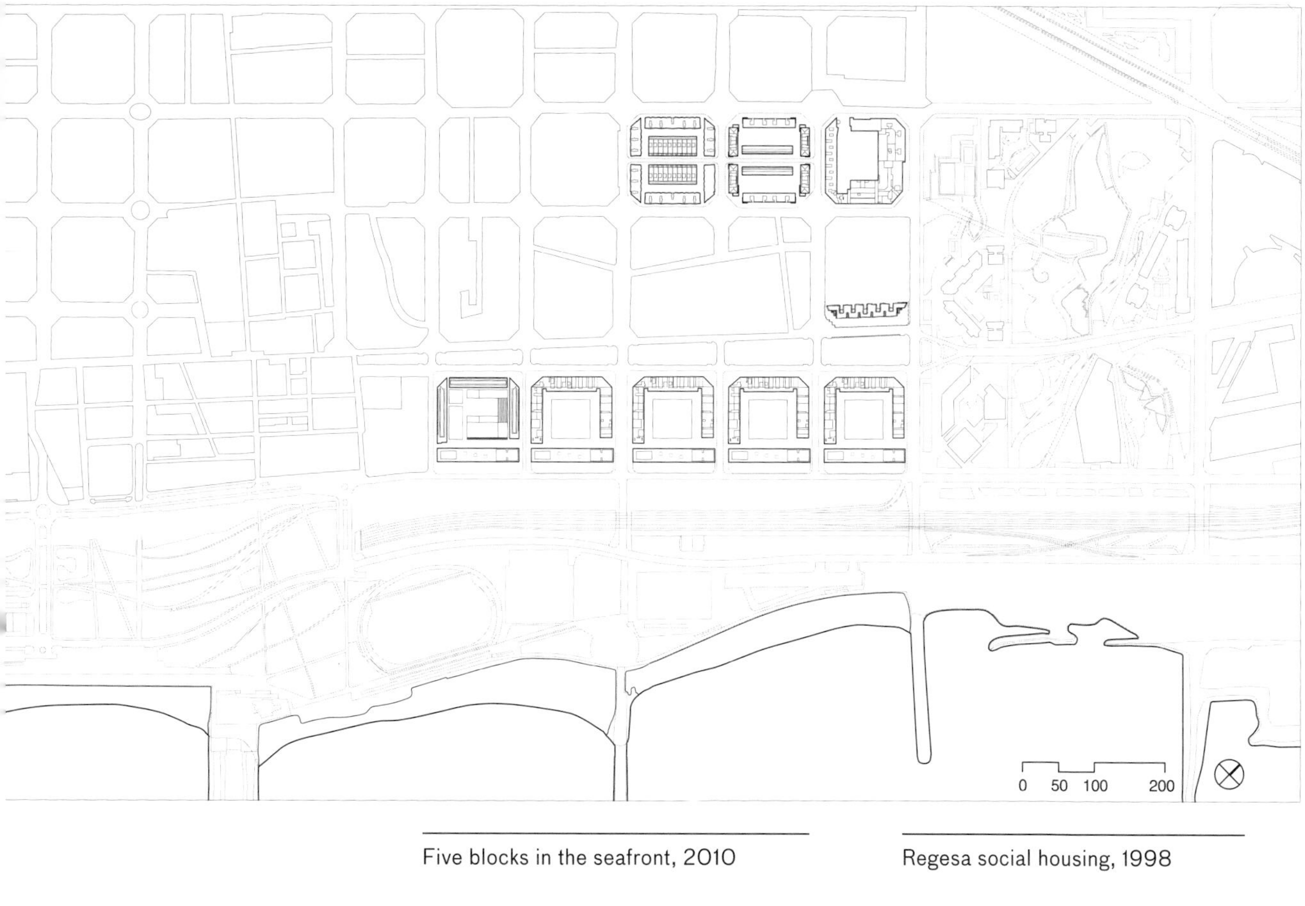

Five blocks in the seafront, 2010

Regesa social housing, 1998

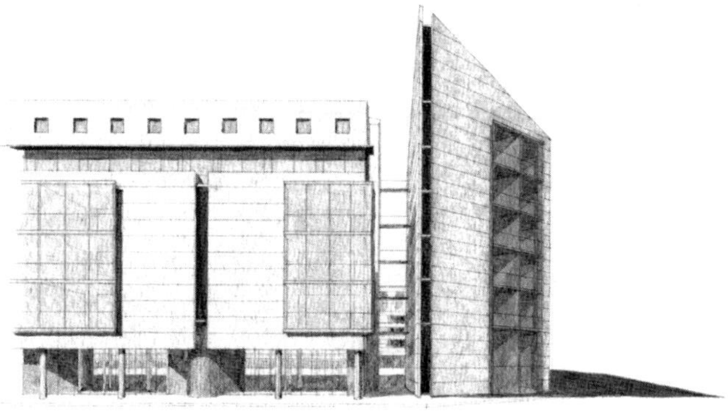

But undoubtedly the team's reflection on the Eixample is particularly interesting when dealing with the definition of new morphologies, for projects that have had the opportunity to present the architectural definition of several entire blocks. This is where taking another glance at the Cerdà project has led to some new dimensions. In fact these are new morphological interpretations already underway, such as, the second Olympic Village in Poble Nou or the Five Blocks on the Seafront.

In either case, the Ferrater team attempts to provide specific solutions for the fact that a project can become involved in a plot larger than that of the architectural site itself and can face up to the logic of the peripheral building and interior space of the block with new commitments.

The first case seeks to rediscover the block courtyard as the centre of the ensemble, producing an aggregate of three blocks that can have their own independent use even though they respond to a logic that allows for a unitary interpretation: To a certain extent, here they seem to recover the start of some passages that intersect and connect several blocks in central Eixample. Within this morphological concept, architecture seeks ways to create singular groups and the typological research is based on interesting principles of constructive rationality. On the other hand, exploration goes from encouraging the "line" of the building to address where the corners meet.

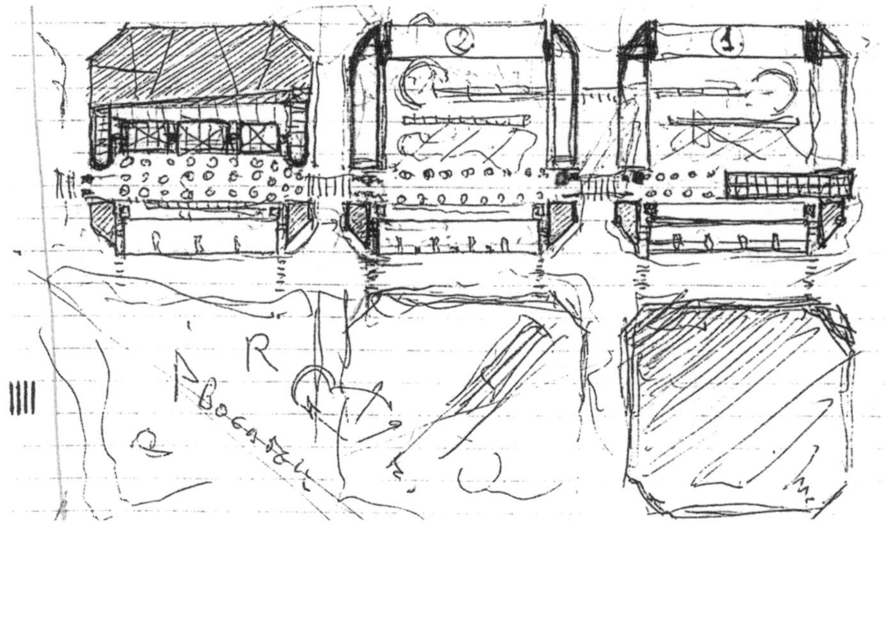

For the Five Blocks on the Seafront, the research is different. Once again, the idea that the closed block must include the perception of an interior courtyard is explored but the commitment lies in distinguishing the front of the block, which is the sea front. This is carried out to formulate a composition that goes beyond the individuality of each block and supports a multi-block composition that plays with large visual seafronts and the possibility that some more unique uses formalise the face of these spaces. This exercise seems to introduce the hybrid block solution as a way of tackling the problem of the singular points. New higher corners, which are now front pieces, let these buildings stand out without turning them into individual pieces, thus drawing attention to the complex.

We should add that the long periods of testing carried out by the Ferrater team on the Eixample verifies the enormous adaptability of the geometric conditions of the blocks proposed by Cerdà. It also demonstrates the team's unwavering commitment to continue to innovate and show how new programmes should come up with new typological answers. Above all we must be concerned about how the different decomposition of a block can introduce different compositional forms from which special morphological commitments are outlined. Despite the individuality of these commitments they continue to maintain a high level of consistency with the organisation of the monumental typology of which the Eixample is a historical legacy.

Eixample Cerdà– Passeig de Gràcia

The Eixample Cerdà has been a testing ground and an endless urban research laboratory for many architects. Its large size and its subtle breaks from the rigidity of a geometrical design has enabled us to interpret different rules for the same board game over 150 years, its different typological, constructive and formal solutions have constituted a high value urban façade with outstanding contributions such as the famous “Illa de la Discòrdia” or synthesis projects from the abstraction such as the façade of *El Noticiero Universal* building by J.M. Sostres.

The urban transformation of Barcelona started in the 80s with the fledgling democracy that allowed our studio to develop a set of project propositions and urban and architecture-based jobs as they worked on the shape and size of the roof at the same time as the interior space of the island creating it as a negative space. Without breaking the basic scheme of the traditional block, issues were addressed, such as buildable depth that would allow for accessible floors and cross ventilation, the permeability of the ground floor linking the road network and the landscaped interiors, the restoration of the terrace roofs as semi-public areas and providing orientation to the block and highlighting the planes and the chamfered corners. This led us to construct an image of cloistered and open interiors through the passages, diagonal perforations and paths that link the different blocks.

For example the project for the 3 blocks in the “Eixample Marítim del Poble Nou” in 1992 or the truncated blocks in the extension of Avda. Diagonal, a result of the consultation-tender planned by the City Council, or the new block created between the streets Ramón Turró and Llull. And in particular the urban proposal, also after an international competition for the Five Blocks on the Seafront in Barcelona, where for the first time a group of blocks from the Cerdà plan was erected in front of the sea. The collaborative work of the architecture critic and historian J.M. Montaner was of great value for the resolution of the majority of these projects.

Alongside these interventions, important for their urban transcendence and size, our studio has experimented with pieces of architecture of different sizes in other locations of Barcelona over the last few years. Such as buildings between party walls, those in the streets Balmes ❷, Còrsega ❸, València ❺, or Gran Vía among others, or the more complex intervention in the *Block in Fort Pienc* by Lucía Ferrater ❻❼❽ with buildings in the streets Alí Bei, Roger de Flor and Nàpols around an interior landscaped island following the old Carretera d’Horta and organised around a small community centre. Although some of the chamfered corner proposals such as Urgell-Sepúlveda or the Casp-Bruc are currently under construction.

Special mention should be given to the rehabilitation carried out on Passeig de Gràcia, both for the quality and centrality of this urban street and for the extraordinary cultural legacy from previously carried out interventions, from modernism, with works of Gaudí, Puig i Cadafalch or Domènech i Muntaner, to valuable environmental and constructive rehabilitation or buildings from the second half of the twentieth century built by architects like Galindo, Tous and Moragas or Fargas.

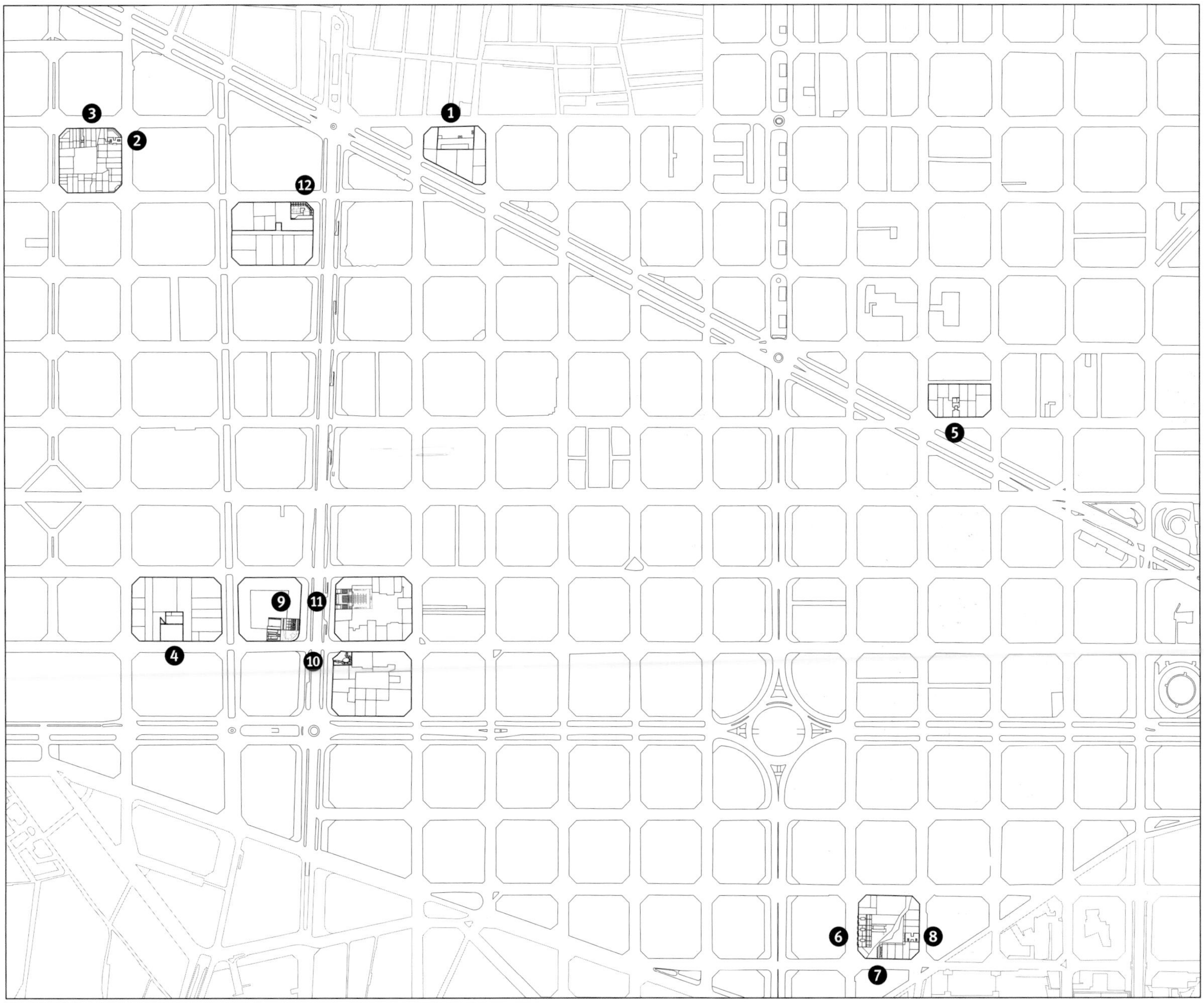

Since our first involvement in the old Cinema Fémina ❾, which ceased to exist after a fire, we have rehabilitated the Passeig de Gràcia sector with an original typological proposal while recovering the façade in Carrer Diputació carried out by Moragas, connecting both volumes to "La Unión y el Fénix Español" building which forms the chamfer.

The complete rehabilitation, along with Lucía Ferrater and Joan Guibernau, of the former BASF Building on the chamfered corner of Rosselló with Passeig de Gràcia ⓬ or the proposal of a new floor plan for the chamfered corner of Diputació-Passeig de Gràcia ❿, carried out by Xavier Martí and Juan Trias de Bes, that Llàtzer Moix baptised "La Pedrera of the 20th century", is complemented by the refurbishment of the former Central Hispano Bank transforming it into the new Mandarin Oriental Hotel ⓫ in collaboration with Juan Trias de Bes.

All these actions and projects have enabled us to understand the importance of taking on the complex cultural heritage, as well as recognising and respecting, the rich morphology, acting as a medium, of the Eixample in Barcelona.

① Còrsega 254
② Balmes 145
③ Còrsega 348
④ Diputació 239–247
⑤ València 381
⑥ Roger de Flor 78
⑦ Alí Bei 57 (Interior)
⑧ Nàpols 89–91
⑨ Passeig de Gràcia 23 / Diputació 259
⑩ Passeig de Gràcia 30
⑪ Passeig de Gràcia 38–40
⑫ Passeig de Gràcia 99

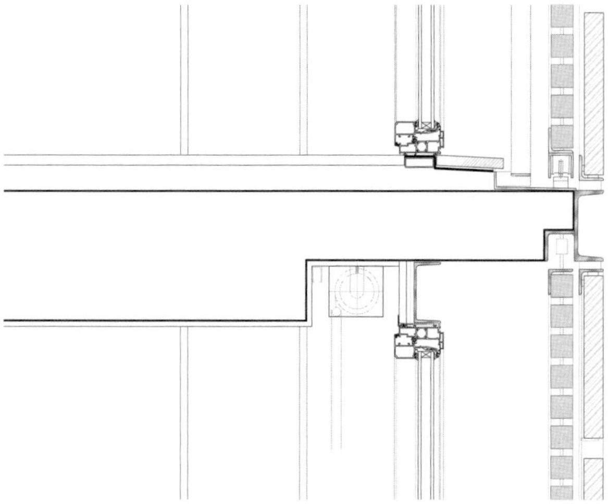

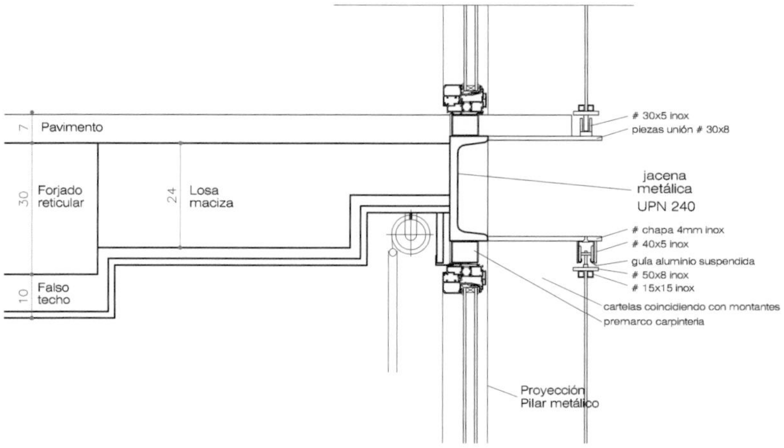

Balmes 145

València 381

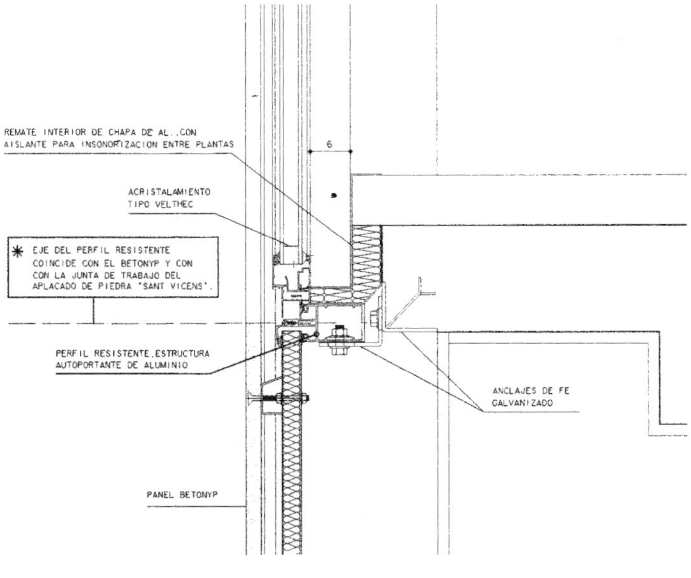
6
REMATE INTERIOR DE CHAPA DE AL.,CON AISLANTE PARA INSONORIZACION ENTRE PLANTAS
ACRISTALAMIENTO TIPO VELTHEC
* EJE DEL PERFIL RESISTENTE COINCIDE CON EL BETONYP Y CON CON LA JUNTA DE TRABAJO DEL APLACADO DE PIEDRA "SANT VICENS".
PERFIL RESISTENTE.ESTRUCTURA AUTOPORTANTE DE ALUMINIO
ANCLAJES DE FE GALVANIZADO
PANEL BETONYP

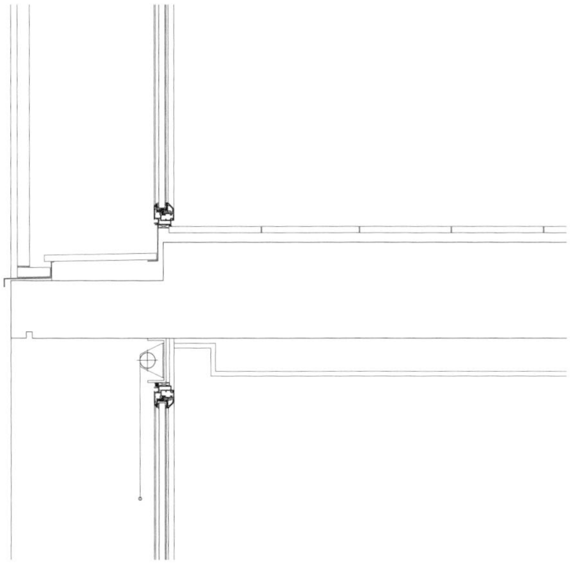

Gran Via 512

Roger de Flor 78

Housing building in Passeig de Gràcia 23 / Diputació 259

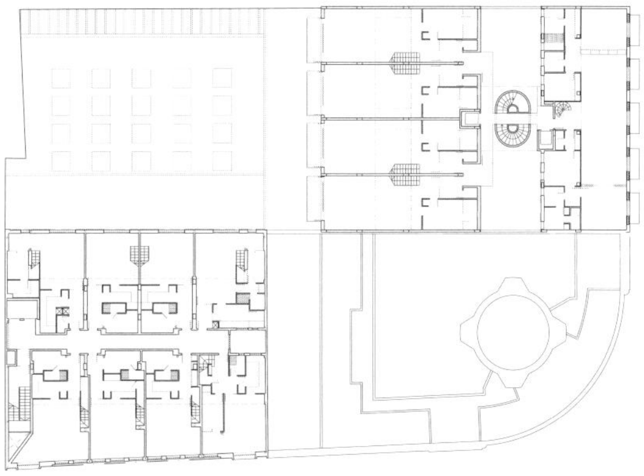

Typical floor plan

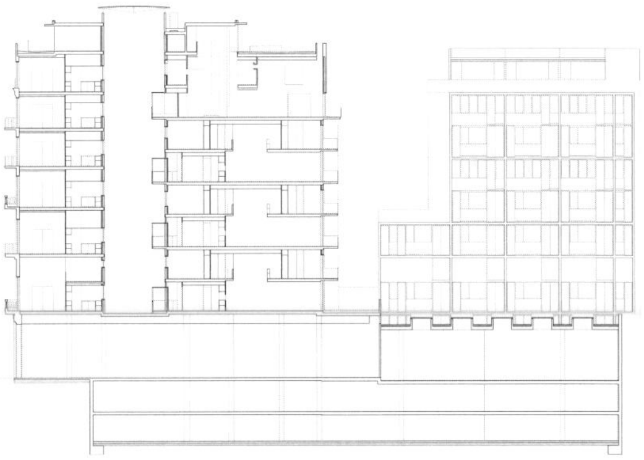

Section

Housing building in Passeig de Gràcia / Rosselló

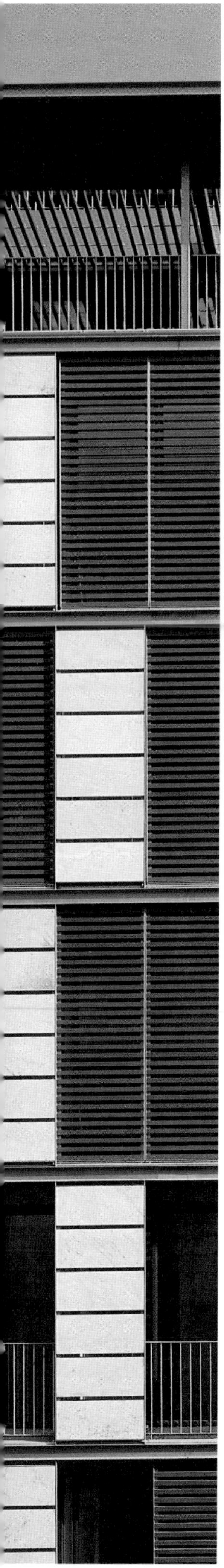

taxi
RABAT

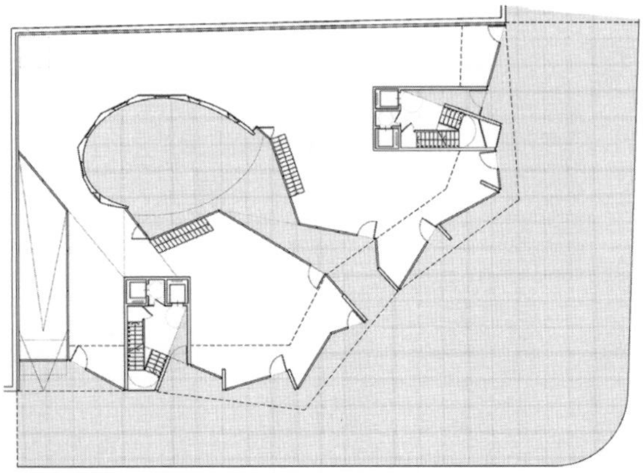

Ground floor plan

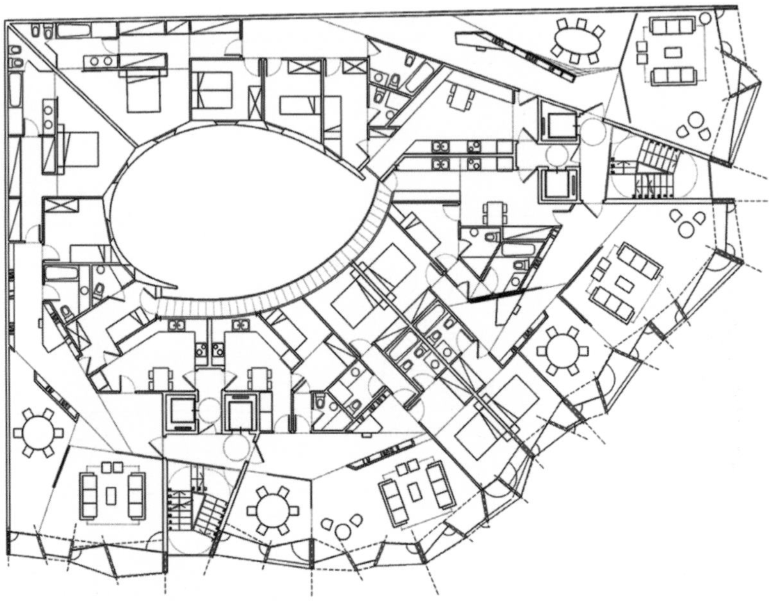

Typical floor plan

IBERIA head office
in Passeig de Gràcia
Barcelona

Housing building in Passeig de Gràcia / Diputació

Hotel Mandarin Oriental

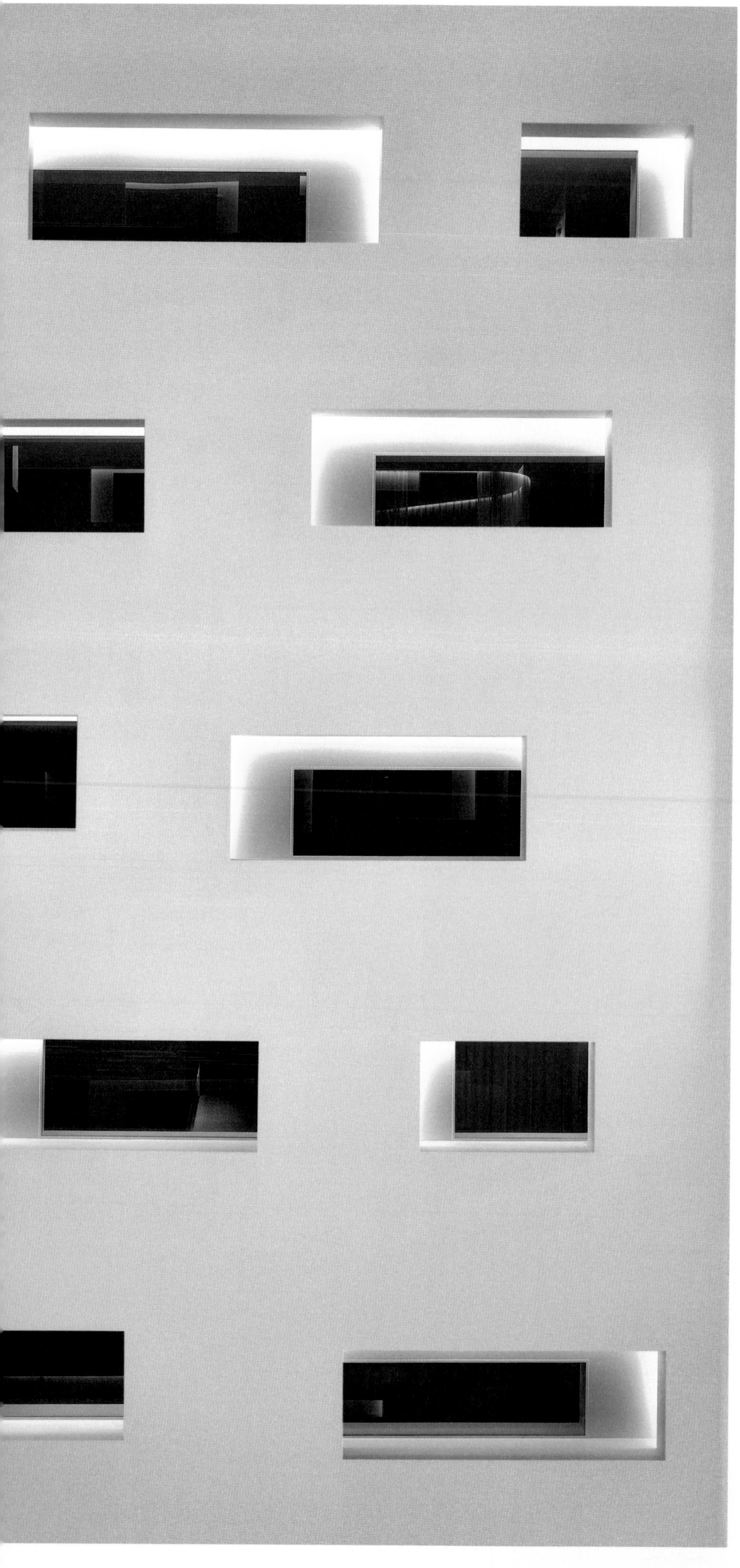

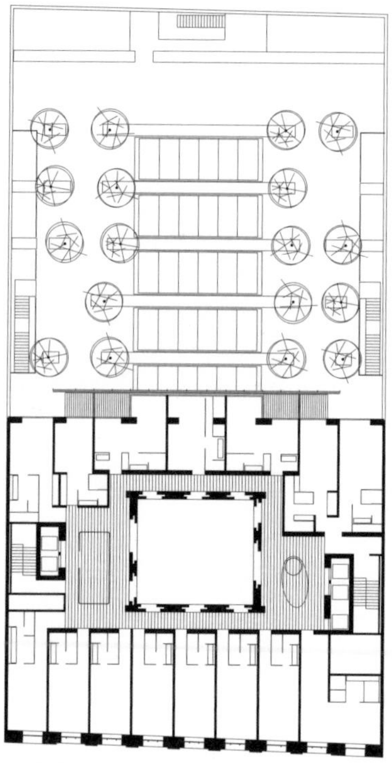

Typical floor plan

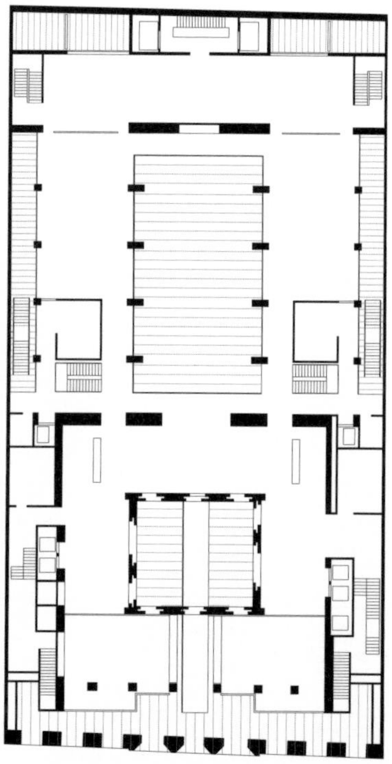

Mezzanine plan

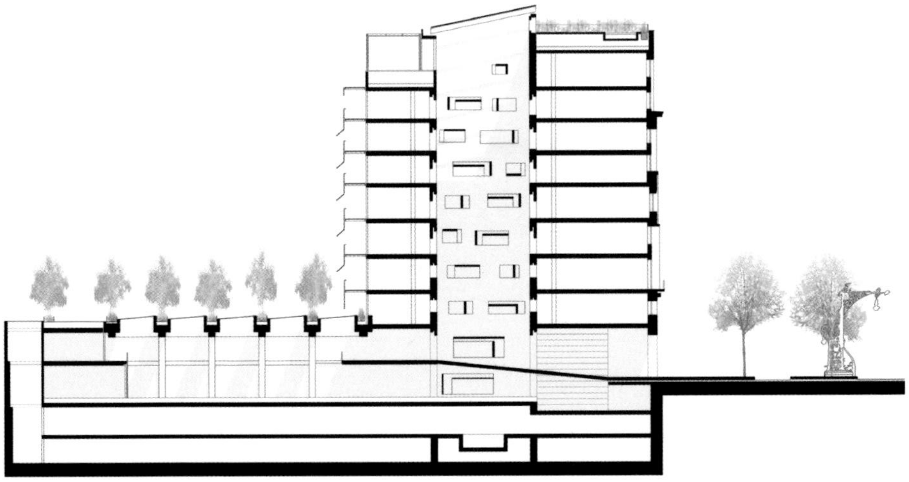

Longitudinal section

5

From the Royal Quarters to the Granada Science Park

Carlos Ferrater

In Granada, a few years after building the Jardines de la Cuba del Cuarto Real next to the Arab district of Realejo, under the direction of Yolanda Brasa Quba, commissioned by the city council, we won the design competition for the extension of the Science Park in Granada, next to the river Genil. The project was conceived as the construction of a single roof with small inflections that looks like an open hand, covering the different programmatic pieces interconnected in a continuous space.

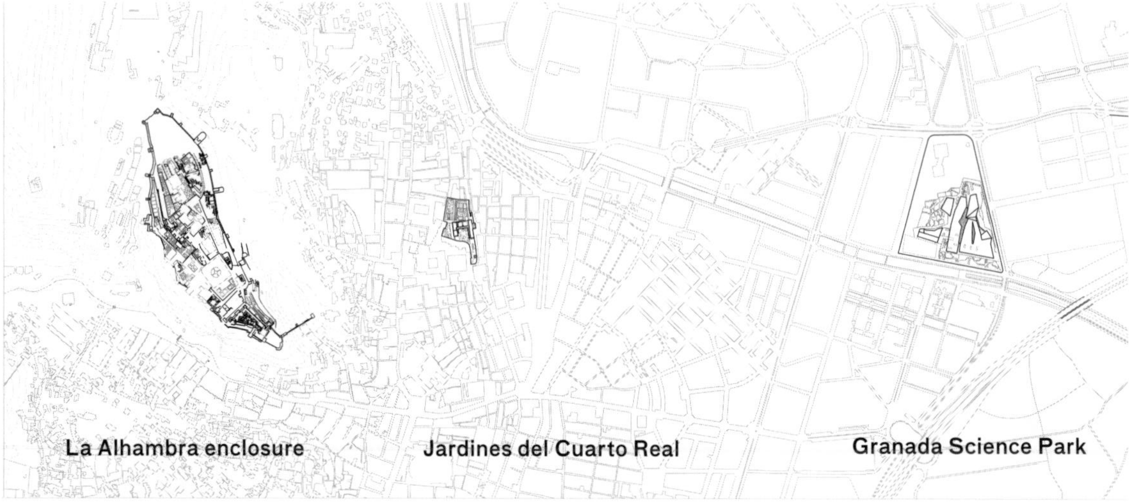

The empty space that connects the large boxes or programme containers: Macroscope, Biodome, Tecnoforum, Health Sciences, Al Andalus, auditoriums and spaces for temporary and permanent exhibitions, structures communications, logistics and relationships with the Park activities. The proposed spatial structure allows for the flexibility of uses and situations that interconnect paths and themes.

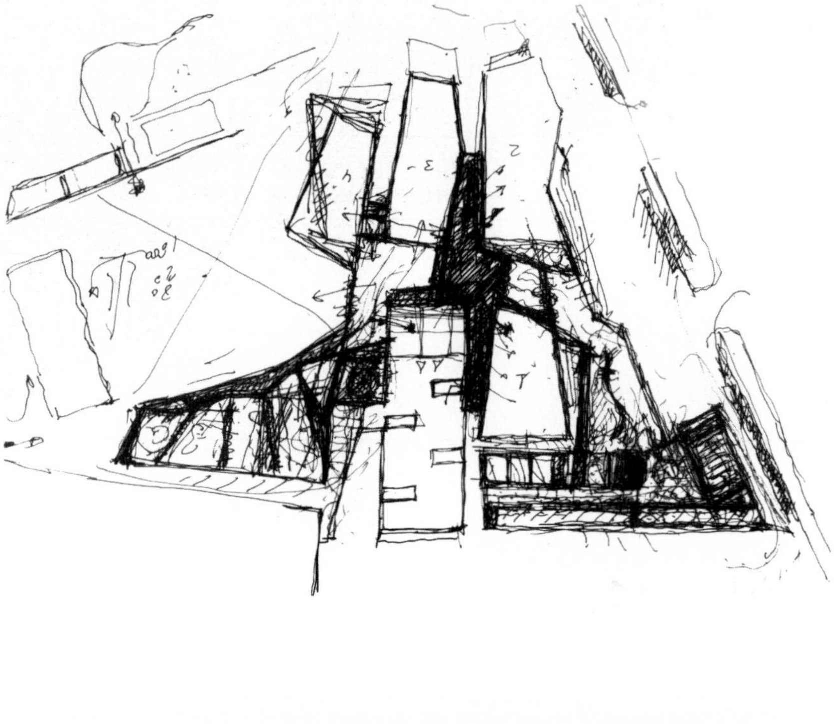

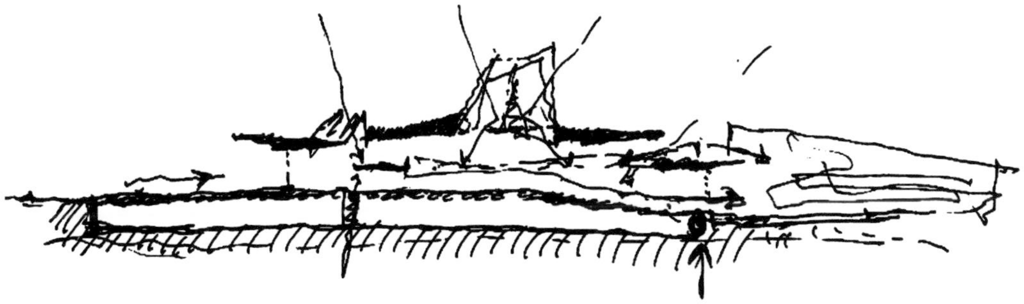

The majority of the projects developed as topographies often substitute the continuous quality of the roof with a succession of planes or different shaped porches. In this way, the space and the roof's constructive autonomy as a continuous element turns into a sequential relation of interconnected spaces.

In Granada, the roof is a folded continuous surface that floats over the inclined plane of the ground level, enclosing the large exhibition spaces between them, highlighting the communication and relation spaces with the light that penetrates between the folded planes.

On its abstraction, the large roof has a profile that is similar to the skyline of the Granada Mountain range. The development of the large topographic roof adapts to the volumetric requirements that create the large, tall, enclosed spaces that house the various programmes in its interior.

The roof flies over the terrain, constructing a new topography that as it folds, organises between folds, the skylights that provide natural light to the circulation and connecting spaces.

The roof mesh is resolved with a double-layer three-dimensional structure that encloses services and technical systems, solving the rain water evacuation. The skylights guide the roof as a continuation of the main structure.

Park and City

The first steps of the Project have been based on understanding the expansion of the Science Park as an opportunity to respond to issues of urban order that transcend the Site and that contribute to shaping an area of great importance to the City.

The relationship with the River Genil and the connection with adjacent spaces of centrality have been the mainspring of the Project's urban dimension. From the start, the latter dismisses the idea of a totem building installed "above the City" and pays attention instead to the various locations of the edges and points of contact with what already exists.

These concerns have configured an organism that houses different types of space beneath a single roof, which, with slight inflections and an outer skin resembling that of a hand, enables the Park and the City to occupy the intermediary spaces -between the fingers -which accommodate the components of the programme. The footbridge linking the opposite bank of the Genil is the arm that brings the City into the Park, a new pedestrian access that connects with points of intense activity, encounter and meeting.

A new way of traversing the Park "hors control" enables us to take in the Complex from a high position and even to cross the lobby over the main Skylight, while appreciating the space and the bustle on the inside, which descending towards the access plaza, leads us to the entrance of the building and the ticket office area.

Interactivity

The idea of interactivity is present on all levels regarding the Park. Spatial continuity and intensification of the interactive potential between Building and City are the Proposal's main theme.

The Enclosure shares its public dimension with the City by means of new urban routes that are interconnected with interior circulations.

Just as the Park focuses its attention on the interactive exhibition of its themed areas, the Project provides all visitors with spaces in which to move with total freedom, accessibility and continuity. Discovering the possible routes among the many options will convert the user into an interested and inquisitive individual who takes on an active role.

Flexibility

The proposed spatial structure allows for total flexibility of use and for diverse configurations interweaving routes and themed areas. This entails converting the experience of the space into an area for games and fun. Intersecting glances, a rapport with the landscape and confined spaces are revealed throughout the visit.

Spatial organisation

The idea of an "enigmatic box" awakens the curiosity and subtly displays its interior as an invitation to be discovered in prolongation with the space of the street.

A single undulating plane floats ten metres high and is sustained by the structure of the programme's huge main boxes, defining in its interstices the vast space of the lobby, a permanent reference for both interior and exterior routes, underlined by the low-angled light of the façade windows and emphasised in the heart of the building by the great glazed fissure identifying the Park on a Metropolitan scale.

The main function of this lobby will be to lead and direct the visitor within the Complex; it receives the flow of people from the access plaza and the Green space next to the River and sends them to the extended open spaces already inside the enclosure: the Nature Plaza or Biodome and the Observatory Plaza.

Suitable programmatic features intensify the porosity surrounding the Complex: mini-cinemas, Internet cafés, a cyber library and shopping areas are set out in continuity with the platform of the public Green Space constituted in the Vestibule of the Cultural Gallery, from where people can also move onto the Macroscopio and the rest of the park. Accessibility is a basic premise of the entire circulation system.

Given its clear identity within the Complex, the Al-Andalus Science Pavilion helps maximise the interactive aspect between the City and the Park. Its entrances are independent and include a public green space nearby. Light is the main rationale for organising the spaces. Four skylights over four courtyards determine the interior, configuring a flexible base for the organisation of the themed spaces.

Sustainability, recycling and collection

The new building becomes a genuine support of these contemporary statements, which are obligatory in large-scale public projects.

The choice of material fulfils technological innovation and energy-saving ecological criteria, supporting and simplifying maintenance and good conservation.

A new urban plane is configured, the large roof, as an abstraction of the furrowed textures of the Vega flatland.

Sections of the roof are adapted to harness solar energy, permitting optimal heating and cooling costs. Other sections are containers for material recycled from building work and other industrial processes: ceramic, plastic, glass, concrete and metal, which will be classified and processed in situ to become ballast and surfacing material.

- 01 Access
- 02 Auditorium
- 03 Cultural Gallery
- 04 Tecno-Forum Hall
- 05 Al-Andalus Pavilion and Science
- 06 Biodome
- 07 Temporary Exhibition Hall
- 08 Pavilion “Travel to the Human Body
- 09 Pavilion “Cultural Hall of Prevention”
- 10 Circulations
- 11 Garden Genil
- 12 Forest of Feelings

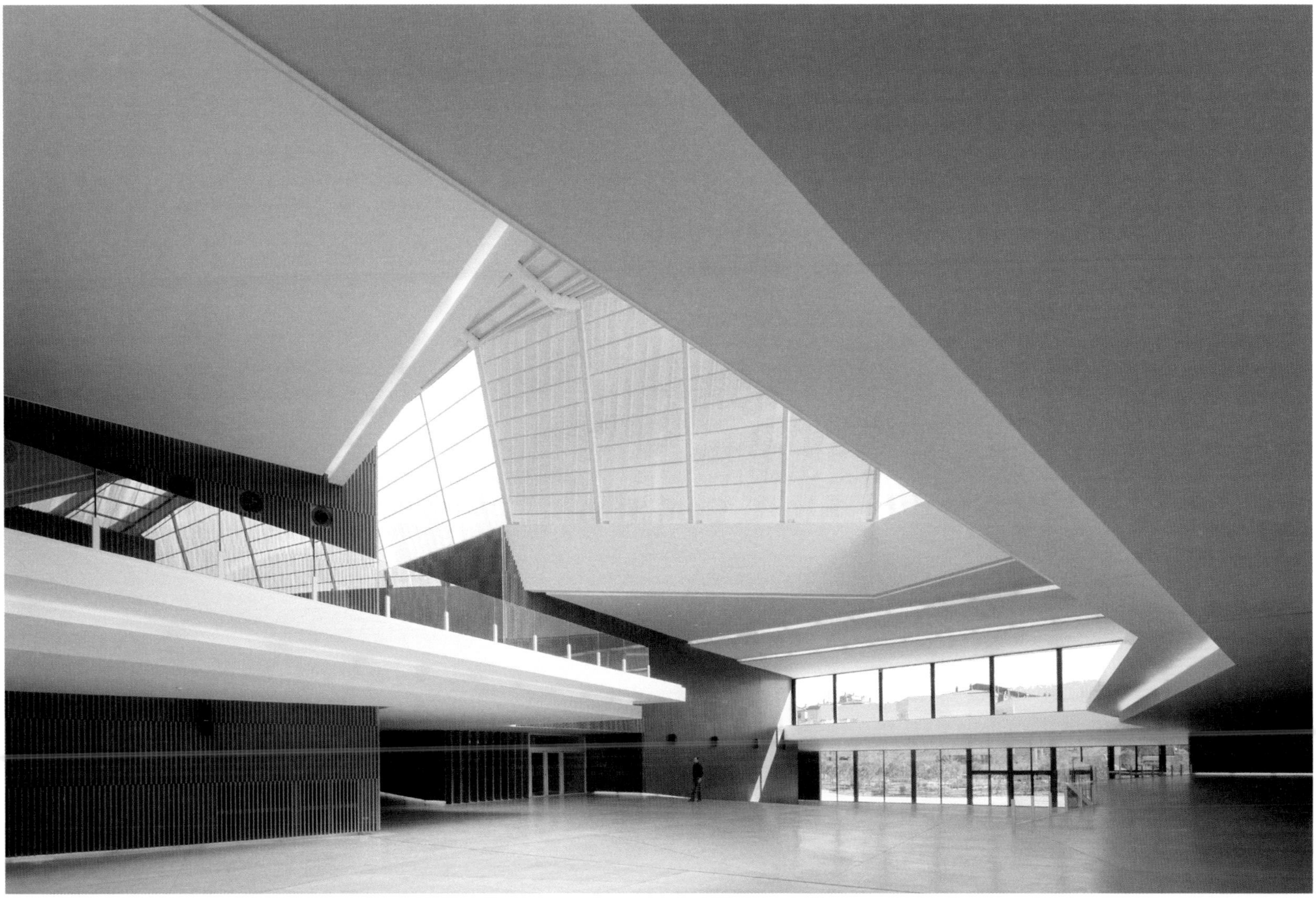

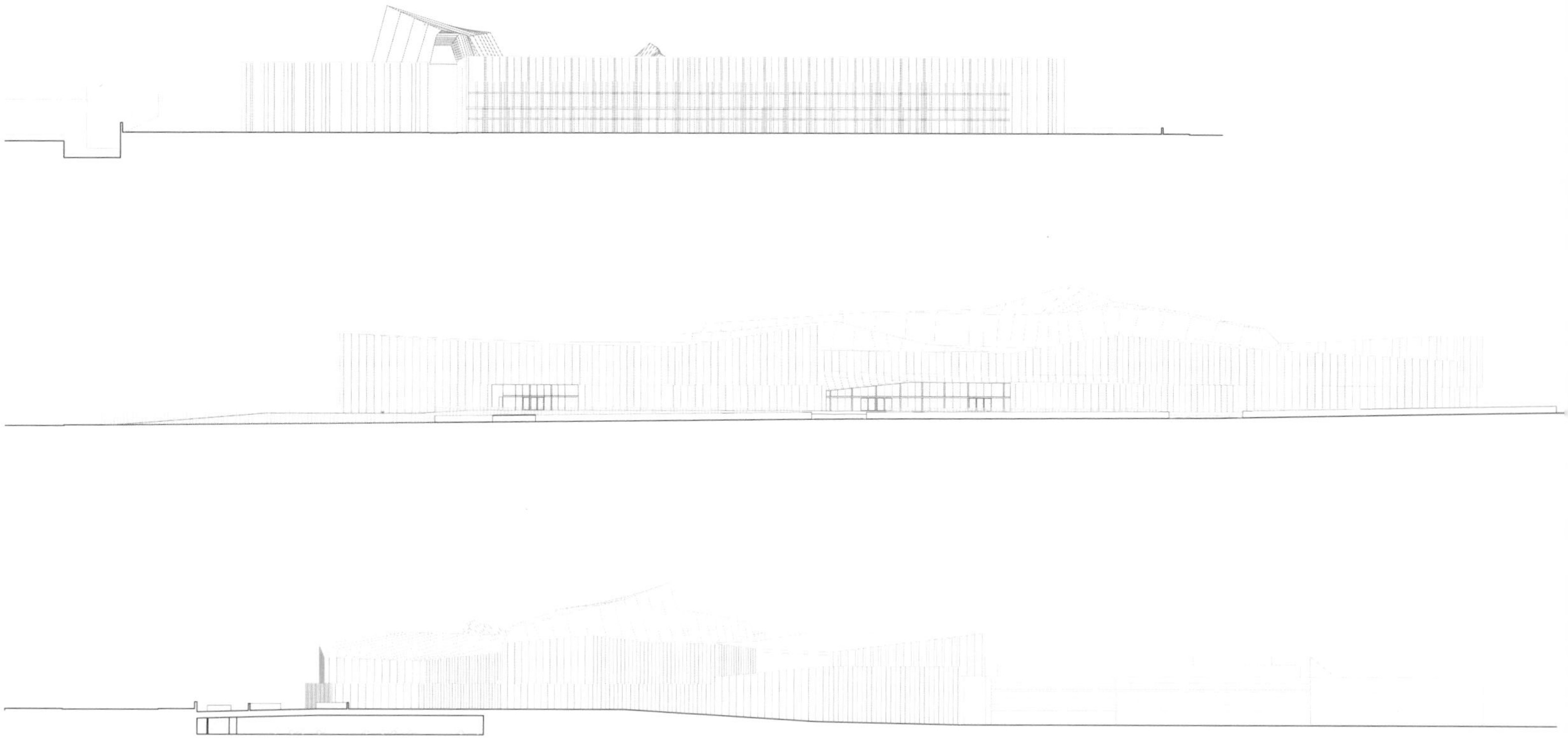

Elevations

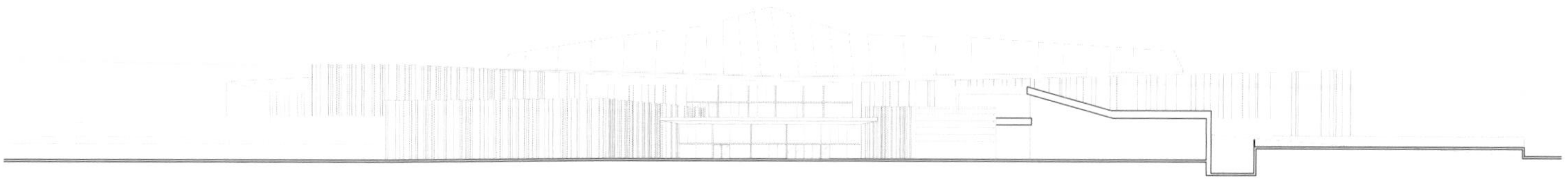

Section

Juan Calvo

The structure of the Science Park of Granada is conceived as a series of rigid concrete blocks that forms each of the showrooms. The presence of these nuclei can adequately resolve the issue of all horizontal structural elements, floors and gateways, using reinforced or prestressed concrete slabs. This structural configuration is adequate in terms of the seismic conditions of the area.

The expansion joints were eliminated from the roof. To do so a large metal structure supported by concrete walls with a certain level of mobility was designed. In addition to mobility, some blocking elements against the action of horizontal forces induced by an earthquake, both longitudinally and transversely were fitted to each of the beams in the roof.

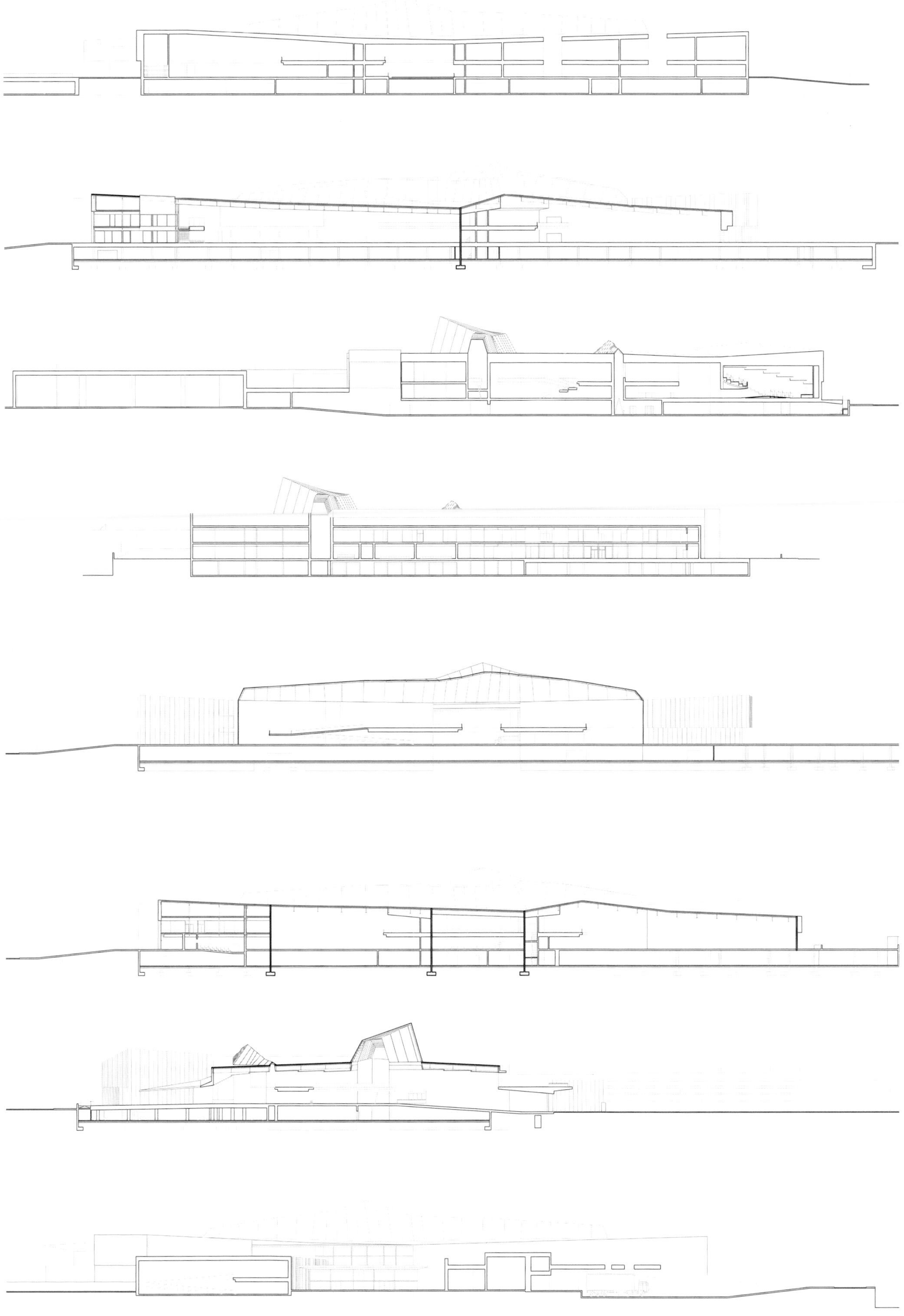

Sections

Ernesto Páramo Sureda

Director of Granada Science Park

Containment and moderation

If you ever see a giant termite the image will stay with you forever. This fabulous animal construction takes over our minds in a mysterious way. Its beauty is geological, mineral, powerful but restrained. Its formal design and incredible efficiency is overwhelming. Some places have that magnetic hold over us, whether it is natural or man-made. We search the world just to experience it. Ayers Rock, the large red rock in Australia or the remote Inca Machu Picchu. Many years later we still remember them with a strange closeness. What is the secret?

With the current technical means and the huge variety of resources and materials available, it is really easy to succumb to stridency and ostentation. This is why it is so great to be able to appreciate both a sober and beautiful building. A true exercise of restraint and sobriety.

I've never been interested in the whole architecture "show". Not only because it often contains a rare blend of technical prowess and banality, but above all because construction clashes with the essence of the show that in order to be so, has a limited duration. We may enjoy a show, provided it doesn't last too long. A building is too long-term for this purpose.

Today the element of surprise is overrated. So much so that more and more buildings are being built in order to surprise rather than for practical purposes and to describe them as functional is often pejorative. I mean really! No one would choose a decorative pacemaker instead of one that works. As this disastrous trend begins to subside, our commitment has been clear and the result is in sight.

In architecture, as in science and communication, we should always have the famous Occam's Razor on hand.

6

The permanence of the ephemeral. The Escher Universe

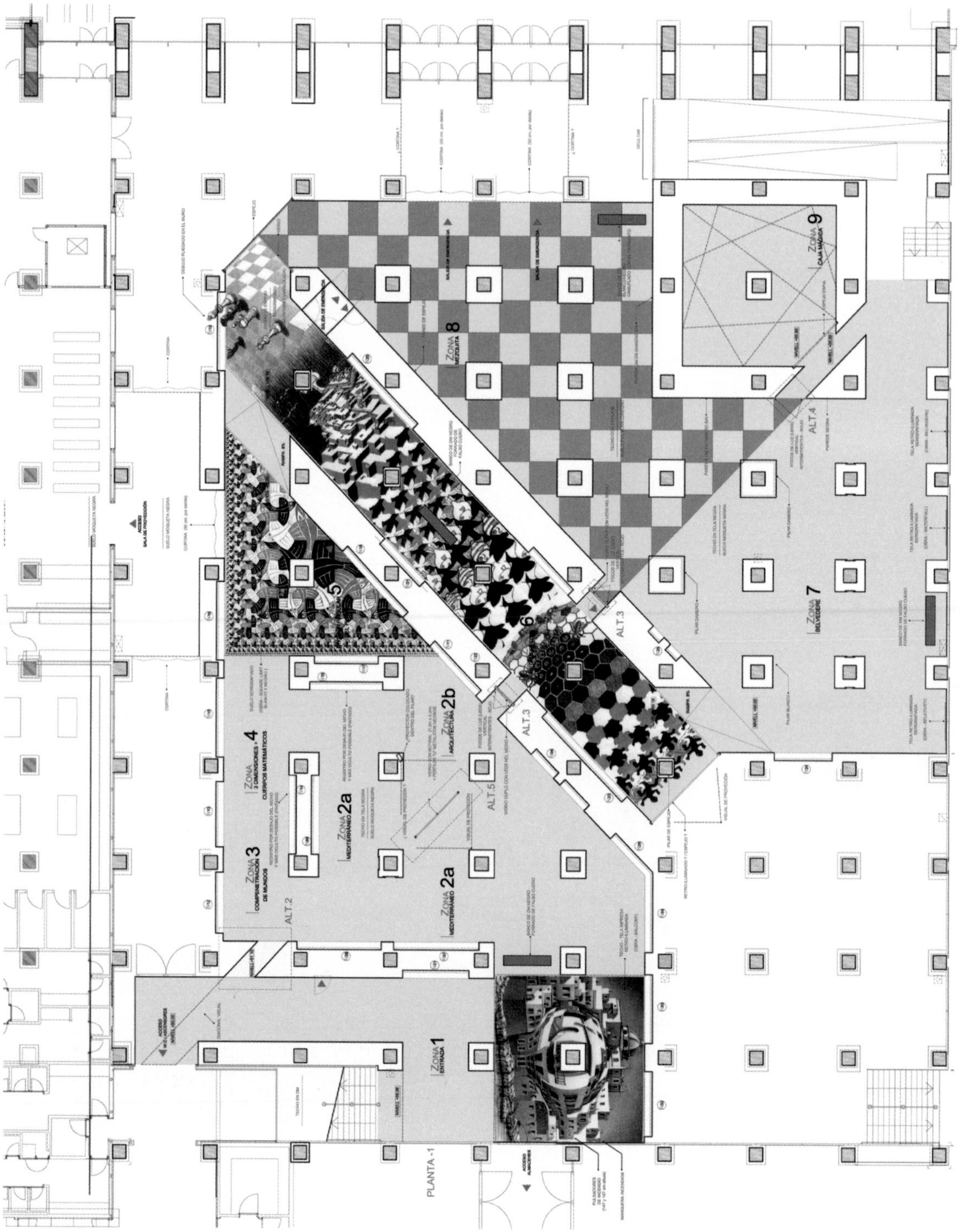

General plan

Frequently throughout the professional career of architects, we receive jobs that initially seem quite far-flung from our professional practice and something that more often than not has to do with a short-lived job that will soon be forgotten about. They are usually jobs parallel to the strict practice of architecture relating to small interventions and greatly linked to the temporary, to events, expositions or small pavilions. We consider them almost like practical exercises which are rapidly conceived and developed.

However, these meetings can bring with them implicit aspects of great importance, as even if we consider them as exploration exercises, thanks to them we develop ideas that perhaps we could not develop under the usual conditioning factors of architecture. In short, they represent a seductive exercise as they symbolise an opportunity to enter into a new, different game in which we can alter, add or eliminate certain rules.

What is curious is that these quick, intensive exercises always leave a trail or a footprint. They are useful as quick lessons to develop innovative concepts and over time they leave their stamp on permanent future projects. Thanks to the intensity and temporary nature of these experiences, the fragmented ideas that remain in the sub-conscience, in some way or another, will unexpectedly re-emerge influencing other projects.

From December 2005 to April 2006, there was an extensive and in-depth exposition in Madrid on the work of the artist Maurits Cornelis Escher, the most important in Spain to date. The OAB studio received the assignment of artistic organisers of the exposition. Already fans of his work, this gave us the opportunity to gain more in-depth knowledge of the artist.

With the appearance of the avant-garde movements, ideological plurality characterised the development of art in the twentieth century. For this reason, when presenting the work of an artist from this century one tends to position him or her within one of these movements. But Maurits Cornelis Escher is difficult to classify.

Escher was a strange artist, difficult to classify, traveller and amateur astronomer, he kept his distance from artistic movements, however, his work quickly became very popular from the 1960s onwards: initially he created a great magnetism between scientists, who used his drawings to explain concepts related to science, and later, very quickly , to find all kinds of interpretations and audiences of all ages.

His professional development began in architecture under paternal guidance, but he soon abandoned his studies and dedicated himself to graphic arts, the medium through which he materialised his ideas. The dedication and effort invested in perfecting his trade were never his principal objectives, as he was fully conscious that technical perfection could be prejudicial for the development of his ideas. This vision made him emphasise the importance of method, both in the process of creation and in that of materialising his ideas and fantasies, leading him to study mathematics.

He was undoubtedly a misunderstood, frustrated artist, not for lack of disciplinary recognition but for the lack of emotion his contemporaries expressed toward his work. Today, years later, now that the study of complex geometries is at the heart of a large part of plastic art and contemporary architecture, Escher is beginning to be recognised and valued for his interdisciplinary qualities.

From 1937 onwards his work lost interest in the real reproduction of nature, his true objective being the manipulation of reality through optical illusion. The interpretative significance of the work took a back seat.

It is through mathematics and, more specifically geometry that Escher constructs his various optical illusions, his studies with reticular three-dimensional mesh and the regular partition of the plane, which gave his work a spatial topicality never previously achieved, overcoming the laws of perspective that had remained untouched since the Renaissance.

Thus some of his works recreate images of three-dimensional objects on flat surfaces, stereometric geometries and topological transformations that allow him to three-dimension the plane and transform cubes into spheres. In this way, his background in architecture is present in his work, as the definition of space becomes the principal argument of his work.

The analysis of his work, as defined by Brunst Ernst, one of his biographers, classifies his work into three basic themes and different categories:

- —The structure of space: including landscapes, understanding of the world and mathematical bodies.
- —The structure of the surface area: Metamorphosis, cycles and approaches to the infinite.
- —The projection of three-dimensional space in the plane: Traditional pictorial representation, impossible perspectives and figures.

From a mathematical point of view, his most daring works are probably those showing non-Euclidean geometry mosaics. These are not just uniform mosaics (they are not only repeated but also to scale). For example, in the "circle limit" series you can recognise the tenets of the hyperbolic plane designed by Henri Poincaré.

Therefore, our project tried to translate into spaces some of the ideas that inspired the artist.

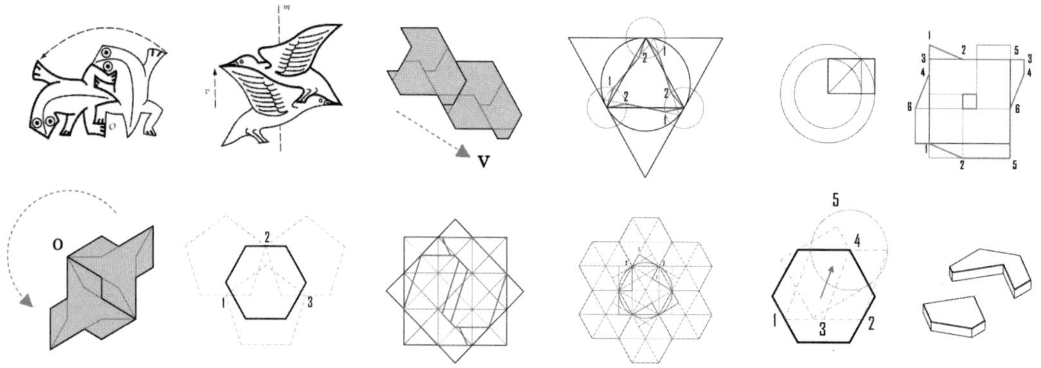

The original space began as an orthogonal grid defined by a grid of columns and was transformed into a labyrinthine space, disrupting the stability of the grid, thus varying geometric rules that originally defined the existing space. Therefore, we sought to introduce the diagonal as a replacement for the orthogonal and thus generate a dual space, transmitting the tension to spectators as they follow the chronological development of his work.

The passing of geometric expressions to animal shapes that live in the plane and could not exist in space, strange mathematical bodies, metamorphosis, impossible worlds and approaches to infinity, make up this Escherian universe.

Right from the start of the project, all the identifying features of the room were eliminated (brick pillars and full-centre arches) in order to give the visitor a totally new and innovative perception of the space regardless of whether this was the second or third visit. To this end, the project always sought to emphasise the visual lines on a diagonal, lower the height of the ceilings, dim the lighting and create three major areas along the exhibition route, just as if this were a film: with a beginning, a middle and an end.

At the start, which shows the beginning stages of the artist, we decided to give the work centre stage thus allowing the visitor to concentrate on the engravings. That is why we decided not to light up the spaces too intensely, to use black to create neutral spaces and to recess niches so that, like in light boxes, the works would float and be better protected.

The Metamorphosis (room 6) was understood as a long straight-lined route for the visitor, and the point of inflection of the exhibition, an experience in transformation where the visitors themselves experience a change.

The Mosque (room 8) was devised in order to express some ideas on which Escher worked. We thought the idea of isotropy was interesting, as currently there are few examples in architecture of truly isotropic spaces. This idea was something that Escher understood when he visited and sketched the mosque at Cordoba. The space was meant to be a true 3D chequerboard. Chess and its relationship with mathematics (impossible moves, the infinite, the repetition of black and white, etc.) were concepts also used by Escher.

The Magic Box (room 9) arose from the idea of recreating different works by the author in a closed yet strange space where reflections intervene to favour the optical illusion of an infinite space and where some of the personages created by the artist come to life. In order to represent these spaces, we worked with the help of mirrored aluminium, backlit screens, videos and audiovisual material all forming part of the exhibition architecture (walls that are audiovisual screens, etc.), a play of mirrors, translucent Perspex, the colour black, white, etc. Throughout this process we used sketches, general scale models, magic box scale models at a 1:10 and 1:20 scale, light scale models for the niches, videos for studying the routes, etc.

Probably anyone who has ever come across one of Escher's works will have focused on his apparently simple drawings at first, and then surprised by something strange, they will have returned their focus to the drawing, played with it, played seriously as Escher would say, and finally wondered about the rest of the work of this Dutch artist.

The group of works that was exhibited was exceptional, and difficult to find outside the Escher Foundation in Holland. Escher's world is presented through 135 of his best works, arranged in different rooms by themes and periods of time. His works were accompanied, at the end of the exhibition, with two "Escherian" spaces specifically tailored for this exhibit: The Mosque and Magic Box.

The exhibition consisted of seven areas and two rooms which could be visited alternately by the visitor as they were designed independently, although a route could also be followed that took a tangential approach to his chronological career.

The short lived experience, lasting only a few months, marked the beginning of various studies, which we have carried out in OAB, and they have remained at the border between the merely theoretical and experimental work (OAB internal research team) and the practice of some projects. Since then we have worked based on regular division of the plane, delving into the design of periodic and a-periodic tilings, entering the amazing world that prompted Escher, Albers, Bill, Penrose etc, understanding the mechanisms of stereometry, the isometry, etc. These studies today represent the foundations of my doctorate. Some of the results of our research have led to specific projects, such as designing a set of precast concrete pavements and the development of systems, going beyond the mere tangential experience to the cornerstone of a possible theory of design.

We are currently working on a major exhibition of MC Escher in Granada sharing the exhibition spatially between the techno-forum of the science park and the crypt of the Palace of Charles V at the Alhambra, where the gigantic stone structures of the palace and the great brick walls of the Nazar palaces intersect. An actual meeting of the impossible Escherian geometry that recall the trips that Maurits Cornelius made to Southern Spain to see the mosque of Cordoba and the Alhambra in Granada, a trip that was the trigger for a radical shift in his work on his way to dividing the plane, the study of tilings and the start of other worlds in his future work.

Borja Ferrater

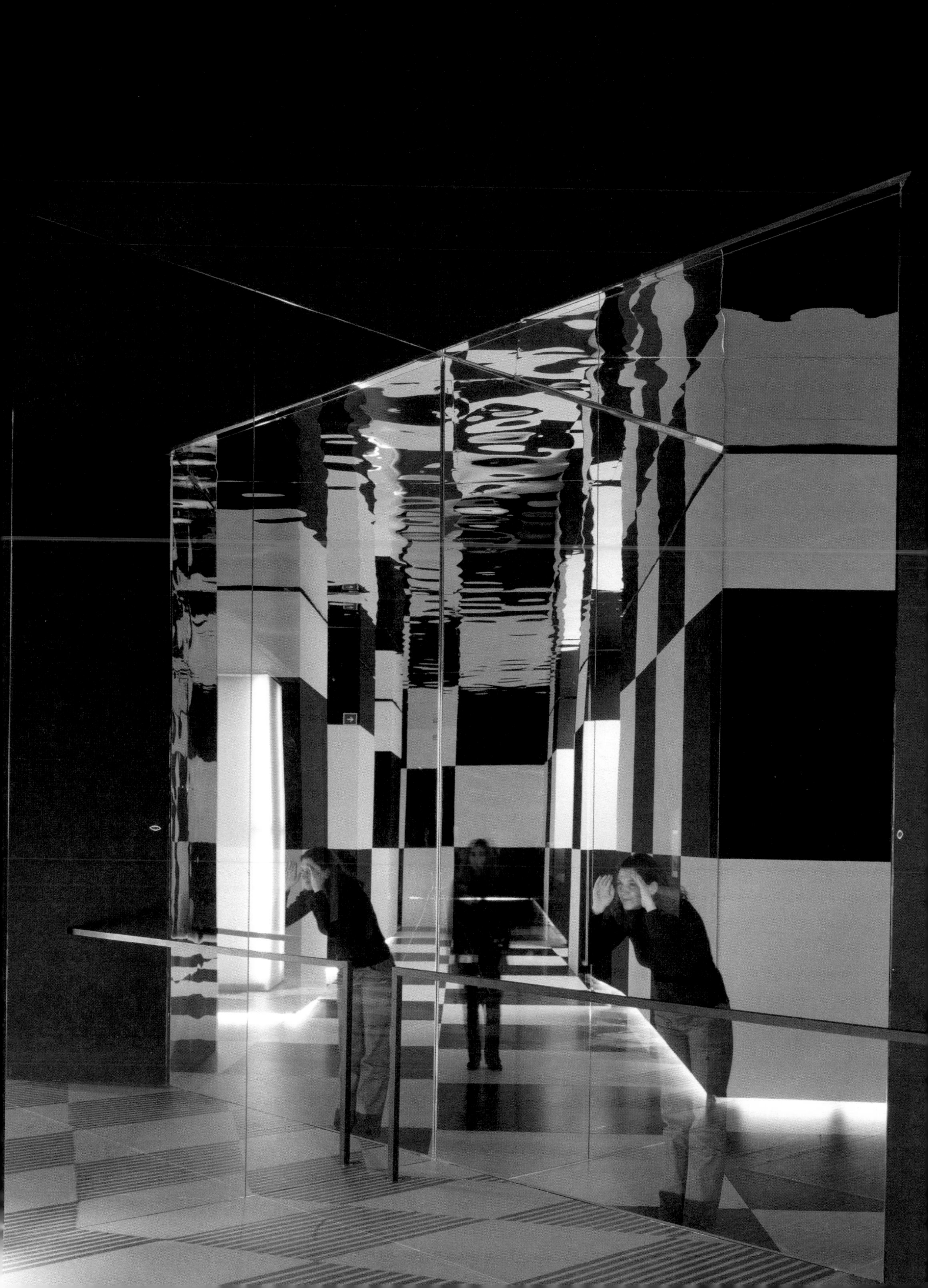

La ilusión que un artista desea crear es mucho más subjetiva y mucho más importante que los medios físicos, objetivos, con los que intenta crearla.
M. C. Escher

Aun si la Tierra dejas

7

Between the sea and the Venetian Lagoon

Carlos Ferrater

The Italian experience

After graduating in the early 70's from the Barcelona school of architecture, virtually paralysed by the political situation of the late Franco regime, trips to northern Italy were a breath of fresh air because there the world of architecture and design led by Gardela, Albini, Peresutti and Rogers, Ponti, Gregotti or Magistretti but also by designers like Sotsass, Colombo, Mendini or Zanusso, seemed to recognise or renew the legacy of the avant-garde rationalists of the 30s following suit from the generation of Terragni, Moretti, Figini and Pollini, Ridolfi and Libera.

New Italian architecture genealogically reconstructed the line of succession while in the school of Venice, Tafuri, Escolari, Aymonino and Rossi formulated the theoretical bases of a new theory of the city, which in a few years would result in dogma blocking the future production of Italian architecture. By breaking the continuity of modern tradition that paradoxically re-emerged in Catalan architecture through the teachings brought to Catalonia by the creators of the School of Barcelona.

The exhibition at the Triennale di Milano by José Antonio Coderch de Sentmenat and in particular the mediation by Oriol Bohigas, Federico Correa and Ignasi de Solà-Morales and a group of young teachers from the school of architecture in Barcelona set the stage and planted the seed that in the 80s and early 90s marked the emergence of Catalan architecture and especially the urban transformation of Barcelona.

My memories of trips to northern Italy in the 70s, preferably Milan and Venice, represent a time of learning, knowledge and familiarity of their cultural and historical models.

In recent years, Italy and in particular the city of Venice has been the most frequent destination of my visits, panels, project corrections and conferences sponsored by Professor Eleonora Mantese in the Venice Institute of Architecture. In the early years, still in the campus of San Polo, she showed us an off-the-beaten track Venice and thus a friendship formed that led us to collaborate in the competition for the extension of "Cimitero de la isola de San Michele". We competed alongside David Chipperfield and Enric Miralles. I remember an extraordinary boat ride along the Venetian Lagoon along with Benedetta Tagliabue in which we were shown the old cemetery, its secrets and problems such as the slow mineralisation of the bodies due to the humidity and pollution of the sludge drained from the Venetian canals used in its construction.

Design competition for the Isola de San Michele cemetery

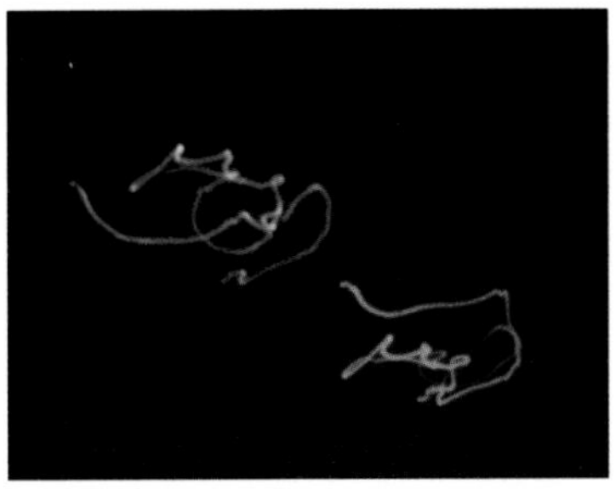

Kites flying in the night skies over Venice

Workshop in Venice with Eleonora Mantese

Years later, in the new Cottonifficcio school, we developed a project workshop in the summer of 2004 with Eleonora Mantese, Christiana Eusepi and Gustavo Carabajal and I remember the exciting night flight of the "aquilones" constructed by students on the canals of Venice. After the academic collaboration, I asked Eleonora and Gustavo to collaborate on the project, sponsored by the Veneto planning consultant, Danilo Gerotto, a private Venetian developer who had the idea to carry out the project from a public-private agreement on the Lido di Jesolo, which consisted of the renovation of public space in the centre of the town and construction of facilities and services that would frame the Aquileia Tower, standing 100 metres high, it would be by far the tallest tower on the Venetian landscape.

Located between the mouth of the River Sile and Piave, between the sea and the lagoon, the project built in part through the efforts and dedication of Gustavo Carabajal, its profile has become the new emblem of the town.

In recent years, after being awarded a Doctor Honoris Causa from the University of Trieste in February 2006, our new studio has been invited to participate in several competitions in various locations in Italy. As a result of this period, we are currently working with Domenico Piemonte on projects such as the remodelling of Castello Borelli and its hydraulic devices in which we proposed the creation of a small residential settlement in the form of a plaza suspended over the sea in a fissure in Monte Piccaro between the towns of Borghetto and Cerialli in the region of Liguria. This project, together with our recent work has been exhibited at the invitation of Ordine degli Architetti di Roma in the magnificent Roman Aquarium in Rione Monti, throughout September, an exhibition curated by Paolo Maselli, one of our studio's partners.

Project for the remodelling of Castello Borelli, Liguria

Throughout the 2009-2010 academic year, together with Alberto Peñín and with the collaboration of Stella Rahola and Jordi Vidal, we have developed proposals for the new port in Venice next to the church of Santa Elena, in the context of the Projects XXI Master's Degree which we teach for the Fundació UPC in the OAB gallery and in the School of Architecture of Barcelona.

For us, Italy has been and will be in the coming years, our favourite destination for our work, both for its cultural proximity and affinity with many young architects who have been carrying out their apprenticeship in our studio, and for their renewed interest in the contemporary project.

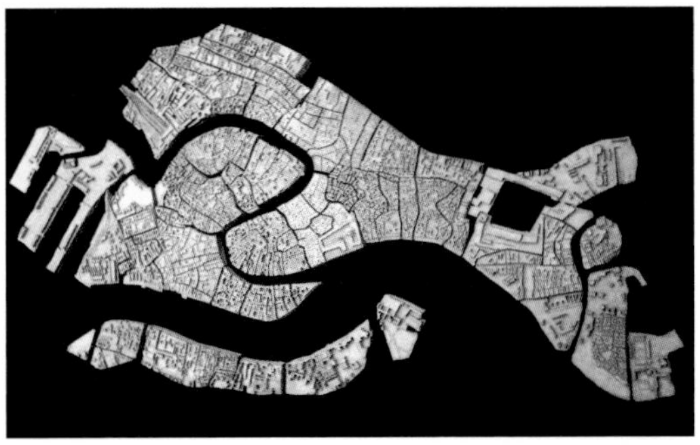

"Projects XXI" Master's Degree. Scale Model of Venice in clay

Gustavo Carabajal

The project falls between the Venice lagoon, the mouth of the Rivers Sile and Piave and the sea, and is integrated through an axis perpendicular to the coastline and extends from the Piazza Internazionale, Via Aleardi, Piazza Mazzini, Via Bafile and the beach, penetrating the sea by four hundred metres. The penetration system is an alternative to the traditional longitudinal system typical of this area.

An underground public car park in Piazza Internazionale with a tree-lined path that alternates between sun and shade, the remodelling of Via Aleardi with the formation of a new public space, the two thousand square metre Piazza Aquileia, surrounded by a two-level building that contains various commercial uses and facilities such as shops, cafes, restaurants and fitness and a sun terrace and pool. A passage serves as the entrance to the underground parking and the logistics of the tower and shopping complex. In the middle of this space surrounded by these buildings stands the Aquileia tower one hundred metres high.

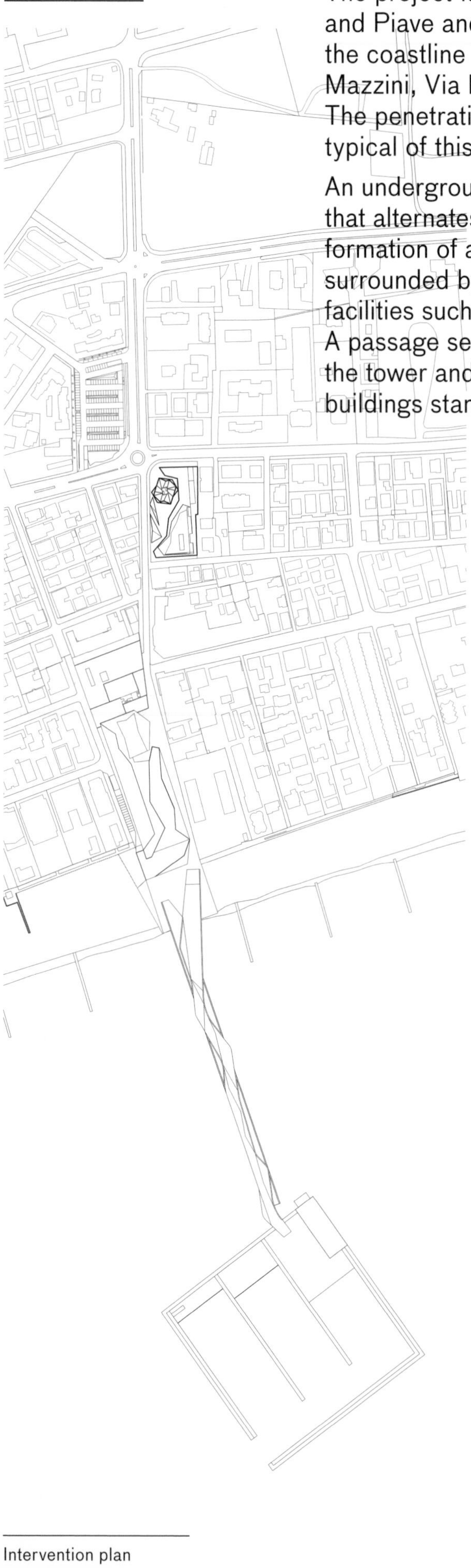

Intervention plan

The project includes the regeneration of the Piazza Mazzini, at the junction of Via Aleardi and Bafile, as a space that organises the intervention. The plaza is thought of as a changing space that supports various uses. This place, paved in stone with trees and lighting, a large bench and a set of sprinklers, sprays and fountains, allows for a multitude of uses and control of the road traffic as well as multiple environmental possibilities. On the south side of the plaza, a large window to the sea, shaped by residential buildings and a quay in the form of a Promenade that penetrates the sea and creates a small dock for the occasional mooring of small boats, completes the intervention.

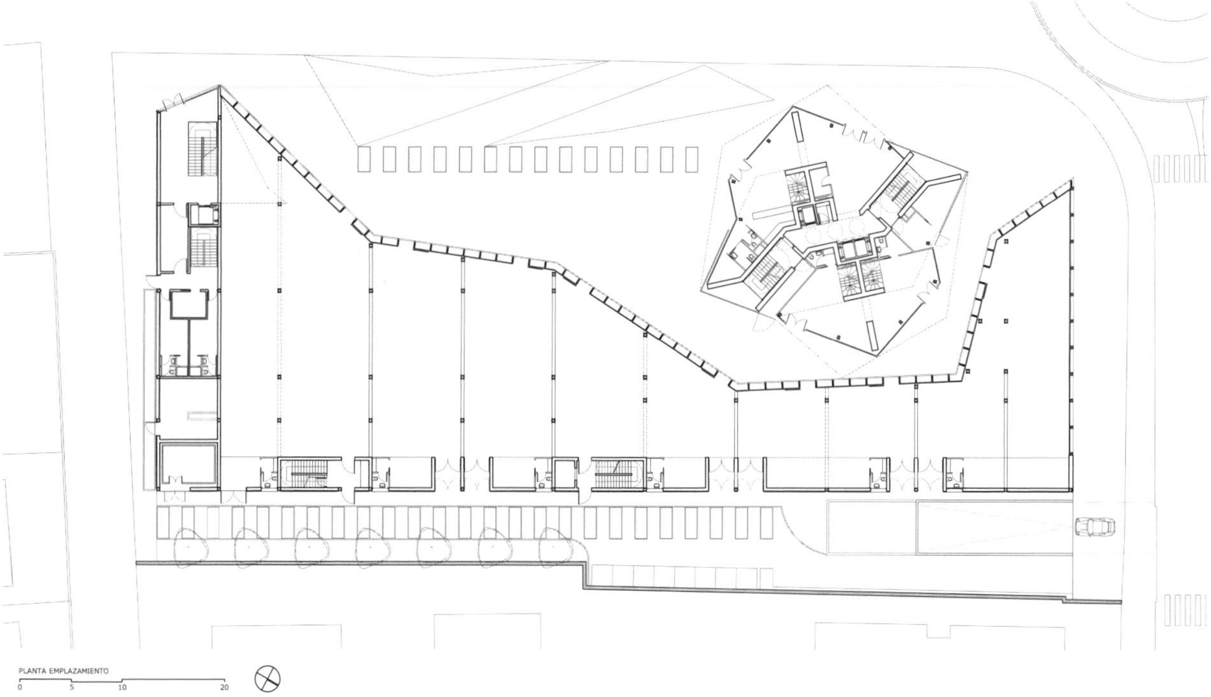

Piazza Aquileia plan

The 24 storey Aquileia tower is structured with a double height ground floor housing the lobby, banks and a cafeteria, two floors for offices and 22 floors with different residential apartments. The polygonal profile organised around the vertical circulation cores, lifts and emergency staircases, provides the four apartments on each floor, of which two are one bedroom and two are two bedrooms,, with views from the terraces of both the sea and lagoon. The houses facing west have views of the campaniles (bell towers) and the city centre of the city of Venice, while the apartments facing east offer views of the rivers and the distant horizon of the Dolomites.

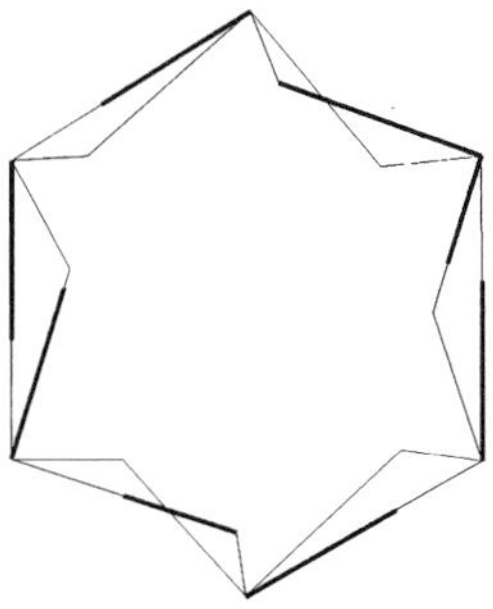

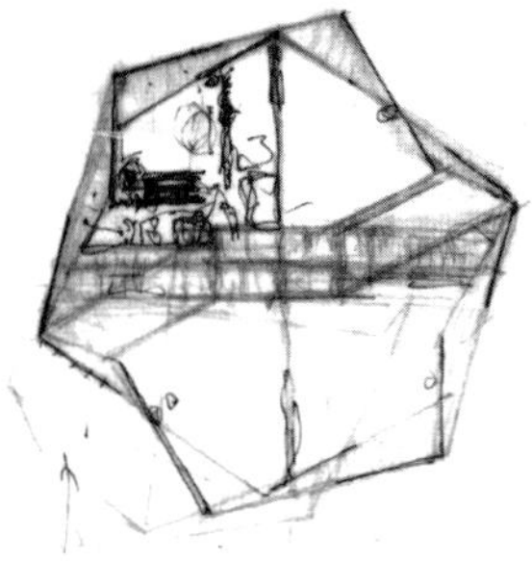

This configuration means that privacy is maintained while allowing for the construction of the intermediate i.e. interior-exterior spaces. These polygonal shaped terraces become living spaces; an extension of the home, their use is made more flexible through sliding glass walls and blinds, becoming a real environmental and climate filter, adjusting the light and shade, and views. The ensemble of the façades is a lightweight, subtle and versatile material that dematerialises the skin, while maintaining the tectonic image of the tower.

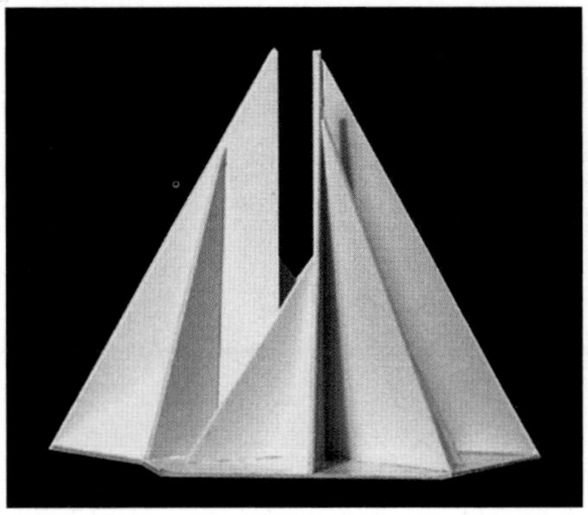

The building is crowned with two outstretched sail-shaped pinnacles, which when lit up at night become a night-time landmark from afar. They act as structural brackets attached to the concrete nucleus, supported through tensors that force the projections of the façades perimeter to work by traction.

On the ground floor, large glass expanses hide the structure and help to balance the volume of the tower with the stony surface of the plaza.

The apartments of sixty and seventy-five square metres with terraces between twenty and thirty square metres consist of an access programme, living room, dining room, kitchen and one or two bedrooms with their respective bathrooms.

In summary, the Aquileia tower project, as an iconic piece throughout Veneto, offers a recognisable profile in an area of low-rise building, playing with the fog and the light of the Adriatic area and becomes the main argument of a new urban system focusing on centrality.

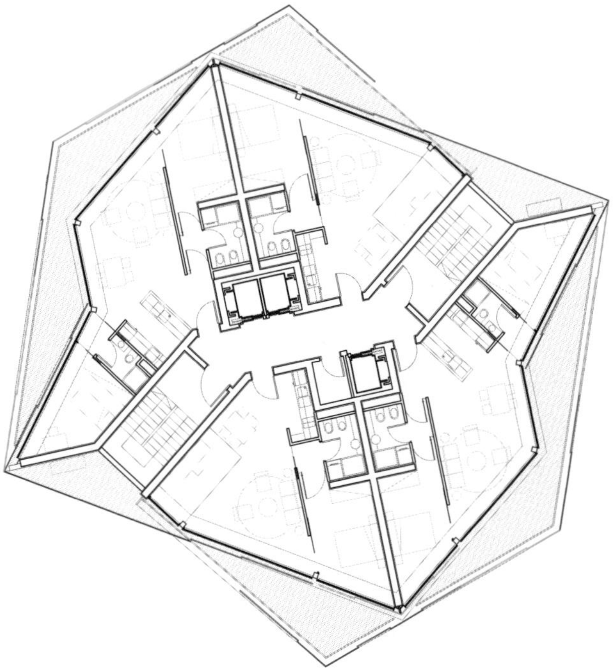

Typical floor plan

Section

8 Confrontation mechanisms. Competitions

José Zabala

If success or failure is the outcome or end of a work process, the design competition is a means to victory or defeat. Winners and losers are two sides of the same coin, the pursuit of a goal through competition. It is the perfect excuse with ingredients such as the spirit of excellence and rivalry, courage in pursuit of confrontation and the achievement of a common goal. But just as in sports, the final is perpetuated by the trophy, a symbol of victory, in architecture it is virtually impossible to point out an end. Winning a competition is the means (or should be) that gives rise to the completion of a project. And the execution (its death?) of the project leads to the materialisation or production of a piece of work to be inhabited, colonised and altered until it perishes due to use, in a kind of continuous future.

The idea, laboratory embryo and creative detonator in OAB

The projects mentioned here share something that makes them familiar, but ultimately, the different conditions under which they were created gives them a distinctive identity. The initial idea could be defined as a space (assuming that architecture =space + time) capable of expanding its properties over time to create new conditions on its periphery, a trigger whose shockwave generates architecture. It is a versatile mechanism common to all competitions presented here and therefore, solely attributable to a work ethic typical of OAB. The fact of transferring, to the very end, the substance of an idea and that it still remains visible in the project, is the expression of the initial radical decision-making.

The proposal developed for the Camp Nou football stadium uses this situation as a starting point where the team (Ferrater-ArupSport-Serra/Vives/Cartagena-Vives) is an indispensable factor for success. Exaequo along with the miraculous[1] proposal by Foster + Partners, takes into account local conditions, the district of Les Corts and the architecture of Mitjans-Soteras and García Barbón. A good alternative to the *traje de luces* (bullfighter's costume) or fake global folklorism a far cry from the representation of football as a community event. OAB's intervention promotes the idea of the large sports complex as an epicentre of urbanity, a mechanism capable of simplifying the organisation of a complex site and able to project the identity of Barcelona to a global landscape.

Futbol Club Barcelona Stadium, 2007

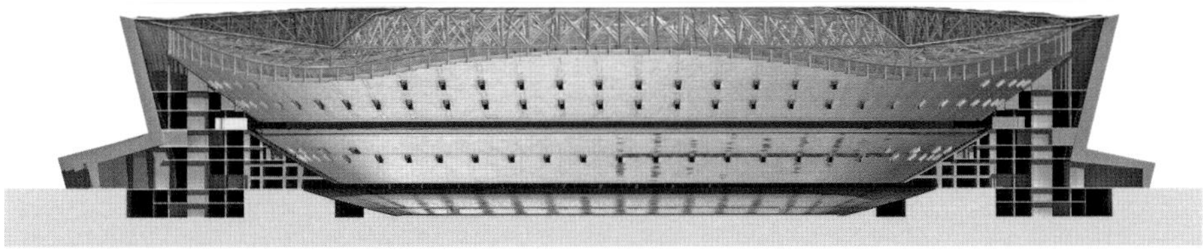

Longitudinal section

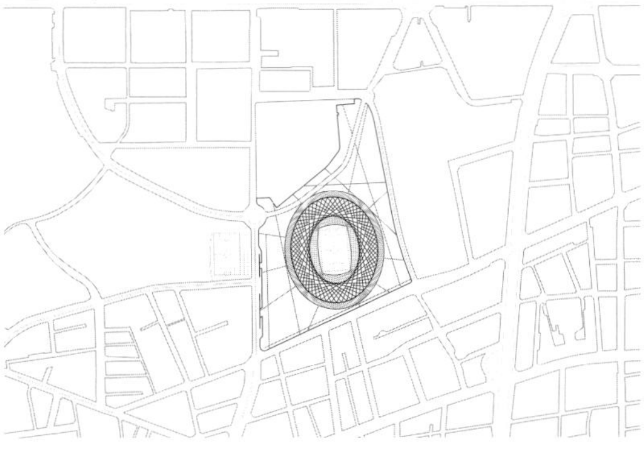

1. Moix, Llàtzer. *Arquitectura milagrosa. Hazañas de los arquitectos estrella en la España del Guggenheim.* Barcelona: Anagrama, 2010.

The Zaragoza CaixaForum Museum acts in the same way as the proposal for the FC Barcelona stadium: compositional concept (unitary character, forms that contain other forms) and geometric simplicity reminiscent of the Mudejar style, a common feature in the historical memoir of the city. Once again, a reflection of the benefits of the collaborative environment in which the proposal was developed. On this occasion, together with José Manuel Broto, founder of Grupo Trama, whose application of the maxim "painting for painting" can be easily applied in this case, "architecture for architecture", a mysterious building crowned with a celestial sphere, container of a universe dedicated to art, a magnet and object of urban desire.

CaixaForum, Zaragoza, 2008

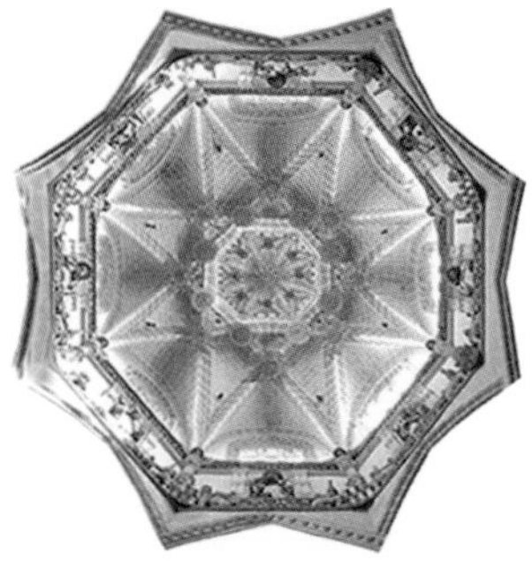

Cimborio of La Seo Cathedral

Ceiling detail in the Aljafería

Dome of The Pillar Basilica

Oratory of the Aljafería

Mozarabic ceiling in Parroquieta de la Seo

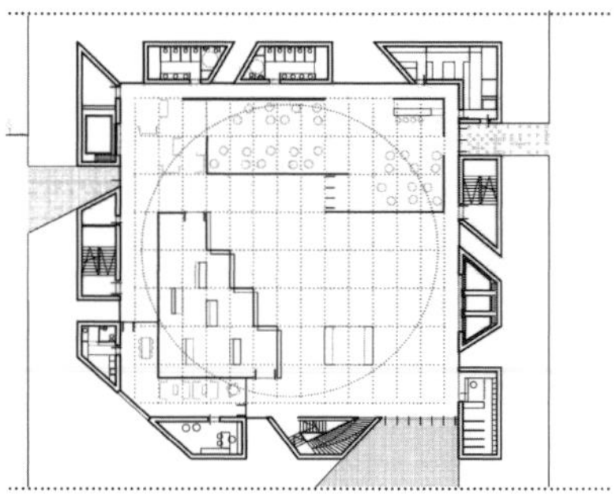

Ground floor plan

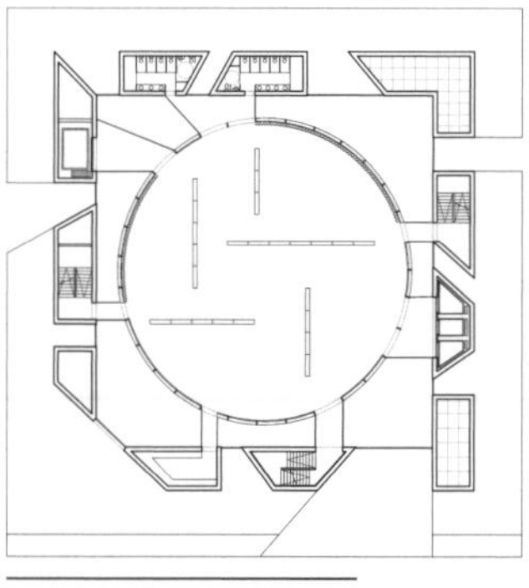

First floor plan

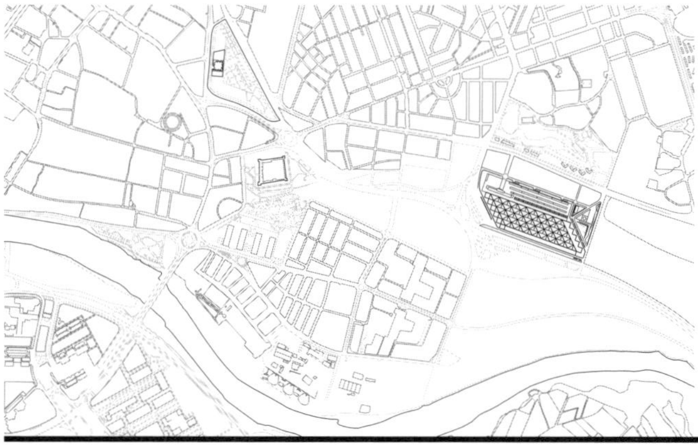

The combination of the circle within a square results in a compact and intense object. A square geometry plan as an exterior perimeter, which defines a portion of terrain and refers to its relationship with the land, while the circle is coverage and continuity, similar to the celestial sphere. From these conditions, the Zaragoza CaixaForum is reminiscent of a permanent and stable architecture, for example a fortified enclosure. A way of expressing the permanence and universality of art.

The proposal for the Barcelona Courthouse building and Court of Appeal contains two intersecting buildings in one volume. Actually it is two blocks connected through a central space. This space, dedicated to the public areas longitudinally, crosses the building, so that the walls are the formalisation of this stimulating idea: two volumes of different heights connected by an intermediate space. A clear and transparent framework, a metaphor of justice just like the hope of citizens.

Courthouse, Barcelona, 2010

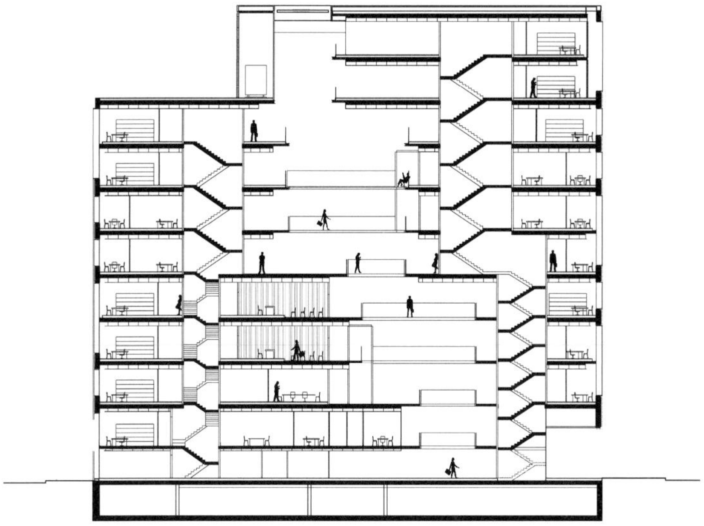

Cross section

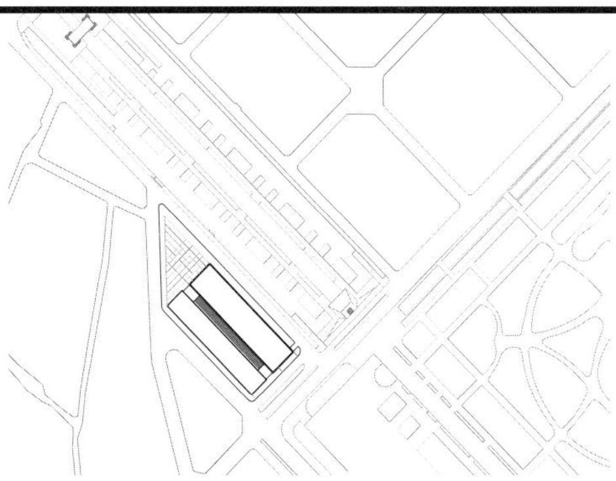

Bilbao is the setting for two projects: the Hospital del Igualatorio Médico Quirúrgico (IMQ) and residential urban development in the area of Garellano. The first, winning proposal by Ferrater-Casares, takes advantage of the opportunity that the plan offers: to create a city landmark at one end of the Peninsula of Zorrotzaurre, part of the Master Plan devised by Zaha Hadid. The part of the programme corresponding to the hospital block is the vertical construction that directs its gaze towards the city. A gesture which claims the social role of the hospital infrastructure and its place in the current Bilbao cityscape.

Igualatorio Médico Quirúrgico, Bilbao, 2008-2012

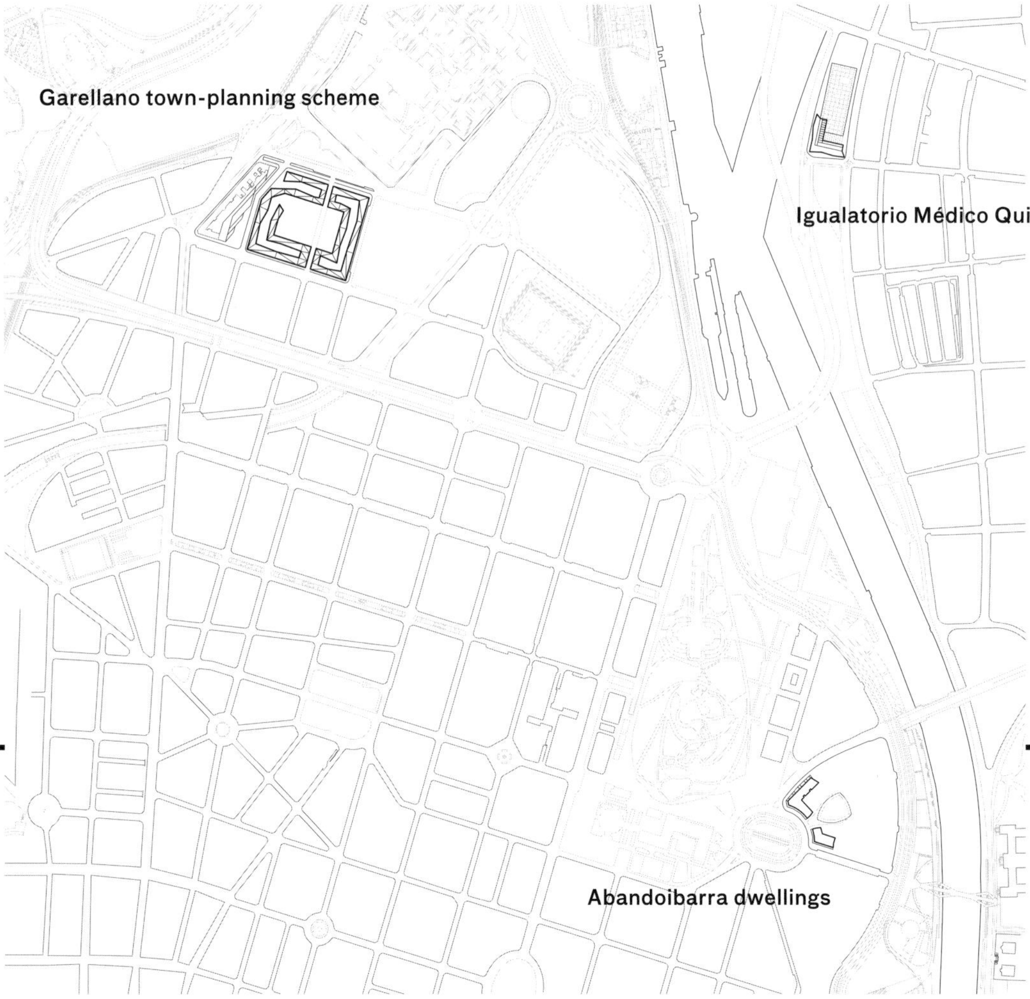

The town-planning scheme for Garellano (OAB-Katsura) shows the possibility of a resistant unitary scheme involving numerous brands of architecture, as well as the idea that the sense of unity prevails so that future action can be easily incorporated into the urban fabric of the Bilbao expansion area.

Distribution of Garellano district, Bilbao, 2009

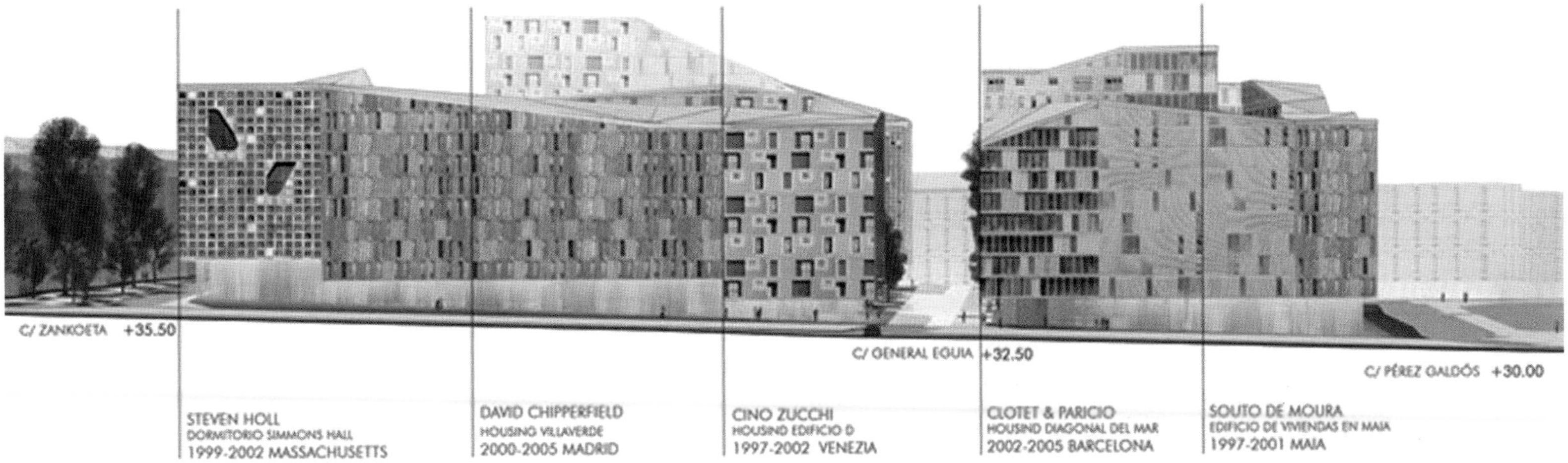

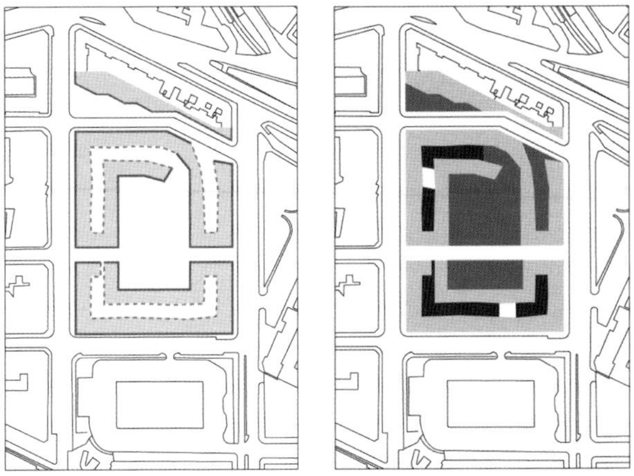

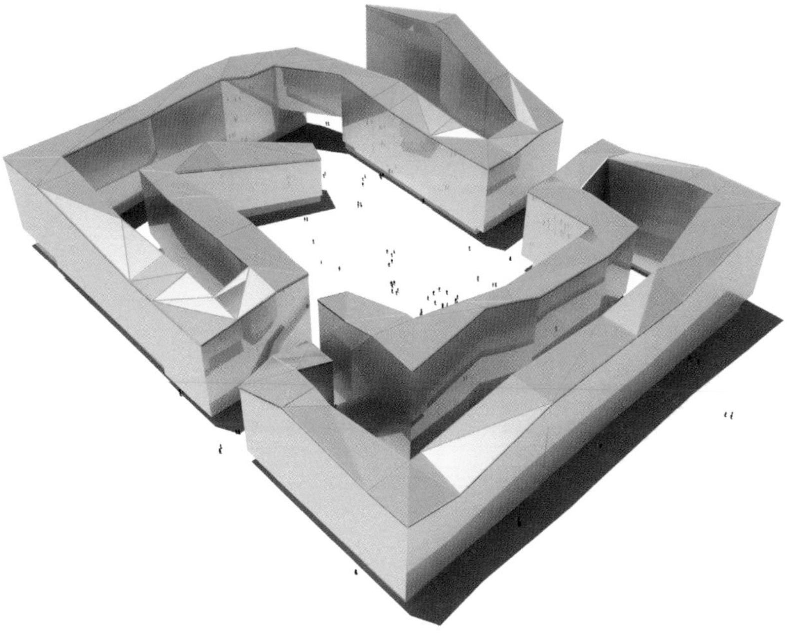

Garellano's principal concern is how to complete an urban space so that it forms part of the landscape. The cityscape, as a part of the city and the natural landscape due to its relationship with a mountain backdrop, in such a way that meeting the proposed density and occupancy requirements are reduced to a simple mathematical exercise: to determine the measurement of the bay of a house that manages to accomplish the proposed density by linear addition. From this moment, this battery of homes can be cut, stretched, compressed and screwed to achieve two purposes: The first, to create a central open space that is both a park and the essence of an urban block, an extension of the fabric of the city. Secondly, to concentrate the expressive load of the volume in the roof, as a representation of the desire for coexistence between architecture and landscape.

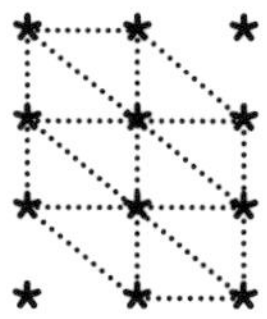

Together with the Garellano project the Frontaura Wineries in Toro share the desire to be objects that participate in the qualities of where they are located. Toro assimilates the rules of the game of the rural plot's grid (in this case, the vineyard as a grid unit) so that the creation of the new building is created from the geometry defined by the vineyards. The building volume is the result of the geometric relationships between the grid points: the line – two points – and the triangle – three points. The amount of programmatic volume and the orientation of the pieces are the conditions that end up finalising the architecture. Toro is a beautiful example of the disappearance of the architect's gesture based on the rules that the locations establish. An attitude that supports the role of nature vs. architecture.

Frontaura wineries, Toro, 2006

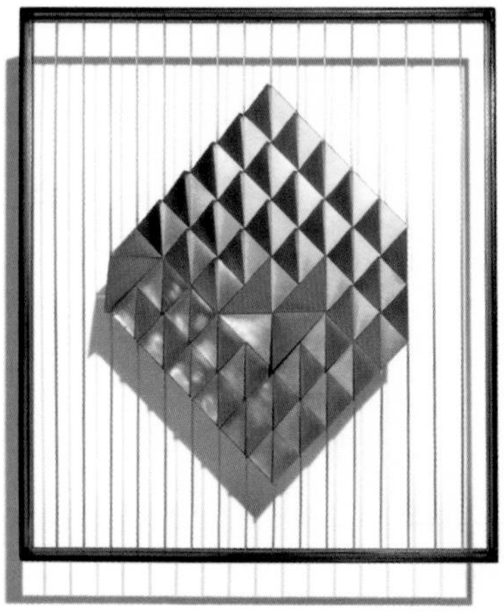

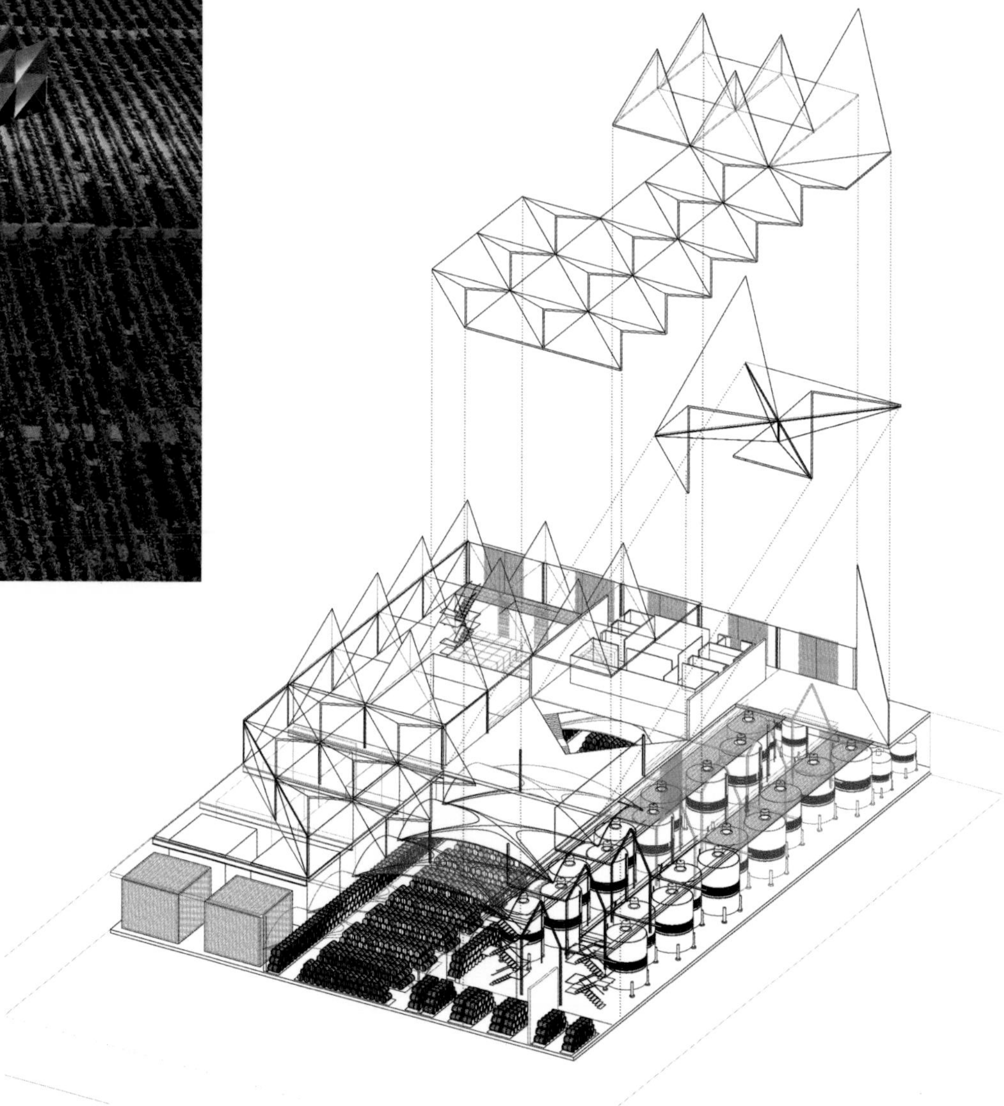

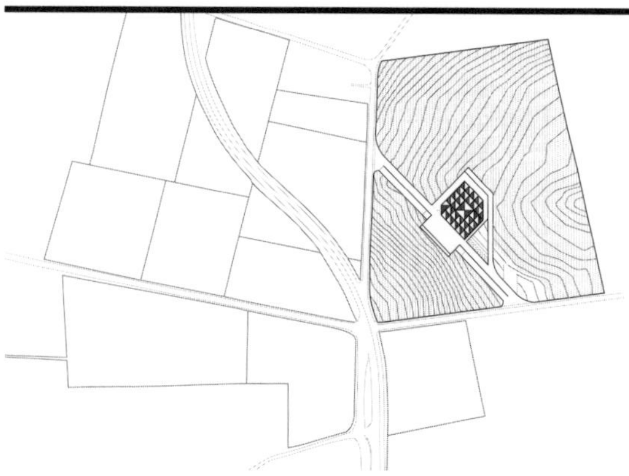

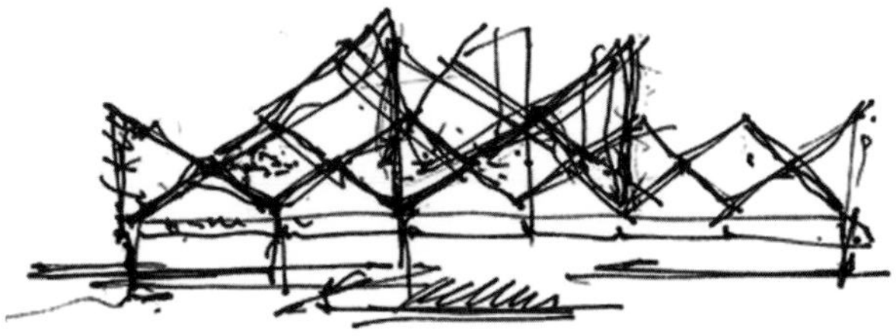

The form of the New Delhi dwelling is derived from its dramatic scenographic setting and the requirements of its singular programme, based on the client's expectations. The result: a versatile layout that exploits the idea of blurring the boundaries between interior and exterior by means of volume diversity – expression of the wealth of possibilites in typology and programme.

Family residence, New Delhi, 2007

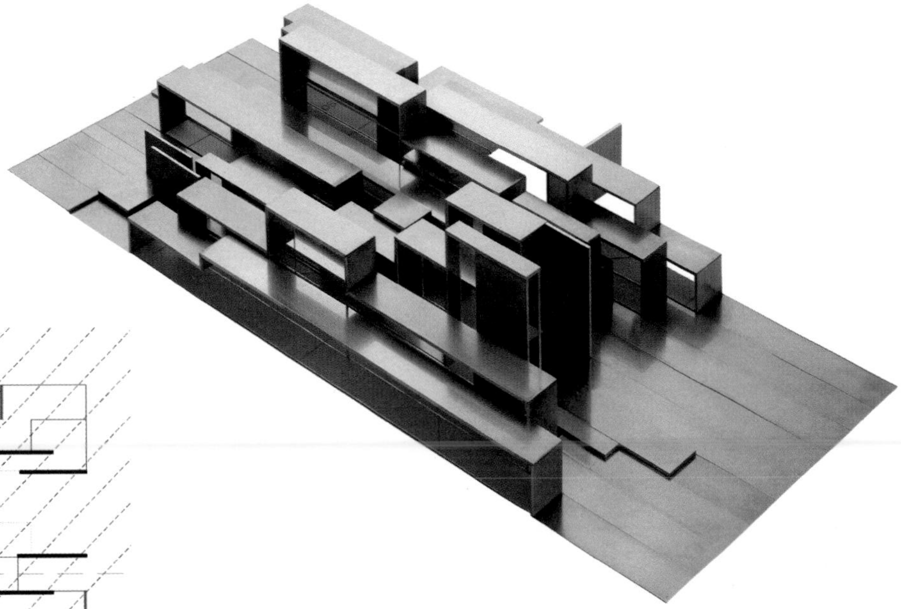

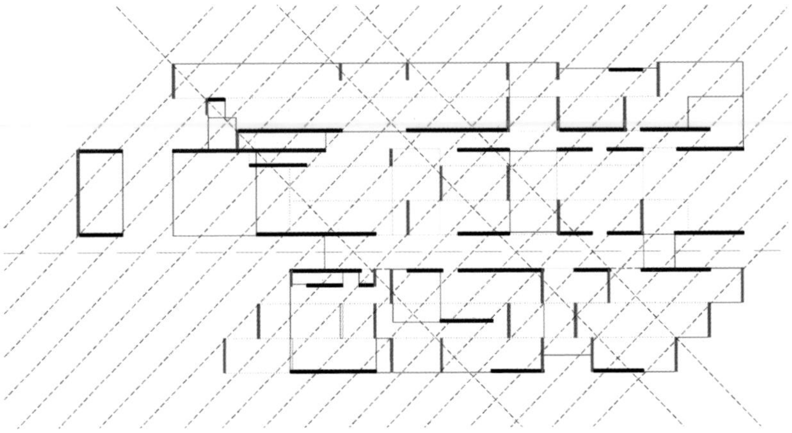

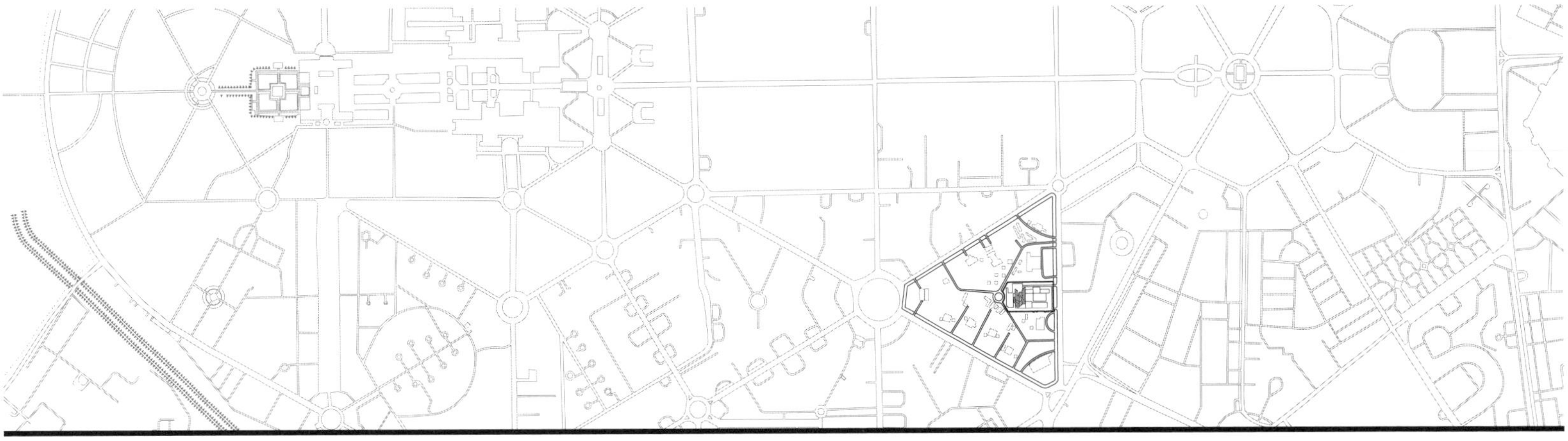

As with the project for the wine cellars, division of the site into a geometric grid creates an identity and enables great organisational flexibility to be incorporated. An in-dpeth reading of this grid reveals the leading role given to diagonal views that cut across different spatial sequences. The volume is broken by courtyards, a vestige of Vastu tradition, and the horizontal planes of the barely-coinciding floor structures, creating a virtual topography on another level – an observatory and a place imbued with ancestral tradition.

9 Azahar. A sustainable building

Grupo Azahar is a group of companies with a strong connection to sustainability and the environment. It provides services of landscaping for public and private spaces, recycling through its waste management plants and environmental consultancy, and other activities including: art sponsorship and cooperation with a foundation on several projects in developing countries.

The parent company is based in Castellón. Given its growth and expansion, it required a head office that reflected its commitment to the environment and the arts, and a programme that incorporated two more actions: greenhouses and exterior plant nursery, and a complementary services building. With this framework, the owners of the Grupo Azahar invited prestigious European architectural practices to design their new headquarters, with the decision in favour of the design created by OAB.

The new building had to be autonomous with respect to the surroundings. This was a way of preserving the integrity of the landscaping on the site. A vast empty triangle without scale, the site is overshadowed by the image of the Maestrazgo Mountains and its proximity to the N-340 highway. Disconnected from the urban fabric and distant from the conditioning factors of conventional legibility, and given the proposed abstraction and geometry of the design, the strategy was for architecture to cross the bounds imposed by discipline to dissolve into the landscape.

The headquarters building has settled into the site, bringing to light the quality of what was already there, camouflaging itself with the setting. To the north and west, the mountainous topography is a backdrop for the building, against which the roof is geometrically cut away. From a distance, its faceted form and profile help to situate it in the landscape. Its tectonic design and image allow it to be described as a sculptural composition, an abstract organisation of solids and voids. The abstraction is the result of the material continuity of the surface and its opaque nature, hiding its supporting structure and the space it envelops.

The planned site layout allows the building to be shown to its best advantage, allowing the perimeter to be traversed entirely and the building to be observed from many different perspectives. Its geometry creates different views, consequence of the interplay of variable light and shade produced over the white folds of the building.

Built on an east-west axis, the building is distributed into two wings joined by a central volume and placed around two open courtyards, each with a different style. The first of these serves as an exterior foyer for receiving visitors and employees; the second is landscaped and has a more private use. Thus, the building is closed off from the distant landscape and establishes a complex interior/exterior relation.

True to the Khanian concept of "Silence and Light", the glass walls facing the courtyards allow the varying tones of natural daylight into the building's interior; they introduce the outside world directly into the interior through these intermediate spaces. Uniform silver daylight bathes the surfaces of the vaults, homogenising the lighting levels inside the building.

The courtyards allow a cross view between the wings through glass walls, with the canopy and the building's orientation helping to keep direct radiation from the inhabitable interior spaces, but allowing in a great deal of controlled light, making artificial lighting practically unnecessary.

The four wings housing different departments of the company converge on a foyer which, besides acting as a distributor, becomes a large representative exhibition space. Once entering through the main doors, not only is the palette of materials changed, but also the criteria behind their handling. While the exterior is predominantly a solid, matt and opaque image, the interior was designed with an eye for the conventions of comfort and recognition. The use of natural materials – stone and wood – offer a counterpoint to the solid abstraction of the exterior.

This foyer receives its light from above; light coming from the north enters the building through a grand skylight above a series of suspended concrete girders, paying tribute to the architects' demolished work; Restaurante Lola.

The ceilings inside reinforce the geometry of the roof and the spatial continuity by means of transparent glass tympani supported on the partitions between the different rooms.

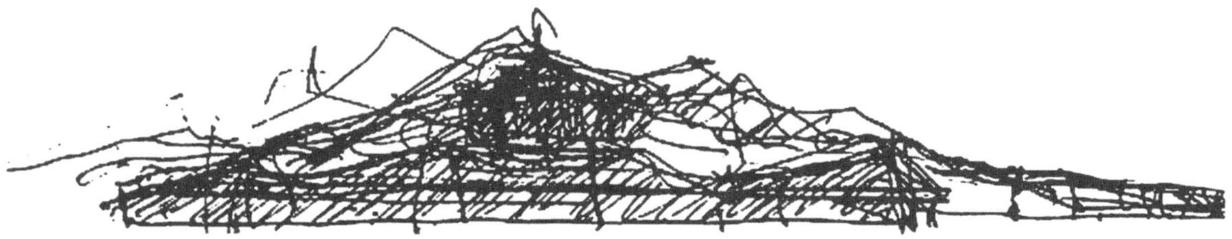

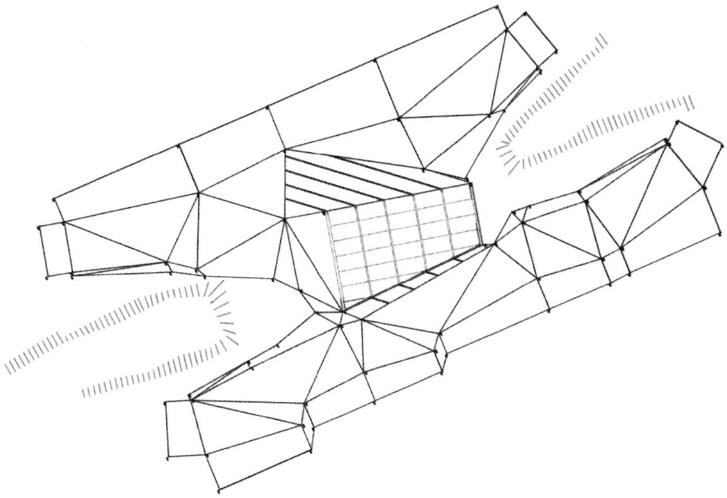

For exterior walls a continuous cladding was chosen that could be applied seamlessly to both façades and roof blurring the lines between them. Collaboration with the R&D department of Parex gave rise to a new material applied to the Coteterm system, with continuity of the thermal insulation the length of the building's perimeter. We intended to achieve maximum energy savings and to find an environmentally-sustainable solution.

The resulting skin is of white flexible and self-cleaning stucco that does not require joints, except for those made during the actual construction measuring 2-3 mm. Special mention should be made of an important aspect – the high energy efficiency we were able to see for ourselves in the interior, given that during the summer months there is no need for supplementary air conditioning.

We find ourselves faced with a building that follows the basic architectural guidelines, what the socio-ecologist Ramón Folch would define as relevant architecture: "It is and wants to be a normal building, because normal means the correct cardinal point orientation, choice of materials based on their extraction-production cost, use and expected duration, the use made of rainwater and greywater, the preeminence of natual daylight and energy efficiency, and a high degree of comfort for the user. But this unusual normal building can be perceived as exceptional."

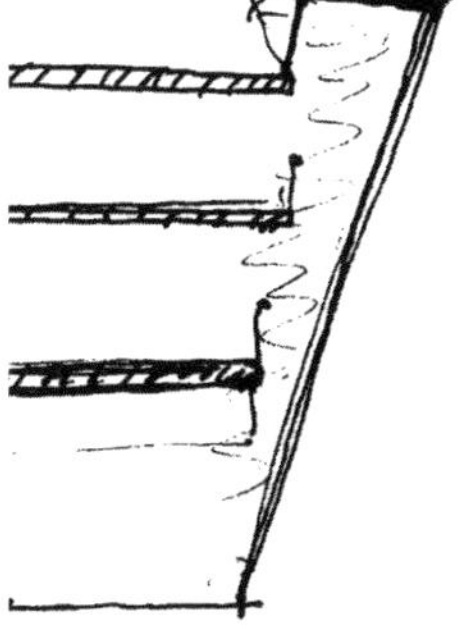

In July 2009, at the Spanish Architecture Conference, we presented the project for the first time and the innovation for the building industry offered by this product, used by OAB in a soon to be finished project for a summer camp complex for the NGO Fundació Catalana de l'Esplai.

One important environmental aspect of the buildings is the rainwater collection from all of the roof areas and the exterior areas into a cistern-pond, for use in watering the gardens and the plant nurseries on the site.

Finally, there is the plant and maintenance building, a 250-m long building with a sloping roof to enhance cross ventilation. It cuts the contours by adapting to the slope while rising in height depending on the uneven nature of the site and the use given to spaces (personnel changing rooms, work areas, plant rooms, store-rooms and garages). The sloping roof holds a landscaped roof terrace with a surface area of 2300 m^2, which serves as a backdrop for the building.

This project won a prize during the 7th Ibero-American Architecture and Town Planning Biennial in April 2010.

Nuria Ayala Prats

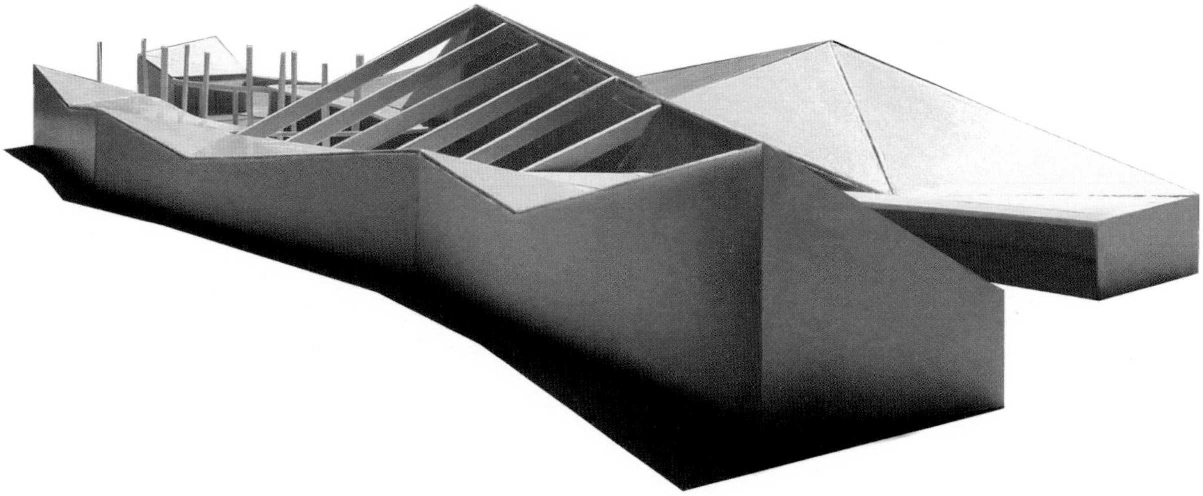

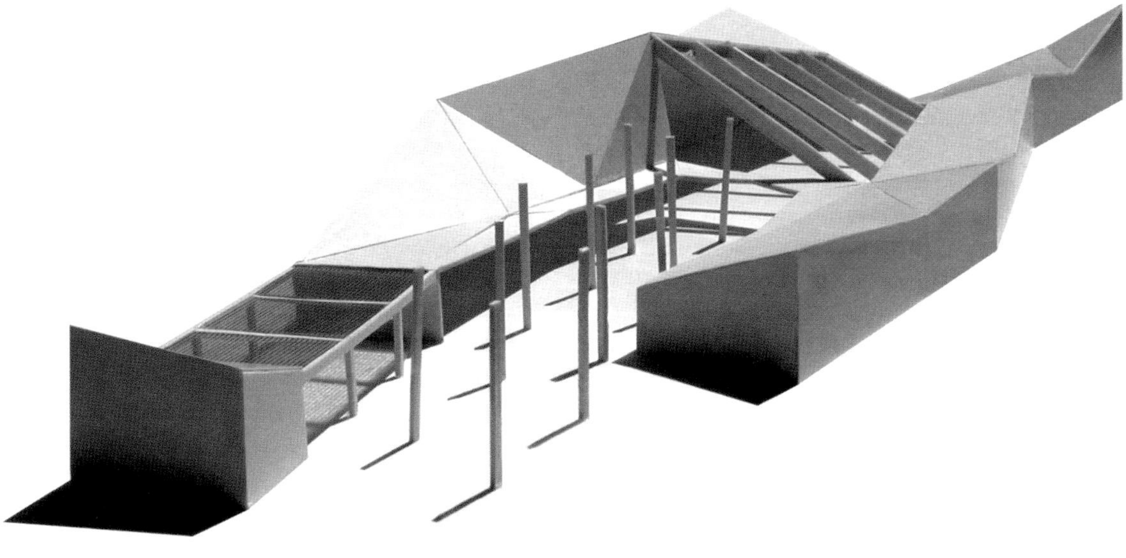

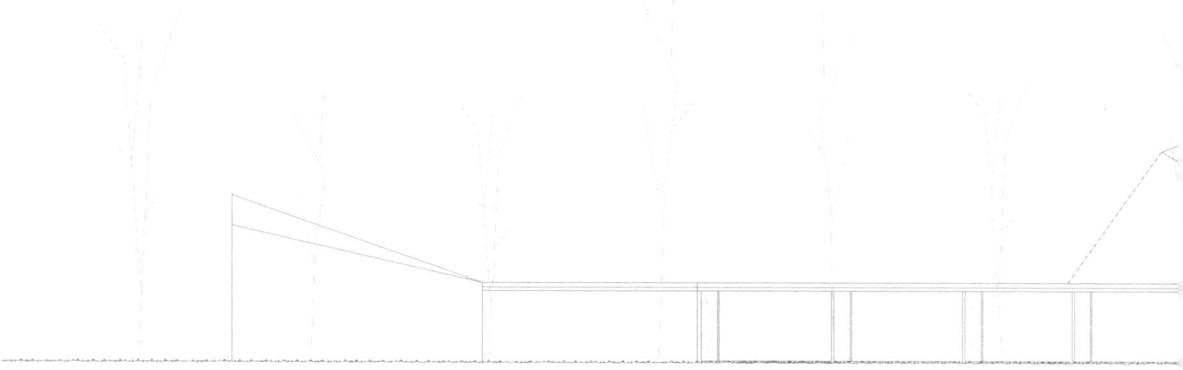

Longitudinal section

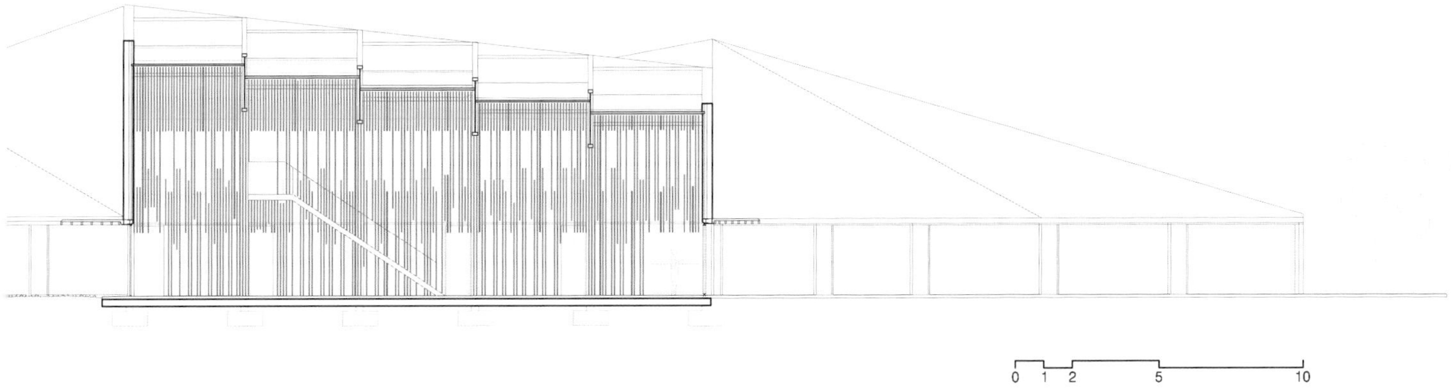
0 1 2 5 10

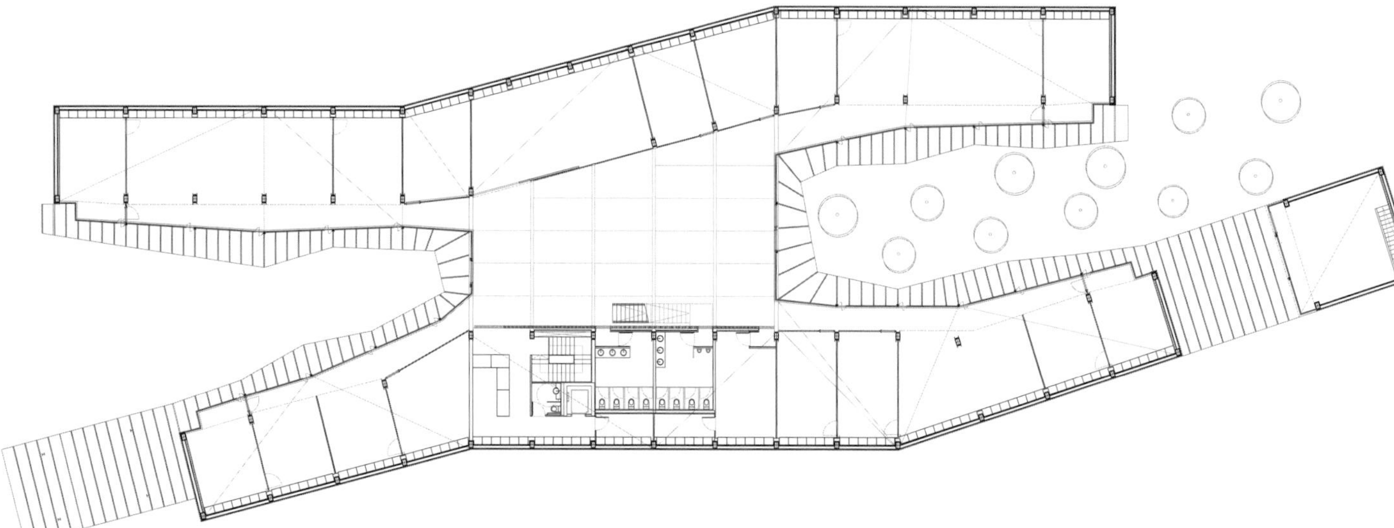

Ground floor plan

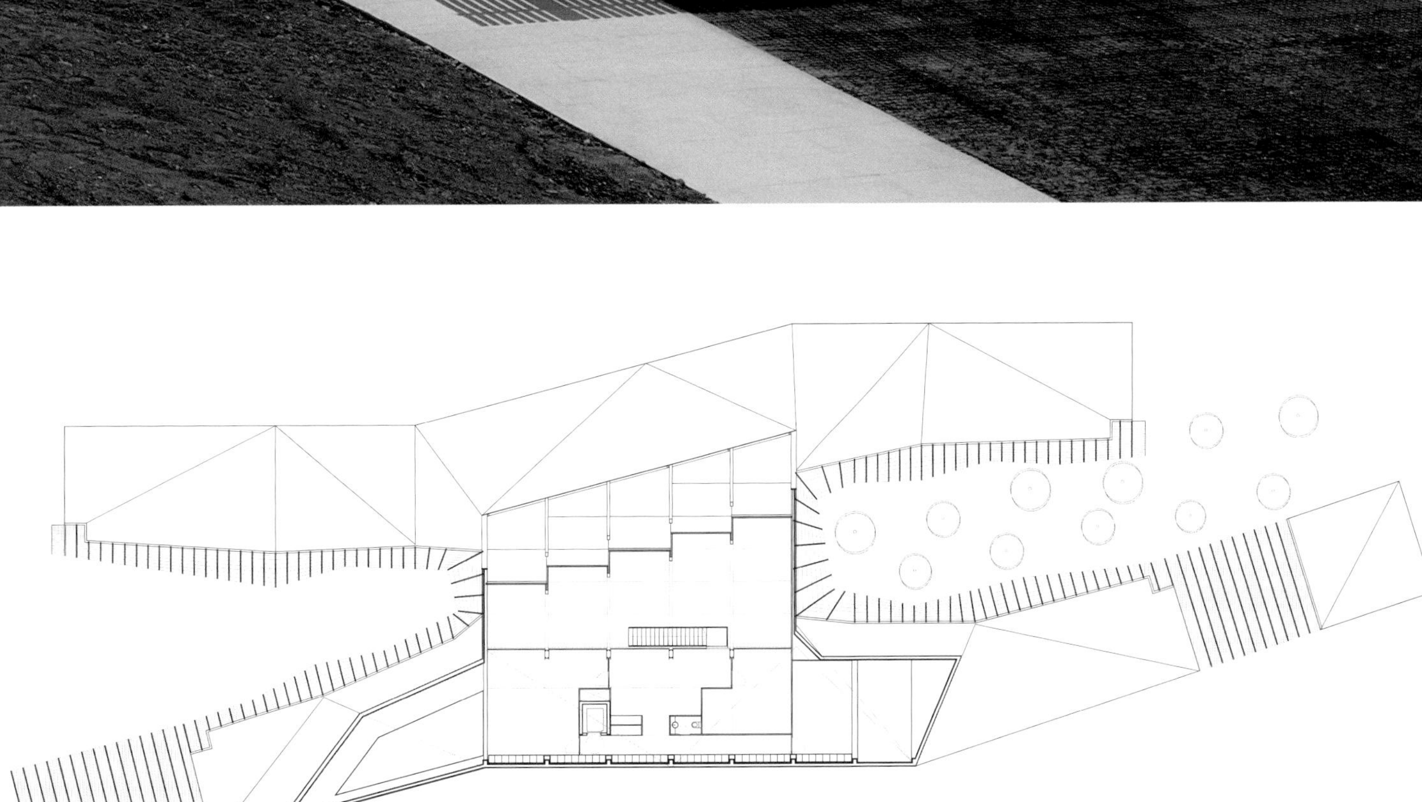

Mezzanine plan

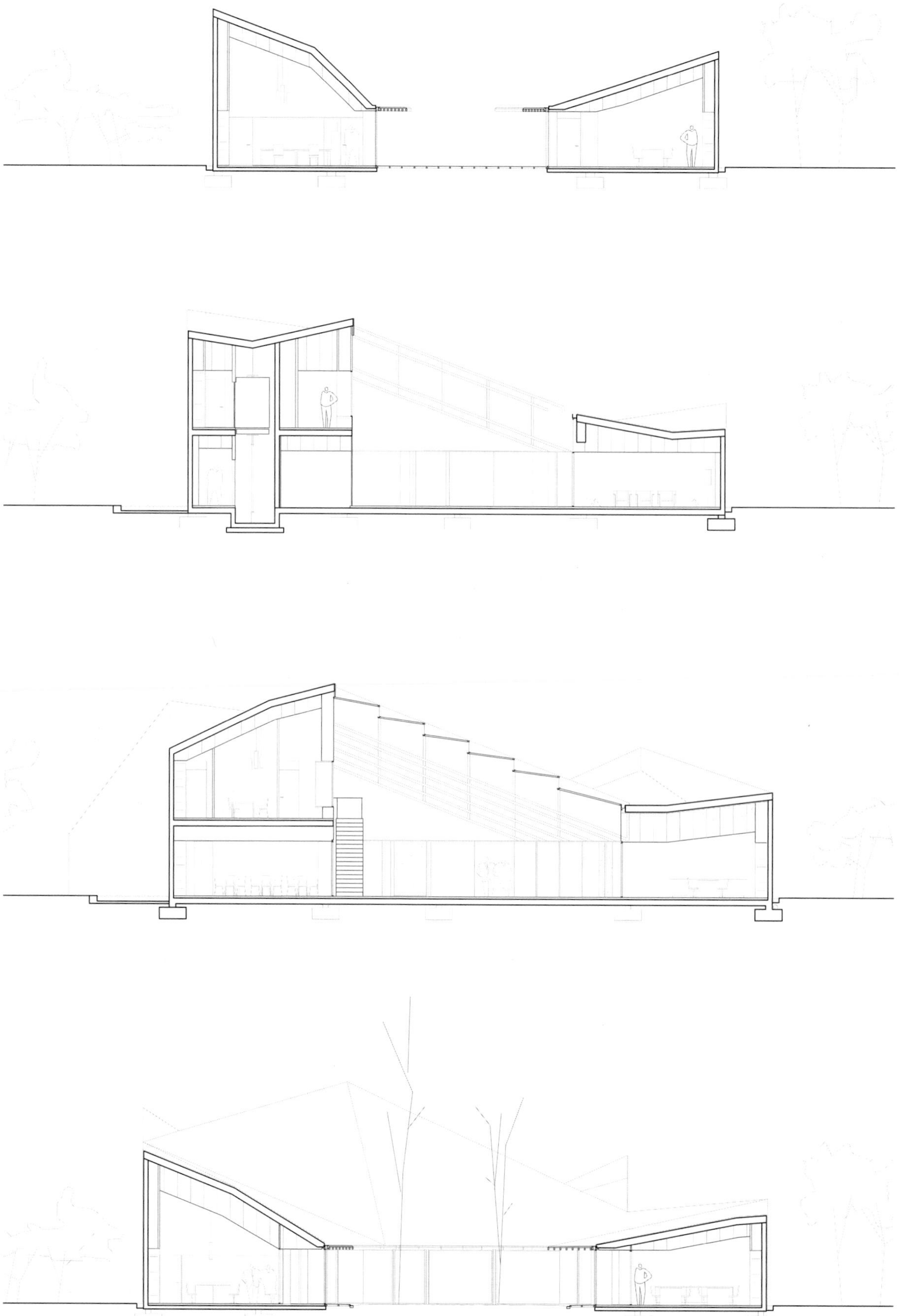

Cross sections

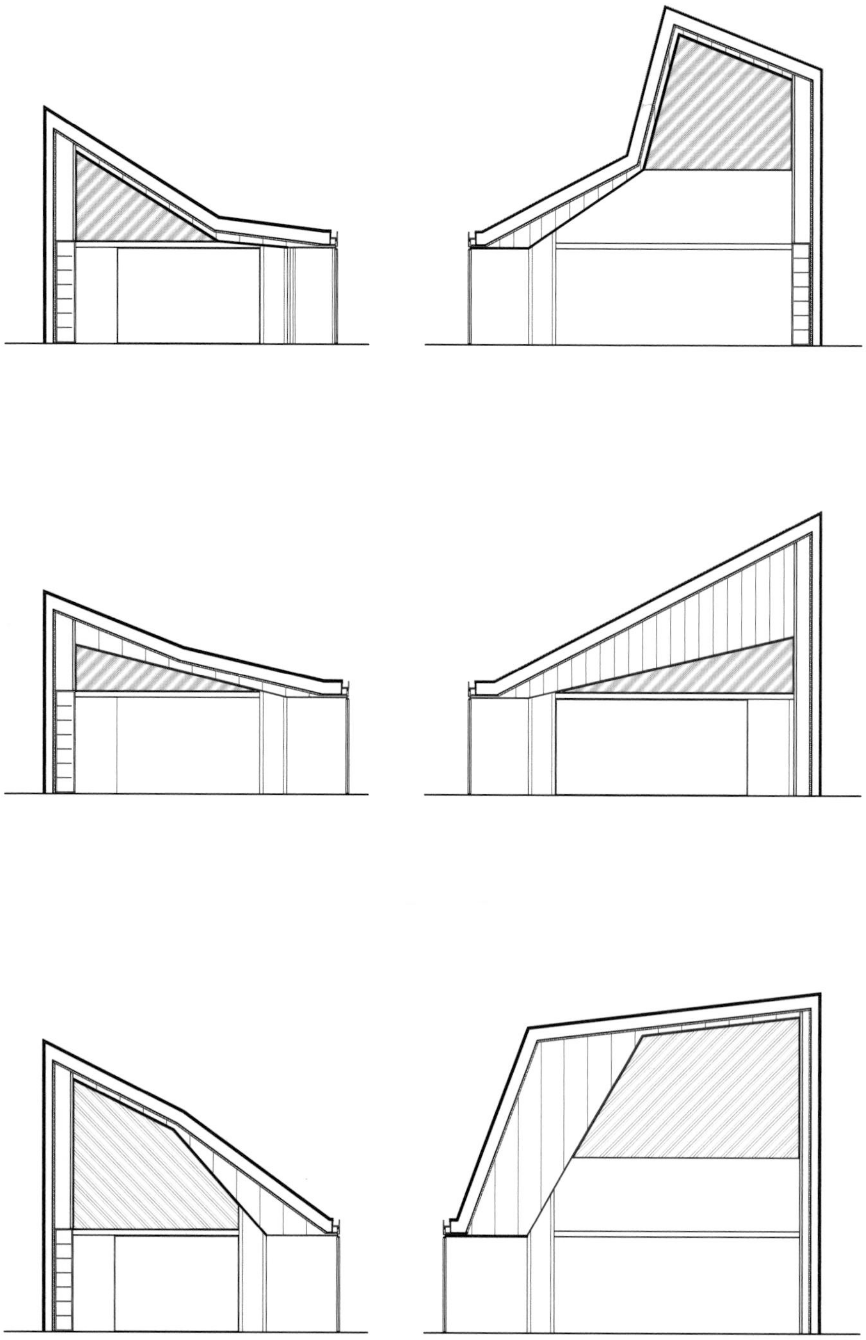

Cross sections

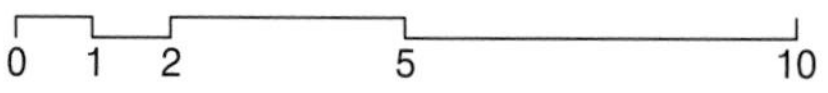

10 Small urban actions

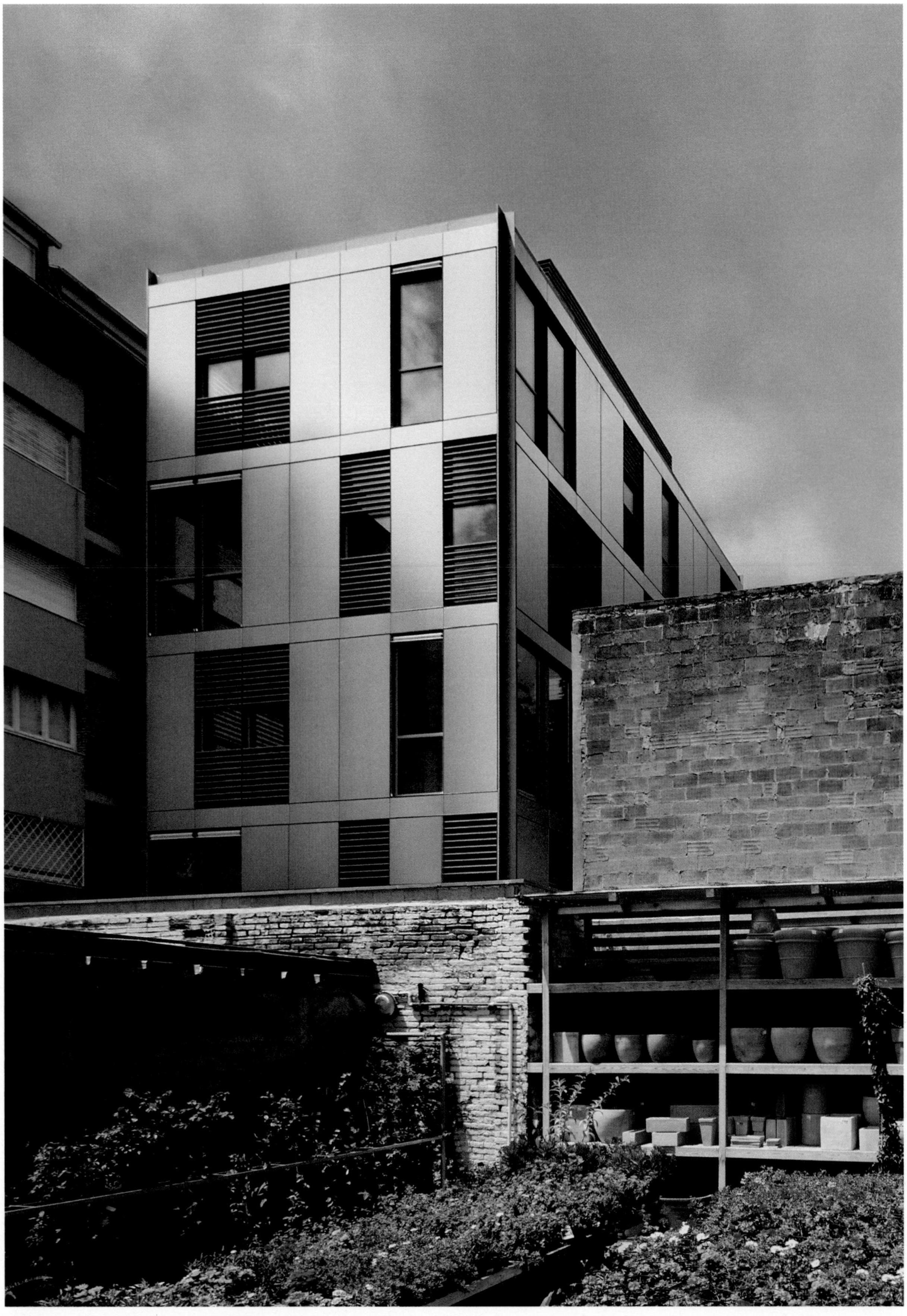

Building in Carrer Dr. Carulla, Barcelona

A series of different actions in the city of Barcelona and other neighbouring urban areas have given rise to different typological designs in which the design strategy was based on strict urban development parameters. Each case is a new way of understanding the immediate environment and of associating the needs of a client with the building that is to be occupied.

One of the projects I took part in during the initial years of OAB was the transformation of a block in the Cerdá's 19th-century Barcelona new town expansion area, the Eixample, for the developers Metro-3, a company with deep roots in the Eixample, and for the public company Pro-Eixample. The transformation involved the regeneration of the interior of the block, which had become overflowing with old workshops and storage areas, as a landscaped public space with a small numer of services, and three residential projects of new construction in the ring around this space.

With a diagonal layout, the route of the former Horta Road provides access to the interior of the block from the opposite streets, becoming the axis for the linear spaces paved in different materials over which the small service facility was suspended following the laws of the garden. It is a modest space, built of concrete, galss and aluminium latticework. It is hermetic during the day and transparent at night. It was chosen years later as one of three projects representing Barcelona in the *On-Site: New Architecture in Spain* exhibition at MoMA in New York.

The three residential buildings completing this action offered us the possibility of researching different typologies. While the building facing Carrer Alí Bei, the walls of which were party walls for the others, and opening onto the garden, was designed with 35 m^2 apartments, the one facing Carrer Roger de Flor was designed to contain apartments with 1+1 and 2+1 bedrooms, with the depths of the living areas varied to create a pattern of volumes on the façade, where the floor slabs were folded and cut out to allow oblique views towards the sea. Meanwhile, the building facing Carrer Nàpols was designed with a dual-aspect typology with larger homes.

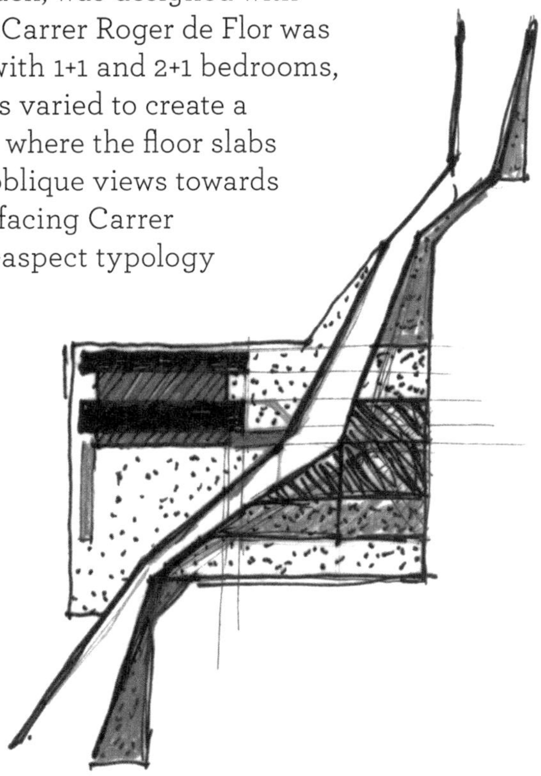

F-3 House is an urban single-family home with a garden, or rather, an urban garden with a home, which was how we designed it. In contrast with the narrow, deep and rectangular site, a series of volumes is laid out according to the requirements of the programme in which each interior space emphasises the exterior spaces. Each part of the house is prolonged towards the exterior creating a sinuous perimeter route that has vegetation as its predominant feature. This series of façades is modulated by a structure erected on the edge of the perimeter, delimiting and pressuring the planes consisting of filled spaces and voids, allowing light to enter intentionally into its open-plan spaces so that a changing interplay of light and shade is recived throughout the day. This house has blind walls built using a drywall system and clad on the outside with limestone, and glazed walls designed to use as few panes as possible.

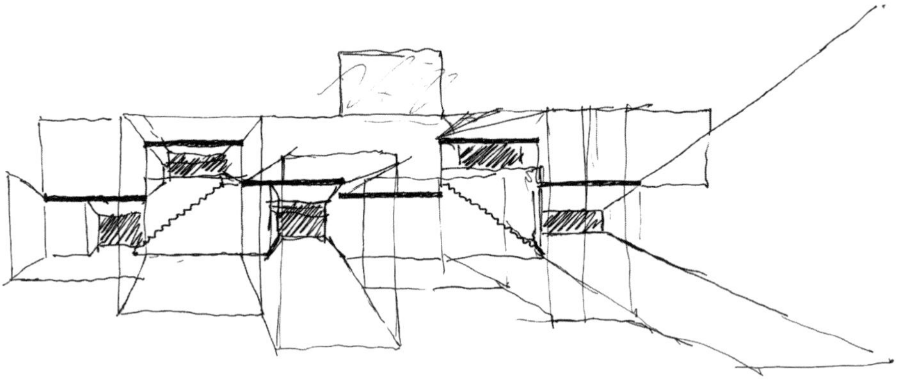

A few streets down, in the same urban setting, in Carrer Doctor Carulla in Barcelona, there is a small site where a small four-storey building has been erected for undefined use – either homes or offices. As with F-3 House, it was built using a drywall system, but unlike the former, the load-bearing structure loses its significance and in its place is an inherent flexible structural system that modulates the façades and allows the elements to be interchanged. In this case, these elements are composite stainless steel and glass panels with concealed aluminium frames and combinable louvres. This construction system is the result of collaboration with the company Technal and with architects Ignacio Paricio and Carlos Ferrater, who designed a system called Fachada Perfectible (Perfectible Façade) for the Barcelona House presented at one of the editions of the Construmat trade show.

In both projects, F-3 and the building in Carrer Doctor Carulla, the client of the former was unknown and the programme for the latter was unspecified. In spite of this, the integration of the building in the garden and the flexible nature of the "perfectible" building have contributed to finding a profile of occupant who have made the project their own immdiately.

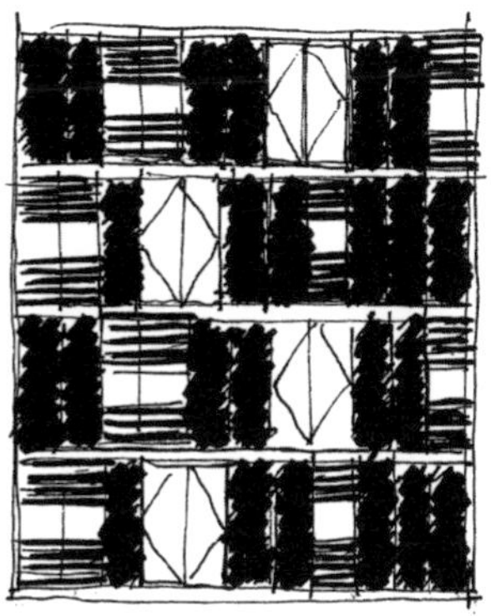

Two projects, completed a few months ago, offered us a strict programme defined by the end users and, particularly, the desire to have a representative and singular building in their urban setting.

The first, a 9-room hotel, is located on the corner of a central square in Sitges, which responds to a layout of narrow and irregular streets lined with low buildings. The location is the famous Carrer 2 de Maig or "Sin Street", so-called because of its night life. The client was a developer and friend, and his young and enterprising daughter who had recently returned from the US and who, after a number of years spent on cruise ships, decided to settle down and take on the family business. The need arose to construct a contemporary building that took into account the Mediterranean tradition and the concepts of the local venacular architecture. The building is an attempt to dignify a public space by enhancing the value of the corner using a sculptural composition of gaps and voids, reflective surfaces and transparency.

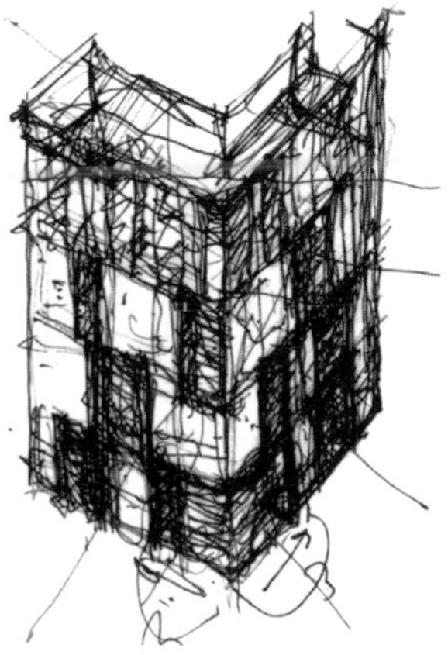

The second is a Protestant church for the United Evangelical Church of Terrassa, an institution with almost one hundred years of history in the city. This community, one of the largest of its kind in Catalonia, had been struggling to find a site for a building that would combine religious and social uses. It needed to house an auditorium and a library for the Protestant Archive of Catalonia, in addition to classrooms, music rooms, a multi-purpose space and a childcare centre to serve the district.

The project took several months to design, during which close contact was maintained with the community, at times with long and large meetings in the office and at others exhibiting the project in churches with 300 people. The new complex was paid for with the sale of the old building, with contributions from members of the community and with a part granted by the government in return for the commitment to a social project they would carry out.

The desire to have an austere but friendly building, without becoming an icon but at the same time unique and a reference point from the distance led us to design a single-storey project without architectural barriers. The height of the building was reduced owing to the slope of the side streets and two cube-shaped volumes were suspended over it, which became representative owing to their size and their skin design. This new complex is located in an area between the peripheral residentail districts and the industrial area where the plots are larger and the streets are wider. It was opened by the former US president and Nobel Peace Prize winner Jimmy Carter.

This church is the last of this overview of different situations we have found in urban centres, where small actions ranging from projects in low-density residential areas to public spaces with diverse programmes have offered us the opportunity to experiment with design approaches involving the economising of means, environmental efficiency, social organisation and respect for the built-up environment and for the city.

Lucía Ferrater

F-3 House, Barcelona

Hotel Alenti, Sitges

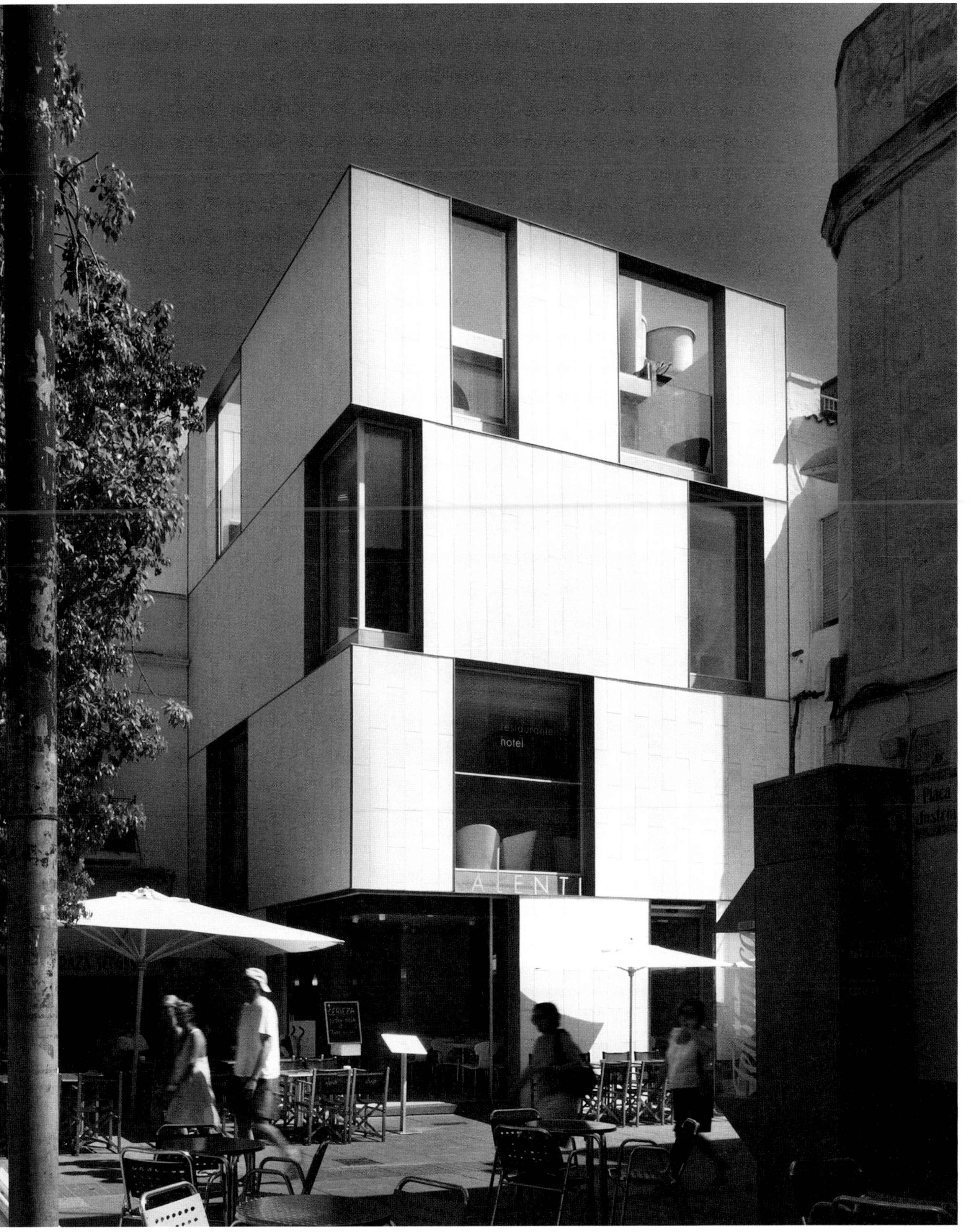
hotel
ALENTI

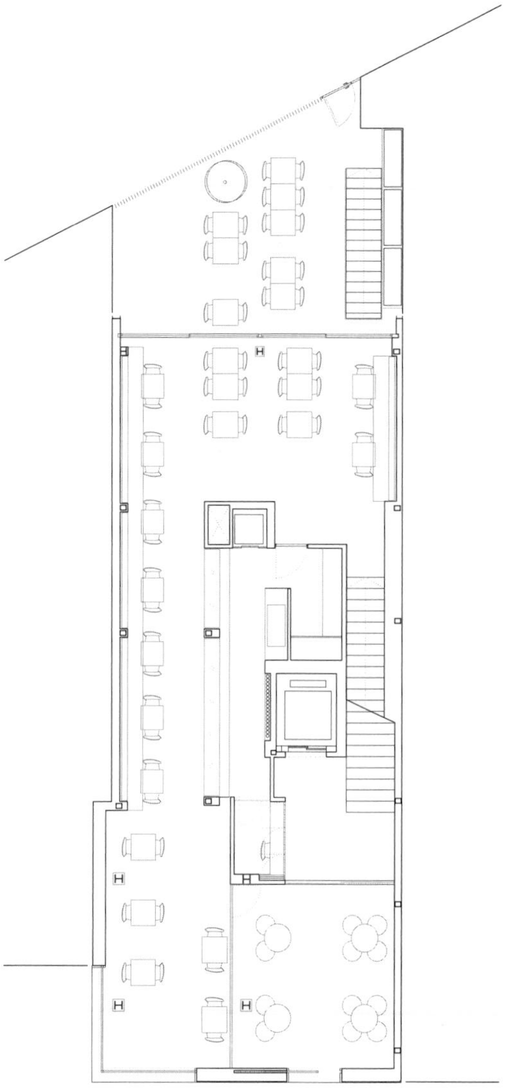

Ground floor plan

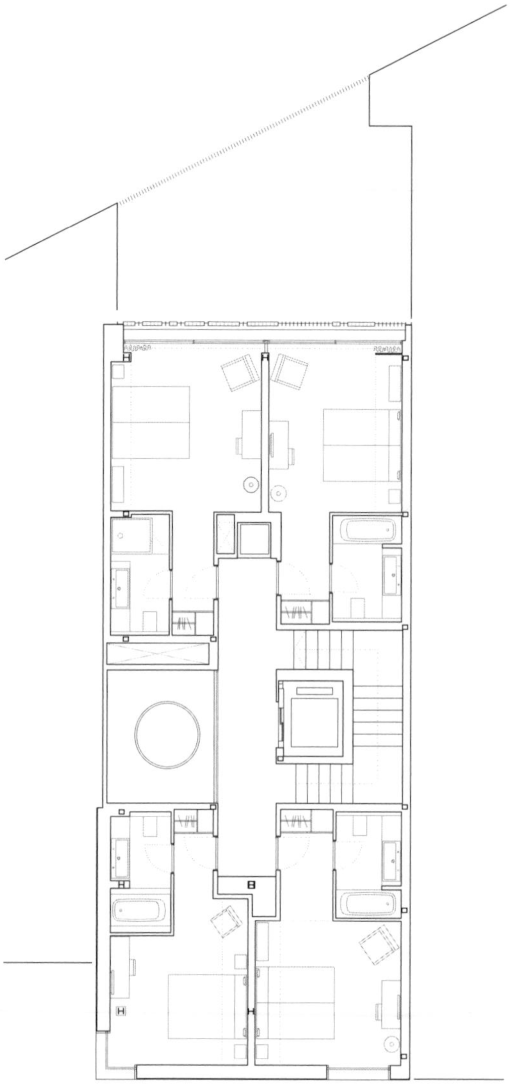

Typical floor plan

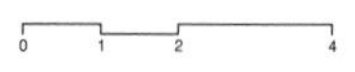

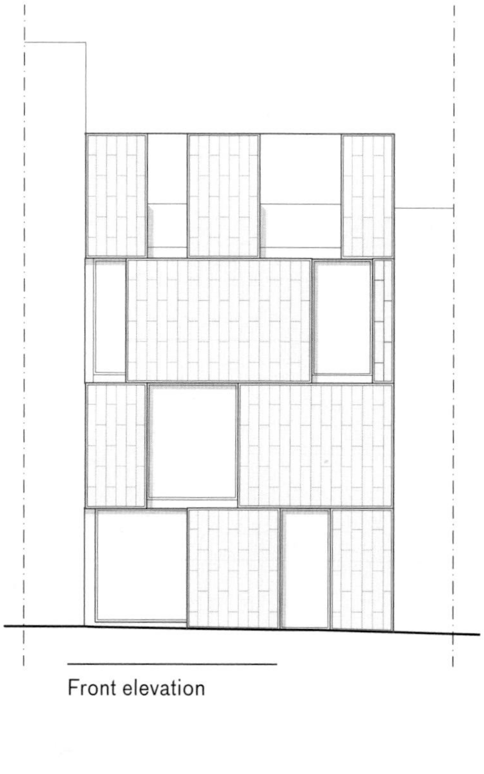

Front elevation

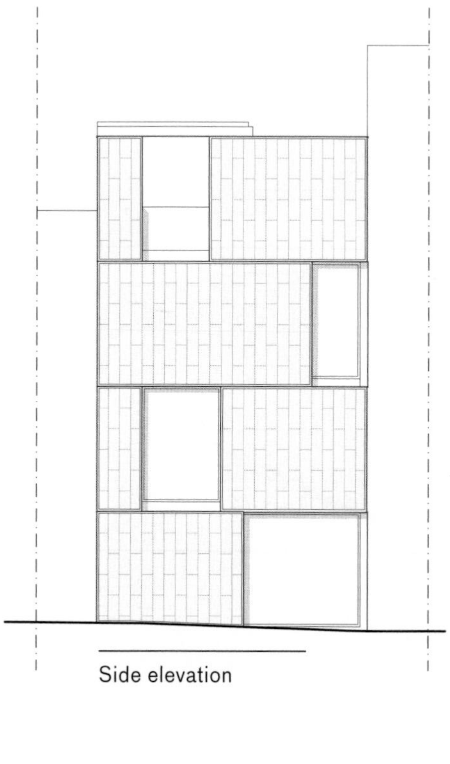

Side elevation

ALENTI
ALENTI

Evangelical Church, Terrassa

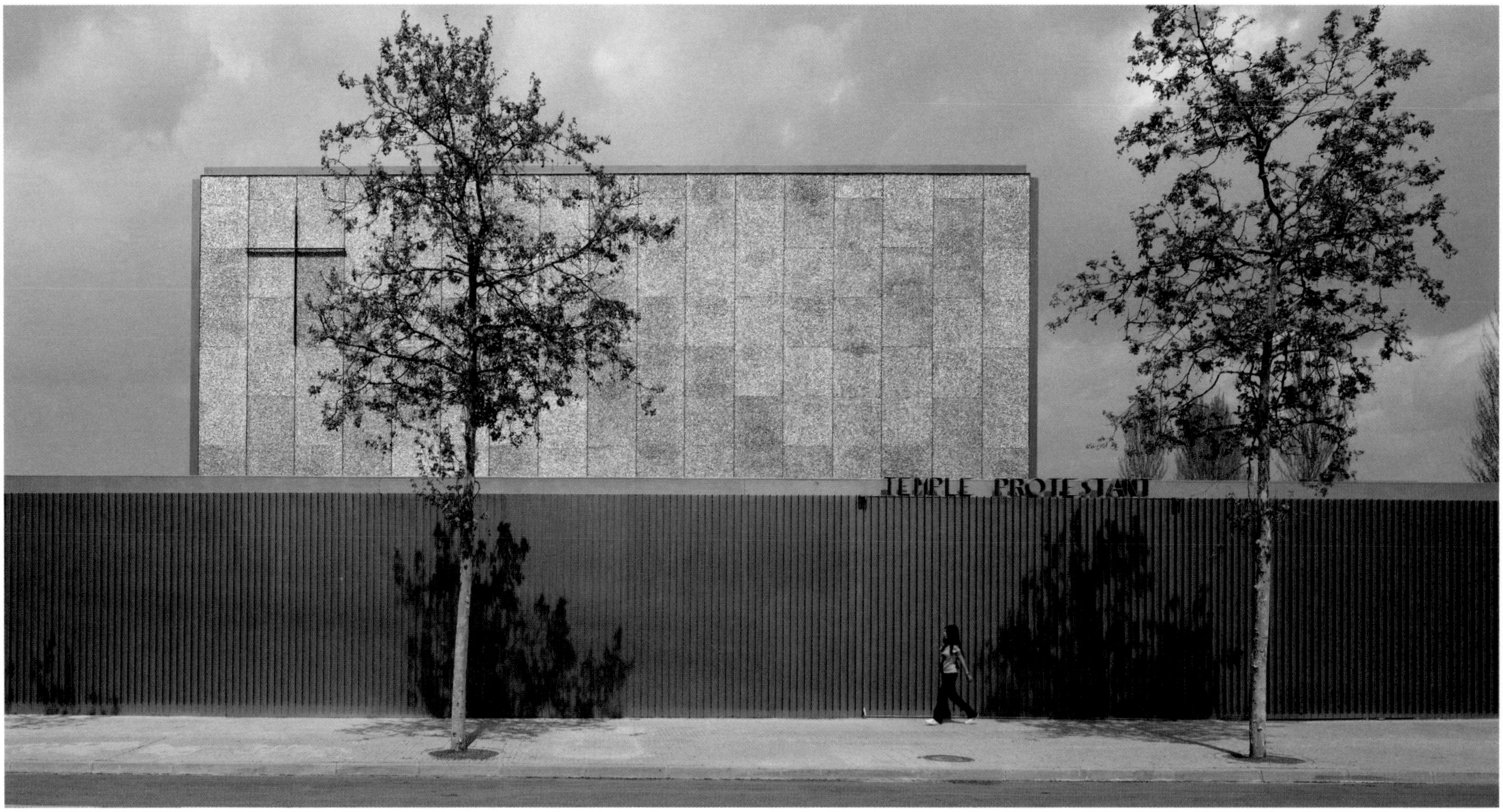

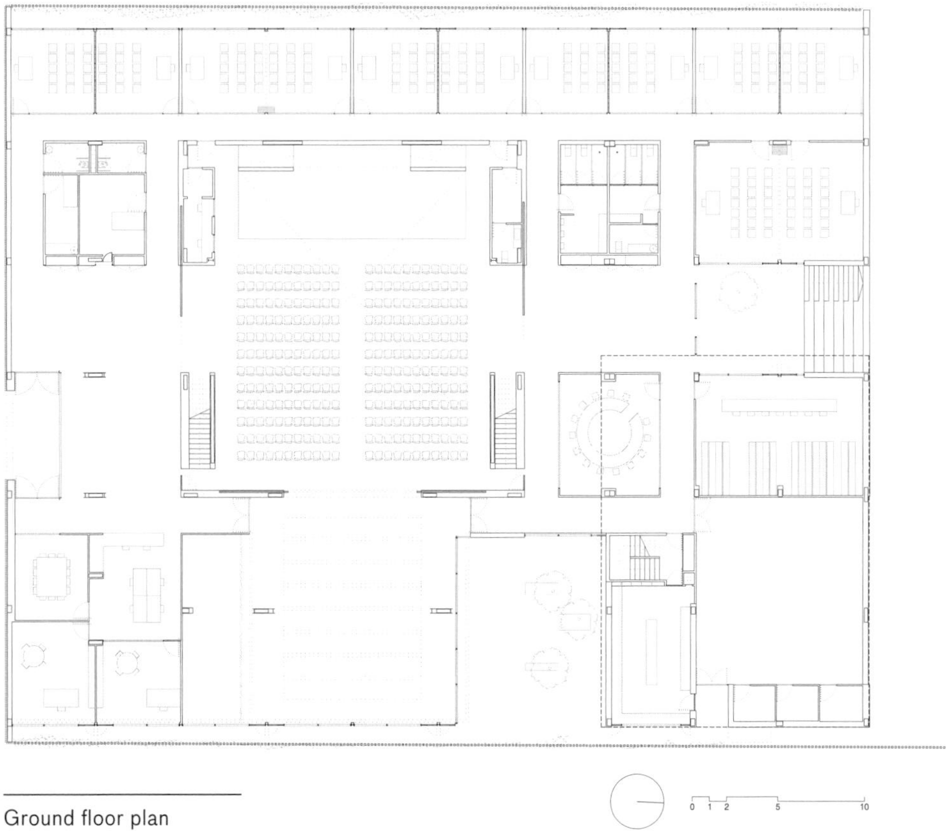

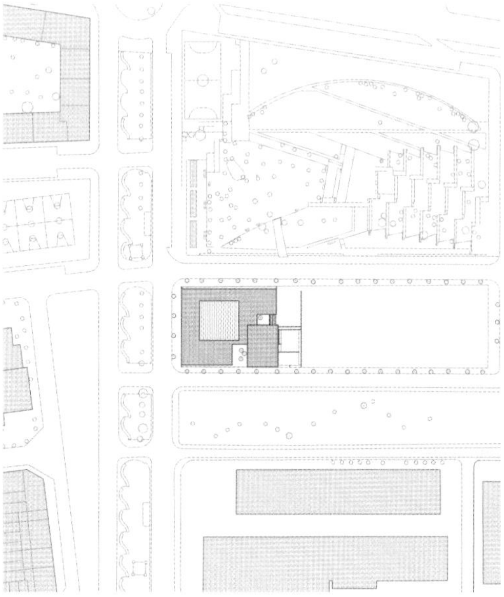

Ground floor plan

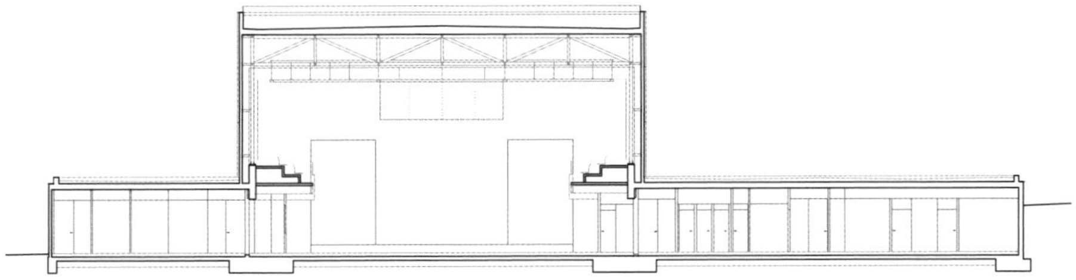

Cross section

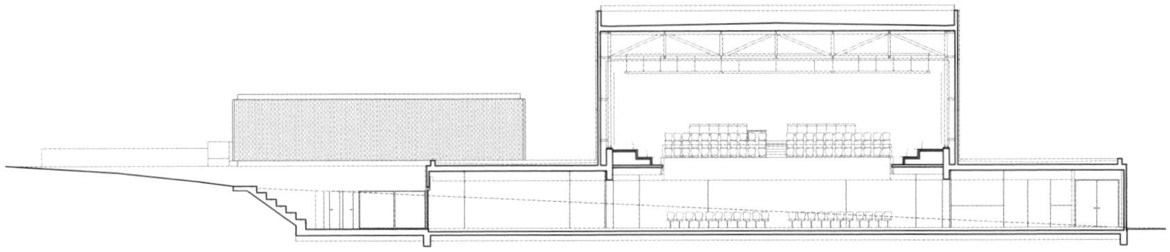

Longitudinal section

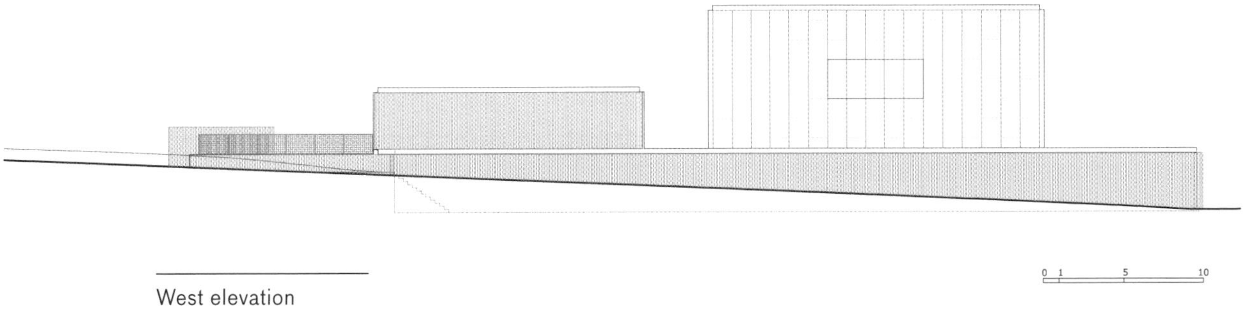

West elevation

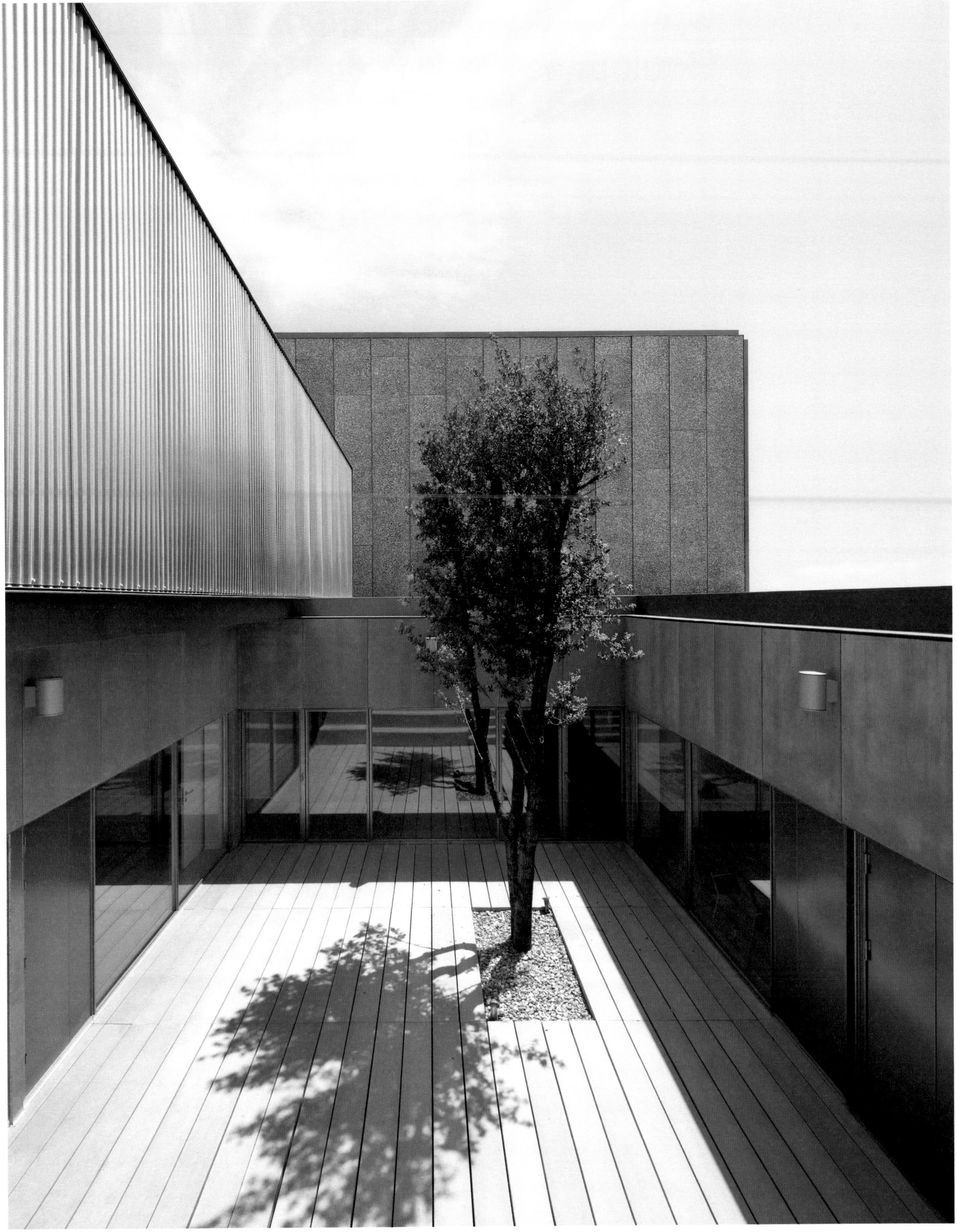

11 Confluence and relations with France. Boulogne

"Jazz" Office Building
Boulogne, Paris

The international design competition for the Museum of Confluences in Lyon that took place in 2000 began a series of OAB designs for France. The competition conditions referred to the North-South cultural encounter that the city's geographical location reflected, and designated the site for its construction on the peninsula where the Rhône and Saône meet. We visited the site together with Bruno Dumétier, our associate architect and urban planner in Lyon. The start of the design was stimulated by the nearby Fourvière Hill. The interpretation of its folds, enhanced during the Festival of Lights by candles placed on the windows of its buildings, brought about the first scale models of the design. Its synthetic qualities were a reflection of the supporting geometry for the project, a series of folds that seemed to be a spatial development of the topography of the Barcelona Botanical Garden.

The museum planned for Lyon connected the city with the park at the confluence of the rivers and presented an interior space similar to the one we would encounter years later in the Science Park in Granada. In turn, it shared the construction base of the firm's projects by turning those folds into structural features that would free up the floor space and provide the fluidity and flexibility required by the programme. Its tectonic effect is achieved by its cladding of cast aluminium panels, vertically grooved to channel away rainwater. Its occasional transparencies allowed the interior of its different folds to be seen; these were frenetic on the side facing the alpine Rhône and languid facing the Saône and the Midi, linked in this way to their respective origins. The design built a landscape through the use of complex geometries; it was more than a building.

Not far from Lyon is the monastery of La Tourette, where we held several university conferences within the framework of the Barcelona School of Architecture (ETSAB) "White Chair" in 2000 and 2001. The encounter with the figure of Le Corbusier was obviously prior to this, but his presence in those years during the visits to La Tourette and others made by Carlos Ferrater to Petit Cabanon and Ronchamp renewed this relationship. As would occur with the Mediapro building (2008), his constructive relevance linked to Mies van der Rohe was pointed out. There is an attitude close to the French-Swiss architect that is present in his way of proceeding with things, in his dense network of collaborators, even in the multiple intellectual roots of his projects. The contemporary and democratic nature of the OAB platform also allows all the architects participating in it to identify fully with his work.

With our sights set on French masters, the architecture of Prouvé in the façade of the Tour Initiale in La Défense was the location of our first meetings with our French clients. The offices of Nexity, one of the most important groups in the property development sector seemed to lead to the design we made together with the firm of Eric Babin and Jean François Renaud for this company in the Boulogne-Billancourt office building (2010). Our relationship with this brilliant and prolific practice run by young Parisians began with the competition we won in 2002 for the Les Jacobins Cultural Centre in Le Mans, which is expected to be built in 2010. Given the presence of the cathedral and Quinconces Park, the design

created continuity between both by means of a partially-covered parvis or courtyard space. The public space produced is introduced between the volume containing cinemas and theatre. at one end of this volume the foyer and public areas are reached through a viewing area opening onto the cathedral.

The attention to the city postulated here is once again the initial argument behind the Boulogne building. Located on a bend in the Seine facing the Meudon Hills and with the Île Séguin as a river port, the former Renault factory site has been designated a regeneration area (Zone de Aménagement Concerté), managed by SAEM Boulogne Billancourt. This gradual redevelopment process will result in a new district that combines density, multiple uses, a restricted variety of building types and the constant presence of the river landscape. It combines different owners and developers together in an operation overseen by the public authorities by means of design competitions for every large-scale development block, architects such as Perrault – precisely with other offices, Nouvel, Foster, Diener&Diener, FOA, Mateo, Barani and Baumschlager-Eberle are involved in the design. The first project designed and built by OAB in France, coordinated by the Belgian architect Stéphane Beel, was the result of one of these competitions.

Located in the avenue leading to Île Séguin, the project reformulates the construction density of the master plan to improve its relationship with the river to the south and to the north with the city of Paris and with the commercial thoroughfare that will connect to the existing densely-populated residential area. Faced with the diversity of the plan in terms of urban development and constructions, the project proposes a classic and restrained modernity, in keeping with the town hall of Boulogne Billancourt, one of the last projects by Garnier (1934) or even with the Institute Français building (1975) by Coderch in Barcelona, in a sort of return trip. Abstraction and timelessness exuded by the building contributes to its integration in the urban setting and is the architects' strategy of working in a responsible and dedicated manner abroad.

The choice of a silvery phyllite stone module measuring 45 x 90 x 3 cm came from the effectiveness on the floor plan of having a row of 1.35-m offices. These modules were submultiples of the 90 x 270-cm window, deeply inset with a 1-cm wide extruded aluminium perimeter frame. The communications core, services, plant and structural frame are laid out along a longitudinal axis, freeing a surface area of 18 x 54.5 m. The façade was built in France in concrete and houses and optimises the rest of the structure. The stone and window modules clad this perimeter over a variable pentagram base, with slight variations and seemingly random gaps which, in some cases such as the cantilever, obey a structural logic.

Subtle changes appear at the top (ninth floor), where the modules are of a greater height and there are brise-soleil; on the corner of the Avenue Île Séguin, where the windows are set at an angle; and on the ground floor, where the vertical proportion of the void is emphasised and the commercial premises are set back for greater protection and depth. The 5.50-m cantilever next to the residential building by Stéphane Beel offers continuity to the landscaped axis that crosses all the blocks enhancing the lively commercial activity desired by the local authorities.

Four canopies are integrated into the building's exterior design to mark the entrance between stainless steel frames. They consist of a horizontal plane suspended by cables, compressing space like an antechamber to the dual-aspect foyer that opens onto the landscaped slope at the heart of the block. The interior design is completed with silvery stone facing on the lifts, matt stainless steel on their frames and joinery, American oak panelling and front desk and the integrated indirect lighting.

The façade becomes an urban texture continuing onto the street, and establishes numerous associations with the Parisian sky and rain, with its material being alive and ambivalent, dark or silvery in line with the weather and light in the city. The quality of the stone, the random lights from offices at night and reflections off the steel canopies and anodised aluminium frames contribute to dematerialise this petrous architecture.

The precise construction of these perimeter frames underscores the way the project was monitored together with Babin-Renaud, with the excellent oversight of their site architect, Mathias Bernard, and the quality of the actual construction process. We experienced the high level of qualification of industry professionals, strict control and management procedures, adherence to tight price and time schedules, and systematisation in meetings between town planners, politicians, clients, supervisors and the many graduate trainees (covering fields as diverse as structural engineering and sustainable development). At times this professionalism meant greater rigidity in the project and having to coexist with a maze of information, official documents and communications. The complexity of the decision-making process owing to the participation of a great many players, from lawyers interpreting urban planning regulations in the early stages to investors who replicated the figure of the client by requesting new inspections at the height of the process, was one of the problems faced by this project. Its strategic value seemed to warrant protecting and clarifying the truly relevant aspects of the design.

The acceptance received by the building encourages the firm to present its architectural designs to public and private competitions in France and its capital. Featuring among these competitions are an office tower in La Défense (with Jean Mas), a convention centre in Nancy (with Barthélémy-Griño) and, more particularly, the Bagnolet Town Hall (2010) in metropolitan Paris. The 2nd prize obtained is high praise for a decidedly urban project we presented together with Babin-Renaud with the incorporation of Xavier Martí.

The design clearly respects the scope of the competition, bringing the old town hall to the focal point of the square fronting it, integrating it and enveloping it in a series of new offices, which also complete a transversal commercial axis and features a municipal information panel at one end. The spiral layout of the rest of the building provides a rich welcoming interior space, the scale of which is suited to the core formed by the old building. The varied series of volumes, their capillarity and adaptation responds to the different town planning requirements. As in Boulogne, the strictly metric design features overwhelming materiality, this time with ceramic louvres and double-height glazed panels in large structural metal frames, in the whitish grey color that is typically Parisian.

A natural environment for growth, France has become a preferential territory for OAB's growing international ambitions and its research into materiality and complex geometries. The monographic exhibition containing them has already visited Chicago, Tel Aviv, Bilbao and Madrid, and is soon expected to visit Paris, where several projects were already present in a collective exhibition – Catalan Architecture at the Maison de l'Architecture (2009), which revealed the Francophile nature of an entire generation of Barcelona architects. The presence of Carlos Ferrater on a number of academic and professional juries, and at recent conferences and events in France is telling, from a disciplinary perspective but also a personal one, of the growing commitment to France of OAB's architecture with the designs that are unfolding in that country. The story of this series of confluences, in other words an almost natural encounter, has, as its first built reality, an office building in Boulogne Billancourt, which is surely a prelude to others.

Alberto Peñin Llobell

Longitudinal section

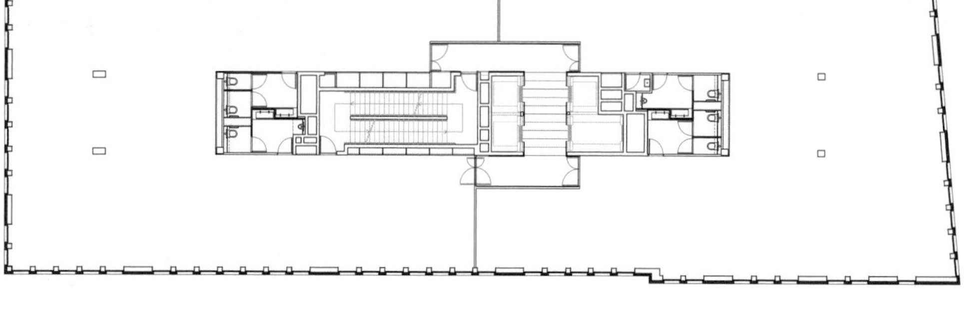

Typical floor plan

GROUPEMENT
TECHNIQUE
GAINES DE VENTILATION

RC

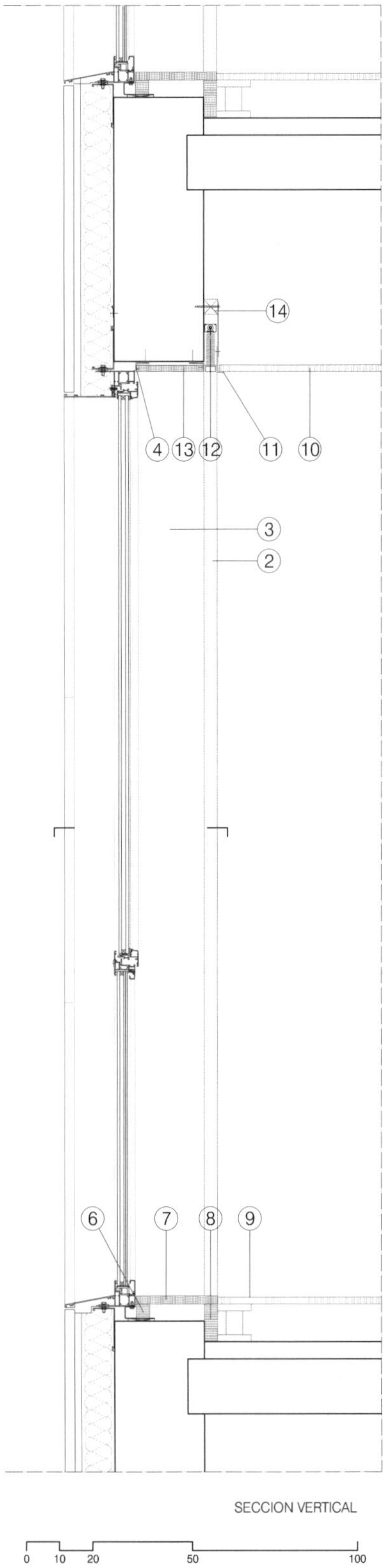

Wall. Vertical section

Quarry stone

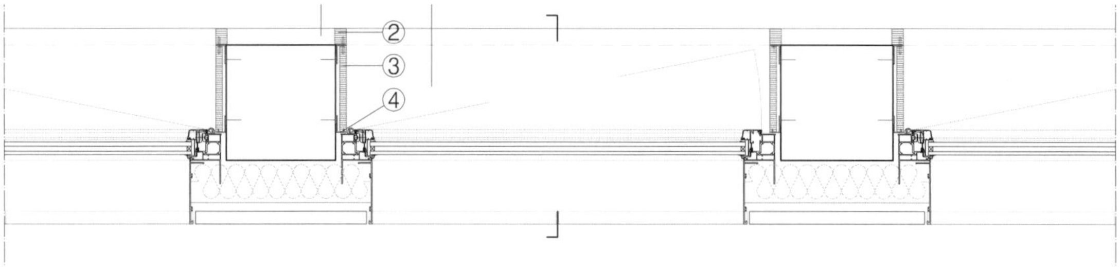

Wall. Plan

1 Bottom Panel lacquered wood. Hidden fixations. 245x24mm
2 Top lacquered wood boards. Fixed on board. 40x28mm
3 Panel lacquered wood. Hidden fixations, 205x16mm
4 Fixing galvanized steel.
5 Base board of lacquered wood. 20x24mm on wooden stick 110x40mm
6 Wooden stick 40x50mm
7 Support on lacquered wood. Hidden fixations. 205x16mm
8 Wooden stick 110x40mm
9 False ground on plots
10 Removable false ceiling
11 Continuous steel side profile, lacquered in white. 20x75mm
12 Stor with adjustable horizontal slats. Metallic silver. Crank
13 Top panel lacquered wood. 205x19mm. Hidden fixations. 205x19mm
14 Fixation of continuous steel side profile over the false ceiling.

12

Audiovisual Campus in 22@ District. Mediapro

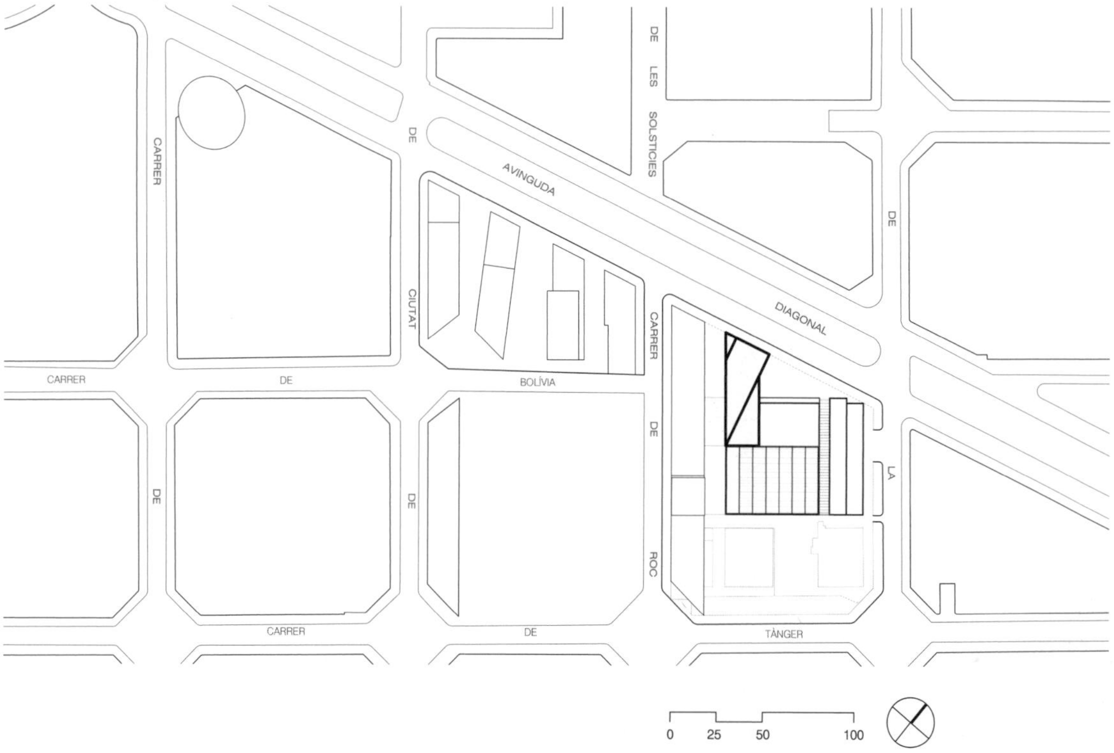

Building with steel

The evolution of architecture throughout time can be understood as a series of innovations in the way of building, and of new materials, which have enabled architects of different times to connect their ideological positions, intellectual challenges and technological advances with the search for new forms of expression.

Exposed steel skeletons became structural diagrams where it was possible to understand the relation of shear, bending, compression and traction, creating new aesthetics in which engineering and architecture turned cast iron and steel into a paradigm of modernity. Hidden skeletons, like that of Adler and Sullivan's Auditorium Building in Chicago, gave rise to standardised construction in order to create density in urban centres, defining a new city model and sacralising verticality as a new formal experience.

Mies van der Rohe rediscovered steel; he rigidified joints and gave rigour, order, proportion and meaning to the metal structural frame. His works in Chicago, New York and Berlin have a steel frame uniting and bringing timelessness to the classicism-modernity binomial, creating in the hidden part of the design process the conditions for the resulting materiality of his buildings.

Given its malleability, and versatility, its ability to support all sorts of shear and the ease with which it is used in construction, steel has also allowed a range of works to be erected masking absurd structures and arbitrary forms behind stone renderings and light metal and glass skins, to produce self-absorbed objects that do not respond to urban situations; they do not build a city; their functional programmes do not respond to proper social organisation and they exceed the limits of the shear-performance ratio, consuming excessive amounts of energy and adding expense to future maintenance requirements.

The sophistication of current finite-element structural calculation systems, technological advances and the modelling capacity of new software applications, together with the combination of mixed structural systems, such as those presented in this issue – combining post-tensioned concrete slabs and steel profile-based reinforcement membranes – allow what had until now seemed unchangeable relations between form and construction to be overthrown by means of geometric processes, as a way of approximating landscape to the urban form.

Experimentation, intellectual risk and formal innovation should allow design to come about from logic and constructive reasoning, although this is not revealed directly in the final form of the project, while at the same time upholding the commitment to the ideological postulates that enlightened modernity.

Carlos Ferrater

Prologue from *TECTONICA* Magazine Issue No. 29. Steel (II)

The stretch of Avinguda Diagonal that passes through 22@ District – the area of the city being reinvented hand in hand with new technologies – is marked by a sequence of buildings which, with the renowned Agbar tower as a backdrop, begins with the new headquarters of the Mediapro media group. Given its location, the design of the new building takes into special account the nature of its urban setting, and its volume has been modelled according to alignment and visual guidelines. Consequently, the main façade has been turned to face the avenue; the four first levels have been perforated to provide an opening for Carrer Bolivia and to direct interest to its perspective. On the lower level, the tower is diverted from the edge of the plot to create a new plane, allowing the adjacent building to be viewed.

These operations give a sculptural feel to the volume, intensified by the cantilevered tower and the resulting arris, and by the horizontal volume with a transparent façade that embraces the new triangular plaza.

The office tower's open plan design provides great flexibility of uses due to the absence of pillars and intermediate frames. The different floors have distinct layouts, allowing certain functional specialisation in their programmes that exceed the mere separation between the horizontal volume, which housed the audiovisual production and training centre, and the tower housing the company's administration.

The versatility of this interior layout is based on the use of a single and repeated window model, developed continuously on all of the façades. They offer good lighting conditions and views of the city from any point of the tower. The glass panes inside the grid stop glare and are protected from direct sun exposure, water and dirt.

The building's skeleton coincides with its final form owing to its perimeter frame. The grid of pillars on the façades and the slabs allow it to be considered a large Vierendeel truss, given that the fusion of membranes or structural diaphragms with the post-tensioned slabs make the large spans possible and provide the structure with rigidity. This system means that areas bearing less of the façade load collaborate to withstand the shear from the more tensioned parts of the grid in a kind of structural democracy. Finally, the greater height of the pillars on the lower levels and at the top – set aside for service installations – and the metallic bronze colour used in the structure and window frames give the building the solid and classic air of a great skyscraper.

The building already adopts sustainable forms from its urban setting alone, and the natural daylight received in all work areas is impeccable. The grid absorbs and spreads daylight uniformly. The structural design was made with strict environmental criteria. The large glazed expanses facing the public plaza are north-facing to avoid excessive exposure to the sun. The roof areas of the lower volume housing the film sets and production areas feature new generation solar panels.

Juan Calvo

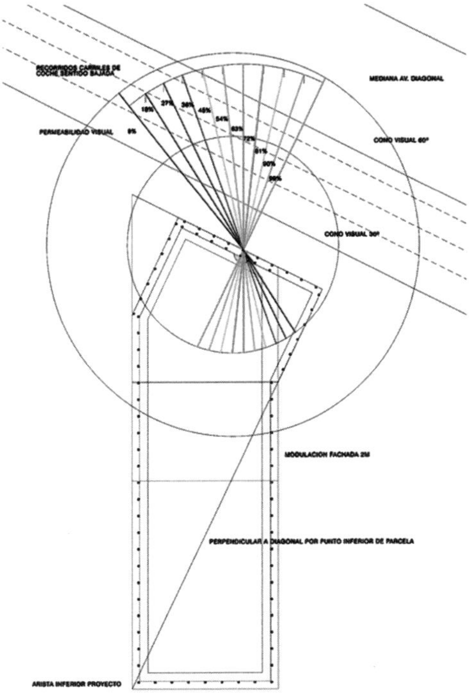

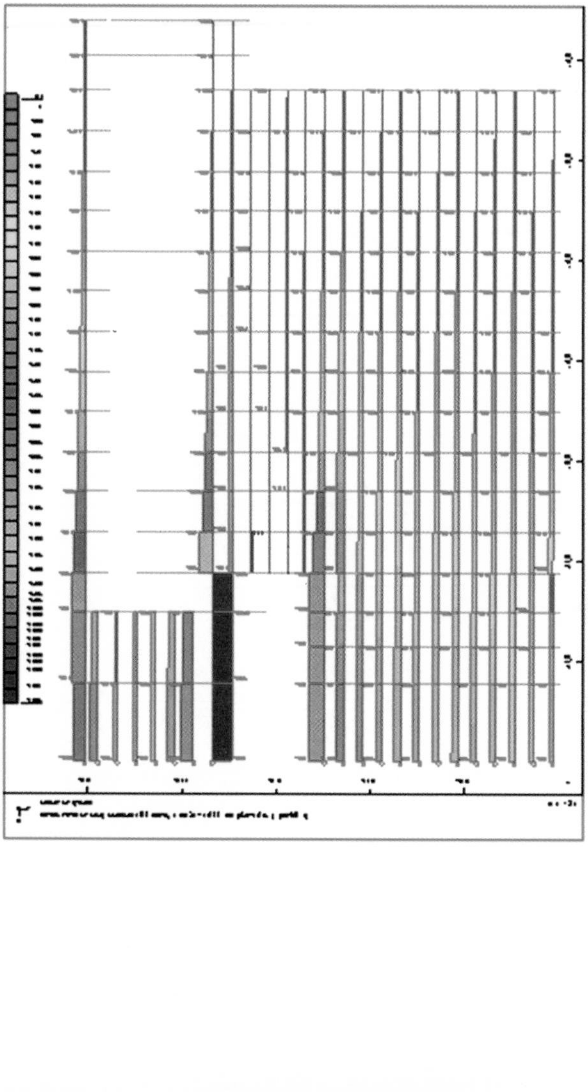

MEDIAPRO

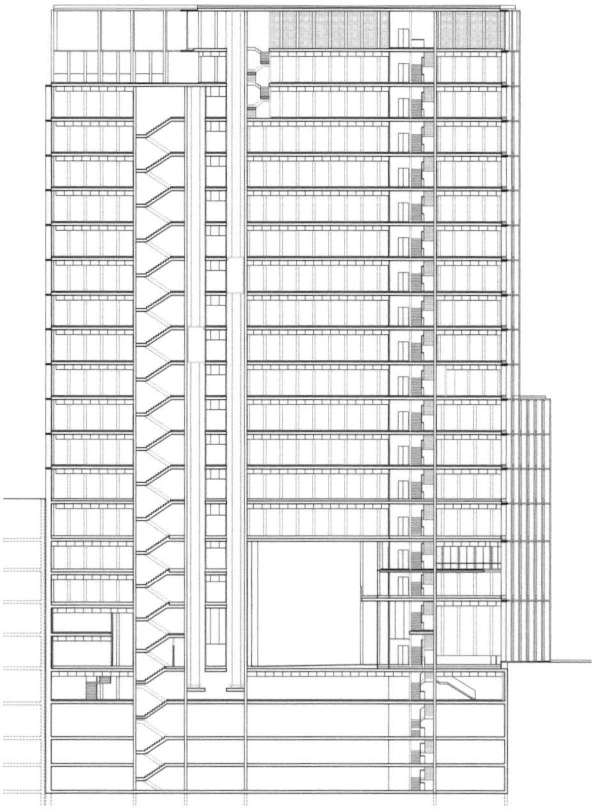

Section

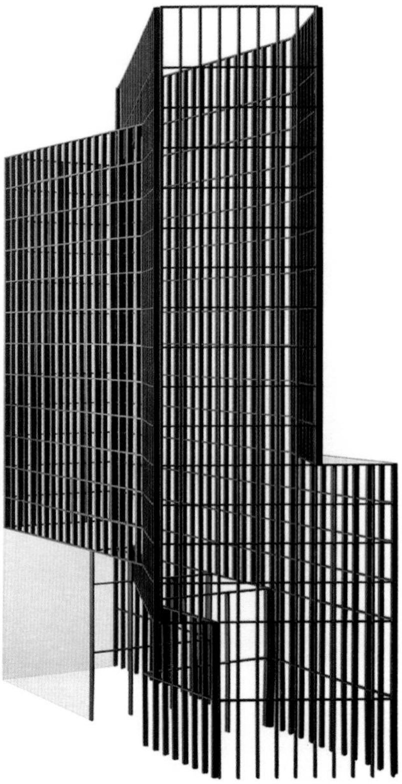

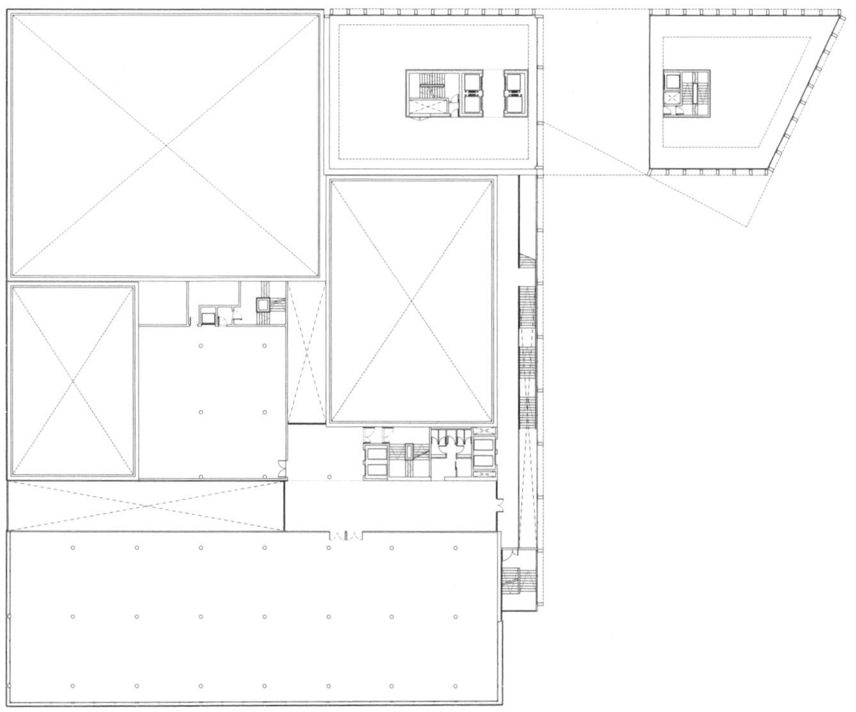

Ground floor plan

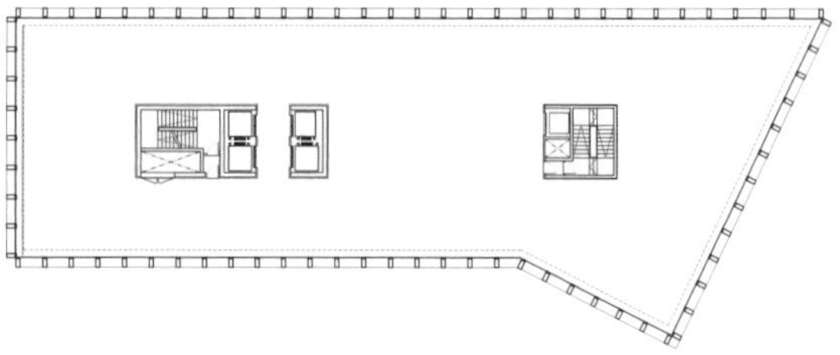

Typical plan of lower floor
with cantilevered overhang

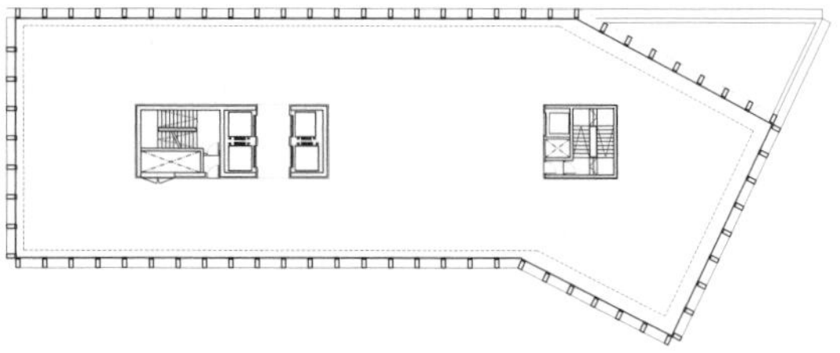

Typical plan of higher floor

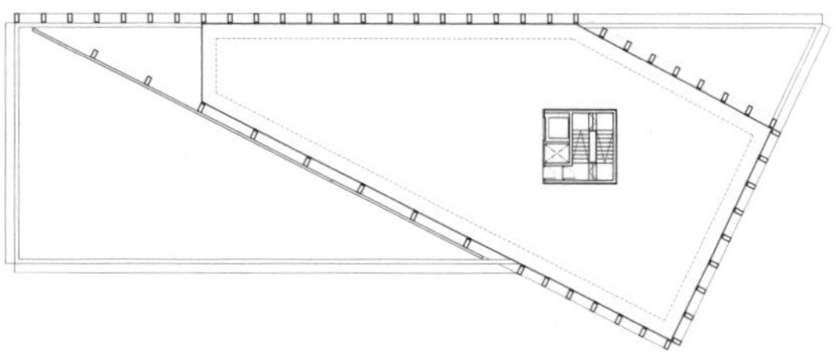

Presidential floor plan

Juan Calvo

The façade contains 112 different pillar alignments. The perimeter of a standard floor has 74 pillars, separated by 1.90-2.05 m, according to the modular design of each façade.

They consist of an outer layer of thick steel plate filled with highly ductile concrete in order to increase their fire resistance time. They all have an external perimeter of 60x30 cm, with only the thickness of the steel wall varying depending on the load (some of them are of solid steel).

Each post-tensioned floor slab in the tower seems to be "sewn" with a series of 3 or 4-strand cables, each one made up of 3 or 4 Ø15-mm super-stabilised steel cables in a sheathe, designed to follow a course made up of straight lines and second-degree parabolas, supported at each metre by the rebars in the floor slab, to guarantee they would not move during concrete pouring.

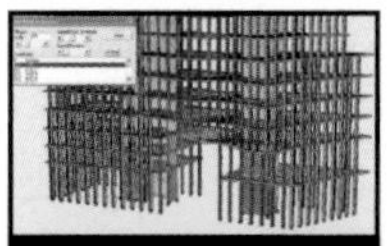

Mediapro Building (structural study)

The tensioning process commences once the concrete has reached a typical resistance of 200Kp/cm^2, with a single tensioning stage of 20 Mp. Once the cables have been tensioned with hydraulic jacks and the required lengthening confirmed, the ends of the cables are cut and sealed with mortar without retracting. Finally, after bleeding the sheathes with water or compressed air, cement mortar is injected into the conduits.

MEDIAPRO

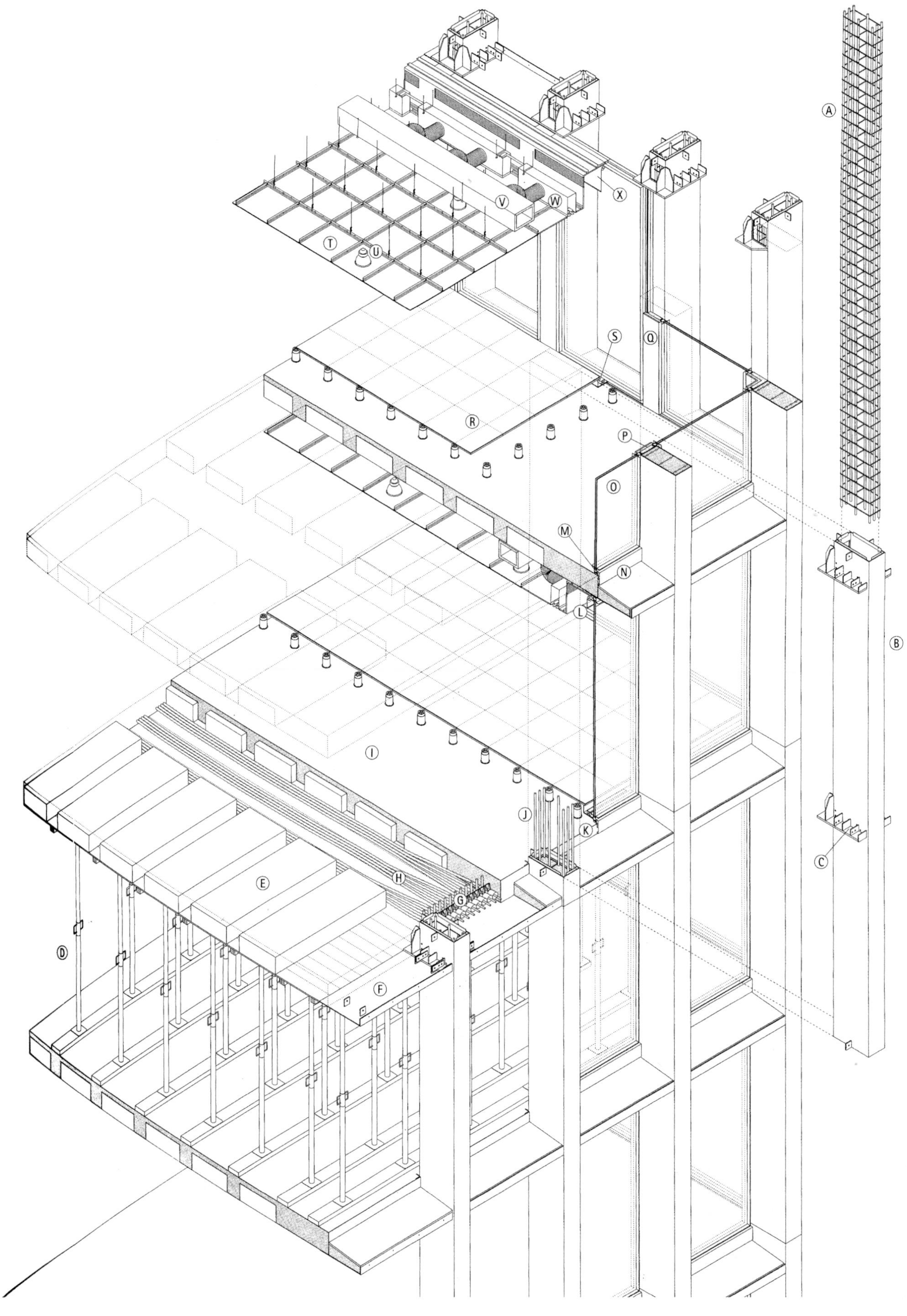

Structure and façade detail. Magazine extract *Tectónica* no.29. Steel (II)

77

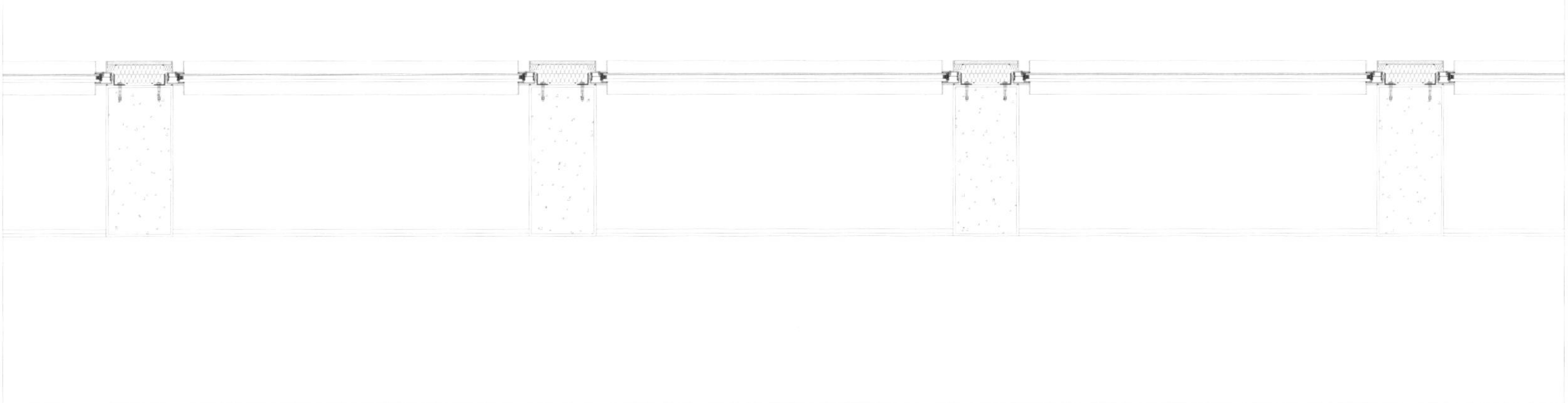

Façade detail section

MEDIAPRO

PLAÇA
GUTENBERG

13

Roca Barcelona Gallery

SINGLES PRO
SINGLES PRO
KENDO

Roca
Barcelona Gallery

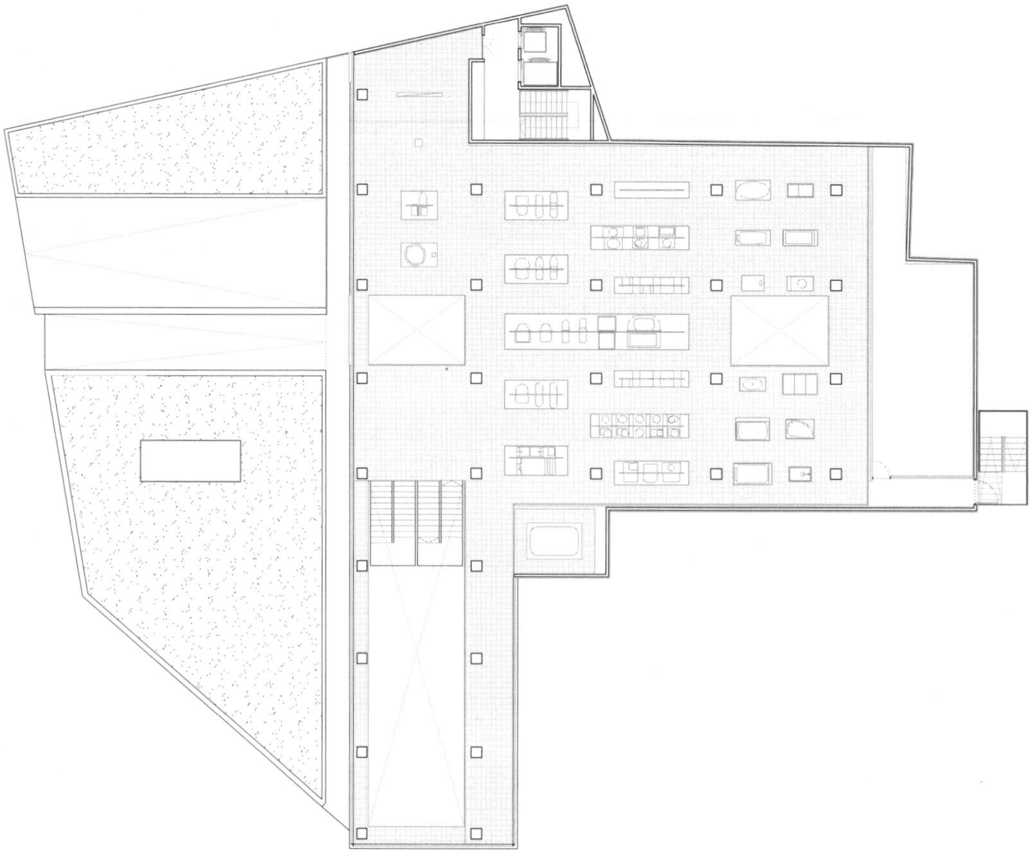

First floor plan

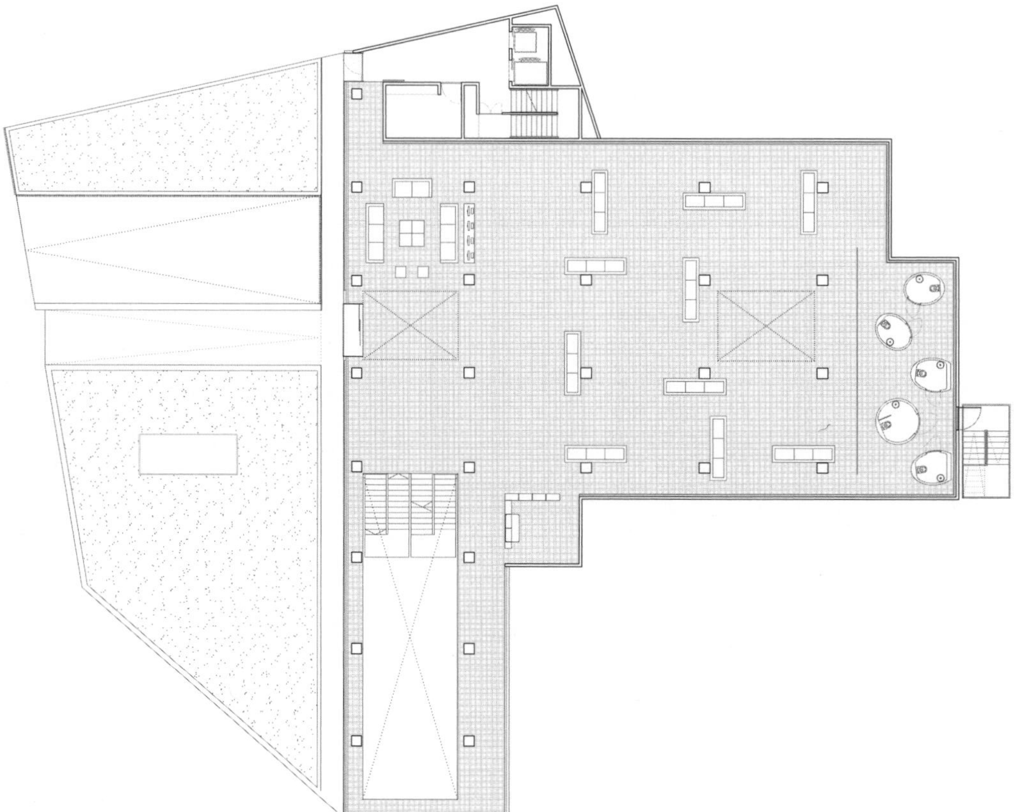

Ground floor plan

Roca Barcelona
Gallery

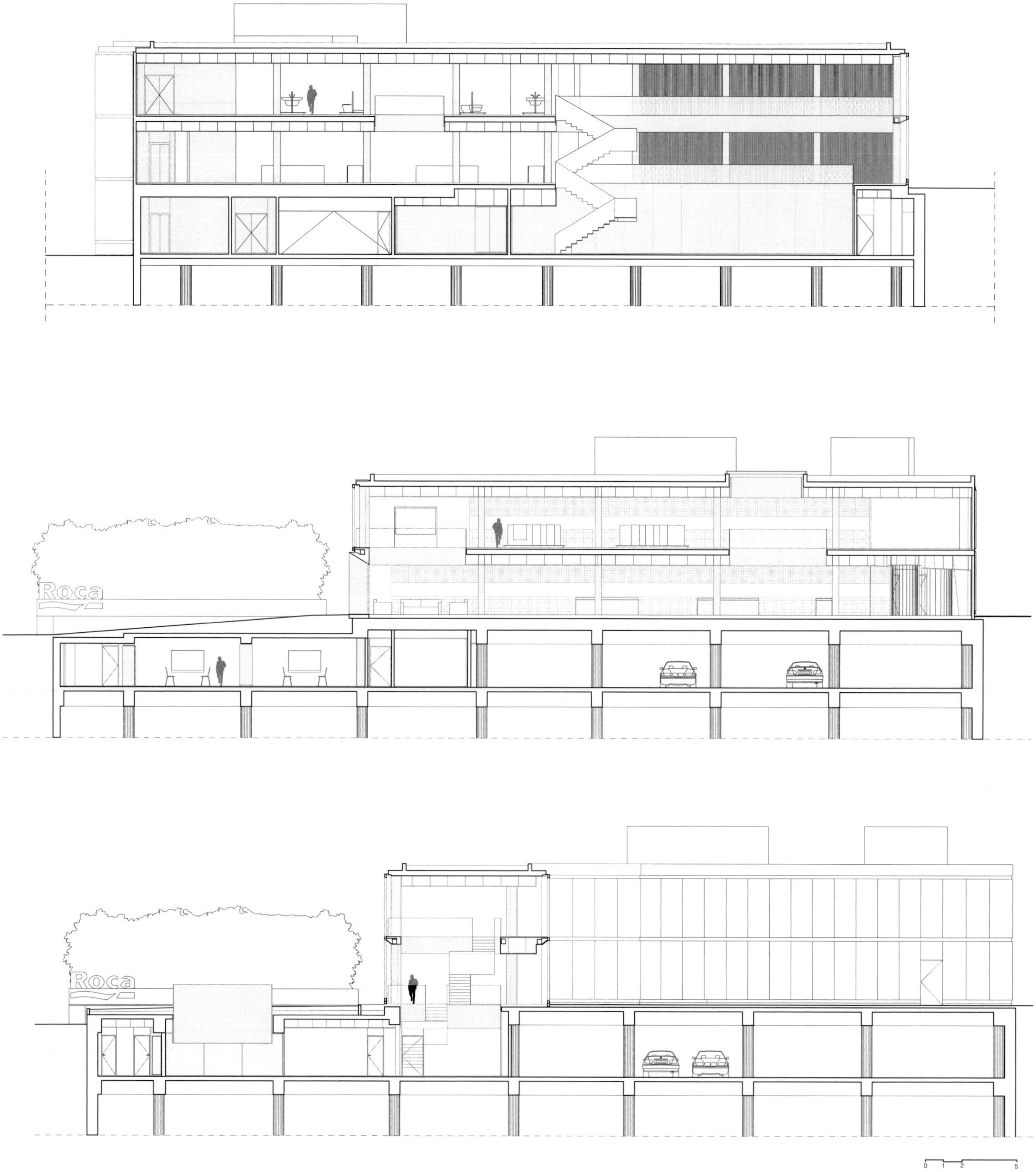

Sections

BAÑO
retrospectiva histórica
THE BATHROOM
a historical retrospective
SISSÍ EMPERATRIZ

SISSÍ EMPERATRIZ
Elisabeth de Wittelsbach (1837-1898)

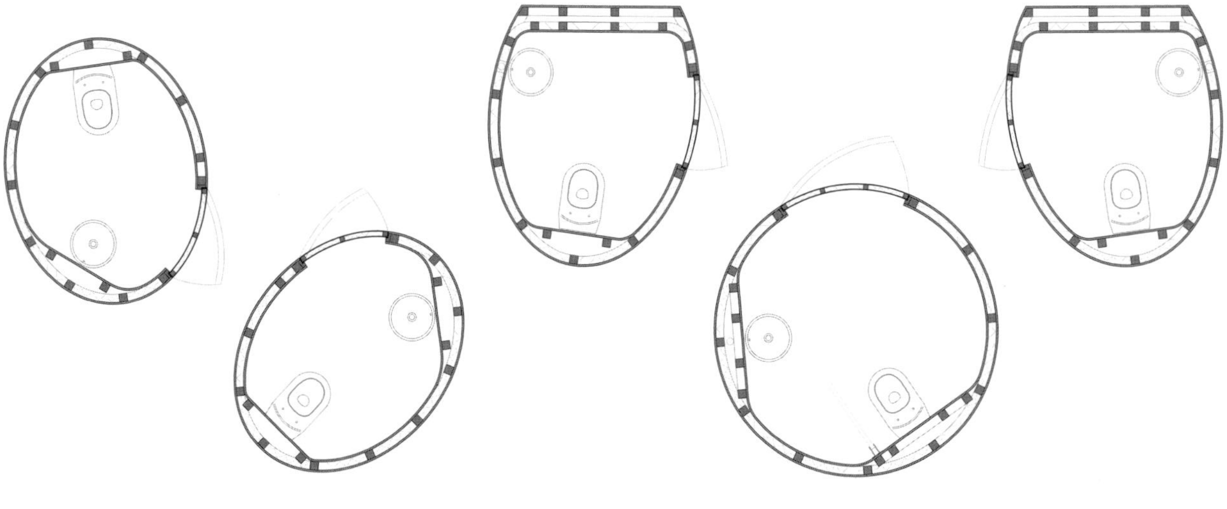

Cabins

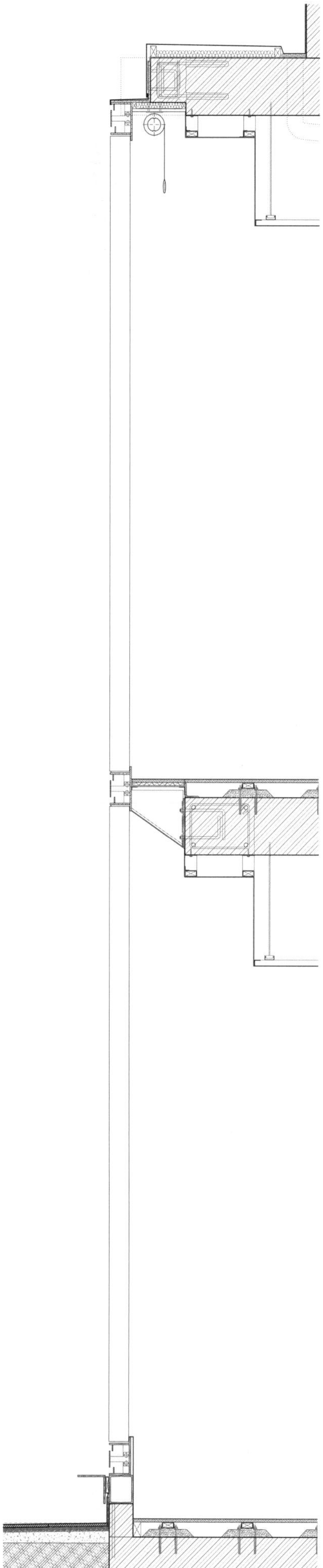

Glass detail on façade

Glass façade automation

14

In the Atapuerca Mountains. Archaeology and landscape

Carlos Ferrater

The Atapuerca Mountains are a landscape bordering on the city of Burgos. It is renowned for the exceptional and authentic nature of its archaeological sites, which have led to it being declared a world heritage site by UNESCO. The project embodies the idea of connecting the two sides of a site running along a trench fourteen metres wide and between six and eight metres deep containing the palaeolontological settlements.

The project consders the construction of a light structure, on a higher level, communicating one side of the site with the other, incorporating a small visitors' centre inside it. While it relates to the topographic section, there is a small abandoned quarry that serves as its support. The strategy consists in using a ramped linear structure, linking both sides to create a covered area and a plaza as a meeting point between the two entrance levels.

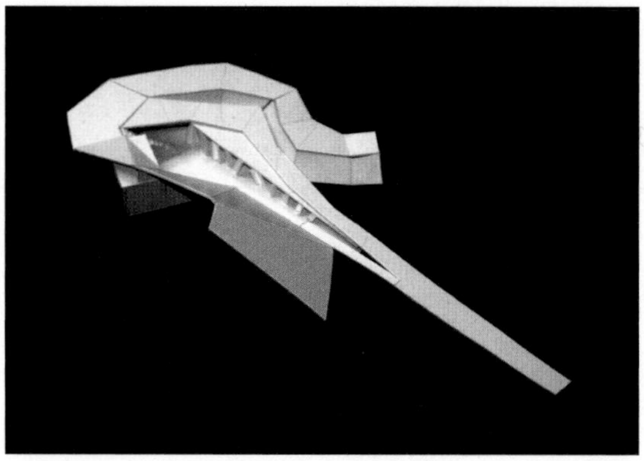

This is the turning point where the project acknowledges the topography and the landscape, maintaining the visual, environmental and archaelogical values of the site. The walkway becomes a transit area and a place to stop, receiving light through the section and taking over the petrous space excavated into the mountain. In this way the different flows are separated and organised by separately coordinating the route taken by the guided tours and the work taking place on the site.

The design is for the minimum expression of a structure, allowing its construction to take place from the air, preventing the need for building operations that harm the landscape.

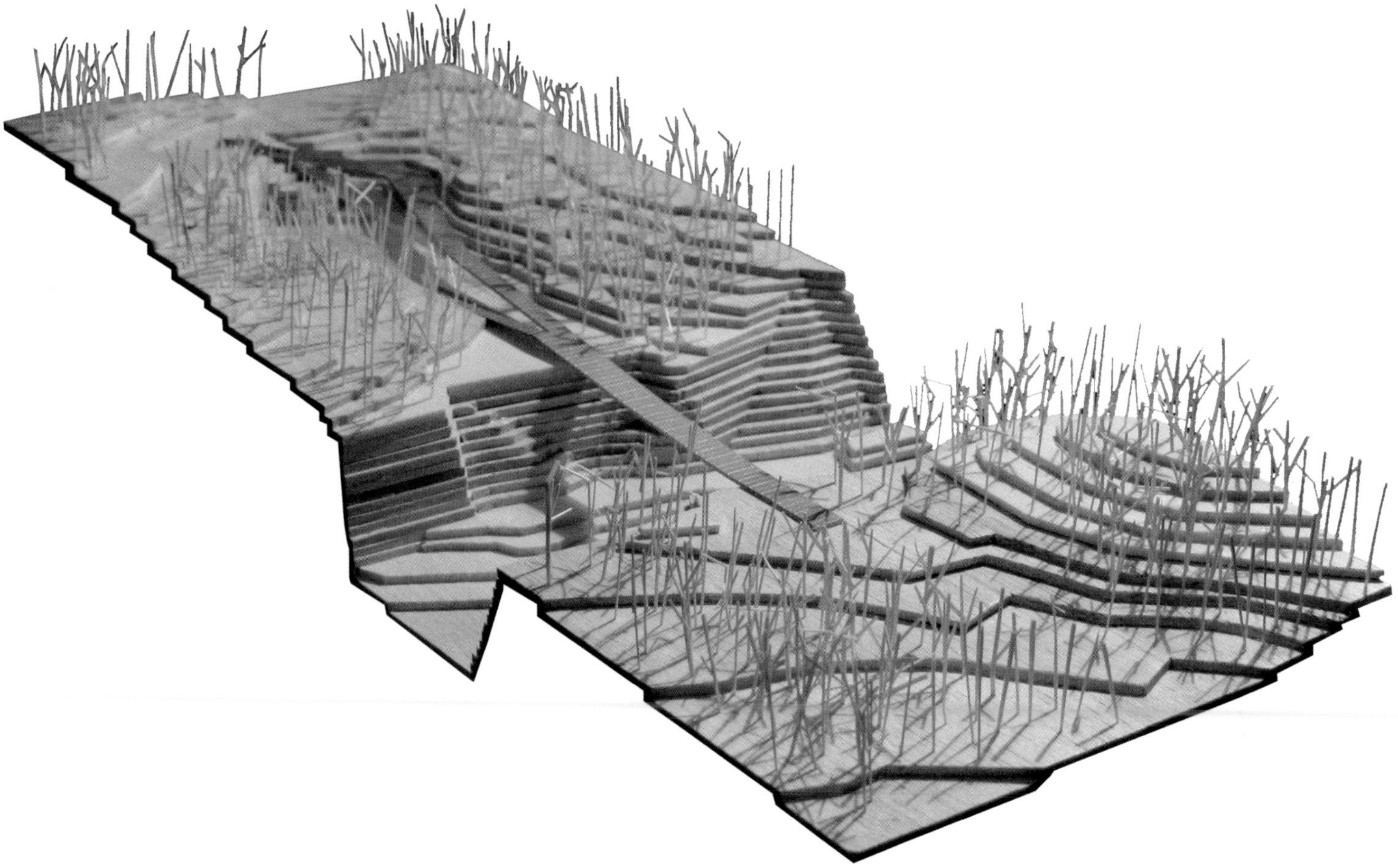

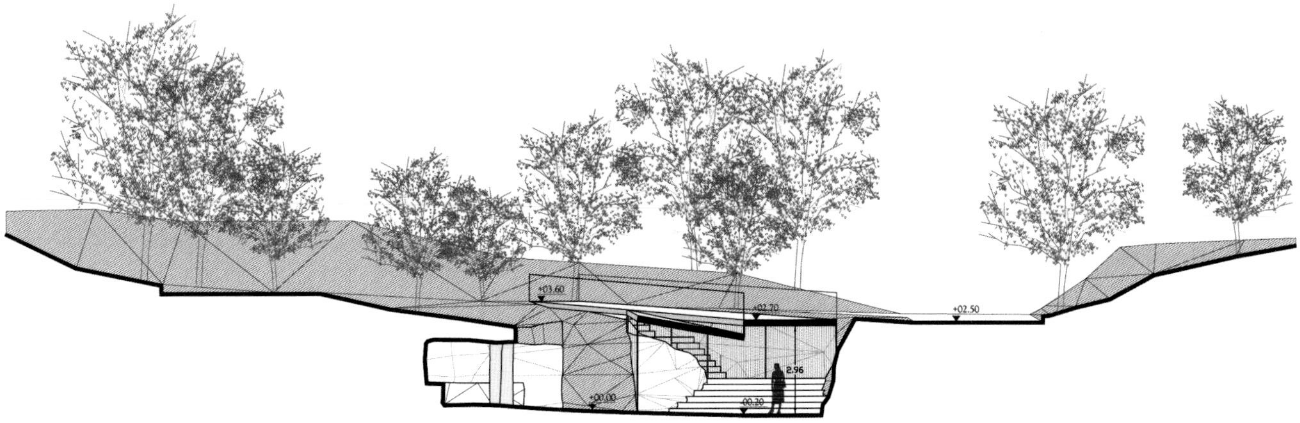
+03.60
+02.70
+02.50
2.96
+00.00
00.20

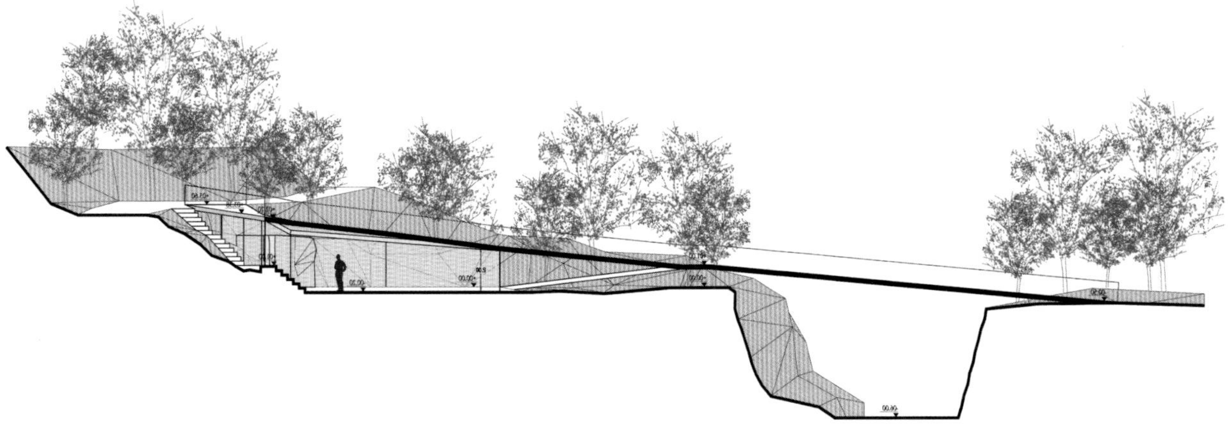

The study scale model made with the techniques used in archaeological models combines and relates the topographical study, the excavation site grid, the Roman numerals signposting on the site and the different stations which, using portable mirrors allow a laser beam to penetrate the model and recreate the different routes traced out through the site with the variations in reflective surfaces of the stations. This establishes numerous itineraries to help visitors discover the site, its vegetation and topography, while recognising the imprint

of the past going back to the Atapuerca man, with Neanderthal and primitive remains on the upper levels, but also Bronze Age remains on uppermost levels, which were later sedimented over. It is a cross-section of humanity. This is all due to the casuistry of the railway route. If it had been diverted by only a few dozen metres, it would have encountered a chasm, making the excavation of the trench unnecessary.

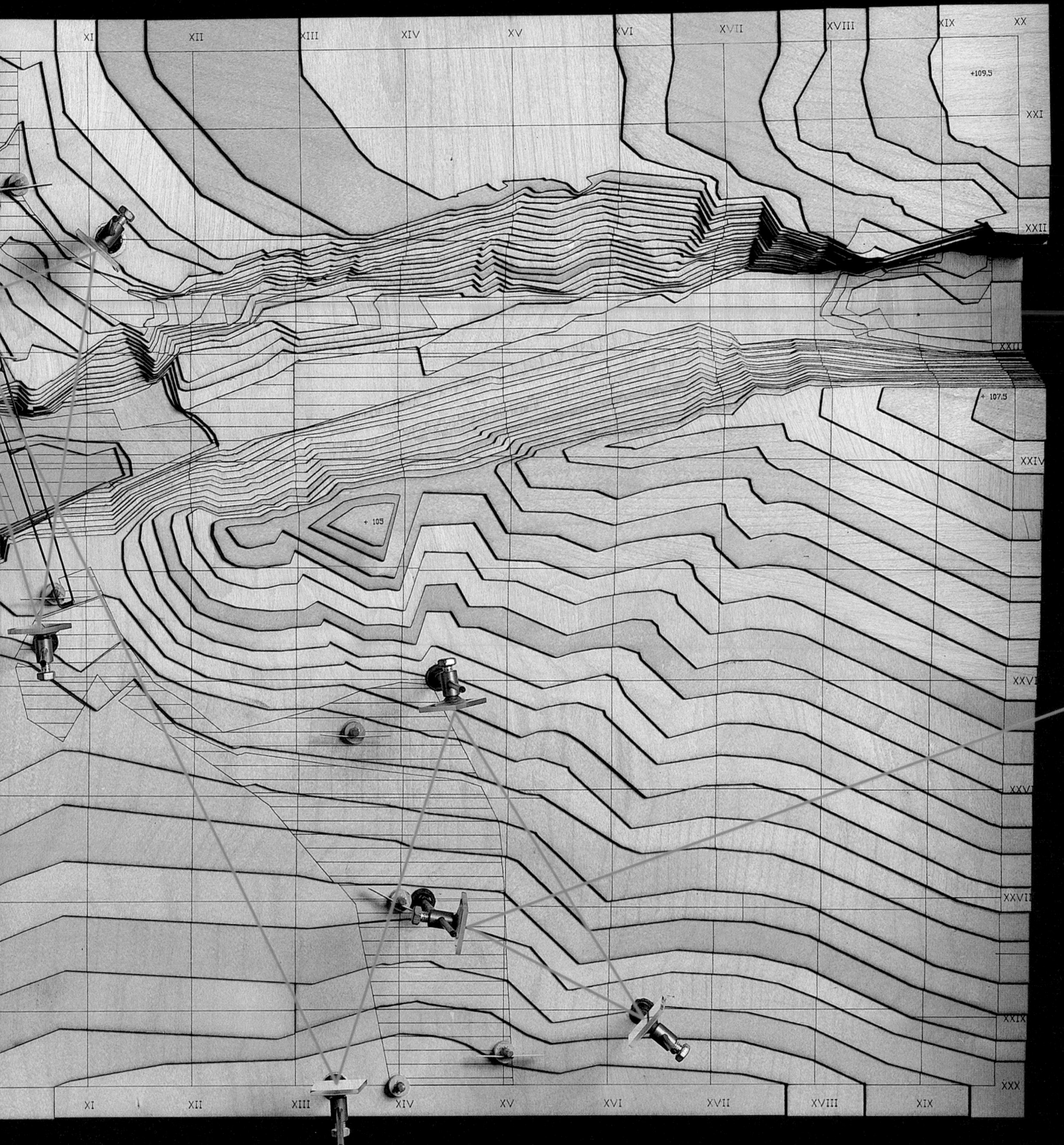

Benidorm West Beach Promenade

The Benidorm urban development model has been criticised for years for its appearance, owing to it being out of keeping; for its choice of encouraging high-rise buildings; for overcrowding and land speculation; for its excessive density; and for its lack of public and community spaces other than its splendid beach.

50 years have passed since that decision taken by the council, and seen now in comparison with the different tourist resorts on the Spanish coast faced with the systematic destruction of the coastline with invasive residential complexes, poor waterfront areas, immense ghost towns that are empty most of the year and which require a consequent effort to maintain infrastructure, roads, services and security, etc. one must wonder whether the Benidorm model in fact turned out to be the most "sustainable" one on the Spanish coast. It occupies very little land, no more than a few hectares, and there is very little use of private transport as everywhere in the town is only a 10-minute walk away from the beach. Most inhabitants have a sea view from their towers. A special feature of the construction involved not sealing the land under asphalt, owing to the respect for the original sloping topography which keeps the natural rainwater channels among the gardens surrounding the apartment tower blocks. There are more than 500,000 people accommodated here during seasonal peaks and the tourist season is year round.

This was the perspective we had with Carlos Ferrater for our participation in the invitation-only design competition for the West Beach promenade, where we considered the possibility of radically restricting vehicular traffic along the waterfront and designing 1.5 km of promenade with a maximum width of 30 m, with a series of overhangs that would not reduce the surface area of the sand and which would be possible because of the 3-4-metre slope between the town and the beach. This would give rise to a large public leisure space that would bring the town into contact with the sea and provide a new seaside promenade for the use of residents and tourists. This new place with such a privileged position between the town and the beach would become a transition space, the border between two worlds.

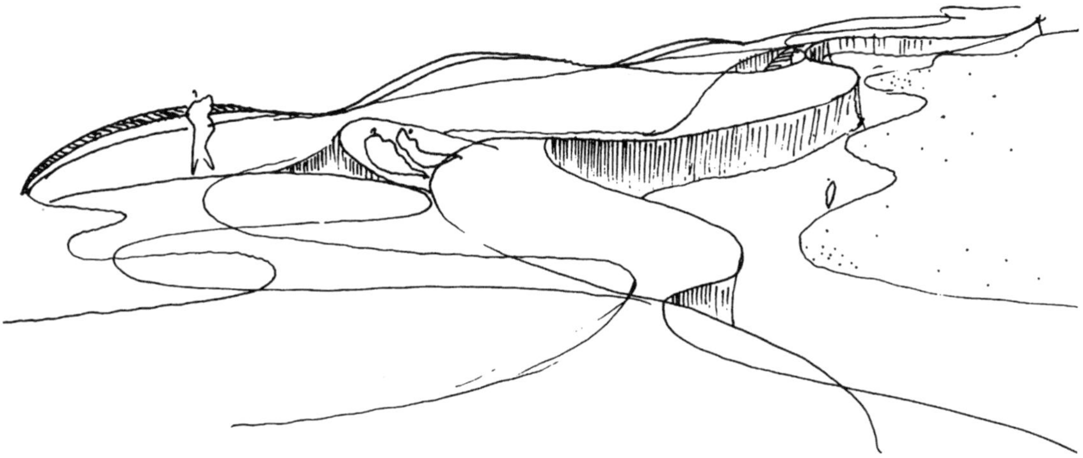

Benidorm now has a natural space built using a sustainable project fused with technology, craftwork using local materials in the Mediterranean sun.

It would be a place for imagination evoking other projects such as that by Clorindo Testa in Mar del Plata and that by Roberto Burle Max in Rio de Janeiro.

The technical and architectural considerations leading to the Benidorm West Beach Promenade responded to a model tying together the cultural characteristics of the place with the intellectual concepts that have been developed inside our practice in recent years. Therefore, the sustainability of the project could be understood as going beyond the application of technological devices to the project. On the contrary, it would arise from the actual qualities of the location (hedonism, leisure, popular traditions, the imprint left by the waves), assimilated by means of a theoretical design that is upheld with the application of geometry to the landscape. This contributed to the first, and perhaps the most important, environmental condition of a project, that of being designed and built using culturally-sustainable criteria.

Geometry and sustainable construction: the concrete membrane

Experimentation with form led to a series of building processes in this project that specifically responded to its qualities, but which also responded to the general laws governing the relation between form and function: The alveolar geometry of the concrete membrane gave the form rigidity, allowing us to reduce the thickness of the concrete layer to only 10 centimetres, which not only significantly reduced the amount of material used, but also made it easy to use, shortening building times. Likewise, the geometric configuration of the slab dissipates the energy of the wind and sea as it does not behave with the rigidity of a continuous wall, which would act as a barrier.

The overhangs resulting from the geometry enabled the surface area of the promenade to be increased by 4,000m^2 without impacting on the surface of the beach, turning the areas protected by them into shady spaces that have been greatly appreciated by beachgoers.

Together with the white concrete, the membrane geometry enhances light, reducing the intensity of lighting required from street lamps, resulting in lower energy costs and demand. Therefore, the need for minimal lighting to provide good illumination not only contributes to lower energy use but light pollution over the beach is also reduced owing to the effects of light on the wall. Consequently, efficient lighting contributed to the environmental sustainability of the project.

The minimalist design of luminaires, railings and benches, which also permit chairs to be incorporated, helped to minimise the use of materials, costs, construction, assembly and maintenance. Plant cover was also improved through the use of native plants and by recycling the pre-existing palm trees, as they are suited to the climate found here.

It is worth mentioning that the variety of forms presented in the project along the length of its 1,500 metres was achieved using differential standardisation. The resulting form was obtained using 55 moulds each with a 5.15-metre lineal length. Owing to alterations in the layout of the moulds, a differential configuration was achieved that produced the different geometries that can be appreciated along the length of the project.

This type of flexibility can also be appreciated in the paving tiles designed for the promenade. The glazed coloured stoneware tiles, developed in collaboration with the ALICER Ceramic Technology Institute and produced by Keramia, adapts to the formal and topographical needs of the project. From a formal perspective, being circular, the tile geometry does not emphasise any particular directionality, facilitating its placement and allowing interchanged use of coloured tiles throughout the interwoven design on the pavement. From at topographic perspective, the tiles adapt to the different changes in level, removing the need for complementary tiles.

Xavier Martí Galí

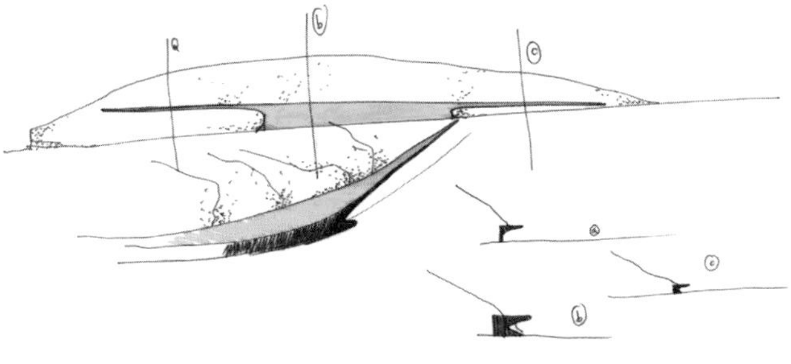

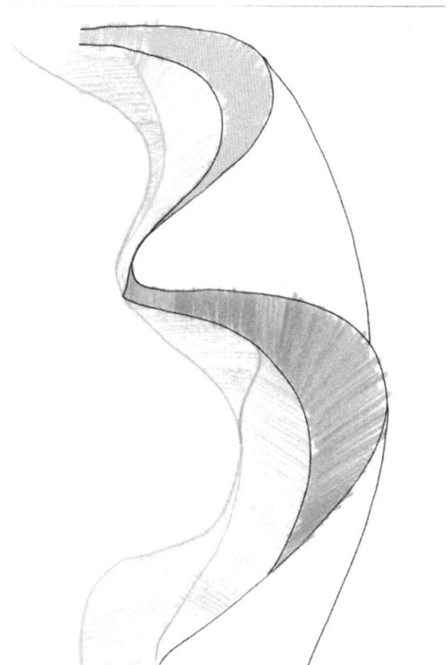

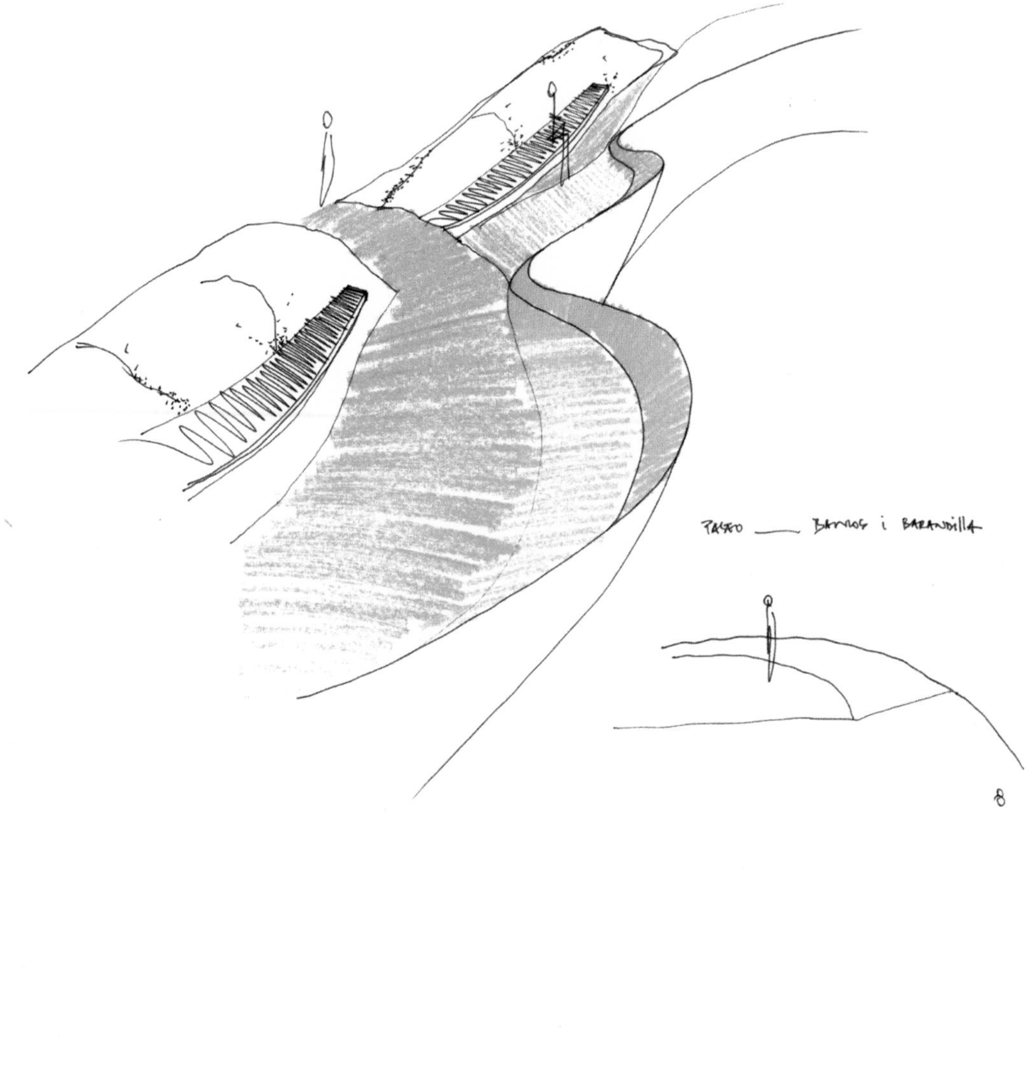
PASEO — BANCOS i BARANDILLA
8

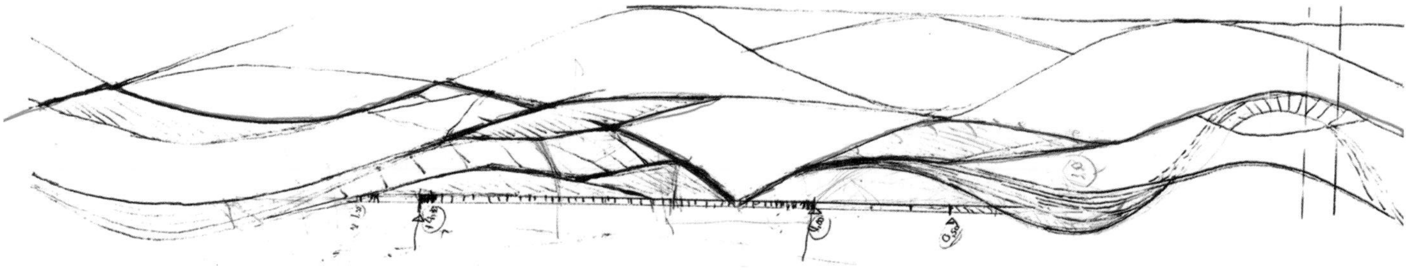

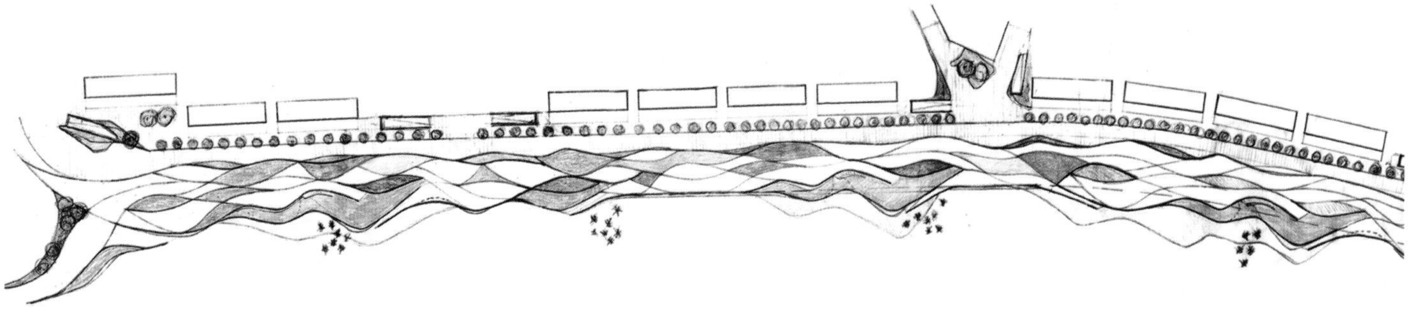

The promenade in Benidorm, a new transitional location between built city and the natural space of sea and beach.

The promenade is not understood as a frontier/borderline but as an intermediary space rendering this transition permeable.

It is structured as a place with a rich topography, as a dynamic space that accommodates the act of strolling and watching the sea, but also organises different areas for stopping and relaxing in.

The promenade subsumes the longitudinal and transverse flows of the different circulations and channels these, allowing easy access to the beach. It eliminates architectural barriers, permitting direct access from parking places.

The promenade thus becomes an architectonic location that molds a new topography and plays with light and shade.

A nexus of sinuous interwoven lines which sets up the different spaces and adopts various natural and organic shapes evocative of the fractal structure of a cliff, as well as the motion of waves and tides.

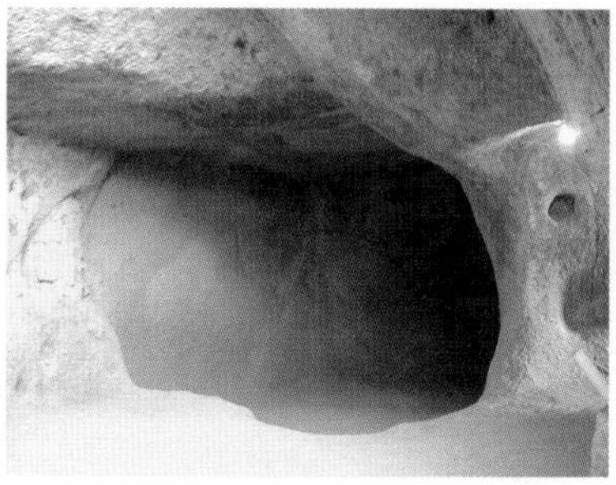

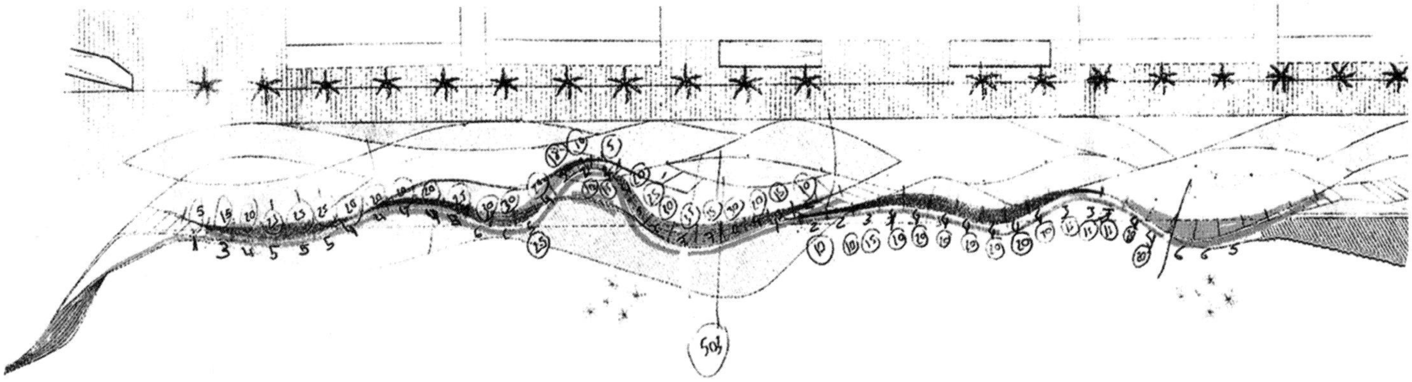

The promenade is structured in different layers: a first structural layer creates the perimeter line in white concrete; another textured layer with paving in different colors; and a last layer of street furniture and natural features like water and vegetation. All these contribute to a homogeneous location with its own personality; as well as being a predecessor to the new architecture of the 21st century by combining building technology and nature in one ensemble.

The new Benidorm promenade is put forward, then, as a new form, one integrating the artificial (or built) and the natural.

The project subsumes three different essences within the organic forms of modernism: the forms of fractal geometry in nature; the latest building technologies; and avant-garde landscape design.

The new promenade leaves nothing to chance but grows out of setting up a number of specific laws, a geometrical ground plan and modulation. A constructional logic is thus established, facilitating its modulation in sections.

The beach partly invades zones previously occupied by the former esplanade, increasing the surface area of sand and reducing that of asphalt.

All the functional aspects are brought together: the promenade, rest and relaxation area, vantage point, transition to the beach, architectural barriers, direct access to parking, rainwater collectors, beach lighting, road communication, integration of street furniture, services infrastructure, and so on.

A new landside frontage is constructed, providing views of the sea and the beach from the upper level of the promenade, and a new borderline established, integrating the different circulations in its undulations and platforms, eliminating a barrier and constructing a place for people to be in.

Waterfront Benidorm

SOROLLA

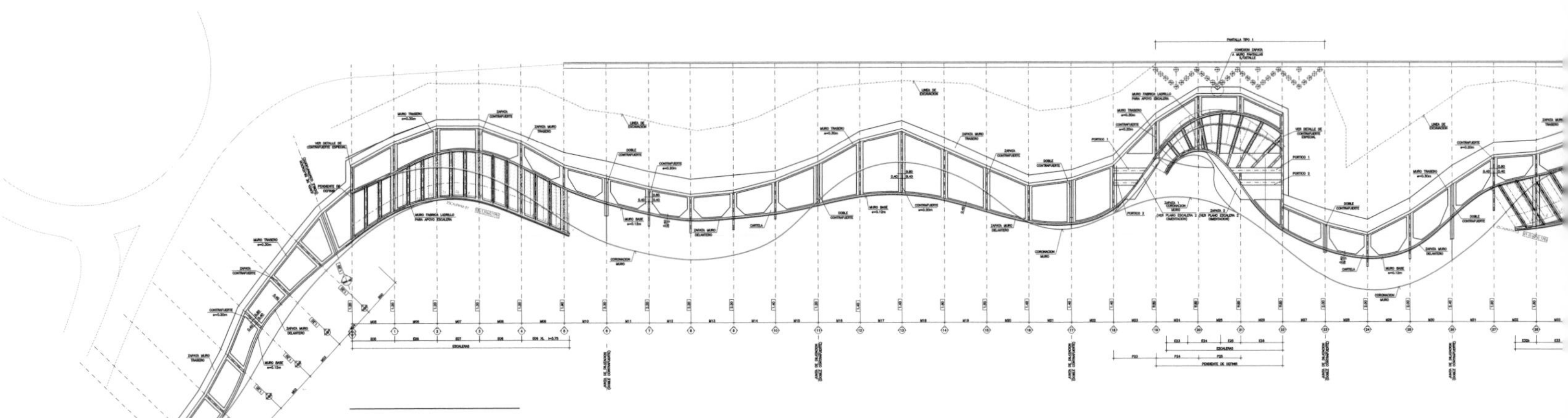

Foundation

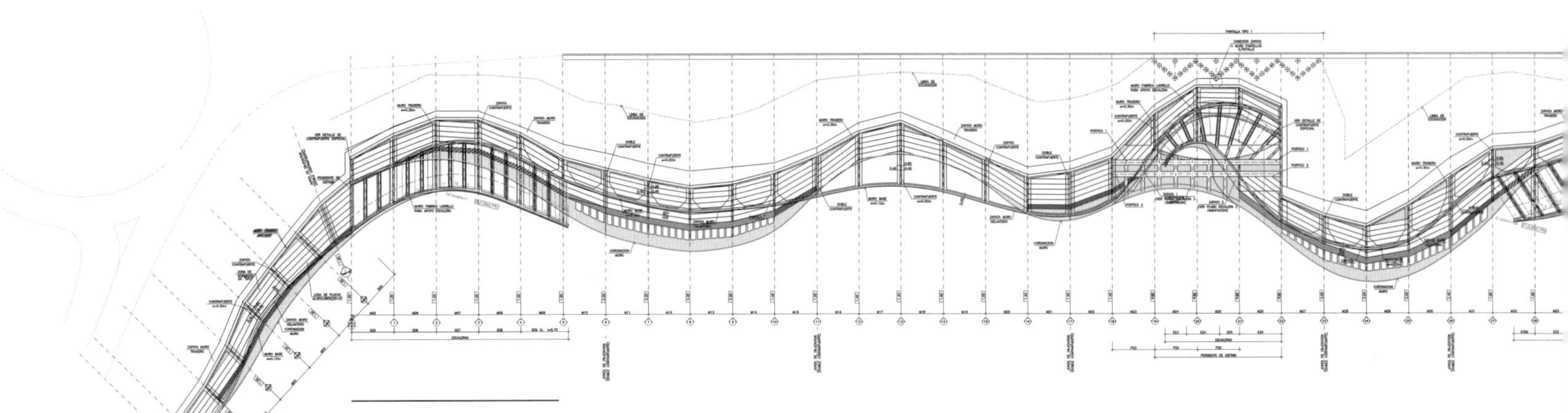

Alveolar panels

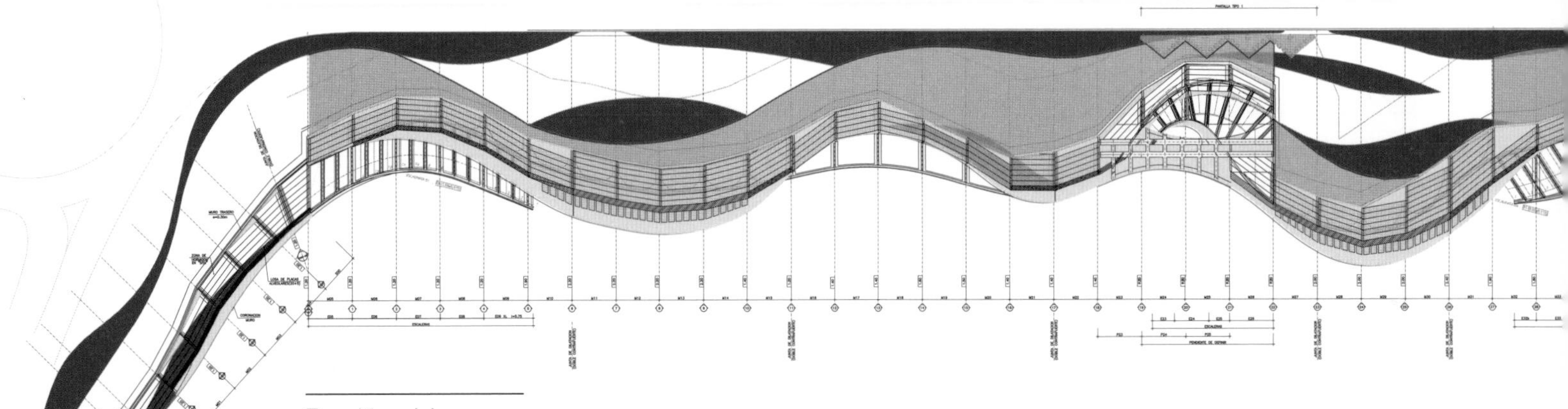

Transition slabs

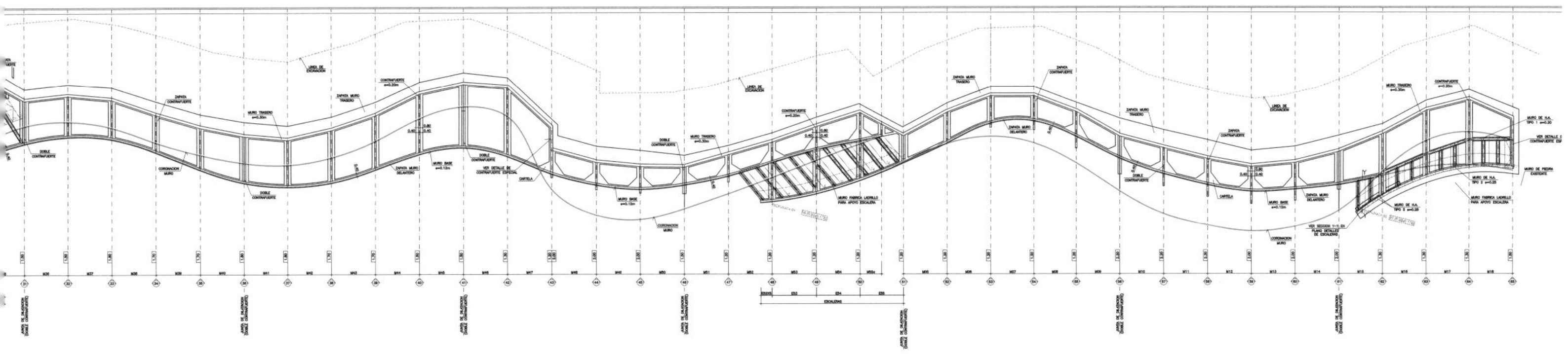

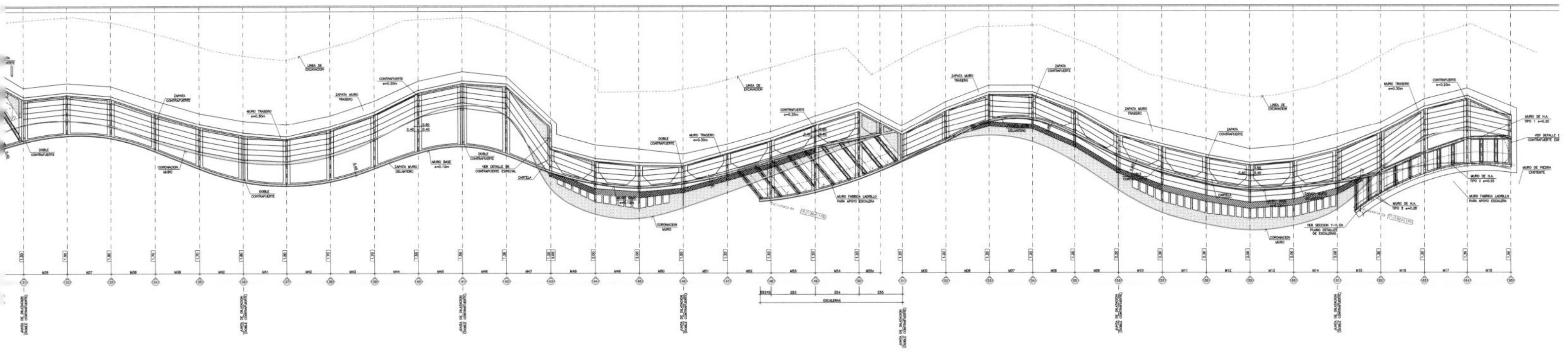

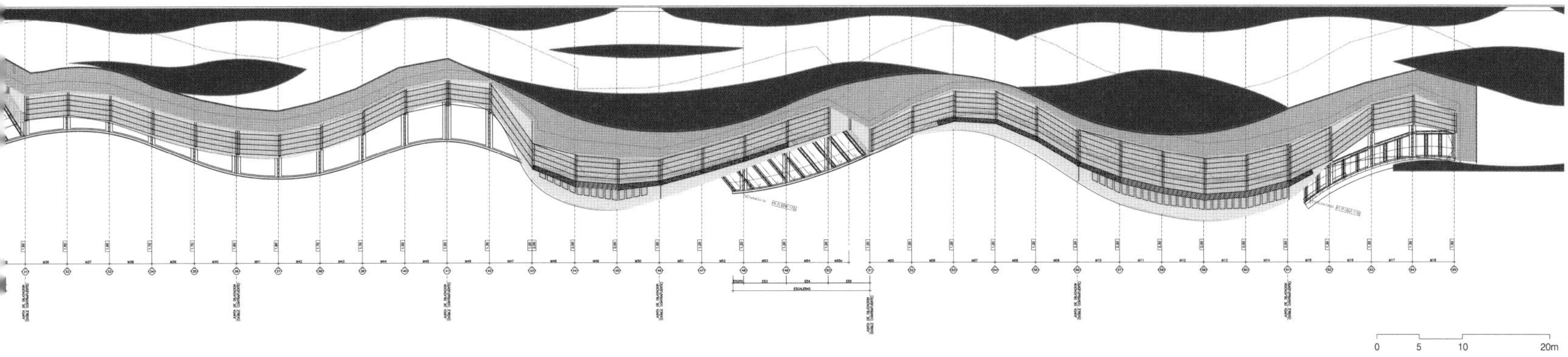
0
5
10
20m

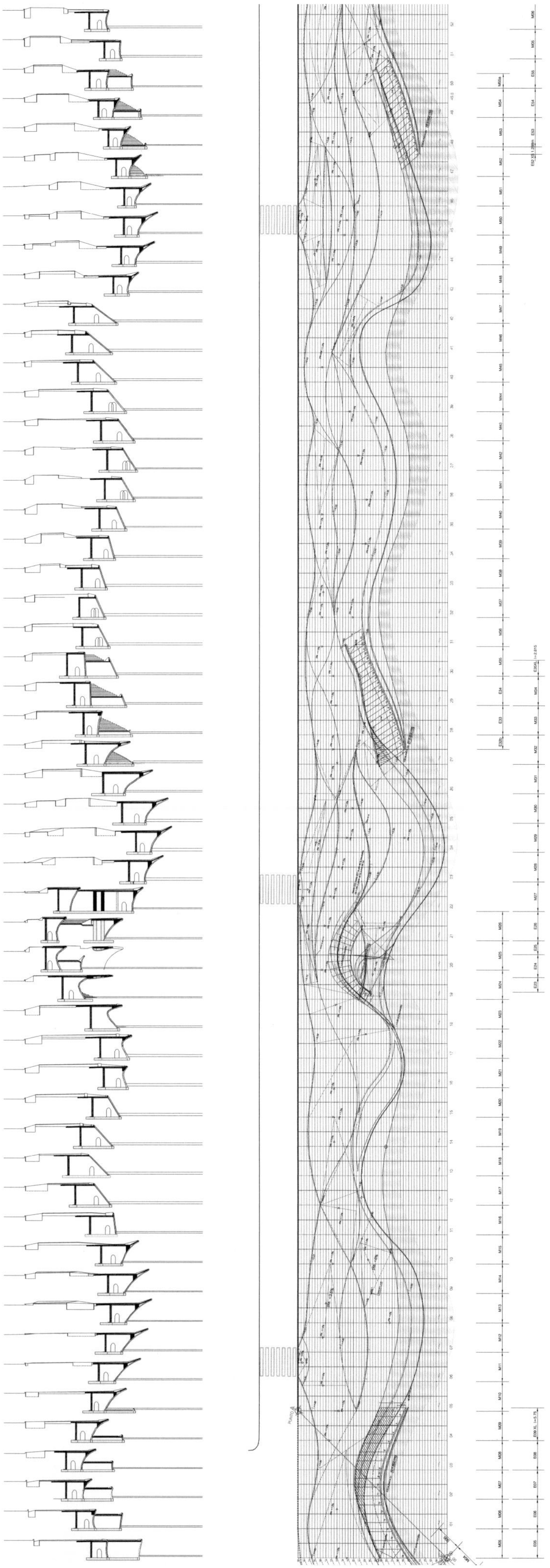

Topographic definition

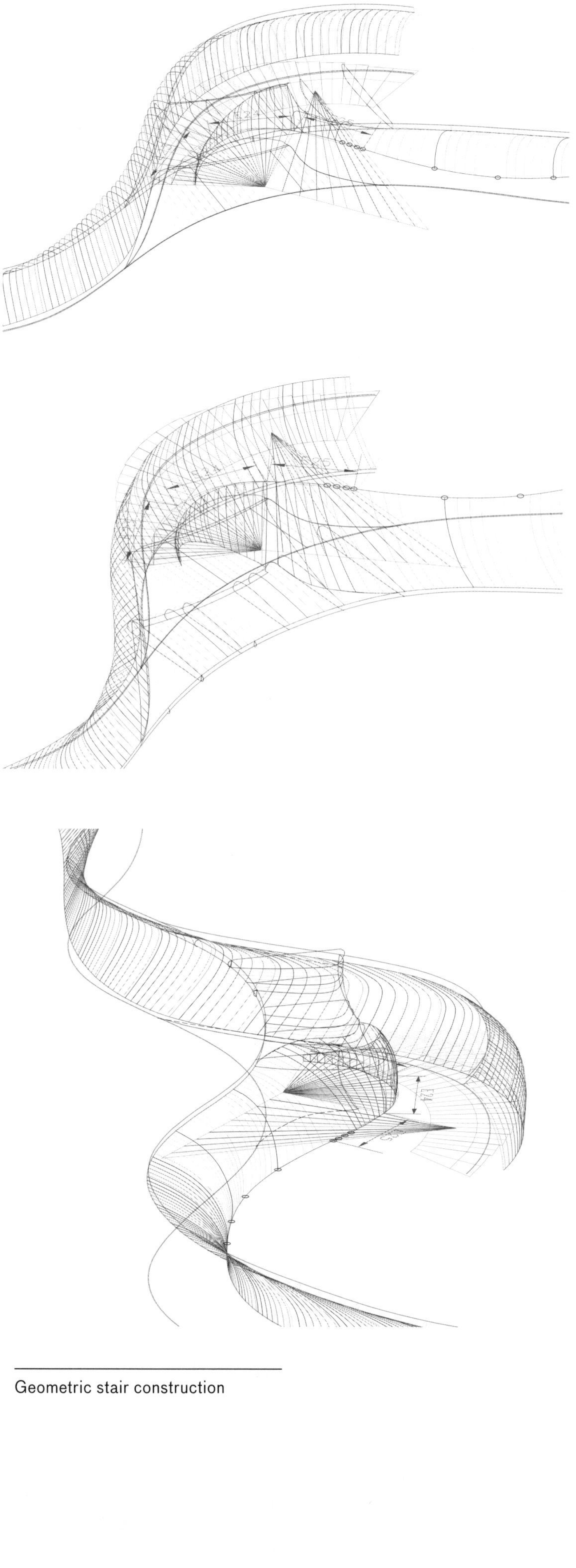

Geometric stair construction

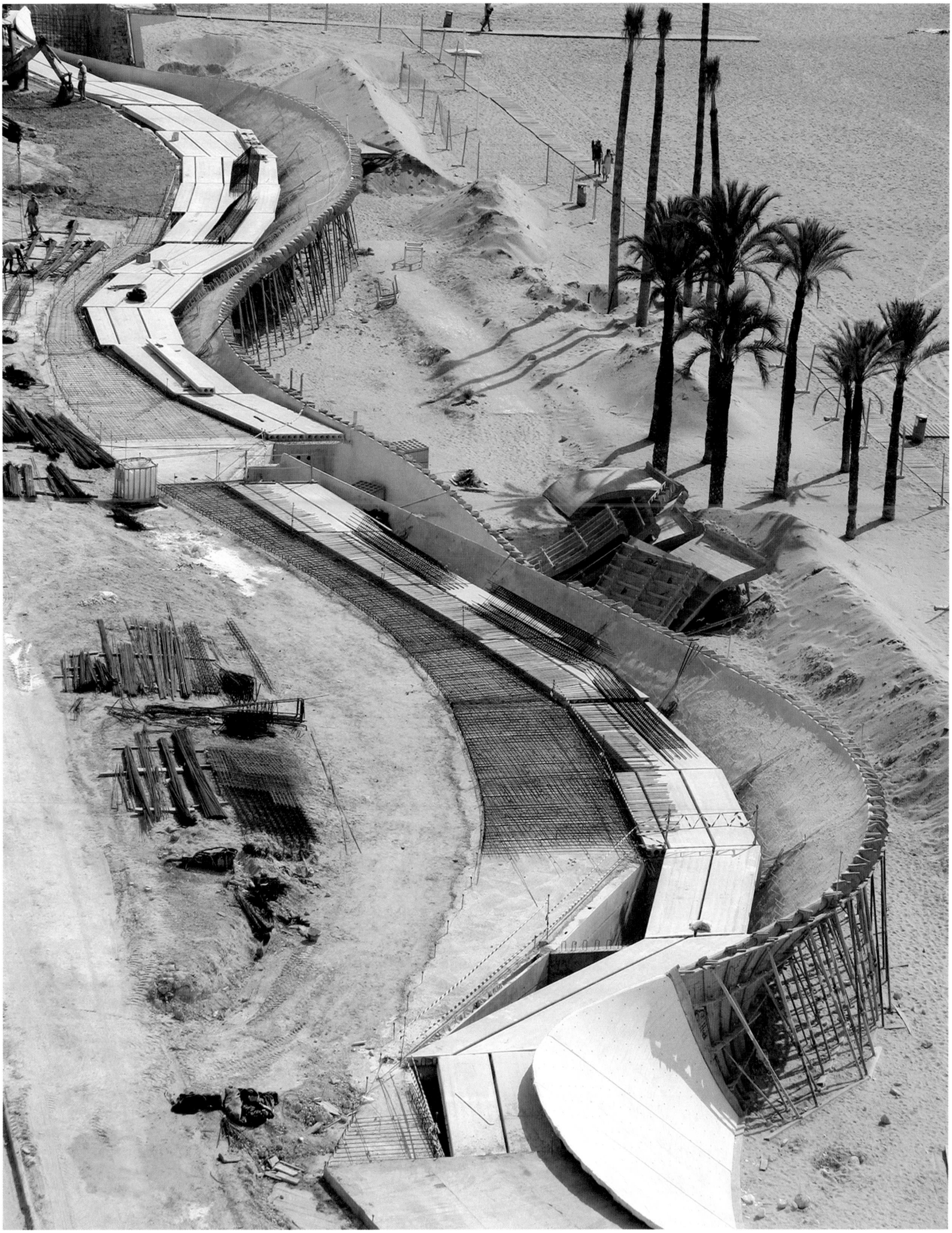

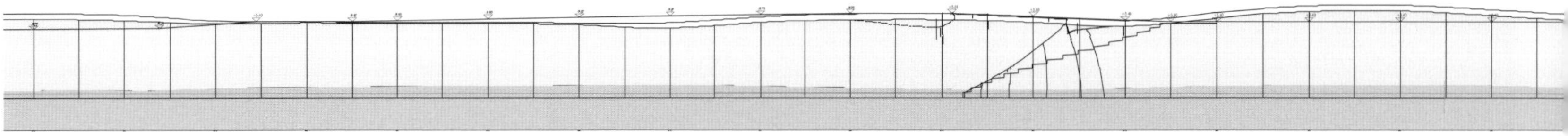

Section

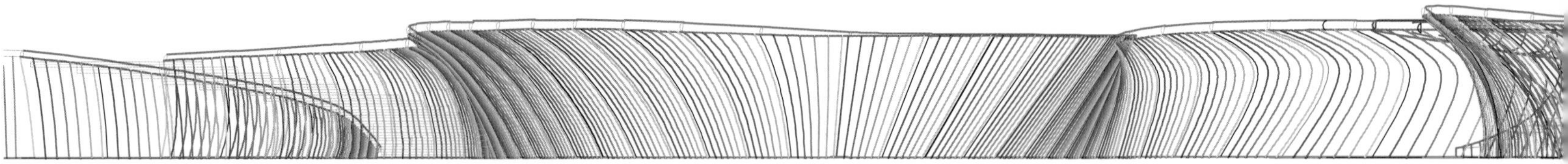

Final elevation

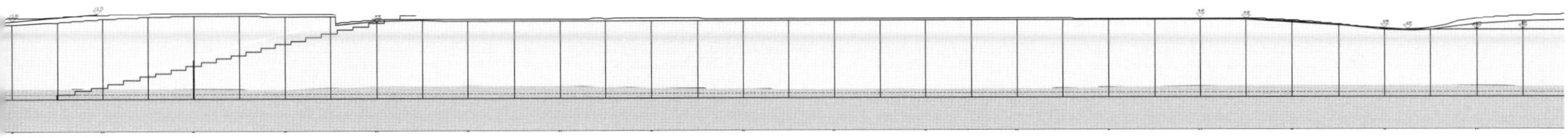

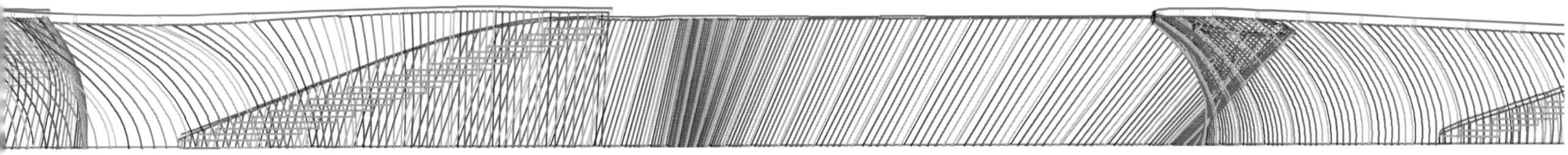

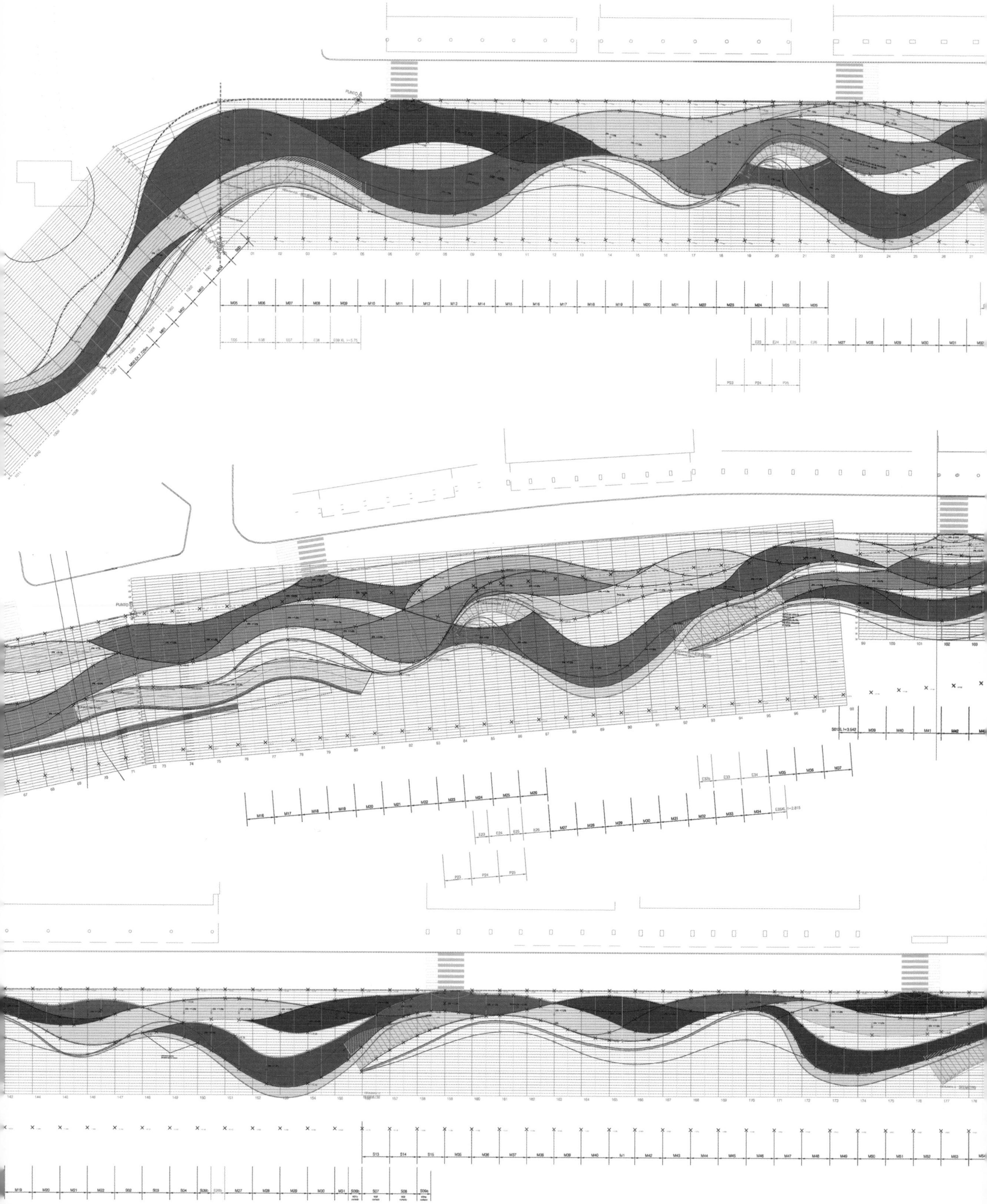

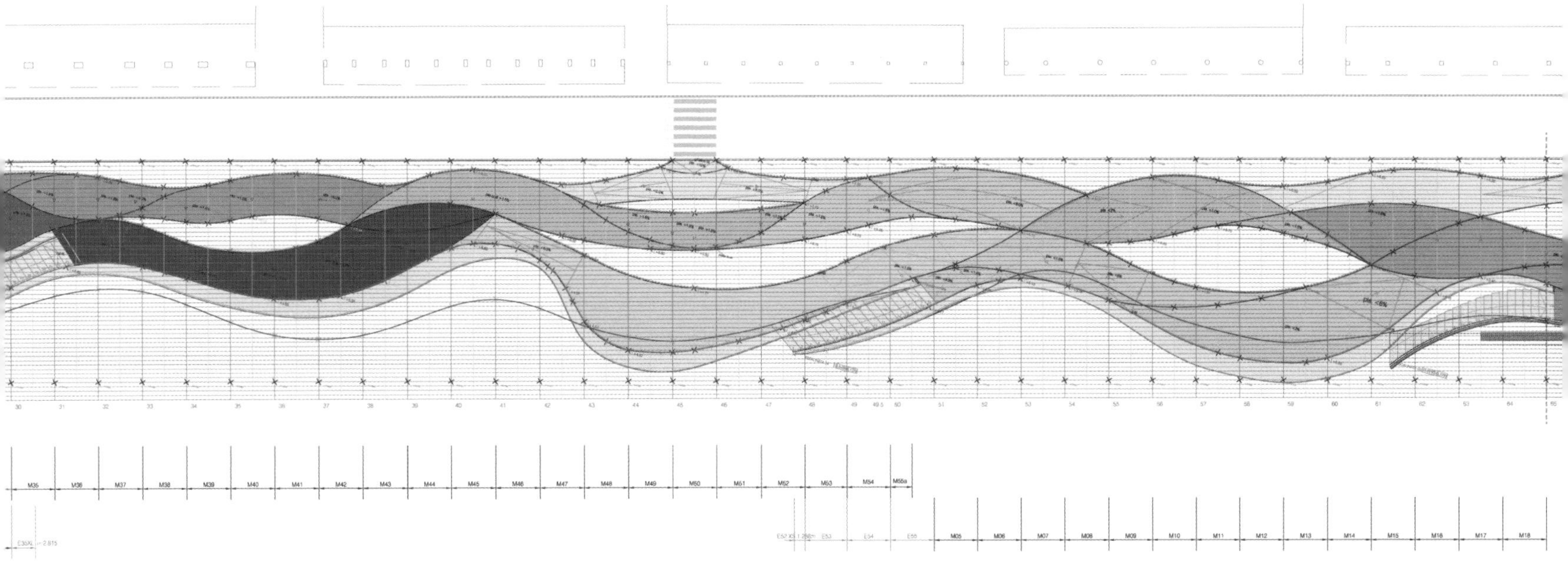

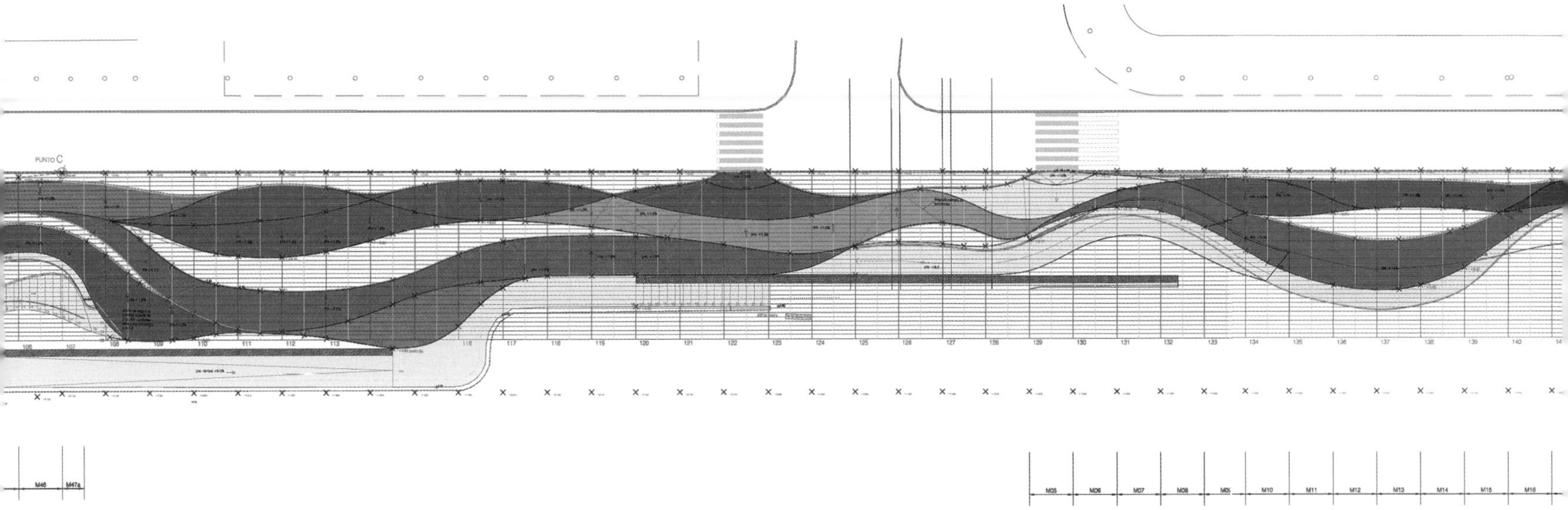

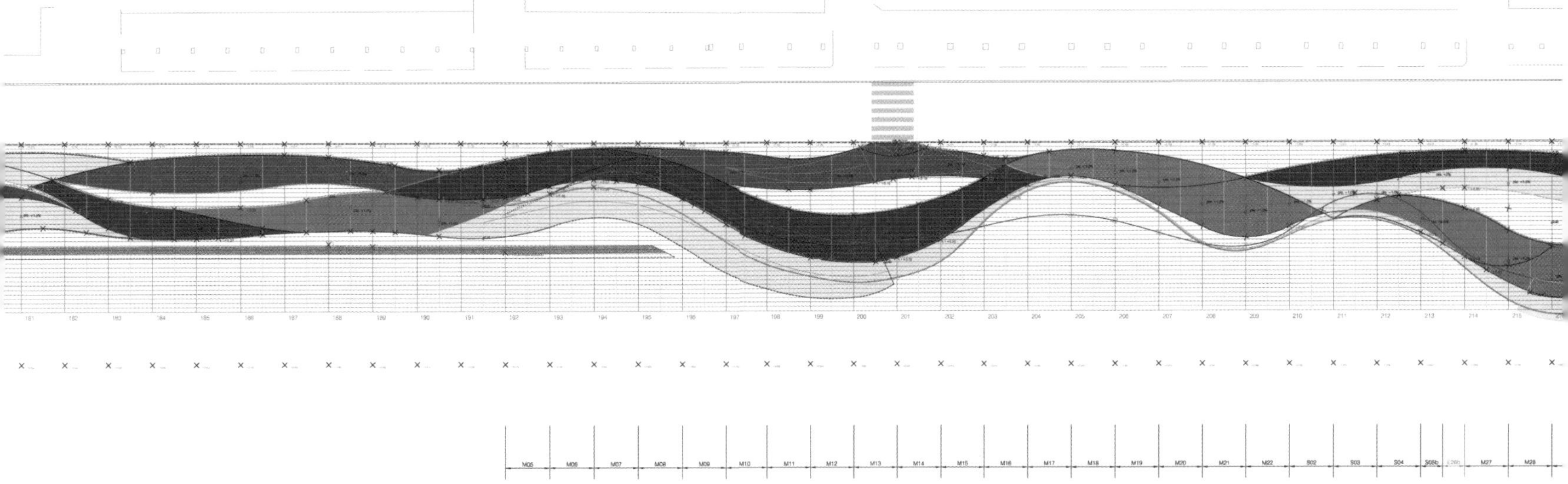

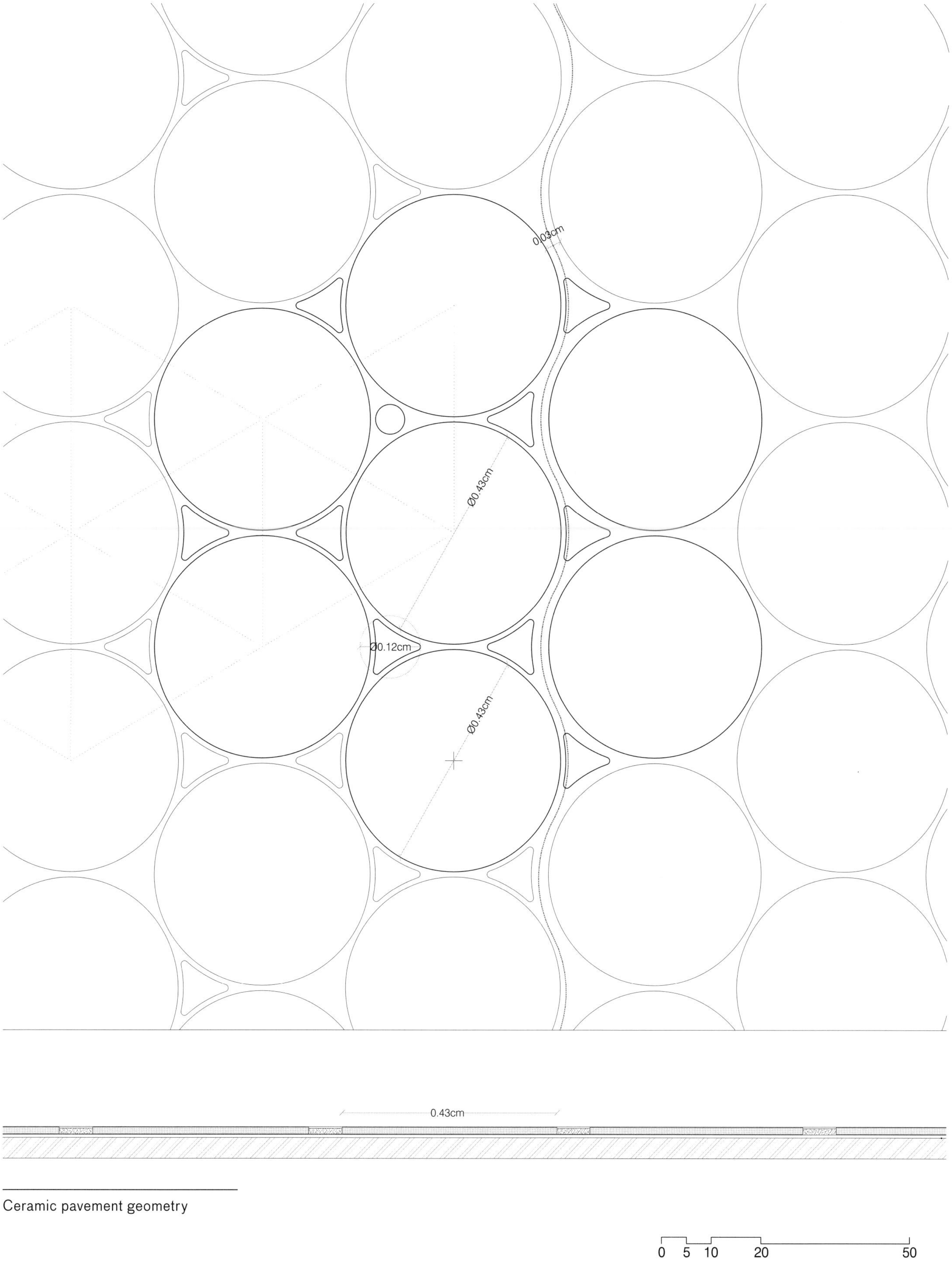

Ceramic pavement geometry

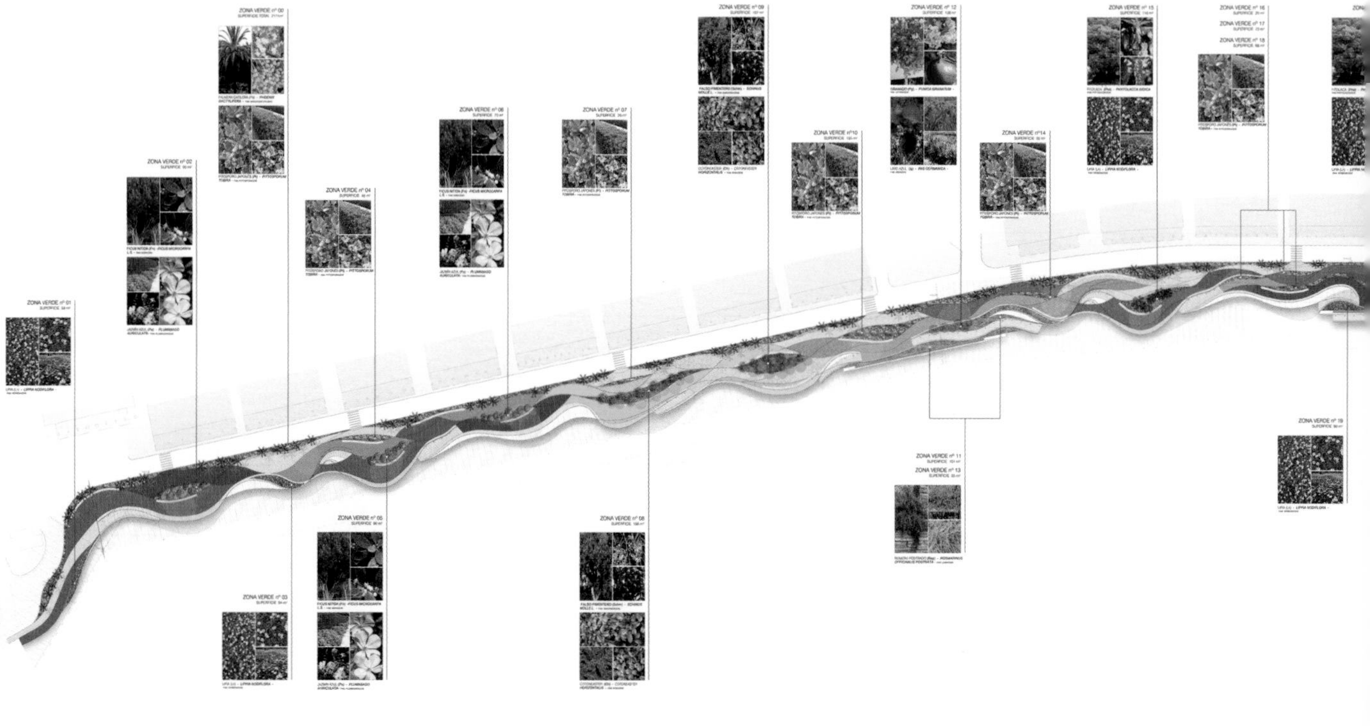

Vegetation plan

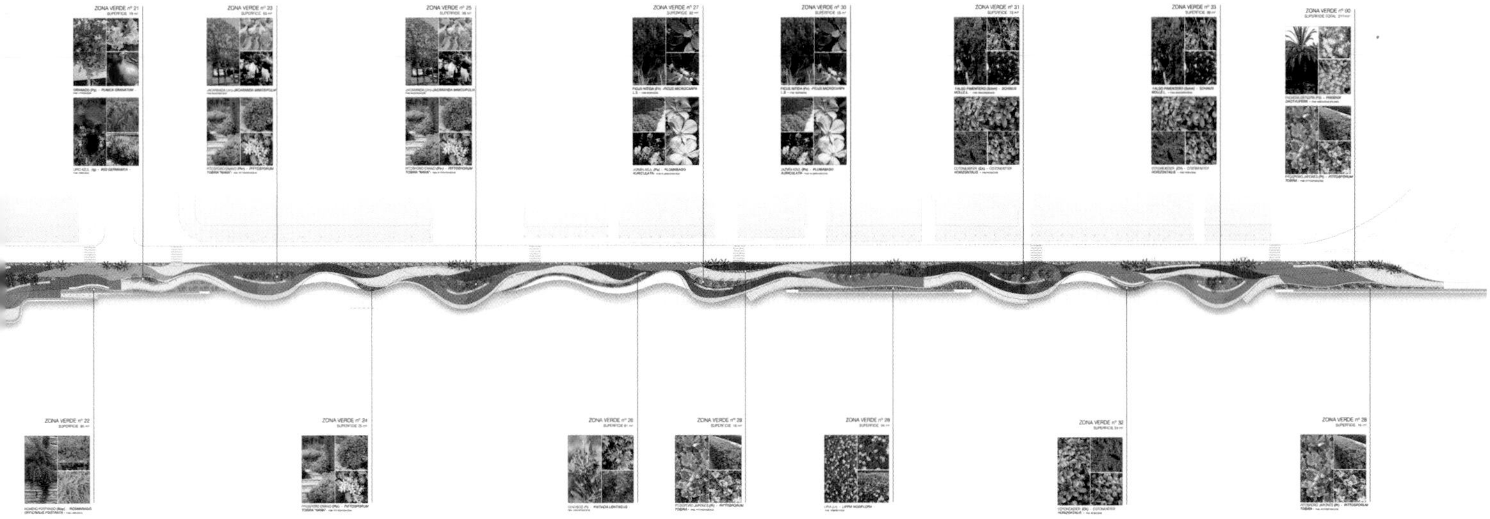

ZONA VERDE nº 21
ZONA VERDE nº 23
ZONA VERDE nº 25
ZONA VERDE nº 27
ZONA VERDE nº 30
ZONA VERDE nº 31
ZONA VERDE nº 33
ZONA VERDE nº 22
ZONA VERDE nº 24
ZONA VERDE nº 32

16

Housing and inhabitants. From Alcanar to the AA House

Carlos Ferrater

Three years ago in Menorca, in August 2007, I wrote a short story about 10 single-family houses built over a period of 30 years with the title *Casas y habitantes* (Homes and occupants) as a tribute to their users and occupants. Two of those houses, one for my brother and AA House, designed together with Xavier Martí and which had not yet been started, put forward two different worlds within the scope of the single-family dwelling and with respect to privacy.

La fàbrica d'Horta (Factory in Horta), 1909
Pablo Picasso

Whereas my brother's second home, the house in Alcanar, was being turned into a self-build exercise for its occupant in the midst of a picturesque landscape of vegetable gardens and orchards by the sea using the fewest possible materials in an attempt to recreate an idea that had emerged from a painting under the splendid light of that place, the large residence in a forest near Barcelona, christened AA House, established a relationship with the past filled with the grand homes of art patrons and leaders from the history of Catalonia. It also allowed us to experiment with typologies and construction processes that would turn its users into the real occupants of their new house. It would seem that the same goal was being pursued along two very different paths.

After a visit to the practically finished AA House with Josep M. Montaner, I received a text from him barely two hours later, written of his own accord and in haste after the visit. Owing to the perceptiveness and intuition of the text, I considered it appropriate for inclusion here.

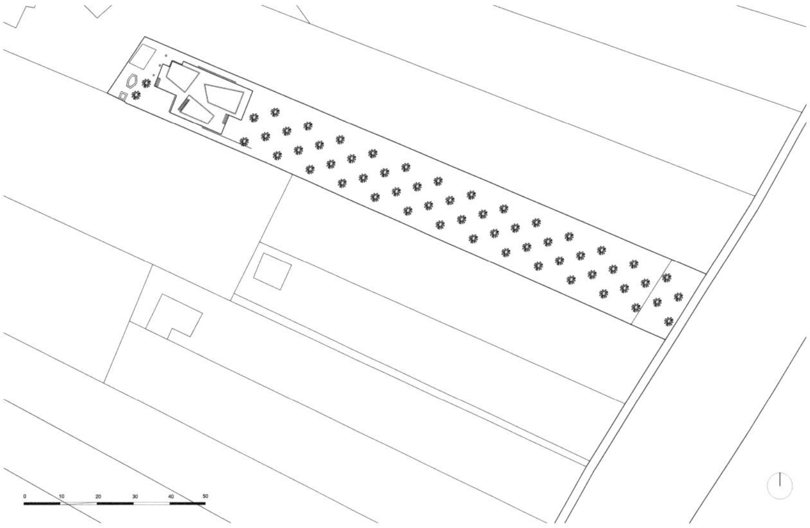

Carlos Ferrater

House for Photographer 2

A plot perpendicular to the sea measuring 250 m in length by 18 m in width. The piece of land lies in an agricultural area that runs back from the beach to a place that forms a backdrop of old ruins, reeds and lemon trees.

The Home for Photographer 2 stands at the back of the site. Built on a platform raised 50 cm over the floodable natural terrain, three small volumes with irregular layouts and elevations create a dialogue through a void with visual distractions.

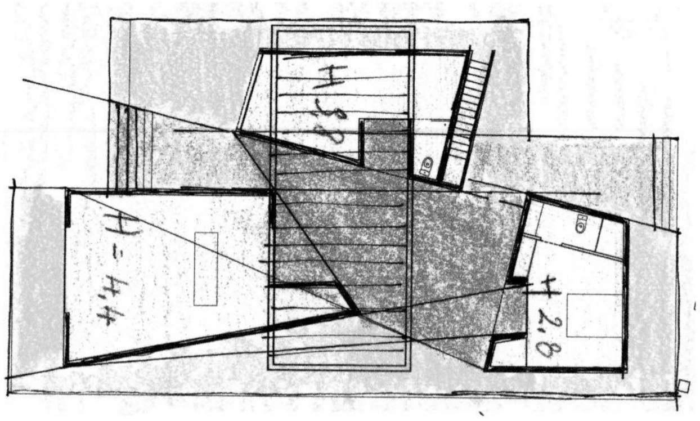

A grove of 51 Washingtonia palms leads from the beach to the house. The deconstructed volumes adapt to the conditions of the landscape, of buildings and light that suggest a painting by Picasso that was painted in the area and now hangs in the Picasso Museum in Paris.

The central void becomes the main space of the home, a tense space geometrically composed in its upper part through the tall, opaque structures of the different pavilions and from the ground up to a height of 2.10 m on a continuous site where the different shaded interior spaces are connected with views of the sea, the lush backdrop and the living areas on the platform.

The set of deconstructed volumes reminds us of Picasso's cubist work. The chiaroscuro and the intense light of this area of the Mediterranean balance the flat landscape of this area of the Ebro Delta.

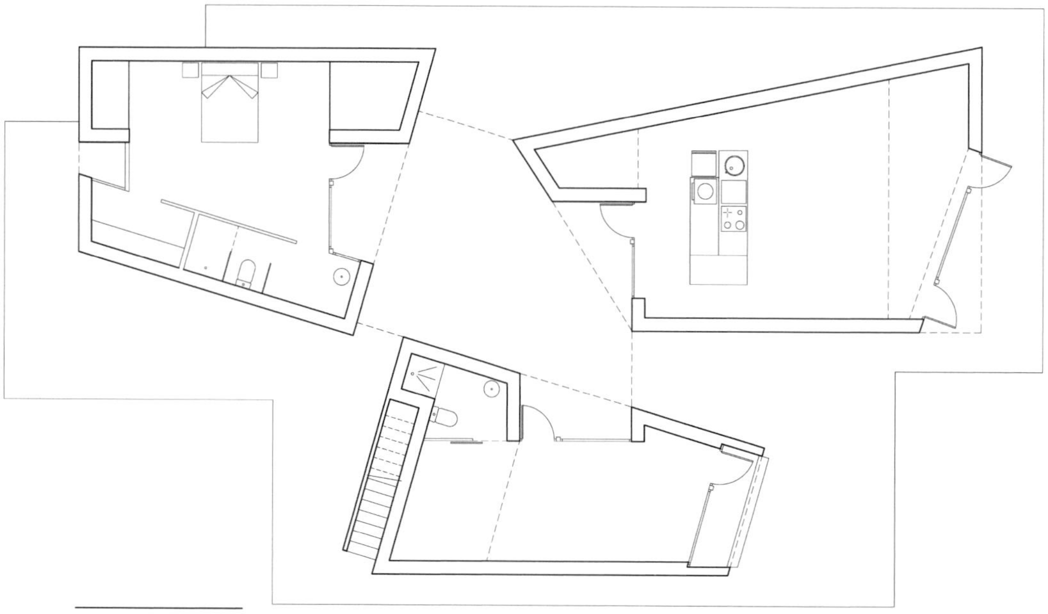

Floor plan

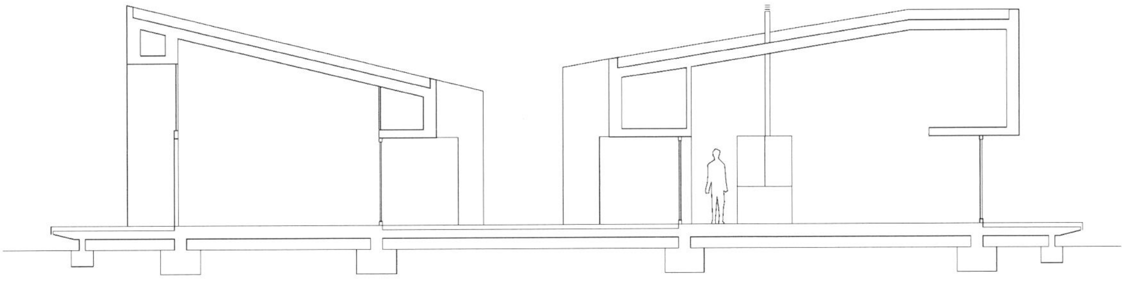

Section

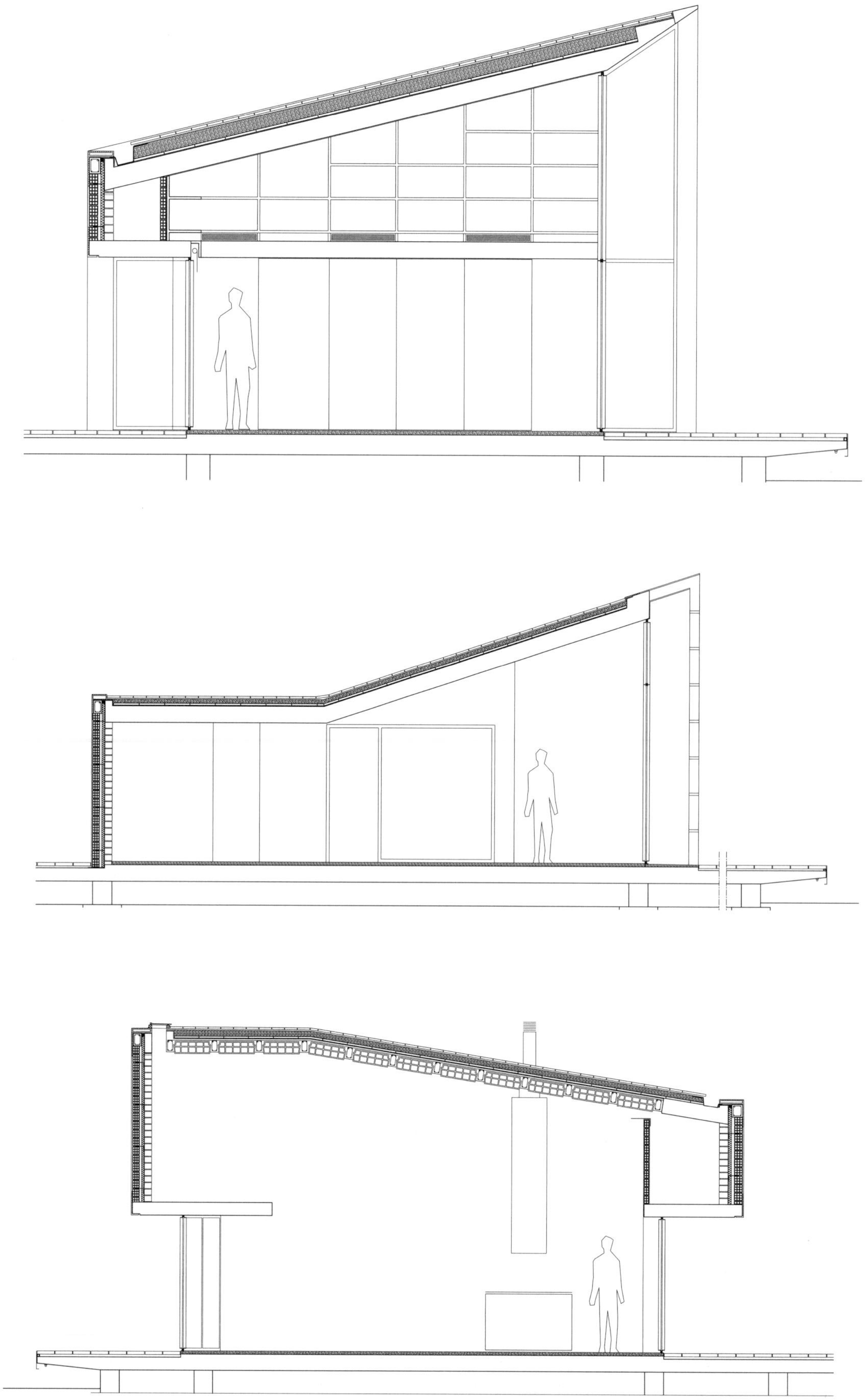

Construction sections

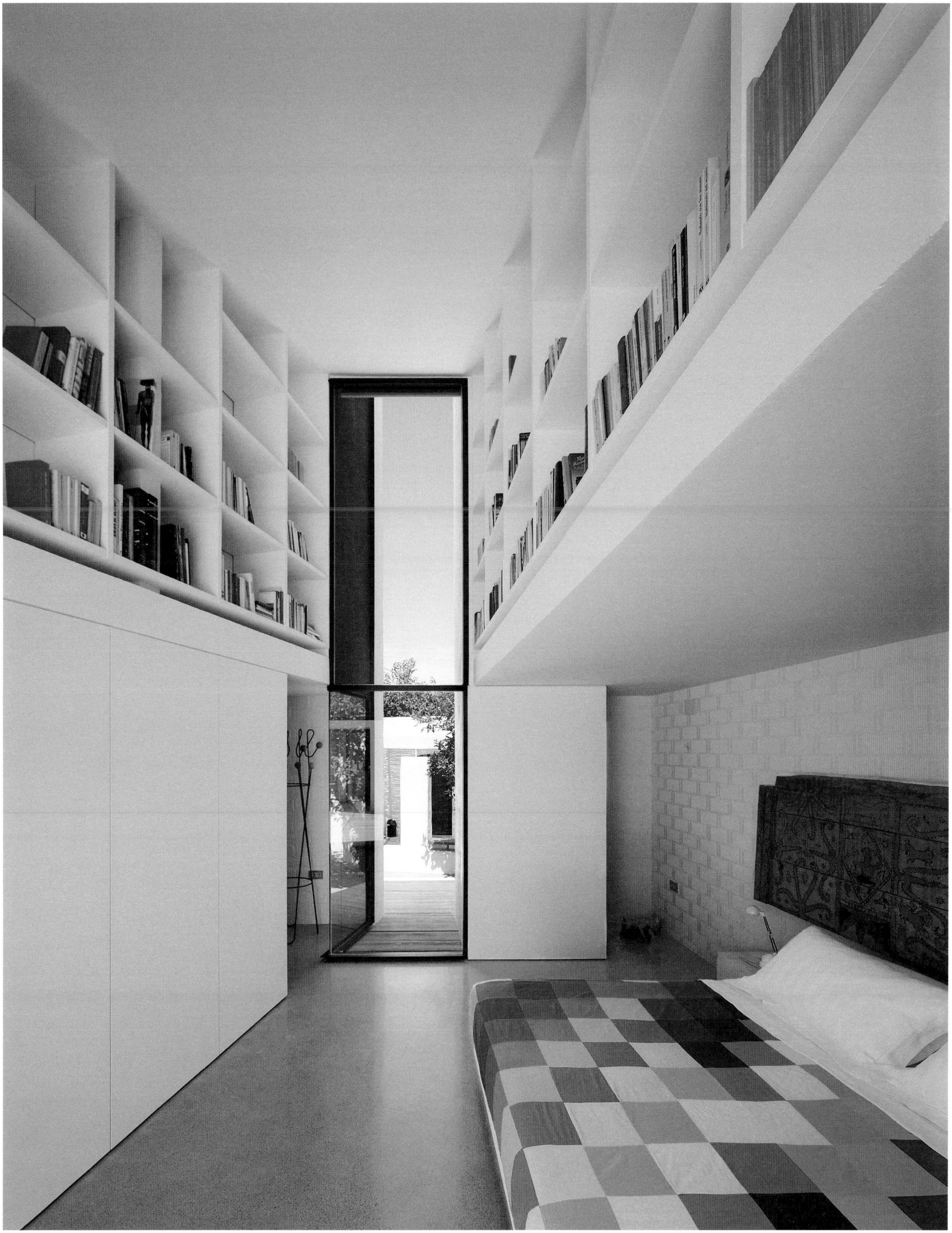

AA House is not one house; it is 4 houses

AA House by Carlos Ferrater and Xavier Martí is one of the most unique and intense single-family homes that has been built in recent times. It establishes a relationship with houses by Louis Khan, Alison and Peter Smithson, and Ray and Charles Eames.

Located in Sant Cugat, next to a forest bordering a golf course, the house rises from the road as a series of sloping roofs among the trees in the garden that form a magnificent belt of picturesque scenery.

On entering, the house greets us with a pool of water, an allegory of one of the four elements and born of a desire for reflections. Before entering, a totally austere plaza is defined. And upon entering, you discover a great longitudinal space, defined by skylights in the sloping roof. This great interior space is at once perfectly on a human scale.

The unique and unsettling fact that there appears to be no staircase and that none of the service facilities of the house are visible, all hidden away on a lower floor, leads us to believe this is not a house but something else; it is many houses at the same time. It is more of a pavilion than a house, given that the only thing to emerge is a large open level of rectangular panels in a bright white, as if it were a temporary Japanese pavilion or a marquee. The house is surrounded by grass, as if it were itself a form of plant life, and floats above it, taking on a mythical and imaginary image. It is reminiscent of the volumes of La Ricarda, the house by Antoni Bonet Castellana.

From the inside, rather than a house to stay in, it becomes a large camera. This sensation owes much to the orthogonal floor plan, perceived as diagonality and dynamicity; the cross section develops into inclined volumes capturing views of the landscaped garden and of the distant landscape beyond, incorporated into the landscape surrounding the house.

In short, it is more than a house, or even a pavilion or a camera; it is like a boat anchored in a green sea of grass. The stairs of this boat are what reveal this secret quality, hidden inside this light and airy house, which seems to be on the point of floating away. The four staircases leading to the lower domains are always hidden and always narrow, like those on a boat. A staircase beside the dining room and kitchen leads directly to the basement. There is a narrow staircase in the bedroom, which, also styled like those on a boat, leads between the walls directly down to the indoor swimming pool and sauna. A light and modern staircase goes from the library directly down to the cinema room, the space for fantasy and dreaming. Finally, there are service stairs leading down from the entrance, next to the kitchen, to the domestic staff apartment.

There are other stairs, also an important feature and, likewise, in the style of a boat, that go up to the higher levels, such as the lightweight contraption that unfolds like a ladder in the library and leads up to a loft where the owner's map collection is kept, the observatory of the world. The kitchen is another house, a world opened completely onto the garden and bathed in natural daylight, a systematic laboratory of nutrition, care, cleaning and work.

It is then that we discover the fourth house, which is the hidden house, the collector's house. It belongs to the collector of cars that are stored in the garage on the lower level. While the visible and representative house, after entering, next to the bar, is the large light-filled living area with piano and library at the back, the truly structuring space, the most private inner sanctum of the house, is not visible. It is the large garage belonging to the collector, where the permanent occupants of the house are to be found: cars, like machines of the subconscious, of desire, and of speed.

It is a house and it is the contrary: telluric and anchored at the base, and yet light and floating like a balloon about to leave the ground. It takes us back to the idea of a "house" as an authentic archetype as understood by Gaston Bachelard and Luís Barragán: with a basement and an attic. With all of its intensity and meaning, this house contains all the symbols. It is a house on pleasant land, all garden, which floats above the grass.

It is not a house. It is many houses. This is what makes it so unique, mythical, archetypal and unsettling. It is a world of illusions: it is a pavilion that floats on a green sea; it is a large camera to capture the surroundings in a thousand ways; it is a boat moored to the trees; it is a balloon about to take to the sky, anchored to the ground by a basement full of machines. it is, in short, the secret world dreamed of by two collectors.

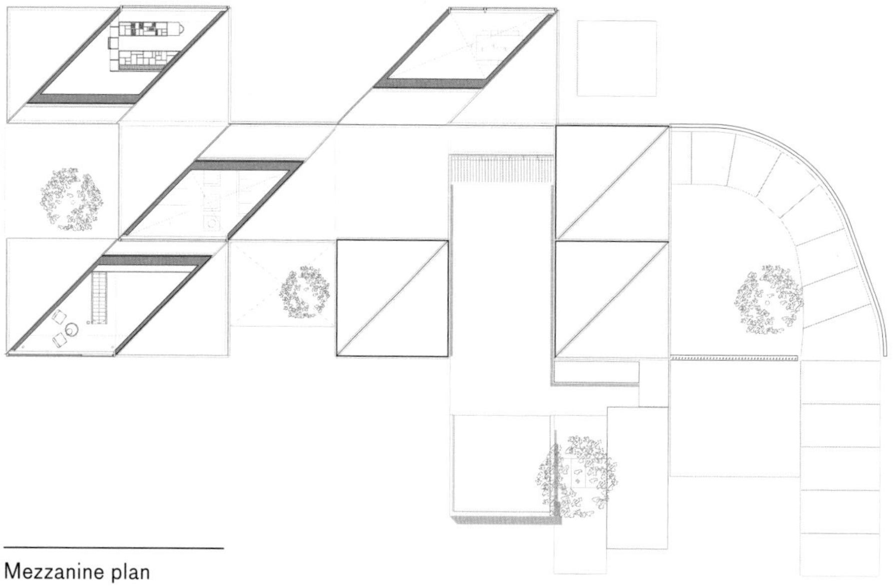

Mezzanine plan

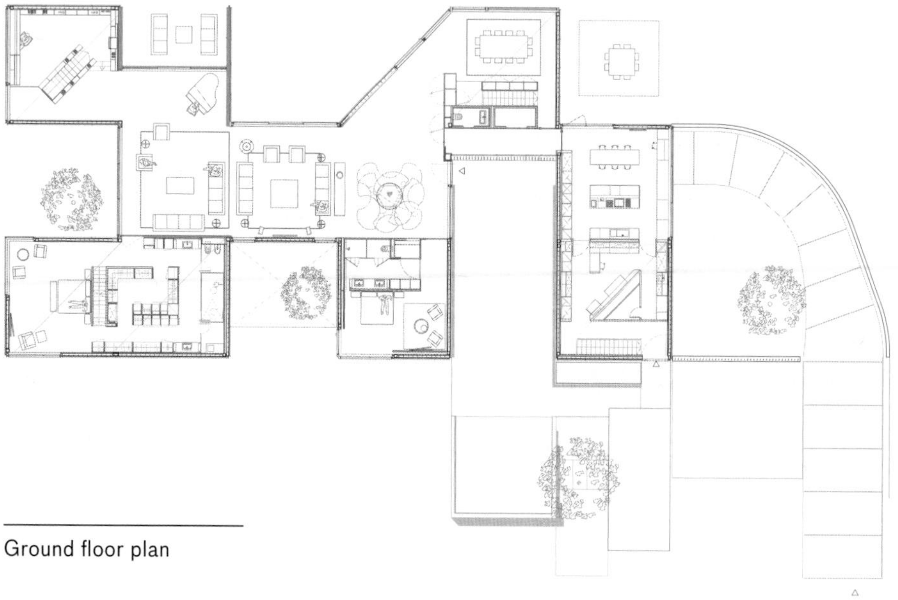

Ground floor plan

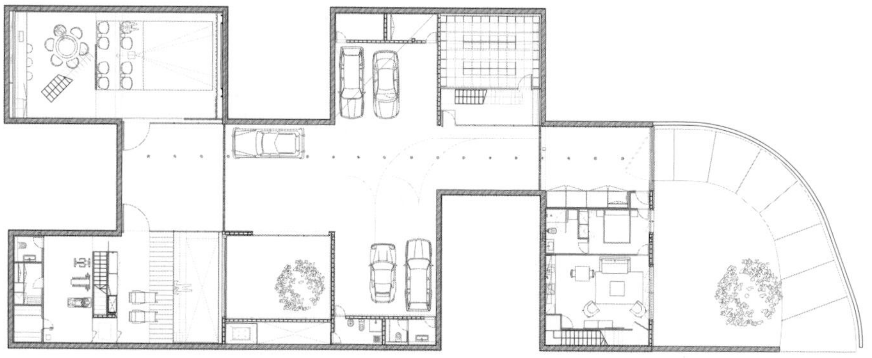

Basement floor plan

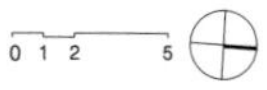

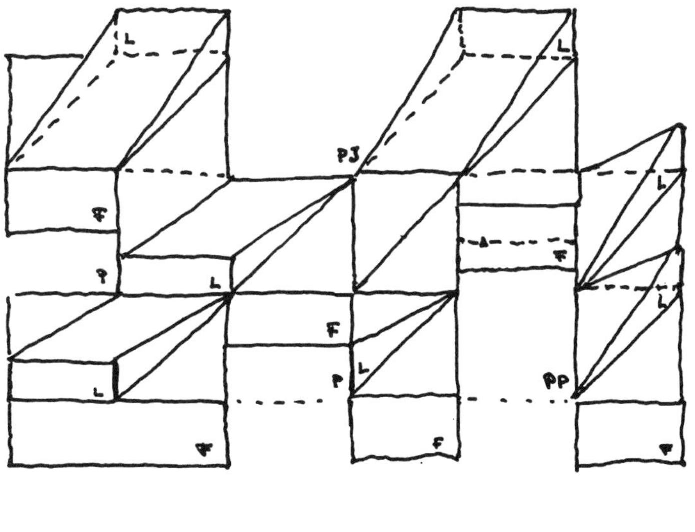
PJ
PP

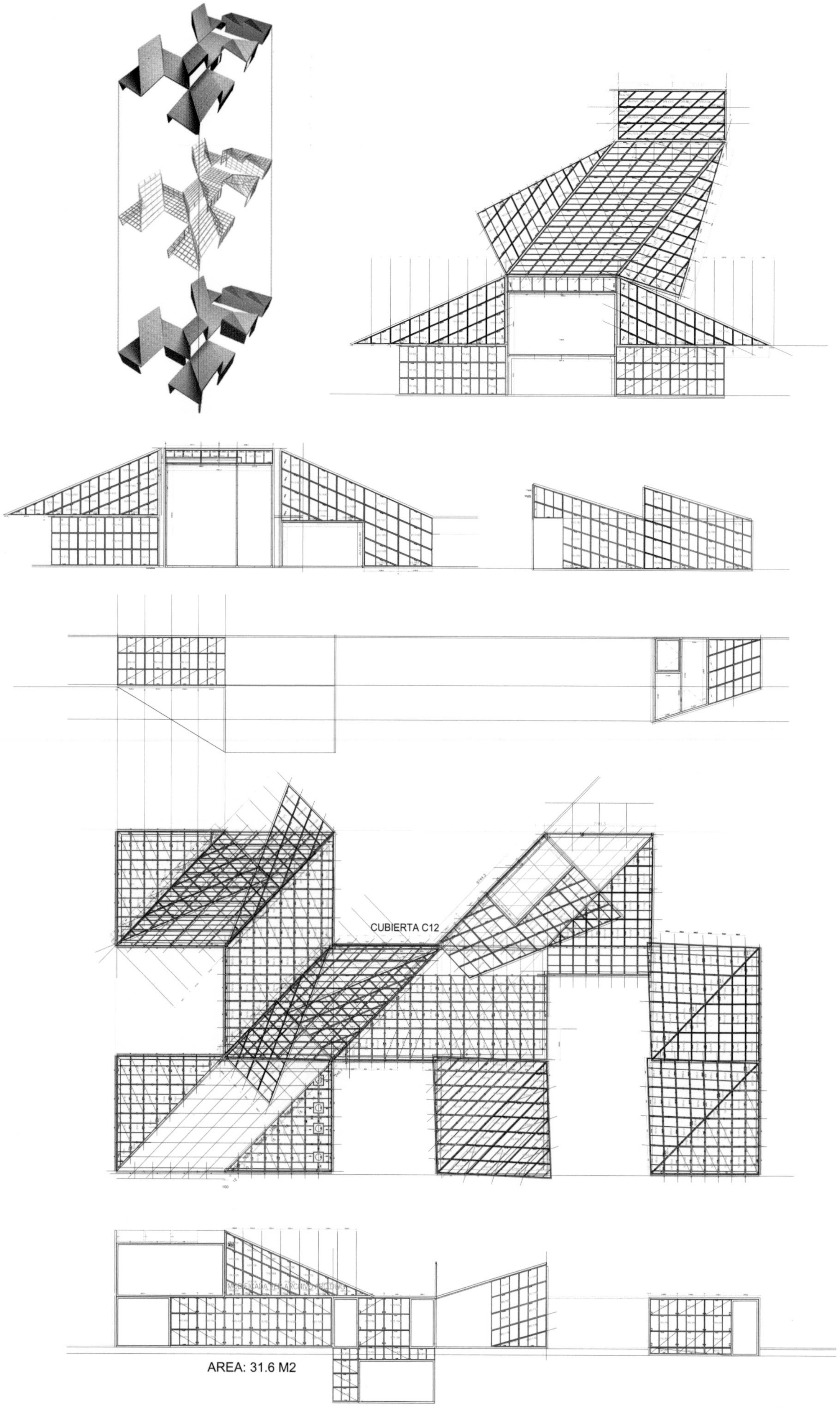

Façade-roof assembly plans. Superimposed sub-structure-cladding

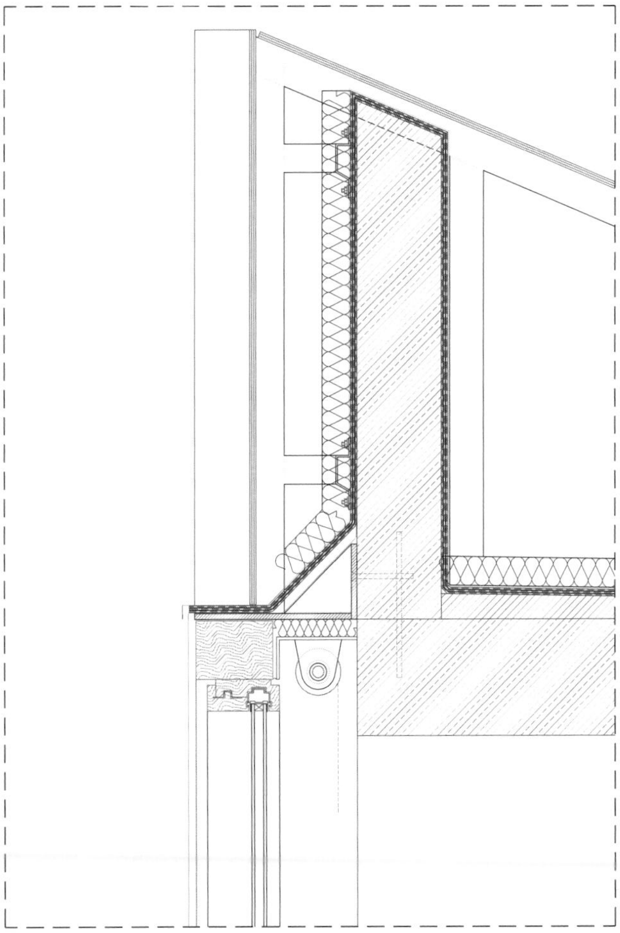

The house follows some basic and very simple rules of geometry, which is where the strength of the project lies:

A 7x7-metre orthogonal network on which the diagonals of this network are overlaid as in a musical staff, the base on which the composition of the project is formed.

The 45º diagonals are the generatrices for the expansions occurring on the roof – skylights in some cases and double heights in others – to produce an artificial topography that rises above that of the terrain.

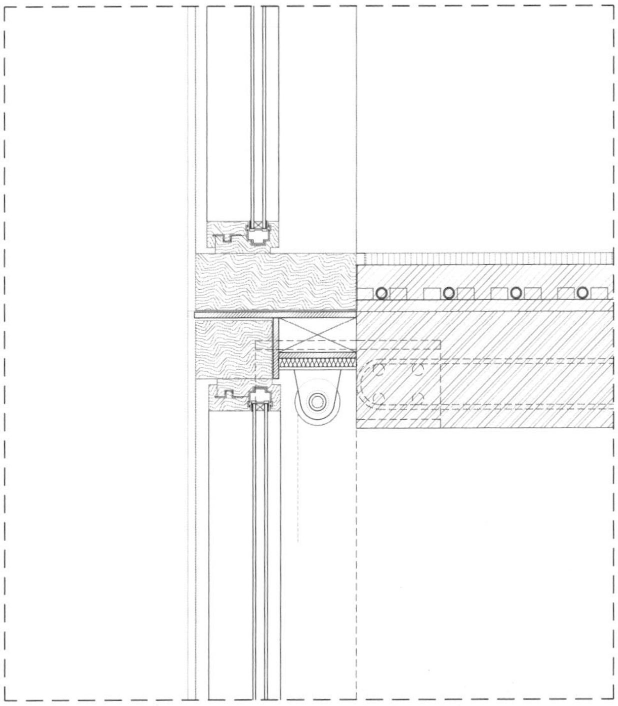

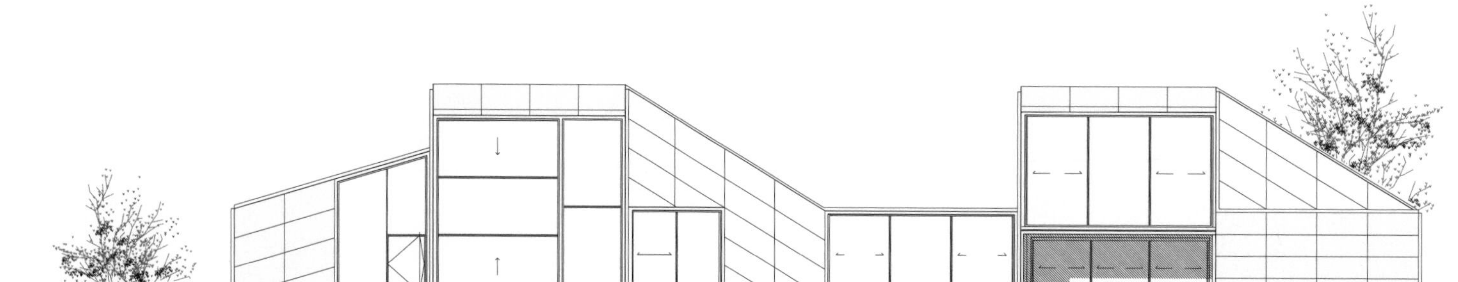

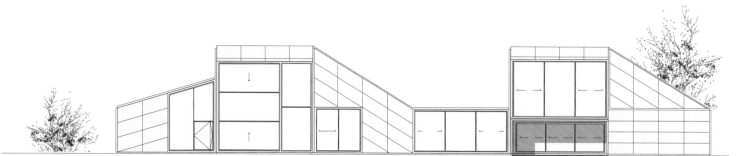

West elevation

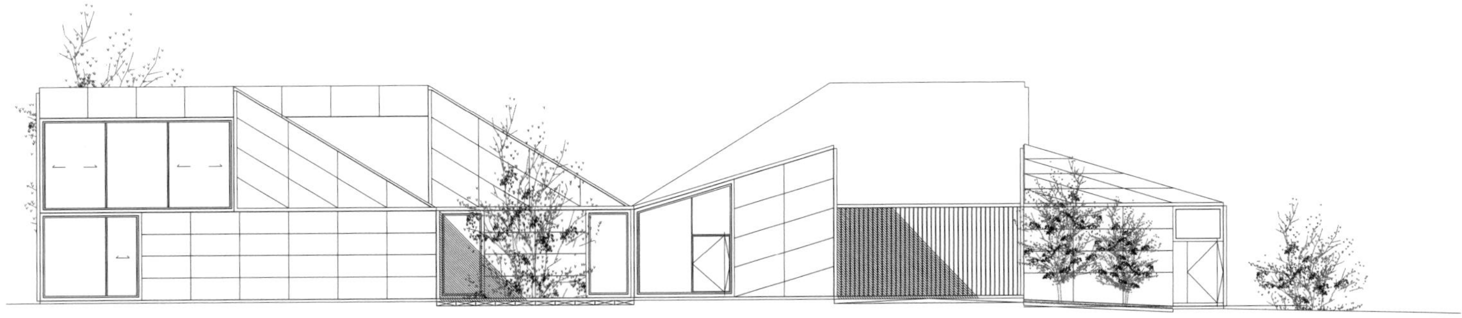

East elevation

MALINCHE
Terenci Moix

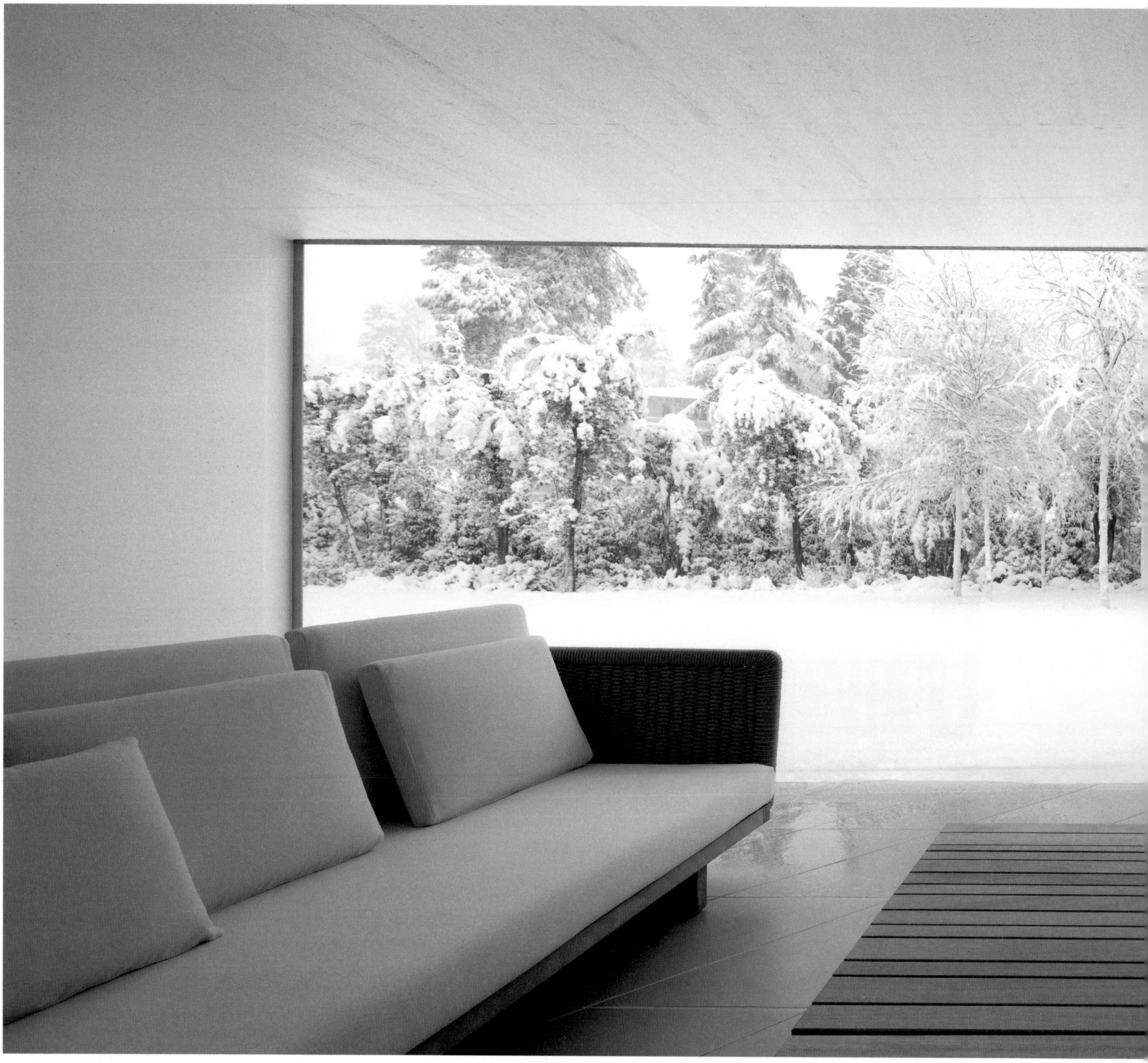

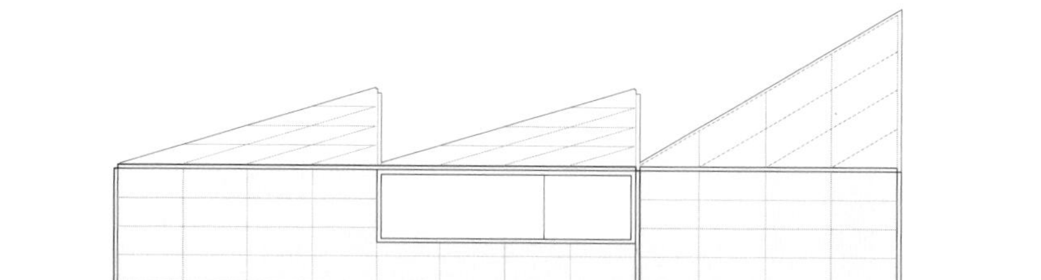

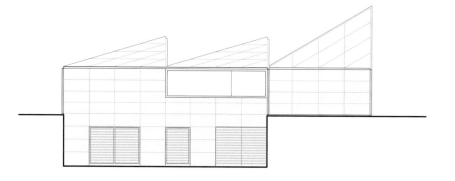

North elevation

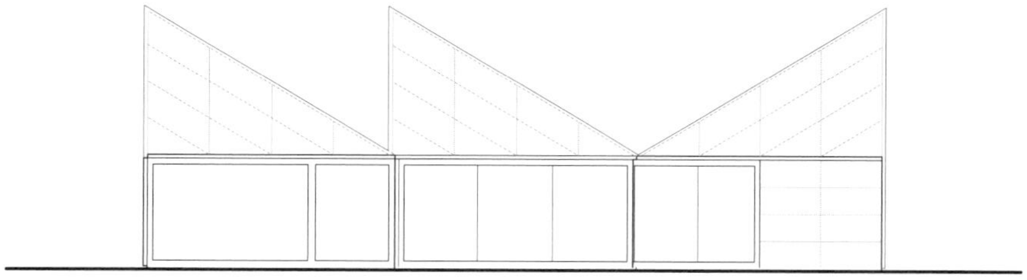

South elevation

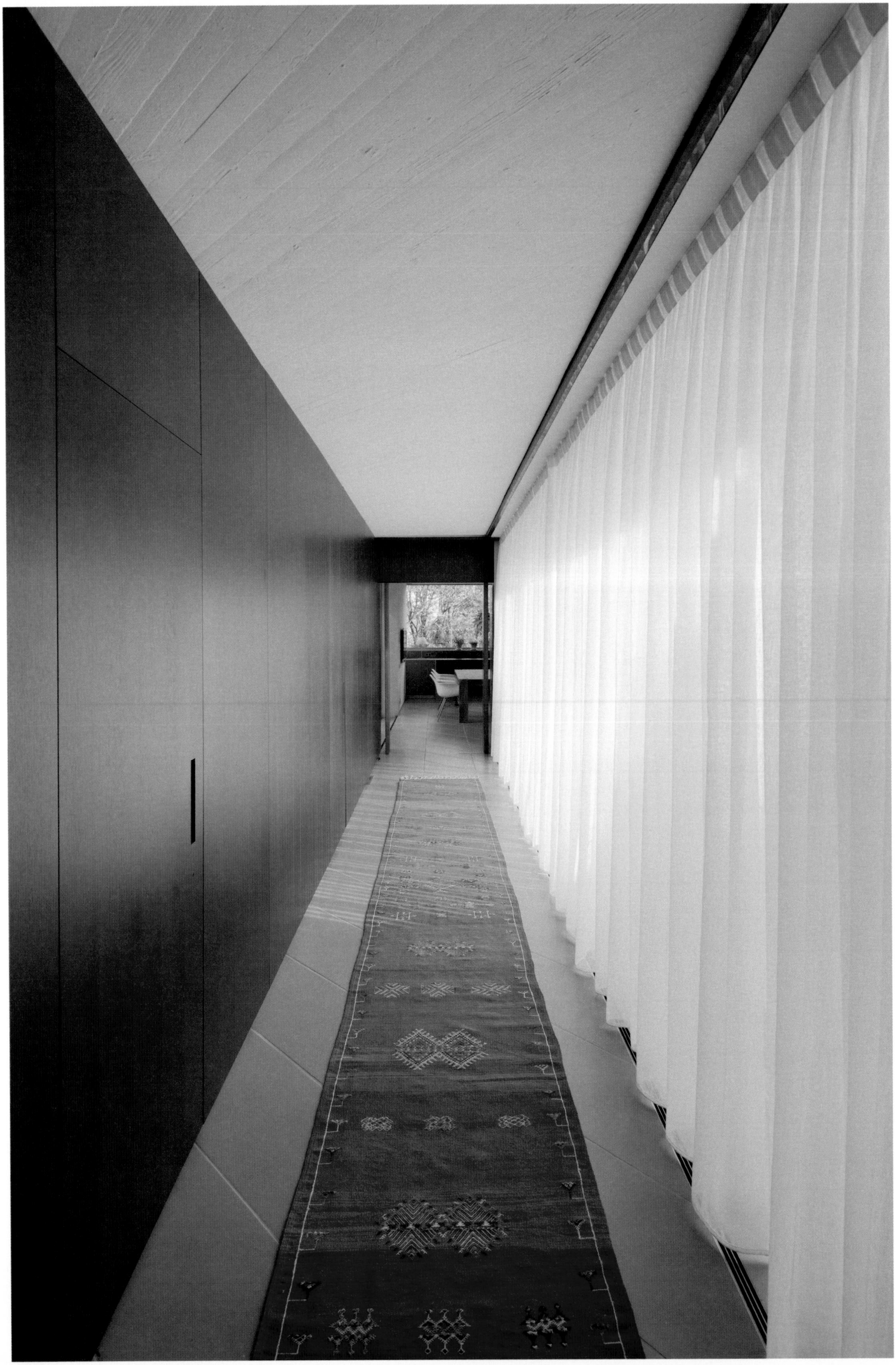

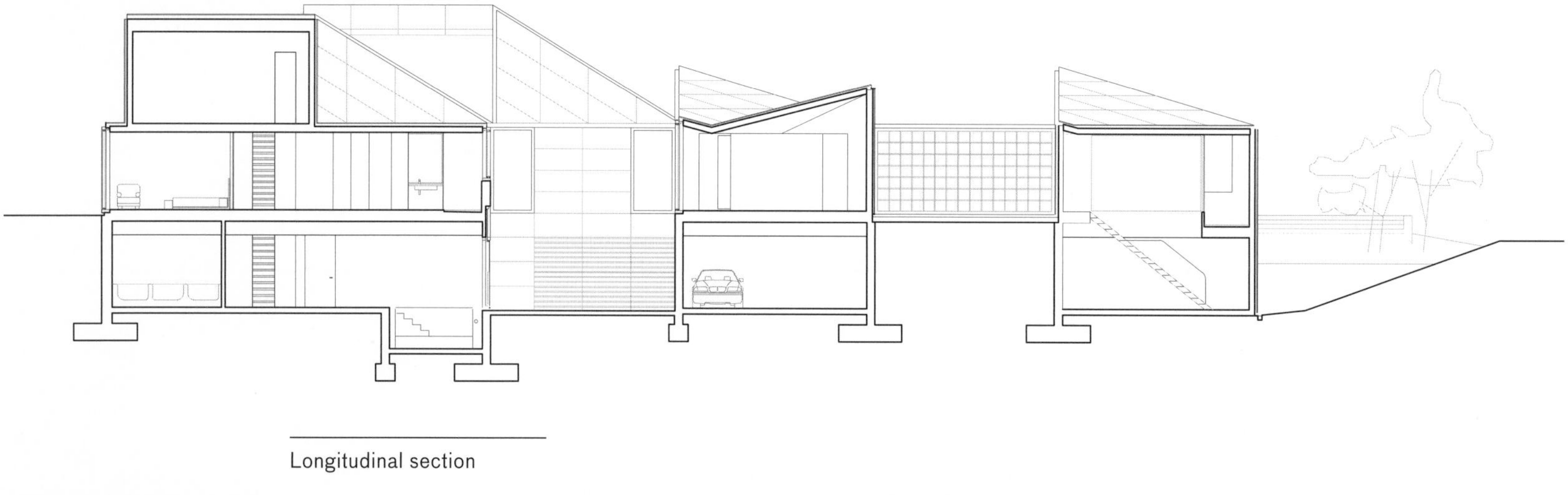

Longitudinal section

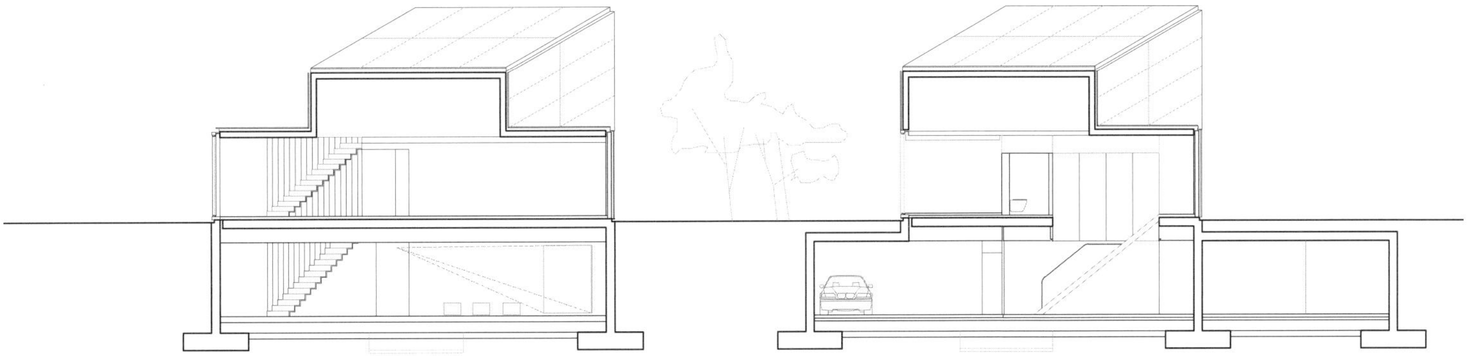

Cross section

Barcelona '92

Rey Juan Carlos I Hotel

Olympic Village in Vall d'Hebron

3 blocks in the Olympic Village

Barcelona Botanical Garden

Early works

Sant Just Park housing building

Instant City

Garbí Building

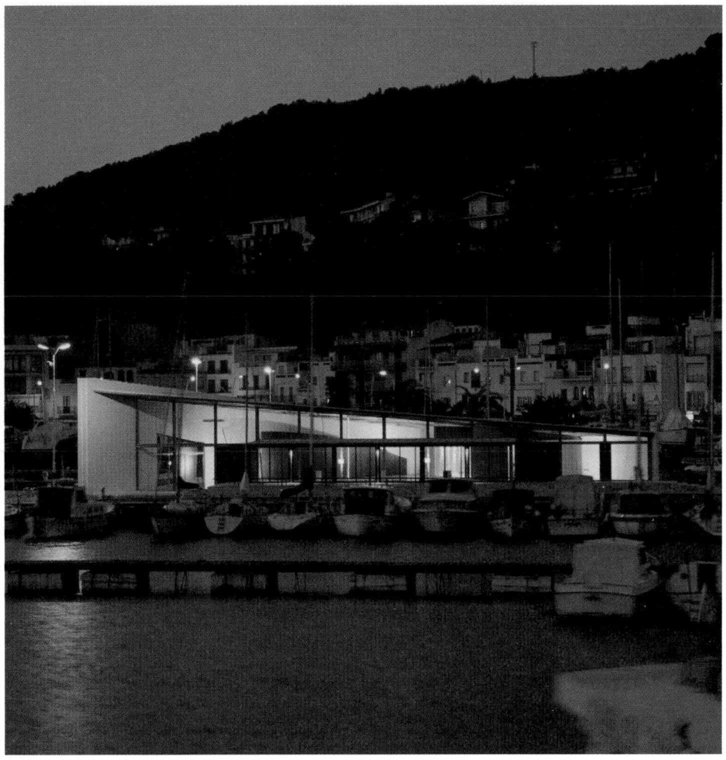

Estartit Yatch Club

Carlos Ferrater

1971–2004

Early works

1 Instant City, Cala San Miguel. Ibiza, 1971
Carlos Ferrater–Fernando Bendito–Jose Miguel de Prada

2 Sant Just Parc housing building, Sant Just Desvern, 1974–1977
Carlos Ferrater

3 Garbí Building, L'Estartit. Girona, 1987–1988
Carlos Ferrater

4 Estartit Yatch Club, L'Estartit. Girona, 1988–1991
Carlos Ferrater–Gerardo Rodríguez–Juan Díaz

Barcelona '92

5 Rey Juan Carlos I Hotel, Avda. Diagonal. Barcelona, 1989–1992
Carlos Ferrater–José Mª Cartañá

6 Olympic Village in Vall d'Hebron, Barcelona, 1990–1992
Carlos Ferrater–José Mª Cartañá

7 3 blocks in the Olympic Village, Barcelona, 1989–1992
Carlos Ferrater with Josep Mª Montaner and Bet Figueras

8 Barcelona Botanical Garden, Montjuïc Mountain. Barcelona, 1989–1999
Carlos Ferrater–Jose Luis Canosa–Bet Figueras

Manifestos

9 House-Studio for a photographer, Llampaies, 1993–1995
Carlos Ferrater

10 IMPIVA Headquarter, Castellón, 1993–1995
Carlos Ferrater–Carlos Bento–Jaime Sanahuja

11 Cinema Studios, Sant Just Desvern. Barcelona, 1995–1997
Carlos Ferrater

12 Fitness Center, Avda. Diagonal. Barcelona, 1993–1996
Carlos Ferrater

2001–2004

13 El Prat Golf Course Clubhouse, Terrassa, 1999–2004
Carlos Ferrater

14 Tagomago House, Ibiza, 1999–2001
Carlos Ferrater

15 Castellón Auditorium and Congress Center, Castellón, 1997–2004
Ferrater–Escura–Martin–Sanahuja

16 Barcelona Botanical Institute, CSIC, Barcelona Botanical Garden, 1999–2003
Carlos Ferrater

2001–2004

El Prat Golf Course Clubhouse

Castellón Auditorium and Congress Center

Barcelona Botanical Institute, CSIC

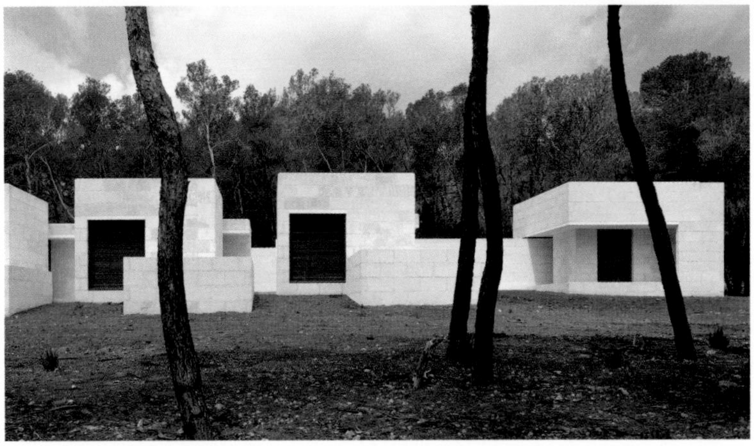

Tagomago House

Manifestos

IMPIVA Headquarter

House-Studio for a photographer

Cinema studio

Fitness Center

OAB

Carlos Ferrater Lambarri Barcelona, 1944

Doctor of Architecture and Professor of Architectural Project Design at the Polytechnic University of Catalonia. Director of the Cátedra Blanca, Barcelona.

Academician-Elect of the Real Academia de Belles Arts de Sant Jordi.

Conferred as Doctor honoris causa by the University of Trieste.

In 2006 he set up, along with Xavier Martí, Lucía Ferrater and Borja Ferrater, the Office of Architecture in Barcelona (OAB), with Núria Ayala as Projects Director.

Awarded the 2009 National Architecture Award by the Spanish Ministry of Housing for his overall career.

Since 2000 he has won five FAD Prizes, the 1999 and 2008 City of Barcelona Prize, the 2005 Brunel International Architecture Award (Denmark) and the 2009 BigMat Prize. He has twice been a finalist for the Mies van der Rohe Award. He has received the City of Madrid Award, the 2001 National Spanish Architecture Award, the 2006 Dedalo Minosse International Prize in Vicenza, the 2006 Decade Award and the 2007 International Flyer Award. The 2008 RIBA International Award was given to his monograph of the editorial MP, among others. He received a mention in the 10th Spanish Architecture and Town Planning Biennial and in the Urban Public Space European Award 2010 for the Benidorm West Beach Promenade which also won the FAD 2010 (City and Landscape Award), Saloni Awards 2010, FOPA 2009, ASCER 2010 Award, COACV 2007-2009, Award and the Chicago Athenaeum International Architecture Award "best global design" 2010. He was a guest exhibitor in the International Pavilion and the Spanish Pavilion at the 2004 Venice Biennale, and was invited by the MoMA, New York, to participate in the exhibition "On-Site: New Architecture in Spain", and to exhibit his work in a one-man show at the Crown Hall at the Illinois Institute of Technology, the Bilbao Fine Arts Museum, the Israel Institute of Technology, the College of Architects of Catalonia, the Foundation of the College of Architects of Madrid, and the Roman Aquarium.

Xavier Martí Galí Barcelona, 1969

Xavier Martí Galí graduated as an architect from the School of Architecture of Barcelona (ETSAB) in 1995.

He joined the Carlos Ferrater studio as an associate architect in 2003. In 2006 he set up the Office of Architecture in Barcelona (OAB) with Carlos Ferrater, Lucía Ferrater and Borja Ferrater, with Núria Ayala as Projects Director.

He is the co-designer with Carlos Ferrater of the West Beach Promenade in Benidorm; the MediaPro Head Office on the District 22@ Audiovisual Campus in Barcelona; a building on the Passeig de Gracia; the World Trade Center Tower in Cornellà; an office building on Carrer Caspe, Barcelona; the AA House in Sant Cugat del Vallès, and The Frontaura winery in Toro, Zamora.

He is currently finalising different apartment buildings in Barcelona, Madrid and Bilbao.

He received the 2008 City of Barcelona Prize as co-designer of the MediaPro Tower in Barcelona.

As co-designer of the Benidorm West Beach Promenade he has received the FAD Award, the first prize in the VIII ASCER Ceramics Awards (2009), the COACV 2007-2009 Award, the FOPA Awards 2009, the Saloni Awards 2010, the APLUS Award 2010, the Chicago Athenaeum International Architecture Award "best global design" 2010, a special mention in the Urban Public Space European Award 2010, and has been finalist in Landscape European Award "Rosa Barba".

Lucía Ferrater Barcelona, 1971

Qualified as an architect in 1997 after studying at the School of Architecture of Barcelona .

In 1998, she became an associate architect for Carlos Ferrater's studio. In 2006, she set up the Office of Architecture in Barcelona (OAB) together with Carlos Ferrater, Xavier Martí, Borja Ferrater and with Núria Ayala as Director of Projects.

Some of her most outstanding works are the renovation of the House-Studio Coderch de Sentmenat in Plaza Calvó, Barcelona, a Social Services Centre in Barcelona's area of urban expansion and a housing development in Plaza Lesseps, Barcelona. She has also worked on various projects, among which an Evangelical Church in Terrassa, different apartment and office buildings in Barcelona, two large houses, the Roca Barcelona Gallery and a hotel in Sitges (Barcelona).

In 2006, she exhibited her work "Social Services Centre in Barcelona's area of urban expansion" in New York's MOMA forming part of the exhibition "On-site: New Architecture in Spain".

She was a finalist in the 2000 FAD Architecture Awards for an apartment block in San Cugat del Vallès.

Wallpaper Design Award in 2010 for the Roca Barcelona Gallery.

She currently teaches Projects V and VI in the School of Architecture (ESARQ) at the International University of Catalonia.

Borja Ferrater Barcelona, 1978

From 1995–1999, Borja studied biology at Temple University (Philadelphia, PA, USA) and the University of Navarre. In 2005 he completed his architecture degree (first class) at the International University of Catalonia.

In 2006, he was the fourth year coordinator and assistant professor for projects 7/8 at the International University of Catalonia. He was also the guest professor at the 'Emotional City' project workshop lead by British architects Sergison & Bates (Sept. 2006). He completed his Master's degree in Biodigital Architecture in January 2010.

He is currently the Assistant Director for culture, publications and international relations in the School of Architecture (ESARQ) at the International University of Catalonia. He also teaches projects, forum and Taller Vertical (Vertical Workshop).

He is the author of the book *Synchronizing Geometry* published by ACTAR which has resulted in several exhibitions in USA, Israel, Italy, and Turkey.

Member and founding partner (January 2006) of OAB (Office of Architecture in Barcelona) together with Carlos Ferrater, Xavier Martí, Lucía Ferrater.

He won the top FAD prize for the "ephemeral architecture" category together with Carlos Ferrater for the Madrid exhibition: "M.C. Escher El arte de lo imposible" and a Wallpaper Design Award 2010 for the Roca Barcelona Gallery designed together with Carlos and Lucía Ferrater. He has also been finalist of the Lamp awards and selected in the 2009 FAD Award in the Interior Design category. He is the author of several projects in the OAB studio including the residential complex and hotel in Turkey, the reception pavilion in the Atapuerca archaeological site, the Barcelona FC stadium and a 3,500 m^2 private residence in New Delhi, India. He is currently working on his doctoral thesis "The Application of complex geometric systems in architecture".

He has also given lectures, participated in round tables and formed part of prize-awarding panels in several cities: Tokyo, Chicago, New York, Boston, Columbus (Ohio), Jerusalem, Stockholm, Saint Petersburg, Hannover, Manchester, Cardiff, Liverpool, Cagliari, Bilbao, Granada, Madrid, Zaragoza and Barcelona.

Núria Ayala Prats Barcelona, 1975

Project Director

Núria Ayala graduated as an architect from the School of Architecture of Barcelona (ETSAB) in 2001. After working in different professional practices after 1997 she joined the Carlos Ferrater studio in the year 2000.

She is the Projects Director, collaborator and co-author of different works, projects and competitions, including the NGO "Centre Esplai" (Special mention in Endesa Awards 2010 at the "More sustainable non-residential promoting"); the Musée des Confluences in Lyons; Casa Nolla; the GISA and FGC institutional headquarters on Via Augusta in Barcelona; Las Palmas de Gran Canaria Promenade; the hotel in the Almodovar Gate in Cordoba; the Azahar Business Group HQ in Castellón; the new City Hall in Palma de Mallorca; the new IMQ Hospital in Bilbao; the development plan for the Garellano area of Bilbao; the La Seda Head Office in Barcelona; the City of Music in Sabadell; the extension to the Barcelona Botanical garden; the project design for Barcelona High Court; the project design for the new Hospital de la Mutua in Terrassa; the extension to Torreblanca Park, plus three holiday camp buildings for the NGO "Fundació Catalana de l'Esplai."

Together with Carlos Ferrater as co-designer of the building Sede del Grupo de Empresas Azahar she received a special mention in the ECOLA Awards, another mention in the COACV 2007-2009 Awards. Azahar headquarters has also been awarded in the VII Ibero-American Biennial of Architecture and Urbanism.

She coordinated and did the graphic design for the "Research Process" in *Synchronizing Geometry*, published by Actar; Editorial MP's monograph *Carlos Ferrater–OAB*, and the book *Casas y habitantes* (Home and Occupants) (Actar).

Juan Calvo Orense, 1963

PONDIO Engineers. Civil Engineer

He graduated from the Polytechnic University of Madrid School of Civil Engineering in 1991 with a degree in Civil Engineering and from the School of Public Works Technical Engineering in 1984 with a degree in Public Works Technical Engineering (3rd National Graduation Prize).

Between 1990 and 1995 he was a Professor of structural analysis for the School of Construction (National University of Distance Learning).

In 1996, he founded PONDIO Engineers, a company dedicated to structural projects from building engineering to civil engineering, of which he is today the Chief Executive.

He participates in various scientific and technical associations in Spain as well as in an international context. He is a member of ACHE (the Scientific Technical Association for Structural Concrete), FIP (International federation for prestressed concrete), IABSE (Internacional Association for Bridges and Structural Engineering), APTA (Association for the Technical Promotion of Steel) and since 1993 founding member of ACIES (Association of Independent Building Structure Consultants).

He collaborates with the Architect Carlos Ferrater on a regular basis and has completed projects such as the New Catalonia Palau de Congresos in Barcelona (Spanish National Architecture Award in 2001), the Convention Centre in Castellón, the Intermodal Station in Zaragoza (FAD Architecture Award 2004), the Granada Science Park, the MediaPro office tower in Barcelona, Houses in the Moraleja area of Madrid, Casa AA in Barcelona and more recently the Playa de Poniente Promenade in Benidorm (The Chicago Athenaeum International Architecture Award 2010).

Catalogued work

Included in this publication

L Location
D Developer
C Constructor
PD Project date
CD Completion Date
A Architects
Col Collaborators
S Structure

**OAB Studio–
Balmes 145 Building**

L c. Balmes, 145, Barcelona
D Metro-3
C Metro-3
PD 2000
CD 2001–2003
A Carlos Ferrater
Col Joan Guibernau, Lucía Ferrater, Núria Ayala

Barcelona Botanical Garden – CSIC Building

L Montjuïc Mountain, Barcelona
D Barcelona City Council
Botanical Garden
PD 1995
CD 1998–1999
A Carlos Ferrater. With Jose Luis Canosa and Bet Figueras
CSIC Building
PD 2000
CD 2001–2003
A Carlos Ferrater. With the collaboration of Joan Guibernau
Extension
PD 2007
CD 2007–2008
A Carlos Ferrater. With the collaboration of Núria Ayala

Horizonscrapers

PD 2002
A Carlos Ferrater
Col Sofía Machado

Vertix Building (68 homes)

L c. Cristòfor de Moura – c. Bac de Roda, Barcelona
D Vertix
C Vertix
PD 2003
CD 2007
A Carlos Ferrater, Xavier Martí (OAB)

Lesseps Building (56 homes)

L c. Velázquez – c. Riera de Vallcarca, Barcelona
D Metro-3
C Metro-3
PD 2004
CD 2007–2008
A Carlos Ferrater, Lucía Ferrater, Xavier Martí (OAB)

Zaragoza-Delicias Intermodal Station

L Avda. Navarra 80, Zaragoza
D Railway Infrastructure Management. Ministry of Public Works
C Fomento de Construcciones y Contratas – Ferrovial, S.A.
PD 2000
CD 2001-2003
A Carlos Ferrater, Jose Mª Valero. With Elena Mateu and Félix Arranz
S Juan Calvo (Pondio)

Intermodal Station at Barcelona Airport

L El Prat Airport, Barcelona
D AENA
PD 2002
CD 2004–2007
A Carlos Ferrater, Ramón Sanabria, Josep Mª Casadevall

3 city blocks in the Olympic Village, Barcelona

L Olympic Village, Barcelona
D Mediterrània de Promocions i Gestions Immobiliàries, S.A.
C Cubiertas MZOV, S.A. – COMSA, S.A. – Const. Padros
PD 1989
CD 1992
A Carlos Ferrater
Col Josep Mª Montaner, Bet Figueras (Landscaper), Josep Samsó

5 city blocks in the seafront Barcelona

L Poble Nou, Barcelona
D Barcelona City Council
PD 1995
A Carlos Ferrater. With the collaboration of Josep Mª Montaner

Housing building in the old Cine Fémina

L Passeig de Gràcia 23 – c. Diputació 259, Barcelona
D Promotores Torma 95
PD 1996
CD 1999
A Carlos Ferrater
Col Joan Guibernau

Casa Masó Building in Passeig de Gràcia

L Passeig de Gràcia 38, Barcelona
PD 2004
A Carlos Ferrater, Juan Trias de Bes, Xavier Martí

Housing building in Passeig de Gràcia

L Passeig de Gràcia 99, Barcelona
D Renta Corporación
C Ferrovial, S.A.
PD 2004
CD 2004–2007
A Carlos Ferrater (OAB)
Col Lucía Ferrater (OAB), Joan Guibernau

Hotel Mandarin Oriental Barcelona

L Passeig de Gràcia 38-40, Barcelona
D Reig Capital
C Dragados
PD 2005
CD 2009–2010
A Carlos Ferrater, Juan Trias de Bes
Col Bet Figueras (Landscaper)

Social Services Centre and block in Fort Pienc

L Interior of the block in c. Nàpols – c. Roger de Flor – c. Alí Bei – c. Ausiàs March
D Barcelona City Council
C Metro-3
PD 2001
CD 2003
A Lucía Ferrater, Carlos Ferrater, Anna Vidal

Office building in c. Còrsega (former Bayer factory)

L c. Còrsega 344–352, Barcelona
D Josel, S.L.
PD 2009
A Carlos Ferrater, Xavier Martí (OAB)

Office building

L c. Casp, 35 – c. Bruc 31, Barcelona
D Peromoinver, S.L.
PD 2007
A Carlos Ferrater
Col Joan Guibernau, Elena Mateu

Gran Via 512 Building

L Gran Via 512, Barcelona
D Metro-3
C Metro-3
PD 1995
CD 1997
A Carlos Ferrater
Col Joan Guibernau

Building in c. Valencia 381

L c. Valencia 381, Barcelona
D Metro-3
C Metro-3
PD 2003
CD 2004
A Carlos Ferrater, Lucía Ferrater, Jaume Monclús

Housing building in c. Diputación

L c. Diputación 239–247
D Rafols Raventós
PD 2008
A Carlos Ferrater, Xavier Martí (OAB)

Royal Quarters of Santo Domingo

L Realejo district, Granada
D Granada City Council
C Construcciones Otero
PD 2000
CD 2004
A Yolanda Brasa, Eduardo Jiménez, Carlos Ferrater

Granada Science Park

L Avda. del Mediterráneo S/N
D Consortium of the Granada Science Park
C Dragados
PD 2004
CD 2005–2008
A Carlos Ferrater, Eduardo Jiménez, Yolanda Brasa
S Juan Calvo (Pondio)

"M.C. Escher. El arte de lo imposible" exhibition

L Paseo de la Castellana, Madrid
PD 2006
CD 2007
A Borja Ferrater, Carlos Ferrater (OAB)

Piccaro sul mare

L Borghetto Santo Spirito, Savona, Italy
D Castello Borelli, s.r.l.
PD 2008
A Carlos Ferrater, Domenico Piemonte

Aquileia Tower in Venice

L Jesolo, Venice, Italy
D BolDrin s.p.a.
C Visedil
PD 2004
CD 2004–2009
A Carlos Ferrater, Gustavo Carabajal, Xavier Martí
Col Eleonora Mantese
S Massimo Majowiecki

Futbol Club Barcelona Stadium refurbishment

L c. Arístides Maillol 12, Barcelona
PD 2007
A Ferrater-OAB, SVC & S.V. & arupsport

Distribution of Garellano district

L Garellano district, Bilbao
D Bilbao City Council and Bilbao Ría 2000
PD 2009
A Carlos Ferrater (OAB). With Luis Domínguez and Núria Ayala (OAB)

New Igualatorio Médico Quirúrgico IMQ Hospital (Zorrotzaure)

L c. Morgan – c. Jon Arrospide, Zorrotzaure, Bilbao
D Sociedad Inmobiliaria del Igualatorio Médico Quirúrgico, S.A.
C Constructora San José, S.A.
PD 2008
CD 2010–2012
A Carlos Ferrater (OAB), Alfonso Casares
Col Núria Ayala (OAB), Antonio Ocaña, Luis Domínguez
S Juan Calvo (Pondio)

CaixaForum Zaragoza

L Zaragoza
D La Caixa
PD 2008
A Carlos Ferrater, Xavier Martí (OAB)
S Juan Calvo (Pondio)

Barcelona Courthouse

L Pg. Lluís Companys, Barcelona
D Conselleria de Justícia, Generalitat de Catalunya
PD 2010
A Carlos Ferrater (OAB). With Núria Ayala (OAB)

Frontaura and Victoria Wineries. D.O. Toro

L Industrial Park 5 Toro, Zamora
D Marqués de Valdelacasa, S.L.
PD 2006
A Carlos Ferrater, Xavier Martí (OAB)
S Juan Calvo (Pondio), Peter Tanner

House in New Delhi

L New Delhi, India
PD 2007
A Borja Ferrater, Carlos Ferrater (OAB)

New headquarter for Grupo de Empresas Azahar

L Carretera Nacional N-340, Castellón
D Grupo de Empresas Azahar
PD 2004
CD 2009
A Carlos Ferrater, Núria Ayala (OAB)

F-3 House

L c. Escoles Pies, Barcelona
D Metro-3, S.A.
C Metro-3, S.A.
PD 2008
CD 2009–2010
A Lucía Ferrater, Carlos Ferrater (OAB)

Building in c. Dr. Carulla

L c. Dr. Carulla 40-42, Barcelona
D Construdive, S.L.
C Xedex, S.A.
PD 2007
CD 2008–2009
A Lucía Ferrater, Carlos Ferrater (OAB)

Hotel Alenti

L c. Indústria – c. 1r de Maig, Sitges
D Sanperhi, S.L.
C Sierra Pintada, S.L.
PD 2007
CD 2009
A Lucía Ferrater, Carlos Ferrater (OAB)

Evangelical Church in Terrassa

L Avda. Béjar, Terrassa, Barcelona
D Església Evangèlica Unida
C Excavaciones Egara
PD 2007
CD 2008–2010
A Lucía Ferrater, Carlos Ferrater (OAB)

Office building in Paris

L Zac Seguin Rives de Seine. Boulogne Billancourt. Macrot Lot B-Lot B2
D Nexity Entreprises
PD 2007
CD 2008–2010
A Carlos Ferrater, Alberto Peñín (OAB). Eric Babin, Jean François Renaud (Atelier 3)
Col Mathias Bernhardt

Mediapro Building in the 22@ Audiovisual Campus

L Avda. Diagonal 177–183. 22@ District, Barcelona
D Mediacomplex, S.A.
C Sacyr S.A.U.
PD 2004
CD 2005–2008
A Carlos Ferrater (OAB), Patrick Genard, Xavier Martí (OAB)
Col Dariela Hentschel
S Juan Calvo (Pondio)

Roca Barcelona Gallery

L c. Joan Güell 211, Barcelona
D Roca Sanitario, S.A.
C Empty
PD 2008
CD 2009
A Borja Ferrater, Carlos Ferrater, Lucía Ferrater (OAB)

Intervention in the archaeological site in Atapuerca

L Sierra de Atapuerca, Burgos.
PD 2008
A Carlos Ferrater (OAB)
Col Borja Ferrater
S Juan Calvo (Pondio) – P. Tanner

Benidorm West Beach Promenade

L Beachfront Promenade, Benidorm
D Generalitat Valenciana-Benidorm City Council
C Ecisa-Dragados
PD 2002
CD 2006–2009
A Carlos Ferrater, Xavier Martí (OAB)
Col Sofía Machado, Luca Cerullo
S Juan Calvo (Pondio)

House for a photographer 2

L Les Cases d'Alcanar, Tarragona
D Jose Manuel Ferrater
C Construcciones PJ 98, S.L.
PD 2003
CD 2006
A Carlos Ferrater with Carlos Escura

AA House

L Sant Cugat del Vallès, Barcelona
C Contratas y Obras Empresa Constructora, S.A.
PD 2006
CD 2007–2009
A Carlos Ferrater, Xavier Martí (OAB)
S Juan Calvo (Pondio)

Bibliography

Works included in this publication

Monographs

Carlos Ferrater. OAB. 2006. Editorial Manel Padura. ISBN: 978-84-934525-6-8. p.282-289; Apartments and offices, OAB Studio

Carlos Ferrater. OAB. 2006. Editorial Manel Padura. ISBN: 978-84-934525-6-8. p.11, 170-179; Barcelona Botanical Garden

2G. Carlos Ferrater. No. 32. 2004. Editorial Gustavo Gili. p.30-33; Barcelona Botanical Garden

Carlos Ferrater. Works and Projects. Intr. A. Pizza. 2002. 1st edition. Editorial Electa, Milan. Phaidon Press. ISBN: 1-9043-1308-6. p.116-129; Barcelona Botanical Garden

Carlos Ferrater. Intr. E. Mantese. 2000. Munilla-Lería. Madrid. ISBN: 84-89150-40-0. p.250-259; Barcelona Botanical Garden

Carlos Ferrater. Intr. W. Curtis. 2000. 2nd edition. Editorial Actar. ISBN: 84-95273-40-3. p.56-71; Barcelona Botanical Garden

Carlos Ferrater. Intr. W. Curtis. 1998. 1st edition. Editorial Actar. ISBN: 84-95273-40-3. p.56-63; Barcelona Botanical Garden

Carlos Ferrater. Ignasi de Solà-Morales. 1995. COAC. p.24-29; Barcelona Botanical Garden

Carlos Ferrater. Obras y proyectos 90's. 1993. Exhibition catalogue, Galería Antonio de Barnola. Editorial Electa. p.5; Barcelona Botanical Garden

El nou Jardí Botànic de Barcelona. 1989. Ajuntament de Barcelona-IMPU. Barcelona Botanical Garden

Carlos Ferrater. OAB. 2006. Editorial Manel Padura. ISBN: 978-84-934525-6-8. p.326-341; Zaragoza-Delicias Intermodal Station

Sincronizar la Geometría. 2006. Carlos Ferrater & Asociados (OAB), Editorial Actar, Barcelona. p.118-127; Zaragoza-Delicias Intermodal Station

2G. Carlos Ferrater. No. 32. 2004. Editorial Gustavo Gili. p.54-69; Zaragoza-Delicias Intermodal Station

Carlos Ferrater. Works and Projects. Intr. A. Pizza. 2002. 1st edition. Editorial Electa, Milan. Phaidon Press. ISBN: 1-9043-1308-6. p.174-181; Zaragoza-Delicias Intermodal Station

Carlos Ferrater. Intr. E. Mantese. 2000. Munilla-Lería. Madrid. ISBN: 84-89150-40-0. p.232-247; Zaragoza-Delicias Intermodal Station

Carlos Ferrater. Intr. W. Curtis. 2000. 2nd edition. Editorial Actar. ISBN: 84-95273-40-3. p.164-167; Zaragoza-Delicias Intermodal Station

Carlos Ferrater. OAB. 2006. Editorial Manel Padura. ISBN: 978-84-934525-6-8. p.260-263; Intermodal Station at Barcelona Airport

Carlos Ferrater. Works and Projects. Intr. A. Pizza. 2002. 1st edition. Editorial Electa, Milan. Phaidon Press. ISBN: 1-9043-1308-6. p.182-189; Intermodal Station at Barcelona Airport

Carlos Ferrater. Intr. E. Mantese. 2000. Munilla-Lería. Madrid. ISBN: 84-89150-40-0. p.112-119; 3 city blocks in the Olympic Village, Barcelona

Carlos Ferrater. Obras y proyectos 90's. 1993. Exhibition catalogue, Galería Antonio de Barnola. Editorial Actar. Barcelona. p.21; 3 city blocks in the Olympic Village, Barcelona

Ferrater. Catálogos de Arquitectura Contemporánea. Intr. W. Curtis. 1989. Editorial Gustavo Gili. ISBN: 84-252-1403-3. p.84-87; 3 city blocks in the Olympic Village, Barcelona

Carlos Ferrater. Intr. W. Curtis. 1998. 1st edition. Editorial Actar. ISBN: 84-95273-40-3. p.92-99; 3 city blocks in the Olympic Village, Barcelona

Carlos Ferrater. Works and Projects. Intr. A. Pizza. 2002. 1st edition. Editorial Electa, Milan. Phaidon Press. ISBN: 1-9043-1308-6. p.44-53; 3 city blocks in the Olympic Village, Barcelona

Carlos Ferrater. Ignasi de Solà-Morales. 1995. COAC. p.50-55; 3 city blocks in the Olympic Village, Barcelona

Carlos Ferrater. Intr. W. Curtis. 2000. 2nd edition. Editorial Actar. ISBN: 84-95273-40-3. p.114-121; 3 city blocks in the Olympic Village, Barcelona

Carlos Ferrater. OAB. 2006. Editorial Manel Padura. ISBN: 978-84-934525-6-8. p.13, 66-73; 3 city blocks in the Olympic Village, Barcelona

Carlos Ferrater. Documentos de Arquitectura. No. 8. 1989. COAAO. p.3-4; 3 city blocks in the Olympic Village, Barcelona

Carlos Ferrater. Intr. W. Curtis. 1998. 1st edition. Editorial Actar. ISBN: 84-95273-40-3. p.86-87; Housing building in Passeig de Gràcia, Barcelona

Carlos Ferrater. Intr. E. Mantese. 2000. Munilla-Lería. Madrid. ISBN: 84-89150-40-0. p.100-103; Housing building in Passeig de Gràcia, Barcelona

Carlos Ferrater. Intr. W. Curtis. 2000. 2nd edition. Editorial Actar. ISBN: 84-95273-40-3. p.108-109; Housing building in Passeig de Gràcia, Barcelona

Carlos Ferrater. OAB. 2006. Editorial Manel Padura. ISBN: 978-84-934525-6-8. p.14, 431; Iberia Building in Passeig de Gràcia, Barcelona

Carlos Ferrater. Intr. W. Curtis. 1998. 1st ed. Editorial Actar. ISBN: 84-95273-40-3. p.86-87; Iberia Building in Passeig de Gràcia, Barcelona

2G. Carlos Ferrater. No. 32. 2004. Editorial Gustavo Gili. p.118-123; Iberia Building in Passeig de Gràcia, Barcelona

Carlos Ferrater. Intr. E. Mantese. 2000. Munilla-Lería. Madrid. ISBN: 84-89150-40-0. p.100-103; Iberia Building in Passeig de Gràcia, Barcelona

Carlos Ferrater. Intr. W. Curtis. 2000. 2nd edition. Editorial Actar. ISBN: 84-95273-40-3. p.108-109; Iberia Building in Passeig de Gràcia, Barcelona

Carlos Ferrater. OAB. 2006. Editorial Manel Padura. ISBN: 978-84-934525-6-8. p.404-413; Social Services Centre in Fort Pienc, Barcelona

2G. Carlos Ferrater. No. 32. 2004. Editorial Gustavo Gili. p.48-53; Social Services Centre in Fort Pienc, Barcelona

Carlos Ferrater. OAB. 2006. Editorial Manel Padura. ISBN: 978-84-934525-6-8. p.370 -375; Granada Science Park

Carlos Ferrater. OAB. 2006. Editorial Manel Padura. ISBN: 978-84-934525-6-8. p.346-351; Royal Quarters of Santo Domingo, Granada

2G. Carlos Ferrater. No. 32. 2004. Editorial Gustavo Gili. p.70-73; Royal Quarters of Santo Domingo, Granada

Carlos Ferrater. Intr. W. Curtis. 2000. 2nd edition. Editorial Actar. ISBN: 84-95273-40-3. p.180-183; Royal Quarters of Santo Domingo, Granada

Carlos Ferrater. Intr. E. Mantese. 2000. Munilla-Lería. Madrid. ISBN: 84-89150-40-0. p.246-249; Royal Quarters of Santo Domingo, Granada

2G. Carlos Ferrater. No. 32. 2004. Editorial Gustavo Gili. p.110-117; Benidorm West Beach Promenade

Carlos Ferrater. OAB. 2006. Editorial Manel Padura. ISBN: 978-84-934525-6-8. p.11, 294-303; Benidorm West Beach Promenade

Carlos Ferrater. OAB. 2006. Editorial Manel Padura. ISBN: 978-84-934525-6-8. p.376-381; New headquarter for Grupo de Empresas Azahar

Carlos Ferrater. OAB. 2006. Editorial Manel Padura. ISBN: 978-84-934525-6-8. p.470-485; House for a photographer 2, Les Cases d'Alcanar

Vivienda Housing. No. 4. 2006. Editorial Manel Padura. p.136-156; House for a photographer 2, Les Cases d'Alcanar

2G. Carlos Ferrater. No. 32. 2004. Editorial Gustavo Gili. House for a photographer 2, Les Cases d'Alcanar

Carlos Ferrater. OAB. 2006. Editorial Manel Padura. ISBN: 978-84-934525-6-8. p.392-395; Aquileia Tower

Chapter in book

Arquittetura e paesaggio costruito. 2010. Documenti di Architecttura. Palerm & Tabares de Nava. Marco Mulazzani. Ed. Mondadori Electa. p.6-13; Barcelona Botanical Garden

Cuaderno de la pequeña dimensión. 1993. Carlos Ferrater Construir el lugar. p.60-61; Barcelona Botanical Garden

Ecological Architecture. 1999. Tendencias bioclimáticas y arquitectura del paisaje en el año 2000. Loft Publicaciones. p.56-59; Barcelona Botanical Garden

Barcelona 1992-2004. 2004. W. Curtis, J.Mª Montaner. Ed. Gustavo Gili. p.110-113; Barcelona Botanical Garden

La nueva sensibilidad ambiental. 2007. Ezequiel Usón Guardiola. Clipmedia Edicions. Barcelona. p.68-75; Barcelona Botanical Garden

Urban Spaces. 2003. Editorial Links. Barcelona. p.42-51; Barcelona Botanical Garden

Rendering para arquitecto. Oct. 2009; Barcelona Botanical Garden

Barcelona Arquitectura Contemporánea. 2006. Ediciones Polígrafa S.A. p.22-33; Barcelona Botanical Garden

Detalles - Barcelona Arquitectura Contemporánea. 2005. Jardin e Instituto Botánico. p.22-33; Barcelona Botanical Garden

Arquitectura Contemporánea a Catalunya. 2005. Josep Mª Montaner. Edificios 62. p.160; Barcelona Botanical Garden

100% Selecció Ruta del Disseny. BCN. 2003. p.83; Barcelona Botanical Garden

Barcelona Stadt und Architektur. 1992. Ed. Tachen. Barcelona Botanical Garden

Lo spazio pubblico in Spagna 1990-2000. 2001. p.50-51; Barcelona Botanical Garden

Arquitecturas recentes 1990-1994. 1994. p.50-53; Barcelona Botanical Garden

Barcelona Futurarquitectura. 2008. p.168-171; Barcelona Botanical Garden

Barcelona Arquitectura y Ciudad 1980-1992. 2004. p.2-3, 130-131; Barcelona Botanical Garden

Las formas del siglo XX. 2002. 206; Barcelona Botanical Garden

Urbanisme a Barcelona. 1999. Ajuntament de Barcelona. p.98-101; Barcelona Botanical Garden

High Architecture Lights. 2008. Shanglin Edition. China. p.98-105; Barcelona Botanical Garden

C3 Topic Public Space II. 2005. p.54; Barcelona Botanical Garden

Archint. No. 7. 1999. Venice, Arian Mostaedi. p.133; Barcelona Botanical Garden

Barcelona 1979 I 2004. Oct. 1999. Del desenvolupament a la ciutat de qualitat. Ajuntament de Barcelona/COAC/CAATEEB. Exhibition catalogue. p.262-263; Barcelona Botanical Garden

Barcelone. May 1992. "Dix années d'urbanisme. La renaissance d'une ville". Guy Henry. Collab. Ida Hounkpatin y Stephan Comby. Editions Du Moniteur. Paris. p.136; Barcelona Botanical Garden

Habitar el presente. Vivienda en España: sociedad, ciudad, tecnologia y recursos. 2006. Viviendas en el Ensanche de Barcelona. p.170-171; Barcelona Botanical Garden

Monjuïc. Barcelona Parc Central. 2007. Liniazero Ediciones. p.86, 96; Barcelona Botanical Garden

Grüne Freiräume in Europas Stëdten. 2002. Ein Netz Aus Dreiecken. p.88-94; Barcelona Botanical Garden

Restauració E. Expertos en restauración y pintura desde 1968. 2008. Zaragoza-Delicias Intermodal Station

Arquitectura Ibérica. No. 9. 2005. Infraestructuras. Ed. Caleidoscópio. ISBN: 972-8801-73-4. p.50-63; Zaragoza-Delicias Intermodal Station

M&T Pencil. No. 1. 2004. Spain Unique Architecture. Editorial M&P Pencil. p.56-79; Zaragoza-Delicias Intermodal Station

En blanco. 2004. Primer Congreso Internacional de Arquitectura Blanca. Ed Biblioteca Tc. ISBN: 8493354023. p.32-49; Zaragoza-Delicias Intermodal Station

Arquitectura Contemporánea a Catalunya. 2005. Josep Mª Montaner. p.154-155; 3 city blocks in the Olympic Village, Barcelona

Sol·lucions constructives per a la arquitectura d'avui. 1993. La construcció de l'espai enjardinat. Jardins Interiors. p.44, 48-49; 3 city blocks in the Olympic Village, Barcelona

100 anys de construcció. 1992. p.114-117; 3 city blocks in the Olympic Village, Barcelona

European Housing Concepts 1990-2010. 2009. p.384-385; 3 city blocks in the Olympic Village, Barcelona

Floor Plan Atlas. 1992. Housing. Ed. Birkhäuser. ISBN: 3-7643-2625-5 / 0-8176-2625-5. p.22-23; 3 city blocks in the Olympic Village, Barcelona

Habitatge, innovació i projecte. 2000. COAC. Barcelona. 3 city blocks in the Olympic Village, Barcelona

Arquitectura a Catalunya. 1996. L'era democràtica 1977-1996. Generalitat de Catalunya. p.176; 3 city blocks in the Olympic Village, Barcelona

Barcelona. La construcción urbanística de una ciudad compacta. 2004. Joan Busquets. Editorial del Serbal. p.400; 3 city blocks in the Olympic Village, Barcelona

Barcelona 1980-1992. 1990. Arquitectura y Ciudad 4. Introducción: O. Bohigas, P. Buchanan, V. Magnano. Ed. Gustavo Gili. p.41; 3 city blocks in the Olympic Village, Barcelona

Vivienda, innovación y proyectos. No. 2. 2000. Tres manzanas en el Ensanche Cerdà. p.105-114; 3 city blocks in the Olympic Village, Barcelona

Habitatge, innovació i projecte. 2000. COAC, Escola Pràctica Josep Lluís Sert. p.112-113; Housing building in Passeig de Gràcia, Barcelona

European Housing Concepts 1990-2010. 2009. p.288-289; Housing building in Passeig de Gràcia, Barcelona

Barcelona Futurarquitectura. 2008. p.45; Housing building in Passeig de Gràcia, Barcelona

Quintaesencia de la excelencia. Dic, 2006. Special edition for Popular Banca Privada. (5.12.06). ISBN: 84-611-3368-4. p.108; Building in Passeig de Gràcia, former BASF company

Arquitectura contemporánea a Catalunya. 2005. Josep Mª Montaner. p.154-155; Iberia Building in Passeig de Gràcia, Barcelona

Habitatge, innovació i projecte. 2000. COAC, Escola Pràctica Josep Lluís Sert. p.112-113; Iberia Building in Passeig de Gràcia, Barcelona

Barcelona 1979 I 2004 1999. Exhibition catalogue, "Del desenvolupament a la ciutat de qualitat". Ajuntament de Barcelona/COAC/CAATEEB. p.154; Iberia Building in Passeig de Gràcia, Barcelona

Minimalismo. 2007. La sobriedad en la Arquitectura. Alex Sánchez. Barcelona - Mexico Df. Reditar Libros S.L. – Loft Publications. p.418-423; Social Services Centre in Fort Pienc, Barcelona

Geometría para turistas. 2009. Las geometrías de Carlos Ferrater. p.72 -73; Frontaura Winery, Toro

Ensayos sobre Arquitectura y Cerámica. Jan., 2010. (Vol.2). Cerámica Variaciones. Jesus Aparicio Guisado. p.9-18; Benidorm West Beach Promenade

La nueva sensibilidad ambiental. 2007. p.76-83; Benidorm West Beach Promenade

Contemporary Public Space Un-Volumetri Architecture. 2006. Aldo Aymonino – Valerio Paolo Mosco. Ed. Skira. p.260-263; Benidorm West Beach Promenade

Contemporary Public Space Un-Volumetri Architecture. 2006. West Beach Promenade In Benidorm. p.260-263; Benidorm West Beach Promenade

En blanco. 2004. Primer Congreso Internacional de Arquitectura Blanca. Ed Biblioteca Tc. ISBN: 8493354023. p.32-49; Benidorm West Beach Promenade

Dinner for Architects. 2003. Waterfront Benidorm. Ed. Winfried Nerdinger. p.29; Benidorm West

Beach Promenade
1st Century Houses. 150 of the World's Best. 2010. House 2 for a Photographer. p.172-173; House for a photographer 2, Les Cases d'Alcanar
Minimalismo. 2008. La sobriedad en la Arquitectura. Les Cases d'Alcanar, España. Alex Sánchez. Barcelona – Mexico D.F.. Reditar Libros S.L. Loft Publications. p.66-73; House for a photographer 2, Les Cases d'Alcanar
Spanish Architecture (1997-2007.) 2008. House in Alcanar, Tarragona, Spain, 2006. Ed. Ca-Group (Shanghai, Madrid, Tokyo) ISBN: 978-7-5083-5690-7. p.80-87; House for a photographer 2, Les Cases d'Alcanar
Arquitectura al detalle. 1997. Casa para un fotógrafo. Fernando Aranda Navarro, Amparo Tarín Martínez. ISBN: 84-7721-462-X 10, p.1-10, 13; House for a photographer 2, Les Cases d'Alcanar

Catalogues

Architecture Catalane 2004 - 2009 Portrait d'époque. Sep, 2009. Edifici d'oficines i habitatge. Apartments and offices, OAB Studio
Madrid - Barcelona. 2005. Exhibition catalogue. 2 ciudades, 40 imágenes en la Fundación COAM. COAM / COAC. Apartments and offices, OAB Studio
Premio de Arquitectura de la Unión Europea. 2001. Premio Mies van der Rohe. p.70-73; Barcelona Botanical Garden
Cerdà 150 anys de modernitat. Nov, 2009. p.239; Barcelona Botanical Garden
Trajectories Metamorph 9. 2004. Mostra Internazionale di Architettura. La Bienale di Venezia. p.161; Barcelona Botanical Garden
2ª Bienal Iberoamericana de Arquitectura e Ingeniería Civil. 2000. Exhibition catalogue. p.120-121; Barcelona Botanical Garden
Arquitectures per al nou segle. 1995. p.10; Barcelona Botanical Garden
Lo spazio pubblico in Spagna 1990-2000. Jun., 2001. Exhibition catalogue. Alinea Editrici. p.50-53; Barcelona Botanical Garden
Barcelona posa't guapa. 1990. Exhibition catalogue. Festival des alluumées. Nantes; Barcelona Botanical Garden
8th International Alvar Aalto Symposium. 2000. p.98-113; Barcelona Botanical Garden
Premis FAD 2000. Arquitectura - Interiorisme. 2000. p.132-135; Barcelona Botanical Garden
Arquitectura per a un nou segle. Apr., 1995. Exhibition catalogue. J.Mª Montaner. Construmat COAC. p.10; Barcelona Botanical Garden
Construyendo la ciudad. Feb., 2010. Colección de la Fundación Mies van der Rohe. p.62-63; Barcelona Botanical Garden
Premios Salón VIII. 2008. Vertix housing building
Arquitectura española 10 proyectos al descubrimiento. 2007. Estación Intermodal de Zaragoza 2002-2003. p.4; Zaragoza-Delicias Intermodal Station
Premio Internazionale Dedalo Minosse. 2006. Mostra Dedalo Minosse. Vicenza, Basílica Palladiana. Alla Comittenza Di Architettura Internacional Prize for Commisioning a Building. Sesta Edizione 2005/2006. p.58-61; Zaragoza-Delicias Intermodal Station
The Brunel Award 05 Copenhagen. 2005. Spain-Ministerio de Fomento - Zaragoza Delicias Station. p.20-21; Zaragoza-Delicias Intermodal Station
Premis FAD 2004. Arquitectura. Interiorisme. 2004. p.74-77; Zaragoza-Delicias Intermodal Station
Cemento Blanco. 2004. El color de la calidad. Folleto Cemento Blanco: http://www.cemex.es/sp/sp_pu.html. Zaragoza-Delicias Intermodal Station
IX Bienal d'Arquitecteura de Valencia 2004. 2004. Estación Intermodal de Zaragoza. p.190-193; Zaragoza-Delicias Intermodal Station
IX Bienal de Arquitectura de Valencia. 2004. Pabellón de España. Corredor de fondo. p.190-193; Zaragoza-Delicias Intermodal Station
Anuario Premis FAD 2008. May, 2009. Arquitectura e Interiorismo. Ed. ArquinFAD. p.162-167; Intermodal Station at Barcelona Airport
Solucions constructives per a l'arquitectura d'avui. Apr., 1993. Exhibition catalogue "La construcció de l'espai ajardinat. Tres illes a l'eixample Cerdà. Jardins Interiors. COAC. p.44, 48-49; 3 city blocks in the Olympic Village, Barcelona
Cerdà i la Barcelona del futur. 2009. CCCB i Direcció de Comunicació de la Diputació de Barcelona. ISBN: 978849833540. p.121; 3 city blocks in the Olympic Village, Barcelona
Cerdà 150 anys de modernitat. Nov. 2009. p.156; 5 city blocks in the seafront, Barcelona
Renta Corporación. 2007. "Cuidamos Los Detalles". Rehabilitación en el Paseo de Gracia. Building in Passeig de Gràcia, former BASF company
Barcelona, 1979 I 2004. 1999. Exhibition catalogue "Del desenvolupament a la ciutat de qualitat". Ajuntament de Barcelona/ COAC/CAATEEB. p.154; Housing building in Passeig de Gràcia, Barcelona
On-Site. Arquitectura en España, hoy. 2005. Exhibition catalogue "Del Centro de Servicios Sociales". p.92-95; Social Services Centre in Fort Pienc, Barcelona
Premis FAD 2004. Arquitectura. Interiorisme. 2004. p.11; Social Services Centre in Fort Pienc, Barcelona
Idees per a l'eixample. 1997. Taula Rodona 1: Idees per projectar a l'Eixample. Ed. Proeixample, S.A. p.22-23; Edificio Gran Via 512
Parque de las Ciencias. Mar., 2009. Memoria 2008. 1; Granada Science Park
Granada Science Park. 2008. Andalucía una nueva especie de museo; Granada Science Park
Anuario Premis FAD. 2007. Expo Escher, Madrid. El Arte de lo imposible. p.454-463; M.C. Escher. El arte de lo imposible
On Diseño. No. 288. 2008. Premis FAD 2008. Barcelona. p.260-273; M.C. Escher. El arte de lo imposible
M.C. Escher. 2007. Exhibition catalogue. Canal de Isabel II, Madrid; M.C. Escher. El arte de lo imposible
Piccinato. 2007. Progettare La complessità Premio per l'urbanistica e la pianificazione territoriale. Il progetto dello spazio pubblico contemporaneo: Piazza Mazzini Jesolo. p.116-117; Aquileia Tower
Idl. No. 48. 2010. Agua, luz y color. Portada; p.52-57; Roca Barcelona Gallery
Nova seu Roca. 2009. Roca inaugura la nova seu-galeria a Barcelona; Roca Barcelona Gallery
Premio Fopa a la mejor obra del año en la provincia de Alicante. May, 2010. Benidorm West Beach Promenade
Cevisama. 2010. Press kit Cevisama 2010. La industria Española de azulejos y pavimentos cerámicos. Premios 14; Benidorm West Beach Promenade
Ceraspaña. No. 24. 2010. Ganadores de los VIII Premios Cerámica de Arquitectura e Interiorismo. p.10-12; Benidorm West Beach Promenade
Ecisa. No. 47. Sep, 2009. Inaugurado el flamante Paseo de Poniente de Benidorm. p.1-3; Benidorm West Beach Promenade
2º Bienal de Canarias Arquitectura, Arte y Paisaje. 2008. p.79; Benidorm West Beach Promenade
Premios Asprima Salón Inmobiliario de Madrid. 2006. Internacional Prize for Commisioning a Building. p.20-23; Benidorm West Beach Promenade
Trajectories Metamorph 9. 2004. 9 Mostra Internazionale di Architettura. p.161, 174; Benidorm West Beach Promenade
VII Edición Premios Saloni de Arquitectura 2007. 2007. Casa para un fotógrafo en el Delta del Ebro. p.1-4; House for a photographer 2, Les Cases d'Alcanar
IX Bienal Española de Arquitectura y Urbanismo. Madrid 2007. Casa en el Delta del Ebro. p.224-231; House for a photographer 2, Les Cases d'Alcanar
Trienal d'Arquitectura de l'Ebre 2004-2006. 2006. Casa para el fotógrafo 2 en el Delta del Ebro. COAC. Demarcació de l'Ebre. p.8-9; House for a photographer 2, Les Cases d'Alcanar

Magazines

Natura. Mar., 2010. Carlos Ferrater Ile Söylesi. p.23; Apartments and offices, OAB Studio
Natura. Mar., 2010. Online version: http://www.naturadergi.com/mart-nisan_2010_natura/natura.html (Turkey) 2; Apartments and offices, OAB Studio
La Vanguardia. Culturas. Nov. 2010. p.19; Apartments and offices, OAB Studio
Diseño Interior. Jun. 2007. Espacios de Trabajo - Carlos Ferrater "Nuestro estudio es una mezcla entre un laboratorio y un

taller". p.16-17; Apartments and offices, OAB Studio
Suma +. No. 83. Nov. 2006. p.164-167; Apartments and offices, OAB Studio
Arquitectura y Urbanismo. May 2006. Brussels. Imágenes y proyectos del desarrollo urbano en Barcelona. (Backpage). p.72; Apartments and offices, OAB Studio
Arquitectura de oficinas. No. 8. 2005. Edificio de viviendas y despachos, Barcelona 2000-2002 (Balmes). p.120-127; Apartments and offices, OAB Studio
Baumaister. No. B6. 2005. 4XI. Poesie und Konstruktion- Balmes Offcina. p.38-43; Apartments and offices, OAB Studio
10 años para un reto. No. 116. 2005. Aguirre Newman. Un espacio para el silencio. p.78-79; Apartments and offices, OAB Studio
Apartamentos en la ciudad. 2005. Architectual Houses. p.108-113; Apartments and offices, OAB Studio
Casa Cor São Paulo. No. 465. 2005. El riesgo creativo; Apartments and offices, OAB Studio
Eme Dos. No. 116. 2005. Agenda de la construcción. Cover; Apartments and offices, OAB Studio
Diseño Interior. No. 155. 2005. Madrid. p.90-94; Apartments and offices, OAB Studio
Detail. May 2004. Munich. p.484-486; Apartments and offices, OAB Studio
Oficinas. No. 246. 2004. p.128-129; Apartments and offices, OAB Studio
2G. Carlos Ferrater. No. 32. 2004. Editorial Gustavo Gili. p.90-99; Apartments and offices, OAB Studio
Via Arquitectura. No. 12. Mar. 2003. p.100-103; Apartments and offices, OAB Studio
INDE. Informació i Debat. Jun. 2003. p.35; Apartments and offices, OAB Studio
L'industria delle construzioni. No. 372. 2003. p.78-81; Apartments and offices, OAB Studio
A+U. No. 394. 2003. Carlos Ferrater - Apartment and Office Building / Carlos Ferrater Studio; Portrait. p.130-133; 139; Apartments and offices, OAB Studio
Area. No. 89. 2003. Housing. Milan. p.72-77; Apartments and offices, OAB Studio
Diseño Interior. No. 135. 2003. p.160-167; Apartments and offices, OAB Studio
Arquitectura. No. 333. 2003. COAM Madrid. (11.01.03 - 11.08.03). Apartments and offices, OAB Studio
Hna. No. 7. 2002. Oficina Balmes. Cover; Apartments and offices, OAB Studio
Oris. No. 3. 2002. Zagreb. p.52-62; Apartments and offices, OAB Studio
Eupalinos. No. 5. Apr. 1999. Al despaxt de Carles Ferrater. p.012-015; Apartments and offices, OAB Studio
Hogares. No. 244. 1988. Un estudio de Arquitectura. p.88-89; Apartments and offices, OAB Studio
Proyecto Contract. No. 64. 2010. Premiso Nacionales de Vivienda y Arquitectura. p.34; Barcelona Botanical Garden
Natura. Mar, 2010. 36-39; Barcelona Botanical Garden
Natura. Mar., 2010. Online version: http://www.naturadergi.com/mart-nisan_2010_natura/natura.html. (Turkey). p.36-39; Barcelona Botanical Garden
L'informatiu. No. 148. Jul. 1999. La fractalitat en la construcció del paisatge. p.27; Barcelona Botanical Garden
CIC. No. 303. Jun. 1999. Paisaje fractal. p.50-59; Barcelona Botanical Garden
Aoa. No. 1. Apr. 2006. Santiago de Chile. p.69-82; Barcelona Botanical Garden
Geo. No. 171. 2001. Madrid. p.110; Barcelona Botanical Garden
AV. No. 81-82. 2000. Monografías, Anuario España. p.112-115, 189; Barcelona Botanical Garden
Casa Vogue. No. 12. 1990. Madrid. p.126-128; Barcelona Botanical Garden
Diseño de la ciudad. No. 23. 2000. Barcelona. p.138-144; Barcelona Botanical Garden
AV Monografías. No. 79-80. 2000. España. Los 90. p.156,159; Barcelona Botanical Garden
AV. No. 79-80. 2000. Monografías España. Los 90. p.156; Barcelona Botanical Garden
Bauwelt. No. 19. 2001. (19.01.2001). p.16-17; Barcelona Botanical Garden
Habitar. No. 41. 1995. Quito. p.18-22; Barcelona Botanical Garden
On Diseño. No. 214. 2000. Barcelona. Premios FAD. p.210-217; Barcelona Botanical Garden
L'informatiu. No. 148. 1999. Barcelona. p.25-34; Barcelona Botanical Garden
AV Monografías. No. 80-81. 2000. Anuario. p.29,112-115,188-189; Barcelona Botanical Garden
Hna. No. 3. 2001. Jardines Mágicos. p.40-42; Barcelona Botanical Garden
Via Arquitectura. No. 6. 1999. Valencia. p.40-45; Barcelona Botanical Garden
La Vanguardia. No. 3. 2004. Cuadernos Cívicos. Cincuenta parques. p.40; Barcelona Botanical Garden
Space. No. 387. 2000. Korea. p.50-71; Barcelona Botanical Garden
Oris. No. 12. 2001. Zagreb. p.52-62; Barcelona Botanical Garden
Selecta Barcelona. No. 3. 2001. New York. p.54-59; Barcelona Botanical Garden
AV Monografías. No. 41. 1993. El huerto ilustrado. p.58-61; Barcelona Botanical Garden
Domus. No. 828. 2000. Milan. p.58-64; Barcelona Botanical Garden
Tsport. No. 226. 2002. L'ultimo ritocco al paesaggio del Montjuic. p.60-64; Barcelona Botanical Garden
Tsport. No. 226. 2002. Verona. p.60-64; Barcelona Botanical Garden
Arquitectos. No. 155. 2000. Información del Consejo Superior de los Colegios de Arquitectos de España. Cuaderno de la pequeña dimensión. Carlos Ferrater. Construir el lugar. p.82-85; Barcelona Botanical Garden
Suma +. No. 49. 2001. Jardí Botànic de Barcelona. Nueva topografía. p.82-89; Barcelona Botanical Garden
Quaderns d'arquitectura i urbanisme. No. 194. 1992. Barcelona. p.96-105; Barcelona Botanical Garden
Nexus. No. 36. 2006. La Catalunya paisatge. A la recerca d'un imaginari contemporani. Fundació Caixa Catalunya. p.98-99; Barcelona Botanical Garden
Topos - European Landscape Magazine. No. 29. 1999. p.11-23; Barcelona Botanical Garden
Cic. No. 396. Jun, 1999. p.56-59; Barcelona Botanical Garden
Suma +. No. 83. Nov, 2006. p.90; Barcelona Botanical Garden
Panorama Architecture Newspaper. No. 1. Jun, 2009. p.2; Barcelona Botanical Garden
A+U. No. 318. 1997. (Tokyo); Barcelona Botanical Garden
Casa Cor São Paulo. No. 465. 2005. El riesgo creativo; Barcelona Botanical Garden
Arquitectos. No. 132. 1993. Información del Consejo Superior de los Colegios de Arquitectos de España. Cuaderno de la pequeña dimensión. Carlos Ferrater. Construir el lugar; Barcelona Botanical Garden
Arquitectura Viva. No. 13. 1990. p.66; Barcelona Botanical Garden
Sites. No. 24. 1992. p.100-103; Barcelona Botanical Garden
Arquitectura Viva. No. 25. 1992. p.12-15; Barcelona Botanical Garden
Arquitectura Viva. No. 30. 1993. p.9; Barcelona Botanical Garden
Eupalinos. No. 5. 1999. p.12-15; Barcelona Botanical Garden
Arquitectura y Crítica. Paisajes. No. 8. 1999. p.22-28; Barcelona Botanical Garden
Barcelona Verda. No. 63. 1999. p.11; Barcelona Botanical Garden
Barcelona Verda. No. 64. 1999. p.11; Barcelona Botanical Garden
Arquitectura Viva. No. 66. 1999. p.9; Barcelona Botanical Garden
L'informatiu. No. 148. 1999. p.25-34; Barcelona Botanical Garden
CIC. No. 330. 1999. p.50-59; Barcelona Botanical Garden
CIC. No. 166. 2000. p.9; Barcelona Botanical Garden
On Diseño. No. 214. 2000. p.210-219; Barcelona Botanical Garden
L'Architecture d'aujourd'hui. No. 330. 2000. p.28; Barcelona Botanical Garden
Space-Korea. No. 387. 2000. p.50-71; Barcelona Botanical Garden
AV Monografías. No. 81-82. 2000. p.112-115; Barcelona Botanical Garden
La Talaia. No. 1. 2001. Portal, p.36; Barcelona Botanical Garden
Suma +. No. 49. 2001. 82-87; Barcelona Botanical Garden
Proyectos 98/99. No. 13-14. 2001. p.98-115; Barcelona Botanical Garden
Da Documentos de Arquitectura. No. 50. 2002. p.44-48; Barcelona Botanical Garden
Inde. Informació i Debat. Dec. 2004. El poder de la Geometría. p.20-21; Barcelona Botanical Garden
El País. Oct. 1999. Babelia, Arquitectura. Barcelona. (16.10.1999). p.20; Barcelona Botanical Garden
Inde. Informació i Debat. Oct. 2003. Voluntat d'innovació. (interview) p.26; p.64; Barcelona Botanical Garden
Inde. Informació i Debat. Jul. 2007. Carlos Ferrater - La

importància del lloc. p.34; Barcelona Botanical Garden
Arquitectura y Urbanismo. May 2006. Bruselas. Imágenes y proyectos del desarrollo urbano en Barcelona. (Backpage). p.73-75; Barcelona Botanical Garden
Investigación y Ciencia. Aug. 2001. Barcelona. p.78; Barcelona Botanical Garden
Inde. Informació i Debat. May 2001. Ponents i projectes: predicar amb l'exemple. p.8; Barcelona Botanical Garden
Inde. Informació i Debat. Jun. 2001. p.22-26; Barcelona Botanical Garden
Inde. Informació i Debat. Jun. 2000. p.22; Barcelona Botanical Garden
Topos - European Landscape Magazine. 1999. Ein Netz Aus Dreiecken. p.24-30; Barcelona Botanical Garden
Inde. Informació i Debat. Mar. 2000. p.42; Barcelona Botanical Garden
Inde. Informació i Debat. May 2001. p.8; Barcelona Botanical Garden
I&D. 2000. Barcelona. p.7; Barcelona Botanical Garden
Topos - European Landscape Magazine. 2002. No. Parks. p.88-94; Barcelona Botanical Garden
Arte y Cemento. Oct. 2000. p.98-104; Barcelona Botanical Garden
El País. May 2007. El viajero. p.12. Barcelona en ocho rutas verdes. (26.05.07); Barcelona Botanical Garden
Architettura Intersezioni. 1998. p.132-133; Barcelona Botanical Garden
Urban Spaces. 2002. p.42-51; Barcelona Botanical Garden
Ecotecture. 1999. p.58-59; Barcelona Botanical Garden
Refer paisatges. 2000. Exhibition catalogue. Caja Arquitectos/ COAC. Barcelona Botanical Garden
Cochlea. 1994. La fractalidad en la construcción del paisaje; Barcelona Botanical Garden
Guies dels parcs de l'Àrea Metropolitana de Barcelona. 2004. Barcelona Botanical Garden
Panorama Architecture Newspaper. No. 3. Oct. 2009. Viviendas en la nueva Diagonal. p.8; Vertix housing building
Viviendas-Housing. No. 3. 2007. Editorial Manel Padura. p.282-293; Vertix housing building
Mimarlik. No. 207. 2007. Turkey. p.98-99; Vertix housing building
Via Inmobiliaria. No. 29. 2004. p.10; Vertix housing building
Salir Urban. Nov. 2008. p.68-74; Zaragoza-Delicias Intermodal Station
Spaincontract. No. 6. 2008. p.78; Zaragoza-Delicias Intermodal Station
Promateriales. No. 19. 2008. p.72-73; Zaragoza-Delicias Intermodal Station
Suma +. No. 93. 2008. p.6-15; Zaragoza-Delicias Intermodal Station
Arquitectura Viva. No. 117. 2008. Zaragoza-Delicias Intermodal Station
Descubrir el Arte. No. 107. 2008. Madrid. p.88; Zaragoza-Delicias Intermodal Station
Mimarlik. No. 207. 2007. Turkey. p.88-89; Zaragoza-Delicias Intermodal Station
Promateriales. No. 2. 2007. Madrid. Editorial Pro-Tiendas. p.16-19; Zaragoza-Delicias Intermodal Station
Pasajes Construcción. No. 14. 2006. Estacion de AVE. p.18-19; Zaragoza-Delicias Intermodal Station
Suma +. No. 83. Nov, 2006. p.94; Zaragoza-Delicias Intermodal Station
Casabella. No. 743. 2006. p.30-41; Zaragoza-Delicias Intermodal Station
Diseñart Magazine. No. 8. 2006. Madrid. p.92-93; Zaragoza-Delicias Intermodal Station
Maquetren. No. 162. 2006. Premio Dedalo Minosse, Estación Intermodal Zaragoza-Delicias. p.92; Zaragoza-Delicias Intermodal Station
Future Architecture. No. 4. 2006. Murcia. p.136-139; Zaragoza-Delicias Intermodal Station
Arquitectura Plus. Nov, 2005. Visión y obra de 44 arquitectos españoles. p.48-49; Zaragoza-Delicias Intermodal Station
Bauwelt. No. 25. 2005. Berlín. p.26-33; Zaragoza-Delicias Intermodal Station
Casabella. No. 737. 2005. p.38-45; Zaragoza-Delicias Intermodal Station
Casa Cor São Paulo. No. 465. 2005. El riesgo creativo. p.20-27; Zaragoza-Delicias Intermodal Station
Via Libre. No. 491. 2005. Madrid. p.13-14; Zaragoza-Delicias Intermodal Station
Inde. Informació i debat. Jul. 2004. Estació Intermodal Zaragoza-Delicias, Premi Ex Aequo. p.16-17; Zaragoza-Delicias Intermodal Station
CIC. No. 396. Jun. 2004. Arquitectura de cristal - Fachada Umaran en la Estación Delicias de Zaragoza. p.78-85; Zaragoza-Delicias Intermodal Station
L'acier pour construir Mar. 2004. París. p.24-27; Zaragoza-Delicias Intermodal Station
Cercha. No. 76. 2004. Zaragoza-Delicias. p.32-44; Zaragoza-Delicias Intermodal Station
Betonart. No. 724. 2004. Turkey. p.20-33; Zaragoza-Delicias Intermodal Station
Vía Construcción. No. 9. 2004. Barcelona. p.32; Zaragoza-Delicias Intermodal Station
Arquitectura Viva. No. 99. 2004. El barrio del AVE Estación Intermodal de Delicias, Zaragoza. p.64-69; Zaragoza-Delicias Intermodal Station
M-Group. No. 1. 2004. p.24-31; Zaragoza-Delicias Intermodal Station
La Llotja de Lleida. No. 11/3-23/4. 2004. Zaragoza-Delicias Intermodal Station
Transporti & Cultura, Pasian de Prato. No. 8. 2004. Anno IV. Italia. p.62-67; Zaragoza-Delicias Intermodal Station
Aragón Rutas. No. 27. 2004. Zaragoza-Delicias-Zaragoza Siglo XXI. p.8-13; Zaragoza-Delicias Intermodal Station
Diseño de la ciudad. No. 52. 2004. p.93-99; Zaragoza-Delicias Intermodal Station
RCT. No. 151. 2004. p.32; Zaragoza-Delicias Intermodal Station
Oficinas. No. 246. 2004. p.136-138; Zaragoza-Delicias Intermodal Station
Anuario de Arquitectura Ibérica. 2004. Premios FAD 2004. p.74-77; Zaragoza-Delicias Intermodal Station
Building on Steel. 2004. p.4-5; Zaragoza-Delicias Intermodal Station
AV Monografías. No. 105-106. 2004. p.56-63; Zaragoza-Delicias Intermodal Station
CIC. No. 399. 2004. p.28; Zaragoza-Delicias Intermodal Station
On Diseño. No. 253. 2004. Premio FAD. p.294-301; Zaragoza-Delicias Intermodal Station
Construire en acier. Nov. 2003. Paris. p.3; Zaragoza-Delicias Intermodal Station
El País. Sep. 2003. Babelia. (06.09.03). Zaragoza-Delicias Intermodal Station
Informes de la construcción. No. 487. 2003. Línea de Alta Velocidad Madrid-Zaragoza-Barcelona-Frontera Francesa, Estación de Zaragoza-Delicias. p.5-11; Zaragoza-Delicias Intermodal Station
Il Giornale dell'Architettura Anno 2 No. 9. 2003. A Saragozza una micro-città "indoor". p.13; Zaragoza-Delicias Intermodal Station
World Architecture. No. 85. 2000. p.34; Zaragoza-Delicias Intermodal Station
Pasajes de Arquitectura y Critica. No. 16. 1999. Zaragoza, punto de encuentro. p.4-6; Zaragoza-Delicias Intermodal Station
Inde. Informació i Debat. Dic, 2009. Nova planta d'equipaments i serveis. p.27; Intermodal Station at Barcelona Airport
Descubrir el Arte. No. 107. 2008. Madrid. p.81; Intermodal Station at Barcelona Airport
On Diseño. No. 297. 2008. p.148-157; Intermodal Station at Barcelona Airport
Vía Construcción. No. 50. 2007. Barcelona. p.14; Intermodal Station at Barcelona Airport
Inde. Informació i Debat. Oct. 2007. p.85; Intermodal Station at Barcelona Airport
El Periódico. Oct. 2007. III Nit de l'Aviació, Premios Flyer 2007 (5.10.06). Intermodal Station at Barcelona Airport
Pasajes de Arquitectura y Crítica. No. 33. 2001. p.9; Intermodal Station at Barcelona Airport
Revista de la Cooperativa Jordi Capell. Sep. 2001. Intermodal Station at Barcelona Airport
Arquitectura Viva. No. 25. Jul. 1992. Puntos críticos. Recorrido por las arquitecturas barcelonesas. Peter Buchanan. p.12, 15; 3 city blocks in the Olympic Village, Barcelona
Construire in Laterizio. No. 27. May 1992. Architettura e urbanistica a Barcellona. J.Mª Montaner. Edit. Peg Spa. p.197; 3 city blocks in the Olympic Village, Barcelona
AV. No. 22-24. Nov. 1990. Monografías de Arquitectura y Vivienda. ISBN 0213-487X. p.52-54; 3 city blocks in the Olympic Village, Barcelona
Arte y Cemento. No. 7. May 1991. p.70-81; 3 city blocks in the

Olympic Village, Barcelona

Construire in laterizio. No. 27. 1992. Viviendas para la Villa Olimpica. p.197; 3 city blocks in the Olympic Village, Barcelona

Noticreto. No. 49. 1998. Colombia. p.20-26; 3 city blocks in the Olympic Village, Barcelona

The Architectural Review - Barcelona Transformed. No. 1146. 1992. Housing, Nova Icària, Carlos Ferrater. p.40-43; 3 city blocks in the Olympic Village, Barcelona

Metropolis. No. 76. 2009. "El Pla 22@ fa una Aposta decidida per l'increment de les edificabilitats, amb l'objectiu d'adequar-se a les noves demandes de l'activitat econòmica de les àrees centrals". p.92-93; 3 city blocks in the Olympic Village, Barcelona

AV Monografías. No. 37. 1992. Dos manzanas y media, unidades de proyecto 1.1/1.5. p.94-96; 3 city blocks in the Olympic Village, Barcelona

Squares. No. 6. 1992. p.220-231; 3 city blocks in the Olympic Village, Barcelona

Nikkei Architecture. No. 8-3. 1992. p.108-109; 3 city blocks in the Olympic Village, Barcelona

A+U. No. 12. 1997. p.62-68; 3 city blocks in the Olympic Village, Barcelona

AU. Apr. 1997. Arquitectura y urbanismo São Paulo. p.62-68; 3 city blocks in the Olympic Village, Barcelona

AD. No. 20. Jun. 1989. p.122-126; 3 city blocks in the Olympic Village, Barcelona

El arte de construir. 1999. Valenciana de Cementos; 3 city blocks in the Olympic Village, Barcelona

Suma +. No. 14. 1995. p.34-43; 3 city blocks in the Olympic Village, Barcelona

A+U. No. 328. 1997. 3 city blocks in the Olympic Village, Barcelona

Area. No. 63. 2002. p.125; 3 city blocks in the Olympic Village, Barcelona

Avui. Oct. 1992. L'obra arquitectònica de C. Ferrater. p.114; 3 city blocks in the Olympic Village, Barcelona

Topos - European Landscape Magazine. 1994. European Landscape Magazine. (07.06.1994). p.77-83; 3 city blocks in the Olympic Village, Barcelona

Axxis Diseño. 1995. Decoración y más. Tras la complejidad de lo esencial. p.8-14; 3 city blocks in the Olympic Village, Barcelona

Metropolis. No. 76. 2009. "La ciutat necessita millorar la integració entre espais privats i publics per trobar formes i programes urbanístics més adients a la condició central que ha anat adquirint l'Eixample". p.86-87; 5 city blocks in the seafront, Barcelona

Baksteen Austeridad. No. 55. Dec. 2008. Witte Geometrie de Reimtelijke Architectuur von Carlos Ferrater (Woningbouw Aan de carrer de Taulat, Barcelona). p.24-25; 5 city blocks in the seafront, Barcelona

Diseño Interior. No. 155. 2005. Madrid. p.90-94; Housing building in Passeig de Gràcia, Barcelona

Quaderns d'Arquitectura i Urbanisme. No. 255. 2008. Barcelona. p.61; Building in Passeig de Gràcia, former BASF company

Premios de Arquitectura Aluminier Technal 2007. 2008. p.130-139, 140-151; Building in Passeig de Gràcia, former BASF company

Arquitectura y Urbanismo. May 2006. Bruselas. Imágenes y proyectos del desarrollo urbano en Barcelona. p.73-75; Building in Passeig de Gràcia, former BASF company

Vía Inmobiliaria. No. 34. 2004. 40; Building in Passeig de Gràcia, former BASF company

Arquine. No. 39. 2007. Mexico. 44-49; Iberia Building in Passeig de Gràcia, Barcelona

Inde. Informació i Debat. Jul. 2007. Carlos Ferrater - La importància del lloc. p.34; Iberia Building in Passeig de Gràcia, Barcelona

Diseño Interior. No. 155. 2005. p.90-94; Iberia Building in Passeig de Gràcia, Barcelona

El País. Apr. 2010. La estrella de los hoteles. Mandarin Oriental Barcelona, un establecimiento exquisito en pleno Passeig de Gràcia (24.04.2010), p.15; Hotel Mandarin Oriental Barcelona

On Diseño. No. 308. Feb. 2010. p.82-89; Hotel Mandarin Oriental Barcelona

Proyecto Contract No. 62. Feb. 2010. El Cielo en la Tierra. 46-65; Hotel Mandarin Oriental Barcelona

Diseño Interior. No. 211. Feb. 2010. Hotel dulce hotel. Ferrater, Trias De Bes y Urquiola. 55, 98-109; Hotel Mandarin Oriental Barcelona

Vía Construcción. No. 76. Jan. 2010. Barcelona cuenta con el primer hotel de la cadena Mandarin. p.17; Hotel Mandarin Oriental Barcelona

Arquitectura y Diseño. No. 110. 2009. Casas estimulantes. Lujo con sabor oriental. p.32-45; Hotel Mandarin Oriental Barcelona

Arquitectura y Urbanismo. May 2006. Brussels. Imágenes y proyectos del desarrollo urbano en Barcelona. p.74; Hotel Mandarin Oriental Barcelona

Inde. Informació i Debat. Ene, 2004. D'un banc a una àrea comercial - Banc Santander Central Hispano. p.42; Hotel Mandarin Oriental Barcelona

Spaincontract. No. 6. 2008. p.83; Social Services Centre in Fort Pienc, Barcelona

Arquitectura y Urbanismo. May 2006. Bruselas. Imágenes y proyectos del desarrollo urbano en Barcelona. p.73; Social Services Centre in Fort Pienc, Barcelona

AOA. No. 1. Apr. 2006. Santiago de Chile. p.69-82; Social Services Centre in Fort Pienc, Barcelona

Vía Construcción. No. 28. 2006. Barcelona. p.4-6; Social Services Centre in Fort Pienc, Barcelona

Arquitectura Viva. No. 104. 2006. p.23; Social Services Centre in Fort Pienc, Barcelona

On-Site. 2006. Arquitectura en España, hoy. p.92-93; Social Services Centre in Fort Pienc, Barcelona

C3 Korea. 2005. Public Space II. p.46-53; Social Services Centre in Fort Pienc, Barcelona

AV Monografías. No. 116. 2005. Vivienda formal. p.38-40; Social Services Centre in Fort Pienc, Barcelona

Werk. No. 12. 2005. Zurich. p.48-49; Social Services Centre in Fort Pienc, Barcelona

On Diseño. No. 100. 1989. Un interior en Barcelona. p.216, 228, 236; Social Services Centre in Fort Pienc, Barcelona

AV Monografías. No. 67 1997. 12 Viviendas en Barcelona, España. p.82-85; Gran Via 512 building

Espacios urbanos. Innovación y Diseño. 2009. Carlos Ferrater+Jiménez-Brasa, Royal Quarters of Santo Domingo. Ed. Links. p.182-193; Royal Quarters of Santo Domingo

Periódico de Arquitectura. No. 5. 2002. Intervención en el Cuarto Real de Santo Domingo. Colegio de Arquitectos de Granada. p.118-119; Royal Quarters of Santo Domingo

Arquitectura Viva. No. 67. 1999. Un tapiz de Ferrater a los pies de la Alhambra. p.7; Royal Quarters of Santo Domingo

Arquitectura Viva. No. 68. 1999. p.28-29; Royal Quarters of Santo Domingo

Musea. Feb. 2009. Museos representativos de la Arquitectura Española en 2008. Online version: www.librospdf.net (15.02.2009); Granada Science Park

Promateriales de Construcción y Arquitectura actual. No. 30. Dec. 2009. Con luz propia. p.7-12; Granada Science Park

Oficinas. No. 279. Sep. 2009. p.56-69; Granada Science Park

Construcción Alimarket. No. 93. May 2009. Ampliación del Parque de las Ciencias de Granada. p.20-23; Granada Science Park

Architecture & Culture. No. 335. Apr. 2009. p.42-55; Granada Science Park

EC. Equipamientos Culturales -Centros de reunión. No. 30. Mar. 2009. p.45-50; Granada Science Park

A10 New European Architecture. No. 26. Mar. 2009. p.50-52; Granada Science Park

Promateriales de Construccion y Arquitectura actual. No. 22. Jan. 2009. Parque de las Ciencias de Granada. p.8-17; Granada Science Park

On Diseño. No. 301. 2009. p.76-83; Granada Science Park

Spaincontract. No. 6. 2008. p.80; Granada Science Park

Salir Urban. Nov. 2008. p.68-74; Granada Science Park

Arquitectura Viva. No. 117. 2008. Ferrater en el Parque de las Ciencias de Granada. p.7; Granada Science Park

Descubrir el Arte. No. 107. 2008. Madrid. p.83; Granada Science Park

Suma +. No. 93. 2008. Buenos Aires. p.44-46; Granada Science Park

AV. No. 129-130. 2008. Anuario. Madrid. p.44-51; Granada Science Park

Andalucía Económica. No. 198. 2008. Ampliando horizontes, Parque de la Ciencia. p.24-38; Granada Science Park

Mimarlik. No. 207. 2007. Turkey. p.98-99; Granada Science Park

Vía Construcción. No. 28. 2006. Barcelona. p.4-6; Granada Science Park

AV Proyectos. No. 1. 2004. Madrid. p.44-45; Granada Science Park

Con luz propia. 2004. Junta de Andalucía. CE. Granada Science Park
Progettare. No. 14. 2004. Milan p.92-97; Granada Science Park
Via Inmobiliaria. No. 29. 2004. p.10; Granada Science Park
Periódico de Arquitectura. No. 4. 2003. Granada. p.48-51; Granada Science Park
Periódico de Arquitectura. No. 1. 2001. Propuesta - Nueva Sede de la Diputación: Carlos Ferrater, Eduardo Jiménez Artacho, Yolanda Brasa Seco. p.20-21; Granada Science Park
Pasajes de Arquitectura y Critica. No. 37. 2001. Concurso para la nueva sede de la Diputación Provencial de Granada. p.26; Granada Science Park
Interior Design. No. 75. 2007. Expo Escher, Madrid. p.294-297; Exposición "M.C. Escher. El arte de lo imposible"
AV Proyectos. No. 18. 2007. M.C. Escher. p.88-89; Exposición "M.C. Escher. El arte de lo imposible"
Inde. Informació i Debat. Sep. 2007. Expo Escher, Madrid. p.76; Exposición "M.C. Escher. El arte de lo imposible"
Arquine. 2007. Escher. El Arte de lo imposible. p.40; Exposición "M.C. Escher. El arte de lo imposible"
El País. Oct. 2007. Babelia. (20.10.07); Exposición "M.C. Escher. El arte de lo imposible"
Al Arquitectura Ibérica. No. 33. Oct. 2009. p.108-117; Aquileia Tower
On Diseño. No. 300. 2009. Torre Aquileia en el Lido, Aquileia Tower on the Lido, Venice, Italy. p.144-149; Aquileia Tower
Domus. No. 930. 2009. Milan. p.31-36; Aquileia Tower
Ait. Oct. 2008. Aussenraumleuchte Fl Jesolo Von Ewo Gmbh. p.9; Aquileia Tower
Mimarlik. No. 207. 2007. Turkey. p.83; Aquileia Tower
Oficinas. No. 262. 2006. Barcelona. p.47; Aquileia Tower
Una finestra tra mare e laguna Apr. 2006. Torre Aquileia. Novaidea Creative Resources. Venezia. Aquileia Tower
A + Arquitectura Plus. No. 8. 2005. p.32-36; Aquileia Tower
Arquitectura Viva. No. 98. 2005. p.38-39; Aquileia Tower
Arquitectura Plus. Nov. 2005. Visión y obra de 44 arquitectos españoles. p.48-49; Aquileia Tower
Progettare il territorio. 2005. Ferrater-Martí-Carabajal-Mantese Le nuove centralità sul mare a Jesolo. p.120-124; Aquileia Tower
2G. Carlos Ferrater. No. 32. 2004. Editorial Gustavo Gili. Aquileia Tower
Salir Urban. Nov, 2008. Ferrater. Sincronizar la geometría. p.68-74; Futbol Club Barcelona Stadium
Arquine. No. 42. 2007. Mexico. p.11; Futbol Club Barcelona Stadium
AV Proyectos. No. 22. 2007. p.46-47; Futbol Club Barcelona Stadium
Inde. Informació i Debat. Nov. 2007. p.44-45; Futbol Club Barcelona Stadium
Inde. Informació i Debat. Oct. 2007. p.54-55, 84; Futbol Club Barcelona Stadium
Arquitectura y Urbanismo. May 2006. Brussels. Imágenes y proyectos del desarrollo urbano en Barcelona. (Backpage). p.73-75; Futbol Club Barcelona Stadium
Deia.Com. Apr. 2010. Pura fachada. Online version: www.deia.com. (12.04.2010); New IMQ Hospital
Vía Construcción. No. 1. Mar, 2010. Grupo San José construye la nueva Clínica IMQ en Bilbao. p.16; New IMQ Hospital
Agencia Efe. Feb. 2010. Online version: Comienza la regeneración de Zorrozaurre con la primera piedra del Centro IMQ. Carlos Ferrater y Núria Ayala. (09.02.2020); New IMQ Hospital
Vasco Press. Feb. 2010. Online version: El IMQ abrirá en 2012 En Zorrozaurre la mayor clínica privada de Euskadi. Carlos Ferrater y Núria Ayala. (09.02.2020); New IMQ Hospital
Europa Press. Feb. 2010. Online version: IMQ coloca en Zorrozaurre la primera piedra de la que será la mayor clínica sanitaria privada de Euskadi. Carlos Ferrater y Núria Ayala. (09.02.2020); New IMQ Hospital
ABC. Feb. 2010. Online version: Comienza la regeneración de zorrozaurre con la primera piedra del Centro IMQ. (09.02.2020). Carlos Ferrater y Núria Ayala; New IMQ Hospital
Diario Vasco. Feb. 2010. Online version: Bilbao abrirá en 2010 la mayor clínica privada de la Comunidad Vasca. Carlos Ferrater y Núria Ayala. (10.02.2020); New IMQ Hospital
El Mundo. Feb. 2010. Online version: El IMQ coloca la priemra piedra de la mayor clínica privada de Euskadi. Carlos Ferrater y Núria Ayala. (09.02.2020); New IMQ Hospital
El País. Feb. 2010. Primera piedra de la futura Clínica del IMQ en Zorrozaure. Carlos Ferrater y Núria Ayala. (10.02.2020). p.4; New IMQ Hospital
Expansión. Feb. 2010. Clínica de IMQ en Zorrozaurre. (10.02.2020). Carlos Ferrater y Núria Ayala. p.16; New IMQ Hospital
ADN. Feb. 2010. Clínica de futuro. Bilbao tendrá el mayor centro privado. (10.02.2020). Carlos Ferrater y Núria Ayala. p.3; New IMQ Hospital
Qué! Feb. 2010. Zorrrozaure. El Igualatorio Médico Quirúrgico colocó ayer en Zorrozaure la primera piedra de su clínica, lo que supone el inicio de la reforma de la península. Carlos Ferrater y Núria Ayala. (10.02.2020). p.7; New IMQ Hospital
El Diario Vasco. Feb. 2010. Bilbao abrirá en 2012 la mayor clínica privada de la Comunidad Vasca. Carlos Ferrater y Núria Ayala (10.02.2020). p.7; New IMQ Hospital
20 Minutos. Feb. 2010. El IMQ pone la primera piedra del futuro de Zorrozaure. Carlos Ferrater y Núria Ayala. (10.02.2010). p.2; New IMQ Hospital
Deia. Feb. 2010. La clínica de bilbao del futuro pone su primera piedra; "Sí a las piezas modernas, pero en una estructura urbana poderosa"; Regresan las botaduras junto a la ría. C. Ferrater y N. Ayala. (10.02.2020). Portada, p.14, 7-8; New IMQ Hospital
El Mundo. Feb. 2010. El IMQ empieza a cumplir el sueño de sus fundadores. Carlos Ferrater y Núria Ayala. (10.02.2020). p.12; New IMQ Hospital
El Correo. Feb. 2010. Primera piedra de la mayor clínica de Euskadi; El Igualatorio pone los cimientos del primer edificio de Zorrozaurre; "Nuestro diseño refleja que Bilbao es una ciudad en movimiento"; colocada en Zorrozaurre, con gran presencia institucional, la primera piedra de la nueva Clínica del IMQ. Carlos Ferrater y Núria Ayala. (10.02.2020). Portada, p.4-5, 7; New IMQ Hospital
Panorama Architecture Newspaper. No. 1. Jun, 2009. p.3; New IMQ Hospital
Vía Construcción. No. 58. 2008. p.8, 16; New IMQ Hospital
AV Proyectos. No. 31. 2009. Ferrater & Martí. p.60-61; CaixaForum Zaragoza
Descubrir el Arte. No. 107. 2008. Madrid. p.83; Frontaura Winery, Toro
Expansión. Nov. 2007. Diursa saca nuevo jugo al suelo. (15.11.2007). p.43; Frontaura Winery, Toro
Expansión. Jun. 2007. Especial Catalunya. Diez autores y sus obras. (26.06.2007). p.43; Frontaura Winery, Toro
AoméΣ. No. 9. 2007. Greece. p.106-111; Frontaura Winery, Toro
Elha. No. 101. 2007. Colegio de Arquitectos de La Rioja. p.18; Frontaura Winery, Toro
Vía Construcción. No. 49. 2007. Barcelona. p.88; Frontaura Winery, Toro
Mimarlik. No. 207. 2007. Turkey. p.91; Frontaura Winery, Toro
Wineries. International Review of Architecture 09/07. Sep. 2007. Frontaura y Victoria Winery, España. p.106-111; Frontaura Winery, Toro
Arquitectura Urbana. Jun. 2010. OAB: Reception Pavillion of Atapuerca. Link: www.arquitectura-urbana.com/OAB-reception-pavillion-of-atapuerca.html (13.06.10); Intervention in the archaeological site in Atapuerca
Designboom. Jun. 2010. Link: www.designboom.com/weblog/cat/9/view/10512/OAB-reception-pavillion-of-atapuerca.html. Intervention in the archaeological site in Atapuerca
Cultura i publicacions Esarq. Mar. 2010. Link: http://publiesarq.wordpress.com/2010/03/15/nueva-sede-del-grupo-de-empresas-azaharoab/ (15.03.10); New headquarter for Grupo de Empresas Azahar
W-A.Pl. Mar. 2010. Link: http://www.W-A.Pl/aktualnosci.php?artykul=1320 (04.03.10); New headquarter for Grupo de Empresas Azahar
Mippin. May 2010. Link: http://m.mippin.com/mip/prev/story.jsp?&id=20798&c=-1&s=6&pv=0&sid=110280317&cat=architecture&check=1&z=1@1269783621591664. New headquarter for Grupo de Empresas Azahar
Arch Daily. May 2010. Link: www.archdaily.com/50548/azahar-group-OAB/. New headquarter for Grupo de Empresas Azahar
Trendhunter Magazine. May 2010. Link: www.trendhunter.Com/trends/azahar-group. New headquarter for

Grupo de Empresas Azahar

Materialdelicius. May 2010. Link: www.Materialicious. Com/2010/02/the-azahar-group-world-headquarters-by-oab-architects.Html. New headquarter for Grupo de Empresas Azahar

Design You Trust. May 2010. Link: http://designyoutrust. Com/2010/02/25/the-azahar-group-world-headquarters-by-oab-architects/ New headquarter for Grupo de Empresas Azahar

Daily Tonic. Mar. 2010. Link: www. dailytonic.com/the-azahar-group-headquarters-by-oab-office-of-architecture-in-barcelona-es/ (02.03.10). New headquarter for Grupo de Empresas Azahar

Thecoolist. May 2010. Link: www. thecoolist.com/azahar-group-headquarters-in-castellon-spain/. New headquarter for Grupo de Empresas Azahar

Cova.Ríos. Feb, 2010. Link: http://covarios.wordpress. com/2010/02/22/oab_sede-del-grupo-azahar/ (22.02.10). New headquarter for Grupo de Empresas Azahar

Existingvisual.com. May 2010. Link: www.existingvisual. com/2010/02/24/the-azahar-group-world-headquarters-by-oab-architects/. New headquarter for Grupo de Empresas Azahar

Concept. No. 133. May, 2010. p.68-73; New headquarter for Grupo de Empresas Azahar

Arquitectura Plus. No. 1. 2010. p.50-52; New headquarter for Grupo de Empresas Azahar

El Cultural. El Mundo. May 2010. Dos nuevos proyectos del último Premio Nacional. Carlos Ferrater, El haz y el envés. (07.05.10). p.38; New headquarter for Grupo de Empresas Azahar

Scalae. May 2010. 38 proyectos, 8 de arquitectos españoles, son los elegidos por el jurado de la VII Bienal Iberoamericana de Arquitectura y Urbanismo, como las mejores obras realizadas en los últimos dos años. Link: http://www. scalae.net/noticia/la-vii-bienal-iberoamericana-elige-los-mejores-proyectos (03.05.2010) New headquarter for Grupo de Empresas Azahar

Inmodiario. Apr. 2010. La VII Bienal Iberoamericana de Arquitectura y Urbanismo elige las mejores obras iberoamericanas. Link: www. inmodiario.com/164/8225/la-vii-bienal-iberoamericana-arquitectura-urbanismo-elige-mejores-obras-iberoamericanas.html (28.04.2010); New headquarter for Grupo de Empresas Azahar

Natura. Mar. 2010. p.30-35; New headquarter for Grupo de Empresas Azahar

Arquitectura Viva. No. 128. Apr. 2010. Cubiertas orgánicas de Ferrater en Castellón. p.11; New headquarter for Grupo de Empresas Azahar

El País. Mar. 2010. Tendencias - Edificios camaleónicos. La última arquitectura y el diseño vanguardista copian al paisaje. (30.03.2010). p.43; New headquarter for Grupo de Empresas Azahar

The Plan. No. 41. Apr. 2010. p.62-72; New headquarter for Grupo de Empresas Azahar

Vía Construccion. No. 79. Apr. 2010. p.6; New headquarter for Grupo de Empresas Azahar

Natura. Mar. 2010. Online version: http://www.naturadergi.com/ mart-nisan_2010_natura/natura. html. (Turkey). New headquarter for Grupo de Empresas Azahar

About:blank. Jan. 2010. The Azahar Group Headquarters. Carlos Ferrater & Núria Ayala. Online version: http://www.aboutblank.pt/ arquitectura/azahar-carlos-ferrater-nuria-ayala/. New headquarter for Grupo de Empresas Azahar

Diario Design. Mar. 2010. Oficinas de inspiración verde; el último proyecto de Carlos Ferrater. Online version: http:// diariodesign.com/2010/03/ oficinas-de-inspiracion-verde-el-ultimo-proyecto-de-carlos-ferrater/ (17.03.2010). New headquarter for Grupo de Empresas Azahar

The Architectural Review. Feb. 2010. Azahar Group Headquarters, Castellon, Spain, by OAB. Online version: http:// www.arplus.com/12538/azahar-group-headquarters-castellon-spain-by-oab/#more-12538. New headquarter for Grupo de Empresas Azahar

Designboom. Feb. 2010. OAB: The Azahar Group Headquarters. Online version: http://www.designboom. com/weblog/cat/9/view/9235/oab-the-azahar-group-headquarters. html. New headquarter for Grupo de Empresas Azahar

Professione Architetto. Feb. 2010. Online version: http://www. professionearchitetto.com/news/en/ news4713.aspx New headquarter for Grupo de Empresas Azahar

Architonic. Feb. 2010. Online version: http://www.architonic. com/aisht/the-azahar-group-headquarters-oab-office-of-architecture-in-barcelona/5100346 New headquarter for Grupo de Empresas Azahar

Newwebpik.com. Feb. 2010. Link: www.newwebpick.com/ publish/story_100221222908.html (21.02.10). New headquarter for Grupo de Empresas Azahar

Design Corner. Feb. 2010. Link: http://designcorner.blinkr.net/ search.php (21.02.10). New headquarter for Grupo de Empresas Azahar

Sigalon's Enviroment / Energy Soup. Feb. 2010. Link: http:// sigalonenvironment.soup.Io/ tag/offices (22.02.10). New headquarter for Grupo de Empresas Azahar

Trends Updates. Feb. 2010. Link: http://trendsupdates.com/office-of-architecture-in-barcelona-designed-the-headquarters-of-azahar-group-castellon-spain/ (24.02.10). New headquarter for Grupo de Empresas Azahar

Style of Design. Feb. 2010. Link: http://www.styleofdesign. com/2010/02/azahar-group-oab/ (22.02.10). New headquarter for Grupo de Empresas Azahar

OComa9. Feb. 2010. Online version: http:// www.0coma9.com/actualidad. php?Id=62&idioma=en&idioma=es. New headquarter for Grupo de Empresas Azahar

Archier. Feb. 2010. Online version: http://www.archier.cn:8080/ archi/705 New headquarter for Grupo de Empresas Azahar

On Diseño. No. 308. Feb. 2010. p.106-113; Hotel Alenti

Diseño Interior. No. 211. Feb. 2010. Carlos Ferrater y Lucía Ferrater Hotel Alenti en Sitges. p.92-97; Hotel Alenti

Diseño Arquitectura. May 2010. Luz y cristal. Link: www.nuevo-estilo.es/extra/diseno/100/2_5. shtml Roca Barcelona Gallery

Expansión.Com. Apr. 2010. Roca lanza una red mundial de edificios singulares. Online version: http:// www.expansion.com/2010/04/01/ catalunya/1270148290.html (01.04.2010); Roca Barcelona Gallery

Vía Construccion. No. 79. Apr. 2010. p.6-7; Roca Barcelona Gallery

Diario Design. Nov. 2009. Roca Gallery, nuevo show-room de Roca diseñado por OAB. Online version: http://diariodesign.com/2009/11/ roca-gallery-nuevo-show-room-de-roca-por-carlos-ferrater/ (18.11.2009); Roca Barcelona Gallery

Diseño Interior. No. 211. Feb. 2010. Ferrater: Ensamblajes en el baño. p.20; Roca Barcelona Gallery

Wallpaper. No. 131. Feb. 2010. Design Awards 2010. Best-Lit Loos. p.76; Roca Barcelona Gallery

Channelbeta Press Release. No.. Feb. 2010. Revista online: http://www.b-e-t-a.net/~channelb/ projects/074roca/index_eng.html Roca Barcelona Gallery

On Diseño. No. 308. Feb. 2010. p.60; Roca Barcelona Gallery

Arquitectura y Diseño. No. 111. Feb. 2010. Llamativo y diferente sin recurrir al espectáculo. p.66; Roca Barcelona Gallery

AV Proyectos. No. 35. Feb. 2010. p.2; Roca Barcelona Gallery

Blueprint. No. 286. Jan. 2010. The leading magazine of Architecture and Design. Art of the bathroom Barcelona. p.56-57; Roca Barcelona Gallery

Designer Magazine. Jan. 2010. http://content.yudu.com/library/ a1kven/designerjanuaryfebru/ resources/index.htm?referrerurl=ht tp%3a%2f%2fwww.yudu.com%2f item%2fdetails%2f118105%2fdesi gner-january--february-2010 Roca Barcelona Gallery

La Vanguardia. Culturas. Jan. 2010. Ruido silencioso. Llàtzer Moix. (29.01.2010). p.35; Roca Barcelona Gallery

Roca Top Professional. No. 6. Jan. 2010. Un novo conveito de Galeria. p.12-15; Roca Barcelona Gallery

Quèfem. Jan. 2010. Roca Barcelona Gallery. Un espai únic al món. (29.01.2010). p.1; Roca Barcelona Gallery

La Vanguardia. Dec. 2009. (21.12.2009). p.65; Roca Barcelona Gallery

Panorama Architecture Newspaper. No. 3. Oct. 2009. Experiencia Roca - Galería Bcna. p.3, 5, 8, 23; Roca Barcelona Gallery

Arquitectura y Diseño. No. 110. 2009. Roca presenta las novedades del 2010. p.170; Roca Barcelona Gallery

Arquitectos asuntos Internos. No. 2. 2009. p.2; Roca Barcelona Gallery

La Vanguardia. Jan. 2008. Roca mima su marca. 21.12.09. p.65; Roca Barcelona Gallery

El Cultural. El Mundo. May 2010.

Dos nuevos proyectos del último Premio Nacional. Carlos Ferrater, El haz y el envés. (07.05.10) p.38; Benidorm West Beach Promenade

Proyecto Contract. No. 64. 2010. Premiso Nacionales de vivienda y Arquitectura. p.34; Benidorm West Beach Promenade

Granada hoy. Apr. 2010. Tres obras de Granada quedan finalistas en los Premios Saloni. Link: http://www.granadahoy.com/article/granada/683392/tres/obras/granada/quedan/finalistas/los/premios/saloni/arquitectura.html (22.04.2010) Benidorm West Beach Promenade

Saloni Cerámicas. Apr. 2010. Finalistas Premios Saloni 2010. Proyecto: Paseo Marítimo de Poniente en Benidorm. Carlos Ferrater y Xavier Martí. Link: www.saloni.com/premios_noticias_detalle.php?news_id=37&l=1. Benidorm West Beach Promenade

AiT. No. 4. Apr. 2010. Cevisama. Fliesenmesse in Valencia. p.26; Benidorm West Beach Promenade

Diseño Interior. No. 213. Apr. 2010. Una topografía a color. Link: http://www.disenointerior.es/index.php/mod.pags/mem.detalle/idpag.3096/cat.2268/chk.91d57f2956cccadcad72de8a0b304562.html. Benidorm West Beach Promenade

On Diseño. No. 310. Apr. 2010. Premios Nacionales de Arquitectura y Vivienda. p.50; 56-63; Benidorm West Beach Promenade

Arquitectura Viva. No. 128. Apr. 2010. 8ª ed. Premios ASCER. p.107; Benidorm West Beach Promenade

Natura. Mar. 2010. p.24-29; Benidorm West Beach Promenade

Public Space. Mar. 2010. Premio Europeo del espacio público urbano de 2010. Mención especial: Paseo Marítimo de la Playa de Poniente de Benidorm. Online version: http://www.publicspace.org/es/premio. Benidorm West Beach Promenade

El País.com. Apr. 2010. El Consell fía al sector privado levantar la ciudad de las lenguas. Link: http://www.elpais.com/articulo/comunidad/valenciana/consell/fia/sector/privado/levantar/ciudad/lenguas/elpepiespval/20100408elpval_11/tes (08.04.2010). Benidorm West Beach Promenade

Scalae. Jul. 2009. Se inaugura el Paseo Marítimo de Poniente en Benidorm. Link: http://www.scalae.net/noticia/se-innaugura-el-paseo-maritimo-de-poniente-de-benidorm (31.07.2009) Benidorm West Beach Promenade

Interiors from Spain. Mar. 2010. Un proyecto de OAB Estudio al borde del mar. Online version: http://www.interiorsfromspain.com/icex/cda/controller/pagegen/0,3346,1559872_5596534_5968335_4306130,00.html (23.03.2010) Benidorm West Beach Promenade

Vía Construccion. No. 79. Apr. 2010. El arquitecto debe convertir nuna idea abstracta en una realidad construida. p.4-5; Benidorm West Beach Promenade

Premios Arquitectura Plus 2010. Mar. 2010. Premio Aoplus a la arquitectura de espacios públicos e infraestructuras. Carlos Ferrater y Xavier Martí (OAB): Paseo Marítimo de Benidorm. Benidorm West Beach Promenade

Public Space. Mar. 2010. Premio Europeo del Espacio Público Urbano de 2010. Mención Especial: Paseo Marítimo de la Playa de Poniente de Benidorm. Online version: http://www.publicspace.org/es/premio Benidorm West Beach Promenade

Lasprovincias.es. Mar. 2010. Costas garantiza la financiación de la segunda fase del Paseo de Poniente. Online version: http://www.lasprovincias.es/v/20100317/alicante/costas-garantiza-financiacion-segunda-20100317.html (19.03.2010). Benidorm West Beach Promenade

Natura. Mar. 2010. Online version: http://www.naturadergi.com/mart-nisan_2010_natura/natura.html. (Turkey). p.1-2, 24-29; Benidorm West Beach Promenade

AV Proyectos. No. 35. Feb. 2010. OAB (Ferrater - Martí). p.66-80; Benidorm West Beach Promenade

Mark. No. 24. Feb, 2010. OAB Catches a wave. p.44-45; Benidorm West Beach Promenade

Baunetz Wissen. Feb. 2010. http://www.baunetzwissen.de/standardartikel/bad-und-sanitaer-strandpromenade-in-benidorm-an-der-costa-blanca-s_939413.html Benidorm West Beach Promenade

On Diseño. No. 308. Feb. 2010. VIII Premios Cerámica de Arquitectura e Interiorismo. p.56; Benidorm West Beach Promenade

Vía Construcción. No. 76. Jan. 2010. Ferrater gana el Premio Cerámica de Arquitectura de ASCER. p.23; Benidorm West Beach Promenade

Diseño Interior. No. 210. Jan. 2010. Una topografía a color. p.16-17; Benidorm West Beach Promenade

Diseño Interior. No. 210. Jan. 2010. Online version: http://www.disenointerior.es/index.php/mod.pags/mem.detalle/idpag.3096/cat.2268/chk.91d57f2956cccadcad72de8a0b304562.html Benidorm West Beach Promenade

CIC. No. 471. Jan. 2010. Arquitectura y Construcción. Pavimento cerámico para un nuevo orden geométrico. p.26-27; Benidorm West Beach Promenade

RCT - Tanitpress. No. 219-220. Jan. 2010. El proyecto del Paseo Marítimo de Benidorm gana el Premio Cerámica de Arquitectura. p.36; Benidorm West Beach Promenade

El País. Jan. 2010. El viajero. Benidorm, la nueva ola. La ciudad de los rascacielos alicantina, abierta al turismo todo el año, estrena un sorprendente y colorista Paseo Marítimo. (30.01.2010) p.2-4; Benidorm West Beach Promenade

Baumaister. No. B1. 2010. Zwischen Sand und Asphalt. p.2, 14-15; Benidorm West Beach Promenade

Arquitectura y Diseño. No. 110. 2009. Premios ASCER. p.168; Benidorm West Beach Promenade

Spain on Spain. 2009. p.1.56-1.61; Benidorm West Beach Promenade

Paisajismo. No. 33. 2009. Revista del paisaje, espacios exteriores urbanos y áreas verdes. Un nuevo Paseo Marítimo de Benidorm. p.8-17; Benidorm West Beach Promenade

Panorama Architecture Newspaper. No. 1. Jun. 2009. p.10; Benidorm West Beach Promenade

Descubrir el Arte. No. 107. 2008. Madrid. Entrevista y fotos. p.79-93; Benidorm West Beach Promenade

Suma +. No. 93. 2008. p.40-43; Benidorm West Beach Promenade

Mimarlik. No. 207. 2007. Turkey. p.82-100; Benidorm West Beach Promenade

Inde. Informació i Debat. Jul. 2007. Carlos Ferrater. La importància del lloc. p.34; Benidorm West Beach Promenade

Suma +. Nov. 2006. p.92; Benidorm West Beach Promenade

L'Architecture d'aujourd'hui. No. 363. 2006. p.104-105; Benidorm West Beach Promenade

Vía Construcción. No. 28. 2006. Barcelona. p.4-6; Benidorm West Beach Promenade

Rodeo. 2004. La Bienal. p.8; Benidorm West Beach Promenade

La Vanguardia. Jun. 2003. Suplemento 51 Cultura. 11.06.03. p.22-23; Benidorm West Beach Promenade

La Vanguardia. Jun. 2003. Espacios: contribuciones al modelo Benidorm. p.22; Benidorm West Beach Promenade

21st Century Houses. 150 of the World's Best. 2010. House 2 for a photographer. p.172-173; House for a photographer 2, Les Cases d'Alcanar

Construire in Laterizio. No. 133. Feb. 2010. House for a photographer 2, Les Cases d'Alcanar

Domus Area. No. 2. Jul. 2009. Casa Duplesis. Hra Sevetla A Stínu. p.76-84; House for a photographer 2, Les Cases d'Alcanar

Architectural Record. No. 4. Apr. 2009. Carlos Ferrater draws on Spain's modern and vernacular traditions for the weekend house for a photographer 2. p.80-85; House for a photographer 2, Les Cases d'Alcanar

On Diseño. No. 304. 2009. Casa en el Delta del Ebro. p.90-97; House for a photographer 2, Les Cases d'Alcanar

C3 Korea. No. 303. 2009. p.86-95; House for a photographer 2, Les Cases d'Alcanar

Suma +. No. 93. 2008. p.34-39; House for a photographer 2, Les Cases d'Alcanar

Inde. Informació i Debat. Sep. 2007. Premis IX Bienal Espanyola. La casa del Delta del Ebro. House for a photographer 2, Les Cases d'Alcanar

El País. Jul. 2007. (01.07.07). p.94-97; House for a photographer 2, Les Cases d'Alcanar

Inde. Informació i Debat. Apr. 2007. Casa per a un fotògraf 2 a Les Cases d'Alcanar. p.70; House for a photographer 2, Les Cases d'Alcanar

Interior Digest. No. 8. 2007. p.152-159; House for a photographer 2, Les Cases d'Alcanar

Decollage. Trends & Design No. 3. 2007. p.34-41; House for a photographer 2, Les Cases d'Alcanar

Barzón. No. 4. 2007. Picasso de vacaciones, casa para un fotógrafo 2. Explorando el mundo contemporáneo. p.126-133; House for a photographer 2, Les Cases

d'Alcanar
Mimarlik. No. 207. 2007. Turkey. p.84-85; House for a photographer 2, Les Cases d'Alcanar
Interior Digest. No. 8. 2007. Mockba. p.152-159; House for a photographer 2, Les Cases d'Alcanar
Diseño Interior. No. 173. 2006. Madrid. p.122-129; House for a photographer 2, Les Cases d'Alcanar
Casa Viva. No. 16. 1998. El refugio del fotógrafo. p.80-87; House for a photographer 2, Les Cases d'Alcanar
Elle. No. 12. 1987. La casa del fotógrafo Ferrater - Un espacio reposado. p.224-227; House for a photographer 2, Les Cases d'Alcanar

Guías

Barcelona, Arquitectura Contemporánea 1979-2004. 2005. Ajuntament de Barcelona. Edicions Polígrafa. Apartments and offices building Studio OAB
Architecture & Design. Barcelona. No. 12. 2004. TeNeues, Ed. Sabina Marreiros. Stuttgart. Office & Industry. Apartments and offices building Studio OAB
Barcelona, Arquitectura Contemporánea 1979-2004. 2005. Ajuntament de Barcelona. Edicions Polígrafa. Barcelona Botanical Garden
Barcelona, A Guide to Recent Architecture. 2002. Ellipsis London. Suzanne Strum. London. Barcelona Botanical Garden
Architecture & Design. Barcelona. No. 38. 2004. TeNeues. Sabina Marreiros (ed.). Stuttgart. Public. Barcelona Botanical Garden
Barcelona: Guia d'Arquitectura Moderna 1860-2002. 2002. Editorial Actar. ISBN: 84-89698-47-3. Barcelona Botanical Garden
Ruta del Disseny BCN. 2003. IMPUIQV. Ajuntament de Barcelona. FAD. p.83; Barcelona Botanical Garden
Arquitectura del Siglo XX. 2005. Una antología personal. Miguel Angel Roca. Cerdá reinterpretado. La manzana como matriz habitacional. p.82-85; 3 city blocks in the Olympic Village, Barcelona
European Masters. No. Tomo 4. 1993. Housing Architecture. 3 city blocks in the Olympic Village, Barcelona
Barcelone. May 1992. Dix années d'urbanisme. La renaissance d'une ville. Guy Henry. Collab. Ida Hounkpatin et Stephan Comby. Editions du Moniteur. Paris. p.153; 3 city blocks in the Olympic Village, Barcelona
La Villa Olímpica. Barcelona 1992. 1991. Jardins de Can Torras. Martorell, Bohigas, Mackay, Puigdomènech. Editorial Gustavo Gili. p.116-119; 3 city blocks in the Olympic Village, Barcelona
Bienal de Arquitectura y Urbanismo de Zaragoza. 1993. Experimenta Edición I. Electa. p.218; 3 city blocks in the Olympic Village, Barcelona
Barcellona 1981-1992. 1992. Transformazione urbane e realizazioni sportive. XXV Giochi Olimpici. Massimo Bianchi/Eugenio Martera/Paolo Setti. Alinea Editrici. p.168; 3 city blocks in the Olympic Village, Barcelona
Atlas de plantas de viviendas. 1997. 3 bloques delimitadores de manzana; p.22-23; 3 city blocks in the Olympic Village, Barcelona
Urban Spaces. Nov. 1994. World Environment Design. Ed. F. Asensio. ISBN 84-8185-004-7 / 84-8185-005-5. p.24-33; 3 city blocks in the Olympic Village, Barcelona
Arquitectura de España 1929-2000. 2000. Carlos Flores – Xavier Güell. Fundación Caja de Arquitectos. p.118; 3 city blocks in the Olympic Village, Barcelona
Paisajistas. 1994. Parques y Jardines entre edificios. Jesús de Vicente/Xavier Carbonell. Ediciones de Horticultura S.L. p.12-19; 3 manzanas en la Vila Olímpica, Barcelona
Barcelona 1929-1994. Apr. 1995. Col. Guía de Arquitectura. Antoni González/Rafael Lacuesta. 3 city blocks in the Olympic Village, Barcelona
Arquitectura de España 1929-1996. 1996. p.118; 3 city blocks in the Olympic Village, Barcelona
Guia de Arquitectura de España. 1996. 3 city blocks in the Olympic Village, Barcelona
Ajuntament de Barcelona. 2005. Edicions Polígrafa. 3 city blocks in the Olympic Village, Barcelona
Barcelona: Guia d'Arquitectura Moderna 1860-2002. 2002. Editorial Actar. ISBN: 84-89698-47-3. 3 city blocks in the Olympic Village, Barcelona
Arquitecture and Design. Barcelona. No. 2. 2004. TeNeues. Sabina Marreiros (ed.). Stuttgart. Living. Housing building in Passeig de Gràcia, Barcelona
La Vanguardia. 2006. Una Pedrera para el Siglo XXI. Llàtzer Moix. (03.03.2006). Iberia Building in Passeig de Gràcia, Barcelona
Architecture and Design. Barcelona. No. 2. 2004. TeNeues. Sabina Marreiros (ed.). Stuttgart. Iberia Building in Passeig de Gràcia, Barcelona
Architecture and Design. Barcelona. 2008. Ed. Daab Gmbh. ISBN: 9783866540293. p.64-69; Social Services Centre in Fort Pienc, Barcelona
Architecture & Design. Barcelona. 2007. Carlos Ferrater. Social Services of Fort Pienc Neighborhood. p.54-69; Social Services Centre in Fort Pienc, Barcelona
Catalunya. Guia d'Arquitectura Moderna 1880-2007. 2007. Maurici Plà. Triangle Editorial. COAC. p.326; House for a photographer 2, Les Cases d'Alcanar
Guia de Arquitectura. España. 2000. Casa para un fotógrafo. p.192; House for a photographer 2, Les Cases d'Alcanar

Videos

Documentos de Arquitectura Contemporánea. 1996. Monography. Prod. 5M. 3 city blocks in the Olympic Village, Barcelona

Published by
ACTAR
Barcelona/New York
Part of ActarBirkhäuser.com
www.actar.com

Edited by
Carlos Ferrater
Núria Ayala

Text supervision
Borja Ferrater

Translation
Cillero & de Motta

Graphic design and production
ActarBirkhäuserPro

Graphic documentation
Estudio OAB

OAB Archive
Gisela Folch
Birgit Eschenlor

Photographs
Alejo Bagué
except
Dani Rovira 14, 15, 72-79, 152-163, 226-227
Roland Halbe 101-105
Alessandra Chemollo 108-115
Lluís Casals
José Manuel Ferrater
Juan Rodríguez 141-145
Estudio OAB, 4-9, 106-107, 192, 196, 202

ISBN 978-84-92861-23-1
DL B-42.296-2010

Printing and bound
in the European Union

Distribution
ActarBirkhäuserD
Barcelona–Basel–New York
www.actarbirkhauser-d.com

Roca i Batlle 2
E-08023 Barcelona
T +34 93 417 49 93
F +34 93 418 67 07
salesbarcelona@actarbirkhauser.com

Viaduktstrasse 42
CH-4051 Basel
T +41 61 5689 800
F +41 61 5689 899
salesbasel@actarbirkhauser.com

151 Grand Street, 5th floor
New York, NY 10013
T +1 212 966 2207
F +1 212 966 2214
salesnewyork@actarbirkhauser.com

This book contains 9 QR codes, which are linked to various audiovisual material. They can also be viewed through the following link:
www.actar.com/ferrater/ferrater_english

Audiovisuals

Botanical Garden Barcelona, Iberia Head Office in Passeig de Gràcia Barcelona, Mediapro Building (structural study)
OAB

Roca Gallery Barcelona
With the permission of Roca

Intermodal Train Station Zaragoza, Science Park Granada,
A production by Carlos López Linares.
With the permission of ArquigramaTV
www.arquigramatv.com

Waterfront Benidorm
With the permission of Studio Banana TV
http://studiobanana.tv

"Jazz" Office Building Boulogne Paris
With the permission of Le Pavillon de l'Arsenal, Collection Paris Architectures

ACTAR

OAB
Office of Architecture
in Barcelona